Ethnic Music on Records

A Discography of Ethnic Recordings Produced
in the United States, 1893 to 1942

RICHARD K. SPOTTSWOOD

VOLUME
5

Mid-East, Far East, Scandinavian,
English Language, American Indian, International

UNIVERSITY OF ILLINOIS PRESS
Urbana and Chicago

The publication of this work has been supported in part by
a grant from the National Endowment for the Humanities
an independent federal agency.

This book is printed on acid-free paper.

Library of Congress Cataloging-in-Publication Data

Spottswood, Richard. (Richard Keith)
    Ethnic music on records : a discography of ethnic recordings
produced in the United States, 1893 to 1942 / Richard K. Spottswood.
        p.   cm. — (Music in American life)
    Includes bibliographical references.
    Contents: v. 1. Western Europe — v. 2. Slavic — v. 3. Eastern
Europe — v. 4. Spanish, Portuguese, Philippine, Basque — v. 5. Mid-
East, Far East, Scandinavian, English language, American Indian,
international — v. 6. Appendix, artist index, title index — v.
7. Record number index, matrix number index.
    ISBN 0-252-01718-8 (set: alk. paper). ISBN 0-252-01723-4 (v. 5 : alk. paper)
    1. Folk music—Discography.   2. Folk-songs—Discography.
3. Popular music—Discography.   4. Sound recordings—United States—
Catalogs. I. Title. II. Series.
ML 156.4.F5S69   1990
016.78162'0026'6—dc20   89-20526
                                                            CIP
                                                            MN

Contents of Volume 5

PART 6: FAR EAST

PART 7: SCANDINAVIAN

PART 8: ENGLISH LANGUAGE

PART 9: AMERICAN INDIAN

PART 10: INTERNATIONAL

PART 5

MID EAST

SECTION 23. ARAB

23.1. Lateefy Abdou *vocal*

6739	Walie Minal Guami-Pt. 1	Mal (12")
6740	Walie Minal Guami-Pt. 2	Mal (12")
6741	Agdadi-Pt. 1	Mal (12")
6742	Agdadi-Pt. 2	Mal (12")
6743	Zabayatal Unsi-Pt. 1	Mal (12")
6744	Zabayatal Unsi-Pt. 2	Mal (12")
6745-A	Zagtoor-Pt. 1	Mal (12")
6746-A	Zagtoor-Pt. 2	Mal (12")
6747-A	Hauvid Min Hona-Pt. 1	Mal (12")
6748	Hauvid Min Hona-Pt. 2	Mal (12")
		NY April 1924
6751	Ya Tayr	Mal (12")
6752	Oumi Tkatari-Pt. 1	Mal (12")
6753-A	Oumi Tkatari-Pt. 2	Mal (12")
6754	Waheed Al-Husni	Mal (12")
6755	Ya Baba	Mal (12")
6756	Hneyona	Mal (12")
6757	Mata Ya Keeram-Pt. 1	Mal 2000(12")
6758	Mata Ya Keeram-Pt. 2	Mal 2000(12)"
6759	Nazari Ila-Pt. 1	Mal (12")
6760	Nazari Ila-Pt. 2	Mal (12")
6761	Da Loona	Mal (12")
6762	Mar Mar Zamani	Mal (12")
6763	Habeebi-Pt. 1	Mal (12")
6764-A	Habeebi-Pt. 2	Mal (12")
6765	Shamil Azhar-Pt. 1	Mal (12")
6766	Shamil Azhar-Pt. 2	Mal (12")
		NY May 1924
6767	Wadin Jameelin-Pt. 1	Mal (12")
6768	Wadin Jameelin-Pt. 2	Mal (12")
6769	Sham Ilzihoor-Pt. 2	Mal (12")
6770	Sham Ilzihoor-Pt. 2	Mal (12")
6771	Hibat Riah-Pt. 1	Mal 3018(12")
6772	Hibat Riah-Pt. 2	Mal 3018(12")
6773	Radeeto Menal Ahibati-Pt. 1	Mal (12")
6774	Radeeto Menal Ahibati-Pt. 2	Mal (12")
6775	Hakaho-Pt. 1	Mal (12")
6776	Hakaho-Pt. 2	Mal (12")
6777	Bil-Aman	Mal (12")

6778	Al-Bahry	Mal (12")
		NY June 1924

Mal 2000 is accompanied by oud;   other accompaniments are untraced.

23.2. Z. **Agob** *soprano*

Zaku Agbt

61565-	test recording	Co
		NY April 12, 1917

Z. Agob

	Lamma Kamani Elhood-Pt. 1	Co E3601
	Lamma Kamani Elhood-Pt. 2	Co E3601
	Lamma Kamani Elhood-Pt. 3	Co E3602
	Lamma Kamani Elhood-Pt. 4	Co E3602
	Yalwatt El-Oursi-Pt. 1	Co E3603
	Yalwatt El-Oursi-Pt. 2	Co E3603
		NY 1917

58823-	Al Bulbul Nagha-Pt. 1	Co E3782
58824-	Al Bulbul Nagha-Pt. 2	Co E3782
58825-	Ha Bibi Ghab-Pt. 1	Co E3783
58826-	Ha Bibi Ghab-Pt. 2	Co E3783
58827-	Gose Elhamam-Pt. 2	Co E3784
58828-	Gose Elhamam-Pt. 2	Co E3784
		NY ca November 1917

23.3. Shehadi **Ashkar** *kanun*

S. Shehadi

44625-	Taxim Hujaz Car	Co E3201
		NY ca January 1917

Shahadi Ashar

6723	Rasd Mahoor	Mal (12")
6724	Takseem Nahawand	Mal (12")
		NY February 1924

23.4. Samy **Attaya** *vocal*

6573-A	Charlotte-Pt. 1	Mal (12")
6574	Charlotte-Pt. 2	Mal (12")
6575	Ya Boo Eeyoon Il Dublana-Pt. 1	Mal (12")
6576	Ya Boo Eeyoon Il Dublana-Pt. 2	Mal (12")
6577	Gamalik Shagil Balik	Mal (12")
6578	Ahl Llgoram	Mal (12")

```
6579        Khifi Ya Oumieal Khalb                      Mal (12")
6580        Ahubiki Ya Salma                            Mal (12")
6581-A      La Paloma-Pt. 1                             Mal (12")
6582        La Paloma-Pt. 2                             Mal (12")
6583        Kainter Fee Wachin Jameelin-Pt. 1'          Mal (12")
6584        Kainter Fee Wachin Jameelin-Pt. 2'          Mal (12")
6585        Ha Hawatha Khatan                           Mal (12")
6586        Ima'l Baria                                 Mal (12")
            'with Mrs. McCormick           NY  February 1923
```

23.5. Aziz

```
6891        Lebanon-Pt. 1                               Mal (12")
6891        Lebanon-Pt. 2                               Mal (12")
                                           NY  March 1925
```

23.6. Rev. Georg Aziz *baritone*

```
39380-1     Sabeho Elrab                                Co E1867
39381-1     Samawty Yabatoulatt                         Co E1867
            vln                            NY  May 15, 1914
```

23.7. Bagdadi *vocal*

```
6833        Wilnabi Youma                               Mal (12")
6834        Inta Sultanil Milah                         Mal (12")
6835        Ya Ladan-Pt. 1                              Mal (12")
6836        Ya Ladan-Pt. 2                              Mal (12")
6837        Koukh Ya Naim                               Mal (12")
6838        In Kunta Tashani                            Mal (12")
                                           NY  December 1924

6847        Beit Abooka-Pt. 1                           Mal (12")
6848        Beit Abooka-Pt. 2                           Mal (12")
6849        Hubik Ya Meesria                            Mal (12")
6850        Fateno'l Gezlan                             Mal (12")
6851        Abattoha                                    Mal (12")
6852        Ya Bood                                     Mal (12")
                                           NY  January 1925
```

23.8. Moses Cohen *vocal*

```
44904-1     Ya Mnanasha-Pt. 1                           Co E3384
44905-1     Ya Mnanasha-Pt. 2                           Co E3384
            El Duzoubia-Pt. 1                           Co E3385
            El Duzoubia-Pt. 2                           Co E3385
            Waslak Wa Hagrak-Pt. 1                      Co E3386
            Waslak Wa Hagrak-Pt. 2                      Co E3386
            vln, oud, kanun                NY  1917
```

B 25439-1	Wana Mali-Pt. 1	Vi 73065
B 25440-1	Wana Mali-Pt. 2	Vi 73065
B 25441-1	Ma Hadi Zayeh-Pt. 1	Vi rej
B 25448-1	Ma Hadi Zayeh-Pt. 2	Vi rej
	vln, oud	NY June 10, 1921

B 25441-2	Ma Hadi Zayeh-Pt. 1	Vi 73148
B 25448-2	Ma Hadi Zayeh-Pt. 2	Vi 73148
	vln, kanun	NY July 1, 1921

23.9. Selim Domani *vocal*

M 451	Ya Salam Al-FLH-Pt. 1	Mal 201
M 452	Ya Salam Al-FLH-Pt. 2	Mal 201
	Naeem Karacand-vln, unk oud, kanun	NY 1920

7977-A	Al Mushal (arr Maloof)-Pt. 1¹	Mal
7978-A	Al Mushal (arr Maloof)-Pt. 2¹	Mal
7979-A	Asmar Illoun (arr Maloof)-Pt. 1¹	Mal 210
7980-A	Asmar Illoun (arr Maloof)-Pt. 2¹	Mal 210
7981-A	Ma Oodishi Maak (arr Maloof)-Pt. 1	Mal
7982-A	Ma Oodishi Maak (arr Maloof)-Pt. 2	Mal
	vln, 'p	NY August 10, 1922

Selim Domani And Mme. Marie

7985-A	Hal-Eeshi Killa Murrah (Maloof)-Pt. 1	Mal
7986-A	Hal-Eeshi Killa Murrah (Maloof)-Pt. 2	Mal
7987-A	Zabata'l Unsi Illyah (arr Maloof)-Pt. 1	Mal 209
7988-A	Zabata'l Unsi Illyah (arr Maloof)-Pt. 2	Mal 209
		NY August 11, 1922

Selim Domani

6533	Tabbassam Washashah-Pt. 1	Mal (12")
6534	Tabbassam Washashah-Pt. 2	Mal (12")
6535	Suhyra Tarckto'l Daer	Mal (12")
6536	Al Hilm	Mal (12")
		NY September 1922

8039	Sah Il-Noum-Pt. 1	Mal
8040	Sah Il-Noum-Pt. 2	Mal
8041	Il Bint De Ambt Tegen-Pt. 1	Mal
8042	Il Bint De Ambt Tegen-Pt. 2	Mal
	orch	NY September 25, 1922

8045	Fulla-Ya-Fulla-Pt. 1	Mal 216
8046	Fulla-Ya-Fulla-Pt. 2	Mal 216
8047-A	Ya-Tamri-Hinna-Pt. 1	Mal
8048	Ya-Tamri-Hinna-Pt. 2	Mal
8049	Seebooni-Ya-Nas-Pt. 1	Mal 217
8050	Seebooni-Ya-Nas-Pt. 2	Mal 217
8051	Habeely-Nasseeby-Pt. 1	Mal

| 8052 | Habeely-Nasseeby-Pt. 2 | Ma1 |
| | oud, kanun | NY September 27, 1922 |

6551	Ya Yaylou Alsab	Ma1 (12")
6552	Atatni Wania	Ma1 (12")
6553	Balaghuha Qasida-Pt. 1	Ma1 221(12")
6554	Balaghuha Qasida-Pt. 2	Ma1 221(12")
6555	Shamil Kookaeen-Pt. 1	Ma1 (12")
6556	Shamil Kookaeen-Pt. 2	Ma1 (12")
6557	O Kathibu Hafsi-Pt. 1	Ma1 (12")
6558	O Kathibu Hafsi-Pt. 2	Ma1 (12")
	Naeem Karacand-vln, unk oud, kanun	NY December 14, 1922

6605-A	Kookieh	Ma1 (12")
6606-A	Shoo Hal Zaman	Ma1 (12")
6607	Tan Lale Ya Habeeli-Pt. 1	Ma1 (12")
6608-A	Tan Lale Ya Habeeli-Pt. 2	Ma1 (12")
6609	Dooma Ya Assal	Ma1 (12")
6610	Masr Al Gadeeda	Ma1 (12")
6611	Seero Lil Harbi-Pt. 1	Ma1 (12")
6612	Seero Lil Harbi-Pt. 2	Ma1 (12")
6613	La Tahsihoo	Ma1 (12")
6614	Shabeehoka Badoil Layl	Ma1 (12")
		NY March 1923

6627	Shadenon-Pt. 1	Ma1 (12")
6628	Shadenon-Pt. 2	Ma1 (12")
6629	Assitni'l Nahli-Pt. 2	Ma1 (12")
6630	Assitni'l Nahli-Pt. 2	Ma1 (12")
6631	Adem Ya Rabina	Ma1 (12")
6632	Ha Busheero'l Bushr	Ma1 (12")
		NY May 1923

6674	Soona-Pt. 1	Ma1 (12")
6675	Soona-Pt. 2	Ma1 (12")
6678	Shakua Mitjawis-Pt. 1	Ma1 (12")
6679	Shakua Mitjawis-Pt. 2	Ma1 (12")
		NY November 1923

6712	Bagdadi Ahan Ala Man	Ma1 (12")
6713	Bagdadi Ya Zain	Ma1 (12")
6714	Ataha Ya Ma Tarat	Ma1 (12")
6715	Ataha Haleeli'l Zain	Ma1 (12")
		NY February 1924

23.10. M. Elhabe *tenor*

	Mehallawy-No. 1	Co E3200
	Mehallawy-No. 2	Co E3200
		NY 1916-7

23.11. M.S. Hawie *spoken*

59610-	Goodbye Whiskey-Pt. 1	Co E5196(12")
59611-	Goodbye Whiskey-Pt. 2	Co E5196(12")
		NY ca 1920

1040	title untraced-Pt. 1	AJM 1696(12")
1041	title untraced-Pt. 2	AJM 1696(12")
		NY 1920s

23.12. W. Kamel *tenor*

44171-1	In Shakout-No. 1	Co E3125
44172-2	In Shakout-No. 2	Co E3125
44173-1	Shakwaty-No. 1	Co E3011
44174-1	Shakwaty-No. 2	Co E3011
44175-1	Salamon Ala-No. 1	Co E3060
44176-1	Salamon Ala-No. 2	Co E3060
	Samahat-No. 1	Co E3010
	Samahat-No. 2	Co E3010
	Salamon Ala-No. 3	Co E3061
	Salamon Ala-No. 4	Co E3061
	Ayn Allaty-No. 1	Co E3430
	Ayn Allaty-No. 2	Co E3430
	Naeem Karacand-vln, unk oud	NY ca July 1916

23.13. Naeem Karacand *tenor, violin*

Syrian-Arabic Instrumental Trio

44199-1	Azrbar Bishro-No. 1	Co E2949
44200-1	Azrbar Bishro-No. 2	Co E2949
44203-1	Al Bulbul Bishro-No. 1	Co E2955
44204-1	Al Bulbul Bishro-No. 2	Co E2955
44205-1	Tatios Bishro-No. 1	Co E2956, E3102
44206-1	Tatios Bishro-No. 2	Co E2956, E3102
44207-1	Bayat Taxim	Co E3012
44208-1	Hujaz Tahmila	Co E3012
	Bitar Bishro-No. 1	Co E2950
	Bitar Bishro-No. 2	Co E2950
	own vln, unk oud, kanun	NY ca August 1916

Co E3102 is a Greek release.

N. Karacand

44626-1	Taxim Seigah [no vo]	Co E3201
		NY ca January 1917

85212-1	Min Seher	Co E4489
85213-1	Onk Elmelech	Co E4489

```
Layaly                                                  Co E4433
Fi Zoli Ahabad Mawol                                    Co E4433
                                                NY  ca May 1919


Violin Solo Flute Imitation                     Macksoud 718(12")
Violin Solo Bird Imitation                      Macksoud 818(12")
oud                                             NY  early 1920s
```

The above are coupled. This musician and NAEEM KAREKIN, a violinist appearing on a number of Turkish recordings, are probably the same.

23.14. Karam *spoken*

```
6669          Telephone Monologue-Pt. 1                     Mal (12")
6670-A        Telephone Monologue-Pt. 2                     Mal (12")
6672-A        Ahlan Bi Arbabil                              Mal (12")
                                                NY  October 1923

6735          Monologue No. 1-Pt. 1                         Mal (12")
6736          Monologue No. 1-Pt. 2                         Mal (12")
                                                NY  March 1924

6793          Monologue-Pt. 1                               Mal (12")
6794          Monologue-Pt. 2                               Mal (12")
6795          Min Rickit Ahl-Pt. 1                          Mal (12")
6796          Agagibtoo-Pt. 2                               Mal (12")
                                                NY  October 1924
```


23.15. Khlil-Zacharia *oud*

```
4367          title untraced                                    LC 14741B1
4368          title untraced [continuation of same song]  LC 14741B2 14741B2
4369          Egyptian March                                    LC 14741B3
              Meliki-Sourou-kanun, Latifi-Haskie-dm, Maria-Lisme-tam
                              Columbian Exposition, Chicago  September 25, 1893
```

LC 14741 is a tape reel on which the original cylinders have been copied.

23.16. Fadwa Kurban *vocal*

```
GEX 2914      Sooria Biladi-Pt. 1                           Mal 37
GEX 2915      Sooria Biladi-Pt. 2                           Mal 37
GEX 2916      Al-Jazayer-Pt. 1                              Mal 39
GEX 2917      Al-Jazayer-Pt. 2                              Mal 39
GEX 2918      Ya Hind-Pt. 1                                 Mal 44
GEX 2919      Ya Hind-Pt. 2                                 Mal 44
GEX 2920      Marhaban-Pt. 1                                Mal
GEX 2921      Marhaban-Pt. 2                                Mal
GEX 2922      Arabic Lullaby-Pt. 1                          Mal 39
GEX 2923      Arabic Lullaby-Pt. 2                          Mal 39
GEX 2924      Ya Hind-Pt. 1 [experimental]                  Mal rej
```

GEX 2925-A	Last Rose Of Summer-Pt. 1		Mal 38
GEX 2926	Last Rose Of Summer-Pt. 2		Mal 38
GEX 2927	Walie Menal Gorami-Pt. 1		Mal
GEX 2928	Walie Menal Gorami-Pt. 2		Mal
	Alexander Maloof-org	NY	March 1932

The Gennett files indicate that Mal 39 was used twice.

GEX 2945	Keefak Keef-Pt. 1		Mal 59
GEX 2946	Keefak Keef-Pt. 2		Mal 59
GEX 2947	Weile		Mal
GEX 2948	Mabrook-Pt. 1'		Mal
GEX 2949	Mabrook-Pt. 2'		Mal
GEX 2950	Home Sweet Home-Pt. 1'		Mal
GEX 2951	Home Sweet Home-Pt. 2'		Mal
	probably Alexander Maloof-p, 'unk vln	NY	June 1932

Matrices GEX 2948-51 are marked "chapel" in the Gennett files, and may have been used for a special funeral parlor series.

23.17. Habib D. Mackouzey *vocal*

W 206042-2	Men Hagebekey-Pt. 1		Co 50006-X(12")
W 206043-2	Men Hagebekey-Pt. 2		Co 50006-X(12")
W 206044-1	In Kanto La Assloo		Co 50010-X(12")
W 206045-2	Lo Can Lee Kalban		Co 50010-X(12")
		NY	October 1928

23.18. Alexander Maloof *piano*

| B 13834-1 | Al-Ja-Za-Yer (A. Maloof) | | Vi 17443 |
| | | NY | July 24, 1913 |

| B 13868-2 | A Trip To Syria-Original Syrian Dance (A. Maloof) | | Vi 17443 |
| | | NY | September 16, 1913 |

Maloof's Oriental Orchestra

M 401	Mt. Lebanon March (Alexander Maloof)		Mal 7002
M 402-2	A Trip To Syria (Alexander Maloof)		Mal 7001
M 403	Cradle Song {Berceuse Orientale} (Alexander Maloof)		Mal 7001
M 404	Egyptian Khedevial March		Mal 7002
M 405	Algerian March		Mal 7003, MO 7
M 408	Bashrof Aleppo		Mal 7003, MO 7
		NY	1920

Mal 7002 as ORIENTAL ORCHESTRA

The following material, made in The Gennett studios, is sparsely documented. Some undoubtedly appears on the artist's Maloof label, though one Gennett issue has been found and appears below. Some items may be piano solos but orchestral performances are more likely.

Orchestra Orientale

8002-A	Valse Petite Orientale (Alex. Maloof)	Mal
8003-B	Syria-Oriental Fox Trot (Alex. Maloof)	Mal
8004-A	On The Beautiful Nile-Oriental Serenade (Alex. Maloof)	Mal

NY August 23, 1922

Alexander Maloof

6544-A	Bashiaf	Mal (12")
6545-A	Ja-Zayer	Mal (12")
8124	Takseem-Pt. 1	Mal
8125	Takseem-Pt. 2	Mal
8126	Bedouin Dance	Mal
8127	Danse Characteristique	Mal

NY December 1, 1922

Alexander Maloof

6559-A	The Sheik	Mal 227(12")
6560-A	America Ya Hilwa-Pt. 1	Mal 225(12")
6561	America Ya Hilwa-Pt. 2	Mal 225(12")
6562	La Matshishe	Mal 227(12")
6562-A	Ghandoora	Mal (12")
8339-A	Pharaoh {Tut-Ankh-Amen}-Egyptian Fox Trot (Maloof)	Ge 5192
8340, -A	Egyptian Glide-Tango Orientale (Maloof)	Ge 5192
8341-A	Ruins Of Balbaak-Valse Orientale (A. Maloof)	Mal
	own p, unk sop sax, cl/ten sax, bells, percussion, vo	

NY April 25, 1923

Ge 5192 as MALOOF AND HIS ORIENTAL ORCH.

| 8381 | Arabian Dance (Maloof) | Mal |
| 8382-A | Hammedieh March (Maloof) | Mal |

NY May 23, 1923

8490-B	Valse Oriental (A. Maloof)	Mal
8491-A	Egyptiana (A. Maloof)	Mal
8492-A	Salome's Dance (A. Maloof)	Mal
8493-A	Echoes Of Luxor (A. Maloof)	Mal
	d P. Floridia	NY August 29, 1923

| 8524-A | The Robin's Serenade (A. Maloof) | Mal |
| 8525 | Adeste Fideles (A. Maloof) | Mal |

NY September 17, 1923

Maloof Band

8813	The Desert Wail-Oriental Cradle Song (A. Maloof)	Mal 7001
8814-A	A Trip To Syria (A. Maloof)	Mal 7001
8815-A	Kurdistan (A. Maloof)	Mal
8816-A	On the Beautiful Nile (A. Maloof)	Mal

NY April 1, 1924

Maloof Trio.

6781	Grecian March	Mal (12")
6782	Medley No. 1	Mal (12")
8975-A	Bashraf	Mal
8976	Dacka	Mal
8977	Doolab	Mal
8978	Medley No. 2	Mal
		NY July 1, 1924

Alexander Maloof

6887	Al-Jazayer	Mal (12")
6888	A Trip To Syria	Mal (12")
		NY March 1925

Maloof's Oriental Orchestra

BVE 34618-1	Call Of The Sphinx-Oriental Waltz (A. Maloof)	Vi 78627
BVE 34619-1	The Desert Wail-Berceuse Oriental (A. Maloof)	Vi 78628
BVE 34620-3	Egyptiana-Oriental Fox Trot (A. Maloof)	Vi 78627
	Somali	Vi 32680
BVE 34621-1	On The Beautiful Nile (A. Maloof)	Vi rej
BVE 34622-2	Kurdistan-Danse Orientale (A. Maloof)	Vi 78628
	2 c, vln, fl, o, sax, vc, tb, p, bj, tuba, traps	
		NY February 15, 1926

Vi 32680 as ORQUESTA ORIENTAL

Alexander Maloof

GEX 2903, N 18545 Abide With Me	Ge 500, Ch 16390, Superior 2796	
GEX 2904-A, N 18546 Nearer My God To Thee	Ge 500, Ch 16390, Superior 2796	
GEX 2905, N 18547 Rock Of Ages	Ge 501	
GEX 2906, N 18548 Jesus Lover Of My Soul	Ge 501	
GEX 2907-A, N 18549 Softly And Tenderly	Ge 502	
GEX 2908, N 18550 Beautiful Isle Of Somewhere	Ge 502	
GEX 2909 Valse Lente	Ge	
GEX 2910 Valse D'Amore	Ge	
GEX 2911 Arabian Shepherd Song	Mal	
GEX 2912 Bashraf	Mal	
pipe org	NY January 1932	

Matrices GEX 2909-10 are marked "for skating rink" in the Gennett files. Ge 502 is uncredited; other issues may be also. Gennett's 500 series were called "chapel transcriptions" and seem to have been intended for use in funeral parlors. Matrices N 18545-50 are studio transfers of the originals.

GEX 2952	God Be With You Till We Meet Again	Ge

```
GEX 2953     My Faith Looks Up To Thee                          Ge
             as before                               NY  June 1932
```

GEX 2953 was the last Gennett matrix made in New York.

23.19. N. Marak *spoken*

```
M 0111-2     Al Sulha 'Ind Al-Khuri-Pt. 1               Mal 400
M 0112-1     Al Sulha 'Ind Al-Khuri-Pt. 2               Mal 400
             male, female voices                       NY  1922
```


23.20. Maria-Lisme *oud*

The identification of this performer is tentative.

```
4371         Scale-first the open strings, then the scale up and down  LC 14741B5
                            Columbian Exposition, Chicago  September 25, 1893
```

LC 14741 is a tape reel on which the original cylinder has been copied.

23.21. Edma Marrache *vocal*

```
100-1        Ya Ouzib Elmershef                     Marrache 100
107-1        Ahob Geyrak                            Marrache 106
             orch d Samy Ashwa                         NY  1920s
```

The above are coupled.

23.22. Andrew Mekanna *vocal*

```
             Lasamto Sagra Azooly-Pt. 1         Macksoud 1000(12")
             Lasamto Sagra Azooly-Pt. 2         Macksoud 1000(12")
             Ya Raab El Ali Shlom               Macksoud 1018(12")
             Nahmo Kawad Keman El Harb          Macksoud 1318(12")
             Naeem Karacand-vln, unk oud            NY  1920s
```

Macksoud 1018 and 1318 are coupled.

23.23. Toufic Moubaid *oud*

```
6721         Takseem Bayat                          Mal  (12")
6722         Takseem Rast                           Mal  (12")
                                              NY  February 1924
```

```
W 205914-2   The Original Algerian March[1]      Co 50002-X(12")
W 205915-2   Bachraf Moubaid[1]                  Co 50002-X(12")
W 205916-1   Takseem Nahat Wand                  Co 50004-X(12")
W 205917-    Takseem Bayat                       Co 50004-X(12")
             [1]Elizabeth Awad-p                    NY  May 1928
```

W 206103-2	Tahmely Hedjab	Co 50007-X(12")
W 206104-2	Daka Wa Nisef	Co 50009-X(12")
W 206105-	Bachraf Bader	Co 50007-X(12")
W 206106-2	Kedivial March	Co 50009-X(12")
	Elizabeth Awad-p	NY December 1928

23.24. Prince Mouhidin *oud*

Martin Schwartz observes that, though the following were isssued as Arabic recordings, spellings and general repertoire are derived from Turkish sources.

6839	Takseem Hejaz	Mal (12")
6840	Takseem Ashak	Mal (12")
9262	Somai-Pt. 1	Mal
9263	Somai-Pt. 2	Mal
9264-A	Running Child	Mal
9265	Caprice Orientale	Mal
		NY January 5, 1925

6877	Takseem Nahawand	Mal (12")
6878	title untraced	Mal (12")
		NY February 1925

6894	Rasid	Mal (12")
6895	Seya	Mal (12")
6896	Kurdi	Mal (12")
6897	Seba	Mal (12")
6898	Ayam	Mal (12")
		NY March 1925

6909	Bashraf	Mal (12")
6910	Samsee	Mal (12")
		NY April 1925

Prince Muhuiddin

W 108208-	Sekah Semai	Co 12-X
W 108209-1	Huzzam Takseem	Co 12-X
W 108210-1	Joguk Havasi; Capricio	Co 13-X
W 108211-2	Kurdili Hijaskar Peshrev	Co 13-X
		NY August 1927

Prince Mohiuddin

W 109262-2	Hedjas Saz Semaissi	Co 20-X
W 109263-2	Hejdaskiar Kurdu Saz Semaissi	Co 20-X
W 109264-2	Nechabourek Saz Semaissi	Co 28-X
W 109265-1	Nechabourek Taxim	Co 28-X
		NY May 1928

Columbia 28-X as PRINCE HOHIUDDIN

W 109972-2	Husseini Saz Semaissi (Tatios)	Co 25-X
W 109973-1	Ferhahfeza Saz Semaissi	Co 45-X
W 109974-2	Ouschak Perchev	Co 37-X
W 109975-3	Chet Araban Saz Semaissi (Jemil Bey)	Co 25-X
W 109976-1	Ouschak Taxim	Co 37-X
W 109977-1	Hedjaz Taxim	Co 45-X
		NY November 1928

23.25. Murad *vocal*

6783	Hawid Min Hina-Pt. 1	Mal (12")
6784	Hawid Min Hina-Pt. 2	Mal (12")
6785	Masria-Pt. 1	Mal (12")
6786	Masria-Pt. 2	Mal (12")
6787	Ya Ward-Pt. 1	Mal (12")
6788	Ya Ward-Pt. 2	Mal (12")
		NY September 1924

6789	Wyack Ya Gazal-Pt. 1	Mal (12")
6790	Wyack Ya Gazal-Pt. 2	Mal (12")
6791	Mowal-Pt. 1	Mal (12")
6792	Mowal-Pt. 2	Mal (12")
		NY October 1924

6814	Ya Meet Masa-Pt. 1	Mal (12")
6815	Ya Meet Masa-Pt. 2	Mal (12")
6816	Bo Kashakish-Pt. 1	Mal (12")
6817	Bo Kashakish-Pt. 2	Mal (12")
		NY November 1924

This artist may be the same as the following.

23.26. Mayer Murad *tenor*

W 206062-1	Ya Na Waem Na Tefah-Pt. 1	Co 50005-X(12")
W 206063-2	Ya Na Waem Na Tefah-Pt. 2	Co 50005-X(12")
		NY October 1928

W 206169-	El Abyadini-Pt. 1	Co 50008-X(12")
W 206170-1	El Abyadini-Pt. 2	Co 50008-X(12")
W 206171-	Taxim Layaly-Pt. 1	Co 50011-X(12")
W 206172-	Taxim Layaly-Pt. 2	Co 50011-X(12")
		NY February 1929

23.27. Sayeg *vocal*

6704	Malick Ya Nayna	Mal (12")
6705	Gawahir Il Hosin	Mal (12")
6706	Amaron Itha Fackarto	Mal (12")
6707	Sharibto Kasa'l Hawa	Mal (12")
6708	Aneeri Makan Badri-Pt. 1	Mal (12")

| 6709 | Aneeri Makan Badri-Pt. 2 | Mal (12") |
| | | NY February 1924 |

6727	Taffah-Pt. 1	Mal (12")
6728	Taffah-Pt. 2	Mal (12")
6729	Fatakato Lahzik-Pt. 1	Mal (12")
6730	Fatakato Lahzik-Pt. 2	Mal (12")
		NY March 1924

23.28. Jamile Sayik *vocal*

58177A-1	Alla Akbar-Moudun Song-Pt. 1	Co E3543
58177B-1	Alla Akbar-Moudun Song-Pt. 2	Co E3543
58178A-1	Acher Surete-Religious Song-Pt. 1	Co E3542
58178B-1	Acher Surete-Religious Song-Pt. 2	Co E3542
	unaccompanied	NY ca April 1917

23.29. Abdul Selim *tenor*

85973-3	Ghaire Ala-Pt. 1	Co E4659
85974-2	Ghaire Ala-Pt. 2	Co E4659
	Fatakat-Pt. 1	Co E4773
	Fatakat-Pt. 2	Co E4773
		NY February 1920

23.30. Serbagi *vocal*

6639-B	Shamay Za Shamay	Mal (12")
6640-A	Rigoletto: Ahzirol Nissa-Act 3	Mal (12")
6641	Ya Shamka	Mal (12")
6642	Yallah-Ya-Habeebi Niskar	Mal (12")
6643	Khadahooka-Pt. 1	Mal (12")
6644	Khadahooka-Pt. 2	Mal (12")
6645	Jalto-Ilykil Hawa-Pt. 1	Mal (12")
6646	Jalto-Ilykil Hawa-Pt. 2	Mal (12")
6647	Salamon-Ala-Ma Assalat-Pt. 1	Mal (12")
6648	Salamon-Ala-Ma Assalat-Pt. 2	Mal (12")
6649	Tarakato-Habeeba-Pt. 1	Mal (12")
6650	Tarakato-Habeeba-Pt. 2	Mal (12")
6651	Zak Zak Il Asfoor-Pt. 1	Mal (12")
6652	Zak Zak Il Asfoor-Pt. 2	Mal (12")
		NY June 1923

6857	Bassara-Pt. 1	Mal (12")
6858	Bassara-Pt. 2	Mal (12")
6859	Nigamatal Layl-Pt. 1	Mal (12")
6860	Nigamatal Layl-Pt. 2	Mal (12")
6861	Fatan-Pt. 1	Mal (12")
6862	Fatan-Pt. 2	Mal (12")
		NY January 1925

6863	Sooria-Pt. 1		Mal (12")
6864	Sooria-Pt. 2		Mal (12")
6865	Ya Baity-Pt. 1		Mal (12")
6866	Ya Baity-Pt. 2		Mal (12")
6867	Bihi Seron-Pt. 1		Mal (12")
6868	Bihi Seron-Pt. 2		Mal (12")
6871	Shemam Hawa-Pt. 1		Mal (12")
6872	Shemam Hawa-Pt. 2		Mal (12")
6873	Bakeeto Shahabi-Pt. 1		Mal (12")
6874	Bakeeto Shahabi-Pt. 2		Mal (12")
6875	Karam-Pt. 1		Mal (12")
6876	Karam-Pt. 2		Mal (12")
		NY	February 1925

23.31. Shamheel

9179	Be Dammi-Pt. 1		Mal rej
9180	Be Dammi-Pt. 2		Mal rej
		NY	November 10, 1924

23.32. Kaziha Shaptini *vocal*

Pshalteemi

X 8564-A	Automobile Story-Pt. 1		Mal
X 8565	Automobile Story-Pt. 2		Mal
		NY	October 22, 1923

A. Shaptini

6671	Ya Ulil Fadl-Pt. 1		Mal 803(12")
6672	Ya Ulil Fadl-Pt. 2		Mal 803(12")
		NY	October 1923

6673-A	Azkurini		Mal (12")
6676	Laura-Pt. 1		Mal (12")
6677	Laura-Pt. 2		Mal (12")
6680-A	Ya Nassom		Mal (12")
		NY	November 1923

6681	Oumi Ya Oumi		Mal (12")
6682	Kuliah Nahsu Nasseebi		Mal (12")
6683-A	Wa Habeebi, Wa Habeebi		Mal 812(12")
6684	Ahaqalbi Kathib (Knashiba)		Mal 811(12")
8627	Oumo Rochoo (Maloof)		Mal
8628	Marhaban		Mal
	orch	NY	November 27, 1923

Maloof 811 and 812 are coupled.

6685	Rozana		Mal (12")
6686	Barhoom		Mal (12")

6687	Lahlahli	Mal (12")
6688	Asfoori	Mal (12")
8638	Ya Mnagrashi (Maloof)	Mal
8639-A	Ezoobia	Mal
	fl, p	NY December 3, 1923

6689	Tbaat Salami	Mal (12")
6690	Yilhaklik-Shakel-Elmaz	Mal (12")
6691-A	Ahwal-Gazal	Mal (12")
6692	Low-Kinta-Dari	Mal (12")
6693-A	Khaherooka	Mal (12")
6694	Jabal Lebnan	Mal (12")
6695	title untraced	Mal (12")
		NY ca January 1924

6710	Ghayri Alal Salwan-Pt. 1	Mal (12")
6711	Ghayri Alal Salwan-Pt. 2	Mal (12")
6716	Bagdadi Ferack Zaman	Mal (12")
6717	Bagdadi Oum Mazih	Mal (12")
6718	Alaba Prtyooni Kazain Massir	Mal (12")
6719	Alaba Ya Nahee	Mal (12")
6725	Bananas	Mal (12")
6726	Bagdadi [in English]	Mal (12")
		NY February 1924

6731	Ya Gameel Ya Nagaf	Mal (12")
6732	Bani Watani	Mal (12")
6733	Allah Hindia	Mal 835(12")
6734	Bali Maak	Mal 834(12")
		NY March 1924

Maloof 834 and 835 are coupled.

6749	O Sole Mio	Mal (12")
6750-A	Mobile	Mal (12")
		NY April 1924

23.33. Malakie Al-Sheich Dahood (Margaret Dahoud) *vocal*

CVE 49042-1	Zabyetah Al {Zabyeta El Onsee}-Pt. 1	Vi 9300(12")
CVE 49043-2	Zabyetah Al {Zabyeta El Onsee}-Pt. 2	Vi 9300(12")
CVE 49044-2	Inneey Marartoo Be {Nasheed} {While Passing Through A Meadow}-Pt. 1	
		Vi 9301(12")
CVE 49045-2	Inneey Marartoo Be {Nasheed} {While Passing Through A Meadow}-Pt. 2	
		Vi 9301(12")
	Prof. Obyad-oud	NY January 4, 1929

23.34. Assad Simon *tenor*

43802-1	Ana Shah Rassi	Co E2837
43803-1	Manazel Khullati	Co E2837
	Kubr-In-Naffs	Co E2838

Zaino Zaino   Co E2838
oud, kanun   NY ca March 1916

23.35. George Simon *tenor*

B 29555-2   Zourooni Bel-Sena Marra {Visit Me Once A Year}
             (Mohammed Asman)-Pt. 1   Vi 77586
B 29556-1   Zourooni Bel-Sena Marra {Visit Me Once A Year}
             (Mohammed Asman)-Pt. 2   Vi 77586
B 29557-2   Balade And Balade {My Country} (G. Simon)   Vi rej
B 29558-1   Asmor Louin {I Like The Dark Girl}   Vi rej
             with chorus, vln, oud   NY February 28, 1924

23.36. Nahum Simon *tenor*

This artist's first name is also given as Nahem, Nahen, Nathem, or simply as N.

39962-1   Himnoo Alalyases El Miskeen-Pt. 1   Co E2332
39963-1   Himnoo Alalyases El Miskeen-Pt. 2   Co E2332
39964-1   Lialee Sultan Jamalak-Pt. 1   Co E2333
39965-1   Lialee Sultan Jamalak-Pt. 2   Co E2333
39966-1   Henyena Ia Hnaina-Pt. 1   Co E2334
39967-1   Henyena Ia Hnaina-Pt. 2   Co E2334
           vln, g   NY March 18, 1915

39968-1   Muskin Hali El Ghareeb   Co E2335
39969-1   Zallat Altana   Co E2335
39970-1   Salamon Ala Abren-Pt. 1   Co E2336
39971-1   Salamon Ala Abren-Pt. 2   Co E2336
           as before   NY March 19, 1915

46009-1   Waddahtoha-Pt. 1   Co E2732
46010-1   Waddahtoha-Pt. 2   Co E2732
46011-1   In Kana Men Zanben Da Hakee-Pt. 1   Co E2733
46013-1   In Kana Men Zanben Da Hakee-Pt. 2   Co E2733
46014-1   Salamon Ala Husnen {Juliet}-Pt. 1   Co E2730
46015-1   Salamon Ala Husnen {Juliet}-Pt. 2   Co E2730
46016-1   Salamon Ala Husnen {Juliet}-Pt. 3   Co E2731
46017-1   Salamon Ala Husnen {Juliet}-Pt. 4   Co E2731
           "Turkish string instruments"   NY September 10, 1915

46024-1   Mawwal Libnan-Pt. 1   Co E2734
46025-1   Mawwal Libnan-Pt. 2   Co E2734
           as before   NY September 14, 1915

46026-1   Mowal Youssef Bey Karan-Pt. 1   Co E2735
46027-1   Mowal Youssef Bey Karan-Pt. 2   Co E2735
46028-1   title untraced   Co rej
           as before   NY September 15, 1915

44081-1   Ashti-Eshtibaky-No. 1   Co E2948
44082-2   Ashti-Eshtibaky-No. 2   Co E2948

	Loan-Elhawagib-No. 1	Co E2947
	Loan-Elhawagib-No. 2	Co E2947
	Bagdadi-Li Damaton Liddima	Co E2954
	Ataba-Hibabi Nazlatte	Co E2954
	oud	NY June 1916
B 18484-1	En Kounto Belgaish-Pt. 1	Vi 69106
B 18485-1	En Kounto Belgaish-Pt. 2	Vi 69106
B 18486-2	Tahayart-Pt. 1'	Vi 69105
B 18487-1	Tahayart-Pt. 2'	Vi 69105
B 18488-1	Al Rosana'	Vi 69104
B 18489-1	Lama Rekebena'	Vi 69104
	kanun, 'vln, oud	NY October 5, 1916
B 18835-1	Mattet Shahidat-Pt. 1	Vi 69194
B 18836-1	Mattet Shahidat-Pt. 2	Vi 69194
B 18837-1	Bent El-Shalabia-Pt. 1'	Vi 69195
B 18838-1	Bent El-Shalabia-Pt. 2'	Vi 69195
B 18839-1	Kalby Youhadossony-Pt. 1	Vi 69196
B 18840-1	Kalby Youhadossony-Pt. 2	Vi 69196
B 18841-1	Nalet Ala Yadeha-Pt. 1	Vi 69197
B 18842-1	Nalet Ala Yadeha-Pt. 2	Vi 69197
B 18843-1	Ga-At Moohazibaty-Pt. 1	Vi 69198
B 18844-1	Ga-At Moohazibaty-Pt. 2	Vi 69198
B 18845-1	Saly El-Nejoom-Pt. 1	Vi 69199
B 18846-1	Saly El-Nejoom-Pt. 2	Vi 69199
B 18847-1	Atait El-Habebat-Pt. 1	Vi 69200
B 18848-1	Atait El-Habebat-Pt. 2	Vi 69200
	vln, oud, kanun, 'chorus by group	NY December 13, 1916
	Nar Ellaza Asha-Bagdadi	Co E2981
	Sadraha Marj Waseh-Ataba	Co E2981
	An Nob An Nob	Co E3062
	Kom Wastameh	Co E3062
	Ghazaltooha Fe Junhi-Pt. 1	Co E3198
	Ghazaltooha Fe Junhi-Pt. 2	Co E3198
	Zainot Iaboz-Zalof-Pt. 1	Co E3265
	Zainot Iaboz-Zalof-Pt. 2	Co E3265
	Iah Migana-Pt. 1	Co E3266
	Iah Migana-Pt. 2	Co E3266
	Ouhibou Min Ajlikom-Pt. 1	Co E3428
	Ouhibou Min Ajlikom-Pt. 2	Co E3428
	Jaat Tamisson-Pt. 1	Co E3429
	Jaat Tamisson-Pt. 2	Co E3429
	Belahi Iah Sadaty-Pt. 1	Co E3544
	Belahi Iah Sadaty-Pt. 2	Co E3544
	Ain Ellatti Aw Hanat-Pt. 1	Co E3600
	Ain Ellatti Aw Hanat-Pt. 2	Co E3600
		NY 1916-7
B 25498-1	Ya Raheb Eldair-Pt. 1	Vi 73329
B 25499-1	Ya Raheb Eldair-Pt. 2	Vi 73329
B 25600-1	Ya Lailo Elsabo-Pt. 1	Vi 73328

B 25601-1	Ya Lailo Elsabo-Pt. 2	Vi 73328
	vln, oud, kanun	NY September 10, 1921
B 25603-2	Rannat Bekhilkhalaha (The Tinkle Of The Anklets)	Vi 73149
B 25604-1	Ataba El Halawa	Vi rej
B 25605-1	Lee Madmaan	Vi rej
B 25606-1	Talabna Min Eleh Elarech (I Prayed To God)	Vi 73149
	vln, kanun	NY September 13, 1921
B 31497-1	Azzebene Fersauf (Torture Me)-Pt. 1	Vi 77934
B 31498-2	Azzebene Fersauf (Torture Me)-Pt. 2	Vi 77934
B 31499-2	Alaya Ayuhal Oushak-Pt. 1	Vi 78008
B 31501-2	Alaya Ayuhal Oushak-Pt. 2	Vi 78008
B 31502-2	Dere Balakia Bnaya-Pt. 1	Vi rej
B 31503-2	Dere Balakia Bnaya-Pt. 2	Vi rej
	oud, kanun	NY December 10, 1924
C 32954-1	Kefabeatlal Salma-Pt. 1	Vi 68708(12")
C 32955-1	Kefabeatlal Salma-Pt. 2	Vi 68708(12")
	own oud, unk kanun	NY July 14, 1925
W 175270-1	test recording	Co
		NY January 18, 1927
W 175669	test recording	Co
		NY ca May 1928
W 205895-2	Halamou Beanni-Pt. 1	Co 50000-X(12")
W 205896-1	Halamou Beanni-Pt. 2	Co 50000-X(12")
W 205897-1	Deeri Balik-Pt. 1	Co 50001-X(12")
W 205898-2	Deeri Balik-Pt. 2	Co 50001-X(12")
W 205899-2	Kaam Baathna-Pt. 1	Co 50003-X(12")
W 205900-2	Kaam Baathna-Pt. 2	Co 50003-X(12")
	Sam Romey-vln, Toufic Moubaid-oud	NY May 1928
W 175883	test recording	Co
		NY October 16, 1928
CVE 48466-2	Nazareth-Pt. 1	Vi V-75000(12")
CVE 48467-2	Nazareth-Pt. 2	Vi V-75000(12")
CVE 48468-2	Sarirokey-Pt. 1	Vi V-75001(12")
CVE 48469-1	Sarirokey-Pt. 2	Vi V-75001(12")
	as before	NY December 14, 1928

23.37. Constantine Souse *tenor*

	Syrian Song	Vi trial
	oud	NY June 2, 1917
B 20720-1	Ana El Sabab-Pt. 1	Vi 69769
B 20721-1	Ana El Sabab-Pt. 2	Vi 69769
B 20722-1	Al Yadi Yadi-Pt. 1	Vi 69826
B 20723-1	Al Yadi Yadi-Pt. 2	Vi 69826

B 20724-1	Boulboul Naga-Pt. 1	Vi 69768
B 20725-1	Boulboul Naga-Pt. 2	Vi 69768
B 20726-1	El Yom Ya Badre	Vi rej
B 20727-1	Wallazi Wallak	Vi rej
B 20728-1	Ya Mayola Al Gossoun	Vi rej
B 20729-1	Saraksi Goson	Vi rej
B 20730-1	Arak Asseyeh El Dameh-Pt. 1	Vi 72743
B 20731-1	Arak Asseyeh El Dameh-Pt. 2	Vi 72743

Naeem Karacand-vln, Abraham Halaby-oud, Shehadi Ashkar-kanun

NY October 8, 1917

B 20739-1	Rahna Nesid-Bagdadi	Vi 69770
B 20740-1	Marmar Zamani	Vi 69770
B 20741-2	Addi Mahobak-Pt. 1	Vi 69825
B 20742-1	Addi Mahobak-Pt. 2	Vi 69825
B 20743-1	Daleel El Hob {Cupid Rules My Heart}-Pt. 1	Vi 73053
B 20744-1	Daleel El Hob {Cupid Rules My Heart}-Pt. 2	Vi 73053
B 20745-1	Ana El Garam-Pt. 1	Vi 72554
B 20746-1	Ana El Garam-Pt. 2	Vi 72554
B 20747-1	Ana El Garam-Pt. 3	Vi 72639
B 20748-1	Ana El Garam-Pt. 4	Vi 72639
B 20749-1	Ana El Gassad-Pt. 1 {Taksim Lalayli}	Vi 72912
B 20750-1	Ana El Gassad-Pt. 2	Vi 72912

as before   NY October 10, 1917

Constantine Sooss

85206-1	Zainat Ya Hoz Zolof-Pt. 1	Co E4434
85207-1	Zainat Ya Hoz Zolof-Pt. 2	Co E4434

NY May 1919

85276-	Ya Beent Ainek-Pt. 1	Co E4774
85277-	Ya Beent Ainek-Pt. 2	Co E4774

NY ca June 1919

	Ma Koont Koolt-Pt. 1	Co E4303
	Ma Koont Koolt-Pt. 2	Co E4303
	Kholy El Aszar-Pt. 1	Co E4490
	Kholy El Aszar-Pt. 2	Co E4490

NY 1919

85977-	Ya Maleeh Al Lama-Pt. 1	Co E4602
85978-	Ya Maleeh Al Lama-Pt. 2	Co E4602
85980-1	Ya Man Gharamack-Bagdadi-Pt. 1	Co E4603
85981-1	Ya Man Gharamack-Bagdadi-Pt. 2	Co E4603
85982-	Ala Ayouha-Pt. 1	Co E7082
85983-	Ala Ayouha-Pt. 2	Co E7082

vln, kanun   NY ca February 1920

C. Souss

8313	Ya Meet Masa-Pt. 1	Mal
8314-A	Ya Meet Masa-Pt. 2	Mal
8315	Michjata'l Sab-Pt. 1	Mal

8316   Michjata'l Sab-Pt. 2   Mal
                                                      NY April 4, 1923

23.38. Syrian Band

44074-   Kadive March   Co E3013
44076-1   Kom Wastameh   Co E3063
44077-   Lake Ettassebih   Co E3013
44078-1   In Kane Baddek Taslack   Co E3063
                                                      NY ca June 1916

23.39. Unknown Pianist

4370   Piano Solo   LC 14741B4
                        Columbian Exposition, Chicago September 25, 1893

LC 14741B4 is a tape reel on which the original cylinder has been copied.

23.40. Uknown Spoken

301   Vocal School In Zaleh By Egyptian Artist' Macksoud unnumbered (12")
302   Faddous & Dorothy {Comic Telephone} [in English and Arabic]
                                                 Macksoud unnumbered (12")
              monolog or 'dialog   NY early 1920s

23.41. Unknown Vocal

36976-1   Om Feeldoga-Pt. 1   Co E5062(12")
36977-1   Om Feeldoga-Pt. 2   Co E5062(12")
              vln   NY May 1914

23.42. Evangelist Andrew D. Urshan *vocal*

L 378-   Sacred Medley   WG U-502
L 379-   Sweet Rays Of Light   WG U-502
              H.E. Haney-p, Wesley Eyres-g   Grafton, WI 1930

23.43. Violin, Canon, Oud And Tambourine

85216-1   Ghazabieh-Pt. 1   Co E4304
85217-1   Ghazabieh-Pt. 2   Co E4304
              probably Naeem Karacand-vln, unk oud, kanun, tam   NY ca May 1919

23.44. Louis Wardiny *tenor*

              Badri Ader Kass   Vi trial
              vln, oud   NY March 14, 1917

B 19799-1	Haje Elgaram		Vi 69471
B 19900-2	Hagarny Habibi		Vi 69471
B 19901-1	El Ozoubiah-Pt. 1		Vi 69610
B 19902-1	El Ozoubiah-Pt. 2		Vi 69610
B 19903-1	Ya Mnagrashi-Pt. 1		Vi 69609
B 19904-1	Ya Mnagrashi-Pt. 2		Vi 69609
B 19905-1	Dondorma		Vi 69470
B 19906-1	Dari Man Tahwa		Vi 69470
B 19907-1	Labat Salamy		Vi 69608
B 19908-1	Gazalaton Agbalat-Bagdadi		Vi 69608
B 19909-1	Ya Zain Tetbah Halak-Bagdadi		Vi 69469
B 19910-1	Yekfa Bena Yazaman-Bagdadi		Vi 69469
	vln, oud, kanun	NY May 16, 1917	
M 427-1	Shams-Il-Shimousi-Pt. 1		Mal 5005
M 428-1	Shams-Il-Shimousi-Pt. 1		Mal 5005
M 437	Zoorooni-Pt. 1		Mal 5009
M 438	Zoorooni-Pt. 1		Mal 5009
	vln, oud, kanun, small cho	NY 1921	
M 461	Walie Menal Gorami (arr Alexander Maloof)-Pt. 1		Mal 6000
M 462	Walie Menal Gorami (arr Alexander Maloof)-Pt. 1		Mal 6000
M 463	Tay Gae-Pt. 1'		Mal 6001
M 464	Tay Gae-Pt. 1'		Mal 6001
	vln, ten sax, p, small cho, oud or 'xyl	NY 1922	
M 465	Ya Malil Sham-Pt. 1		Mal 6002
M 466	Ya Malil Sham-Pt. 2		Mal 6002
M 467	Soorya Alwatan-Pt. 1		Mal 6003
M 468	Soorya Alwatan-Pt. 2		Mal 6003
	Alexander Maloof-p, unk vln, oud small cho	NY 1922	
M 504	Ya Mariya-Pt. 1		Mal 6005
M 505	Ya Mariya-Pt. 2		Mal 6005
	fl, p, oud, d Munid Wakrul	NY 1922	
6653	Ya Rabrabi		Mal (12")
6654	Adeste Fideles-Pt. 1		Mal (12")
6655	Adeste Fideles-Pt. 2		Mal (12")
6656	Ya Ayni (A. Maloof)-Pt. 1		Mal 6008(12")
6657	Ya Ayni (A. Maloof)-Pt. 2		Mal 6008(12")
6658-A	Ya Boab		Mal (12")
	orch	NY July 1923	
6795-A	Hakeeni Bil Telephone-Pt. 1		Mal (12")
6796-A	Hakeeni Bil Telephone-Pt. 2		Mal (12")
6799	Shamis Il Shoumousy		Mal (12")
6800	Sooria		Mal (12")
6801	Zooroomi		Mal (12")
6802	Bol Zelof		Mal (12")
6803-A	Okalbu Oumi-Pt. 1		Mal (12")
6804-A	Okalbu Oumi-Pt. 2		Mal (12")
6805	Tay Jay		Mal (12")

| 6806 | Ya Malil Sham | Mal (12")
NY October 1924 |

6820	Ya Banat-Pt. 1	Mal (12")
6821	Ya Banat-Pt. 2	Mal (12")
6822-A	Shanta-Pt. 1	Mal (12")
6823	Shanta-Pt. 2	Mal (12") NY November 1924

6841	Takseem Layali	Mal (12")
6842	Mowal	Mal (12")
6843	Habeebi Gab-Pt. 1	Mal (12")
6844	Habeebi Gab-Pt. 2	Mal (12")
6845	Mali Malo	Mal (12")
6846	Rishna Miswar	Mal (12") NY January 1925

| 6879 | Yasmin | Mal (12") |
| 6880 | Rahil Alameen | Mal (12")
NY February 1925 |

| 6889 | Racka Unsin-Pt. 1 | Mal (12") |
| 6890 | Racka Unsin-Pt. 2 | Mal (12")
NY March 1925 |

Louis Wardini

| | Haleeshy Kola Mourra | AJM 920A |
| | Ya Kalti Abi Jarah | AJM 1020A
NY 1920s |

The above are coupled.

Louis Wardiny

	Ya Meet Massa-Pt. 1	AJM 1216(12")
	Ya Meet Massa-Pt. 2	AJM 1216(12")
	Zaynat Ya Bouzolof-Pt. 1	AJM 1316(12")
	Zaynat Ya Bouzolof-Pt. 2	AJM 1316(12")
	Souriya Ya Helwa-Pt. 1	AJM 1320(12")
	Souriya Ya Helwa-Pt. 2	AJM 1320(12")
	Naeem Karacand-vln, unk oud	NY 1920s

Louis Warding

M 506	Bol-Zelof-Pt. 1	Newphone 505
M 507	Bol-Zelof-Pt. 2	Newphone 505
	fl, cym	NY 1920s

23.45.   Al-Zahir *tenor*

37224-1	Nasseem Es Soba-Pt. 1	Co E5111(12")
37225-1	Nasseem Es Soba-Pt. 2	Co E5111(12")
	Naeem Karacand-vln	NY March 1915

23.46.   M. Zaineldeen *tenor*

44509-3	Tair An Nia-Bagdadi-Pt. 1	Co E3431
44510-3	Tair An Nia-Bagdadi-Pt. 2	Co E3431
	Khafaratt-Pt. 1	Co E3123
	Khafaratt-Pt. 2	Co E3123
	Lagi Ala Addarr-Pt. 1	Co E3124
	Lagi Ala Addarr-Pt. 2	Co E3124
	Ya Rakiban	Co E3199
	Biabi Ajfan	Co E3199
	Ramatin Soulaima-Pt. 1	Co E3264
	Ramatin Soulaima-Pt. 2	Co E3264
	Allahu Akbar-Pt. 1[1]	Co E3383
	Allahu Akbar-Pt. 2[1]	Co E3383
	vln, kanun, [1]probably unaccompanied	NY ca December 1916

SECTION 24. ARMENIAN

24.1. Sh**on Arslen *tenor*

W 205715-3	Atemee Baghladem	Co 71005-F(12")
W 205717-2	Kurdi	Co 71000-F(12")
W 205720-2	Diarbekir Divan	Co 71001-F(12")
	Stephan Simonian & Co.: vln, cym, dumbeg	NY ca November 1927

24.2. Jack Aslanian *violin*

AFS 4245A1	Armenian Soldiers' March[2] [3] [4]	LC
AFS 4245A2	Tuning	LC
AFS 4245B1	Song Of Freedom[2] [3] [4]	LC
AFS 4244A1	Camel's Caravan[1] [2] [3] [4]	LC
AFS 4244B1	Three Dances[2]	LC
	own vln/[1]vo, [2]Mesroub Takakjian-cl, [3]Archie Krotlian-oud, [4]Bedros Haroutunian-kanun	Fresno, CA April 23, 1939

The above are listed in the order they were recorded.

24.3. Ruben J. Baboyan *vocal*

AFS 4234A1	Kélé-Kélé-Dance Song	LC
AFS 4234A2	Ham Gül Ham Vart {Both Rose And Narcissus}-Dance Song [in Turkish and Armenian]	LC
AFS 4234B1	Yes Saren Gukiji {As I Came From The Hill}	LC
AFS 4234B2	Alagaz Bartzer Sare {Alagaz Mountain}	LC
AFS 4235A1	Yar Ounei {I Had A Sweetheart}-Soldier's Song	LC
AFS 4235A2	Googen Ara {I Took The Earthen Jar To The Well}	LC
AFS 4235B1	Inchoo Bingól Medar {Why Did You Enter Bingol?}-Dance Song	LC
AFS 4235B2	Godou {Bird's Song}	LC
AFS 4236A1	Alagaz {Alagaz Mountain}	LC
AFS 4236B1	Mogatz Mirza {Lament For Mogatz Mirza}	LC
AFS 4236B2	Dele Yaman	LC
AFS 4237A1	Hey Nazanem {Those Coy Darlings}-Dance Song	LC LBC-6(33)
AFS 4237A2	Yayloughs {The Kerchief}-Dance Song	LC
AFS 4237B1	Andooni {The Homeless}-Orphan's Song	LC
AFS 4237B2	Erivan Baghem Arer {I've Kissed At Erivan}	LC
		Fresno, CA April 16, 1939

24.4. Hosrof Bagraduni *vocal*

BVE 34267-1	Dule Yaman	Vi 78538
BVE 34268-2	Siroon Ahtchig (A. Tigranian)	Vi 78538
BVE 34269-2	Duee Duee! (R. Melikian)	Vi rej
	orch d Bruno Reibold	NY January 11, 1926

BVE 34269-5	Duee Duee! (R. Melikian)	Vi 78541
BVE 34508-1	Whyry Zaghig (R. Melikian)	Vi 78541
BVE 34509-3	Im Chenary Yaru (Gomidas Vartabed)	Vi 78621
	as before	NY January 28, 1926

BVE 34927-1	Vart {Rose} (R. Melikian)	Vi 78645
BVE 34928-3	Vertchin Vart {Last Rose} (Sarkisian)	Vi 78645
BVE 34929-3	America High Aghchigner {U.S. Armenian Girls} (Hosrof Bagraduni)	
		Vi 78621
	as before	NY March 2, 1926

W 108229-2	Hovivi Erku	Co 28002-F
W 108230-2	Ambern Egan	Co 28003-F
W 108231-2	Barza Sarer-Operatic Song	Co 28002-F
W 108232-2	Siretzi Yars Daran	Co 28004-F
W 108233-2	Sev Gakavig	Co 28003-F
W 108234-2	Hokis Murmoor	Co 28004-F
		NY ca August 1928

24.5. John Barberian *vocal*

This artist also played the oud, though none is evident here. His name is also spelled BERBERIAN.

Z 244	Nerdefandan	Margosian's 63
Z 258	Der-Zor	Margosian's 63
	Vartan Margosian-vln, Bogos Boghosian-kanun	NY early 1920s

24.6. Joe Bedrosian *zourna*

AFS 4241A1	Tuning	LC
AFS 4241A2	Yankee Doodle	LC
AFS 4241A3	Mountains Of Ezeroum	LC
AFS 4241B1	Turkish March	LC
AFS 4241B2	Daki-Tezlana	LC
		Fresno, CA April 24, 1939

24.7. Hachik Berberian *vocal*

W 111961-1	Barsir Ahpuir	Co 28023-F
W 111962-1	To Pecge Kamin	Co 28023-F
W 111963-2	Badme Inzi Hayrenikian	Co 28024-F

W 111964-1   Zinvor Ganchtesin Darin   Co 28024-F
               Oriental Orchestra   NY April 1930

24.8. Torcom Bézazian *baritone*

39812-1   Voh, Intch Anouche (H. Simanian)   Co E2296
39813-1   Dalvorig (H. Simanian)   Co E2296
39814-1   Pandargialy (Effendi Faltis)   Co E2297
            orch   NY February 2, 1915

39817-1   Nor-Oror   Co E2297
39818-1   Pamp Vorodan (H. Simanian)   Co E2298
39819-1   Arig Haigazounnk (H. Simanian)   Co E2298
39820-1   I Puir Trainitz   Co rej
            orch   NY February 5, 1915

39925-1   Mesrobian-Hymne   Co
39926-1   Ai Varte   Co
            orch   NY March 9, 1915

39944-2   La Marseillaise (De L'Isle) [in French]   Co rej
39945-1   Le Rêve Passé (Helmeret Krier) [in French]   Co E2323, E2454
            band   NY March 13, 1915

39820-2   I Puir Trainitz   Co
            orch   NY March 19, 1915

45670-   Hayasdan   Co
            orch   NY May 21, 1915

39944-3   La Marseillaise (De L'Isle) [in French]   Co E2322
45700-1   Le Régiment De Sambre Et Meuse (R. Planquette) [in French] Co E2453
45701-1   Le Chant Du Départ (Mehul) [in French]   Co E2453
45702-1   Les Gars De La Marne (P. Letombe) [in French]   Co E2454
45703-1   Chantons L'Amour (R. Desmoulins) [in French]   Co E2452
            band   NY May 26, 1915

45815-1   Oublions Le Passé (Dickson) [in French]   Co E2452
            orch   NY June 23, 1915

46037-1   Pensée D'Automne (Massenet) [in French]   Co E2577
46038-1   Toujours Toi [in French]   Co E2743
            orch   NY September 20, 1915

46082-2   La Chanson De Martha (Gustave Chiron) [in French]   Co E2691
            orch   NY October 6, 1915

B 16704-1   Boulanger March {En Revenant De La Revue} (Henry Duprato)
               [in French]   Vi 67542
B 16705-2   Mon Soldat (Louis Payette) [in French]   Vi 67537
B 16706-2   Marche Du Triomphe (L. Cailliet) [in French]   Vi 67542
B 16707-2   La Bataille (L. Cailliet) [in French]   Vi 67537
            orch d Walter B. Rogers   NY October 21, 1915

46180-2	La Bataille (L. Cailliet) [in French]		Co E2690
46181-1	Mon Soldat (L. Payette) [in French]		Co E2691
	orch	NY	November 6, 1915

43575-1	Chargez! (Merelly) [in French]	Co E2690
43619-3	Le Roi Héros-Monologue [in French]	Co E2741
43668-	Le Crucifix (Faure)' [in French]	Co E3210
43676-1	Le Beau Rêve [in French]	Co E2743
43678-1	Leretz Ambéren (Faltis Eff.)	Co E2793
43679-1	Mair Araxi (H. Simanian)	Co E2793
43693-1	Fauvette (Remi Lormes) [in French]	Co E2742
43694-1	Vieux-Tu Savoir (Remi Lormes) [in French]	Co E2742
43695-1	Le Clairon: Chant Du Soldat (E. André) [in French]	Co E2741
43698-	Les Vieux Priseurs' [in French]	Co E3210
	'with Tadeusz Wroński	NY 1915-6

43734-1	Phrynette [in French]		Co E2794
43735-1	Quand Tu M'Amais [in French]		Co E2794
43752-1	Hardi Les Gars [in French]		Co E2795
43753-	Marche Boulanger {En Revenant De La Revue} (Dupramo) [in French]		
			Co E2795
43799-	Le Dernier Tango-Chanson Argentine (Doloire) [in French]		Co E3211
43800-	Quand Les Papillons (Vercolier) [in French]		Co E3211
		NY	March 1916

B 18462-2	Pamp Vorodan-March (arr H. Simanian)		Vi rej
B 18463-2	Nor Oror (K. Proft-Kalfaian)		Vi 69102
	King's Orchestra	NY	September 26, 1916

B 18462-3	Pamp Vorodan-March (arr H. Simanian)		Vi 69102
B 18603-2	Chargez (Louis Niallo'h-Ch. Merelly) [in French]		Vi 69129
	as before	NY	October 11, 1916

| B 18615-2 | La Marseillaise (de L'Isle) [in French] | | Vi rej |
| | as before | NY | October 18, 1916 |

| B 18615-4 | La Marseillaise (de L'Isle) [in French] | | Vi 69129 |
| | as before | NY | October 24, 1916 |

B 18804-2	Arik Haygazounk (H. Simanian)		Vi 69202
B 18805-3	I Piur Tzainitz (H. Simanian)		Vi 69202
B 18806-3	Dalvorig (H. Simanian)		Vi 69189
	as before	NY	December 6, 1916

B 18824-2	Loussine Ga (V. Faltis Eff.)		Vi 69201
B 18825-1	Voh Intch Anouche (H. Simanian)		Vi 69190
B 18826-2	Dzovague (V. Faltis Eff.)		Vi 69190
B 18827-1	Hayasdan (V. Faltis Eff.)		Vi 69189
	as before	NY	December 8, 1916

B 18850-2	Té Tév Ounéi (arr Edna White)		Vi 69201
B 18851-2	Haratch Entenank (arr Edna White)		Vi 69207
	as before	NY	December 14, 1916

```
B 18859-1    La Marseillaise (de L'Isle) [in Armenian]             Vi 69207
             as before                                 NY  December 20, 1916

B 18864-2    Gardons Notre Amour Pour Le Retour Des Vainqueurs
             {Keep The Home Fires Burning} (R. Brisson-Ivor Novello)
             [in French]                                           Vi 17705
B 18865-2    Katcheri Bar (arr V. Faltis Eff.)                     Vi 69208
B 18866-2    Leretzi Amberen (arr V. Faltis Eff.)                  Vi 69208
             as before                                 NY  December 21, 1916

B 19007-2    Le Crédo Du Paysan (G. Goublier) [in French]          Vi 69270
B 19008-3    Le Clairon (Émile André) [in French]                  Vi 69270
B 19009-2    Le Rêve Passé (Armand Foucher-Ch. Helmer-G. Krier) [in French]
                                                                   Vi rej
             as before                                 NY  January 4, 1917

B 19009-4    Le Rêve Passé (Armand Foucher-Ch. Helmer-G. Krier) [in French]
                                                                   Vi 69278
B 19059-2    Rosalie (Theodore Botrel) [in French]                 Vi 69272
B 19060-2    La Française (Miguel Zamacois-Camille Saint-Saens) [in French]
                                                                   Vi 69278
B 19061-1    Groung (K. Proff-Kalfaian)                            Vi 69325
             as before                                 NY  January 18, 1917

B 19204-1    Pandarguiale Ar Dzidzernag (arr V. Faltis Eff.)       Vi 69325
             as before                                 NY  February 20, 1917

44638-       Haratch Entanank                                      Co E3458
44639-       Katchéri Bar                                          Co E3458
44706-       Pamp Vorodan (H. Simanian)                            Co E2298
44707-2      Marche Du Triomphe (Cailler) [in French]              Co E3702
44708-2      La Française-Chanson Marche [in French]               Co E3452
44709-1      Gardons Notre Amour Pour Le Rétour Des Vainqueurs-Chanson Marche
             [in French]                                           Co E3452
44734-2      Ne Touchez Pas Á La France (Jules De Bouliel) [in French]  Co E3702
                                                 NY  February-March 1917

B 19253-2    Le Dernier Tango-Chanson Argentine (A. Foucher-E. Doloire)
             [in French]                                           Vi rej
B 19254-3    Quand Les Papillons (R. Gael-J. Vercolier) [in French]   Vi rej
             King's Orchestra                          NY  March 8, 1917

B 19253-3    Le Dernier Tango-Chanson Argentine (A. Foucher-E. Doloire)
             [in French]                                           Vi 69347
B 19254-5    Quand Les Papillons (R. Gael-J. Vercolier) [in French]   Vi 69347
B 19407-1    Fleurettes De Trianon (Andre Piedallu-Henry Fevrier) [in French]
                                                                   Vi 69488
             as before                                 NY  March 22, 1917

B 19723-2    Le Roi Héros (X. Granier) [in French]                 Vi 69488
             as before                                 NY  April 30, 1917
```

B 19977-2	Aimons-Nous (C. Saint-Saens) [in French]	Vi 77936
B 19978-1	Désir D'Amour (C. Saint-Saens) [in French]	Vi rej
	as before	NY June 6, 1917
B 19978-4	Désir D'Amour (C. Saint-Saens) [in French]	Vi 77936
	as before	NY November 28, 1917
85090-1	Noël De Déliverance-Patriotic Christmas Song [in French]	Co E4324
85091-1-2	Tu Renaîtras' [in French]	Co E4324
	Edna White-tp, unk org	NY ca April 1919
85105-2	Quand Madelon-March Song [in French]	Co E4323, 34262-F
85107-1-2	La Madelon De La Victoire-Patriotic Song' [in French]	
		Co E4323, 34262-F
	orch, 'including Edna White-sop	NY April 1919
B 22756-1	Tu Renaîtras (T. Dronchat) [in French]	Vi 72377
	Nathaniel Shilkret-org	NY May 1, 1919
B 22757-3	Noël De Déliverance (T. Dronchat) [in French]	Vi 72377
	as before	NY May 2, 1919
85275-1	Aimer' [in French]	Co E4523
85290-1-3	Les Cent Vierges [in French]	Co E4523
	orch, 'including Edna White-sop	NY ca June 1919
59568-2	Barbiere Di Siviglia: Place Au Factotum [in French]	Co E5191(12")
59571-	Carmen: Chanson Du Toréador (Bizet) [in French]	Co E5191(12")
59572-	Benvenuto: Arioso (Díaz) [in French]	Co E5192(12")
59591-	Faust: Invocation [in French]	Co E5192(12")
	orch	NY ca July 1919
7121	Se Vous L'Aviez Compris! (Denza) [in French]	Ed rej
	orch	NY January 19, 1920
7125	La Chanson De Martha (Chiron) [in French]	Ed rej
	orch	NY January 21, 1920
7130	Les Cent Vierges-Vals Chantée (Lecocq) [in French]	
		Ed 74015, 27192(4 min)
	orch	NY January 26, 1920
7133	Quand Les Papillons (Vercolier) [in French]	Ed 74012, 27193(4 min)
	orch	NY January 28, 1920
7121	Se Vous L'Aviez Compris! (Denza) [in French]	Ed 74013, 27203(4 min)
7125	La Chanson De Martha (Chiron) [in French]	Ed 74012, 27195(4 min)
7139	Le Dernier Tango-Chanson Argentine (Doloire) [in French]	
		Ed 74014, 27197(4 min)
7140	Aimons-Nous (St. Saens) [in French]	Ed 74015, 27202(4 min)
	orch	NY January 30, 1920

7191	Manon: A Quoi Bon L'Économie? {What's The Good Of Economy?} (Massenet) [in French] orch	Ed 82214 NY March 1, 1920	

7191   Manon: A Quoi Bon L'Économie? {What's The Good Of Economy?}
                (Massenet) [in French]   Ed 82214
     orch   NY March 1, 1920

7201   Lakmé: Stances (Délibes) [in French]   Ed 82210
     orch   NY March 8, 1920

7268   Hamlet: Chanson Bachique (Thomas) [in French]   Ed 82203
     orch   NY April 6, 1920

7310   Aimer [in French]   Ed rej
     orch   NY April 21, 1920

7321   Ce N'est Pas Vrai (Mattei) [in French]   Ed rej
     orch   NY April 26, 1920

7334   Le Moulin De Maître-Jean {Master John's Mill} (w: Bertal-Marnois,
               m: Ch. Borel-Clerc) [in French]   Ed 58022, 27196(4 min)
     orch   NY April 30, 1920

7310   Aimer [in French]   Ed 74014
7321   Ce N'est Pas Vrai (Mattei) [in French]   Ed 74013, 27194(4 min)
     orch   NY May 24, 1920

86902-2   Tashnagtzagan Ghoump   Co E7083, 28021-F
86903-2   Antranig   Co E7083, 28021-F
                                       NY December 1920

87007-   Santa Maria (J. Faure) [in French]   Co E7043
87009-   Élégie (Massenet) [in French]   Co E7043
     orch with Edna White-tp   NY January 1921

87732-1   Cherie [in French]   Co E7383
87737-2   Le Loup De Mer [in French]   Co E7382
87738-2   Peggy O'Neil [in French]   Co E7383
87739-1-2   Le Carillonneur (Daniderff) [in French]   Co E7382
87740-   La Ou Le Misssissippi {Where The Mississippi Flows} [in French]
                                                   Co E7384
87741-   Lisou-Lisette (Borel-Clerc) [in French]   Co E7384
     orch   NY September 1921

24.9. E. Boghosian *vocal*

319   Gnig Goozem   Ph P550
320   Harsin Douvin   Ph P550
321   Ardems Knatz Pjishkin   Ph P549
322   Pessan Zokamchin Kove   Ph P549
VB 324   Namaget Ari   Ph P553
VB 326   High Yeridasartner   Ph P553
     vln, oud, p, d Gulazian   NY ca 1927

24.10. Vahan Boyajian *vocal*

89571-2	Darelmadja Yiuk-Canto [in Turkish]	Co 32000-F
89572-1	Martinim Oumouzoumda-Canto [in Turkish]	Co 32000-F
89573-1	Neva Gazel [in Turkish]	Co 32001-F
89574-1	Telegrafin Telerine [in Turkish]	Co 32001-F
	cl, oud	NY ca December 1923

A 0025-1	Derzor Desdanaci	Bilbil 2
A 0026-1	Georgina Shirki (Damdan Deuslidin Dalgaleniyorim}	Bilbil 2
	vln, oud	NY early 1920s

A 0027-1	Jurjina Sharki	Bilbil 4
A 0028-1	Gazel	Bilbil 4
	vln, kanun	NY early 1920s

A 0031-1	Germeyenge Saba Idemen-Gargeghar Canto'	Bilbil 6
A 0032-1	Sayillim Geldim Kapoona-Rast Gazel	Bilbil 6
	vln, 'oud	NY early 1920s

Bilbil was the singer's own label.

W 205721-1	Bayisi Berbademy-Rast Canto [in Turkish]	Co 75020-F(12")
W 205722-2	Tatly Tatly Sezlerine-Huzam Canto [in Turkish]	Co 75017-F(12")
W 205723-1	Bahtse Douvarene Achdim-Duyek Charki [in Turkish]	Co 75020-F(12")
W 205724-1	Debrely Hasan-Jourgina Charki [in Turkish]	Co 75016-F(12")
W 205725-1	Bir Gulin Meftouneyem-Garib Hijaz Gazel [in Turkish]	Co 75017-F(12")
W 205726-2	Dideden Chekmez Hayalin-Nihavend Gazel [in Turkish]	Co 75016-F(12")
	as before	NY ca December 1927

24.11. A. Chah-Mouradian *tenor (1878-1939)*

Some issues spell this name as SHAH-MOURADIAN.

	Krisdos Badarakial; Hindoo Song	Vi trial
	Edward T. King-p	NY June 19, 1916

58297-1	Hayasdan-National Song	Co E3459, 28014-F
58298-2	Pam Porodan-National Song	Co E3459, 28014-F
58299-2	Mayr Araksie-National Song	Co E3460, 28015-F
58300-2	Sirouhis	Co E3460, 28015-F
58315-1	Hishestsouk-Kisheri-Religious Song	Co E3506, 28016-F
58316-1	Krisdos Badarakyal-Religious Song	Co E3461, 28019-F
58317-1	Amen Hayr Sourp-Religious Song	Co E3461, 28019-F
58318-2	Ourakh Ler-Religious Song	Co E3506, 28016-F
		NY May 1917

58645-1	Kele Kele	Co E4201, 28020-F
58646-1	Gantche Groung	Co E3929, 28022-F
59542-2	Aror Dadrak	Co E5175(12")
59543-2	Andouni	Co E5175(12")
		NY 1917

84315-2	Alagez, Khungi Dzar	Co E3929, 28022-F
84316-2	Goujn Ara, Kina Kina	Co E4201, 28020-F
84341-1	Hov Arek	Co E4009, 28018-F
84342-2	Giligia	Co E4009, 28018-F
	vln, vc, p	NY April 1918

171-1	Ov Zarmanali (Komitas Wardapet)	ACM 1
172-1	Nor Alagiaz (V. Servantsdiantz)	ACM 2
173-1	Dele Yaman (V. Servantsdiantz)	ACM 2
174-1	Yes Saren Gookai (Komitas Wardapet)	ACM 1
	vln, fl, p	NY ca 1926

24.12. M. Douzjian *vocal*

160A-2	Anarad Aghchig	MGP 530, Ph 530
161A-2	Hokvov Siretzi	MGP 530, Ph 530
		NY 1920s

101	Shad Anoush'	Ph 561, Yeldez 301
102	Neshanvadz Degha'	Ph 561, Yeldez 301
103	High Aghchig'	Ph 562
104	Hura! Hura!'	Ph 562
105	Kizem Sona Alayim-Canto	Ph 563
106	Kalpageny Eymishin-Canto	Ph 563
307	Kurd Havassi [in Kurdish]	Ph P545
308	Yandi Djanim	Ph P545
379	Aman Aman Maritza'	Ph 564
380	Ah Im Aghvor Meg Hadik'	Ph 564
385-1	Toumboulik Aghchik'	Ph P569
387-1	Sevoulik Manchour'	Ph P569
	vln, 'oud	NY ca 1927

Pharos 564 as M. DUZJIAN

24.13. Nouart Dzeron-Koshkarian *vocal*

B 23619-2	Aletcharchar {Like A Wave Tossed Ship} (Proff Kalfaian)'	Vi rej
B 23620-3	Groung {The Crane} (Komitas Vartabed)	Vi 78666
	fl, vc, p or 'org	NY January 9, 1920

B 24038-2	Manir-Manir Im Jakharag {Chant Du Rouet}	Vi 72727
	vln, vc, p	NY May 6, 1920

B 24050-1	Gnatz Ashoon, Yegav Garoune (K. Boyajian)	Vi 72727
	orch d Nathaniel Shilkret	NY May 11, 1920

B 24299-2	Jan Gulum {Jeanne Guillin} {Violet Song} {My Adorable} (arr K. Boyajian)	Vi 78666
	King's Orchestra	NY September 30, 1920

24.14. Rev. S.K. Emurian *vocal*

1-2	The Lord's Prayer [in English]	Special unnumbered
2-2	The Lord's Prayer [in Armenian]	Special unnumbered
	p	Chicago(?) early 1920s

Label note: Rodeheaver Record Company, Chicago

24.15. Mary Goshtigian *vocal, oud*

AFS 4238A1	Kirgus Dan Maral Ahtchik {I Take Maral In My Arms}	LC
AFS 4238A2	Tuning And Modal Scale	LC
AFS 4238B	Heliné {Helene}	LC
AFS 4239A	Taksim And Sha'ki [no vo]	LC
AFS 4239B	Taksim And Sha'ki¹	LC
	¹Hargop Goshtigian-vln	Fresno, CA April 17, 1939

24.16. Music By Gulazian's

382-1	Havouz Bashi	Ph P568
388-1	Highgagan Bar¹	Ph P568
	vln, oud, vc, p, or ¹vln, oud, dumbeg	NY ca 1927

24.17. Bedros Haroutunian *instrumental*

AFS 4242A1	Tuning; Taksim; Wedding Dance	LC
AFS 4242B	Keri Yerk	LC
AFS 4243A1	Solo¹	LC
AFS 4243A2	Tuning On Open Strings¹	LC
AFS 4243B1	Tuning-Complete Scale¹	LC
	kemancha or ¹kanun solos	Fresno, CA April 22, 1939

File note: [The kemancha is] a knee fiddle with 4 strings and 4 sympathetic strings.

24.18. Kaspar Janjanian *vocal*

175-A	Harpootun Yazelary-Harpoot Havissi (Janjanian)	Yeprad 1000
176	Maya (Janjanian)	Yeprad 1000
	K. Geljookian & Co	NY 1920s

24.19. H. Karagosian *vocal, dumbeg*

Z2	Kashlarun Inja Inja	Margosian's 30
	Vartan Margosian-vln	NY early 1920s

24.20. A. Kevorkian *vocal*

W 110266-2	Gigo	Co 28009-F
W 110267-1	March Of Antranig	Co 28009-F
W 110268-2	Shivari	Co 28010-F
W 110269-1	Telephone Arnem	Co 28010-F
	Mesroub Takakjian-cl, unk vln, oud	Los Angeles January 1929

Kevorkian & Co.

RA 1145	Areve Dzakets	Rec-Art 1938
RA 1148	Ounkeri Gamari Bes	Rec-Art 1938
	vln, cl, dm	Los Angeles(?) 1930s

24.21. Koushnarian's Orchestra

109-1	Arshin Mal Alan: Selection (Act 3)	So 5
113-2	Arshin Mal Alan: Shamili Bari	Ph 7
		NY 1920s

24.22. Alice Kurkjian *soprano*

W 106134-2	Karoon {Spring}	Co 28001-F
W 106135-4	Mair Araxe	Co 28000-F
W 106136-2	Vart {The Rose} (R. Melekian)	Co 28000-F
W 106137-2	Haistan-Patriotic Song	Co 28001-F
	orch	NY December 1925

24.23. S. Maghalian *vocal*

154-1	Bar Dance And Chors [no vo]	So 24
155-1	Ay Khanoum, Khanoum	So 24
	vln, tar, dumbeg	NY early 1920s

24.24. Vartan Margosian *vocal, violin*

	Te Hairenyats	A&T 5
	Emyeress	A&T 17-A
		NY early 1920s

The above are coupled.

ZA	Karpoot Govandi [no vo]	Margosian's 21
ZB	Boo Daghlar Koryet	Margosian's 21
ZE	Ateme Baghadem	Margosian's 23
ZF	Dertli Kerem [in Turkish]	Margosian's 23
ZL	Hayoon Voshre'	Margosian's 27
ZM	Teran Arghev Noush Gella	Margosian's 27
ZP	Aghchig Serma Mazert	Margosian's 29

ZQ	Boyed Neman Er Marmare	Margosian's 29
ZT	Trumpa Caproosee	Margosian's 31
ZU	Aman Doctor [in Turkish]	Margosian's 30
ZV	Bayala Kash; Bashirin	Margosian's 31
ZY	Yarem Sizlar	Margosian's 2
	Karpoot Mayasee	Margosian's 22
	Galammi Yar	Margosian's 22
	own vo/vln, H. Karagosian-dumbeg or ¹unaccompanied	NY early 1920s
Z 208	Hay Aghchig	Margosian's 37
Z 214	Bardezrt Vartere	Margosian's 37
	cl, oud	NY early 1920s
Z 234	Karpoot Mayasi	Margosian's 2
	own vo, K. Takakjian-cl	NY early 1920s
Z 251	title untraced	Margosian's 5
	own vo, John Barberian-oud, Bogos Boghosian-kanun	NY early 1920s
Z 254	title untraced	Margosian's 5
	own vo, unk cl, dumbeg	NY early 1920s
Z 265	Aravod Looso	Margosian's 52
Z 266	Asek Shinafor¹	Margosian's 52
	own vo/vln, H. Karagosian-dumbeg or ¹unaccompanied	NY early 1920s
Z 274	Koonede Artuncer²	Margosian's 50
Z 275	Me-Haranar¹ ³	Margosian's 50
	own vo/¹vln, ²John Barberian-oud, ³Bogos Boghosian-kanun, H.	
	Karagosian-dumbeg	NY early 1920s
Z 294	Karpooton Yazulari [in Turkish]	Margosian's 3
Z 295	title untraced	Margosian's 1
Z 296	Kasook Mayasee [in Turkish]	Margosian's 7
	own vo, D. Perperian-cl, Bogos Boghosian-kanun, H. Karagosian-dumbeg	
		NY early 1920s

Margosian's 3 and 00 (by D. PERPERIAN) are coupled.

143-1	Mer Khentzorin Dzar	So 16
	own vo/vln, unk cl, oud	NY 1920s
195-3	Sheg Mazerover¹	So 37
196-1	An Ko Achgeret	So 37
	own vo/vln, unk oud, ¹cl	NY 1920s
311	Shirvany	Ph P546
315	Darsim	Ph P546
	own vo, Stepan & Haigaz-vln, p (it is not known who plays which)	
		NY 1920s

24.25. Garabet Merjanian *tenor, oud*

Merdjian Garabet, Eff.

58754-	Isvahan Sharki Sendemi Halea [in Turkish]	Co E3744
58755-1	Shevkinle Hayalin [in Turkish]	Co E3785
58769-2	Kesinin Baghlari {Atma, Anam} [in Turkish]	Co E3785
58770-1	Bulbul Olsam [in Turkish]	Co E4696
59521-	Halima [in Turkish]	Co E5168(12")
59527-2	Nenny-Tchifte Telli Ghazel [in Turkish]	Co E5168(12")
	Kemany Minas-vln, unk kanun	NY November 1917

Garabet Merjanian

W 205808-2	Surmeli Canto [in Turkish]	Co 75019-F(12")
W 205810-1	Ges Kisheroon	Co 71002-F(12")
W 205811-1	Yeni Nenni [in Turkish]	Co 75019-F(12")
W 205813-2	Loosin Tchikar	Co 71002-F(12")
	Ay Koon, Ay Koon	Co 71003-F(12")
	Yar Ouneyi	Co 71003-F(12")
	Te Hayrenyatz	Co 71004-F(12")
	Ayriin Voghpe	Co 71004-F(12")
	Nishan Sedefjian-vln, S. Mostitsian-oud	NY February 1928

24.26. Zabella Panosian *soprano*

This artist's first name is also spelled ZABELLE.

58167-3	Caroun	Co E3505
58168-	Der Getso	Co E3504
58169-	Mir Khor Babge Kerezman	Co E3504
58171-5-7	Groung	Co E3503, 28017-F
58172-4-5	Im Sireli Zavagounks	Co E3503, 28017-F
	vln, p	NY ca April 1917

58359-4	Tzain Dour Ov Dzovag	Co E3505
		NY 1917

84457-2	Mi Lar Pibool'	Co E4202, E4660
84458-1	Khavarel Yem	Co E4010
84463-2	La Perle De Brasil: Charmant Oiseau [in French]	Co E4660
84465-1	Togh Tcherke Blbool	Co E4010
	Kilikia	Co E4202
	orch or 'vln, vc, p	NY June 1918

24.27. Helen Paul *soprano*

84274-	Tzanie Hentchetz	Co E4661
84275-	Mer Hairenik	Co E4661
		NY April 1918

24.28. D. Perperian *clarinet*

Z 291	Arabker Havasee	Margosian's 000
Z 292	Tamzara	Margosian's 7
Z 293	Jezaier	Margosian's 00
	Bogos Boghosian-kanun, H. Karagosian-oud	NY early 1920s

Margosian's 00 and 3 (by VARTAN MARGOSIAN) are coupled.

24.29. Karekin Proodian *tenor*

43719-	Kurd Havasy-Pt. 1 [in Turkish]	Co E2841
	Nihavend-Canto [in Turkish]	Co E2786
	Oglan Yayly-Canto [in Turkish]	Co E2786
	Hijaz Gazel [in Turkish]	Co E2842
	oud, kanun	NY February 1916
44021-1	Mushkil Imish-Hidjaz Sharki [in Turkish]	Co E3064
44022-1	Sharab Itchdim-Hidjaz Canto [in Turkish]	Co E3064
44023-	Iprev Ardziv {Song To Antranig}'	Co E3065
44024	Sevdim Gazel-Canto' [in Turkish]	Co E3065
44027-	Mahmour Bakishin' [in Turkish]	Co E3067
44028-1	Felik Nitchin Keydin-Saba Canto' [in Turkish]	Co E3067
44161-1	Chifta Telly Canto' [in Turkish]	Co E3127
44163-1	Chifta Telly Gazel' [in Turkish]	Co E3127
	Kiaghedkhané Zemane-Canto' [in Turkish]	Co E3066
	Nérdé Benim Shivekarem' [in Turkish]	Co E3066
	fl, kanun, or 'unk	NY 1916
B 18807-1	Ghitdy Ghenchlik-Rast Sharky [in Turkish]	Vi 69174
B 18808-2	Kakidhana Zemany-Ooshak Canto [in Turkish]	Vi 69173
B 18809-1	Felek Bana-Saba Canto [in Turkish]	Vi 69175
B 18810-1	Pek Juda Duchdim-Husseiny Sharky [in Turkish]	Vi 69176
B 18811-1	Iftilahy Derdi Ashkin-Hijaz Sharky [in Turkish]	Vi 69177
B 18812-2	Dayanilmion Daktor-Neva Canto [in Turkish]	Vi 69178
	Kemany Minas-vln, Morene Eff.-oud, Hagop-kanun	NY December 6, 1916
	Chiefta Tally [in Turkish]	Vi trial
	oud	NY December 5, 1921
31-1	Hasagt Partsr	MGP 1
	Hasaguet Partzer	Ph 501
32-1	Akh Atsn Glorig Manche	MGP 1
	Guelorig Manche	Ph 501
	Hovsep Shamlian-oud, unk kanun	NY 1920s
103A-1	Khal Ellim	MGP 503, Ph 503
103B-1	Gamavor Zenvor	MGP 502, Ph 502
104A-1	Keriyin Yerke	MGP 503, Ph 503
104B-1	Ouy Janem	MGP 502, Ph 502
125A-1	Mazer Ounis Shahmaran	MGP 519, Ph 519
126A-1	Tzerkis Kenaren	MGP 519, Ph 519

127A-1	Akh Anoush	MGP 520, Ph 520
128A-1	Vartanoush	MGP 520, Ph 520
160-1	Shirazle Kantose	Oriental 207
161-1	Shinanam Kantose	Oriental 207
	vln, oud	NY 1920s

24.30. Riza Bey *vocal*

136-A	Felekden Hijazkiar Kurdi Sharki	MGP 523, Ph 523
137-A	Geschdi Hayalem-Suzinak Canto	MGP 523, Ph 523
		NY 1920s

24.31. Maksoud Sariyan (Karakash) *vocal, oud*

| Z 223 | Tamzara [no vo] | Margosian's 42 |
| | M. Paraskevos-vln | NY 1920s |

Margosian's 42 as M.S. KARAKASH

| Z 228 | Hairenikis Siroon | Margosian's 47 |
| | Vartan Margosian-vln, K. Takakjian-cl | NY early 1920s |

142-A	Aman Minosh-Hijaz Canto [in Turkish]	MGP 526, Oriental 209, Ph 526
143-A	Nehmem-Oushak Canto [in Turkish]	MGP 526, Oriental 209, Ph 526
	unk vln	NY 1920s

24.32. Miss H. Sarkisian & Vartan Margosian *vocal*

| Z 235 | Door Yaylooghes | Margosian's 47 |
| | K. Takakjian-cl, Maksoud Sariyan (Karakash)-oud | NY early 1920s |

24.33. George Shah-Baronian *tar*

190-1	Ouzoun Dara Dance	So 33
192-1	Yetim Segya[1]	So 33
332-	Russian Rag-Fox Trot	Ph 559
333-A	Romance	Ph 559
	[1]with vo	NY 1920s

24.34. Hovsep Shamlian *vocal, oud*

144-1	Sona Yar	So 17
146-1	Degha Degha Char Degha	So 17
	vln	NY early 1920s

| 1006-1 | Manni | Shamlian unnumbered |
| | vln | NY 1927 |

```
1008-          Inch Anem                                          Shamlian unnumbered
1010-          Yegour Balas                                       Shamlian unnumbered
               vln, fl, dumbeg                                             NY   1927

1015-1         Le Yaman-Khempagan Bar                             Shamlian unnumbered
               nai (flute), dumbeg                                         NY   1927

1018-A         Bala Jan                                           Shamlian unnumbered
1020-A         Gananch Daleneret Siren                            Shamlian unnumbered
               vln, dumbeg                                                 NY   1929
```

Couplings use matrices 1006/1015, 1008/1010 and 1018/1020.

24.35. Mrs. Siranoosh Shapazian *vocal*

```
AFS 4265B3     Tsakig, Makig {The Gosling}                                      LC
AFS 4266A1     Vairy Zagig {Wild Flower}                                        LC
AFS 4266A2     Nashkoon Gakavig {Coloured Dove}                                 LC
AFS 4266A3     Karoon Agav {The Spring Came}                                    LC
AFS 4266A4     Mangig Ev Turtchnig {Boys And The Bird}-Children's Game Song     LC
                                              Fowler, CA   October 30, 1939
```

24.36. Vartan S. Shapazian *vocal*

```
AFS 4265A1     Aror, Aror {Plough, Plough}                                      LC
AFS 4265A2     Sevga Kavig {Black Dove}                                         LC
AFS 4265B1     Jan Jan Sarer {Dear Mountain}                                    LC
AFS 4265B2     Golkozi Atchik {Girl Of The Kolghoz}                             LC
AFS 4266B1     Groong Jan {Messenger Swallow}                                   LC
AFS 4266B2     Derzor Chollerenda {Armenian Exiles In The Desert Of Derzor}
               [in Turkish]                                                     LC
                                              Fowler, CA   October 30, 1939
```

24.37. T. Shatinian *kavoll (syrinx)*

```
AFS 4240A1     Yerp Alaygutz {Escape By Sea From The Turks}                     LC
AFS 4240A2     Solo                                                            LC
AFS 4241A4     Tuning, Open and Chromatic Scales                                LC
                                              Fresno, CA   April 24, 1939
```

24.38. Stephan Simonian & Co. *instrumental*

```
W 205716-2     Almaya Daldan Aldem                             Co 71005-F(12")
W 205718-2     Hale Makam                                      Co 71000-F(12")
W 205719-1     Haygagan Makam                                  Co 71001-F(12")
               vln, cym, dumbeg                           NY  ca November 1927
```

24.39. Mrs. S. Siroonian *vocal*

Z 272	Eanash Dam	Margosian's 33
Z 273	Aslan Yarem	Margosian's 33
	probably: Vartan Margosian-vln, John Barberian-oud, Bogos	
	Boghosian-kanun	NY 1920s

24.40. Mr. Sourapian *vocal*

102-2	Arshin Mal Alan	So 2
103-1	Arshin Mal Alan	So 2
104-2	Arshin Mal Alan	So 4
	orch d Prof. Koushnarian	NY early 1920s

"Arshin Mal Alan" is an opera.

119-2	Yar Ouneyi	So 9
	vln, p	NY early 1920s

24.41. Mrs. Sourapian *soprano*

101-2	Arshin Mal Alan: Selection (Act 3)	So 5
107-1	Arshin Mal Alan: Selection (Act 2)	So 1
108-2	Arshin Mal Alan: Selection	So 4
	orch d Prof. Koushnarian	NY early 1920s

122-2	Yerevan Bagh Em Arel	So 9
	p	NY early 1920s

24.42. Sourapian Duet *vocal*

106-2	Arshin Mal Alan: Selection (Act 1)	So 1
115-2	Arshin Mal Alan: Pogh Ounis, Ha! Ha!	So 7
	orch d Prof. Koushnarian	NY early 1920s

24.43. Mesroub Takakjian *clarinet*

AFS 4240B1	The Dark Clouds; Caucasian Folk Dance	LC
		Fresno, CA April 23, 1939

24.44. M.O.S. Tashjian *tenor*

4100-1	Him...Llerenk, Lretz A... (Keep Silence For Awhile)	Co E529
		NY 1909

24.45. Tashjian Brothers *vocal duet*

4954-1	Mir Heyrenik (S. Shah Azizian)	Co E658
4964-1	Tartsial Paylitz-Fedayi Yeraze	Co E658
4971-1	Aznif Ungert (S. Shah Azizian)	Co E661
4973-1	Menk Bedk E Gurvink-Fedayi Yeraze	Co E661
	tp, vln, p	NY ca July 1910

24.46. Unknown Vocal, Instrumental

	Verkerov Li	Ph 551
	Antranik (Iprev Ardziv)	Ph 551
	Markahednin Mech	Ph 552
	Katzek Dessek	Ph 552
	Hampertzoum Yaila	Ph 557
	Lejin Mech Navage	Ph 557
	Genige	Ph 558
	Telli Yarim	Ph 558
	Varte	So 10
	Oror Nazigin	So 10
	Sinetzi Yares Daran	So 12
	Intz Vor Hartzenes Genga	So 12
	Dele Yaman	So 23
	God Ou Gess	So 23
	Kini Litz Akhber	So 25
	Aghchig Mi Heranar	So 25
	Oghi Da	So 28
	Vosgi Areve	So 28
	Yerevantzi	So 29
	Ararayi Zinvore	So 29
	High Aghchig	So 38
	Zov Kisher	So 38
		NY 1920s

24.47. S. Vartian *tenor*

142-1	Jahel Em Gnig Chunim	So 16
	vln, cl, oud	NY 1920s

SECTION 25. PERSIAN

25.1. J. Alexander *vocal*

W 111302-1	Salanebam Gidan Dilbar	
W 111303-2	Achildy Tarlalar	
	tar	

Co 42006-F
Co 42006-F
Chicago   December 1929

25.2. **Muresa Daniels** *soprano*

Shahimis Boyurobter[1]
Tabrisdan Chikhanda[1]
Khamta Najeb
Bkha M'Nyomany
Npilee Lara
Urmee-Urmee
[1]with J. Alexander And S. More Co.

Co 42008-F
Co 42008-F
Co 82000-F(12")
Co 82000-F(12")
Co 82001-F(12")
Co 82001-F(12")
Chicago   ca December 1929

According to Martin Schwartz, the 10" Columbias are both sung in Azari, an Azerbaijani Turkish dialect. The 12" Columbias are in Assyrian (Neo-Aramaic or Neo-Syriac), the language of Christians from Azerbaijan in Northwest Iran. The following is sung in genuine Persian.

25.3. **Haroot Maroot** *vocal*

431	Tasnif Aloo-Aloo	
432	Tasnif Ma Digar	
	George Shah-Baronian-tar	

Ph 000(12")
Ph 000(12")
NY   1920s

SECTION 26. TURKISH

26.1. Marko Melkon Alemsherian *vocal, oud*

Marko Melkon

129-A	Endamin-Huzam Sharky	MGP 516, Ph 516
	Endamen Hayalin	MGP 536, Ph 536
303-A	Karib-Hijaz Taksim	MGP 516, Ph 516
	vln	NY 1920s

Melkon Effendi

672-A1	Daghda Fustik-Hidjaz Canto	Harry's 672
	Harry Edward Effendilar-vln	NY 1920s

Harry's 672 and 303 (by HARRY EDWARD EFFENDILAR) are coupled.

Oudi Melkon Eff Alemsherian

VB 413-B	Oushak Taksim [no vo]	Ph P806(12"), Rounder 1051(33,C,CD)
VB 414-	Shed Araban Taksim (with Soultanieh) [no vo]	Ph P806(12")
		NY 1926-7

Marko Melkon

BS 04849-1	Oglan, Oglan	Orth S-2831, Vi 26-2053
		NY February 15, 1937

26.2. Avny Bey *(Aomi Beg); violin (keman)*

45993-1	Sabah Djtaresaim	Co rej
45999-1	Ushak Taxim	Co E2617
		NY September 8, 1915

Co E2617 is uncredited.

26.3. D. Baghdadlian *vocal*

Z 111-A	Chello	Baghdadlian unnumbered
Z 112-A	Chello	Baghdadlian unnumbered
	vc	NY early 1920s

26.4. Manafsha G. Demoorjian *tenor*

43705-1	Kassook	Co E2789
43707-1	Urfa Agzy	Co E2789
43708-1	Bashiry	Co E2790
43709-1	Maya	Co E2790
	Husseiny Gazel	Co E2840
	Shirvany	Co E2840
	kanun	NY February 1916

26.5. Dikran Eff. *vocal*

38258-1	Merdini Dideme-Hidjaz Sharki'	Co E1110
38267-1	Oushak Gazel	Co E1109
38269-1	Iki De Keklik-Hidjazkiar Sharki'	Co E1108
	vln, kanun, 'with Naeem Karekin	NY September 13, 1912

The above are listed in the CBS files as M.G. PARSEKIAN & CO.

26.6. Oady Farajy *oud*

43717-	Saba Taxim	Co E2843
	Hijazkiar Kurdy Taxim	Co E2842
		NY late 1915

26.7. Garbis *vocal, kanun*

This artist's full name is Garbis Bakirjian.

Canoni Garbis Effendi

101-A	Seuyletme Beni-Ouchak Charki	Stamboul 400
102-B	Gazel Tourna-Ouchak Canto	Stamboul 400
103-A	Kesi Beghlare	Stamboul 402
104-B	Tatle Minoch-Hedjaz Canto	Stamboul 401
105-A	Nitchun Kustun Bana-Hedjaz Canto	Stamboul 401
106-A	Yuri Dilber Yuri-Hedjaz Yosma Cantose	Stamboul 402
110-A	Kashlaren Inje Inje	Stamboul 405
116-B	Neva Rast Gazel'	Stamboul 405
	vln, oud, or 'vln only	NY ca 1927

26.8. Harry Edward Effendilar *violin*

	Shad Araban Shaz Semaisy'	Harry's 301(12")
	Hoosaiy Saz Semaisy'	Harry's 301(12")

```
                 Neva Hidjaz Taksim                          Harry's 303
                 'probably Marko Melkon Alemsherian-oud        NY  1920s
```

Harry's 303 and 672 (by MARKO MELKON ALEMSHERIAN) are coupled.

26.9. Ibrahim Effendi *vocal*

```
190-A        Salla Salla                                       Ge (12")
                                                     NY  February 1924

191-A        Aman Kodzadzigim                                  Ge (12")
                                                     NY  March 1924

192-A        Endamin                                           Ge (12")
                                                     NY  April 1924

195-A        Tomboul Memeli Cante                              Ge (12")
                                                     NY  October 1924

196-A        Neva Oushak Canto                                 Ge (12")
                                                     NY  December 1924
```

The above were possibly made for the Maloof label.

```
150-A        Kessi Baglarina-Nevah Oushak Canto      MGP 529, Ph 529
                                                     NY  1920s
```

26.10. Jemal Bey (Oody) *vocal, oud*

```
B 22491-1    Huseiny Uzery Saba                                Vi 72865
                                                     NY  October 8, 1919

B 23339-1    Rast Gazel (Jemal Bey)                            Vi 72526
B 23340-2    Yeny Memo (Jemal Bey)                             Vi 72526
B 23341-1    Yeny Kessick Kerem (Jemal Bey)                    Vi 72865
             Avny Bey-vln, T. Kappas-kanun          NY  November 18, 1919
```

Vi 72526 as HAIRY BEY "OODY"

26.11. Naeem Karekin Effendy *vocal*

```
38315-2      Ibrahim Ghazel                                    Co E1200
             vln, kanun, octorino                   NY  October 7, 1912

38369-1      Shirvani                                          Co E1200
38371-1      Huzzam Gazel                                      Co E1201
38372-1      Kharpoot Mayasy                                   Co
38373-1      Eky Telly Gazal                                   Co rej
38374-1      Ov Dzedzernag [in Armenian]                       Co
```

| 38375-1 | Ibrahimi | Co E1200 |
| | vln, kanun, tchegertna | NY October 24, 1912 |

Matrices 38315 and 38375 have both been reported on Co E1200.

	Kessik Koshma	Co E5029(12")
	Husseini Gazel	Co E5029(12")
		NY 1912

26.12. H. Karagosian *vocal*

| Z 219 | Oglan, Oglan | Margosian's 42 |
| | vln, cl, oud | NY ca 1924 |

26.13. K. Kevo *vocal*

44162-1	Huzam Gazel	Co E3128
44164-1	Ushak Gazel	Co E3128
	kanun	NY ca July 1916

26.14. Leadet Hanim-Sinem Effendy *soprano, tenor*

| 45988-1 | Ben Bir Fendekdiéyem-Canto | Co E2619 |
| | vln, kanun | NY September 7, 1915 |

The above is described as a "soprano solo," but both voices can be heard.

45992-1	Debedji Kantosi	Co rej
45994-1	Osman Agha-Canto	Co E2619
	as before	NY September 8, 1915

26.15. Tamboory Looder Eff. *violin*

| 58741- | Neva Taksim | Co E3743 |
| | | NY November 1917 |

26.16. Haffiz Maher *vocal*

B 27643-1	Nihavent Gazel {Lost Love}	Vi 77327
B 27644-1	Neva Gazel {His Doubt}	Vi 77328
B 27645-2	Neva Canto	Vi rej
B 27646-1	Nihavent Sharki {Only One Girl In The World}	Vi 77327
B 27647-2	Huzam Gazel {Song Of Songs}	Vi 77328
B 27648-2	Huzam Charki	Vi rej
	James Sadaka-oud	NY March 7, 1923

Hafiz Maher

B 28333-2	Ushack-Gazel	Vi 77006
B 28334-2	Ushack-Sharcki	Vi 77006
B 28335-1	Rast-Gazel	Vi 77007
B 28336-1	Rast-Sharki	Vi 77007
B 28337-1	Hijaz Gazel {My Heart Is Broken}	Vi 77008
B 28338-1	Hijaz Sharcki {A Suitor's Doubt}	Vi 77008
	as before	NY August 1, 1923

26.17. Kosrof Malool *baritone*

Khusrev Effendi

38370-1	Rast Gazel	Co E1201
	vln, kanun, tchegertna	NY October 24, 1912

Kosroff Eff.

43706-1	Navrooz	Co E2843
43710-	Kurd Havasy-Pt. 2'	Co E2841
	kanun, 'vln	NY February 1916

Kosrof Malool

2001-A	Anadol Hevasi Shirvani	Oriental 101
2002-B	Anadol Kourd Hevasi [in Kurdish]	Oriental 101
	vln, oud	NY early 1920s

The assumption that the above are all by the same person is likely, though not certain.

26.18. Kemany Minas *tenor, keman (violin)*

B 18813-1	Memo-Neva Sharky	Vi 69173
B 18814-1	Chifta Telly Gazel'	Vi 69178
B 18815-1	Ben Neler-Hijaz Gazel'	Vi 69177
B 18816-1	Koozy-Husseiny Gazel'	Vi 69176
B 18817-1	Nezerimda Yena-Saba Gazel	Vi 69175
B 18818-1	Beny Sermez Bilirim-Rast Gazel	Vi 69174
	oud, or 'unaccompanied	NY December 6, 1916

58742-1	Nazarimda Yine Afak[2]	Co E4250
58743-1	Oushak Ghazel	Co E3786
58744-	Sabah Ghazel	Co E3744
58753-	Nihavend March [no vo]	Co E3787
58756-1	Karshouda Kurd Evlery	Co E4250
58757-1	Conialy Cantosou	Co E3745
58758-1	Denesli Cantosou {Develli Cantosou}	Co E4696
58759-1	Bulbul Canto	Co E3786
58760-1	Seni Geordukje	Co E4249, 32011-F
58761-1	Nine Nine Cantosou	Co E3745

58763-1	Eghin Havasi[2]	Co E4249, 32011-F
58772-	Djezair March [no vo]	Co E3787
58773-	Osman Bey Pesrefi [no vo]	Co E4430
58774-	Mahour Semayi [no vo]	Co E4430
59521-1-2	Halima[1]	Co E5168(12")
59522-1	Mavili Cantosou	Co E5169, 75023-F(12")
59523-1	Memo	Co E5272, 75022-F(12")
59524-1	Sheker Oghlan Cantosou	Co E5169, 75023-F(12")
	oud, kanun, [1]Garabet Merdjian-vo or [2]unaccompanied	NY November 1917

Co E3787 and E4430 as KEMAN, OUD AND CANOON; Co E3787 states "recorded in Europe".

26.19. Moustafa Haffouz *vocal*

| 197-A | Nechapourek Gazel | Mal |
| | | NY December 1924 |

26.20. K. Nodar *vocal*

38261-1	Oushak Kanto {Guzal Darom}[1]	Co E1109
38266-1	Ne Zeman Rahm-Sabah Gazel	Co E1108
38268-1	Tchare Boulan-Hidjaz Charki	Co E1110
	vln, kanun, [1]with Dikran Eff.	NY September 13, 1912

The above are listed in the CBS files as M.G. PARSEKIAN & CO.

26.21. Orchestre

	Marche Vatan Silistria	Jupiter 2075
	Marche Osman Pacha	Jupiter 2077
		NY(?) 1910s

Though the label states "Jupiter Record U.S.A.," this coupling may be European.

26.22. M.G. Parsekian & Co. *vocal, instrumental*

38259-1	Micheulmich	Co rej
38260-1	Rahme Ale Bana	Co rej
38262-1	Turkish March	Co rej
38263-1	Dugiah Kanto {Duarbakir Kanto}	Co E1107
38264-1	Kanto {Urfa}	Co E1107
38265-1	Husani Gazal	Co rej
	vln, kanun	NY September 13, 1912

Matrix 38263 as EKDEM VÉ NEVDAD, 38264 as NEVDAD VÉ DIKRAN; the kanun is not present on Co E1109. "Nevdad" appears in a 1919 catalog as NODAR.

38304-1	Hidjaz Sharke {Mashrabi Avarami}	Co E1132
38305-2	Hidjaz Kanto-Sevdim Gazel	Co rej
	as before	NY September 30, 1912

38310-1	Husseini Peshrav	Co E1131
38311-1	Husseini Gazel	Co E1131
38312-1	Husseini Sharke	Co E1130
38313-1	Hidjaz Gazel	Co E1132
38314-1	Navrouz Gazel	Co E1130
	vln, kanun, octorino	NY October 7, 1912

26.23. Soultana K. Poulou *vocal*

452-3	Ah! Varamadem Amerikaya-Canto	Ph 812(12")
453-2	Kadife Yasdigim Yok-Bahrie Cifte Telli	Ph 812(12")
	vln, oud, kanun	NY 1926-7

26.24. Riza Bey *vocal*

136-A	Felekden Hijazkiar Kurdi Sharki	MGP 523, Ph 523
137-A	Geschdi Hayalem-Suzinak Canto	MGP 523, Ph 523
		NY 1920s

26.25. Nishan Sedefjian *violin*

Kemany Nishan Effendi

CVE 39987-2	Tsifte Telli Taxim	Vi 68872(12")
CVE 39988-1	Hidjaz Taxim	Vi 68872(12")
	Achilleas Poulos-oud	NY August 17, 1927

Nishan Sedef, Effendi

	Nihavent	Co 75015-F(12")
	Tsifte Telli¹	Co 75015-F(12")
	Kurd Havasi¹	Co 75018-F(12")
	Sabahi	Co 75018-F(12")
	Kashik Havasi¹	Co 75021-F(12")
	Taxim Hidzaskiar Kurdi	Co 75021-F(12")
	¹probably Achilleas Poulos-oud, unk cym	NY ca 1928

26.26. Sinem Effendy *baritone*

45987-1	Neva Gazel	Co E2618
	Avny Bey-vln	NY September 7, 1915

45989-1	Kashi Gueormeyeidim-Huzzam Sharki	Co E2615
45995-1	Zemani Kar-Huzzam Sharki	Co E2616
45996-1	Ghamlé Keymetdar-Ushak Sharki	Co E2615
45997-1	Mubtelayi Derd Ashken-Hidjaz Sharki	Co E2618
45998-1	Pekdjuda Dushdum-Husseini Sharki	Co E2616
46000-1	Hugan	Co rej
46001-1	Ushak Pishrev¹ [no vo]	Co E2617

46002-1	Nast Genstermole	Co rej
	kanun, 'Avny Bey-vln	NY September 8, 1915

Co E2617 is uncredited.

Sinam Eff.

43550-1	Hidjaz Gazel	Co E2839
43551-1	Rast Gazel	Co E2839
	vln	NY late 1915

26.27. Smyrna Quartette *vocal, instrumental*

	Bilmen Gui Beni (Morris Levy)	Vi trial
	Zaibek; Tchifte	Vi trial
		NY March 18, 1925
B 32925-2	Leprenguine-Rast Sharki	Vi 78556
B 32926-2	Yuzelim Kararmisin-Rast Canto	Vi 78556
B 32927-2	Tchifate Teh'	Vi 78193
B 32928-2	Telegrafin Teleri-Neva Canto	Vi 78193
B 32929-2	Dilseni {Unreturned Love}-Nehavent Sharki'	Vi 78194
B 32930-3	Zaibek Havassi {Mountaineer's Dance} [no vo]	Vi 78194
	vln, oud, kanun, unk or 'Moise Effendi-vo	NY June 25, 1925

26.28. Stamboul Quartet *vocal, instrumental*

BVE 35102-2	Nazli Y Ouzei-Hidjazkiar Canto'	Vi 78829
BVE 35103-2	Aman Done-Neva Canto[3]	Vi 78596
BVE 35104-2	Nitchun Kiustun-Hidjaz Canto'	Vi 78656
BVE 35105-1	Tchalguidjilik-Neva Hidjaz Canto[3]	Vi 78656
BVE 35106-1	Yeni Sevdaya Doshdum-Neva Canto'	Vi 78596
CVE 35107-2	Kashlarin Indje Indje-Neva Canto[3]	Vi 68744(12")
CVE 35108-2	Hadji Duba-Huzam Canto'	Vi 68744(12")
BVE 35109-2	Yoynumu Ihia Iden-Hidjaz Canto[2]	Vi rej
BVE 35110-3	Ishtim Soyunu-Ousseini Canto[2]	Vi rej
BVE 35111-1	Hedjazkiar Taxim [no vo]	Vi 78829

Maurice Ganon-vln, Isaac Angel, Louis Matalon, M. Cazas-2 of whom play
oud and kanun, 'Isaac Angel, [2]Louis Matalon, [3]M. Cazas-vo

Camden, NJ February 22, 1926

BVE 35109-3	Yoynumu Ihia Iden-Hidjaz Canto'	Vi 78830
BVE 35110-4	Ishtim Soyunu-Ousseini Canto[2]	Vi 78830
	as before, 'M. Cazas, [2]Isaac Angel-vo	Camden, NJ March 12, 1926

The Stamboul Quartette

W 106798-1	Tchiktim Bey Oglou Bashine-Sabah Canto	Co 32004-F
W 106799-2	Beyim Hosh Yeldin-Neva Hidjaz Canto	Co 32002-F
W 106800-2	Seni Boyle-Sabah Canto'	Co 32002-F
W 106801-2	Alsan Yarimi Ele-Neva Hidjaz Canto'	Co 32005-F
W 106802-1	Yormedim Aolmende Vefa-Huzam Sharki	Co 32003-F

```
W 106803-2    Missirli Cantossi-Rast Canto'              Co 32003-F
W 106804-2    Kiz Seni Bilmezdim-Neva Hidjaz Canto       Co 32005-F
W 106805-3    Bilmen Ki Neden-Rast Sharki'               Co 32004-F
              as before, Isaac Angel or 'M. Cazas-vo     NY  May 1926


              Bilirim Sen Kiutchdjuksin Hedjaz Canto     Co 75000-F(12")
              Aarifem Hidjiazkiar Kurdi Sharki           Co 75000-F(12")
              Meyhane-Neva Canto                         Co 75001-F(12")
              Uch Yil-Nehavent Sharki                    Co 75001-F(12")
              Vayered Ashem [in Hebrew]                  Co 78000-F(12")
              Avino Malqueno [in Hebrew]                 Co 78000-F(12")
              Bezohri [in Hebrew]                        Co 78001-F(12")
              Ayom Arad Olam [in Hebrew]                 Co 78001-F(12")
                                                         NY  ca May 1926
```

Co 78000-F and 78001-F are the only issues in a "Spanish-Hebrew" series.

26.29. Tom Stathis *tenor*

```
12110-B       Soular Tashkein                            Ge rej
12111-B       Halime Kanto                               Ge rej
12112-B       Sabah Gazel Ey Fellek                      Ge rej
12113-B       Huzom Gazel                                Ge rej
                                       Richmond, IN  December 30, 1924

12121         test recording                             Ge
                                       Richmond, IN  January 10, 1925

12144-B       Soular Tashkein                            Ge 20095
12145-B       Gene Aksan                                 Ge 20094
12146-A       Sabah Gazel Ey Fellek                      Ge 20095
12147-A       Huzom Gazel                                Ge 20094
                                       Richmond, IN  January 28, 1925
```

26.30. Mary Steele *soprano*

```
              Kulkin Beklem                              Vi trial
              cl, cym, finger cymbals          NY  October 2, 1919
```

Mme. S. Mary And Co.

```
B 23309-1     Yababa Gowizany {Father I Want To Get Married} (M. Steele)
                [in Syrian]                              Vi 72566
B 23310-2     Al Rosana {My Rose} (M. Steele) [in Syrian]  Vi 72566
B 23311-2     Nina (M. Steele)                           Vi 72533
B 23312-2     Nara! Nara! {Fire! Fire!} (M. Steele)      Vi 72533
              cl, cym                          NY  October 27, 1919
```

Matrix B 23312 is sung in a "mixture of dialects: Turkish, Armenian, Syrian, Kurdish etc."

B 23320-3	Flamuri {The Flag} (M. Steele) [in Albanian]	Vi 72562
B 23321-3	Cuchawaki {The Gamblers} (M. Steele) [in Greek]	Vi rej
B 23322-2	Ismenenyes (M. Steele) [in Greek]	Vi rej
B 23323-1	Ardhi Koha A Bekuar {Hurrah For The Nation} [in Albanian]	Vi rej
	as before	NY November 3, 1919

B 23321-5	Cuchawaki {The Gamblers} (M. Steele) [in Greek]	Vi rej
B 23322-4	Ismenenyes (M. Steele) [in Greek]	Vi rej
B 23323-3	Ardhi Koha A Bekuar {Hurrah For The Nation} [in Albanian]	Vi rej
	Antoniou Brothers-cl, cym	NY November 19, 1919

B 23321-7	Cuchawaki {The Gamblers} (M. Steele) [in Greek]	Vi rej
B 23322-6	Ismenenyes (M. Steele) [in Greek]	Vi rej
B 23323-5	Ardhi Koha A Bekuar {Hurrah For The Nation} [in Albanian]	Vi 72562
	as before	NY December 4, 1919

B 23322-9	Ismenenyes (M. Steele) [in Greek]	Vi rej
B 23323-7	Ardhi Koha A Bekuar {Hurrah For The Nation} [in Albanian]	Vi rej
	as before	NY December 24, 1919

Mme. Mary Steele

87263-2	Shemi Husnun-Sharki	Co E7171
87265-1	Severim Tzanim Kibi-Canto	Co E7422
87266-2	Nare	Co E7171
	vln, oud, san	NY March 1921

87427-2	Dareldime Tzitzim Bana	Co E9030
87428-2	Yeni Tsifte Telli'	Co E7422
	vln, cym, or 'cl, san	NY May 1921

26.31. Tambour And Kemanche *instrumental*

138-A	Kurdi Hijazkiar Peshrof-Pt. 1	MGP 524, Ph 524
139-A	Kurdi Hijazkiar Peshrof-Pt. 2	MGP 524, Ph 524
		NY 1920s

26.32. Unknown Instrumental

	Lebebitzu-Horos	Ph 815(12")
	Mars Tou Sardar	Ph 815(12")
		NY mid-1920s

26.33. Unknown Oud Solos

4374	Turkish Song-Pt. 1	LC 14741B8
4375	Turkish Song-Pt. 2	LC 14741B9
	Columbian Exposition, Chicago	September 25, 1893

LC 14741 is a tape reel on which the original cylinders have been copied.

Huseini	Ph 808(12")
Oushak Taxim	Ph 808(12")
	NY mid-1920s

26.34. Unknown Vocal

Turkish Song	Ber 1301(7")
Turkish Speech On America	Ber 1400(7")
Turkish Serenade	Ber 1402(7")
	NY(?) ca 1896

26.35. Unknown Vocal, Instrumental

4372	Turkish National Hymn-Pt. 1	LC 14741B6
4373	Turkish National Hymn-Pt. 2	LC 14741B7
	vln, oud, tam, dm Columbian Exposition, Chicago September 25, 1893	

LC 14741 is a tape reel on which the original cylinders have been copied.

Rast Gazel	Co E5026(12")
Kurd Havasi	Co E5026(12")
	NY 1912

Tombouli Memeli Gelin	MGP 518, Ph 518
Sentiki Giosler-Canto	MGP 518, Ph 518
Tamzara	MGP 522, Ph 522
Enishde Kantosi	MGP 522, Ph 522
Roum Havasi	Ph 556
Dondourmaji Kantosi	Ph 556
	NY 1920s

26.36. Hafooz Yashar *vocal*

Yiashar Haffous

188-A	Dil Hanemi Yiktiny	Mal
189-A	Ralmi Yiok Bir Yara	Mal
		NY December 1923

193-A	Telegrafin Telleri Neva Canto	Mal
		NY May 1924

194-A	Neva Hedjaz Gazel	Mal
		NY June 1924

Hafooz Yashar Bey

151-B	Ben Nasil Ah Etmyem-Nihavent Gazal	MGP 529, Ph 529
		NY 1920s

26.37. Yoosoof Eff. *tenor*

43713-1	Saba Sharky	Co E2787
43716-1	Huzain Gazal	Co E2787
	oud, kanun	NY February 1916

PART 6

FAR EAST

SECTION 27.   CHINESE

27.1.   Cantonese Orchestra

M 1773   Tak Ai Men {Open The Doors Wide}   Mon 1773, Vi 7184, 42480
                                                          NY November 17, 1902

See note at this chapter's end for discussion of other material made on this and
nearby dates.

27.2.   Chinese Band

          Hoo Su Sung Do {To Celebrate Long Life And Present A Son}-Pt. 1
                                                          Ed 12777(2 min)
          Hoo Su Sung Do {To Celebrate Long Life And Present A Son}-Pt. 2
                                                          Ed 12778(2 min)
          Hoo Su Sung Do {To Celebrate Long Life And Present A Son}-Pt. 3
                                                          Ed 12779(2 min)
          Hoo Su Sung Do {To Celebrate Long Life And Present A Son}-Pt. 4
                                                          Ed 12780(2 min)
          Seow Toi Mon   Ed 12781(2 min)
          Mong Lung-Pt. 1   Ed 12782(2 min)
          Mong Lung-Pt. 2   Ed 12783(2 min)
          Ba Ton {To Prepare A Dinner}-Pt. 1   Ed 12784(2 min)
          Ba Ton {To Prepare A Dinner}-Pt. 2   Ed 12785(2 min)
          Lung Quon {To Persuade a King}   Ed 12786(2 min)
                                                  San Francisco   late 1902

27.3.   Chinese Novelty Orchestra

85544-2   Chinese One-Step-Pt. 1   Co E4506
85545-2   Chinese One-Step-Pt. 2   Co E4506
                                                  NY(?)   ca October 1919

27.4.   Chinese Orchestra

This entry appears in the Edison payment books for the following dates: July 28-9,
1909, January 6, 10, 11, 12, February 2, 10 and July 1, 1910. Material from
these sessions was released but remains untraced.

27.5. Lee Fee Fung *vocal; Cantonese*

BVE 50984-1	Man Toy-Pt. 1'		Vi 43857
BVE 50985-1	Man Toy-Pt. 2'		Vi 43857
BVE 50986-1	Man Toy-Pt. 3'		Vi 43858
BVE 50987-2	Man Toy-Pt. 4'		Vi 43858
BVE 50988-2	Man Toy-Pt. 5'		Vi 43859
BVE 50989-1	Man Toy-Pt. 6'		Vi 43859
BVE 50990-2	Fa Shum Tip Chick Mock Kan Fu-Pt. 1		Vi 43860
BVE 50991-1	Fa Shum Tip Chick Mock Kan Fu-Pt. 2		Vi 43860
BVE 50992-1	Chook Ying Toy Hook Ling-Pt. 1		Vi 43861
BVE 50993-2	Chook Ying Toy Hook Ling-Pt. 2		Vi 43861
BVE 50994-2	Chook Ying Toy Hook Ling-Pt. 3		Vi 43862
BVE 50995-2	Chook Ying Toy Hook Ling-Pt. 4		Vi 43862

> Chinese Orchestra: 2 Chinese vln, foreign vln, Chinese fl, Chinese md, Chinese p, woodblocks, 'with Gee Eng Hawk NY March 29, 1929

BVE 55893-2	Jair Yuk Eus Sing Chew Kee {Mun Night Burn Clothes}-Pt. 1		Vi 43866
BVE 55894-2	Jair Yuk Eus Sing Chew Kee {Mun Night Burn Clothes}-Pt. 2		Vi 43866
BVE 55895-1	Jair Yuk Eus Sing Chew Kee {Mun Night Burn Clothes}-Pt. 3		Vi 43867
BVE 55896-2	Jair Yuk Eus Sing Chew Kee {Mun Night Burn Clothes}-Pt. 4		Vi 43867
BVE 55897-1	Jair Yuk Eus Sing Chew Kee {Mun Night Burn Clothes}-Pt. 5		Vi 43868
BVE 55898-2	Jair Yuk Eus Sing Chew Kee {Mun Night Burn Clothes}-Pt. 6		Vi 43868
BVE 55899-2	Leung Wu Ti Hay Hoo Chiu One Key {Queen Snake Body}-Pt. 1		Vi 43863
BVE 57000-2	Leung Wu Ti Hay Hoo Chiu One Key {Queen Snake Body}-Pt. 2		Vi 43863
BVE 57001-1	Leung Wu Ti Hay Hoo Chiu One Key {Queen Snake Body}-Pt. 3		Vi 43864
BVE 57002-2	Leung Wu Ti Hay Hoo Chiu One Key {Queen Snake Body}-Pt. 4		Vi 43864
BVE 57003-1	Leung Wu Ti Hay Hoo Chiu One Key {Queen Snake Body}-Pt. 5		Vi 43865
BVE 57004-2	Lueng Wu Ti Hay Hoo Chiu One Key {Queen Snake Body}-Pt. 6		Vi 43865

> 2 Chinese vln, American vln, Chinese bj, woodblocks
> NY October 15, 1929

27.6. Li Jenkung *vocal*

BS 101118-1	The Street Vendors; Kites Are Flying; Lanterns Glowing (arr Stella Marek Cushing, from "Music Highways And Byways," pub. Silver Burdett Company) {Trips Abroad-China}	Vi 25380
BS 101119-1	Fisherman's Song; Lullaby (arr Stella Marek Cushing, from "Music Highways And Byways," pub. Silver Burdett Company) {Trips Abroad-China}	Vi 25380

> Lucia Dunham-p NY March 25, 1936

27.7. Sher Doy Wong *spoken*

Muck Mul-Comic Recitation-Pt. 1	Ed 12762(2 min)
Muck Mul-Comic Recitation-Pt. 2	Ed 12763(2 min)
Muck Mul-Comic Recitation-Pt. 3	Ed 12764(2 min)
Comic Recitation	Ed 12774(2 min)
Foong Woong Ga {Foong Woong Song}-Comic Recitation	Ed 12775(2 min)

> San Francisco late 1902

27.8. Theodore B. Tu *tenor; Mandarin*

	Take Time To Be Holy	`Vi trial
	Clifford Cairns-p	NY March 20, 1924

B 30188-2	Take Time To Be Holy	Vi rej
B 30189-1	How Shall The Young Secure Their Hearts	Vi 43315
B 30190-2	Praise Ye The Saviour's Grace	Vi 43312
B 30191-2	Abide With Me	Vi rej
B 30192-3	What A Friend We Have In Jesus	Vi 43314
	Leroy Shield-org	NY June 13, 1924

B 30188-4	Take Time To Be Holy	Vi rej
B 30191-4	Abide With Me	Vi 43315
B 30438-1	Nearer My God To Thee (transcribed by Rev. W.A.P. Martine, D.D., m: Lowell Mason)	Vi 43313
B 30439-3	There Is A Green Hill Far Away (transcribed by Rev. H.D. Porter, D.D., m: George C. Stebbins)	Vi rej
	as before	NY June 30, 1924

B 30446-1	Lead Kindly Light (transcribed by C. Goodrich, D.D., m: John B. Dykes)	Vi 43313
B 30447-2	O Day Of Rest And Gladness (transcribed by Rev. H.D. Porter)	Vi 43312
B 30448-2	Thou Didst Leave Thy Throne (transcribed by C. Goodrich, D.D., m: Ira D. Sankey)	Vi 43314
	as before	NY July 1, 1924

27.9. Unknown Vocal

Jom Se Moan {To Destroy The Four Gates}-Pt. 1	Ed 12741(2 min)
Jom Se Moan {To Destroy The Four Gates}-Pt. 2	Ed 12742(2 min)
Jom Se Moan {To Destroy The Four Gates}-Pt. 3	Ed 12743(2 min)
Jom Se Moan {To Destroy The Four Gates}-Pt. 4	Ed 12744(2 min)
Jom Se Moan {To Destroy The Four Gates}-Pt. 5	Ed 12745(2 min)
Jom Se Moan {To Destroy The Four Gates}-Pt. 6	Ed 12746(2 min)
Jom Se Moan {To Destroy The Four Gates}-Pt. 7	Ed 12747(2 min)
Jom Se Moan {To Destroy The Four Gates}-Pt. 8	Ed 12748(2 min)
Jom Se Moan {To Destroy The Four Gates}-Pt. 9	Ed 12749(2 min)
Jom Se Moan {To Destroy The Four Gates}-Pt. 10	Ed 12750(2 min)
Jom Se Moan {To Destroy The Four Gates}-Pt. 11	Ed 12751(2 min)
Jom Se Moan {To Destroy The Four Gates}-Pt. 12	Ed 12752(2 min)
Ga Fu Cha Man {A Widow's Lament}-Pt. 1	Ed 12753(2 min)
Ga Fu Cha Man {A Widow's Lament}-Pt. 2	Ed 12754(2 min)
Ga Fu Cha Man {A Widow's Lament}-Pt. 3	Ed 12755(2 min)
Sa Hon Ti Wy {Assembly On A Sand Bank}-Pt. 1	Ed 12756(2 min)
Sa Hon Ti Wy {Assembly On A Sand Bank}-Pt. 2	Ed 12757(2 min)
Sa Hon Ti Wy {Assembly On A Sand Bank}-Pt. 3	Ed 12758(2 min)
Sa Hon Ti Wy {Assembly On A Sand Bank}-Pt. 4	Ed 12759(2 min)
Sa Hon Ti Wy {Assembly On A Sand Bank}-Pt. 5	Ed 12760(2 min)
Sa Hon Ti Wy {Assembly On A Sand Bank}-Pt. 6	Ed 12761(2 min)
Swa Hi {The Nest In a Shoe}	Ed 12765(2 min)

Fong U {To Visit A Friend}   Ed 12766(2 min)
U Si Wo {Travelling By The West Lake}   Ed 12767(2 min)
Chu Leong Sudo {Chu Leong Collects Rent}   Ed 12768(2 min)
Lo Yon Ti Se {An Old Valet Carries A Letter}   Ed 12769(2 min)
Sut Junk Yen {A Wise Man In The Snow}-Pt. 1   Ed 12770(2 min)
Sut Junk Yen {A Wise Man In The Snow}-Pt. 2   Ed 12771(2 min)
Quing Ming Qu Heng {The Death of Loong Ming}-Pt. 1   Ed 12772(2 min)
Quing Ming Qu Heng {The Death Of Loong Ming}-Pt. 2   Ed 12773(2 min)
Wong Dan Su Yeo {The Wizard Captures a Demon}-Comic Recitation
                                                             Ed 12776(2 min)
orch   San Francisco late 1902

27.10. Professor Wei Chung Loh *of the Ta Tung National Music Research Institute*
of Shanghai

RS 737-A   Soliloquy Of A Convalescent (Liu T'ien Hua)   Musicraft 1139
RS 738-A   March (Liu T'ien Hua)   Musicraft 1139
            er-hu solos   NY 1939

RS 739-E   Dance Prelude (Liu T'ien Hua)   Musicraft 1140
RS 740-C   Flying Flowers Falling Upon Emerald Green Grass   Musicraft 1140
            pi-pa solos   NY 1939

RS 741-A   The Drunken Fisherman   Musicraft 1141
RS 742-C   Parting At Yang Kwan (Wang Wei)   Musicraft 1141
            7-string ching solos   NY 1939

RS 743-B   Temple Meditation   Musicraft 1142
RS 744-A   The Flight Of The Partridge'   Musicraft 1142
            hsiao (phoenix flute) or 'ti-tze (horizontal flute) solos   NY 1939

The above are in album 44.

27.11. Yau Hok Chau *violin, vocal; Cantonese (1880-1942)*

BVE 59712-1   Wu Kwai Tse Presenting His Sword-Pt. 1   Vi 56128
BVE 59713-2   Wu Kwai Tse Presenting His Sword-Pt. 2   Vi 56128
BVE 59714-2   Wu Kwai Tse Presenting His Sword-Pt. 3   Vi 56129
BVE 59715-2   Wu Kwai Tse Presenting His Sword-Pt. 4   Vi 56129
BVE 59716-2   Pooi Gut {Strolling In The Moonlight} (Prof. Yau Hok Chau)-Pt. 1
                                                                     Vi 56130
BVE 59717-2   Pooi Gut {Strolling In The Moonlight} (Prof. Yau Hok Chau)-Pt. 2
                                                                     Vi 56130
BVE 59718-1   Happy Go Lucky World (Prof. Yau Hok Chau) [no vo]   Vi 56131
BVE 59719-2   The Rain Dropping on The Banana Tree (Prof. Yau Hok Chau) [no vo]
                                                                     Vi 56131

        Chan Chi Ping-dulcimer, Wong Heung Ting-bj, Lui Pak Wing-lute
                                                    NY March 21, 1930

27.12. Julius Yee

10593-	Chinese #1	Ba
10594-	Chinese #2	Ba
10595-	Chinese #3	Ba
10596-	Chinese #4	Ba

NY April 24, 1931

Although surviving documents are unclear and incomplete, Victor appears to have made Chinese records on several occasions during 1902-3 in New York City. Fagan and Moran report the following numbers and dates:

```
1557-1576  August 1902
1769-1789  November 17, 1902  (renumbered M 7160-M 7180)
1864-1885  1902  (renumbered M 7201-M 7222)
1941-1942  February 2, 1903
1956 February 10, 1903  (renumbered 7242-7253)
1957 February 10, 1903  (renumbered 7254-7262)
2128-2145  March 31-April 1, 1903
2302-2324  1903  (renumbered 7241-7303)
```

Higher numbers appear to have been made during recording expeditions to China. The reason for larger quantities appearing in the renumbered sections above is not clear. The files also indicate recordings on November 17, 1902 and February 2, 1903 by ROSALIA CHALIA, as soloist and in duets with baritone S.H. Dudley, using numbers identical to those for the Chinese discs. None were released.

SECTION 28. EAST INDIAN

28.1. Satyabala Devi (Sara Swati Avtar) *vocal, vina (b. 1892)*

19128-1	Dipuck	Co N1
19129-1	Sam-Veda	Co N1
19130-1	title untraced	Co rej
		NY November 22, 1910
19146-1	Aliya	Co N2
19147-1	Thumri	Co N2
19148-1	Kaffi Tapa	Co
	vln	NY December 5, 1910
19264-1	Damru¹	Co N3
19265-1	Bhairavi	Co N3
19266-1	Tilak Kamod	Co rej
	vln, org, or ¹vina solo	NY March 23, 1911
19369-1	Bhairavi Tappa	Co N4
19370-1	Kaffi Hori	Co N4
		NY May 15, 1911
19463-1	Kaffi	Co N5
19464-1	Bhairavi	Co N5
19465-1	Kasida-I-Samsh¹	Co N6
19466-1	Gazal-Natia¹	Co N6
19467-1	Dhurpad-Sindura	Co N7
19468-1	Turvat-Kedara	Co N7
	¹with Ustad Piaremian	NY July 17, 1911
19600-1	Natmalari	Co N8
19601-1	Dance Of God Mahadeo {Tandeo Paran} { Radha Dance}	
	{Dha Kitiak Dha Tit}	Co N8
19604-1	Bihag	Co N10
19605-1	Bhimpasasi	Co N10
	vln, org	NY October 18, 1911
19606-1	Geet-Govind {Gita Govind Jayo Deo Shastri} {Pralaya Payodhi Jale}	
		Co N11
19609-1	Kaffi	Co N13
19610-1	Khamach	Co N13
19611-1	Dhurpad-Pilu	Co rej
		NY October 20, 1911

```
19618-1        Coronation Song-Emperor George V
                   {Crowning Of Emperor George Vth At Delhi} {Jio Jio Delhi Pati}
                                                                     Co N11
               org                                         NY  October 24, 1911


19645-1        Dhurpad-Pilu                                         Co rej
19646-1        Ragini Malar                                        Co rej
               org                                         NY  November 2, 1911


19645-2        Dhurpad-Pilu'                                        Co N24
19646-2        Ragini Malar                                        Co N24
19666-1        Tilak Kamod                                               Co
19667-2        Devgiri                                                   Co
               harmonium, tabla, 'vln                     NY  November 16, 1911
```

28.2. Dulal, Sisir And Rabindra

```
BS 04967-1     Raga Mishra-Kaphi                                   Vi  1834
               sarode, esraj, tabla-banya                NY  February 22, 1937
```

Vi 1834 is in album M 382.

28.3. Prof. Ustad Chamman Khan   *vocal*

```
19612-1        Gazal Nashim                                        Co N14
                                                          NY  October 20, 1911


19620-1        Miaun, Miaun                                        Co N15
19621-1        Nakda                                               Co N15
               p                                          NY  October 23, 1911


19619-1        Brandy                                              Co N14
                                                          NY  October 24, 1911


19626-2        Dhurpad Inayat; Rag Bahar                           Co N17
19629-1        H.H. Maharaja Yackwar Jubilee Song                  Co N17
               org                                        NY  October 31, 1911


19638-         Pusto Gazal                                              Co
               org                                        NY  November 1, 1911


19639-2        Lavini Inayat                                            Co
19640-1        Gazal Natia                                         Co rej
19641-1        Maulud Shariff-Pt. 1                                     Co
19642-1        Maulud Shariff-Pt. 2                                Co rej
               org                                        NY  November 2, 1911


19642-2        Maulud Shariff-Pt. 2                                     Co
19665-1        Kalandari                                                Co
               org                                        NY  November 16, 1911
```

28.4. Prof. M.R. Pathan *piano*

19647-1   Dussek Sonatina (J.L. Dussek)   Co N22
                                                          NY November 2, 1911

19672-1   Sonata (Mozart)   Co N22
                                                          NY November 17, 1911

28.5. Ustad Piaremian *vocal*

This artist's name is spelled PIAREMIA on at least some issues.

19602-1   Kavali Kudus   Co N9
19603-1   Gazal Mistur   Co N9
            vln, org   NY October 18, 1911

19607-1   Gazal-Orbal   Co N12
19608-1   Gazal-Akdass   Co N12
                                                          NY October 20, 1911

19622-1   Kassida Kudsi   Co N16
            org   NY October 23, 1911

19627-1   Ganja-Jumuna; Kassida Inayat   Co rej
19628-1   Gazal Amir Minai {Ankho Me Noor Tera}   Co N18
19630-1   Gazal Sufia {Rag Sarang} {Gazal-I-Faiz} {Kare Hum Kiski Pooja}
                                                                        Co N18
            org   NY October 31, 1911

19634-1   Bhajan-Swami Surdas   Co N19
19635-   title untraced   Co
19636-1   Labu Kushakjan   Co N19
19637-1   Bhajan Inayat   Co
            org   NY November 1, 1911

19643-1   Nate Kchbube Khuda   Co
19644-1   Kassida-E-Makdum   Co rej
            org   NY November 2, 1911

19627-2   Ganja-Jumuna; Kassida Inayat   Co N16
            org   NY November 16, 1911

Michael S. Kinnear's article "Columbia Double Disc--An Unusual Indian Series" in
TALKING MACHINE REVIEW, No. 73 (February 1988), pp. 2124-7, provides interesting
background for Columbia's East Indian N series.

28.6. Uday Shan-Kar *dancer*

Uday Shan-Kar And His Company Of Hindu Dancers And Musicians

CS 04960-1   Raga Tilanga   Vi 14506(12")
              fl, sitar, sarode, esraj, tabla-banya, saranga, gongs, d Vishnudass
              Shirali   NY February 22, 1937

CS 04961-1   Raga Bahar   Vi 14506(12")
              fl, sitar, sarode, tabla-banya, saranga, d Vishnudass Shirali
                                                               NY February 22, 1937

CS 04962-2   Danse Gandharva {Raga Malkounsa}   Vi 14507(12")
              sitar, sarode, esraj, saranga, d Vishnudass Shirali
                                                               NY February 22, 2937

CS 04963-1   Danse Ramachandra {Ragas Sinhendra, Maddhyama & Hansaddhwani}
                                                                         Vi 14507(12")
              fl, tanapura, sitar, sarode, mridunga, khunkhuni, d Vishnudass
              Shirali   NY February 22, 1937

CS 04965-1   Danse Kartikeyya {Raga Malkounsa}   Vi 14508(12")
              fl, jala-taranga, sarode, saranga, mridunga, gongs, shankha, zhanzha,
              d Vishnudass Shirali   NY February 22, 1937

BS 04966-1   Danse Indra {Raga Bhairava}   Vi 1834
              fl, sitar, sarode, tabla-banya, esraj, sarange, d Vishnudass Shirali
                                                               NY February 22, 1937

BS 04968-1   Danse Snanum {Ragas Durga & Khamaj}   Vi 1835
              fl, jala-taranga, sitar, sarode, madal, khol, khunkhuni, d Vishnudass
              Shirali   NY February 22, 1937

28.7. Vishnudass Shirali *vocal, drums*

CS 04964-2   Tabla-Taranga {Raga Adana}   Vi rej (12")
BS 04969-1   Bhajana-Religious Song   Vi 1835
              own vo, unk fl, sitar, sarode, tabla-banya, karatal, or 'dm solo
                                                               NY February 22, 1937

The above are in album M 382; a similar performance to that on matrix CS 04964 was
issued on Vi 14508 and drawn from HMV matrix 2EA 5455-1.

SECTION 29. JAPANESE

29.1. Ara Kasen *vocal*

PBVE 54893-2	Shure Bushi-Pt. 1A	Vi
PBVE 54894-2	Shure Bushi-Pt. 1B	Vi
PBVE 54895-2	Shure Bushi-Pt. 2A	Vi
PBVE 54896-1	Shure Bushi-Pt. 2B	Vi
	samisen	Hollywood July 24, 1930

29.2. Fujiwara Yosie *tenor (1898-1976)*

BVE 33809-1	Oki-no-Kamone-Fisherman's Song	Vi 1175, 4048
BVE 33810-1	Kojo-nu-Tsuki {Moon On Ruined Castles}	Vi 1175, 4048
	Leroy Shield-p	NY October 26, 1925
BVE 37650-2	Sea Port {Na Kayama}-Boatman's Song	Vi 1230, GJ16
BVE 37651-1	Reminiscence {The Old Home} (Saito)	Vi 1231, GJ17
	as before	Camden, NJ January 28, 1927
BVE 37652-2	Séssésé	Vi 1231, GJ17
BVE 37653-1	Outgoing Ship {Goodbye}-Boatman's Song	Vi 1230, GJ16
BVE 37654-1	Sakura, Sakura {Cherry Blossom}	Vi 1232, GJ18
BVE 37655-2	Nana No Uta {Flower Song}	Vi 1232, GJ18
	as before	Camden, NJ January 29, 1927
PBVE 42051-2	Sendo Uta {Youthful Boatman} (Yuji Itow)	Vi 4043, GJ13
PBVE 42052-2	Hoko O Osamate-Whaler's Song (Nakayama)	Vi 4043, GJ13
PBVE 42053-2	Gombei Sow {Gombe Ga Tane Maku} (Yuji Itow)	Vi 4045
	as before	Oakland, CA March 3, 1928
PBVE 42054-1	Shinoda No Yabu {Tale Of Mother Fox} (Pujii)	Vi 4041
PBVE 42055-1	Port Of Habu {Habu So Mitvato} (Nakayama)	Vi 4042, GJ12, NK3001
PBVE 42056-1	Chidori {Plovers} (Kenoye)	Vi 4041
PBVE 42057-2	Aki Na Uta {Song Of Autumn} (Sugiyama)	Vi 4044
PBVE 42058-2	Hono: Susukippo {Pampas Grass} (Yanada)	Vi 4044
PBVE 42059-2	Le Violette (Alessandro Scarlatti) [in Italian]	Vi rej
PBVE 42060-2	Caro Mio Ben (G. Giordani) [in Italian]	Vi rej
PBVE 42061-2	Sleepy Head {Asane} (Hirota)	Vi 4042, GJ12
PBVE 42062-2	Yoimachigusa {Lament} (Ohno)	Vi 4045
	as before	Oakland, CA March 4, 1928
BVE 42559-1	Waga Namida {My Dear} (Sugiyama)	Vi 4047, GJ14
BVE 42560-2	Otosan To Boya {Where Is Mother?} (Inoue)	Vi 4046
BVE 42561-1	Hakone Hachiri-Mountaineer's Song	Vi GJ11

```
BVE 42561-2   Hakone Hachiri-Mountaineer's Song              Vi 4046, NK3001
BVE 42562-2   Funa Uta-Boatman's Song (Konoye)                   Vi 4047, GJ14
              Maxim Schapiro-p                    Camden, NJ  March 22, 1928

BS 06439-1    Carmela (De Curtis)                                          Vi
BS 06440-1    Tokaino (Inouye)                                             Vi
BS 06441-1    The Old Refrain (Kreisler)                                   Vi
BS 06442-1    Folk Song Of The Spanish Californians                        Vi
              orch d Alfredo Cibelli                    NY  March 23, 1937
```

29.3. Hokutosai-Kennyuh *vocal*

```
PBVE 219-1    Hidari Jingoro-Pt. 1                                   Vi 45534
PBVE 220-2    Hidari Jingoro-Pt. 2                                   Vi 45534
PBVE 221-2    Ohtake Jubei {Ancient Warrior} (Kennyuh)-Pt. 1        Vi 45535
PBVE 222-2    Ohtake Jubei {Ancient Warrior} (Kennyuh)-Pt. 2        Vi 45535
              samisen                          Los Angeles  May 13, 1926
```

29.4. Ichijeo Mariko *vocal, samisen*

```
PBVE 54890-2  Oiski Yamaga Okuri-Pt. 1A                                    Vi
PBVE 54891-2  Oiski Yamaga Okuri-Pt. 1B                                    Vi
                                               Hollywood  July 21, 1930
```

29.5. Ishigami Takane *vocal*

```
PBVE 225-3    Hato-Poppo; American Hatopoppo; O Tamajiakushi        Vi 45537
PBVE 226-3    Usagi-to-kame; Momotaro                               Vi 45537
PBVE 227-1    Kakitsubata; Sakura Sakura                            Vi 45538
PBVE 228-1    Urashima Taro; Kagashi                                Vi 45538
              Nanbu-2d vo, Leroy Shield-p        Los Angeles  May 13, 1926
```

29.6. Kawafuku-Tei Hatsune *vocal*

```
PBVE 223-2    Stuttonton-Bushi                                      Vi 45536
PBVE 234-3    Ohryokko-Bushi                                        Vi 45536
              2 samisen                         Los Angeles  May 13, 1926
```

29.7. Kawata Seiairo *tenor*

```
BS 010678-1   Song To Oshima (arr Stella Marek Cushing, from
              "Music Highways And Byways," pub. Silver Burdett Company)
              {Trips Abroad-Japan}                              Vi 25384
              dm                                   NY  June 17, 1937
```

Two other tracks on matrix BS 010678 are by SAITO YOSHIKO

29.8. Koyke Hizi *soprano*

BS 82599-   Suwani Gawa No Uta {Old Folks At Home} (S. Foster)   Vi
BS 83300-   Minnetonka No Kohan {By The Waters Of The Minnetonka}
                (Thurlow Lieurance)   Vi
BS 83301-   La Traviata: Tsuba Kihime, A Sowa Kanohitoka {Ah, Fors 'E Lui}
                {The One Of Whom I Dreamed} (Verdi)   Vi
BS 83302-   La Traviata: Tsubakihime-Tawamure Yoite {Sempre Libera Deggio}
                {I'll Fulfill The Round Of Pleasure} (Verdi)   Vi
            orch d Alfredo Cibelli   NY   June 11, 1934

Recorded for the Victor Talking Machine Company, Japan

29.9. Kudzuoka Sokichi *vocal*

> Kimigayo-National Anthem of Japan   Ed 12813(2 min)
> Suruganaru-Song Of Mount Fiji   Ed 12814(2 min)
> Imayo {Song Of The Four Seasons}   Ed 12815(2 min)
> Hotaru No Hikari {The Firefly's Light} (melody: Auld Lang Syne)
>   Ed 12816(2 min)
> Ukikumo {Fleecy Clouds}   Ed 12817(2 min)
> Omoi Izureba {A Student's Thoughts Of Home} (melody: Bonny Doon)
>   Ed 12818(2 min)
> Ware No Kami Ni {Nearer My God To Thee}   Ed 12819(2 min)
> Komori Uta-Lullaby   Ed 12822(2 min)
> Hitotsutoya-New Year's Song   Ed 12823(2 min)
> Kii No Kuni {Song To The God Of Rice}   Ed 12824(2 min)
> Dodoitsu-Three Love Songs   Ed 12825(2 min)
> Kappore-Dancing Song   Ed 12826(2 min)
>   NY   early 1903

Catalog note: "Selections 12822-12823-12824-12825-12826 are accompanied with an
instrument similar to the mandolin; the others are accompanied with piano." The
artist recorded for Edison again on April 17, 1905, probably to remake one or more
of these titles.

29.10. Kyoyama Hanachiyo *vocal, samisen*

PBVE 54886-2   Takumino Kami Tamurate-Study Song-Pt. 1A   Vi
PBVE 54887-2   Takumino Kami Tamurate-Study Song-Pt. 1B   Vi
PBVE 54888-2   Takumino Kami Tamurate-Study Song-Pt. 2A   Vi
PBVE 54889-1   Takumino Kami Tamurate-Study Song-Pt. 2B   Vi
                                              Hollywood   July 21, 1930

29.11. Naganuma Sisters (Setsuko & Masako) *vocal*

PBVE 61009-2   Anzen Daiichi (K.I. Okada)   Vi rej
PBVE 61010-2   Kutsu Canaru-Children's Songs; Onsen Machikara   Vi rej
            Fukushima T.-hca, Naganuma Michiko-p   Hollywood   August 20, 1930

PBVE 61009-4 Anzen Daiichi (K.I. Okada)   Vi
PBVE 61010-4 Kutsu Canaru-Children's Songs; Onsen Machikara   Vi
       as before   Hollywood August 22, 1930

29.12. Nakagawa Makizo *tenor*

BS 78233-1 Am Meer (Schubert)   Vi
BS 78234-1 Chatsumi Musume (T. Tsuyaki)   Vi
BS 78235-1 Nostalgia (H. Hoasu)   Vi
BS 78236-1 The Two Grenadiers   Vi
       tp, 2 vln, cl, o, vla, tb, bsn, p, sbs, d Alfredo Cibelli
                                    NY October 18, 1933

29.13. Saito Yoshiko *soprano*

BS 010678-1 Lullaby; Cherry Bloom (arr Stella Marek Cushing, from
            "Music Highways And Byways," pub. Silver Burdett Company)
            {Trips Abroad-Japan}   Vi 25384
BS 010679-1 Kinnyamonya; Over Mt. Hakone (arr Stella Marek Cushing, from
            "Music Highways And Byways," pub. Silver Burdett Company)
            {Trips Abroad-Japan}   Vi 25384
       p   NY June 17, 1937

One further track on matrix BS 010678 is by KAWATA SEIAIRO

29.14. Sekiya Toshiko *soprano*

CRC 71814-2 Lo Here The Gentle Lark (Shakespeare-Sir Henry Bishop) [in English]
                                         Vi rej (12")
BRC 71815-1 La Serenade (Schubert, tr Keizo Horiuchi)   Vi
BRC 71816-1 Wiegenlied {Komoriuta} (F. Schubert, op. 98, tr Mr. Naito)   Vi
       orch d Nathaniel Shilkret   NY February 4, 1932

BRC 71818-2 Clavelitos {Carnations} (Estic-J. Valverde) [in Spanish]   Vi
BRC 71819-1 Estrellita (M.M. Ponce, arr Nathaniel Shilkret) [in Spanish] Vi
BRC 71820-2 Indian Love Call, from "Rose Marie"
            (Otto Harbach-Oscar Hammerstein II-Rudolf Friml)   Vi rej
       as before   NY February 5, 1932

CRC 71840-2 Santa Lucia-Neapolitan Barcarole [in Italian]   Vi (12")
BRC 71841-2 Sansashigure-Song Of Congratulations (Toshiko Sekiya)   Vi
BRC 71842-2 Ariake {Dawning}   Vi
BRC 71843-1 Uguisiu {The Nightingale} (J. Hullah, arr Toshiko Sekiya)   Vi
       as before   NY February 9, 1932

CRC 71814-4 Lo Here The Gentle Lark (Shakespeare-Sir Henry Bishop) [in English]
                                         Vi (12")
BRC 71820-3 Indian Love Call, from "Rose Marie" (Otto Harbach,
            Oscar Hammerstein II-Rudolf Friml)   Vi
BRC 71845-2 Yaei No Akatsuki {Dawn Of The Camp} (Swiss Melody,
            arr Toshiko Sekiya)   Vi

BRC 71846-1   Hitorigoto {Memories} (Rynko Kawaji-Toshiko Sekiya)   Vi
          as before   NY February 10, 1932

The above were made for the Victor Talking Machine Company, Japan.

29.15. Sugimachi Miyashi *(Wyate Moore); vocal*

PBS 68601-2   Yanagi {Trees} (Oscar Rasbach)   Vi rej
PBS 68602-1   Wakaki Hi No Yume {The Dream Of A Young Day} (Cloud Lapham) Vi rej
          2 vln, vc, p   Hollywood October 26, 1933

PBS 79496-   Yo Shi Ki Ki (Ryutaro Hirota)   Vi
PBS 79497-   Aoi Su Sumki (Shimpe Nakayama)   Vi
PBS 79498-   Yo Fu Ke Te Uta O Ru {The Midnight Song} (Chosei Motoori)   Vi
PBS 79499-   Atsui Namda {Tears} (Tei Harita)   Vi
PBS 79500-   Matsushima Ondo   Vi
          2 vln, fl, o, bsn, harp, traps   Hollywood December 23, 1934

29.16. Susuki Yoneyakki *vocal*

BVE 50812-2   Yoneyama Jinku {Hauta With Naniwabushi}   Vi 50840
BVE 50813-2   Dodoitsu   Vi 50840
BVE 50814-1   Yoneyama Jinka Naniwabushiiri   Vi
BVE 50815-1   Oryokko-Bushi; Dodoitsu   Vi 50841
BVE 50816-1   Yasugi-Bushi; Los-Bushi   Vi 50841
          Yoshikawa Chiyoko-samisen, unk 2d voice   Hollywood April 12, 1929

BVE 50818-1   Ikanaya-Matsugoro (Yoneyakki Susuki)-Pt. 1   Vi 50842
BVE 50819-2   Ikanaya-Matsugoro (Yoneyakki Susuki)-Pt. 2   Vi 50842
BVE 50820-2   Ikanaya-Matsugoro (Yoneyakki Susuki)-Pt. 3   Vi 50843
BVE 50821-1   Ikanaya-Matsugoro (Yoneyakki Susuki)-Pt. 4   Vi 50843
BVE 50822-1   Sakanaya-To-Hondako-Pt. 1   Vi 50844
BVE 50823-1   Sakanaya-To-Hondako-Pt. 2   Vi 50844
BVE 50824-1   Sakanaya-To-Hondako-Pt. 3   Vi 50845
BVE 50825-2   Sakanaya-To-Hondako-Pt. 4   Vi 50845
          as before   Hollywood April 13, 1929

29.17. Royden Tatsuo Susumago *tenor*

BVE 616   Sakura, Sakura   Vi trial
          p   NY January 21, 1929

BVE 51929-2   Sakura Sakura {Cherry Blossoms} (Kosack Yamada)   Vi rej
BVE 51930-2   Kin-Gna-Mon-Gna (Kosack Yamada)   Vi rej
BVE 51931-1   Oshi Hi Bari {The Dumb Lark}-Children's Song (Ruitaro Hirota) Vi
BVE 51932-1   Hama Chi Dori {The Plover}-Children's Song (Ruitaro Hirota)   Vi
BVE 51933-1   Hana No Uta {Flower Song}; Oshima Bushima   Vi
BVE 51934-2   Kuraka, Kuraka {Will You Come} (Kosack Yamada)   Vi rej
          Pauline Corliss-p   NY April 26, 1929

```
BVE 53437-1   A Shi Ta {Tomorrow}-Children's Song (Riutaro Hirota)            Vi
BVE 53438-1   Shikararete {Being Scolded}-Children's Song (Riutaro Hirota)    Vi
BVE 51929-3   Sakura Sakura {Cherry Blossoms} (Kosack Yamada)                 Vi
              as before                                       NY  May 24, 1929
```

29.18. Tamaki Miura *soprano (1884-1946)*

Presumably a portion of the following are sung in Italian.

```
61854-        test recording                                                 Co
                                                      NY  September 11, 1917
```

```
49260-1       Madame Butterfly: Un Bel Dì, Vedremo (Puccini) [in Italian]
                                   Co 49260, 60005-D(12"), HMV RL5743(33)
              orch                                      NY  October 16, 1917
```

Tamaki Miura-Theodore Kittay

```
49265-2       Madame Butterfly: Love Duet (Act 1) (Puccini) [in Italian]
                                                            Co 49265(12")
              orch                              NY  October-November 1917
```

Tamaki Miura

```
77496-1       Don't Tie The Pony To The Cherry Tree {Saita Sakura}    Co E4222
77497-1       Waiting {Kuru Ka Kuru Ka}-Fisherman's Song              Co E4222
              orch                                    NY  November 9, 1917
```

```
BVE 51695-2   Madame Butterfly: Un Bel Dì, Vedremo {Some Day He'll Come} (Act 2)
                   (G. Puccini)                                      Vi rej
BVE 51696-2   Madame Butterfly: Butterfly's Death Scene (Act 2) (G. Puccini)
                                                                     Vi rej
BVE 51697-2   Mignon: Connais Tu Le Pays? {Knowest Thou The Land?} (Thomas)
                                                                     Vi 4147
              orch d Rosario Bourdon                    NY  May 10, 1929
```

```
BVE 51698-2   Last Rose Of Summer                                   Vi 4147
BVE 51699-1   Children's Song (Tamaki Miura)                        Vi 4148
BVE 53500-2   Kinnia Monnia; Sedono Danbatake                       Vi 4148
              orch d Bruno Reibold                      NY  May 16, 1929
```

```
BVE 51695-4   Madame Butterfly: Un Bel Dì, Vedremo {Some Day He'll Come} (Act 2)
                   (G. Puccini)                                      Vi 4149
BVE 51696-5   Madame Butterfly: Butterfly's Death Scene-Act 2 (G. Puccini) Vi 4149
              orch d Rosario Bourdon                    NY  May 31, 1929
```

29.19. Tanaka Otake *vocal*

```
              Kappore-Dancing Song                          Ed 12820(2 min)
              Suiryo Bushi-Two Love Songs {Think It Over}    Ed 12821(2 min)
              samisen                                   NY  ca April 1905
```

29.20.   Unidentified Vocal

1490	title untraced¹	Phono-Cut 5216
1494	title untraced	Phono-Cut 5216
	samisen, dm, female or ¹male singer	Boston(?) 1913

29.21.   Yoshida Naramaru   *vocal*

B 20402-1	Yoshitomo's Miyako Ochi	
	{From Kyoto To Noma No Utsumi 700 Years Ago}-Pt. 1	Vi 50172
B 20403-1	Yoshitomo's Miyako Ochi	
	{From Kyoto To Noma No Utsumi 700 Years Ago}-Pt. 2	Vi 50172
B 20404-1	Yoshitomo's Miyako Ochi	
	{From Kyoto To Noma No Utsumi 700 Years Ago}-Pt. 3	Vi 50173
B 20405-1	Yoshitomo's Miyako Ochi	
	{From Kyoto To Noma No Utsumi 700 Years Ago}-Pt. 4	Vi 50173
B 20406-1	Yoshitomo's Miyako Ochi	
	{From Kyoto To Noma No Utsumi 700 Years Ago}-Pt. 5	Vi 50174
B 20407-1	America Miyage {From Japan To America}-Pt. 1	Vi rej
B 20408-1	America Miyage {From Japan To America}-Pt. 2	Vi rej
B 20409-1	America Miyage {From Japan To America}-Pt. 3	Vi rej
B 20410-1	America Miyage {From Japan To America}-Pt. 4	Vi rej
B 20411-2	Adzuma No Hana-Biogrqphy Of Sakuragawa Gorozo-Pt. 1	Vi rej
B 20412-1	Adzuma No Hana-Biography Of Sakuragawa Gorozo-Pt. 2	Vi rej
B 20413-1	Adzuma No Hana-Biography Of Sakuragawa Gorozo-Pt. 3	Vi 50179
B 20414-1	Adzuma No Hana-Biography Of Sakuragawa Gorozo-Pt. 4	Vi 50179
B 20415-1	Adzuma No Hana-Biography of Sakuragawa Gorozo-Pt. 5	Vi 50180
B 20416-1	Adzuma No Hana-Biography of Sakuragawa Gorozo-Pt. 6	Vi 50180
B 20417-1	Katsuda Shinaemon, from "Chiushin Gishi"-Pt. 1	Vi 50181
B 20418-1	Katsuda Shinaemon, from "Chiushin Gishi"-Pt. 2	Vi 50181
B 20419-1	Katsuda Shinaemon, from "Chiushin Gishi"-Pt. 3	Vi 50182
B 20420-2	Katsuda Shinaemon, from "Chiushin Gishi"-Pt. 4	Vi 50182
	Mrs. Toyoto Yoshida-samisen	NY July 20, 1917

B 20411-2	Adzuma No Hana-Biography Of Sakuragawa Gorozo-Pt. 1	Vi 50178
B 20412-2	Adzuma No Hana-Biography Of Sakuragawa Gorozo-Pt. 2	Vi 50178
B 20421-1	Biography Of Lincoln-Pt. 1	Vi 50183
B 20422-1	Biography Of Lincoln-Pt. 2	Vi rej
B 20423-1	Taira No Kagekiyo-Pt. 1	Vi 50184
B 20424-1	Taira No Kagekiyo-Pt. 2	Vi rej
B 20425-1	Taira No Kagekiyo-Pt. 3	Vi 50185
B 20426-1	Taira No Kagekiyo-Pt. 4	Vi 50185
B 20427-1	Taira No Kagekiyo-Pt. 5	Vi rej
B 20428-1	Taira No Kagekiyo-Pt. 6	Vi 50186
B 20429-1	Taira No Kagekiyo-Pt. 7	Vi 50187
B 20430-1	Taira No Kagekiyo-Pt. 8	Vi 50187
B 20431-1	Tokiwano Mae	Vi rej
B 20444-1	Yato Uemonshichi No Chiugi (Ako Gishi)-Pt. 1	Vi rej
B 20445-1	Yato Uemonshichi No Chiugi (Ako Gishi)-Pt. 2	Vi 50188
B 20446-1	Yato Uemonshichi No Chiugi (Ako Gishi)-Pt. 3	Vi 50189
B 20447-1	Yato Uemonshichi No Chiugi (Ako Gishi)-Pt. 4	Vi 50189
	as before	NY July 24, 1917

B 20407-2	America Miyage {From Japan To America}-Pt. 1		Vi 50175
B 20408-2	America Miyage {From Japan To America}-Pt. 2		Vi 50175
B 20409-2	America Miyage {From Japan To America}-Pt. 3		Vi 50176
B 20410-2	America Miyage {From Japan To America}-Pt. 4		Vi 50176
B 20450-1	America Miyage {From Japan To America}-Pt. 5		Vi 50177
B 20451-1	America Miyage {From Japan To America}-Pt. 6		Vi 50177
B 20422-2	Biography Of Lincoln-Pt. 2		Vi 50183
B 20424-2	Taira No Kagekiyo-Pt. 2		Vi 50184
B 20427-2	Taira No Kagekiyo-Pt. 5		Vi 50186
B 20431-2	Tokiwano Mae		Vi 50174
B 20444-2	Yato Uemonshichi No Chiugi (Ako Gishi)-Pt. 1		Vi 50188
	as before	NY July 25, 1917	

PART 7

SCANDINAVIAN

SECTION 30. DANISH

30.1. Per Bjørn *bass-baritone*

39768-	Den Store Hvide Flok (Grieg)	Co E2247
39769-	Bøn For Danmark (Hornemann)	Co E2247
39770-	Paa Søen Naar Den Skummer Vred (Heiberg)	Co E2248
39771-	Ørnen Løfter Med Stærke Slag {Arnes Sang} (Heise)	Co E2248
39772-1	Den Spillemand Snapped Fiolen Fra Væg (Miskow)	Co E2249
39773-1	Bergmanden {Bergvæg, Brist Med Larm Og Brag} (Heise)	Co E2249

orch   NY January 13, 1915

9628	Sang Af "Tycho Brahes Spaadom" {The Reader Of The Stars} (C.E.F. Weyse)	Ed 59010
9629	Vær Hilset, Mit Gamle Fædreland! {I Salute Thee, My Fatherland} (Niels W. Gade)	Ed 59008
9630	Danmark, Dejligst Vang Og Vænge {Denmark, The Land Of Green Meadows} (P.E. Rasmussen)	Ed 59008

orch   NY July 14, 1924

9631	Skøn Jomfru! Luk Dit Vindue Op {Open Thy Window, Pretty Maiden} (C.E.F. Weyse)	Ed 59009
9632	Der Staær Et Slot I Vesterled {Evening Song} (C.E.F. Weyse)	Ed 59009
9633	Nattens Dæmrende Taager {Coming Of The Night Fog} (T. Mortensen)	Ed 59010

p   NY July 21, 1924

30.2. Paul Bjørnskjold *tenor*

	Polsk Fædrelandssang	Vi trial
	H. Trolle-unk instrument	NY May 29, 1918

84432-2	Den Lille Ole Med Paraplyen	Co E4090
84440-2	Ved Fremmed Kyst Paa Fjerne Strand	Co E4012
84441-1	Jylland Mellem Tvende Have (Heise-Anderson)	Co E4012
84444-2	To Drosler Sad Paa Bøgekvist (Dedekan-Bruun)	Co E4066
84445-1	Livet Kan Være Forbandet Nok	Co E4066
84446-	God Aften, God Aften	Co E4090
84447-	Det Er Saa Yndigt At Følges Ad (Weyse-Grundtvig)	Co E4167
84448-	Du Er Rig, Du Er Dejlig, O Syd (R. Bay)	Co E4167
84449-	I Gaar Jeg Fik Min Trøje!	Co E4461
84450-	Selma	Co E4461
	Valkyrien: Sigmunds Elskovssang (Wagner)	Co E4011
	Mestersangerne: I Arnekrog Ved Vintertid (Wagner)	Co E4011
	Den Gang Jeg Drog Afsted	Co E4065

	Der Er Et Land Dets Sted Er Højt Mod Norden (Weyse-Boye)	Co E4065
	Den Dag Jeg Første Gang Dig Saa	Co E4089
	Du Spørger, Min Dreng (Lumbye-Glückstadt)	Co E4089
	Slumrer Sødt I Slesvigs Jord (Hartmann-Holst)	Co E4166
	Slesvig Vort Omstridte Elskede Land (Thaulow)	Co E4166
	Du Skønne Fortryllende Kirsten (Bøgh)	Co E4284
	I Natten Klam Og Kold (Hornemann-Recke)	Co E4284
	orch	NY ca June 1918

B 23542-2	Herre Konge, Bliv Her! (P. Heise)	Vi rej
B 23543-2	Dansken Har Sejr Vundet	Vi 72559
B 23544-2	Taaren (Sofie Dedokam)	Vi rej
B 23545-2	Nu Vil Jeg Synge {En Gadevise}	Vi 73217
	orch d Rosario Bourdon	NY December 22, 1919

B 23542-4	Herre Konge, Bliv Her! (P. Heise)	Vi rej
B 23561-3	Agnete Og Havmanden	Vi 72559
B 23562-2	Til Den Lille By {Det Gaar Atter Hjemad}, from "Verdens Herkules"	
		Vi 72945
B 23563-2	Nattens Dæmrende Taager	Vi rej
B 23564-1	Hvorfor Svulmer Weichselfloden (Niels W. Gade)	Vi rej
	as before	NY January 2, 1920

B 23544-3	Taaren (Sofie Dedokam)'	Vi 72945
B 23564-3	Hvorfor Svulmer Weichselfloden (Niels W. Gade)	Vi rej
B 23565-2	Min Hakke, Min Slovl Og Min Spade (Johannes Torrild)	Vi rej
B 23566-1	Et Bondebryllup (E. Hornemann)	Vi 73217
	as before	NY January 5, 1920

85789-	Naar Maanens Straaler Forsølver Staden	Co E4816
85790-	Vort Modersmaal Er Dejligt	Co E4664
85791-	Jomfru, Vil De Med I Skoven?	Co E4664
85792-	Dejlige Danmark	Co E4665
85793-	Skriv Hjem Til Mor	Co E4665
85794-	Der Var En Svend Med Sin Pigelil	Co E4816
85795-	Roselil Og Hendes Moder	Co E4604
85796-	Lille Ellen	Co E4605
85797-	Gutter Om Bord	Co E4605
85801-	En Sekstur, Ak, I Det Lille Ord	Co E4604
85802-	De Sønderjydske Piger	Co E4737
85803-2	Julia, Julia Hopsasa	Co E4521
85804-2	Ser I Hvem Der Kommer Her?	Co E4521
85805-	Kærlighed Fra Gud'	Co E4736
85806-	Kirkeklokke! Ej Til Hovedstæder'	Co E4894
85807-	Dejlig Er Jorden'	Co E4736
85808-	Herr Peder Kasted Runer Over Spange	Co E4737
85809-	Skærsommersangen	Co E4894
85810-	Bedstefars Uhr	Co E4522
85811-	En Sømands Brud Har Bølgen Kær	Co E4522
	orch or 'org	NY ca January 1920

87069-	Det Kimer Nu Til Julefest-Christmas Song (Balle-Grundtvig)	Co E7284

87070-	Julen Har Bragt Velsignet Bud-Christmas Song (Weyse-Ingemann)	
		Co E7284
	org, glockenspiel	NY ca February 1921

87104-1	Hvor Nilen Vander (H. Rung)	Co E7285
87105-2	Skamlingsbanken {On The Banks Of The Wabash} (Ved. P. Wurck)	
		Co E7285
	as before	NY February 1921

B 27086-3	Hils Fra Mig Derhjemme (Elith Worsing)	Vi rej
B 27639-2	Ved Øresunds Kyst (Wilhelm Hansen)	Vi 73782
	orch d Ted Levy	Camden, NJ March 7, 1923

B 27086-6	Hils Fra Mig Derhjemme (Elith Worsing)	Vi 73782
	orch d Nathaniel Shilkret	NY March 20, 1923

30.3. Fred Bliss *tenor*

W 106075-2	Vaagn Af Din Slummer	Co 2004-F
W 106076-1	Paa Søndag Aften	Co 2004-F
W 106077-2	Har Man Ungdomskræfter	Co 2005-F
W 106078-2	Sømandssang	Co 2005-F
	harp trio	NY November 1925

30.4. Florence Bodinoff *mezzo-soprano*

B 21176-2	Aa, Farvel, Og Vær Velsignet (Rosenfeld); Tal Du Sagte, Unge	
	Nattergal (Borreson)	Vi rej
	King's Orchestra d Nathaniel Shilkret	NY December 13, 1917

5929	Flyv, Fugl! {Fly, Birdie, Fly} (w: Chr. Winter, m: S.P.E. Hartmann)	
		Ed 77001, 78008
5930	Den Tapre Landsoldat {The Brave Soldier} (E. Horneman)	
		Ed 77001, 78008
	orch	NY December 17, 1917

B 21198-1	Der Er Et Yndigt Land {Fædrelandsang}	
	(H.E. Krøyer-A. Oehlenschläger)	Vi rej
	King's Orchestra d Nathaniel Shilkret	NY December 20, 1917

B 21176-3	Aa Farvel, Og Vær Velsignet (Rosenfeld); Tal Du Sagte, Unge	
	Nattergal (Borreson)	Vi 72170
B 21198-3	Der Er Et Yndigt Land {Fædrelandsang}	
	(H.E. Krøyer-A. Oehlenschläger)	Vi rej
B 21524-2	De Vog Dem, Vi Grov Dem (Hillebrandt)	Vi 72170
	as before	NY February 15, 1918

30.5. Gudrun Carlson *soprano*

B 4115-1	Jocelyn: Berceuse (Godard)	Vi 3715, 15193, 63414
E 4116-1	Vuggesang (Ploug-Hartmann)	Vi 3714, 15192(8")

B 4117-1	Hjemwee (Rudolph Bay)	Vi 3717, 15195, 63415
E 4118-1	De To Katte (Tofft)	Vi rej (8")
B 4119-1	Champagnevise (N. Hansen)	Vi 3716, 15194, 63414
	p	NY December 7, 1906

Vi 15192-15195 were never released.

30.6. Dansk Infanteri Band (Danish Military Band)

44165-	Aarhus Tappenstreg-March Polka (C.Møller)	Co E2969
44166-	Den Gamle Soldats Minder Fra Kriget 1848 (Selling)	Co E2969
44167-	Patriotisk Fire Blade Klöver (arr Selling)	Co E2970
44168-	I Kongelunden-Vals (Heiberg)	Co E2970
	d C.M. Selling	NY ca July 1916

Scandinavian Infantry Band

44880-	Potpourri Af Norske Sange (C.M. Selling)	Co E3351
44881-	To Springdanse (Bergen-Aamot)	Co E3351
44916-	Potpourri Över Svenska Folksånger (Selling)	Co E3355
44917-1	Fjällnäs Polka {Trekarlspolka} {Dwie Mazur Polka}	
	{Two Polka-Mazurka}	Co E3338
44918-1	Militär Rheinländer {Military Dance} {Wojskowy Taniec "Rheinlander"}	
		Co E3338
44919-	Marsz-Polka {Jodler Marsch-Polka} {March-Polka}	Co E3337
44920-	Mazur-Polka {Polska-Mazurka} {Polka-Mazurka}	Co E3337
	Paa Rundreise (Selling)	Co E3894
	as before	NY early 1917

Co E3337 and E3338 as COLUMBIA BAND, E3894 as DANSK INFANTERI BAND

Dansk Infanteri Band

58209-2	De Danske Matroser-Samling Af Orloos-Sange (C.M. Selling)	Co E3396
58211-2	Hedvig Polka (Ramsöe-Selling)¹	Co E3396, E3474
	Jadwigapolka	Co E3474
	De Danske Skytter	Co E3395
	Kombinations Dans	Co E3395
	as before, ¹Benjamin Klatzkin-tp solo	NY April 1917

Co E3474 (International and Polish) as COLUMBIA BAND, with Polish copies
(Jadwigapolka) as ORKIESTRA COLUMBIA

Danish Military Band

58951-2	Vagtparaden Paa Amalienborg	Co E3819
58952-2	Champagne Galop (Lumbye)	Co E3819
		NY October 1917

Scandinavian Military Band

4527-2	Kongliga Kronobergs Regementes Parad-Marsch (arr Selling)	Em 18007
4528-1	Herliga Land; Marschen Gar Till Tuma; Vart Fosterland; Glad Sasom	
	Foglen (arr Selling)	Em 18007
	Riberhus Marsch	Em 18006
	Gamle Danmark	Em 18006
		NY ca October 1919

Selling's Militär Tanzkapelle

41482-2	Manover Polka	Em 19017
41483-3	Ella-Rheinländer	Em 19017
		NY ca October 1920

Fanfaren Kapelle

41515-3	Potpourri (arr C.M. Selling)	Em 19018
41516-2	Medley Of Christmas Songs	Em 19018
	d C.M. Selling	NY November 1920

41592-2	Lustige Brüder: Donauwellen; Wiener Blut; Künstler Leben-Potpourri	Em 19023
41593-3	Ein Flotter Studio-Marsch	Em 19023
		NY ca December 1920

30.7. Carl Friberg *vocal*

CVE 47795-2	Gurre (Hvor Nilen Vander Ægypterens Jord} (Henrik Rung)	Vi rej (12")
CVE 47796-3	Skærsommersangen	Vi rej (12")
	2 vln, fl, vc, p, sbs, d Leonard Joy	NY October 20, 1928

30.8. Johannes Herskind *vocal*

B 4100-1	Gold Er Den Jord: Sang Af Tordenvejr (Heise)	Vi 3705, 15183, 63410
B 4101-1	Liden Karen (Heise)	Vi 3702, 15180, 63409
B 4102-1	Den Spillemand Snapped Fiolen Fra Væg (Miskow)	Vi 3708, 15186, 63411
B 4103-1	Majsang (G.A. Lembcke)	Vi 3711, 15189, 63412
E 4104-1	Du Lille Zuzu (Dougherty)	Vi rej (8")
B 4105-1	La Mascotte: Duk Duk {Gobble Duet} (Audran)[1]	Vi 3718, 15196, 4977
B 4106-1	Lykkebranet Jag: Tilstaa Noa (Audran)[1]	Vi rej
B 4107-1	Tambour Majorens Datter {Drum Major's Daughter}: Legende	
	(Offenbach)[1]	Vi 3721, 15199, 63416
B 4108-1	Bellman Og Wessel (Offert Jespersen)[1]	Vi 3719, 15197, 63415
B 4109-1	Fritz Og Lise (Offenbach)[1]	Vi 3720, 15196, 63416
E 4110-1	Eventyr Paa Fodrejsen (Bruun)	Vi 3704, 15182(8")
B 4111-1	Det Ved Jeg Lille Mor (Juel-Fredericksen)	Vi 3709, 15187, 63411
B 4112-1	Den Kjærlighed Som Jeg Mon Hære {Kelserens Nye Klæder} (Kjerulf)	
		Vi 3707, 15185, 63410
B 4113-1	Midsommervise (Lange-Muller)	Vi 3703, 15181, 63409
E 4114-1	Kender Du Danmark (Bachgarde)	Vi 3701, 15179(8")
	p, [1]with Gudrun Carlson	NY December 6, 1906

E 4120-1	Til Ungdommen (O. Jacobsen)	Vi 3706, 15184
B 4121-1	Sommernat (Bæckers-Munkel)	Vi 3713, 15191, 63413
E 4122-1	Bryllup I Skoven	Vi 3700, 15178(8")
B 4123-1	Serenade Af Molboerne (Offert Jespersen)	Vi 3712, 15190, 63413
B 4124-1	Gammel Kjærlighed (Hildebrand)	Vi 3710, 15188, 63412
	p	NY December 7, 1906

Vi 15178-15199 were never issued.

	Vi Elske Vort Land	Co E400
	Eventyr Paa Fodrejsen	Co E400
		NY 1900s

30.9. Axel Jorgenson *baritone*

	Dagen Gaar Med Raske; Vaagn Af Din Slummer	Vi trial
	Ted Levy-p	NY December 23, 1916

B 19023-2	Danmark, Vor Elskede Gamle Mor!-Patriotic Song	Vi 69260
B 19024-1	Kongernes Konge-Patriotic Song (Horneman)	Vi 69288
B 19025-3	O Margareta-Romance (Gounod)	Vi rej
B 19026-2	Der Var En Svend (Heise)	Vi rej
B 19027-2	Vuggesang {Cradle Song} (Hartmann)	Vi rej
B 19028-2	Hvor Nilen Vander (Rung)	Vi rej
	King's Orchestra	NY January 9, 1917

B 19031-2	Flyv, Fugl Flyv!	Vi 69288
B 19032-1	Valdemar Og Tove (w: I.R. Jacobsen)	Vi 69260
B 19037-2	Dagen Gaar Med Raske Fjed-Hymn'	Vi rej
B 19038-2	Kirkeklokke-Hymn'	Vi rej
	King's Orchestra or 'Edward T. King-org	NY January 10, 1917

30.10. Mischa Leon *tenor*

B 19452-2	Serenade, from "Der Var Engang" (P.E. Lange-Muller, op. 25)	Vi 69411
B 19453-2	Arme Hjerte! Er Du Træt (P. Heise)	Vi 69412
B 19454-1	Venetiansk Serenade (John Paulsen-Johan Svendsen, op. 24 no. 3)	Vi 69412
B 19455-2	Det Gamle Kristianshavn (Holger Drachmann-Charles Kjerulf, op. 30 no. 4)	Vi 69411
	King's Orchestra	NY April 6, 1917

B 19919-2	Ved Solnedgang (P.E. Lange-Muller, op. 14 no. 1)	Vi rej
B 19920-1	Liden Karen (P. Heise)	Vi 69672
B 19921-1	Jens Vejmand (Carl Nielsen)	Vi 73783
B 19922-2	Jeg Elsker Dig (Edvard Grieg)	Vi rej
	as before	NY May 17, 1917

B 19959-2	Lær Mig! (J.P.E. Hartmann)	Vi rej
B 19960-1	Vuggesang (Emil Hartmann)	Vi 69672
B 19961-2	Vaagn Af Din Slummer (P. Heise)	Vi 73783

B 19962-2   Faust: Siebels Arie (Ch. Gounod) [in French]   Vi rej
             King's Orchestra d Rosario Bourdon   NY May 29, 1917

30.11. Einar Linden *tenor*

43691-	Eventyr Paa Fodrejsen-"Ja Hvis I Skovens Hal"	Co E2737
43692-	Naar Pisken Den Knalder (Weyse)	Co E2737
	Paa Söndag Aften	Co E2736
	Jeg Kom Bag Plankeværket	Co E2736
	orch	NY late 1915

30.12. Enrico Palmetto *tenor*

45798-1	Ak' Kæreste Hr. Guldsmed {Oh! Dearest Mr. Goldsmith} (N.W. Gade)	
		Co E2451
45799-1	Husker Du I Høst {Do You Remember The Harvest Time?} (P. Heise)	
		Co E2451
45800-1	Gud Har Min Sjæl (Slapisson)	Co E2631
45801-1	Vuggesang (I.P. Hartmann)	Co E2634
	orch	NY June 21, 1915

45802-1	Den Spillemand Snapped Fiolen Fra Væg (Sextus Miskow)	Co E2450
45803-1	I Danmark Er Jeg Født {Danmark Mit Fædreland} {In Denmark I Am Born}	
	(Henrik Rung)	Co E2632
45809-2	Lyksalig Hver Sjæl Som Har Fred (Berggren)	Co E2449
45810-1	En Engel Har Rørt Ved Din Pande (Lange-Muller)	Co E2449
45811-2	Kornmodsglansen (Lange-Muller)	Co E2634
45812-1	Flyv, Fugl, Flyv {Fly Birdie Fly} (I.P. Hartmann)	Co E2633
45813-1	Hvor Skulte Jeg	Co rej
	orch	NY June 22, 1915

45816-1	Kongernes Konge (Hornemann)	Co E2631
45817-2	Sømandsang (J. Beckgaard)	Co E2633
45818-2	Serenade Venetienne (J.S. Svendsen)	Co E2635
45819-2	Majsang; Skin Ud Klare Solskin (G.A. Lembke)	Co E2450
45820-2	Danmark Skal Staa {Denmark Shall Stand, Though Waves Roll On}	
	(G.A. Lembcke)	Co E2632
	orch	NY June 23, 1915

46576-1	I Pagliacci: Canios Sang (Leoncavallo)	Co E2635
	orch	Chicago August 1915

58601-	Dejlig Er Den Himmel Blaa-Christmas Song'	Co E3549
58602-	Højt Fra Træts Grønne Top-Christmas Song'	Co E3550
58603-	Ole Og Margrette	Co E3893
58604-	Glade Jul Dejlige Jul-Christmas Song'	Co E3549
58605-	Et Barn Er Født I Betlehem-Christmas Song'	Co E3550
58606-	Det Er Et Yndigt Land-National Song	Co E3551
58607-	Kong Kristian Stod Ved Højen Mast-National Song	Co E3551
58608-	Vift Stolt Paa Kodans Bølge (R. Bay)	Co E3656
58609-	Den Tapre Landsoldat-Soldier Song (Hornemann-Faber)	Co E3656

58610-	Nattens Dæmrende Taager (Mortensen-Ploug)	Co E3656
	orch or 'org	NY ca August 1917

30.13. Siegfried Philip *baritone*

	I Know Of Two Eyes	Vi trial
	For You Alone	Vi trial
	Edward T. King-p	NY February 9, 1917

B 20532-2	Skin Ud, Du Klare Solskin (P.E. Lange-Muller, op. 18 no. 4)	Vi 69697
B 20533-1	Den Danske Sang (P. Lauritson-Robert Henriques)	Vi 69697
	King's Orchestra d Rosario Bourdon	NY August 16, 1917

B 20542-2	Jeg Ved Mig To Øjne (August Enna)	Vi rej
	as before	NY September 6, 1917

B 20548-3	Knud Lavard (m: N.W. Gade, w: Carsten Hauch)	Vi rej
B 20553-2	Ved Land (Julius Bechgaard)	Vi rej
B 20554-2	En Sangers Bøn (F.A. Reissiger)	Vi rej
	as before	NY September 11, 1917

B 20542-3	Jeg Ved Mig To Øjne (August Enna)	Vi rej
B 20554-4	En Sangers Bøn (F.A. Reissiger)	Vi 72368
B 20578-2	Hjemkomsten {From Sømands Liv} (Julius Bechgaard)	Vi rej
	King's Orchestra	NY September 20, 1917

B 20583-1	Kirkeklokke Ej Til Hovedstæder (N.F.S. Grundtvig-H. Rung)	Vi 72368
	as before	NY September 21, 1917

30.14. Jacob Saxtorph-Mikkelsen *baritone*

	Den Jydske Lyng	Co E3657
	Den Blanke Aa (G. Knudsen-J. Aakjær)	Co E3657
	Bal I Provinsen	Co E3658
	Kjesten Og Kræn Kresten	Co E3658
	orch	NY 1917

58746-2	Havren	Co E3719
58747-2	Pæ' Søwren	Co E3720
58748-	Mads Tammesens Maren	Co E3718
58749-	Ole Ligeglads Viser No.1	Co E3812
58750-2	Forspil Til Rugens Sange	Co E3719
58752-	Stille Hjerte	Co E3812
58765-	Klokken	Co E3718
58767-1	Æ Gammel Smed'	Co E3720
	orch, or 'spoken	NY ca November 1917

30.15. Axel Schutz *vocal*

9659 K-K-K-Ketty {K-K-K-Katy} (w: Axel Andreasen, m: Geoffrey O'Hara)
                    Ed 59011
9660 Dejlige Fjord {By The Beautiful River} (w: Sofus Peterson,
    m: H. Christine)   Ed 59011
  John F. Burckhardt-p   NY August 5, 1924

30.16. Estrid Terkelsen *contralto*

B 20799-2 Vuggevise (H. Bodenhoff)   Vi 72660
B 20900-2 Droslen Slog I Skov Sin Klare Trille (Joseph Glæser) Vi 72660
  King's Orchestra   NY October 19, 1917

B 21336-2 Nær Kysten Paa Fyen (Caroline Recke Madsden)   Vi rej
B 21337-2 Slesvig, Vort Elskede, Omstridte Land (Th. Thaulow) Vi rej
  orch d Nathaniel Shilkret   NY January 4, 1918

B 21336-3 Nær Kysten Paa Fyen (Caroline Recke Madsden)   Vi 73296
B 21337-4 Slesvig, Vort Elskede, Omstridte Land (Th. Thaulow) Vi 73296
  as before   NY January 24, 1918

SECTION 31. FINNISH

31.1. Lillian Aho *vocal*

AFS 2379B1   Matkamies Matkalla   LC
AFS 2389A1&2 Oi Terve Pohjola Isäimme Kotimaa'   LC
             unaccompanied, or 'with Peter Aho, unk kantele
                                              Calumet, MI   September 1938

31.2. Jukka Ahti *tenor (b. 1897)*

This artist's original name was Jukka Hietanen.

BVE 57114-2   Kulkiessani Vainiolla {Strolling In The Meadow}   Vi V-4060
BVE 57115-2   Siniharjulla {On The Blue Ridge}   Vi V-4060
BVE 57116-2   Tienraivaaja {The Pioneer} (Olavi Hirvonen)   Vi V-4055
BVE 56117-2   Proletaarilapsen Laulu {Song Of The Proletariat}   Vi V-4055
             vln, vc, p, d Alfredo Cibelli   NY   October 24, 1929

BVE 59150-1   Vapaa Venäjä {Free Russia}   Vi V-4068
BVE 59151-2   Ole Armollinen {Be Merciful} (N.R. Bakaleinikow)   Vi V-4070
BVE 59152-1   Mustalais Romanssi {Gypsy Romance} {Lyö Ystäväin,
                  Nyt Kanssain Kättä}   Vi V-4070
BVE 59153-1   Kansainvälinen {Internationale} {Song Of The Laborers} (Degeyter)
                                                                     Vi V-4068
             c, vln, fl, cl, tb, p, tuba, tr, d Alfredo Cibelli
                                                     NY   February 5, 1930

BVE 62228-1   Villiruusu {Wild Rose} (Evert Suonio)   Vi V-4091, V-4151, 26-6004
BVE 62229-2   Kevät Laulu {Spring Song}, from "Kun Kevät Kutsuu" (Wm. E. Stein)
                                                                     Vi V-4081
BVE 62230-1   Vapauden Aamu {Morning Of Freedom} (arr Alfredo Cibelli)
                              Vi V-4091, V-4151, 26-6004, RCA PL40115(33)
BVE 62231-2   Leimun Laulu {Song Of The Flame} (Herbert Stothart-G. Gershwin)
                                                                     Vi V-4081
             tp, vln, fl, cl, tb, p, tuba, d Alfredo Cibelli   NY   May 15, 1930

BRC 69698-1   Lautta Laulu (w: J. Virtanen)   Vi V-4129
BRC 69699-1   Sua Lemmin {I Love Thee}, from "Kun Kevät Kutsuu" (w: Wm. E. Stein)
                                                                     Vi V-4110
BRC 69700-1   Vanhan Merenkävijän Laulu (Francois)   Vi V-4129
             Alfredo Cibelli-md, unk g   NY   June 8, 1931

BRC 69936-1   Oi Älä Vaadi Multa   Vi V-4120
BRC 69937-1   Oli Silloin (Wm. E. Stein)   Vi V-4120

2565

BRC 69938-1   Tarina Ruususta {The Tale Of The Rose} (m: Jukka Ahti)   Vi V-4115
BRC 69939-1   Serenadi (tr Jukka Ahti, m: E. Toselli)   Vi V-4115
              vln, cl, vc, p, sbs, d Alfredo Cibelli   NY June 15, 1931

BRC 69948-1   Kevät Pohjolassa {Springtime In The Northland}
              {Springtime In The Rockies} (tr Jukka Ahti)   Vi V-4110
                                                                     NY June 16, 1931

On matrix BRC 69948, Ahti is accompanied by a recording (BVE 63380-2) by Alfredo
Cibelli's Orchestra, originally issued as V-60 by the TIVOLI NOVELTY ORCHESTRA

31.3. Jennie Anderson *soprano*

W 105826-2   Laula Tyttö   Co 3014-F, 16173
W 105827-2   Kevät Laulu   Co 3014-F, 16173
             orch   NY ca August 1925

W 109534-2   Tuutulaulu (Emil Kauppi)   Co 3163-F
W 109535-1   Vanha Raita (Martti Nisonen)   Co 3163-F
W 109536-1   Soita Somer, Helkä Hiekka! (Emil Kauppi)   Co 3120-F
W 109537-4   Etsiessä (Aaro Vallinmäki)   Co 3120-F
             orch   NY July 1928

31.4. Anderson Ja Söderlund *accordion duet*

The second artist is Matti Söderlund.

84866-1   Kielan Jäähyvaste   Co E4350
84867-2   Tunturin Kellot   Co E4226
84869-1   Koiviston Polska   Co E4226
                                                             NY ca October 1918

31.5. B.S.S. Clubin Orkesteri

The abbreviation stands for "Brooklynin Suomalainen Sosialisti Clubi".

W 109484-1   Venäläinen Surumarssi (M.L. Lake)
                                     Co 3094-F, 16171, Eteenpäin ETLP-301(33)
W 109485-2   Vapaa Venäjän Marssi (W.N. Rostakowsky)   Co 3084-F, 3174-F, 16067
W 109486-2   Kansainvälinen Marssi (Adolphe De Geyter)   Co 3084-F, 16067
             d Oskar Tofferi   NY July 1928

31.6. Waldemar Carlson *accordion*

BVE 41744-2   Waldemar Valssi (arr Waldemar Carlson)   Vi rej
BVE unnumbered-1 Perhonen {Butterfly}-Sotissi   Vi rej
                                                          NY February 16, 1928

31.7. Marjorie Edgar *vocal*

AFS 3247A4   Wake Up   LC
AFS 3247A5   The Carvers Of The Hour   LC
                      National Folk Festival, Chicago May 1937

The singer is from Maria on St. Croix, MN.

31.8. John M. Eriksen *vocal*

B 4637-1   Suomen Laulu (Pacius)   Vi 3915
E 4638-1   Honkain Keskellä (Wegelius)   Vi 3900(8")
B 4639-1   Sä Kasvoit Neito Kaunoinen   Vi 3916
E 4640-1   Tuoll' On Mun Kultani   Vi 3901(8")
B 4641-1   Yksin Istun Ja Lauleskelen   Vi 3917
E 4642-1   Oi Maamme Suomi (Pacius)   Vi 3902(8")
E 4643-1   Aamulla Varhain   Vi 3903(8")
E 4644-1   Oi, Jos Ilta Joutuisi   Vi 3904(8")
            p   NY July 8, 1907

E 4646-1   Voi Äiti Parka Ja Raukka   Vi 3905(8")
E 4647-1   Minun Kultani Kaukana Kukkuu   Vi 3911(8")
E 4648-1   Taivas On Sininen   Vi 3907(8")
B 4649-1   Savolaisen Laulu (Collan)   Vi 3908
B 4650-1   Voi Minua Poika Raukka   Vi 3918
E 4651-1   Yksi Ruusu On Kasvanut Laaksossa   Vi 3909(8")
E 4652-1   Kesä-Ilta   Vi 3910(8")
E 4653-1   Minun Kultani Kaunis On   Vi 3906(8")
B 4654-1   Mustalaiseks Olen Syntynyt¹   Vi 3919
E 4655-1   Tula Tuulan Tula Tuli Tei (Merikanto)¹   Vi 3912(8")
E 4656-1   Punasarafaani   Vi 3913(8")
E 4657-1   Täällä, Tääll' On Ihanaista¹   Vi 3914(8")
            p or ¹unaccompanied   NY July 9, 1907

31.9. Finnish American Elite Choir

B 13432-2   Suomen Laulu (F. Pacius)   Vi 65420
B 13433-1   Suomis Sång (F. Pacius) [in Swedish]   Vi rej
B 13434-1   Björneborgarnes-Marsch (arr F. Pacius) [in Swedish]   Vi rej
B 13435-1   Iloa Ja Surua {Joy And Sorrow} (w: Runeberg, arr E. Sivori) Vi 65418
B 13436-2   Terve Suomeni Maa (E. Genetz)   Vi 65418
B 13437-2   Hälsning Till Hemlandet {Greetings To My Native Land} (Kromer)
                      [in Swedish]   Vi rej
B 13438-1   Myrsky-Yo Merellä   Vi 65419
B 13239-1   Lugn Hvilar Sjön (Pfeil) [in Swedish]   Vi rej
B 13240-2   Maamme {Our Country} (Runeberg-Pacius)   Vi 65419
B 13241-1   Porilaisten {Björneborgarnes}-Marssi (Runeberg-Pacius) Vi 65420
                                              NY June 16, 1913

31.10. Group From De Kalb *instrumental*

AFS 3248A4&B1	Vedän Verkaa Kudon Sarkaa	LC
AFS 3248B2	30-Vuotisen Sodan Marssi	LC
AFS 3248B3	Me Marssimme Yli Vuorten	LC

National Folk Festival, Chicago May 1937

31.11. Ilona Hallinen *vocal*

AFS 2399B1	Liian Nuori Olin Minä Ijältäni	LC
AFS 2399B2	Hyvästi Nyt Kaikki Hyvästi Isänmaa	LC

Allouez, MI September 30, 1938

31.12. Hänninen Ja Williams *instrumental*

W 109820-2	Hännisen Polka-Monio	Co 3138-F, DI49
W 109821-1	Hännis-Masurkka	Co 3138-F, DI49
	vln, acn	NY October 1928

31.13. Ilmari Hautala *vocal*

W 111946-3   Sakilaisten Laulu (arr J. Guilbert)

Co 3149-F, DI96, Sävel SÄLP 663(33)

W 111947- (W 194842) Ikä-neito Pelastusarmeijassa

Co 3149-F, DI96, Love LXLP505(33)

orch d Antti Kosola   NY ca April 1930

31.14. Amanda Heikkinen *vocal*

AFS 2394B3   Kaura Pellon Pientareella Kasvoi Kaunis Kukka   LC

Calumet, MI September 29, 1938

31.15. Lauri Herranen *accordion*

W 107822-2	Keskiyö-Valssi	Co 3053-F, 16158, Sävel SÄLP 663(33)
	Vid Midnatt-Vals	Co 22086-F
W 107823-2	Laurin Sotiisi	Co 3051-F, 16156
W 107824-2	Katkenneet Kielet-Valssi	Co 3051-F, 16156
W 107825-2	Salon Ruusu-Masurkka	Co 3053-F, 16158
		NY April 1927

Co 22086-F as ERIC NILSSON

W 108638-2	Klarinetti Polkka	Co 3070-F, 7803
W 108639-2	Muistojen Valssi	Co 3070-F, 7803
		NY January 1928

31.16. Leo Hill *(Länsimäki Vesteri) accordion (1895-1987)*

BVE 59613-1	Lämäskä-Polkka	Vi V-4069
BVE 59614-1	Kulkurin Kaiho {Vagabond's Regret}-Valssi	Vi V-4069
		NY March 5, 1930

BVE 59528-1	Muisto {Memory}-Sotiisi	Vi V-4084
BVE 59529-1	Väärä Ja Kiero Viitonen {Crooked And Askew}-Polkka	Vi V-4084
BVE 59530-1	Haaskin-Sotiisi	Vi V-4099
BVE 59531-1	Rukkaset-Valssi	Vi V-4099
	Eugenio Cibelli-g	NY March 18, 1930

31.17. Wäinö Hirvelä *vocal*

AFS 2423B	Tuonne Taakse Metsämaan, Sydämmeni Palaa¹	LC
AFS 2424A1	Minä Seisoin Korkealla Vuorella¹	LC
AFS 2424A2	title untraced	LC
	¹with kantele	Ironwood, MI October 9, 1938

AFS 2467B2	Kalevala (fragment)	LC
AFS 2468B2	Tuonne Taakse Metsämaan, Sydämmeni Palaa¹	LC
	¹with kantele	Ironwood, MI October 15, 1938

AFS 2424B2	Sa Kasvoit Neito Kaunoinen¹	LC
AFS 2467A1&2	Elämä Vieläkin Paratiisi Ois	LC
AFS 2467B1	Minne Käy Tuulen Ilmassa Tie	LC
	¹with kantele	Ironwood, MI October 1938

31.18. Henry Holm *vocal* ·

BVE 56155-2	Suomalaisen Cowboyn Laulu {Song Of The Finnish Cowboy}	
	(Martti Nisonen)	Vi V-4052
BVE 56156-2	Ristilukki {The Spider} (J. Sibelius)	Vi V-4052
BVE 56157-1	Mist On Tuo Joukko Valkoinen {The Vast Unnumbered Throngs}	Vi V-4067
BVE 56158-2	Sotilas Poika {The Soldier Boy} (F. Pacius)	Vi V-4067
	Alfredo Cibelli-vc, unk vln, p	NY September 26, 1929

31.19. Jallu Honkonen *(John Jalmari) baritone (b. 1883)*

W 111139-2	Mirri Sairastaa; Tiu Tau Tilhi	Co 3129-F, DI30
W 111140-3	Mamman Oma Matti; Satu Ihmeellisestä Vuoresta	Co 3129-F, DI30
W 111141-1	Turlita Tuohitorveen	Co 3146-F, DI64
W 111142-2	Yksin-Valssi (Herman Sjöblom)	Co 3146-F, DI64
	orch	NY October 1929

31.20. Adolf Hovi *tenor*

W 108197-2	Vappulaulu	Co 3056-F, 16172
W 108198-2	Orjan Kevät	Co 3056-F, 16172
	orch	NY July 1927

W 109836-3	Milloin Raukka Onnen Saa (E. Kauppi)	Co 3103-F, 16119
W 109837-2	Inarin Järvi (Evert Suonio-Z. Topelius)	Co 3103-F, 16119
W 109842-	Valtion Varsalla-Marssi (A. Similä)	Co 3105-F, 16192
W 109843-2	Suruhan Se Sorti Nuoren Pojan (A. Similä)	Co 3105-F, 16192
	orch	NY October 1928

31.21. Esteri Hukari *vocal*

W 113504-1	Vanha Kirkko (Yrjö Kilpinen)	Co 3206-F
W 113506-1	Kesäyö (Yrjö Kilpinen)	Co 3206-F
	Columbia Soitin Trio	NY April 1932

31.22. John Hyvönen *vocal*

AFS 2395B1	Pääsky Lintu Taivaan Lintu	LC
	Penabic, near Hancock, MI September 29, 1938	

AFS 2401A	Nyt Otan Kynän Käteeni Ja Laulun Kirjoitan	LC
	Penabic, near Hancock, MI September 30, 1938	

31.23. Pahka Jaakko *tenor*

B 21334-1	Kerran Ma Rakastuin Tyttöön {Once I Loved A Girl}	Vi rej
B 21335-2	Pikkuinen Poika {As A Little Boy}	Vi rej
	King's Orchestra d Nathaniel Shilkret	NY January 4, 1918

B 21334-3	Kerran Ma Rakastuin Tyttöön {Once I Loved A Girl}	Vi rej
B 21335-4	Pikkuinen Poika {As A Little Boy}	Vi rej
	as before	NY February 21, 1918

B 21334-4	Kerran Ma Rakastuin Tyttöön {Once I Loved A Girl}	Vi rej
B 21335-6	Pikkuinen Poika {As A Little Boy}	Vi 72552
	orch d Nathaniel Shilkret	NY April 23, 1918

B 21334-5	Kerran Ma Rakastuin Tyttöön {Once I Loved A Girl}	Vi 72552
	as before	NY June 27, 1918

31.24. Maikki Järnefelt Palmgren *soprano (1871-1929)*

	Summer Evening	Vi trial
	Selim Palmgren-p	NY August 29, 1921

B 25873-1   Polska (arr Selim Palmgren)   Vi 73184
B 25874-1   Pai Pai Paitaressu-Cradle Song (Oskar Merikanto)   Vi 73184
             orch d Nathaniel Shilkret   NY December 16, 1921

Vi 73184 as MAIKKI JÄRNEFELT

B 26015-2   En Vårvisa (Spring Song) (Selim Palmgren) [in Swedish]   Vi rej
B 26016-3   Liljekonvaljen (Lily Of The Valley) (Selim Palmgren)' [in Swedish]
                                                                        Vi rej
             orch d Nathaniel Shilkret, or 'Selim Palmgren   NY January 4, 1922

31.25. Jousinen Ja Stein *instrumental*

45746-1   Järven Polka   Co E2416
45747-1   Häämarssi Tippan   Co E2416
45748-1   Itin Tildu [Schottische]; Kalastajan Valssi   Co E2417
45749-1   Laihijian Polska (Lampaan Polska)   Co E2417
45750-1   Nuoren Vaimon Soitto   Co E2639
45751-1   Kissan Saakeli   Co E2639
45752-   Voi Äiti Parka Ja Raukka   Co rej
             probably: Jousinen-vln, William E. Stein-p   NY June 4, 1915

31.26. Aapo Juhani *vocal*

AFS 2387B1   Oi Armas Taisto Kun Olet Kerran Nähnyt   LC
                                          Calumet, MI September 27, 1938

31.27. Matti Jurva *baritone (1898-1943)*

BVE 40932-1 Hawaiji Idylli (Hawaiian Idyll)   Vi 80411, HMV AL1034
BVE 40933-1 Pikku Leilamme (Little Leilamme)   Vi 80411, HMV AL1034
             Leroy Shield-p, unk fl   Chicago November 21, 1927

BVE 40376-2 Maantien Varrelta (By The Roadside) (w: Einola, m: Matti Jurva)
                                                                     Vi 80586
BVE 40377-2 Maija Laulu   Vi 80586
BVE 40378-2 Hei, Hei (w: Matti Jurva)   Vi 80633
BVE 40379-2 Peräkylän Matti (Matti Jurva-Dr. Nortamo)   Vi 80788
             Cortese-p   Camden, NJ January 30, 1928

BVE 40380-2 Kun Eukko Menee Sinne (My Wife's On Her Vacation) (Matti Jurva)
                                                                     Vi 80788
BVE 40381-2 Lehmäkauppias Kaikkonen (The Finland Market) (Matti Jurva) Vi 80633
             as before   Camden, NJ January 31, 1928

BVE 45125-2 Kiertolainen (The Wanderer) (Selim Palmgren)   Vi 81447
BVE 45126-1 Petollinen Julia (Unfaithful Julia) (Borenius-Nortamo) Vi 81447
             vln, sax, p, g   NY May 9, 1928

W 109303-2   Kylpymatka   Co 3096-F, 16078
W 109304-2 (W 130534) Missä Sä Vietit Yösi (Kosola)'   Co 3200-F

W 109306-1 Ilta Pienessä Kaupungissa   Co 3096-F, 16078
        Antti Kosola Trio or 'Antti Kosola-acn, unk g NY May 1928

BVE 51152-2 Nämäkin Jalat {My Wonderful Feet} {These Feet Of Mine} Vi V-4046
BVE 51153-1 Kuinka Maailma Muuttuu {How The World Changes}   Vi V-4046
BVE 51154-2 Soita Vielä Se Neeker-Jazz {Play That Jazz Again}
                     Vi V-4027, RCA PL40115(33)
BVE 51155-2 Anna Mun Uinua {Let Me Dream}'   Vi V-4027
        acn, sax, g, vln or 'c   NY April 11, 1929

BVE 62108-1 Suur-Kaupungin Lapsi {Big Town Children}-Valssi (Matti Jurva)
                          Vi V-4080
BVE 62109-1 Sitä Eihän Luulis {Unbelievable} (w: Matti Jurva) Vi V-4080
BVE 62110-1 Piikalikka Nilsiästä {A Maid From Nilsiä} (w: Matti Jurva) Vi V-4088
BVE 62111-1 Runoa Ja Proosaa {Poetry And Prose}   Vi V-4088
BVE 62112-1 Lauantai-Illan Valssi (Matti Jurva)   Vi V-4133
BVE 62113-1 Meripoika Kuivalta Maalta (w: Matti Jurva)   Vi V-4133
        c, acn, g   NY April 23, 1930

W 111969-2 Kun Pusta Uinuu (E. Kalman-Matti Jurva)   Co 3152-F, DI72
        orch d Antti Kosola   NY April 1930

W 112032-2 Kulkijan Kaiho-Valssi   Co 3147-F, DI94
W 112033-2 Antin Hää-Polkka   Co 3147-F, DI94
W 112034-1 Kuti, Kuti-Waltz Comic Song   Co 3162-F, DI164
W 112035-2 Pidetty Mies-Fox Trot'   Co 3162-F, DI164
        orch d Antti Kosola, 'with chorus   NY ca April 1930

W 112081-2 Kahdenlainen Suudelma, from "Miranoco" (T. Palmroth) Co 3152-F, DI72
W 112082-2 En Sitä Koskaan Voi Tietää   Co 3191-F
W 112083-1 Kielon Hyvästijättö (O. Lindvall)   Co 3172-F
W 112084-2 Meripoikain Lähtölaulu (H. Borenius)   Co 3172-F, DI201
W 112086-1 Pihlajapuun Alla   Co 3191-F
        orch d Antti Kosola   NY ca May 1930

        Suomi-Slowfox   Co DI264
        as before   NY 1930

31.28. Leo Kauppi *baritone*

W 107133-1 Kuuliaiset Kottilassa   Co 3040-F, 13352, Sävel SÄLP 662(33)
W 107134-2 Maailman Matti   Co 3032-F, 13351
W 107135-2 Helmi Ja Kalle   Co 3040-F, 13352, Love LXLP505(33)
W 107136-1 Rivakka Polkka   Co 3032-F, 13351, Sävel SÄLP 662(33)
        Willi Larsen-acn, unk g   NY September 1926

W 107889-2 Laulu On Iloni Ja Työni   Co 3049-F, 16155
W 107890-2 Kallaves'   Co 3052-F, 16157
        vln, p   NY May 1927

W 107891-2 Heitä Huolet Pois   Co 3049-F, 16155
W 107892-3 Salkolan Syntymäkemut Co 3052-F, 16157, Sävel SÄLP 663(33)
        vln, acn   NY May 1927

```
W 108267-1   Kulkijaksi Luotu-Sotiisi                    Co 3058-F, 16161
W 108268-2   Renk' Jussi Palajaa Sodasta-Sotiisi
                                     Co 3060-F, 16163, Sävel SÄLP 663(33)
W 108269-1   Juhannustanssit Paksulassa-Polkka
                                     Co 3058-F, 16161, Sävel SÄLP 663(33)
W 108270-2   Herra Petteri-Merimiehen Laulu             Co 3060-F, 16163
             Antti Kosola-acn                           NY  August 1927

W 108587-2   Meren Aallot (A. Kosola)¹     Co 3067-F, 7790, Sävel SÄLP 663(33)
W 108588-2   Oi Tyttö Tule¹                             Co 3067-F, 7790
W 108589-2   Sjöman Andersson-Pt. 1²                    Co 3069-F, 7802
W 108590-1   Sjöman Andersson-Pt. 2²                    Co 3069-F, 7802
             ¹Antti Kosola Trio, ²vln, alt sax, p       NY December 1927

W 109031-2   Laivan Kannella (Emil Kauppi-Pasi Jääskeläinen)
                                     Co 3083-F, 16066, Sävel SÄLP 662(33)
W 109032-2   Aika Poika (J. Alfred Tanner)  Co 3083-F, 16066, Sävel SÄLP 662(33)
W 109033-2   Talkoo Polkka¹                 Co 3079-F, 13414, Sävel SÄLP 662(33)
W 109034-2   Honolulu¹                      Co 3079-F, 13414, Sävel SÄLP 662(33)
             Antti Kosola-acn or ¹Antti Kosola Trio: acn, uke, g   NY April 1928

W 110127-1   Mun Eukkoni On Maalla (J.A. Tanner)        Co 3101-F, 16117
W 110128-1   Ma Odotan Sua (J.A. Tanner)                Co 3101-F, 16117
W 110129-1   Pikku Liisa (J.A. Tanner)                  Co 3106-F, 16193
W 110130-1   Yhteinen Susannamme (S. Foster-J.A. Tanner)
                                     Co 3106-F, 16193, Sävel SÄLP 663(33)
             Antti Kosola-acn                           NY December 1928

W 110330-2   Herra Adamson-Comic Song                   Co 3114-F, 16228
W 110331-2   Elämään Kyllästymisestä                    Co 3123-F, 16236
W 110332-2   Kesälaitumelta-Comic Song                  Co 3114-F, 16228
W 110333-2   Mikko Ja Miina                             Co 3123-F, 16236
             orch d Antti Kosola                        NY  January 1929

W 110566-2   Amalia                                     Co 3161-F
W 110567-1   "Ei Tule Suvi..."
                       Co 3141-F, DI52, Sävel SÄLP 662(33), Love LXLP505(33)
W 110568-1   Meripoika                                  Co 3170-F
W 110569-2   Tytön Huivi (J.A. Tanner)                  Co 3170-F
             Antti Kosola Trio                          NY  April 1929

W 111167-1   Kalle Parka                                Co 3141-F, DI52
W 111168-2   Oi, Aino¹                                  Co 3161-F, DI187
W 111169-1   Villiruusu-Waltz Song (Evert Suonio)¹      Co 3135-F
W 111170-1   Emma-Comic Song                            Co 3135-F
             orch or ¹trio, d Antti Kosola              NY  October 1929

W 112846-3   Me Nuoret Meripojat, from "Meripoika" (Toivo Kuula-Teuvo Pakkala)
                                                        Co 3179-F, DI210
W 112847-2   Meripojan Kaipaus (Yrjö Kyllönen)          Co 3179-F, DI210
W 112848-2   Nujulan Kaupungin Historia (J. Alfred Tanner)  Co 3195-F, DI246
W 112849-  (W 130347) Kulkurin Heila-Schottische        Co 3195-F, DI246
             orch d Antti Kosola                        NY  March 1931
```

31.29. Wäinö Kauppi *cornet*

Wäinö Kauppi Ja Hänen Suomi Orkesteri

BVE 39625-1	Syysruusuja {Autumn Roses}-Valssi (Herman Sjöblom, op. 4)	
		Vi 80141, 80252
BVE 39626-2	Kulkurin-Masurkka (Herman Sjöblom, op. 4)	Vi rej
	own c, unk vln, tb, vc, p, traps	NY July 5, 1927
BVE 39914-2	Sotamarssi {War March} (Kajanus); Suomen Ratsuväen {Cavalry March}	
		Vi V-4004
BVE 39915-1	On A Beautiful Summer Night {Kesäilta}	Vi 20871
BVE 39916-2	Honeysuckle Polka	Vi 20871
BVE 39917-2	Yksin {Alone} {Ida}-Valssi	Vi 80141, 80252
	as before	NY July 28, 1927

Vi 80252 (Polish) as ORKIESTRA APOLLI

31.30. Erik Kivi *violin, vocal*

Finnish Folk Song-Polka	Vi trial
Finnish Folk Song-Mazurka	Vi trial
	Camden, NJ July 9, 1926

The file entry for the above trials describes Erik Kivi's instrument as a "toothpick violin".

BVE 36108-1	Laula Kukko {Sing Rooster}-Polka [no vo]	Vi 78907, RCA PL40115(33)
BVE 36109-2	Masuska {Mazurkka} [no vo]	Vi 78907
BVE 36110-1	Porin Poika {Hobo Fishing Song}	Vi 78882
BVE 36111-1	Merimiehen {Sailor Boy}-Valssi	Vi 78882
		NY August 9, 1926
BVE 36530-2	Vintelska-Hungarian Dance [no vo]	Vi 80069
	Wengerka-Hungarian Dance	Vi 80253
BVE 36531-3	Batespan {Pas d'Espagne}-Spanish Waltz [no vo]	Vi 80069, 80253
BVE 36532-2	Sepänsälli-Sotiisi [no vo]	Vi 79091
BVE 36533-1	Kivi Erkin Polkka [no vo]	Vi 79091
BVE 36534-1	Sotiisi {Schottische} [no vo]	Vi 79316
BVE 36535-2	Masuska {Masurkka} [no vo]	Vi 79316
		NY October 8, 1926

Vi 80253 (Polish) as KIRI KIRI

BVE 36690-1	Sini Aaltoset {Blue Waves}	Vi 79149, Love LXLP505(33)
BVE 36691-1	Puna Liivi {Red Vest}	Vi 79149, Love LXLP505(33)
BVE 36692-1	Matin Maija	Vi 79195
BVE 36693-1	Hotelli Laulu {Hotel Song}	Vi 79258
BVE 36694-1	Mankin Laulu {Vankin Laulu} {Prisoner's Song}	Vi 79055
BVE 36695-2	Lapsuuden Koti {Baby At Home}	Vi 79055
BVE 36696-2	Suutari Otto {Otto The Shoemaker}	Vi 79258

BVE 36697-1   Fitchburgin Akkain Kahvipolkka {Fitchburg Women Coffee Polka}
Vi 79195
Camden, NJ November 16, 1926

31.31. C.A. Koljonen *vocal*

AFS 4260A1   Isontalon Antti {Andrew Isontalon}   LC
AFS 4260A2   The Disgusted Swede [in English]   LC
Central Valley, CA September 4, 1939

31.32. Charles Korvenpää *vocal*

AFS 2407A1   Kutojan Tanssi   LC
AFS 2407B1   Nyt Laulaa Vaan Ma Tahdon   LC
AFS 2407B2   Marssi   LC
AFS 2409A2   Tyttö Meni Niitylle Ruohoja Leikkaamaan¹   LC
"sung and played with group" or ¹unaccompanied
Green, MI October 1, 1938

31.33. Juho Koskelo *tenor*

B 9174-1   Soi Vienosti Murheeni Soitto (Merikanto)   Vi 16615
B 9175-1   Niin Kauvan Minä Tramppaan (Kuula)   Vi rej
B 9176-1   Se Oli Yksi Lauvantaki-Ilta   Vi 16616
B 9184-1   Itkevä Huilu (Merikanto)   Vi 16615
B 9185-1   Miksi Laulan (Merikanto)   Vi 16614
B 9186-1   Kun Päivä Paistaa (Merikanto)   Vi 16610
B 9187-1   Ingalill (Lejdström) [in Swedish]   Vi 16618
Thompson-p   NY July 18, 1910

B 9188-1   Linjaali Rattaat   Vi 16611
B 9189-1   Eikä Sita Sanoa Saisi   Vi 16611
B 9190-1   Illalle (Sibelius)   Vi 16612
B 9191-1   Uskoton-Saksalainen Kansan Laulu   Vi rej
B 9192-1   Kaks' Neitoa Käveli   Vi 16616
as before   NY July 19, 1910

C 9195-1   Laula Laula (Järnefelt)   Vi 35131(12")
C 9196-1   Kesäpäivä Kangasalla (Linsen)   Vi 35131(12")
B 9197-1   Sotilas Poika (Pacius)   Vi 16613
B 9198-1   Oi Muistatko Vielä Sen Virren (Merikanto)   Vi 16614
B 9199-1   Joutsen (Ehrström)   Vi rej
as before   NY July 20, 1910

B 9316-1   Stjernan (Collan)   Vi 16618
B 9317-1   Syntymistään Sureva   Vi 16613
B 9318-1   Reppurin Laulu (Merikanto)   Vi 16610
as before   NY July 21, 1910

B 9175-2   Niin Kauvan Minä Tramppaan (Kuula)   Vi rej
B 9191-2   Uskoton-Saksalainen Kansan Laulu   Vi 16617

| B 9199-2 | Joutsen (Ehrström) | Vi 16612 |
| | as before | NY July 22, 1910 |

19157-1	Itkevä Huilu (Oskar Merikanto)	Co E708, E2636
19158-2	Soi Vienosti Murheeni Soitto (Oskar Merikanto)	Co E709
19159-2	Ingalill [in Swedish]	Co E710
19160-1	Spindelen [in Swedish]	Co E711
	p	NY December 12, 1910

19169-1	Det Gingo Två Flickor I Rosendelund [in Swedish]	Co rej
19170-1	Tuulan Tei (Oskar Merikanto)	Co E712, E2637
	p	NY December 21, 1910

	Oi, Muistatko Vielä Sen Virren (Merikanto)'	Ed 20723(2 min)
	Itkevä Huilu (Merikanto)	Ed 20724(2 min)
	Soi Vienosti Murheeni Soitto! (Merikanto)	Ed 20725(2 min)
	Tuulan Tei (Merikanto)	Ed 20726(2 min)
	Se Oli Yksi Lauvantaki Ilta	Ed 20727(2 min)
	Niin Kauvan Minä Tramppaan	Ed 20728(2 min)
	p or 'orch NY December 22-23, 1910, possibly January 6, 1911	

| 19177-1 | Bland Fjellen [in Swedish] | Co E713 |
| | orch | NY December 30, 1910 |

19184-1	Till Norden-Swedish National Song [in Swedish]	Co E714
19185-1	Stjernan [in Swedish]	Co E715
19186-1	Allt Under Himmelens Fäste [in Swedish]	Co E716
19187-1	Sotilas Poika (Pacius-Runeberg)	Co E717, E2637
19188-1	Waasan Marssi (Collan)	Co E718, E2638
19189-1	Oi, Muistatko Vielä Sen Virren (Merikanto)	Co E719, E2638
	orch	NY January 5, 1911

	Suomen Laulu (Pacius)	Ed 11550(4 min), 11700(4 min)
	Kolme Veljestä	Ed 11551(4 min), 11701(4 min)
	Laula, Laula! (Järnefelt)	Ed 11552(4 min), 11702(4 min)
	Kesäpäivä Kangasalla (Linsén)	Ed 11553(4 min), 11703(4 min)
	Sotilas Poika (Pacius)	Ed 11554(4 min), 11704(4 min)
	Porilaisten Marssi-National Song	Ed 11555(4 min), 11705(4 min)
	Waasan Marssi (Collan)	Ed 11556(4 min), 11706(4 min)
	orch	NY January 6, 1911

19208-1	Drick Ur Ditt Glas [in Swedish]	Co E748
19209-1	Till Österland Vill Jag Fara [in Swedish]	Co E749
19210-1	Kristallen Den Fina [in Swedish]	Co E807
19211-1	Det Gingo Två Flickor I Rosendelund [in Swedish]	Co E808
	p	NY January 17, 1911

19212-1	Jag Går I Tusen Tankar [in Swedish]	Co E809
19213-1	Morgonsång [in Swedish]	Co E810
	p	NY January 21, 1911

	Till Norden-Festival Song [in Swedish]	USE 5780(2 min)
	Till Österland Vill Jag Fara (Now Far Eastward I'll Hie Me)	
	[in Swedish]	USE 5781(2 min)

Jag Går I Tusen Tankar (A Thousand Things I Ponder) [in Swedish]
USE 5782(2 min)
Allt Under Himmelens Fäste (In Heaven's Vault Above Me) [in Swedish]
USE 5783(2 min)
Waasan Marssi   USE 5960(2 min)
Linjaali Rattaat (Fun And Sorrow)   USE 5961(2 min)
Lypsäjän Laulu   USE 5962(2 min)
Stjernan (Star In Heaven) [in Swedish]   USE 21570(4 min)
Det Gingo Två Flickor I Rosendelund [in Swedish]   USE 21571(4 min)
Porilaisten Marssi   USE 21750(4 min)
Kesäpäivä Kangasalla (A Summer Day At Kangasalla)   USE 21751(4 min)
Sotilas Poika-Soldier Song   USE 21752(4 min)
NY   1911

39671-1	Suomen Salossa	Co E2163
39672-1	Kreivin Sylissä Istunut	Co E2163
39673-1	Kesä-Ilta	Co E2164
39674-1	Toivova-Önskan	Co E2164
39675-1	Rannalla Istuja	Co E2165
	orch	NY December 4, 1914

39680-1	Tuomen Juurella; Lypsäjän Laulu	Co E2165
	orch	NY December 7, 1914

39691-1	Kansainvälinen	Co E2166
39692-1	La Marseillaise	Co E2166
	orch	NY December 15, 1914

45770-1	Vankilaan Mennessä	Co E2420
45771-2	Kahvia	Co E2420
45772-1	Tallella	Co E2418
	orch	NY June 14, 1915

45773-1	Kesäillalla	Co E2419
45774-1	Varis	Co E2419
45776-1	Köyhä Poika; Isäntä Emäntä Renki	Co E2418
	orch	NY June 15, 1915

43620-	Käy Kotiin-Religious Song	Co E2739
43621-	Lähteellä-Religious Song	Co E2739
43622-1	Dawidin 137 Psalmi-Church Song	Co E2738
43623-1	Sun Haltuus Rakas Isäni-Church Song	Co E2738
	org	NY 1915-6

43724-	Onnelliset (Merikanto)	Co E2848
43725-	Linjaalirattaat	Co E2848
43726-1	Suomen Laulu (Pacius)	Co E2846
43727-1	Huraa Me Suomen Meripojat	Co E2847
43728-1	Illalla	Co E2847
43729-1	Savolaisen Laulu	Co E2846
	orch	NY March 1916

43964-2	Työväen Marssi-Socialist Song (Merikanto-Tuokko)	Co E2968
43965-1-2	Warshavjanken-Socialist Song	Co E2968

2577

43966-1	Hosianna-Christmas Song	Co E2966, 3142-F, DI53
	orch	NY May 1916

44042-2	Joulu-Virsi-Christmas Song	Co E2966, 3142-F, DI53
	orch	NY June 1916

44144-1	Kaakuri	Co E2967
44145-1-2	Kaurapellon Pientareella	Co E2967
	acn	NY ca June 1916

59464-	Laula, Laula (Järnefelt)	Co E5138(12")
59465-	Kesäpäivä Kangasalla (Linsen)	Co E5138(12")
	orch	NY ca 1916

44578-1	Maamme-Patriotic Song (Pacius)	Co E3552
44579-3	Se Oli Yksi Lauvantaki Ilta; Miksi Laulan (Merikanto)	Co E3167
	orch	NY January 1917

44609-1	Karjalaisten Laulu (Hannikainen)	Co E3166
44610-	Orvon Kyyneleet	Co E3223, 3154-F, DI100
44611-2	Merellä	Co E3433
44612-1	Kymmenen Virran Maa (Merikanto)	Co E3166
44613-	Mustalainen	Co E3223, 3154-F, DI100
44614-1	Porilaisten Marssi	Co E3167
	orch	NY ca February 1917

44926-1	Hankoniemen Silmä	Co E3432
44927-1	Lapsuuden Ystävälle	Co E3432
	orch	NY 1917

58515-1	Joutsen	Co E3553
58516-1	Vienan Rannalla	Co E3659
58517-2	Laulu Suomessa	Co E3553
58518-1	Suomen Walta	Co E3552
58519-2	Tuuti Lasta Tuonelahan	Co E3659
	orch	NY August 1917

84095-	Sunnuntai	Co E3927
84096-	Laps Suomen (Pacius)	Co E3927
84097-	Kun Päivä Paistaa	Co E3928
84098-	Luostarin Kellot-Kansanlaulu	Co E3928
	orch	NY ca December 1917

84694-2	Työväen Joukot	Co E4168, Eteenpäin ETLP-301(33)
84695-2	Weljet Siskot Rientäkäämme Jo	Co E4168
	Mökin Poika	Co E4169
	Tuima On Tuuli	Co E4169
	orch	NY ca October 1918

B 22349-2	Kun On Hätä Matkallamme	Vi rej
B 22350-2	Luoja Taivasten (F.J. Hannikainen)	Vi rej
	Edward T. King-org	NY December 17, 1918

```
B 22349-4    Kun On Hätä Matkallamme                                    Vi rej
B 22350-4    Luoja Taivasten (F.J. Hannikainen)                        Vi rej
B 22364-2    Joulu Laulu {Oi Sä Riemuisa}-Christmas Song (A. Delfage)' Vi 72409
             as before, 'Nathaniel Shilkret-chimes       NY January 21, 1919

B 22585-2    Hosianna (G.J. Vogler)                                    Vi rej
B 22586-2    Köyhä Poika                                               Vi 72276
B 22587-2    Tämän Kylän Poikien Laulu                                 Vi rej
             orch d Rosario Bourdon              NY  February 13, 1919

B 22585-5    Hosianna (G.J. Vogler)                                    Vi rej
B 22587-4    Tämän Kylän Poikien Laulu                                 Vi 72276
             as before                               NY  March 19, 1919

B 22349-7    Kun On Hätä Matkallamme                                   Vi rej
             Edward T. King-org                       NY  April 2, 1919

B 22585-6    Hosianna (G.J. Vogler)                                    Vi 72409
B 22861-1    Marseljeesi {The Marseillaise} (Rouget De Lisle)
                                        Vi 72396, Eteenpäin ETLP-301(33)
B 22862-2    Kansainvälinen {Internationale} (arr J. Paananen)
                                        Vi 72396, Eteenpäin ETLP-301(33)
             orch d Rosario Bourdon                  NY  May 19, 1919

B 23154-3    Lauluja; Tukkijoella (Oskar Merikanto)                    Vi 72765
B 23155-2    Vallinkorvan Laulu (Oskar Merikanto)                      Vi 72765
             as before                          NY  September 19, 1919

85628-5      Torpparien Marssi                                        Co E4524
85629-       Ja Nythän On Taasen Helluntai                            Co E4738
85631-       Ruusu Laaksossa                                          Co E4738
             orch                                NY  ca October 1919

85812-1      Iltalaulu                                                Co E4524
             orch                               NY  ca December 1919

7407         Laula, Laula! {Sing!, Sing!} (w: S. Killinen, m: Armas Järnefelt)
                                                                       Ed rej
7408         Etelästä Tuulee {When The Southern Breezes Blow}         Ed rej
             orch                                  NY  June 16, 1920

7414         Savolaisen Laulu {Song Of Savo} (K. Collan)              Ed rej
7415         O Hellas Barn {Child Of Finland} (F. Pacius)             Ed rej
             orch                                  NY  June 21, 1920

7407         Laula, Laula! {Sing, Sing!} (w: S. Killinen, m: Armas Järnefelt)
                                                                       Ed 59301
7408         Etelästä Tuulee {When The Southern Breezes Blow}         Ed 59300
7414         Savolaisen Laulu {Song Of Savo} (K. Collan)  Ed 59301, 11711(4 min)
7415         O Hellas Barn {Child Of Finland} (F. Pacius) Ed 59300, 11712(4 min)
                                                  NY  July 9, 1920

7546         Aittalaulu; Heilani Kammari (Emil Kauppi)                Ed 59302
             orch                               NY  September 26, 1920
```

7551   Soi Vienosti Murheeni Soitto; Kullan Murunen (Oskar Merikanto)
                                                                        Ed 59302
                 orch   NY September 29, 1920

B 24712-1   Kulkurin Valssi (J. Alfred Tanner)   Vi 72910
B 24713-2   Etelästä Tuulee; Plakkarikello   Vi 72910
B 24714-2   Oma Kulta   Vi rej
                 orch d Nathaniel Shilkret   NY December 1, 1920

87483-   Naapurin Likka   Co E7242
87484-   Sorsa (Emil Kauppi)   Co E7242
87485-1-2   Kulkurin Valssi (J.A. Tanner)   Co E7241, 3156-F
87486-1-2   Reisu-Poika   Co E7241, 3156-F
                 orch   NY ca June 1921

B 25485-2   Luttis Jussi   Vi 73163
B 25459-1   Vanhapoika   Vi 73163
                 acn   NY July 11, 1921

88413-   Lammen Laine   Co E7572
88416-   Kaks' Neitoa   Co E7572
                 orch   NY March 1922

B 26610-2   Kuinka Se Joki; Tule Tule Kultani   Vi rej
                 c, cl, p, d Nathaniel Shilkret   NY June 5, 1922

89149-2   Orpopojan Valssi   Co E9032, 3157-F
89150-4   Kalle Aaltonen   Co E9032
                 orch   NY April 1923

B 27859-2   Orpopojan Valssi {The Orphan's Waltz} (w: J. Alfred Tanner) Vi 73870
B 27860-2   Kalle Aaltonen {Song Of Kalle Aaltonen} (w: J. Alfred Tanner)
                                                                       Vi 73870
B 27861-1   Liisa Ja Lassi (w: J. Alfred Tanner)   Vi rej
                 orch d Nathaniel Shilkret   NY April 30, 1923

89246-1   Pikkuinen Poika   Co E9003, 3157-F
89247-1   Luttis Jussi   Co E9003
                 acn   NY ca May 1923

31.34. Antti Kosolan Orkesteri

W 111948-4   Lancastria-Valssi (A. Kosola)   Co 3148-F, DI95
W 111949-5   Atlantin Polkka {Härmän & Forssin Polkat}   Co 3148-F, DI95
                 Antti Kosola (1896-1972)-acn, others unk   NY 1930

31.35. Cecilia Kuitunen *vocal*

AFS 3270B1   Minä Seisoin Korkealla Vuorella   LC
AFS 3270B2   Voi, Äiti Parka Ja Raukka   LC

AFS 3271A1   Voi, Äiti Parka Ja Raukka   LC
              vln   Ely, MN August 17, 1937

31.36. Wiljo H. Kujala *tenor*

CO 30250-1   Laulu Tulipunaisesta Ruususta {Song Of The Fire Rose}
              (U. Hurmerinta)   Co 3243-F
CO 30251-1   Sillanpään Marssilaulu {Sillanpää March Song} (Aimo Mustonen)
                                                                       Co 3242-F
CO 30252-1   Merimies Laulu-Finnish Soldier's Song (Kosti Vehanen)   Co 3242-F
CO 30253-1   Siskosein {Krevitär Maritza} {Sister Mine}, from "Countess Maritza"
              (Emmerich Kalman)   Co 3243-F
              Columbia Orkesteri   NY April 15, 1941

31.37. Arthur Arkadius Kylander *vocal (1892-1968)*

CVE 40100-2   Muistojen Valssi {Memory Waltz} (A. Kylander)
                                         Vi 68901(12"), RCA PL40115(33)
CVE 40101-1   Muistoja Alaskasta {Memories Of Alaska} (A. Kylander) Vi 68901(12")
BVE 40102-1   Selkärenka Tohtori {Chiropractor} (A. Kylander)   Vi 80185
BVE 40103-2   Lumber Jäkki {Lumber Jack} (A. Kylander)   Vi 80185
              acn, p   NY September 19, 1927

BVE 41201-1   Neekeri Mailla Afrikassa {In Africa} (Kylander) Vi 80520, HMV AL1019
BVE 41202-1   Paitaressu Vihtori {Victor} (Kylander)   Vi 80520, HMV AL1019
BVE 41203-2   Ylioppilas Suomesta {Student Of Finland} (Arthur Kylander) Vi 80556
BVE 41204-1   Nyt Minä Reissaan Vanhaan Maahan   Vi 80556
              as before   NY December 6, 1927

BVE 43150-1   Lehto Lapsi {Child Of The Primrose Path} (A. Kylander)¹
                                                         Vi 80712, HMV AL992
BVE 43151-1   Vahingossa Syntynyt {Unintentionally Produced} {The Foundling}
              (A. Kylander)   Vi 80712, HMV AL992
BVE 43152-2   Ennen Ja Nyt {Past And Present} (A. Kylander)   Vi 81507
BVE 43153-2   Siirtolaisen Ensi Vastuksia {The Immigrant's First Difficulties}
              (A. Kylander)   Vi 81507, RCA PL40115(33)
              vln, xyl, p, ¹xyl omitted   NY March 19, 1928

BVE 48356-1   Rakastuneiden Valssi {Lover's Waltz} (A. Kylander)¹
                                                         Vi V-4019, HMV AL1168
BVE 48357-1   Iloinen Caballero {Gay Caballero} (F. Crumit) Vi V-4019, HMV AL1168
BVE 48358-1   Kuinka Heikki Munitti Kanoja {How Henry Made His Hens Lay}
              (Kylander)   Vi V-4058
BVE 48359-2   Merimiehen Elämää {Sailor's Life} (Kylander)   Vi V-4058
              c, vln, cl, p, sbs, traps, d Alfredo Cibelli, ¹with Julia Kylander
                                                  NY February 13, 1929

The files show Frank Crumit as composer for both sides of Vi V-4058.

BVE 50710-1   Suomalainen Ja Sauna {Finn And Sauna} (Arthur Kylander)
                                         Vi V-4021, V-4171, 26-6016
BVE 50711-2   Oi! Kuinka Engeliksi Mielin {We'll Be Angels Bye And Bye} Vi V-4037

BVE 50712-2   Turun Tytön Laulu {Aboe Girl's Song} (A. Kylander)
                        Vi V-4021, V-4171, 26-6016, RCA PL40115(33)
BVE 50713-1   Kulkuri {The Wanderer} (A. Kylander)   Vi V-4037, RCA PL40115(33)
              2 vln, fl, cl, vc, sbs, traps   NY March 4, 1929

31.38. Hannes Laine *instrumental (1890-1937)*

Laine-Toppila Orkesteri

BVE 57435-1   Lännen {Western}-Polkka (H. Laine)'   Vi V-4138, V-4170, 26-6015
BVE 57436-1   Tähti {Star}-Polkka'   Vi V-4063
BVE 57437-1   Kukko {Rooster}-Polkka'   Vi V-4138, V-4170, 26-6015
BVE 57438-1   Venäläinen {Russian}-Sotiisi'   Vi V-4063
BVE 57439-1   Kukkii Nyt Tuomet Taas {The Flowers Are Blooming Again}   Vi V-4064
BVE 57440-1   Laulu On Iloni Ja Työni {Songs Are My Joy And Work} (A. Tanner)
                                                                    Vi V-4064

              Hannes Laine, Walter Toppila-acn, xyl (it is not known who plays
              which), 'unk bj   Chicago November 21, 1929

31.39. Katri Lammi *soprano*

BVE 49610-2   Soi Viserrys, Soi {Sing, Bird, Sing}   Vi V-4009
BVE 49611-2   Terveheksi {Best Regards} (L. Koski)   Vi V-4013
BVE 49612-2   Lemmi Mua {Love Me And The World Is Mine} (tr Sola) Vi V-4009
BVE 49613-1   Mä Tahtoisin {I Wonder} (Antti Palen)   Vi V-4013
              vln, fl, cl, vc, p, sbs, d Alfredo Cibelli   NY December 31, 1928

W 111147-1   Urali (Ralph Erwin)   Co 3127-F, DI28
W 111148--2   Pikku Äiti (Igor Borganoff)   Co 3127-F, DI28
              Suomalainen Taiteilija-Yhtymä, d Stein-Östman   NY October 1929

W 112428-2   Särkynyt Onni-Valssi (Georg Malmsten)   Co 3167-F
W 112429-2   Tummat Silmät   Co 3171-F
W 112430-   Kadun Lapsi {Bublitshki} (Bogomazow)   Co rej
W 112431-   Valencia (Boyer-Charles-J. Padilla)   Co rej
              as before   NY November 1930

W 112430-6   Kadun Lapsi {Bublitshki} (Bogomazow)   Co 3167-F
W 112431-5   Valencia (Boyer-Charles-J. Padilla)   Co 3171-F
              as before   NY November 1930

W 112967-1   Raatajille (Rykin-J. Ahti)   Co 3185-F
W 112968-2   Kasakkaleirillä-Fox Trot (Anna M. Kluchansky-Jukka Ahti)   Co 3190-F
W 112969-2   Minä Muistelen Sinua   Co 3190-F, DI252
W 112970-2   Syksyn Tuulet-Valssi (Jules Sylvain)   Co 3185-F, DI252
              orch d William E. Stein   NY June 1931

31.40. Lampi Trio *instrumental*

BVE 62124-1	Ajatelmat {Thoughts}-Valssi (arr A. Williams)	
		Vi V-4078, V-4154, 26-6005
BVE 62125-1	Meidän {Hours}-Sotiisi (arr A. Williams)	Vi V-4078, V-4154, 26-6005
BVE 62126-1	Pitkät Päivät {Long Days}-Waltz (arr A. Williams)	Vi V-4087
BVE 62127-1	Kissalan Aapelin {Abel From Kissala}-Sotiisi	Vi V-4087
BVE 62128-1	Wahinko Valssi	Vi V-4132
BVE 62129-1	Maalais-Sotiisi	Vi V-4132
	acn, sax, xyl	NY April 28, 1930

31.41. Elmer Lamppa *tenor (1894-1974)*

BVE 39072-1	Saukkosen Avioero	Vi 80072
BVE 39073-1	Viinatrokarin Laulu	Vi 80072, Sävel SÄLP 663(33)
BVE 39074-2	Suomalainen Kansanlaulu¹	Vi 80062
BVE 39075-2	Kulkurin Laulu (Martti Nisonen)¹	Vi 80062
	Eddy Jaakala-acn or ¹p	Chicago July 2, 1927

Elmer Lamppa-H. Saarinen

BVE 40968-2	Markkinamatka {Market Song}	Vi 80789
BVE 40969-2	Poliisina Ollessani {Policeman Song}	Vi 80789
BVE 40970-2	Pelti-Liisa {Ford Song}	Vi 80467
BVE 40971-2	Pois Sormet Taikka (Martti Nisonen)	Vi 80467
	H. Saarinen-acn	Chicago November 29, 1927

Elmer Lamppa

BVE 41322-1	Kehtolaulu {Russian Lullaby} (Irving Berlin-E. Lamppa)	
		Vi 80549, HMV AL1033
BVE 41323-2	Syömmesi Kamarissa {In Your Heart}¹	Vi 80549, HMV AL1033
	p or ¹acn	Chicago December 5, 1927

31.42. Willi Larsen *accordion (b. 1885)*

87623-2	Merellä-Valssi	Co E7328
87624-1-2	Lammen Laine-Valssi	Co E7328
87626-1	Kymmentä Kynttä-Polka	Co E7399
87628-1	Suomen Ent. Kaartin Marssi	Co E7399
		NY July 1921

Willy Larsen

W 105816-2	Kaipuu Valssi (H. Sjöblom)¹	Co 3015-F, 16127
	Na Bregovih Drave	Co 25029-F
W 105817-2	Lyytin Polkka; Surut Pois-Polkka	Co 3018-F, 16128
W 105818-1	Kerenski²	Co 3015-F, 16127

W 105819-1   Tyttöjen Vienti-Schottische   Co 3018-F, 16128
             with ¹vln or ²sax   NY ca August 1925

Co 25029-F as FRAN GRDINA

W 106204-2   Yksin-Waltz   Co 3021-F, 16131
W 106205-1   Pohjalais Polkka¹   Co 3020-F, 16130
             Österbottnisk Polka¹   Co 22029-F
W 106206-2   Taika Yö-Waltz   Co 3020-F, 16130
W 106207-2   Heilini Kanssa-Polka¹   Co 3021-F, 16130
             Med Min Älskling¹   Co 22029-F
             ¹with cl   NY December 1925

W. Larsen-O. Tolonen

W 106742-2   Syys Tunnelma {Autumn Dreams}-Valssi (Joyce)   Co 3030-F, 16139
W 106743-2   Suomen Polkka   Co 3027-F, 16137
W 106744-2   Rakkauden Kaiho-Valssi   Co 3027-F, 16137
W 106745-   Helmi-Sottiisi   Co rej
             own acn, O. Tolonen-vln   NY May 1926

W 106745-3   Helmi-Sottiisi   Co 3031-F, 16140
W 107072-1   Viimeinen Valssi {The Last Waltz}   Co 3031-F, 16140
W 107073-1   Evelina-Polka   Co 3035-F, 16143
             as before   NY August 1926

William Larsen-Stanley Lutz

BVE 38478-2   Syysruusuja Valssi   Vi 79357, HMV AL1029
BVE 38479-1   Elämä Juoksuhaudassa-Valssi   Vi 79357, HMV AL1029
             own acn, Stanley Lutz-vln   NY April 21, 1927

BVE 38807-3   Majani Kanssa-Sotiisi (Willi Larsen)   Vi 79403, HMV AL1030
BVE 38808-2   Turun Polkka (Willi Larsen)   Vi 79403, 80179, HMV AL1030
             own acn, Stanley Lutz-vln, W. Dorn-xyl   NY May 17, 1927

Willy Larsen

BVE 43548-2   Kyllikin Valssi (arr Willy Larsen)   Vi 80717, HMV AL991
BVE 43549-2   Jää Hyvästi Isänmaa {Farewell My Fatherland}-Marssi (H. Konno)
                                         Vi 81446, HMV AL991
BVE 43550-1   Kultani Kainalossa {In My Sweetheart's Arms}-Masurkka   Vi 81446
BVE 43551-2   Lukkari Heikin Polkka {Finnish Polka Medley}   Vi 80717
                                        NY April 10, 1928

W 109760-1   Elokuun Kuutamo-Valssi (H. Sjöblom)   Co 3092-F, 16169
W 109761-2   Säk' Järven Polkka   Co 3092-F, 16169
             Den Drömmande Vintergöken-Polka   Co 22086-F
W 109762-1   Muistoja Synninlaaksosta-Sottiisi   Co 3110-F, 16204
W 109763-1   Muistoja Pohjolasta (Sam Sihvo) Co 3110-F, 16204, Sävel SÄLP 663(33)
                                        NY ca October 1928

Willy Larsen Trio

W 111705-2	Muistoja Karpaateilta-Valssi	Co 3139-F, DI50
	Spomin Iz Ljubljane	Co 25175-F
W 111706-2	Seurasaaren Polkkia	Co 3139-F, DI50
	Vecerni Polka	Co 25175-F
W 111707-2	Soittajan Kohtalo-Valssi	Co 3151, DI162
W 111708-2	Poikain Vienti-Sottiisi	Co 3151-F, DI162
		NY February 1930

Co 25175-F as ACCORDION ORCHESTRA

W 112726-2	Sydänsuru-Valssi (K. Niemi)	Co 3175-F, DI199
	Skors Serdtza-Vals	Co 20256-F
	Walc "Slawcia"	Co 27319-F
W 112727-2	Viipurin Sottiisi (Willy Larsen)	Co 3194-F, DI245
W 112728-2	Lemmenkaipuu-Valssi	Co 3194-F, DI245
W 112729-1	Hattulan Polkkia	Co 3175-F, DI199
	Russkaya Polka	Co 20256-F
	Mostynska Polka	Co 27319-F
	own acn, unk vln, g	NY ca December 1930

Co 20256-F as INSTRUMENTALNOYE TRIO, 27319-F as UKRAINSKA NARODNA ORCHESTRA

31.43. Saima Laurila-Newland *soprano*

W 108376-2	Vilja "Iloinen Leski" (F. Léhar)	Co 3066-F, 7789
W 108377-2	Tuomien Valkoiset Tertut, Mustalaislaulu (M. Steinberg)	
		Co 3066-F, 7789
	orch	NY October 1927

W 110027-2	Oi Bajadeeri, from "Bajadeeri" (E. Kalman)	Co 3098-F
W 110030-3	Oikeaan Ja Vasempaan, from "Bajadeeri" (E. Kálmán)	Co 3098-F
	orch	NY November 1928

31.44. Lilly Leeman-Lehtimäki *soprano*

BVE 45207-1	Hennan Keinulaulu {Midsummer Night} (Oskar Merikanto)	Vi 81508
BVE 45208-2	Mustalais Ruhtinatar {Riemu Mielin Ninha Tahtoo}	
	{"Czardas Princess"} (E. Kálmán)	Vi 81508
BVE 45209-1	Vanha Sanna {The Old Mother} (E. Polon)	Vi 81304
BVE 45210-1	Kerjäläisen Laulu {Beggar's Song} (Frank Lindros)	Vi 81304
	Schmidt-vln, Lennartz-vc, Charles Linton-p Camden, NJ May 24, 1928	

| BVE 53620-2 | Minä Muistelen Sinua (Antti Palen) | Vi rej |
| | vln, fl, cl, vc, p, sbs, traps, d Alfredo Cibelli NY May 15, 1929 | |

31.45. Walfrid Lehto *tenor*

W 107387-2	Heilini Soitteli (Erkki Melartin)	Co 3042-F, 16149
W 107388-3	Aikoja Entisiä (Erkki Melartin)	Co 3042-F, 16149
	orch	NY December 1926

Volpi Leuto

BVE 46918-2	Vanha Mummo {Old Mother Grand} (O. Merikanto, op. 2 no. 2)	Vi V-4010
BVE 46919-2	Angela Mia {My Angel}, ftmp "Street Angel" (Lew Pollack-E. Rapee)	
		Vi 81620
BVE 46920-2	Maria, Mari! (E. Di Capua)	Vi 81620
	orch d Alfredo Cibelli	NY August 20, 1928

BVE 49275-2	Volgan Venemiesten Laulu {Song Of The Volga Boatmen}	Vi V-4010
	as before	NY December 18, 1928

BVE 48512-2	Aurinkoinen {O Sole Mio} {My Sunshine} (Di Capua-Volpi Leuto)	
		Vi V-4018
BVE 48513-	Siirtolaisen Kaiho {La Paloma} {The Dove} (Yradier)	Vi V-4018
	orch	NY December 24, 1928

BVE 51663-2	Sä Olet Mielestäin Kaunihimpi {You Are the Most Beautiful To Me}	
		Vi V-4045
	2 vln, fl, cl, vc, p, sbs, d Alfredo Cibelli	NY April 26, 1929

BVE 53621-1	Tuule, Tuuli Leppeämmin {Blow Ye Winds}	Vi V-4045
	vln, fl, cl, vc, p, sbs, traps, d Alfredo Cibelli	NY May 15, 1929

BVE 55102-2	Pääsky {La Golondrina} (La Forge)	Vi V-4047
BVE 55103-1	Pyhä Napoli {Santa Lucia} (w: V. Leuto)	Vi V-4047
	Alfredo Cibelli-md, unk fl, acn, g, traps	NY July 5, 1929

31.46. Anna Leino *spoken*

AFS 3271B1&2	Hammassäryn Ja Palohaavan Parantamis Loitsu	LC
AFS 3271B3	Hikkataudin Parantamis Loitsu	LC
AFS 3273A1	Kalevala Runo, Lines 11-25 And 37-45	LC
AFS 3273B1	Velisurmaaja	LC
		Ely, MN August 17, 1937

31.47. Soittokunta Louhi (Louhi's Band)

B 22520-2	Maamme-National Hymn (F. Pacius)	Vi 72203
	Pois Rannoilta Suomen (F. Pacius)	Vi trial
	6 c, fl, 7 cl, o, 3 sax, 3 fr hn, 2 bar hn, 4 tb, bs cl, 2 bsn, 2	
	tuba, 2 dm	NY July 5, 1918

31.48. Ida Lovardi *mezzo-soprano*

W 108378-2	Paimen Poika	Co 3063-F, 16165
W 108379-1	Antti Tanssitti Mua	Co 3063-F, 16165
	orch	NY October 1927

31.49. Maki Trio *instrumental*

BVE 49676-2	Minun Kultani {My Sweetheart}-Sotiisi	Vi V-4014
	Moja Luba-Schottische	Vi V-16055
BVE 49677-2	Sorretun Elämä {The Life Of The Opressed}-Waltz (H. Reinikainen)	
		Vi V-4020
BVE 49678-2	Caspian Polka	Vi V-4014, V-14018
	Nad Wisła {By The Vistula}-Polka	Vi V-16055
BVE 49679-2	Polkkia Pohjoos Maalta {Medley Of Polkas From The Northland}	
	(Herman Mäki)	Vi V-4050
BVE 49680-2	Barrikadi {Barricade}-Marssi¹	Vi rej
BVE 49681-2	Syysajatus {Autumn Caprice}¹	Vi rej
	Arvo Vähämäki-acn, Signe Vähämäki-sax, Sulo Vähämäki-dm, unk bj, or	
	¹acn only	NY January 23, 1929

Vi V-14081 as MAKI TREJETAS, V-16055 as MAKIŃSKA TRÓJKA

BVE 48317-1	Maatyttöjen {Country Girls}-Sotiisi	Vi V-4050
BVE 48318-2	Waasan Polkka (Herman Maki)	Vi V-4020
BVE 48319-2	Mennyt Ilo {Lost Happiness}-Valssi	Vi V-4036
BVE 48320-2	Espanjatar {La Spagnola}-Valssi (Di Chiarra)	Vi V-4036
	as before	NY January 29, 1929

BVE 57415-1	Juhannus {Midsummer Day}-Sotiisi (Arvo Maki)	Vi V-4065
BVE 57416-2	Se Hulivili Polkka {That Gay Polka} (Arvo Maki)	Vi V-4065
BVE 57417-2	Särkyneet Unelmat {Broken Dreams}-Valssi	Vi V-4071
BVE 57418-1	Intolan Polkka (Arvo Maki)	Vi V-4071
BVE 57419-2	Haitari {Accordion}-Sotiisi	Vi V-4093
BVE 57420-2	Liina Polkka	Vi V-4093
	unk bj omitted	Chicago November 16, 1929

31.50. Emil Mäki *vocal*

AFS 2336A1	Nyt Aion Laulun Laulella	LC
		Newberry, MI September 1938

31.51. Jukka Mäki *baritone*

	Aamulaulu	Vi trial
	Edward T. King-p	NY March 19, 1917

B 19731-2	Aittalaulu (Emil Kauppi)	Vi rej
B 19733-2	Aamulaulu (Toivo Kuula)	Vi 69468
	King's Orchestra d Rosario Bourdon	NY May 1, 1917

B 21504-2   Maanpakolaisten Jäähyväislaulu   Vi 78257
             King's Orchestra d Nathaniel Shilkret   NY February 5, 1918

B 21512-2   Rauhattoman Rukous (w: Eino Leino, m: J. Tuuri)   Vi rej
             as before   NY February 7, 1918

B 21512-3   Rauhattoman Rukous (w: Eino Leino, m: J. Tuuri)   Vi 78257
             as before   NY   March 26, 1918

31.52. Mrs. Marttila *vocal*

AFS 2367B2   Siellä Se Kukkii Se Tulipunaruusu   LC
                                        Calumet, MI September 27, 1938

31.53. Marie Moilanen *vocal*

AFS 3275A1   Nyt Ylös Sieluni   LC
AFS 3275A2   Herraa Hyvää Kiittäkäät   LC
AFS 3275B1   Mä Herätessäin Aamulla   LC
AFS 3275B2   Jo Joutuu Armas Aika Ja Suvi Suloinen   LC
                                      Mountain Iron, MI September 19, 1937

31.54. Annie Mörk *vocal (1887-1959)*

BVE 53543-2 Muistathan Kai? {Do You Remember?}, from "Muistathan Ruhtinatar"
                (E. Kalman)'   Vi V-4035
BVE 53544-2 Mirjamin Laulu {Miriam's Song} (E. Melartin)   Vi V-4062
BVE 53545-2 Jai Mama {Oh Mama}, from "Muistathan Ruhtinatar" (E. Kálmán)
                                                             Vi V-4062
BVE 53546-2 Mikä Onneansa Etsii? {Why Look For Happiness?} (E. Kálmán) Vi V-4035
                2 vln, fl, cl, vc, p, sbs, d Alfredo Cibelli, 'with Volpi Leuto
                (Walfrid Lehto)   NY   June 6, 1929

31.55. Josefina Mustonen *soprano*

                Suomen Lapsi (Pacius)   Ed 11707(4 min)
                                                            NY   July 23, 1913

Sanfrid Ja Josefina Mustonen

                Talkoo; Tyttöjen; Poikien; Talkoo, from Saimaan Rannalla (Pacius)
                                                            Ed 11708(4 min)
                Tukkijoella; Annin Ja Huotarin Vuoro (Merikanto)   Ed 11709(4 min)
                Juhannustulilla; Hennan Keinulaulu; Hennan Ja Manun Vuoro
                                                            Ed 11710(4 min)
                                                            NY   July 23, 1913

"Tyttöjen" is a solo by Josefina Mustonen; "Poikien" and "Hennan Ja Manun Vuoro"
are solos by Sanfrid Mustonen.

31.56. Siimi Mustonen *soprano*

89626-1	Kevä Laulu	Co 3001-F
89627-1-2	Äiti Äiti Älä Soimaa	Co 3001-F
	orch	NY January 1924

31.57. New Yorkin Laulumiehet *male chorus*

W 110881-2	Karjalainen Marssi (O. Merikanto)	Co 3119-F, 16224
W 110882-2	Kullan Ylistys	Co 3119-F, 16224
W 110883-2	Uusi Kulta Ja Vanha Kulta; Kitkat, Kitkat	Co 3164-F, DI178
W 110884-2	Satu; Tii Tii Tikanpoika	Co 3164-F, DI178
		NY June 1929

31.58. Hilda Olvinen *vocal*

AFS 2416A	The Morning Star [in Polish]	LC
AFS 2416B1&2	Bywaj Mi Zdrowa Dziewczyno Kochana {Farewell, Beloved Girl} {Goodbye My Dear Girl} [in Polish]	LC
AFS 2417A3	Polka	LC
AFS 2418A1	Karjan Kellot Kilvan Kalkattaa	LC
		Bessemer, MI October 7, 1938

31.59. Östman-Stein Orkesteri

BVE 45687-2	Ramona (w: A. Vuorisola, m: Mabel Wayne)[1]	Vi 81417
BVE 45688-2	Oira, Oira-Polkka (J.X.)	Vi 81691, 81696
BVE 45689-1	Elokuun Kuutamo-Valssi (Herman Sjöblom)	Vi 81691
	Augustinatt-Vals	Vi 81696
BVE 45690-2	Kulkurin Masurkka {Tramp's Mazurka} (Herman Sjöblom)	Vi 81417

William E. Stein-p, Urho Östman, unk instrument, unk vln, cl/sax, acn, traps, [1]Volpi Leuto (Walfrid Lehto)-vo   NY July 6, 1928

Stein-Östman Orkesteri

W 109769-2	Suru-Valssi	Co 3095-F, 16077
W 109770-2	Moskova Marssi	Co 3095-F, 16077
W 109771-1	Taika Yö-Valssi (Tomnikowski)[1]	Co 3093-F, 16170
W 109772-2	Mustalaisen Kaipaus (Herbert-Vuorisola)[1]	Co 3093-F, 16170
	[1]Allie Ronka-sop	NY October 1928

W 109994-2	Merenneito-Sottiisi	Co 3104-F
W 109995-1	Hawaijan Yö-Valssi (Lee S. Roberts)	Co 3099-F, 16115
	Hawaiian Nights-Waltz	Co 12110-F
W 109996-2	Honolulun Kuutamo-Valssi (Fr. Lawrence)[1]	Co 3104-F, 16120

W 109997-2   Aamullinen Koi (Arthur A. Penn)'   Co 3099-F, 16115
              'unk vo   NY November 1928

Co 12110-F as COLUMBIA NOVELTY ORCHESTRA

Östman-Stein Orkesteri

BVE 48448-   Joutsen {Swan}-Sotiisi   Vi V-4033
              Svanen-Schottische   Vi V-20043, V-20063, 26-0011
BVE 48449-   Tatjana-Valssi   Vi V-4033
              Tatjanas-Waltz   Vi V-20043, V-20063, 26-0011
              Tatiana-Waltz   Vi V-131, 25-0028
BVE 48450-1   Elomme Päivät-Marssi'   Vi V-4029, V-4150, 26-6003, HMV AL1086
BVE 48451-1   Hyvästi Jää (Aloha Oe)'   Vi V-4029, V-4150, 26-6003, HMV AL1086
              William E. Stein-p, unk vln, sax, acn, bj, sbs, traps, 'Volpi Leuto
              (Walfrid Lehto)-vo   NY December 10, 1928

BVE 51683-2   Tunnustettu Rakkaus {Confessions Of Love}-Valssi (arr W.E. Stein)
                                                                        Vi V-4057
BVE 51684-2   Laura-Valssi (A. Wirzenius)   Vi V-4057
BVE 51685-2   Idän Ruusut {Oriental Roses}-Valssi (I. Ivanovici)   Vi V-4044
BVE 51686-2   Entis' Ajan {Old Times}-Polkka (W.E. Stein)   Vi V-4044
              Alfredo Cibelli-md, William E. Stein-p, unk vln, sax, acn, g, sbs,
              bells   NY May 6, 1929

31.60. Ernest Paananen *baritone, violin (1879-1951)*

              Song Of The Loggers   Vi trial
              Wedding Procession And Dance [no vo]   Vi trial
              p   NY May 24, 1923

Paananen Ja Kump.

BVE 56713-1   Naimahommia-Pt. 1: Alkutoimituksia (Ernest Paananen)   Vi V-4049
BVE 56714-1   Naimahommia-Pt. 2: Aitan Oven Takana (Ernest Paananen)   Vi V-4049
BVE 56715-2   Naimahommia-Pt. 3: Lemmen Lurituksia (Ernest Paananen)   Vi V-4053
BVE 56716-2   Naimahommia-Pt. 4: Kuokkavieraita (Ernest Paananen)
                                                        Vi V-4053, RCA PL40115(33)
BVE 56717-2   Naimahommia-Pt. 5: Kuokkimista (Ernest Paananen)   Vi V-4056
BVE 56718-2   Naimahommia-Pt. 6: Kuuliaistanssit (Ernest Paananen)
                                                        Vi V-4056, RCA PL40115(33)
              own vln, unk acn, p, traps, 4 men and 1 woman-vo
                                                        NY September 25, 1929

Ernest Paananen

W 111145-2   Mennäästä Poijat   Co 3132-F, DI39
W 111146-2   Harmiaveden Rannalla   Co 3132-F, DI39
              Suomalainen Taiteilija-Yhtymä, d Stein-Östman   NY October 1929

W 112371-2   Hei Varsalla Vain (Ernest Paananen-A. Kosola)   Co 3178-F
W 112372-2   Lauluni Kannel Nyt Soi (Ernest Paananen-A. Kosola)   Co 3178-F

W 112373-1   Muistatko Vielä Illan Sen-Waltz Song (Ernest Paananen-A. Kosola)
                                                        Co 3165-F, DI179
W 112374-2   Liukkaalla Jäällä-Polka (Ernest Paananen-A. Kosola) [no vo]
                                                        Co 3165-F, DI179
        Paananen-Kosola Orkesteri: own vln, Antti Kosola-acn, others unk
                                                        NY December 1930

31.61. Alex Pasola *bass*

            Kuinka Maasta Isien'   Vi trial
            Häämatka   Vi trial
            Edward T. King-p, 'with Jukka Mäki   NY March 19, 1917

B 19730-3   Kuinka Maasta Isien, from "Naytelmästä Hardangerin Harjulla"'
                                                          Vi 69468
B 19732-2   Juomalaulu   Vi 69467
B 19734-2   Hevospaimenen Häämatka   Vi 69467
        King's Orchestra d Rosario Bourdon, 'with Jukka Mäki   NY May 1, 1917

B 21372-1   Aika Poika   Vi 77219
B 21373-2   Tampereen Tyttö   Vi rej
B 21374-2   Viuliulei   Vi 77219
        King's Orchestra d Nathaniel Shilkret   NY January 17, 1918

Alex Pasola-Jukka Mäki

B 21398-2   Tullos Lippumme Luo (Wm. E. Stein)   Vi rej
B 21399-2   Kun Kevät Koittaa (G. Wennerberg)   Vi 77218
            as before   NY January 31, 1918

B 21398-4   Tullos Lippumme Luo (Wm. E. Stein)   Vi 77218
            as before   NY March 26, 1918

31.62. Tatu Pekkarinen *vocal (1892-1951)*

BVE 40924-1   Riijuu Rallatus   Vi 80339, HMV AL1031
BVE 40925-1   Posetiiviveisu Suomesta   Vi 80339, HMV AL1031
BVE 40926-1   Kyllä Tästä Selvitään   Vi 80364, HMV AL1032
BVE 40927-1   Meidän Talon Haitari   Vi 80364, HMV AL1032
BVE 40928-1   Ramperi Kesäleskenä {Ramperi, The Summer Widower}
                                                  Vi 80466, HMV AL1018
BVE 40929-1   Jussi Laulaa Heilastaan {Jussi, Singing Of His Sweetheart}
                                                  Vi 80466, HMV AL1018
BVE 40930-1   Vanhanpojan Veisu   Vi 80555
BVE 40931-1   Savon Ukon Esitelmä Rakkaudesta'   Vi 80555
            fl, p, or 'spoken   Chicago November 21, 1927

BVE 40372-3   Meijän Kylän Tyttäret {The Lover}   Vi 80713, HMV AL993
BVE 40373-2   Jutikaisen Jussi {The Surprised Farm Hand}   Vi 81448
BVE 40374-2   Kirkonkylän Tanssit {Barn Dance} (Pekkarinen) Vi 80713, HMV AL993

BVE 40375-2   Vanhat Viinaveikot {Prohibition Song} {Prohibition In Finland}
                   (Pekkarinen)   Vi 80631
               Clement Barone-fl, Matti Jurva-p   Camden, NJ January 30, 1928

File note: An extra man (Cortese) called but not used as Pekkarinen wanted Matti
Jurva to play for him.

BVE 40382-2   Laulu Almanakasta {Song Of The Almanac} (w: Tatu Pekkarinen)
                                                                         Vi 80631
BVE 40383-2   Uusi Hattu {New Hat}   Vi 81448
               Matti Jurva-p   Camden, NJ January 31, 1928

BVE 45122-2   Muistoja Suomesta {Memories Of Finland}   Vi V-4001
BVE 45123-1   Helsingin Heila Muistelee Iivanaa {A Helsingfors Girl's Love}
                                                                         Vi 81689
BVE 41524-1   Iita Ja Minä {Ida And I}   Vi V-4001
BVE 41527-1   Renkipojan Reisupolkka {A Farmer's Farewell Polka} (Tatu Pekkarinen)
                                                                         Vi 81689
BVE 45128-1(2R) Meripojan Juttuja {Sailor's Stories} (Tatu Pekkarinen)   Vi 81305
BVE 45129-1(2R) Savon Ukko Helsingissä {A Farmer From Savo Visits Helsingfors}
                                                                         Vi 81305
                   vln, sax, p, g   NY May 9, 1928

Tatu Pekkarinen-Matti Jurva

CVE 45130-2   Jahvetti Autolla Helsingissä {Jahvet In An Automobile}-Pt. 1
                   (Tatu Pekkarinen)   Vi 59023(12")
CVE 45131-2   Jahvetti Autolla Helsingissä {Jahvet In An Automobile}-Pt. 2
                   (Tatu Pekkarinen)   Vi 59023(12")
                   acn, g   NY May 9, 1928

31.63. Elsa Perälä *vocal*

AFS 3298B1   Pohjola On Kaunis Suomi   LC
                                               Mountain Iron, MN September 1937

This artist may be the same as the following.

31.64. Mrs. Matti Perälä *vocal*

AFS 3275A3   Kataja Se Marjoja Kasvaa Ilman Kukkimata   LC
                                            Mountain Iron, MN September 19, 1937

31.65. Fina Petersen *vocal*

AFS 4260A3   Rekilaulu {Sleigh Song}   LC
AFS 4260B1   Kalliolle Kukkulallen {Rocky Hills}[1]   LC
AFS 4260B2   Lauvantaki Ilta {Saturday Night}[1] [2]   LC
AFS 4260B3   Honkain Keskella {Deep In The Forest}[1] [2]   LC
                   with [1]Celia Koljonen, [2]Mary Salonen   Central Valley, CA September 4,
                                                                                         1939

31.66. Aina Pohjala *vocal*

AFS 2379A1	Ja Sen Silkkihuivin Jonka Mulle Annoit	LC
AFS 2379A2	Nätti Poika Rinnallani, Kuolemankin Hetkellä	LC
	Calumet, MI	September 26, 1938

31.67. Otto Pyykkönen *tenor*

89624-1	Lapsuuden Koti (P. Würck-V. Sola)	Co 3002-F
89625-2	Aamu-Laulu (T. Kuula-Eino Leino)	Co 3002-F
	orch	NY January 1924

89637-1	Se Oolanin Sota	Co 3000-F
89638-1	Isotalo Ja Rannanjärvi	Co 3000-F
	acn	NY ca January 1924

B 29999-1	Hurraa Nyt Komppania (Hurray! Now Comes The Regiment)	Vi 77556
B 30100-2	Laivapojat (Sailor's Song) (arr E. Kauppi)	Vi 77556
	orch d Leroy Shield	NY May 13, 1924

B 30202-3	Minäpä Olen Laulajapoika (I'm A Boy Who Sings)	Vi 77747
B 30203-2	Kun Kävelin Kesäillalla (I Walked On A Summer Night)	Vi 77747
	as before	NY May 21, 1924

9542	Syystunnelma (Autumn Sensation) (w: Eino Leino, m: Toivo Kuula)	
		Ed 59303
9543	Aamulaulu (Morning Song) (w: Eino Leino, m: Toivo Kuula)	Ed 59303
	John F. Burckhardt-p	NY June 2, 1924

9548	Kesäillalla (A Summer Night)'	Ed 59304
9549	Soipa Kieli (w: Ilmari Calamnius, m: O. Merikanto)	Ed 59304
	orch or 'John F. Burckhardt-p	NY June 3, 1924

105279-1	Älä Itke Tyttöni Pieni-Valssi	Co 3003-F, 16058, Sävel SÄLP 662(33)
105280-1	Vapaa Wenäjä (Free Russia)	Co 3003-F, 16058, Eteenpäin ETLP 301(33)
	orch	NY ca November 1924

105331-1	Yks' Haamu Seisoi Marjaanan Ovella	Co 3004-F
105332-1	Korjat Poijat Ja Tytöt	Co 3005-F
105333-2	Laivapoikain Laulu	Co 3004-F
105334-2	Kosken-Laskijan Morsiamet	Co 3005-F
	vln, p	NY ca January 1925

105420-2	Matalasta Torpasta	Co 3007-F
105421-	Anssin Jukka Ja Härmän Häät	Co 3007-F
	acn	NY ca February 1925

105464-2	Syystunnelma (Kuula)	Co 3008-F, 16200
105465-1	Yks' Lauantaki-ilta	Co 3008-F, 16200
105466-1	Tuomet Valkeina Kukkii (Kilkka)	Co 3006-F
105467-1	Kesä-illalla (Oskar Merikanto)	Co 3006-F

```
105468-1    Lemminkäisen Laulu                                      Co 3009-F
105469-1    Näytelmästä "Pohjalaisia"                               Co 3012-F
105470-1    Tuuli Se Taivutti Koivun Larvan                         Co 3012-F
105471-1    Poijat Kun Raitilla Laulelee                            Co 3009-F
            2 vln, p                                      NY  February 1925
```

```
W 106698-2  Vangin Laulu {The Prisoner's Song} (Guy Massey)    Co 3026-F, 16136
W 106699-2  Viaporin Valssi         Co 3026-F, 16136, Eteenpäin ETLP 301(33)
            orch                                             NY  April 1926
```

```
18288       Istontalon Antti Ja Rannanjärvi                         Ed 59305
18289       Anssin Jukka Ja Härman Häät                             Ed 59306
18290       Matalasta Torpasta {Humble Peasant House}               Ed 59305
            vln, acn, p                                 NY  March 5, 1928
```

```
18294       Wiaporin Valssi                                         Ed 59307
18295       Lauvantaki Ilta {Saturday Evening}                      Ed 59306
18296       Silloin Se Ilma {Southern Winds}                        Ed 59307
            orch                                        NY  March 8, 1928
```

31.68. Elmer Ronka And His Finnish Orchestra

```
W 110873-1  Unkarilainen Tanssi No. 5 {Hungarian Dance No. 5} (Joh. Strauss)
                                                                    Co 3125-F
W 110874-2  Venäläinen Fantasia {Grand Russian Fantasy} (Jules Levy)  Co 3125-F
            Elmer Ronka-tb, others unk                       NY  June 1929
```

31.69. Aino Saari *soprano*

```
W 107223-2  Sorakumpujen Vainajille (F. Lindros)
                            Co 3039-F, 16147, Eteenpäin ETLP-301(33)
W 107224-2  Inga Pieni (Leijdström)                            Co 3044-F, 16150
W 107225-2  Mustalaisruhtinatar (Emmerich Kalman)              Co 3044-F, 16150
W 107226-2  Tehtaassa                                          Co 3039-F, 16147
            orch                                             NY  October 1926
```

```
BVE 40470-1  Ei Kyytimies Kiirettä Oo {Driver Do Not Whip Your Horses}
                              (J. Feldman)                            Vi 80521
BVE 40471-1  Kesävirkistystä {Summer Idyll} (Wm. E. Stein)  Vi 80632, Viking V-10
            orch d Bruno Reibold                       Camden, NJ  November 9, 1927
```

```
BVE 40472-2  Sulle {To You}, from "Lehtimajan Kukka" (Wm. E. Stein)
                                                       Vi 80632, Viking V-10
BVE 40473-1  Merellä {The Sea} (Oskar Merikanto, op. 47 no. 4)        Vi 80521
            as before                             Camden, NJ  November 10, 1927
```

```
W 108709-2  Babette {Horatio Nicholls}                         Co 3071-F, 7831
W 108710-2  Venäläinen Kehtolaulu {Russian Lullaby} (I. Berlin)  Co 3071-F, 7831
W 108711-2  Kuutamo Yö, from "Lehtimajan Kukka" (Wm. E. Stein)   Co 3075-F, 7888
W 108712-2  Soita Mustalainen Soita, from "Countess Maritza" (E. Kálmán)
                                                            Co 3075-F, 7888
            orch                                           NY  January 1928
```

31.70. Hannes Saari *tenor*

W 105804-2	Iloinen Meripoika (E. Kauppi)	Co 3013-F, 16126, Sävel SÄLP 663(33)
W 105805-2	Kulkurin Masurkka	Co 3013-F, 16126, Sävel SÄLP 662(33)
	orch	NY ca August 1925

W 107155-3	Volgan Aallot	Co 3034-F, 16142
W 107156-3	Tämä Maa	Co 3034-F, 16142
W 107157-2	Chrysanthemum (Wm. E. Stein)	Co 3036-F, 16144
W 107158-2	Meripojan Heilat (R.F. Strange)	Co 3036-F, 16144
	William E. Stein-p	NY September 1926

BVE 39267-2	Espanjatar	Vi 79442
BVE 39268-1	Ruski Iivana Pakolaisena Suomessa	Vi 79442
BVE 39269-1	Tilta Tuohimaa	Vi 80063
BVE 39270-2	Bellona Ja Rodrigo	Vi 80063
	Willi Larsen-acn	NY June 17, 1927

W 108253-2	Valkotuomet	Co 3059-F, 16162
W 108254-1	Ei Kyytimies Kiirettä Oo	Co 3059-F, 16162
W 108255-2	Kehtolaulu, from "Laivan Kannella"	Co 3065-F
W 108256-1	Meripojan Tervehdys-Comic Song	Co 3065-F
	orch	NY August 1927

W 108414-2	Sonja (Eugène Bartós)	Co 3064-F, 7787, Sävel SÄLP 663(33)
W 108415-2	Raatajan Serenaadi (A. Virtanen)	
		Co 3064-F, 7787, Eteenpäin ETLP-301(33)
W 108416-1	Oi Mistäs Saataisiin	Co 3062-F, 7786, Sävel SÄLP 663(33)
W 108417-2	Saukkosen Avioero	Co 3062-F, 7786, Sävel SÄLP 662(33)
	Trio Finnish Program Society Orchestra	NY October 1927

W 108723-3	Sinikellot (Frändilä)	Co 3072-F, 7832
W 108724-2	Musta Ratsu	Co 3072-F, 7832
W 108725-2	Pois Sormet (M. Nisonen)	Co 3076-F, 7889
W 108726-2	Viivin Jenkka	Co 3076-F, 7889, Love LXLP505(33)
	Antti Kosola Trio	NY January 1928

W 109122-2	Korven Raivaajille (John Doyle)	Co 3080-F, 13413
W 109123-2	Proletaarit Nouskaa, Aatteellinen	
		Co 3080-F, 13413, Eteenpäin ETLP-301(33)
W 109124-1	Lähtö	Co 3078-F, 13401
W 109125-2	Vanha Madrid {In Old Madrid}	Co 3078-F, 13401
W 109126-2	Punavangin Laulu, Aatteellinen	
		Co 3086-F, 16069, Eteenpäin ETLP-301(33)
W 109127-2	Volgan Lotjamiesten Laulu {Song Of The Volga Boatmen}	
		Co 3086-F, 16069
	orch	NY March 1928

W 109440-2	Laivan Kannella (E. Kauppi)	Co 3088-F, 16167
W 109441-1	Uskoton Ja Petollinen Julia (E. Borenius)	Co 3088-F, 16167
W 109442-2	Lontoon Jenny	Co 3082-F, 16002
W 109443-2	Juomarin Laulu	Co 3082-F, 16002

| W 109444-2 | Priki Efrosiina (A. Törnudd)-Pt. 1 | Co 3109-F, 16203 |
| W 109445-2 | Priki Efrosiina (A. Törnudd)-Pt. 2 | Co 3109-F, 16203 |

with Columbian Suomalainen Mieskvartetti, including William E.
Stein-p NY June 1928

W 110572-3	Kaunis On Kesä¹	Co 3115-F
W 110573-2	Armas Vanhaksi Jo Käyn {Silver Threads Among The Gold} (H.P. Danks)¹	
		Co 3115-F
W 110574-1	Tonavan Aallot-Waltz Song	Co 3131-F, DI38
W 110575-2	Iltalaulu²	Co 3131-F, DI38

orch, with ¹mixed choir or ²male quartet NY April 1929

W 110927-2	Kaivosmies (F. Hakala)	Co 3144-F, DI62
W 110928-3	Armahani (Edward G. Simon)	Co 3122-F, 16235
W 110929-1	Muisto-Valssi (V. Korpela)	Co 3122-F, 16235
W 110930-2	Tienraivaaja (O.A. Hirvonen)	Co 3144-F, DI62

V. Frändilän Orkesteri NY ca July 1929

W 112183-1	Jos Pietari Sen Tietäis¹	Co 3166-F
W 112184-1	Liisa Ja Lassi¹	Co 3166-F
W 112185-2	Oi Sulle Vain-Valssi (Pugatschow-Martti Vuori)	Co 3159-F
W 112186-2	Tytön Huolet-One Step (V. Korpela)	Co 3159-F

orch d Werner Koivunen, ¹with Alli Anttila NY ca June 1930

31.71. Sahlman-Trio *instrumental*

W 111255-1	Kesäilta; En Koskaan Voi Unhoittaa Sua	Co 3130-F, DI37
	One Summer Night; I Will Never Forget You	Co 12124-F
W 111256-2	Elokuun Kuutamo-Valssi (Herman Sjöblom)	Co 3130-F
W 111257-2	Czardas (W. Hrimaly)	Co 3160-F
W 111258-2	Nina {Tre Giorni} (G.B. Pergolesi)	Co 3160-F, 12124-F

NY November 1929

31.72. Vilma Salmi And Lillian Forester *vocal*

| AFS 2404B1 | Olin Minä Ennen Vaalia Poika | LC |
| AFS 2405A1 | Löysin Minä Lankakerän | LC |

Laurium, MI October 1, 1938

31.73. Hiski Salomaa *vocal (1891-1957)*

| W 175281-1 | test recording | Co |

NY February 2, 1927

| W 107622-2 | Tiskarin Polkka | Co 3045-F, 16151, CBS 25197(33), Love LRLP17(33) |
| W 107623-2 | Askon Kolmerivinen | Co 3045-F, 16151, CBS 25197(33), Love LRLP17(33) |

acn NY February 1927

| W 108729-2 | Laulu Taiteilioista | |
| | Co 3073-F, 7833, CBS 25197(33), Love LRLP17(33), IFLP 2(33) | |

W 108730-2   Vanhanpiian Polkka (Hiski Salomaa)
                           Co 3073-F, 7833, CBS 25197(33), Love LRLP17(33)
                                                           NY January 1928

W 109293-2   Savonpiijan Amerikkaan Tulo
                           Co 3081-F, 16001, CBS 25197(33), Love LRLP17(33)
W 109294-1   Emännät Piknekissä Co 3081-F, 16001, CBS 25197(33), Love LRLP17(33)
              vln, acn   NY May 1928

W 110495-2   Vapauden Kaiho   Co 3137-F, DI48, Love LRLP17(33)
W 110496-2   Elisan Valssi   Co 3137-F, DI48, Love LRLP17(33)
W 110497-2   Häät Remulassa   Co 3111-F, 16225, CBS 25197(33), Love LXLP505(33)
W 110498-2   Dahlmannin Paartit Co 3111-F, 16225, CBS 25197(33), Love LXLP505(33)
              Hännisen Orkesteri   NY March 1929

W 112128-2   Lännen Lokari-Sottiisi (Hiski Salomaa-W. Kauppi)   Co 3158-F, DI163,
                           Electro E3135, De SD3135, CBS 25197(33), FM MFLP-37(33),
                           MFMC-37(C), Finnlevy SFK-2010(33), Helmi HK-812(33),
                           Love LRLP17(33), RD VPS-1007(33), Rytmi R-6432(33),
                           RN-4020(45), RLP-8043(33), RILP-7035(33), RILP-7060(33)
W 112129-1   Talvella Maa On Valkoinen (Hiski Salomaa)
                           Co 3169-F, DI186, CBS 25197(33), Love LRLP17(33)
W 112130-3   Kemppaisen Avioelämä (Hiski Salomaa)
                           Co 3169-F, DI186, CBS 25197(33), Love LRLP17(33)
W 112131-2   Iitin Tiltu-Polkka (Hiski Salomaa-W. Kauppi)
                           Co 3158-F, CBS 25197(33), Love LRLP17(33)
W 112132-1   Auvisen Akkahommat   Co 3202-F, CBS 25197(33), Love LXLP505(33)
              Wäinö Kauppi, Larsen & Co.   NY May 1930

W 112992-2   Ryöstöpolkka (Hiski Salomaa)
                           Co 3189-F, CBS 25197(33), Love LXLP505(33)
W 112993-1   Taattoni Maja   Co 3202-F, CBS 25197(33)
W 112994-2   Värssyjä Sieltä Ja Täältä (Hiski Salomaa)
                           Co 3189-F, LC LBC-10(33), CBS 25197(33), Love LXLP505(33)
              Kosolan Orkesteri: William Syrjälä-tp, Antti Kosola-acn, Frankie
              Stenbacka-g   NY ca June 1931

31.74. Maija Särkipato *violin*

AFS 3272A1   Koiviston Polska   LC
AFS 3272A2   Ei Ole Rosvoa Lainkaan   LC
AFS 3272A3   En Minä Kaikkia Rahojani Juonut   LC
                                              Ely, MN August 17, 1937

31.75. Mary Särkipato *vocal*

AFS 3270A1   Taivas On Sininen   LC
AFS 3271A2   Kesä Ilta   LC
              vln   Ely, MN August 17, 1937

31.76. Otto Särkipato *vocal*

AFS 3271B4	Keskellä Lahtea	LC
AFS 3271B5	Lähetäämpäs Pojat Soutelemaan	LC
		Ely, MN August 17, 1937

31.77. Kuuno Sevander *vocal (b. 1898)*

W 110848-2	Poika Oli Pohjan Torniosta	Co 3199-F
W 110849-2	Tanssit Tarvaisen Torpassa	Co 3121-F, 16234
W 110850-1	Kuutamossa Venäjän (Meyer Gusman)	Co 3118-F, 16220
W 110851-1	Erien Rannalla (John Doyle)	Co 3118-F, 16220
	orch	NY June 1929

W 110933-2	Tuletko, Tyttö Tanssiin?-Waltz Song	Co 3134-F, DI41
W 110934-2	Römperin Tanssit	Co 3134-F, DI41
W 110945-1	Helsingin Kulkurin Huolia	Co 3199-F
W 110946-2	Kiikalan Polkka	Co 3121-F, 16234
	orch	NY ca July 1929

W 111681-1	Elontiellä (John Doyle)	Co 3140-F, DI51
W 111682-3	Kataja Se Matala-Sottiisi	Co 3168-F, DI181
W 111683-1	Lempi, Sun Säveleesi Soi {Love, Your Magic Spell Is Everywhere}	Co 3140-F, DI51
W 111684-2	Ain' Merta Mer' Mies Rakastaa	Co 3168-F, DI181
	orch	NY February 1930

31.78. Julius Siik *baritone*

W 112062-1	Viulu-Sampan Laulu (O. Merikanto); Häilyvä Nainen (Rossini)	
		Co 3153-F
W 112063-2	Ähä-Ähä	Co 3153-F
	Lypsäjan Laulu	Co 3150-F
	Jannen Hanuripolkka	Co 3150-F
	Liimatainen-Loya	Chicago May 1930

The missing matrix numbers are probably W 112060 and W 112061.

W 112772-1	Heilani Soitteli (Erkki Melartin)	Co 3198-F
W 112773-1	Heinässä (K.W. Kilkka)	Co 3176-F
W 112774-1	Oravan Jäljillä (Erkki Melartin)	Co 3198-F
W 112775-1	Tukkipoikia Tulossa (Emil Kauppi)	Co 3176-F
	orch	Chicago ca February 1931

W 113155-2	Sempä Tähden	Co 3205-F
W 113294-2	Toisen Oma	Co 3205-F
W 113295-2	Wenehessä Soutelen; Paljo Olen Maata Kulkenut (Jääskeläinen)	
		Co 3203-F
W 113296-2	Minä Laulan Sun Iltasi Tähtihin (Linnavuori)	Co 3208-F
W 113297-2	Ikävissä; Lemmenhetki (Merikanto)	Co 3203-F

```
W 113298-2    Wirran Rannalla (Tuuri)                               Co 3208-F
              Soitin-Trio                            Chicago  ca December 1931
```

31.79. Matt Simi *vocal*

```
AFS 3268A1    Vilho Ja Bertta
AFS 3268A2    Pium Paum Kehto Heilahtaa                                      LC
AFS 3268B2    Kukkuu Kukkuu Kaukana Kukkuu                                   LC
                                                                            LC
                                               Cloquet, MN  August 16, 1937
```

31.80. Sue And Olga Simi *vocal*

```
AFS 3268B1    Lemminkäisen Äiti
                                                                            LC
                                               Cloquet, MN  August 16, 1937
```

31.81. Martti Similä *baritone*

```
W 107231-2    Hallin Janne                                    Co 3038-F, 16146
W 107233-2    Ostron Tyttö                                    Co 3038-F, 16146
W 107234-2    Härmän Pojat                                    Co 3041-F, 16148
W 107235-2    Marjalunnin Jussi                               Co 3041-F, 16148
         p                                                     NY  October 1926

W 107840-2    Merimiehen Hyvästi Jättö; Meripojan Koti        Co 3048-F, 16154
W 107841-2    Sepän Sälli                                     Co 3054-F, 13354
W 107842-2    Aamu Tunnelma; Talon Tyttö Ja Torpan Tyttö      Co 3048-F, 16154
W 107843-1    Jos Kaikki Suomen Järvet                        Co 3054-F, 13354
         orch                                                  NY  April 1927
```

31.82. Matti Söderlund *accordion*

Matti Söderlund-John Homan

```
              Port Arthur-March                                      Vi trial
              John Homan (1891-1977)-2d acn        NY  September 5, 1916
```

Söderlund Ja Larsen

```
85878-1-2     Lehtein Väreily
85880-1       Elisabetin Jänka                                     Co E4818
85881-1-2     Vuori Kaikuja-Masurka                                Co E4667
85883-2       Apostol Schottische                                  Co E4818
              Willi Larsen-2d acn                                  Co E4667
                                                   NY  ca February 1920
```

Matti Söderlund-John Homan

```
B 24535-2     Isänmaan Kaiho {Longing For My Country}-Marssi        Vi rej
B 24536-2     Manchurian Kukkuloilla {On The Hills Of Manchuria}-Valssi  Vi 73475
B 24537-2     Kolka-Mazurkka                                       Vi 72849
B 24538-1     Piknikki-Polkka                                      Vi 72849
```

```
B 24539-2      Laura-Valssi                                            Vi rej
               John Homan-2d acn                          NY  October 19, 1920
```

Matti Söderlund-Fritz Ericson

```
B 26067-2      Tunturin Kellot {Mountain Bells}-Schottische            Vi 73475
               Bergsklockor-Rheinländer                                Vi 73476
B 26068-2      Taika Yö {Seeing Things}-Waltz                          Vi rej
               Fritz Ericson-2d acn                      NY  February 1, 1922
```

Vi 73476 is Swedish.

Matti Söderlund

```
B 26608-2      Taika Yö {Magic Night}-Waltz                            Vi rej
B 26609-3      Naisten {Ladies}-Polka                                  Vi rej
               Nathaniel Shilkret-p, unk c, cl            NY  June 5, 1922
```

```
W 109982-1     Punkaharju-Valssi             Co 3107-F, 16194, Sävel SÄLP 662(33)
W 109983-2     Paraati-Marssi                               Co 3133-F, DI40
W 109984-2     Aamurusko-Sottiisi¹                          Co 3133-F, DI40
W 109985-2     Lappeenrannan Rakuna-Polkka¹                 Co 3107-F, 16194
               ¹g                                         NY  November 1928
```

31.83. John Soininen *vocal*

```
AFS 4274A1     Juomalaulu-Sailor's Drinking Song                           LC
AFS 4274A2     Syntymistään Sureva {Oh That I Had Never Been Born}         LC
AFS 4274A3     Illalla Myöhään {Late In The Evening}                       LC
AFS 4274B1     Velisurmaaja {The Brother-Murderer}                         LC
AFS 4274B2     Minun Kultani {My Sweetheart}                               LC
AFS 4275A1     Aikoja Entisiä {Times Gone By}                              LC
AFS 4275A2     Älä Itke, Äitini {Don't Cry, Mother}                        LC
AFS 4275A3     Kesä-ilta {Summer Evening}                                  LC
AFS 4275B1     Vaka Vanha Väinämöinen {Steady Old Väinämöinen} (Kalevala, XL Runo,
                    lines 221 ff.)                                         LC
AFS 4275B2     Kanteleelle {Song For The Kantele}                          LC
                                             Berkeley, CA  November 5, 1939
```

31.84. Wäinö Sola *tenor (1883-1961)*

```
W 106001-2     Soitin Pillillä                             Co 3016-F, 16174
W 106002-1     Sain Paljon Luojalta Armahain (K.W. Kilkka) Co 3022-F, 16132
W 106003-2     Se Rakkaus                                  Co 3016-F, 16174
W 106004-1     Heilallein Minä Laulelen                    Co 3022-F, 16132
                                                         NY  November 1925
```

```
BVE 34932-1    Yö (A. Pushkin-A. Rubinstein)                          Vi 78614
BVE 34933-3    Suru {Elegie} (J. Massenet)                            Vi 78614
               orch d Rosario Bourdon               Camden, NJ  March 4, 1926
```

```
BVE 34934-3    Karjapihassa {In The Stockyard} (w: Larin Kyösti, m: Toivo Kuula,
                   op. 31 no. 2)                                      Vi 78775
BVE 34935-1    Kevätlaulu {Spring Song} (Martti Nisonen)             Vi 78775
               as before                             Camden, NJ  March 5, 1926

W 109881-2     Sotamiehen Laulu "Daniel Hjort" (J.J. Wecksell)       Co 3097-F, 16079
W 109882-2     Sinä Sanoit (Wm. E. Stein)                            Co 3100-F, 16116
W 109883-1     Kaunein Keijukainen (Th. A. Arne-Wm. E. Stein)        Co 3097-F, 16079
W 109884-1     Hyvästi {Goodbye} (P. Tosti-Wm. Stein)                Co 3100-F, 16116
               orch                                            NY  November 1928
```

31.85. Otto Strid *accordion*

```
BRC 70164-1    Postimies {Postilionen} {Postman}-Valssi             Vi V-4113
BRC 70165-1    Heinäsirkat {Grasshopporna} {Grasshopper}-Polka      Vi V-4113
                                                      NY  August 12, 1931

BRC 70181-1    Miranda-Valssi (arr Otto Strid)                      Vi rej
BRC 70182-1    The Flag Of Victory-March (Von Bleu-arr Otto Strid)  Vi V-4130
BRC 70183-1    Poranek-Valssi (arr Otto Strid)                      Vi V-4130
                                                      NY  August 26, 1931
```

31.86. Elli Suokas *soprano*

```
B 17920-2      Pai, Pai, Paitaressu {Bye Bye Baby}-Cradle Song (Oskar Merikanto)
                                                                     Vi 67945
B 17921-1      Tuuti, Mun Vauvani, Nukkukaa! {Baby Go To Sleep}; Tipu, Tipu,
                   Kuuleppas! {Chickie, Chickie, Little Friend} (Oskar Merikanto)
                                                                     Vi 67945
B 17922-1      En Voi Sua Unhoitaa {I Can't Forget You} (Carl Gehrmans); Ainoa Olen
                   Talon Tyttö {I Am The Only Farmer's Daughter} (A.E. Lindgren)
                                                                     Vi 67946
B 17923-2      Käen Kukkuessa {Coo Coo} (Emil Kauppi)                Vi 67946
               King's Orchestra                         NY  June 23, 1916

B 17932-2      Joululaulu {Christmas Song} (Selim Palmgren, op. 34 no. 1)   Vi rej
B 17933-2      Syystunnelma {Herbststimmung}-Fall Song (Toivo Kuula, op. 2 no. 1)
                                                                     Vi 69075
B 17934-2      Kyyhkynen Kylpee {Bathing Doves} (Otto Kotilainen)   Vi rej
B 17935-1      Taivas On Sininen Ja Valkoinen {The Sky Is Blue And White} Vi 67980
B 17936-1      Ei Taivahan Alla; Polska                             Vi 67980
B 17937-2      Oi Sinä Korkia Kuningasten Kuningas; Sydämestäni Rakastan  Vi rej
               as before                               NY  June 27, 1916

B 17932-3      Joululaulu {Christmas Song} (Selim Palmgren, op. 34 no. 1)  Vi 69051
B 17934-3      Kyyhkynen Kylpee {Bathing Doves} (Otto Kotilainen)   Vi 69051
B 17937-3      Oi Sinä Korkia Kuningasten Kuningas; Sydämestäni Rakastan  Vi 69075
B 18423-2      Rida Ranka {Riding On A Pony} (A. Ekenberg)          Vi 69561
                                                      NY  September 13, 1916

B 18428-2      Irmelin Rose (W. Peterson-Berger, op. 3 no. 3)       Vi rej
                                                      NY  September 14, 1916
```

44574-4	Laulu Lapista; Talon Tyttö	Co E3222
44576-1	Sureva	Co E3434
44577-3	Pai, Pai, Paitaressu (Oskar Merikanto)	Co E3222
	orch	NY ca January 1917

B 19493-2	Tiroler Sind Lustig {The Folk Of The Tyrol Are Happy And Gay}, from	
	"Der Tiroler Wastl" (Jacob Haibel) [in German]	Vi rej
B 19494-2	Schweizerlied {Swiss Song} [in German]	Vi rej
B 19495-1	Des Glockenthurmers Tochterlein {The Belfry Warden's Daughter}	
	(w: Ruckert) [in German]	Vi rej
	King's Orchestra d Rosario Bourdon	NY April 17, 1917

B 19495-2	Des Glockenthurmers Tochterlein {The Belfry Warden's Daughter}	
	(w: Ruckert) [in German]	Vi 73070
	as before	NY April 26, 1917

B 19980-2	Suomen Lapsi (F. Pacius)	Vi 69501
B 19981-2	Isänmaalle (J. Sibelius)	Vi 69501
	King's Orchestra	NY June 7, 1917

58394-1	Erkki Paimen	Co E3660
58395-1	Varpunen Jouluaamuna	Co E3660
58396-	Käen Kukkuessa	Co E3554
58397-	Mirjamin Laulu	Co E3554
	orch	NY ca June 1917

B 20102-1	Ballaadi Kaarle Kuninkaan Metsästyksestä (Fredrik Pacius)	Vi 69603
B 20103-2	Ah, Mikä Taitaa Olla Mun	Vi rej
B 20104-2	Rannalla Istuja (Ilmari Hannikainen, op. 5)	Vi rej
B 20105-2	Hymni Suomelle (Fredrik Pacius)	Vi 69603
	King's Orchestra	NY June 12, 1917

B 18428-3	Irmelin Rose (W. Peterson-Berger, op. 3 no. 3)	Vi 69561
B 19493-3	Tiroler Sind Lustig {The Folk Of The Tyrol Are Happy and Gay}, from	
	"Der Tiroler Wastl" (Jacob Haibel) [in German]	Vi 69646
B 19494-4	Schweizerlied {Swiss Song} [in German]	Vi rej
B 20150-2	Nouse Rienna Suomen Kieli-Finnish Patriotic Hymn (Joseph Haydn)	
		Vi rej
B 20151-1	Varpunen {The Sparrow} (Armas Järnefelt)	Vi 72517
	King's Orchestra d Rosario Bourdon	NY June 21, 1917

B 19494-6	Schweizerlied {Swiss Song} [in German]	Vi 69646
B 20103-4	Ah, Mikä Taitaa Olla Mun	Vi rej
B 20104-5	Rannalla Istuja (Ilmari Hannikainen, op. 5)	Vi 72517
	King's Orchestra	NY August 9, 1917

B 21303-2	Kullan Ylistys {Praising Her Sweetheart}	Vi 72768
B 21304-1	Iloa Ja Surua {Happiness And Sorrow}	Vi 72768
	King's Orchestra d Nathaniel Shilkret	NY December 26, 1917

B 21314-2	Kesäpäivä Kangasalla (G. Linsen)	Vi rej
B 21315-2	Ajan Aallot (J.H. Erkko-Armas Järnefelt)	Vi rej
	as before	NY December 27, 1917

Elli Suokas-Steinback

86516-	Hei, Henttuni Sinisillä Silmillä	Co E4817
86517-	Venehessä Vetten Päällä	Co E4817
86519-1	Laulu Tulipunaisesta Kukasta	Co E7006
86520-2	Lintuselle	Co E7006
	orch	NY ca September 1920

31.87. Suomalainen Kvartetti *vocal quartet*

39676-1	Sota Marssi	Co E2168
39677-1	Kosioretki	Co E2168
39678-1	Kansan Laulu	Co E2167
39679-1	Ii, Ii, Illall'	Co E2167
		NY December 7, 1914

31.88. Suomalainen Soittokvartetti *instrumental*

86060-1	Vanhaa Polskaa	Co E4666
86061-1	Polkka No. 3	Co E4666
86062-1	Palpankilli	Co E4739
86063-1	Kansallinen Valssi	Co E4739
	vln, cl, vc, p	NY March 1920

Co E4666 as FINNISH INSTRUMENTAL QUARTETTE

31.89. Suomalainen Taiteilija-Yhtymä *instrumental*

W 111143-3	Kelluvalla Pinnalla-Polkka	Co 3128-F, DI29
W 111144-2	Koko-Maailman Valssi	Co 3128-F, DI29
	d Stein-Östman	NY ca October 1, 1929

31.90. Suomalainen Tanssi Orkesteri (Finnish Dance Orchestra)

B 22785-1	Maa {Country}-Polka	Vi 72470
	Kaimo Polka	Vi 72486
B 22786-1	Tunnustettu Rakkaus {Confession Of Love}-Waltz	Vi 72330
	Meiles Išpažintis-Valcas	Vi 72486
B 22787-2	Augusti Eeklevi-Schottische	Vi 72330
B 22788-2	Alma-Masurkka	Vi 72470
	J.H. Greenberger-vln, Nathaniel Shilkret-cl, Juho Koskelo-vc, William	
	E. Stein-p	NY May 28, 1919

Vi 72486 (Lithuanian) as KAUNO KAPELIJA

B 23679-3	Suomi {Finland}-Masurkka (arr Nathaniel Shilkret)	Vi rej
B 23680-2	Tildun-Polkka {Tilda's Polka} (arr Nathaniel Shilkret)	Vi rej
B 23681-3	Kuutamo-Valssi (arr Nathaniel Shilkret)	Vi rej

B 23682-1   Vuoriston Kaunotar-Sottiisi (arr Nathaniel Shilkret)   Vi 72664
      as before   NY February 18, 1920

B 23679-5   Suomi {Finland}-Masurkka (arr Nathaniel Shilkret)   Vi 73521
B 23680-5   Tildun-Polkka {Tilda's Polka} (arr Nathaniel Shilkret)   Vi 73521
B 23681-5   Kuutamo-Valssi (arr Nathaniel Shilkret)   Vi 72664
      as before   NY March 22, 1920

31.91. Suomi Orkesteri

W 107706-2   Saksan Polkka   Co 3046-F, 16152
W 107707-2   Mä Oksalla Ylimmällä-Vals   Co 3046-F, 16152
W 107708-2   Sikermä Suomi Lauluja-Pt. 1   Co 3050-F, 7785
W 107709-1   Sikermä Suomi Lauluja-Pt. 2   Co 3050-F, 7785
      Wäinö Kauppi-c, others unk   NY March 1927

31.92. Kirsti Suonio *spoken*

BVE 38710-2   Kävi Maantiellä Tanssi {Dance On The Country Lane}
                                Vi 79358, HMV AL1040
BVE 38711-2   Kissanpoika {The Kitten}; Jaska Ja Miina {Jack And Mina}
                                Vi 79358, HMV AL1040
BVE 38712-2   Kolme Akkaa Ahteessa; Kaupungin Luutnantti   Vi 80070
BVE 38713-2   Hyvää Yötä   Vi 80070
      p   NY May 2, 1927

W 107912-1   Maitojuna; Romaani   Co 3055-F, 16159
W 107913-2   Pekkalan Veljet; Kova Pää   Co 3055-F, 16159
                                      NY May 1927

31.93. Sointu Syrjälä *baritone*

W 109712-1   Minun Enkelini {Angela Mia} (Rapee-Vuorisola)
                              Co 3090-F, 3091-F, 13439
W 109715-1   Sireenien Kukkiessa {Jeannine, I Dream Of Lilac Time}
           (L. Wolfe Gilbert-A. Vuorisola)   Co 3090-F, 3091-F, 13439
      orch   NY September 1928

Co 3091-F and 13439 as OTTO LAURINEN. Co 3090-F was withdrawn on November 11, 1928 and remaining copies were scrapped, according to a file note.

31.94. Antti Syrjäniemi *vocal*

BVE 51225-2   Viola Turpeinen Tanssit Kiipillä
           {Viola Turpeinen's Dance On Cape Ann} (Syrjäniemi)
                              Vi V-4040, RCA PL 40115(33)
BVE 51226-2   Päivän Tapahtumia {Happenings Of The Day} (Syrjäniemi)   Vi V-4040
BVE 51227-2   Hämmästys Kekkerit {The Surprise Party} (Syrjeniemi)-Pt. 1 Vi V-4028
BVE 51228-2   Hämmästys Kekkerit {The Surprise Party} (Syrjeniemi)-Pt. 2 Vi V-4028

BVE 51229-2   Daytonin Apinajuttu {The Dayton Evolution Trial} (Syrjäniemi)
                                      Vi V-4092, LC LBC-10(33), Love LXLP505(33)
        Willi Larsen-acn, unk g   NY April 15, 1929

Vi V-4028 as ANTTI SYRJENIEMI

31.95. Kosti Tamminen *vocal*

BVE 38480-1   Hei Heilini (Esther Helenius)   Vi 79404, Sävel SÄLP 662(33)
BVE 38481-2   Työttömän Valssi {Come Around Again}
                                      Vi 79344, Eteenpäin ETLP-301(33)
BVE 38482-2   Laulu On Iloni   Vi 79344
BVE 38483-2   Hoobo Valssi (Arthur Kylander)   Vi 79404
        own g, Willi Larsen-acn   Camden, NJ April 21, 1927

BVE 46949-2   Puuseppä {The Carpenter} (Jaakko Pulli)-Pt. 1
                                              Vi 81690, RCA PL 40115(33)
BVE 46950-1   Puuseppä {The Carpenter} (Jaakko Pulli)-Pt. 2
                                              Vi 81690, RCA PL 40115(33)
BVE 46951-1   Viimeinen Valssi {The Last Waltz}   Vi V-4002
BVE 46952-2   Aatami Paratiisissa {Adam In Paradise}   Vi V-4002
        as before   NY August 27, 1928

BVE 59773-2   Vieraan Kylän Pojat {Boys From The Neighboring Village}
                  (arr Kosti Tamminen)   Vi rej
BVE 59774-1   Lappeenrannan Kasarmilaulu {Soldier's Song}
                  {Lappeenranta Calvalry Song} (arr Kosti Tamminen)   Vi V-4079
BVE 59775-2   Kulkijan Kaiho {Vagabond's Longing} (arr Kosti Tamminen) Vi V-4079
BVE 59776-2   Lukkari {Directus Cantus Polka} (Kosti Tamminen)   Vi rej
        Finnish Four: tp, vln, acn, g   NY April 30, 1930

31.96. Johan Alfred Tanner *baritone (1884-1927)*

J. Alfr. Tanner

B 30255-1   Tuhatjärvien Lumien Maa {Land Of Snow And A Thousand Lakes} Vi 77789
B 30257-1   Kymmenen Pientä Neekeripoikaa {Ten Little Negroes}   Vi 77647
B 30258-2   Oi Sä Hellä Helsinkimme {Dear Old Helsingfors} (J.A. Tanner)
                                                                         Vi 77610
B 30259-1   Nujalan Talkoopolkka {Harvest Polka At Nujala} (J.A. Tanner)
                                                                         Vi 77610
B 30260-1   Viimeinen Lautta {The Last Raft}   Vi 77647
B 30261-2   Jannen Hanuripolkka {John's Accordion Polka}   Vi 77789
        John Witzmann-vln, William E. Stein-p   Camden, NJ June 9, 1924

31.97. Thanlow Soitto Kwartet *instrumental*

W 107195-2   Mustalainen   Co 3037-F, 16145
W 107196-1   Kehtolaulu (A. Järnefelt)   Co 3037-F, 16145
        2 vln, fl, p   NY October 1926

31.98. Jean Theslöf *baritone*

43607-1	Näckens Polska [in Swedish]	Co E2784
43608-2	I Småland Där Ä De Så Gutt, Gutt, Gutt [in Swedish]	Co E2784, E4127
43609-	Kultani Kukkuu	Co E2740
43635-	Tääll' On Mun Kultani (M. Wegelius)	Co E2740
	A Jänta Å Ja [in Swedish]	Co E2785
	Ja Sjunger Å Dansar [in Swedish]	Co E2785, E4127
	orch	NY 1916

84323-3	Voi Äiti Parka Ja Raukka	Co E4068
84324-1-3	Suomalaisen Ratsuväen Marssi	Co E4067, 3155-F
84325-2	Markkinapoika	Co E4067, 3155-F
84326-3	Rekilauluja	Co E4068
	orch	NY April 1918

B 21888-2	Voi, Voi, Kuin Kullallein	Vi rej
B 21889-2	Sunnuntaina (Arnas Järnefelt)	Vi rej
B 21890-2	Porilaisten Marssi (Björneborgarnes)	Vi 73865
	orch d Nathaniel Shilkret	NY June 6, 1918

B 21888-4	Voi, Voi, Kuin Kullallein	Vi rej
	as before	NY June 28, 1918

84707-2	Å Jänta Å Ja [in Swedish]	Co E4199
84708-1	Näckens Polska [in Swedish]	Co E4199
	orch	NY ca August 1918

84959-1	Minä Tahdon Laulun Laulella	Co E4350
84972-1	Pellavan Kitkijä	Co E4225
84973-3	Tuonne Taakse Metsämaan	Co E4225
	orch	NY ca October 1918

	Soldatvisa [in Swedish]	Co E4388
	Athenaenes Sång (Sibelius) [in Swedish]	Co E4388
		NY 1918

B 22430-2	Sunnuntaina (Armas Järnefelt)	Vi 73865
B 22431-2	Pellavan Kitkijä (Erkki Melartin, op. 15 no. 3)	Vi rej
	orch d Rosario Bourdon	NY November 26, 1918

B 22376-1	Jouluvirsi-Christmas Hymn	Vi 72424
	Nathaniel Shilkret-org	NY February 7, 1919

B 22582-2	Juomalaulu, from "Regina Von Emmeritz" (Soderman)	Vi 72316
B 22583-1	Voi, Voi, Kuin Kullallein; Kultaselle	Vi 78354
B 22584-2	Ateenalaisten Laulu (Jean Sibelius, op. 21 no. 3)	Vi 72316
	orch d Rosario Bourdon	NY February 13, 1919

B 31253-1	Mennähän Pojat	Vi 77952
B 31254-2	Jääkärin Laulu (Sam Sihvo)	Vi rej
B 31255-1	Olannin Sota	Vi 77952
	orch d Charles Prince	NY December 5, 1924

```
B 31254-4     Jääkärin Laulu (Sam Sihvo)                                Vi 78104
B 32202-1     Läksin                                                    Vi 78104
B 32203-2     Vainiolla                                                 Vi 78354
B 32204-1     Härmän Häät (The Wedding In Harma)                        Vi 78056
B 32205-2     Isoo-Antti Ja Rannanjärvi (Big Andy And Rannanjärvi)      Vi 78056
              orch d Leroy Shield
                                                      NY   March 16, 1925
```

Vi 78056 as MUHOKSEN JANNE

```
W 105942-1    Pappani Maja                                  Co 3017-F, 16175
W 105943-2    Pohjolan Häät                                 Co 3019-F, 16129
W 105944-1    Oulun Susiteetissa                            Co 3019-F, 16129
W 105945-2    Rekiretki                                     Co 3017-F, 16175
                                                            NY   October 1925
```

```
CVE 33998-2   Sotaveikot (The Two Grenadiers) (Heinrich Heine-Robert Schumann)
                                                            Vi 68748(12")
              orch d Rosario Bourdon            Camden, NJ  December 14, 1925
```

Muhoksen Janne

```
BVE 33697-2   Meripojan Kotiinpaluu (The Sailor's Homecoming) Vi 78615, HMV AL1039
BVE 33698-1   Se On Ylösotettu (It Is Reserved)
                              Vi 78615, HMV AL1039, Sävel SÄLP-663(33)
BVE 33699-2   Tavaristshin Svobodaseikkailut (Comrade's Freedom Adventures)
                                                            Vi 78574
BVE 33700-3   Heppu Helsingistä (Helsingin Heppu) (Guy From Helsingfors)  Vi 78574
              Eddy Jahrl-acn                     Camden, NJ  February 10, 1926
```

```
W 106537-2    Juomalaulu-Comic Sketch           Co 3024-F, Sävel SÄLP 662(33)
W 106538-2    Merimiesrakkautta-Comic Sketch               Co 3024-F, 16134
              as before                                    NY   March 1926
```

Jean Theslöf

```
CVE 35413-2   Volga Lautta Miesten Laulu (Ei Uknem) (Song Of The Volga Boatmen)
                    (Chaliapin-Koeneman)                    Vi 68748(12")
              orch d Bruno Reibold               Camden, NJ  April 19, 1926
```

```
W 106582-2    Heikki Hautala                               Co 3029-F, 16176
W 106583-1    Illalla Kävelin (Kilpinen)                   Co 3029-F, 16176
                                                           NY   April 1926
```

```
BVE 35610-3   Kanteleeni (Erkki Melartin)                  Vi 78911
BVE 35611-2   Jo Joutuu Ilta (Jouluvirsi) (J. Sibelius)'   Vi rej
              2 vln, vc, org, 'fl, chimes, d Nathaniel Shilkret  NY  May 18, 1926
```

```
W 106750-2    Vanha Mustalainen (E. Kondor)                Co 3028-F, 16138
W 106751-1    Mustalaisen Surulaulu                        Co 3028-F, 16138
              orch                                         NY   May 1926
```

```
BVE 35172-4   Skyddskärs Marsch (Björck) [in Swedish]      Vi 79206
```

BVE 35173-4   Björneborgarnes Marsch (Pacius) [in Swedish]   Vi 79206
            orch d Bruno Reibold   Camden, NJ June 3, 1926

BVE 35611-5   Jo Joutuu Ilta {Jouluvirsi} (J. Sibelius)'   Vi 78911
            2 vln, vc, tuba, traps, d Nathaniel Shilkret   NY September 13, 1926

W 110409-2   Tieni Kulkee Mandaljaan {On The Road To Mandalay}
            (Oley Speaks-R. Kipling)   Co 3108-F
W 110410-2   Nichavo {Nothing Matters} (Manne Zucca)   Co 3108-F
W 110411-   Nuijamiesten Marssi (Martti Nisonen)   Co rej
W 110412-   Laulu Tulipunaisesta Kukasta   Co rej
                                         NY February 1929

W 110411-4   Nuijamiesten Marssi (Martti Nisonen)   Co 3126-F
W 110412-3   Laulu Tulipunaisesta Kukasta   Co 3126-F
                                         NY October 1929

31.99. Heikki Tuominen *vocal*

W 112594-2   Oi Donna Klara (Petersburshki)   Co 3173-F, DI201
W 112595-2   Donin Tyttö (Stephan Kamensky)   Co 3173-F
W 112730-2   Särkyneet Toiveet (R. Hirviseppä)   Co 3197-F
W 112731-2   Hae Pois Vaan Sormukses (Toivo Kuula)   Co 3177-F
W 112732-2   Mua Millä Muistat Miellä? (Jaako Tuuri)'   Co 3177-F
W 112733-2   Hawaijin Kuningatar (Pekka Ukkonen)   Co 3197-F
            Columbia Orchestra or 'acn   NY ca January 1931

31.100. Viola Turpeinen *accordion (1909-1958)*

Viola Turpeinen Ja John Rosenthal

W 108652-2   Hämärä Sottiisi   Co 3074-F, 7887
W 108653-2   Hollolan Polkka   Co 3074-F, 7887
W 108654-1   Kulkurin Serenaadi   Co 3077-F, 13402
W 108655-2   Vanhanmaan Sottiisi   Co 3077-F, 13402
            John Rosendahl-vln   NY January 1928

John Rosendahl-Viola Turpeinen

BVE 41657-2   Emman {Emma}-Valssi, from "Rykmentin Saittaja"   Vi 80587, V-4100
BVE 41658-2   Kaustisen Polkka   Vi rej
BVE 41659-1   Kauhavan-Polka   Vi 80587, V-4100, RCA PL40115(33)
BVE 41660-1   Violan Polkka'   Vi 80790
BVE 41661-1   Penttilän Valssi {Pentilla's Waltz}   Vi 80634, Love LXLP505(33)
BVE 41662-2   Jukan Sottiisi {Jake's Schottische}   Vi 80634
BVE 41663-2   Jäähyväis Valssi   Vi 80790
            as before, or 'Turpeinen only   NY January 30, 1928

Viola Turpeinen-John Rosendahl

BVE 48600-2	Hanuri Marssi (Accordion March)	Vi V-4025
BVE 48601-2	Pääskys (Swallow)-Valssi	Vi V-4025
	as before	Chicago November 19, 1928

BVE 48603-2	Hymy Huulilla (Sweet Smiles)-Mazurka	Vi V-4005, V-4177, 26-6019
BVE 48604-2	Suomi Sottiisi	Vi V-4043
BVE 48605-2	Neekeri Mailla (In The Land Of Negroes)	Vi rej
BVE 48606-2	Violon (Viola's)-Masurkka[1]	Vi V-4008
BVE 48607-2	Ihanne (Ideal) Valssi[1]	Vi V-4008
BVE 48608-1	Jalasjärven Polkka[1]	Vi V-4005, V-4177, 26-6019
	John Rosendahl-vln, or [1]Turpeinen only	Chicago November 20, 1928

BVE 51291-1	Viulu Polkka	Vi V-4051
BVE 51292-1	Soittajan Polkka[1]	Vi V-4048
BVE 51293-1	Mustalaisen Sottisi	Vi V-4048
	as before	NY May 7, 1929

BVE 51991-1	Ihana Maa-Masurkka	Vi V-4034
BVE 51992-2	Tähti Valssi[1]	Vi V-4051
BVE 51993-2	Kaustisen Polkka[1]	Vi V-4034, RCA PL40115(33)
BVE 51994-2	Iloinen Polkka[2]	Vi V-4043
	own acn, John Rosendahl-[1]vln, [2]bj	NY May 10, 1929

Viola-Sylvia-John

BRC 70144-1	Kaikuja Tanssisalista-Polkka (arr John Rosendahl)[1]	Vi V-4114
	Eko Polka[1]	Vi V-20055, 26-0009
BRC 70145-1	Merellä-Valssi (arr John Rosendahl)	Vi V-4112, V-4155, 26-6006
BRC 70146-1	Mikkelin-Polkka (arr John Rosendahl)	Vi V-4112, V-4155, 26-6006
BRC 70147-1	Iloiset Päivät (Merry Days)-Sottisi (arr Viola Turpeinen)[1]	Vi V-4114
	Luftslott-Schottish[1]	Vi V-20055, 26-0009
BRC 70148-1	Ilonen Leski-Valssi[1] [2]	Vi rej
BRC 70149-1	Neuvoja Naimattomille[3]	Vi V-4117
	own acn, [1]Sylvia Polso-2d acn, John Rosendahl-vln or [2]bj [3]vo	
		NY August 3, 1931

Vi V-20055 and 26-0009 as SKANDINAVSKA TRIO

Viola Turpeinen Trio

BS 83317-1	Surun Kaiho-Yö (Sorrow's Longing Night)-Valssi (Werner A. Birch)	
		Vi V-4145, V-4168, 26-6013
	Natt Av Sorg-Vals	Vi V-24086, 26-1004
BS 83318-1	Hei Stop! Stop! Luuta Tanssi (Hey Stop Broom Dance)-Sottiisi	
	(Werner A. Birch)	Vi V-4145, V-4168, 26-6013
	Hej Stop-Schottis	Vi V-24086, 26-1004
BS 83319-1	Peukalon (Thumb)-Polkka (arr Viola Turpeinen)	Vi V-4147, 26-6002
	Tumme-Polka	Vi V-24088, 26-1006, 443-1000
BS 83320-1	Tip Top-Hambo (Ivar Nygard, arr Viola Turpeinen)	
		Vi V-4147, V-24088, 26-1006, 26-6002, 443-1000
BS 83321-1	Aland-Schottische (Turpeinen-Syrjala)	Vi V-4149, V-24090, 26-1008

BS 83322-1   Asikkalan Polkka (arr Viola Turpeinen)   Vi V-4149, V-24090, 26-1008
              own acn, William Syrjälä-tp, Werner A. Birch-p   NY June 18, 1934

Viola Turpeinen

BS 027971-1   Unelma Valssi (Vili Syrjälä)   Vi V-4175, 26-6018, RCA PL40115(33)
BS 027972-1   Kahden Venheessa   Vi V-4175, 26-6018
              vo, acn   NY October 24, 1938

31.101. Tom Vehkaoja *baritone*

W 109698-2   Nuor Vaimoni Sai Poikasen (Szirmai Albert)   Co 3112-F, 16226
W 109699-1   Hevospaimenen Häämatka   Co 3112-F, 16226
              orch   NY September 1928

W 110856-2   Minä Olen Härmän Kankahanpäästä   Co 3136-F
W 110857-2   Niin Kauvan Minä Tramppaan   Co 3136-F
W 110858-2   Kasakan Laulu-Patriotic Song   Co 3124-F
W 110859-2   Sotilaan Laulu, from "Regina Von Emmeritz" (Aug. Söderman) Co 3124-F
              orch   NY June 1929

31.102. Frank Viita *vocal*

AFS 2366B, 2367A1 Yhteis Rintamaan Meitä Veljet Kutsutaan   LC
                                              Amasa, MI September 23, 1938

31.103. Hilja Vilonen *soprano*

W 109232-1   Kaipaava   Co 3087-F, 16166
W 109233-2   Vanha Sanna   Co 3087-F, 16166
W 109234- (W 130645) Venehessä   Co 3201-F
W 109235- (W 130646) Hiihdellessä Konnunsuolla   Co 3201-F
              orch   NY April 1928

31.104. Margherita Violante *vocal*

Margherita Violante-Volpi Leuto

Volpi Leuto is a pseudonym for Walfrid Lehto.

BVE 50920-2   Soipa Kieli {Sounding Chord} (P. Merikanto)   Vi V-4026
BVE 50921-2   Äiti Ja Kulkuripoika {Mother And the Beggar Boy} (Oskar Merikanto)
                                                                       Vi V-4026
BVE 50922-2   Tuoll' On Mun Kultani {There Is My Sweetheart} (Sov. Selim Palmgren)
                                                                       Vi V-4066
BVE 50923-2R Oi Kiitos Sa Luojani Armollinen (Oskar Merikanto)   Vi V-4066
              2 vln, fl, cl, vc, p, sbs, d Alfredo Cibelli   NY March 7, 1929

Margherita Violante

BVE 53618-1   Kehtolaulu-Lullaby (Kauppi)   Vi V-4075
BVE 53619-2   Mustalaistyttö {My Gypsy Girl} (V.I. Shapstek)   Vi V-4075
          vln, fl, cl, vc, p, sbs, traps   NY May 15, 1929

31.105. Akseli Vuorisola *baritone*

BVE 41258-2   Pikku Lola (arr Wm. E. Stein)   Vi 80465
BVE 41259-2   Kai Muistat (Järvinen-Nortamo)   Vi 80465
          orch d Alfredo Cibelli   NY December 21, 1927

W 109528-1   Sorjosen Ryyppyreissu   Co 3117-F, 16219
W 109529-2   Katinka-Fox Trot (Henry Tobias)   Co 3085-F, 16068, Love LXLP505(33)
W 109530-2   Hoo Hii O Hei   Co 3117-F, 16219
W 109531-1   Alaska-Fox Trot   Co 3085-F, 16068, Sävel SÄLP 663(33)
          Willi Larsen-acn   NY July 1928

31.106. Aili Ja Lyyli Wainikainen *instrumental*

W 112800-2   Kasakka-Polkka   Co 3182-F, DI212, NW 264(33)
          Polka "Tchornyj Ostrov"   Co 20259-F
W 112801-2   Kulkuripojan Sotiisi   Co 3192-F
W 112802-2   Kulkijan Unelma-Valssi   Co 3182-F, DI212
          Finlandskyj Vals   Co 20259-F
W 112803-2   Lydia-Mazurka (Wäinö M. Warvikko)   Co 3192-F
          vln, acn   NY February 1931

Co 20259-F as HARMONIA I SKRIPKA

SECTION 32.   ICELANDIC

32.1.   Otto Bardarson   *vocal*

AFS 3845A1   Heimfórin Til Íslands-1930 {A Trip Home To Iceland-1930}
       (w: Sigurd Bardarson, Seattle)
                        LC
AFS 3845A2   Rymur {Rhymes}
                        LC
               Carmel, CA   January 17, 1939

32.2.   Sigurd Bardarson   *vocal; age 89*

AFS 4278A   Rimur   LC
AFS 4278B   Rimur {Rima Of The Flower-Bedecked Tournament Field In Italy}   LC
AFS 4279A   Rimur   LC
AFS 4279B   Rimur   LC
    with Leo Bardarson   Carmel, CA   April 28, 1940

AFS 4280A1   Verses (Sigurd Bardarson)   LC
AFS 4280A2   Verses (Sigurd Bardarson)   LC
AFS 4280B   The Looks Of A Girl; Mt. Baker, Washington-Verses (Sigurd Bardarson)
                        LC
AFS 4281A&B1   Two Old Ladies In Winnipeg Had A Fight-Verses (Sigurd Bardarson) LC
AFS 4281B2   Rimur   LC
AFS 4282A1   For An Old Lady On Her Departure From Winnipeg-Verses
        (Sigurd Bardarson)
                        LC
AFS 4282A2   A Girl To Work In The House-Verses (Sigurd Bardarson)   LC
AFS 4282A3   To A Friend In Winnipeg-Verses (Sigurd Bardarson)   LC
AFS 4282A4   Sailing On Lake Winnipeg-Verses (Sigurd Bardarson)   LC
AFS 4282A5   A Man Trying To Get A Dog Out Of The Church In Winnipeg-Verses
        (Sigurd Bardarson)
                        LC
AFS 4282B1   Rimur   LC
               Carmel, CA   April 29, 1940

32.3.   Sigridur Benonys   *vocal*

AFS 3829A5   Bi Bi Og Blaka-Cradle Song   LC
AFS 3829A6   Björt Mey Og Hrein {Maiden Fair And Pure}   LC
AFS 3829B1&2   Ó Blessud Vertu Somarsól {O Blessed Summer Sun} (m: Ingri Larusson)
                        LC
AFS 3829B3   Ólafur Reid Med Björgum Fram-Dance Song[1]   LC
    [1]with chorus   Berkeley, CA   May 25, 1938

32.4. Thodur Einarsson *vocal*

AFS 3830A1	Pietr {Peter In The High Chair}	LC
AFS 3830A2	Póstular Kjörir Kristur Thrá {The Twelve Apostles}	LC
AFS 3830A3	Pilatus {Pontius Pilate}	LC
AFS 3830A4	Upp, Upp Mín Sál {Up, Up, My Soul}	LC

San Francisco May 25, 1938

File Note: From "Passíupsálmer" (Passion Psalms), a kind of play in verse, sung in church or at prayers on farms. Texts by Hjallgrímur Pétursson (about the middle of the 16th century).

AFS 4267A	Petur Þar Sat Í Sal {Peter In The High Seat Of The Hall} (verses 1-10)	LC
AFS 4267B	Petur Þar Sat Í Sal {Peter In The High Seat Of The Hall} (verses 11-20)	LC
AFS 4268A1-3	Upp, Upp Mín Sál {Up, Up, My Soul}	LC
AFS 4268B1	Petur Þar Sat Í Sal {Peter In The High Seat Of The Hall} (verses 20-29)	LC

San Francisco November 11, 1939

From the "Passíupsálmer" as before.

32.5. Einar Hjaltested *tenor*

58839-	Ólafur Og Álfamærin (Ísl. Þjóðlag)	Co E3730
58840-	Vorgydjan (Guðm. Guðmundsson-Arni Thorsteinsson)	Co E3730
58867-1	Rósin (Guðm. Guðmundsson-Arni Thorsteinsson)	Co E3731
58868-1	Björt Mey Og Hrein (Stefán Olafsson-Ísl. Þjóðlag)	Co E3731
	orch	NY October 1917

32.6. Maria Markan *vocal*

BS 071529-	Draumalandið (Guðm. Magnusson-Sigfus Einarsson)	Vi PR-830
BS 071530-	Svanasöngur Á Heiði (Stgr. Thorst.-Sigv. S. Kaldalóns)	Vi PR-830
	Beryl Blanch-p	NY October 3, 1941

Label note: Dedicated by Miss Markan to the Canadian Forces on active service in Iceland.

Vi PR-830 is a Canadian issue.

32.7. John Olafson *vocal*

AFS 3828B2	Stodum Tvö I Tuni {Saying Goodbye To Your Sweetheart}-Ryma No. 6	LC
AFS 3828B3	Tobag's Bankur {Admiring The Snuffbox}	LC
AFS 3828B4	Upp I Malar Skola Skina {Teaching Girls To Cook And Sew}	LC
AFS 3828B5	Reid Eg Grána {The Gray Horse}	LC
AFS 3838B6	Likafron Og Lagsmenn Tveir {The Two Young Men}	LC
AFS 3828B7	Thvi Vill Granda Tholgidi {The Boatman Carried From The Shore}	LC

AFS 3828B8	A Jeg Ad Halda Afram Lengra {The Discouraged Poet}	LC
AFS 3829A1	Ad Sigla {To Sail A Boat}-Ryma No. 7	LC
AFS 3829A2&3	Ifir Kaldan Eydtisand {The Vagabond}	LC
AFS 3829A4	Boom-fa-la-la	LC

San Francisco May 25, 1938

File note for AFS 3828B4: Satire on an Iceland budget appropriaton of about 1900,
for teaching girls to sew; for AFS 3828B8: He went from Iceland to Greenland in
1837 and was disgusted with his poems on the subject of the war between Lombardy
and Rome.

32.8. Oddrun Sigurdsson *vocal; 87 years old*

AFS 3827A1	Viglunder-Ryma, No. 1	LC
AFS 3827A2	Trausta-Ryma, No. 2	LC
AFS 3827A3	Eina Stund {Once Upon A Time}-Ryma No. 3	LC
AFS 3827A4	Frosta Frone {Freezing Weather}	LC
AFS 3827A5&B3	Helgi Saga {Ballad Of Helgi}	LC
AFS 3827B1	Eina Stund {Once Upon A Time}-Ryma No. 4	LC
AFS 3827B2	Ó Thala Thràd-Spinning Song	LC
AFS 3827B3	Helgi Saga {Ballad Of Helgi}	LC
AFS 3828A1&2	Budar Ei Lofti {Up In The Store}-Lullaby	LC
AFS 3828A3	Gjase Ei Paradise {The Goose In Paradise}	LC
AFS 3828A4	Stod Jeg Uti Tungljos {The Moonlight}	LC
AFS 3828A5	Egill's Saga	LC
AFS 3828B1	Thorgrymur Prudy {Viglander's Father}-Ryma No. 5	LC

San Francisco May 25, 1938

SECTION 33. NORWEGIAN

33.1. Arne Arnesen *violin*

Norwegian Airs   Vi trial
unaccompanied   Camden, NJ July 15, 1921

B 26002-2   Eg Ser Deg Ut For Gluggjin {I See Your Shadow Yonder}; Aa Ola, Ola
                  Min Eigan Onge {Oh, Ole, Ole, I Loved You Dearly};
                  Halling-Norske Melodier No. 1 (arr N. Shilkret)   Vi 73194
B 26003-1   Ho Ragna Va Fattig {Poor Ragna}; Halling-Norske Melodier No. 2
                                                      Vi 73194
            Nathaniel Shilkret-p   NY December 23, 1921

33.2. Augustana College A Capella Choir *Sioux Falls, South Dakota*

W 148697-1	Jeg Ved En Vei (arr Carl R. Youngdahl)[1]	Co 26100-F
W 148698-1	Jesus Du Min Glaede (J.S. Bach)	Co 26100-F
	Ye Are Not Of The Flesh	Co 69000-F(12")
	Wake Awake	Co 69000-F(12")
	[1]Clifford J. Olsen-soloist	NY June 15, 1929

33.3. W.J. Barthold *baritone/bass*

	Hei Huskon I Hei	Co 17001-F
	Se Norges Blomsterdal	Co 17001-F
	Gud Signe	Co 17002-F
	Moder, Jeg Er Træt	Co 17002-F
		NY ca 1923

W 106943-2	Det Gamle Ærværdige Kors-Evangelistik Sang	Co 17007-F
W 106944-2	Alt, Men Ikke Jesus-Evangelistik Sang	Co 17007-F
W 106945-3	Naar Eg Aa Jesus Aaleine Er	Co 17008-F
W 106946-1	Alt Som Glæder Mig Er Jesus-Evangelistik Sang	Co 17006-F
W 106947-2	O, Hvor Herligt Min Synd (Hos. E. Anderson)	Co 17008-F
W 106948-2	Naar Solen Daler-Evangelistik Sang	Co 17006-F
W 106949-2	Jesus, Du Som Har Mig Kjær (A. Anderson)	Co 17009-F
W 106950-2	Klæder I Glids Frelse	Co 17009-F
		NY July 1926

2617

33.4. Sigvart Borgen *vocal*

B 22028-1	Lars Olsens Afsked	Vi 72144
B 22029-1	Bonde Guttens Frieri {Anne Maria Bakken}	Vi 72394
B 22030-2	I Verden For Jeg Rundt Omkring [in Norwegian and English]	Vi 72394
B 22031-1	Skal Vi Gaa {Home To Norway} [in Norwegian and English]	Vi 72144

orch d Nathaniel Shilkret   NY June 21, 1918

33.5. Mildrid R. Bruns *vocal*

B 21535-2	Til Fredens Hjem (Prins Gustaf-Agata Rosenius)	Vi rej
B 21536-2	Kun Et Skridt (H.A. Urseth-F. Melius Christiansen)	Vi rej

Edward T. King-org   NY February 20, 1918

B 21537-2	Vuggevise For Lillegut-Cradle Song	Vi rej
B 21538-3	Syng Mig Hjæm {Sing Me Home} (Bjornsterne Bjornson-Edm. Neupert, op. 26 no. 1)	Vi rej
B 21539-2	Fly Som En Fugl {Flee As A Bird}	Vi 72473
B 21540-1	Til Fredens Hjem {To The Home Of Peace} (Prins Gustaf-Agata Rosentius)	Vi 72473
B 21541-2	Kom Du Bedrovede (Thomas Moore-Samuel Webbe)	Vi rej

King's Orchestra d Nathaniel Shilkret   NY February 21, 1918

33.6. Erik Bye *baritone (1883-1953)*

	Norrønakvadet	Vi trial

Nathaniel Shilkret-p   NY March 25, 1920

B 23988-2	Norrønakvadet, from "Sigurd Jorsalfar" (E. Grieg)	Vi 72700
B 23989-1	Kongekvadet, from "Sigurd Jorsalfar" (E. Grieg)	Vi 72700
B 23990-2	Serenade Venetienne {Kom Karina} (Victor Wilder-Johan S. Svendsen)	Vi 73385, HMV X1814

orch d Rosario Bourdon   NY May 3, 1920

B 24033-2	Saa Danser Jeg Dig Imøde (Barbara Larssen)	Vi 72763

orch d Nathaniel Shilkret   NY May 5, 1920

B 24144-2	Barndomsminne Fra Nordland (Adolf Thomsen)'	Vi 73385, HMV X1814
B 24145-2	Hei, Huskom I Hei! (Thelemarken)	Vi 72763
B 24146-1	Dæ Va Irlands Kongje Bold	Vi 73849
C 24147-2	Den Heliga Staden {The Holy City} (Stephen Adams) [in Swedish]	Vi 68599, HMV Z139(12")

orch d Rosario Bourdon   NY May 27, 1920

	Der Soldat {Es Geht Beigedämpfter Trommel Klang'} [in German]	Co E7488
	Einsam Bin Ich Alleine [in German]	Co E7488

NY 1921-2

86249-	Norrønakvadet	Co E7028
86263-	Ved Rundarne (Grieg-Vinje)	Co E4758

86264-	Norge	Co E4758
86265-	Kongekvadet	Co E7028
86273-	Evangelimanden¹	Co E4834
86274-	Der Flyver Saa Mange Fugle¹	Co E4834
59620-	Mor	Co E5219(12")
59621-	Rhenvinets Lof	Co E5219(12")
59645-1	Tannhäuser: O Du Mein Holder Abendstern (Wagner) [in German]	

		Co E5230(12")
59646-	An Der Weser (Schubert) [in German]	Co E5227(12")
59648-	Am Meer (F. Schubert) [in German]	Co E5231(12")
59649-	Du Bist Die Ruhe (F. Schubert)	Co E5231(12")
59653-2	Der Wanderer (F. Schubert) [in German]	Co E5232(12")
59654-2	Der Erlkönig (F. Schubert) [in German]	Co E5224(12")
59675-1	Tannhäuser: Blick Ich Umher (Wagner) [in German]	Co E5230(12")
59676-	Das Zauberlied (Meyer-Helmund) [in German]	Co E5227(12")
	Jeg Er Fra Norge Og Jeg Er God	Co E7110
	Serenade	Co E7110
	orch or ¹org	NY May-June 1920

B 24147-2	Den Heliga Staden {The Holy City} (Stephen Adams) [in Swedish]	
		Vi rej
	orch d Nathaniel Shilkret	NY June 10, 1920

88452-	Wenn Die Rösen Blümen (Luise Reichardt) [in German]	Co E7692
88453-	Ein Rheinisches Mädchen (Paul Hoppe) [in German]	Co E7692
	orch	NY ca April 1922

C 26777-2	I Gröna Palmers Skrud {The Palm Trees} (J. Faure, arr H. Millard,	
	tr Dr. L. Holmes) [in Swedish]	Vi 68599, HMV Z139(12")
B 26778-2	Jeg Lagde Mig Saa Sildig	Vi 73849
	orch d Nathaniel Shilkret	NY September 14, 1922

Erich Bye

9905	Grüsse An Die Heimat (Kromer) [in German]	Vo 14607, 10038
9907/8	Edelweiss (Teichmann-Penschel) [in German]	Vo 14607, 10038
	orch	NY September 1922

W 175266-1	test recording	Co
		NY January 12, 1927

33.7. Otto Clausen *baritone*

Den Store, Hvide Flok (Grieg)	Ed 9200(4 min), 9225(4 min)
Or Ræven Laa Under Birkerod	Ed 9201(4 min), 9226(4 min)
Aa Kjøre Vatten Aa Kjøre Ve	Ed 9202(4 min), 9227(4 min)
Bor Jeg Paa Det Høje Fjeld	Ed 9203(4 min), 9228(4 min)
Eg Ser Deg Ut For Gluggjin	Ed 9204(4 min), 9229(4 min)
Kan Du Glemme Gamle Norge	Ed 9205(4 min), 9230(4 min)
Tilfjelds Over Bygden	Ed 9206(4 min), 9231(4 min)
Nu Fylkes Vi Nordmænd (Teilman)	Ed 19900(2 min)
Ola Glomstulen	Ed 19901(2 min)
Den Friske Vind	Ed 19902(2 min)

```
                  Blandt Alle Lande                              Ed 19903(2 min)
                  Kjölstad-Gutten                                Ed 19904(2 min)
                  Astri, Mi Astri                                ED 19905(2 min)
                  orch                            NY   June 16, 26, 29, 30, 1911
```

33.8. De Forenede Skandinaviske Sangere I New York (United Scandinavian Singers
Of New York)

```
CVE 33528-1   Olaf Trygvason (F.A. Reissiger)                        Vi 68723(12")
CVE 33529-2   Naar Fjordene Blaaner {When The Fjords Are Like Violets Blue}
              (Alfred Paulsen)                                       Vi 68723(12")
BVE 33530-2   Sangerhilsen {Singer's Greeting} (Edvard Grieg)           Vi 78359
BVE 33531-2   Ja, Vi Elsker Dette Landet {Yes, We Love This Land}-Norwegian
              National Hymn (Rickard Nordraak)                          Vi 78359
              20 1st ten, 20 2d ten, 25 1st bs, 28 2d bs, d Ole Windingstad
                                                           NY   October 1, 1925
```

33.9. Gudrun Ekelund *soprano*

```
W 403751-     Jeg Kunde Slet Ikke Sove (Halfdan Kjerulf)                Ok 25090
W 403752-A    Jeg Heter Anne Knutsdatter                                Ok 25090
W 403753-B    Hvis Du Har Varme Tanker (H. Børreson)                    Ok 25089
W 403754-B    Blåklokker-Tango (Kristian Hanger)                        Ok 25089
              North Star Trio                            NY   February 1930
```

33.10. Astrud Fjelde *soprano*

```
B 25926-1     Hjem, Hjem Mit Kjære Hjem {Home Sweet Home} (m: Sir Henry R. Bishop)
                                                                        Vi 73318
B 25927-3     Sommerens Sidste Rose {Last Rose Of Summer}               Vi rej
              orch d Rosario Bourdon                     NY   December 28, 1921

B 25927-4     Sommerens Sidste Rose {Last Rose Of Summer}      Vi 73724, HMV X1856
B 26405-3     Elsk Mig Lidt! {Love Me} (m: Mrs. Frederikke Fjelde, op. 3) Vi 73318
              as before                                   NY   April 10, 1922

B 27294-2     Synnøves Sang (w: B. Bjornson, m: Halfdan Kjerulf)
                                                              Vi 73724, HMV X1856
              Where My Caravan Has Rested [in English]'           Vi trial
              Nathaniel Shilkret-org, unk vln, cl, fl, or 'own p
                                                          NY   November 13, 1923
```

33.11. Magnhild Fjelheim *(The Radio's Singing Lady); soprano*

```
W 113779-4    Sol Paa Havet {Torna E Sorriento} (E. De Curtis)        Co 22172-F
W 113780-4    Lailas Kjærlighetssang, ftmp "Laila"
                        (E. Ellgen-Freo Bjonner-Kr. Hauger)           Co 22172-F
              Harold Ekeland (The Accordion Master)-acn   NY   ca January 1934
```

33.12. Mr. Forster *accordion*

AFS 2385A1	Polka	
AFS 2385A2	The Orphan Girl	LC
AFS 2385B2	Polka	LC
AFS 2385B3	Over The Waves	LC
		LC

Calumet, MI   September 1938

33.13. Alfred Halvorsen *baritone*

B 20191-2	Norske Folkmelodier-Pt. 1	Vi 69559
B 20192-1	Norske Folkmelodier-Pt. 2	Vi 69559
B 20193-2	Perdicans Sang (m: Rudolph Bay)	Vi rej
B 20194-2	En Fri Og Freidig Sanger (m: T.W. Naumann)	Vi rej
B 20195-1	Konge For En Dag (m: Ad. Adam)	Vi rej
	King's Orchestra d Rosario Bourdon	NY July 3, 1917

B 20194-4	En Fri Og Freidig Sanger (m: T.W. Naumann)	Vi rej
B 20195-3	Konge For En Dag (m: Ad. Adam)	Vi rej
B 20210-2	Skivise (w: Th. Caspari, m: Max Ræbel)	Vi rej
B 20211-2	Østerdalsmarschen (w: Ivan Mortenson, m: Johan Halvorsen)	Vi rej
	as before	NY July 10, 1917

B 20234-2	Jed Længter Mot Sol Og Sommer (w: Robert Loennecken, m: Rudolph Moller)	Vi rej
B 20235-1	Jeg Tænkte, Jeg Blev Noget Riktig Stort (w: B. Bjornson, m: Peter Lindeman op. 3 no. 2)	Vi 72575
B 20239-2	Midsommervise (w: Holger Drach, m: P.E. Lange-Muller)	Vi 69749
B 20240-2	Herrens Bon (m: Emil-Juel Frederiksen)	Vi rej
	as before	NY July 19, 1917

B 20194-6	En Fri Og Freidig Sanger (m: T.W. Naumann)	Vi 72285
B 20195-5	Konge For En Dag (m: Ad. Adam)	Vi 72575
	as before	NY July 24, 1917

B 20234-3	Jed Længter Mot Sol Og Sommer (w: Robert Loennecken, m: Rudolph Moller)	Vi 69749
B 20240-4	Herrens Bon (m: Emil-Jiel Frederickson)	Vi rej
B 20252-2	Vis Dig Ven Vinduet-Serenade (m: Louis Gregh, m: A. Queyriaux)	Vi rej
B 20254-2	Jule Nat-Christmas Song (Ad. Adam)	Vi rej
B 20255-2	Havet Er Skjønt (m: F.A. Reissiger, w: S.O. Wolff)	Vi 72285
	as before	NY July 26, 1917

33.14. Rolf J. Hammer *tenor (1868-1922)*

B 14758-1	Venevil (B. Bjornson-H. Kjerulf, op. 6 no. 6)	Vi 65930
B 14759-1	Venetiansk Serenade (John Paulsen-Johan S. Svendsen)	Vi 65928
B 14760-1	Træt (The Tree) (B. Bjornson-Nordraak, op. 2)	Vi 65928
B 14761-1	Fyrsestev (m: Christian Sinding, op. 26 no. 2)	Vi rej

```
B 14762-1    Kom Med Visor, from "Smyra" (m: Christian Sinding, op. 25 no. 2)
                                                                    Vi rej
B 14763-1    Ingrid's Vise {Ingrid's Song} (B. Bjornson-H. Kjerulf, op. 6 no. 4)
                                                                    Vi 67079
B 14764-1    Vær Hilset, I Damer {I Greet You Ladies} (Drachman-E. Grieg,
                op. 49 no. 3)                                       Vi rej
C 14765-1    Sidste Reis {Sailor's Last Voyage}
                (Henrik Wergeland-E. Yvindo Alnæs, op. 1)      Vi 68451(12")
B 14767-1    Tillags Aat Alla; Han Ole¹                             Vi 65931
             Katherine Pike-p, or ¹unaccompanied          NY   April 24, 1914

39347-1      Venevil                                             Co E1836
39349-2      Ingrids Vise                                        Co E1836
             p                                             NY   May 2, 1914

             Sidste Reis-Hymn                               Co E5055(12")
             Vær Hilset, I Damer-Ballade                    Co E5055(12")
             Gamle Norge                                    Co E5056(12")
             Han Mass Aa'n Lasse                            Co E5056(12")
                                                           NY   ca May 2, 1914

B 14761-2    Fyrsestev (m: Christian Sinding, op. 26 no. 2)        Vi 67079
B 14762-2    Kom Med Visor-from "Smyra" (m: Christian Sinding, op. 25 no. 2)
                                                                    Vi 65932
B 14764-2    Vær Hilset, I Damer {I Greet You, Ladies} (Drachman-E. Grieg,
                op. 49 no. 3)                                       Vi 65930
B 14793-1    Gamle Norge                                            Vi 65929
B 14794-1    For Norge Kjæmpers Fodeland {To Norway, Mother Of The Brave}
                (A. Grétry)                                         Vi 65929
B 14795-1    Det Norske Flag {Norway's Flag} (L.M. Isben)           Vi rej
B 14796-1    Millom Bakkar Og Berg Utmed Havet
                {'Mong The Rocks By The North Sea's Blue Waters}
                (w: Ivan Aasen)                                     Vi rej
C 14797-1    Den Store Hvide Flok (E. Grieg)                   Vi rej (12")
C 14797-3    Den Store Hvide Flok (E. Grieg)¹              Vi 68451(12")
C 14798-1    Han Mass Aan Lasse²                                    Vi 65931
             Katherine Pike-p, ¹Edward T. King-org, or ²unaccompanied
                                                           NY   May 5, 1914
```

33.15. Nathalie Hansen *soprano*

```
B 19075-2    Hvor Skulde Jeg (Sophus Michælis)                     Vi rej
B 19076-2    Sæterjentens Sang (Hansen)                            Vi rej
B 19077-2    Mit Hjerte Og Min Lyre (Thomas Moore, op. 16 no. 2-Halfdan Kjerulf)
                                                                    Vi
             King's Orchestra                          NY   February 13, 1917

B 19091-1    Ifjor Gatt' Eg Geitinn' {Last Year I Tended The Goats}
                (H.A. Wergeland, arr Halfdan Kjerulf)              Vi 69326
B 19092-2    Aftenstemming-Norwegian Romance (Halfdan Kjerulf)     Vi rej
             as before                                 NY   February 16, 1917
```

B 19217-2	Blåbær-Li (Edward Grieg, op. 67)	Vi 69326
B 19218-2	Lind (Agathe Backer Grondahl)	Vi rej
	as before	NY February 23, 1917
B 19076-4	Sæterjentens Sang (Hansen)	Vi rej
B 19221-2	Paa Fjellet (Louise Michæli)	Vi 69324
B 19222-2	Liden Kirsten (Eyvind Alnæs, op. 2 no. 4)	Vi 69324
	as before	NY February 27, 1917
B 19075-3	Hvor Skulde Jeg (Sophus Michælis)	Vi 69538
B 19076-5	Sæterjentens Sang (Hansen)	Vi 69413
B 19077-3	Mit Hjerte Og Min Lyre (Thomas Moore, op. 16 no. 2-Halfdan Kjerulf)	
		Vi 69413
B 19092-4	Aftenstemming-Norwegian Romance (Halfdan Kjerulf)	Vi rej
B 19218-4	Lind (Agathe Backer Grondahl)	Vi rej
	as before	NY April 10, 1917
B 19092-6	Aftenstemming-Norwegian Romance (Halfdan Kjerulf)	Vi 69641
B 19218-5	Lind (Agathe Backer Grondahl)	Vi 69538
B 19935-2	Hvis Du Har Varme Tanker (Hakon Børreson, op. 2 no. 4)	Vi 69641
B 19936-2	En Svane (Edvard Grieg)	Vi 69707
	as before	NY May 23, 1917
B 20164-2	Aagots Fjeldsang, Aagots Berglied (H.A. Bjerregaard)	Vi rej
B 20165-2	Vejviseren Synger {Der Wegweiser Syngt} (J.S. Welhaven,	
	op. 6 no. 1-Halfdan Kjerulf)	Vi rej
	as before	NY June 26, 1917
B 20289-1	Aften Er Stille (Bjornsterne Bjornson-A.B. Grondahl)	Vi 69635
B 20290-1	Herrens Bon (m: A. Klewe)	Vi 69635
	as before, d Rosario Bourdon	NY August 7, 1917
B 20572-3	Jule Nat-Christmas Song (Ad. Adam)	Vi 69707
	as before	NY September 18, 1917
B 20788-2	De To Drosler (Sophie Dedeham)	Vi rej
B 20789-2	Den Første Kjerlighed (Fru G. Recke)	Vi rej
	King's Orchestra	NY October 18, 1917
B 21319-2	Taaren {Tears} (H.O. Anderson-Sophie Dedeham)	Vi rej
B 21320-3	I Rosens Doft {Fragrance Of A Rose} (Prinds Gustaf)	Vi rej
	King's Orchestra d Nathaniel Shilkret	NY December 28, 1917
B 21320-4	I Rosens Doft {Fragrance Of A Rose} (Prinds Gustaf)	Vi rej
B 22034-1	En Digters Sidste Sang (H.C. Andersen-E. Grieg)	Vi rej
	orch d Nathaniel Shilkret	NY June 21, 1918
B 22316-2	Det Kimer Nu Til Jule Fest-Hymn	Vi 72411
B 22317-1	Deiling Er Den Himmel Blaa-Hymn	Vi 72411
	Nathaniel Shilkret-org, Edward T. King-chimes	NY September 20, 1918

33.16. Gudrun Ring Henning *contralto*

W 403639-	Minne (Gudrun Ring Henning)		Ok 25087
W 403640-	Synnøves Sang (Halfdan Kjerulf)		Ok 25088
W 403641-	Eg Veit Ei Liti Gjenta (Catherinus Elling)		Ok 25088
W 403642-	Det Var Dans Bort I Vägen (Helfrid Lambert)		Ok 25087
	Edward Bernath-vln, Einar Hoff-p	NY	January 1930

33.17. Herman Ivarson *vocal*

BS 065079-1 Ja, Vi Elsker {Yes, We Love With Fond Devotion} (Nordraak,
                arr Herman Ivarson); Sønner Av Norge {Sons Of Norway} (Blom,
                arr Herman Ivarson)   Vi V-15066, 25-8024

BS 065080-1 Jeg Vil Værge Mit Land {Fatherland's Song} (Tischendorf,
                arr Herman Ivarson); Gud Signe Norigs Land
                {God Bless The Land Of Norway} (Halverson, arr Herman Ivarson)
                                          Vi V-15066, 25-8024

BS 065081-1 Aa Kjøre Vatten Aa Kjøre Ve {Fra Romeike} {Oh, Haul The Water}; Per,
                Spelman {The Fiddler} (arr Herman Ivarson)   Vi V-15067

BS 065082-1 Jeg Lagde Mig Saa Silde {I Lay Me Down So Softly}   Vi V-15067
        tp, vln, Hammond org   NY May 5, 1941

33.18. Sofus Kjeldsen *baritone*

	Den Store Hvide Flok (Grieg)	Vi trial
	Edward T. King-p	NY April 14, 1914

B 19231-3	Eg Elskar Voggande Tonar! (Chr. Depsoe)		Vi 69543
B 19232-2	Naar Fjordene Blaaner Som Markens Fiol (Wilfred Paulsen)		Vi rej
B 19233-2	Der Stod Sig Et Slag Udi Kjøgebugt (Johan Halvorsen)		Vi 69401
	King's Orchestra	NY	March 1, 1917

B 19296-1	Endnu Et Streif Kun Af Sol (Agathe Backer Grondahl)		Vi rej
B 19232-3	Naar Fjordene Blaaner Som Markens Fiol (Wilfred Paulsen)		Vi 69401
	as before	NY	March 20, 1917

B 19296-3	Endnu Et Streif Kun Af Sol (Agathe Backer Grondahl)		Vi rej
B 20121-2	Gamle Mor {My Dear Old Mother} (Edward Grieg)		Vi rej
B 20122-2	Du Spørger, Mit Barn, Eften Broder Din (Johan Halvorsen)		Vi 69543
	as before, d Rosario Bourdon	NY	June 14, 1917

B 19296-4	Endnu Et Streif Kun Af Sol (Agathe Backer Grondahl)		Vi rej
B 20121-4	Gamle Mor {My Dear Old Mother} (Edward Grieg)		Vi rej
	as before	NY	August 2, 1917

33.19. Kris Kristoffersen *vocal*

BVE 39891-1	Overmaade Fuld Af Naade	Vi 80597
BVE 39892-2	Jeg Ser Dig Søde Lam	Vi 80258
BVE 39893-2	Hvad Es Du Dog Skjon	Vi 80597

```
BVE 39894-2    I Himmelen
BVE 39895-2    Den Store Hvide Flok                                     Vi 80257
BVE 39896-1    Jesus, Dein Forening At Smage                            Vi 80257
               Sophus Kristofferson-p                                   Vi 80258
                                              Camden, NJ  October 14, 1927
```

33.20. Erling Krogh *tenor*

```
W 81961-B      Sidste Reis (Eyvind Alnas)
W 81962-B      Naar Fjordene Blaaner (w: John Paulsen, m: Alfred Paulsen)  Ok 25084
W 81963-B      Kan Du Glemme Gamle Norge                                   Ok 25081
W 81964-B      Der Aander En Tindrende Sommerluft (Halfdan Kjerulf)        Ok 25082
               Carl Soyland-p                                              Ok 25081
                                                       NY  December 27, 1927
```

```
BVE 41427-1    Sønner Av Norge, Det Ældgamle Rige {Sons Of Norway} (C. Blom)
                                                                        Vi 4029
BVE 41428-2    Ved Rundarne {Mountains Of Norway} (E. Grieg)            Vi 4030
BVE 41429-1    Tonerne {Tones} (C.L. Sjoberg)                           Vi 4030
               orch d Bruno Reibold                          Camden, NJ  December 28, 1927
```

```
BVE 41430-2    Kjærlighed Fra Gud {Love From God} (Schorring)           Vi 4033
BVE 41431-1    Kimer, I Klokker {Ring Ye Bells}                         Vi
BVE 41432-2    Paaskemorgen Slukker Sorgen {Easter Sunday} (Lucy M. Lindeman)
                                                                        Vi 4032
BVE 41433-1    Kirken Den Er Et Gammelt Hus {The Church Is An Old House}
               (Lucy M. Lindeman)                                       Vi 4033
BVE 41434-3    Sol Paa Havet {Torna E Surriento} {Sun On The Sea} (E. Di Curtis)
                                                                        Vi 4031
BVE 41435-2    Kun For Dig {For You Alone}                              Vi 4031
BVE 41436-2    Norrøna Folket {The Norse People}, from "Sigurd Jorsalfar"
               (B. Bjornson-Edvard Grieg, op. 22)                       Vi 4029
               as before                                     Camden, NJ  December 29, 1927
```

```
W 81976-B      Barndomsminne Fra Nordland (Adolf Thomsen)               Ok 25085
W 81977-B      Solefaldssang, from "Svein Urad" (Ole Olsen)             Ok 25082
W 81978-B      Livets Blomster (Otto Bruun)                             Ok rej
W 81979-B      Broderens Sang (Baard Heradstveit)                       Ok rej
W 81980-B      En Sangers Bon (F.A. Reissiger)                          Ok rej
               Carl Soyland-p                                NY  December 30, 1927
```

```
W 81985-B      Solvet (Tho. Lammers)'                                   Ok 25084
W 81986-B      Barnets Vaardag (Agathe Backer Grondahl)'                Ok 25083
W 81987-B      Fa Vi Elsker Dette Landet (R. Nordrask)                  Ok rej
W 81988-B      Olaf Trygvason (F.A. Reissiger)                          Ok 25085
W 81989-B      Den Store Hvide Flok (Edward Grieg)                      Ok 25083
               as before, 'Walter Biedermann-vln                NY  January 3, 1928
```

33.21. Sverre Larsen *vocal*

```
B 27878-2      To Storlygare {Two Great Liars} (w: Sverre Larsen)       Vi 73868
B 27879-2      Lise's Kjærlighetsbrev Til Per Rekrut
               {Lise's Love Letter To Her Recruit} (w: Sverre Larsen)
                                                                        Vi 73868
```

B 27880-2	Gamle Marit {Old Marit} (Sverre Larsen)	Vi 73907
B 27881-2	Ola Husmands Frieri {The Courtship Of Ola Bondsman}	
	(w: Sverre Larsen)	Vi 73907
	c, vln, fl, cl, p, tuba, d Nathaniel Shilkret	NY May 3, 1923

B 28840-2	Kari Og Jeg Paa Amerikareise {Kari And I Go To America}	
	(Sverre Larsen)	Vi 77434
B 28841-1	Telefonvisen {Over Telephone} (Sverre Larsen)	Vi 77434
B 28842-2	Jens Pedersen Hos Doktoren {Jens Pedersen And The Doctor}	
	(Sverre Larsen)	Vi rej
B 28843-2	Da Lars Vilde Gifte Sig {Lars To Be Married} (Sverre Larsen)	Vi rej
	orch d Leroy Shield	Camden, NJ November 16, 1923

33.22. Christian Mathisen *tenor*

	Hvor Skulde Jeg	Vi trial
	Edward T. King-p	NY May 1, 1917

B 19759-2	Kan Du Glemme Gamle Norge {Can You Forget Old Norway}	Vi 69606
B 19760-1	Mor {Mother} (w: Anton Kristen, m: Heinrich Martens)	Vi 69480
B 19761-1	Per's Sang {Per's Song}, from "Til Sæters" (w: P.C. Riis,	
	m: F.A. Reissiger)	Vi 69464
B 19762-2	Halvor's Sang {Halvor's Song}, from "Til Sæters" (w: P.C. Riis,	
	m: F.A. Reissiger)	Vi 69464
B 19763-1	Jeg Saa Dig {I Saw You} (w: Andreas Hansen, m: Eugene Lunggren)	
		Vi rej
	King's Orchestra	NY May 8, 1917

B 19763-2	Jeg Saa Dig {I Saw You} (w: Andreas Hansen, m: Eugene Lunggren)	
		Vi 69480
B 19774-2	En Bøn {A Prayer} (w: V. Bergsoe, m: F.A. Reissiger)	Vi rej
B 19775-2	Norges Fjelde {The Mountains Of Norway} (w: Henr. Wergeland,	
	m: Halfdan Kjerulf)	Vi rej
B 19776-1	Paal Paa Haugen {Paul On The Hill} (w: R.B. Anderson)	Vi 72581
	as before	NY May 11, 1917

B 19787-1	Aa Kjøre Vatten Aa Kjøre Ve {Come Haul The Water And Haul The Wood}	
		Vi 72581
B 19788-2	Jeg Vil Værge Mit Hand-National Hymn (Lichendorf)	Vi 69606
B 19789-2	Glade Jul, Hellige Jul! {Silent Night} (Franz Gruber)	
		Vi 69662, HMV X742
B 19790-2	Norrøna Kvadet, from "Sigurd Jorsalfar" (w: B. Bjornson,	
	m: Edvard Grieg, op. 22)	Vi rej
B 19791-1	Eg Ser Deg Ut Før Gluggjin {I See Your Shadow Yonder}	Vi 73087
B 19792-2	Længsel (Halfdan Kjerulf)	Vi rej
B 19793-2	Nu Takker Alle Gud-Hymn	Vi 69750
B 19794-2	Sørg O Kjære Fader Du (L.M. Lindeman)	Vi rej
B 19795-2	Vor Gud, Han Er Saa Fast En Borg (Martin Luther)	Vi 69750
B 19796-1	Jeg Synger Julekvad	Vi 69662, HMV X742
	as before	NY May 15, 1917

B 19917-2	Konge Kvadet, from "Sigurd Jorsalfar" (w: B. Bjornson,	
	m: Edvard Grieg, op. 22)	Vi rej

| B 19918-3 | Ola Glomstulen (arr L.M. Lindeman) | Vi 73087 |
| | as before | NY May 18, 1917 |

B 22836-3	Hvor Salig Er Den Lille Flok (L.M. Lindeman)	Vi 73201
B 22837-2	En Sangers Bon {The Singer's Prayer} (F.A. Reissiger)	Vi rej
	Mendoza-vln, William Feder-vc, Nathaniel Shilkret-org	
		NY March 11, 1920

B 23848-3	I Denne Sode Juletid-Christmas Hymn	Vi 72800
B 23849-2	Gud Skal Alting Mage (L.M. Lindeman)	Vi 72800
	Nathaniel Shilkret-org	NY March 15, 1920

Christian Mathiesen

86075-	Norge, Norge!	Co E4681
86076-	Og Ræven Laa Under Birkerod	Co E4681
86077-	Hjem Kjære Hjem	Co E4759
86078-	Hvor Skulde Jeg	Co E4759
	orch	NY March 1920

33.23. Wm. C. Nettenn *tenor*

| 85640- | Majsang | Co E7372 |
| | orch | NY November 1919 |

33.24. Alf Nilssen *vocal*

AFS 3853B1&2	Eg Ser Deg Ut For Gluggjin {I Knew You By Your Shadow}	LC
AFS 3853B3	Paal Paa Haugje {Paul On the Hill}	LC
AFS 3854A1	Eg Gjoette Tulla I Femten Aar {I Cared For Tulla For Fifteen Years}	
		LC
AFS 3854A2	Ola Glomstulens Brudeferd {Ola Glomstulen's Wedding}	LC
AFS 3854A3	Aa Kjøre Vatten Aa Kjøre Ve {Hauling Water And Hauling Wood}	LC
AFS 3854A4	Paa Fjallet {On The Mountain} (w: Kristofer Janson, b. 1841,	
	m: Halfdan Kjerulf)	LC
		Carmel, CA February 18, 1939

33.25. Ester Olsen *soprano*

85556-	Hvis Du Har Tanker	Co E4918
85557-	Ventende Paa Far	Co E4918
85558-	Lyngbloms	Co E7158
85559-	Sørg Kjære Fader Du	Co E7158
85561-	Spørgsmaal	Co E7372
	orch	NY ca November 1919

33.26. Eleanora Olson *contralto*

| | O Herre (Axel Lindgren)[1] | Vi trial |
| B 22448-1 | Sognekjærring-Pt. 1 | Vi 72183 |

2627

B 22449-1   Sognekjærring—Pt. 2   Vi 72183
                  spoken or 'Edward T. King—org   Camden, NJ March 11, 1918

B 21576-2   Bissam, Bissam Baadne (arr E. Grieg); Killebukken, Lammet Mit
                  (R. Nordraak)   Vi 72412
B 21577-2   Mot Kveld {Eventide} (Agathe Backer Grondahl)   Vi 72077
B 21578-2   Byssan Lu, Byssan Lei (Agathe Backer Grondahl)   Vi 72412
B 21579-2   Syng Kun I Din Ungdoms Vaar (Silcher)[1]   Vi 72077
                King's Orchestra d Nathaniel Shilkret, 'with Ethel Olson
                                                NY March 14, 1918

B 21580-2   Jeg Trænger Dig Hver Stund (Annie S. Hawks—Robert Lowry)   Vi rej
B 21581-1   O Herre (V. Krag—Erkki Melartin, op. 13 no. 1)   Vi 72323
B 21582-2   Bliv Hos Mig Mestai {Abide With Me} (Henry F. Lyte—Wm. Henry Monk)[1]
                                                      Vi 72323
                Edward T. King—org, 'with Ethel Olson   NY March 15, 1918

Florence Fleming

6179   A Perfect Day (C.J. Bond) [in English]   Ed 80538
                Robert Gayler—p   NY May 15, 1918

Eleanora Olson

B 23683-2   Herre Mit Hjerte   Vi rej
B 23685-2   Et Er Nodigt, Dette Ene {One Thing Needful}   Vi rej
B 23686-2   Nu Hviler Mark Og Enge {Now Rest Between Night's Shadow} (arr Bach)
                                                      Vi rej
                Mendoza—vln, Nathaniel Shilkret—org   NY February 19, 1920

B 23694-1   Övfer Kaffekopparna {Naa Me Drikke Kaffe} {Over The Coffee Cups}
                  (Eleanora Olson)   Vi 77517
B 23695-2   Naa De Brente Hos Kniperuds {The Fire At Kniperuds}   Vi rej
                spoken   NY February 20, 1920

7178   Gurie Paa Farmen {Gurie On The Farm}   Ed 59007
                spoken   NY February 25, 1920

7182   Gurie Kommer Til Byen (Gurie In Town)   Ed 59007
7183   Syng Kun I Din Ungdoms Vaar {Sing While You Are Young}
                (w: P.A. Jensen, m: Silcher)[1] [2]
                                                        Ed 59006
7186   Længsel (Kjerulf)[1] [3]   Ed 59006
                spoken, or 'sung with Ethel Olson; Robert Gayler—[2]p, or [3]org
                                              NY February 26, 1920

Ed 59006 as THE MISSES OLSON

B 23810-2   I Kveld Er Eg Glad {Tonight I Am Happy}   Vi 73086
B 23811-2   Du Gutten Min {My Boy} (Lepsoe)   Vi rej
                King's Orchestra   NY February 26, 1920

B 23695-4   Naa De Brente Hos Kniperuds {The Fire At Kniperuds}   Vi 73086
                as before   NY February 27, 1920

| B 23812-3 | Praise To The Lord The Almighty [in English] | Vi rej |
| | Nathaniel Shilkret-org | NY February 28, 1920 |

11795/6	Sogne Kjerring	
	(A Woman From Sogne Telling About Her Sweethearts)-Pt. 1	
		Br 40053
11797/8	Sogne Kjerring (A Woman From Sogne Telling About Her Troubles)-Pt. 2	
		Br 40053
	spoken	NY November 3, 1923

11807/8/9	Aa, Ola, Ola, Min Eigen Onga (Oh, Ole, Ole, I Loved You Dearly)	
		Br 40055
11810/1	Og Jeg Vil Ha Mig En Hjærtenskjær (I Want A Sweetheart), from	
	"Til Sæters"	Br 40055
	Ralph Mazziotta-p	NY November 5, 1923

B 28837-2	The Ladies Aid	Vi 77517
B 28838-2	At The Radio	Vi rej
B 28839-2	Trial Marriage	Vi 77286
	spoken	Camden, NJ November 6, 1923

89510-1	Aa Jeg Vil Ha Mig En Hjertens Kjær	Co 17003-F
89512-1	Naar Solen Ganger Til Hvile	Co 17003-F
89513-1	Vuggevise For Lillegut-Cradle Song (Winge)	Co 17005-F
89514-2	Listening In On The Radio¹ [in English]	Co 22026-F
89515-3	Byssan Lu, Byssan Lu	Co 17005-F
	¹with Ethel Olson	NY ca November 1923

Co 22026-F as OLSON SISTERS

	Gurie On The Farm	Co 22005-F
	Gurie In Town	Co 22005-F
	spoken	NY 1923

33.27. Ethel Olson *soprano*

This artist's monologs are in English, as are her Edison releases.

B 21695-1	A Norwegian Woman Using The Telephone	Vi 72060
B 21696-1	A Norwegian Woman At The Beach	Vi 72060
	spoken	NY March 11, 1918

Ethel Fleming

| 6178 | Thais: Meditation | Ed 80509 |
| | Robert Gayler-p | NY May 15, 1918 |

| 6201 | Cantilena | Ed 80509 |
| | as before | NY June 5, 1918 |

Ethel Olson

	Syng Mig Hjæm; Sole Gaan Aaser Ne Nathaniel Shilkret-p	Vi trial NY May 20, 1919
	Hver Skulde Jag; Sporgsmaal as before	Vi trial NY June 12, 1919
B 23450-3 B 23451-3	Sæterjenten {Song For Children} Fiskarvalsen (David Hellstrom) orch d Rosario Bourdon	Vi 72772 Vi 72772 NY November 3, 1919
B 23687-1 B 23688-2 B 23689-2 B 23690-2	The New Book Case (Ethel Olson) The Laughing Girl At The Photographers (Ethel Olson) The New Piano (Ethel Olson) The Piano Lesson (Ethel Olson) spoken	Vi 72930 Vi 72930 Vi rej Vi 72657 NY February 19, 1920
7176 7177	Larsen Kids Go Bathing Laughing Girl Has Her Picture Took spoken	Ed 50942, 4601(4 min) Ed 50844, 4558(4 min) NY February 25, 1920

Ethel Fleming

7181	Adoration Robert Gayler-p	Ed 80538 NY February 26, 1920

Ethel Olson

B 23689-4	The New Piano (Ethel Olson) spoken	Vi 72657 NY February 27, 1920
89516-2	The Baseball Game spoken	Co 22026-F NY October 1923
11792/3/4	A Norwegian Woman On The Telephone spoken	Br 40052 NY November 3, 1923
11799/800 11801/2 11804 11806 11812/3	Preparations For Mabel's Wedding-Pt. 1: The Search For The Dressmaker Preparations For Mabel's Wedding-Pt. 2: Discussing Her Suitors Story Of The Book Case The Ball Game Laughing Record spoken	 Br 40054 Br 40054 Br 40051 Br 40051 Br 40052 NY November 5, 1923
B 28834-2 B 28835-2 B 28836-2	The Baseball Game A Delicatessen At The Movies spoken	Vi 77251 Vi 77286 Vi 77251 Camden, NJ November 6, 1923
	Mabel's Wedding-Pt. 1 Mabel's Wedding-Pt. 2	Co 22002-F Co 22002-F

A Norwegian Woman   Co 22003-F
A Busy Piano Teacher   Co 22003-F
spoken   NY   1923

33.28. Inga Ørner *soprano (ca 1875-ca 1962)*

            Jeg Reiste; Norsk Folkvise   Vi trial
            Fred Bachman-p   Camden, NJ October 9, 1913

39642-2   Liden Karen   Co rej
39643-1   Rose Marie; Ensam I Skogen [in Swedish]   Co E2134
39644-1   Mot Kveld "Alle De Duguaate Blomster" (A. Backer-Grondahl) Co E3045
39645-1   Majsang; Vær Hilset Min Sol   Co E2133
39646-1   När Jag Blef Sjutton År [in Swedish]   Co E2134
39647-1   Serenade; Maanen Lyser Øver Søen   Co E2132
39648-1   Flickan Kom Från Sin Alsklings Möte [in Swedish]   Co E2161
            orch   NY November 27, 1914

39642-3   Liden Karen; Husker Du I Høst   Co E2133
39651-1   Jeg Reiste En Deilig Sommerkveld   Co E2160
39652-1   Ola! Ola! Min Eigen Onge   Co E2132
39653-1   Eit Syn; Ei Jente Jeg Saag   Co E2160
39654-1   Spinn, Spinn [in Swedish]   Co E2161
            orch   NY November 30, 1914

39693-1   Irmelin Rose (Peterson-Berger)   Co E3045
            p   NY December 15, 1914

37082-1   Jeg Elsker Dig; Jeg Vill Ha Mig En Hjertenskjær   Co E5082(12")
37081-1   Johanne "En Fillehyte Var Dit Bo"   Co E5082(12")
            orch   NY 1914

B 19950-2   Godnat {Good Night} (Per Lasson); God Morgen {Good Morning}
               (E. Grieg)   Vi rej
B 19951-3   Rav {Amber} (Christian Sinding)   Vi rej
B 19952-2   Arnes Sang {Arne's Song} (P.A. Heise)   Vi rej
B 19953-2   Syng, Syng! {Sing, Sing!} (Halfdan Kjerulf); Sovner {Slumber}
               (Halfdan Kjerulf)   Vi rej
            King's Orchestra d Rosario Bourdon   NY May 24, 1917

B 19963-2   Soen (Wilh. Kloeg); Eg Vil Deg Kje Elske (Christian Sinding) Vi rej
B 19964-1   Kom Kjyra!-Norwegian Echo Song (W. Thrane)   Vi 69483
B 19965-2   Vandring I Skoven {Woodland Fancies} (Edvard Grieg) Vi rej
            as before   NY May 29, 1917

B 19952-4   Arnes Sang {Arne's Song} (P.A. Heise)   Vi rej
B 19969-1   En Drøm {A Dream} (Edvard Grieg)   Vi 69607
B 19970-2   Min Elskte, Jeg Er Bunden {A Magic Power} (Halfdan Kjerulf) Vi 69483
B 19971-3   Vidste Du Hvor Hjertet Skjælver {Could'st Thou Know} (Carl Warmuth)
                                                                 Vi rej
            as before   NY May 31, 1917

B 19965-3   Vandring I Skoven {Woodland Fancies} (Edvard Grieg)   Vi 69607
B 19994-2   Naar Jeg Kommer Hjem {Keep The Home Fires Burning Till The Boys Come
            Home} (Ivor Novello)   Vi 69493
B 19995-1   Dengang Jeg Drog Af Sted {Den Tapre Landsoldat} (E. Horneman)
                                                                             Vi 69493
            King's Orchestra   NY June 8, 1917

B 19952-7   Arnes Sang {Arnes Song} (P.A. Heise)   Vi rej
            King's Orchestra d Rosario Bourdon   NY June 12, 1917

33.29. Ole Paullsen *vocal*

            Længsel   Ed 12171(2 min)
            Noekken   Ed 12172(2 min)
            Norske National Song   Ed 12173(2 min)
                                                                             NY 1901

33.30. Adolph Petersen *vocal*

A 512-1   Der Foerstedhe (Hjetus)   Vi 2502(7")
B 512-1   Der Foerstedhe (Hjetus)   Mon 2502
A 513-1   Des Mondes Silber (Kjerulf)   Vi 2503(7")
B 513-1   Des Mondes Silber (Kjerulf)   Mon 2503
A 514-1   Gipsy John (Clay) [in English]   Vi rej (7")
B 514-1   Gipsy John (Clay) [in English]   Mon rej
A 515-1   God Morgen (Kjerulf)   Vi 2501(7")
B 515-1   God Morgen (Kjerulf)   Mon 2501
            p   NY October 7, 1903

33.31. Hjalmar E. Røren *baritone*

B 3535-1   Aa Ola Ola Min Ejgen Ongje   Vi 3503
B 3536-1   Jeg Lagde Mig Saa Sildig   Vi 3504, 63395
B 3538-1   Sønner Af Norge (Blom)   Vi 3506, 63396
E 3539-1   For Norge, Kjæmpers Føderland (Grétry)   Vi 3500(8")
B 3540-1   Det Norske Flag (L.M. Ibsen)   Vi 3507, 63396
B 3541-1   Sæterjentens Søndag (Ole Bull)   Vi 3508, 63397
B 3542-1   Millom Bakkar Og Berg Ut Med Havet   Vi 3509, 63397
E 3543-1   Syng Kun I Din Ungdoms Vaar (Silcher)   Vi 3501(8")
E 3544-1   Studentersang   Vi 3502(8")
B 3546-1   Ja Vi Elsker (Rikard Nordraak)   Vi 3505, 63395
            p   NY July 17, 1906

Matrix number B 3546 was also used for Vi 3155 and 62187 by SR. CAMPO (Spanish).

            Sæterjentens Sondag (Ole Bull)   Ed 19113(2 min)
            Aa Ola, Ola, Min Eigen Onge!   Ed 19114(2 min)
            Ja, Vi Elsker Dette Landet (R. Nordraak)   Ed 19115(2 min)
            En Sangers Bøn (F.A. Reissiger)   Ed 19116(2 min)
            Mens Nordhavet Bruser (L.M. Ibsen)   Ed 19117(2 min)
            Sønner Af Norge, Det Ædgamle Rige (C. Blom)   Ed 19118(2 min)

Du Gamla, Du Friska   Ed 19119(2 min)
Vi Vil Os Et Land (Christian Sinding)   Ed 19120(2 min)
                                               NY   May 15 and July 29, 1907

33.32. Morton Sherdahl *baritone*

W 107331-1   På Roines Strand (K. Collan) [in Swedish]   Co 26043-F
W 107332-1   Ack Värmeland, Du Sköna [in Swedish]   Co 26043-F
             orch   NY   November 1926

Morton Sherdal

W 107507-2   Af Høiheden Oprunden Er (Phi Nicolai)   Co 17010-F
W 107508-2   Vor Gud Han Er Saa Fast En Borg (Martin Luther)   Co 17010-F
W 107509-2   Zions Vægter Hæver Røsten (Phi Nicolai)   Co 17011-F
W 107510-1   Lover Den Herre, Den Mægtige Konge (J. Neander)   Co 17011-F
                                                            NY   December 1926

Morton Sherdahl

BVE 37609-2   Och Jungfrun Gick Åt Killan {The Maiden Hied Her To The Well}
                (arr Gustav Haag) [in Swedish]   Vi 79158
BVE 37610-3   Det Står Ett Ljus I Österland {There Is A Light In Easterland}
                (arr Gustav Haag) [in Swedish]   Vi 79158
              orch d Bruno Reibold   Camden, NJ   January 6, 1927

33.33. Thorstein Skarning *accordion*

             Old Comrades March   Vi trial
                                                            NY   May 5, 1918

84420-1   Vår Kyssen-Vals   Co E4158
84421-   Norsk Arie   Co E4620
84422-   Vosserull   Co E4476
84424-   Seasons Coming   Co E4476
                                                            NY   June 1918

Thorsten Skarning And His Old Time Orchestra

TC 6420   The Caller {Lokkeren}   Br 477
TC 6421   Maybelle Schottische   Br 477
                                               Chicago   October 1930

33.34. Gunleik Smedal *hardanger violin*

BVE 48621-2   Guro Heddelid-Halling   Vi V-15001
BVE 48622-2   Giboens Minde {Giboens Memory}   Vi V-15001
BVE 48623-1   Sagafossen {Saga Falls}-Springar   Vi V-15002
BVE 48624-2   Nes Haugen-Halling   Vi V-15002
                                               Chicago   November 23, 1928

33.35. Robert Sterling *(Halfdan Meyer) vocal (1877-1946)*

| | Norwegian Song; Det Rode | Vi trial |
| | Edward T. King-p | NY   July 10, 1917 |

B 20510-2	Nikoline (Christine)	Vi 69645
B 20511-2	Liten Eva; Spansk Elskovstragedie (Waldteufel)	Vi 69834
B 20512-2	Jeg Følger I Min Faders Fotspor {Following In Father's Footsteps}	
	(E.W. Rogers)	Vi 69752
B 20513-2	Da Smeltestykket Sprang	Vi rej
	King's Orchestra d Rosario Bourdon	NY August 14, 1917

B 20530-2	Mit Første Rendezvous	Vi rej
B 20531-1	La Madrilena	Vi 69645
	as before	NY August 16, 1917

B 20513-3	Da Smeltestykket Sprang	Vi 69752
B 20530-4	Mit Første Rendezvous	Vi 69834
B 20547-1	Gammel Norsk Sjømandsvise	Vi 72259
	as before	NY September 7, 1917

B 20792-2	Från Engeland Te Scottland [in Swedish]	Vi rej
B 20793-2	Champagne Charley	Vi 72259
B 20794-2	En Sandpærdig Historie	Vi rej
B 20795-2	Ship Ahoy (m: Bennet Scott)	Vi 69955
B 20796-2	Han Kom Aldrig Igjen	Vi 69955
	as before	NY October 18, 1917

| 62090-1 | test recording | Co |
| | | NY   January 30, 1918 |

	Nicoline	Co E3761
	Følger I Faders Fotspor	Co E3761
	Jeg Maa Gaa Hjem Ikveld	Co E3762
	Da Smeltestykket Sprang	Co E3762
	La Madrilena (Daniderff-Dybwad)	Co E3763
	Mit Første Rendezvous (A. Dybwad)	Co E3763
	Sterling Er Giftesyk	Co E3877
	Gammel Sjømands Vise	Co E3877
	Fy Mette	Co E3878
	Manden Som Hængte Sig	Co E3878
	orch	NY 1918

33.36. Carl Struve *tenor*

| | Syng, Syng | Vi trial |
| | Nathaniel Shilkret-p | NY   March 5, 1920 |

B 23874-2	Kjærlighed Fra Gud-Hymn (Schorring)	Vi rej
B 23875-1	Du Herre, Som Er Sterk Og Stor (E. Grieg, op. 61 no. 7)	Vi 73201
B 23876-2	Liden Karen (P.A. Heise)	Vi 72723

B 23877-2   Sylvelin (Christian Sinding, op. 55 no. 1)   Vi 72723
             orch d Nathaniel Shilkret   NY March 31, 1920

33.37. S.T. Svenningsen *vocal*

88433-1   Nu Sju Og Forti   Co 17004-F
88434-2   Oslo Rekrutten   Co 17004-F
                                                          NY ca March 1922

33.38. Aalrud Tillisch *alto*

B 11480-1   Aa Ola, Ola, Min Eigen Onge {Oh Ole Ole I Love You Dear}-Folkevise
                Fra Vegaardsheien   Vi 63618
B 11481-1   O Herre {O Father} (Signe Lund, op. 28 no. 1)   Vi rej
B 11482-1   Eg Gjætte Tulla {My Tullar}-Folkvise Fra Hitterdal   Vi 63620
B 11483-1   Astri! Mi Astri {Astri My Astri} (w: H. Hansen)   Vi 63618
B 11484-1   Jeg Vil Ud! {I Must Fly} (Catherinus Elling, op. 45 no. 4) Vi rej
B 11485-1   Der Skreg En Fugl {There Cried A Bird} (Christian Sinding) Vi 63619
B 11486-1   Jeg Elsker Dig {I Love You} (Edw. Grieg)   Vi 63621
B 11487-1   Og Jeg Vil Ha Mig En Hjærtenskjær {I Will Have Me A Sweetheart}
                (Edw. Grieg)   Vi 63620
B 11488-1   Høsts Tormen {Autumn Gale}   Vi 63619
B 11489-1   Vuggesang {Cradle Song}   Vi 63621
             Charles Albert Baker-p   NY January 18, 1912

B 11481-2   O Herre {O Father} (Signe Lund, op. 28 no. 1)   Vi
             as before   NY February 24, 1912

             I Rosens Doft (Prince Gustav, Duke Of Upland)   USE 21575(4 min)
                                                          NY ca 1912

B 20732-2   Vesele Gutten Uppi Bakken {The Little Boy On The Hill Top}
                (arr Agathe Backer Grondahl)   Vi 73759
B 20733-2   Guten Va Trett {The Tired Boy} (Huldrevkas)   Vi rej
B 20734-3   Hugen {Thoughts} (Christian Sinding, op. 28 no. 6)   Vi rej
B 20735-2   So Lokka Me Over Den Myra   Vi 72618
             King's Orchestra   NY October 8, 1917

B 20736-2   Go Kvell, Mi Mari, Her Æe (arr Grieg)   Vi rej
B 20737-3   Kari Aa Mari, Stata Op Naa (Østerdalen)   Vi 72618
             as before   NY October 10, 1917

B 20751-2   Alverden Skal Synge {All The World Shall Sing}
                (Agathe Backer-Grondahl op. 31)   Vi rej
B 20752-2   Die Princessen {The Princess} (Grieg)   Vi 73759
B 20755-2   Hei, So Dansa Jenta Mi (arr Agathe Backer-Grondahl); Per Spelmann
                Han Hadde Ei Einaste   Vi rej
B 20756-2   Fola, Fola, Blakken (E. Grieg)   Vi rej
             as before   NY October 11, 1917

33.39. Tor Van Pyk *tenor*

973-	Tro Ej Glädjen Tro Ej Sorgen [in Swedish]	Co 973
	Tro Ej Glädjen Tro Ej Sorgen [in Swedish]	Co 31913(2 min)
974-	Mit Hjerte Og Min Lyre (Kjerulf)	Co 974
	Mit Hjerte Og Min Lyre (Kjerulf)	Co 31927(2 min)
975-2	Polska Från Uppland [in Swedish]	Co 975(7")
975-2	Polska Från Uppland [in Swedish]	Co 975, E797
	Polska Från Uppland [in Swedish]	Co 31914(2 min)
976-	Fågeln I November [in Swedish]	Co 976
	Fågeln I November [in Swedish]	Co 31915(2 min)
977-	Jeg Elsker Dig (E. Grieg, op. 5 no. 3)	Co 977
	Jeg Elsker Dig (E. Grieg, op. 5 no. 3)	Co 31928(2 min)
978-	Det Første Møde	Co 978
	Det Første Møde	Co 31929(2 min)
979-	Det Första Mötet [in Swedish]	Co 979
	Det Första Mötet [in Swedish]	Co 31916(2 min)
980-2	Romans Af Rotschild [in Swedish]	Co 980
	Romans Af Rotschild [in Swedish]	Co 31917(2 min)
981-	Margaretes Vuggesang (Grieg)	Co 981
	Margaretes Vuggesang	Co 31930(2 min)
982-1	Du Gamla, Du Friska, Du Fjällhöga Nord (w: R. Dybeck) [in Swedish]	Co 982
	Du Gamla, Du Friska, Du Fjällhöga Nord (w: R. Dybeck) [in Swedish]	Co 31918(2 min)
983-2	Vårt Land, Vårt Land [in Swedish]	Co 983(7")
983-1	Vårt Land, Vårt Land [in Swedish]	Co 983
	Vårt Land, Vårt Land [in Swedish]	Co 31919(2 min), Busy-Bee 349(2 min)
984-	Glädjens Blomster I Jordens Mull [in Swedish]	Co 984
	Glädjens Blomster I Jordens Mull [in Swedish]	Co 31920(2 min)
985-	Allt Under Himmelens Fäste [in Swedish]	Co 985
	Allt Under Himmelens Fäste [in Swedish]	Co 31921(2 min)
986-1	Mandom, Mod Och Morske Män [in Swedish]	Co 986
	Mandom, Mod Och Morske Män [in Swedish]	Co 31922(2 min)
987-	Klara Stjerna [in Swedish]	Co 987
	Klara Stjerna [in Swedish]	Co 31923(2 min)
988-	Hvi Skull Du Fjeran Vara [in Swedish]	Co 988
	Hvi Skull Du Fjeran Vara [in Swedish]	Co 31924(2 min)
989-	Djupt I Hafvet På Demantehällen [in Swedish]	Co 989(7")
989-3	Djupt I Hafvet På Demantehällen [in Swedish]	Co 989
	Djupt I Hafvet På Demantehällen [in Swedish]	Co 31925(2 min)
990-	Krigarn Hvilar Sig I Mark Och Skog [in Swedish]	Co 990
	Krigarn Hvilar Sig I Mark Och Skog [in Swedish]	Co 31926(2 min)
1011-	Ja Vi Elsker Dette Landet	Co 1011
	Ja Vi Elsker Dette Landet	Co 31951(2 min)
1044-1	Min Elskte Jeg Er Bunden	Co 1044, E410
	Min Elskte Jeg Er Bunden	Co 31984(2 min)
1045-	Vidste Du Vej	Co 1045
	Vidste Du Vej	Co 31985(2 min)
1046-	Længsel	Co 1046
	Længsel	Co 31986(2 min)
1047-	I Søde Blege Kinder	Co 1046

	I Søde Blege Kinder	Co 31987(2 min)
1048-	Ingrids Vise	Co 1048
	Ingrids Vise	Co 31988(2 min)
1049-	Ved Sven	Co 1049
	Ved Sven	Co 31989(2 min)
1063-	Jeg Vil Ud	Co 1063, E410
	Jeg Vil Ud	Co 32002(2 min)
1064-	Brudefærden I Hardanger	Co 1064
	Brudefærden I Hardanger	Co 32003(2 min)
1071-	Den Førstefødte	Co 1071
	Den Førstefødte	Co 32011(2 min)
1096-	Norges Fjelde	Co 1096
	Norges Fjelde	Co 32036(2 min)
1110-	Af Maanens Sølverglod	Co 1110
	Af Maanens Sølverglod	Co 32046(2 min)
	p	NY ca 1902

All discs above were recorded in both 7" and 10" sizes.

33.40. August Werner *baritone*

	I Himmelen, I Himmelen	Vi trial
	Nathaniel Shilkret-p	NY October 5, 1918

B 22743-2	Overmaade Fuld Av Naade (arr C. Elling)	Vi rej
B 22744-3	Den Blide Tanke	Vi 72855
	Reidar Haugan-vc, Gertrude Gunsten-org	NY April 15, 1919

B 22832-1	Norge, Deu Hvis Høvdingord	Vi 72499
B 22833-1	Kjølstadgutten	Vi 72355
B 22834-1	Liljekonvallens Farvel (Otto Lindwall)	Vi 72355
	orch d Rosario Bourdon	NY May 6, 1919

B 22743-3	Overmaade Fuld Av Naade (arr C. Elling)	Vi 72855
B 22908-3	Bølgeskvulp {White Caps} {Dashing Waves}	
	(Kr. Randers-Catherinus Elling, op. 45 no. 2)	Vi 78181
	Nathaniel Shilkret-cl, Gertrude Gunsten-org	NY June 10, 1919

B 23418-2	Den Fyrste Sang {The First Song} (Lars Soraas-Per Sivle)	Vi 73408
B 23422-2	I Rosenlund {Under Sagas Hall} {In The Rosedale} (J.S.C. Welhaven)	
		Vi 78181
B 23423-1	Sang Til Bergen {Song To Bergen} (Johan Nordahl Brun)	Vi 72499
	orch d Rosario Bourdon	NY October 17, 1919

C 24013-2	Min Sjæl, Min Sjæl Lov Herren! {My Soul, Now Bless Thy Maker}	
	(m: L.M. Lindeman, 1812-1887, w: J. Grauman, 1540, transcribed	
	by M.B. Laudstad, 1861)	Vi 68609(12")
C 24014-3	O Salige Stund {Oh Blessed Moment} (w: J. Hahnrast,	
	m: Kl. Wendelberg)	Vi 68609(12")
	Nathaniel Shilkret-org	NY April 21, 1920

| B 24132-2 | Markje Grønast | Vi 73025 |

B 24133-1	Hjemreise Fra Sætern {Os Na Gjort}	Vi 73025
	orch d Rosario Bourdon	NY May 25, 1920
B 24610-2	Her Er Det Land Som Hugar Meg Best (w: Ivar Aasen)	Vi 73408
B 24611-2	Var Det En Drøm? (R. Thommessen)	Vi rej
C 24612-2	Det Var Kun En Drøm (D. Mackim)	Vi rej (12")
	orch d Nathaniel Shilkret	NY October 5, 1920
B 24611-5	Var Det En Drøm? (R. Thommessen)	Vi 73474
B 26578-3	Barndomshjemmet (P. Wurch)	Vi 73474
	orch d Rosario Bourdon	Camden, NJ July 7, 1922
B 28208-2	Dukken Lise (Elith Worsing)	Vi rej
B 28209-2	Hils Fra Os Derhjemme (Elith Worsing)	Vi rej
	orch d Nathaniel Shilkret	NY June 2, 1923
B 28208-4	Dukken Lise (Elith Worsing)	Vi 73960
B 28209-4	Hils Fra Os Derhjemme (Elith Worsing)	Vi 73960
	as before	NY July 2, 1923
B 28276-2	Kristenfolkets Julehelg (Sigvald Skavland-Carsten Solheim)	Vi 77111
	as before	NY July 12, 1923
B 28558-1	Jeg Er Saa Glad Hver Julekveld	Vi 77111
	vln, bsn, p, org, traps, d Nathaniel Shilkret NY September 12, 1923	
B 29741-1	Han Er Opstanden {He Is Risen} (Ph. Nicolai)	Vi 77880
B 29742-1	Paaskemorgen Slukker Sorgen {Easter Morning Quench The Sorrow}	
	(N.F.S. Grundtvig-Lucy M. Lindeman)	Vi 77880
	orch d Leroy Shield	NY March 27, 1924
B 29967-2	Frøken, Giv Mig Himlens Numer (Chas K. Harris)	Vi 77596
B 29968-3	Sjømandevals {Hal Topsail Min Pige} {Sailor's Waltz}	
	(Riedar Thommessen)	Vi 77648
	as before	NY May 6, 1924
B 30099-2	Skjørsommersangen {The Song Of Midsummer} (Claribel)	Vi 77648
B 30200-2	Hymne	Vi rej
B 30201-1	Sommersol Til Sisste Stund {Silver Threads Among The Gold}	
	(H.P. Banks-E. Rexford)	Vi 77596
	orch d Charles Prince	Camden, NJ May 20, 1924
B 32256-2	Sol Over Seil {Sun And White Sails} (Reidar Thommesen, op. 39)	
		Vi 78058
B 32257-3	Eventerland {Fairyland} (Arth. B. Sars, op. 4)	Vi 78058
	orch	NY March 26, 1925
BVE 32792-1	Norge, Mit Norge {Norway My Norway} (Max Ræbel, op. 33 no. 7)	
		Vi 78404, V-15037, 25-8004
BVE 32793-2	Jeg Elsker Dit Smil {I Love Your Smile} (Reidar Thommessen)	
		Vi 78404, V-15037, 25-8004
BVE 33105-2	Herr Kommer Dine Arme Smaa {Here Come Your Poor Small Ones}	
	(J.A.P. Schulz)	Vi 78263

| BVE 33106-2 | O Jul Med Din Glæde {O Christmas Of Gladness} | Vi 78263 |
| | orch d Rosario Bourdon | Camden, NJ July 24, 1925 |

BVE 34090-1	Getsemane (Caroline Schytte Jensen)	Vi 78527
BVE 34091-3	Paaskehymne (Carl Sander-P.A. Jensen)	Vi 78527
	Morris Braun-vln, Christian Klus-vc, Leroy Shield-org	
		Camden, NJ January 14, 1926

BVE 34442-2	Se Solens Skjønne Lys Og Pragt	Vi 80448
BVE 34443-3	Om Nogen Til Ondt Mig Lokke Vil	Vi 80448
BVE 34444-3	Les Rameaux {The Palms} (m: J. Faure)	Vi rej
	Fred Cook, Leon Arkless-2 vln, unk org Camden, NJ January 29, 1926

BVE 34906-3	Det Var Kun En Drøm {It Was But A Dream} (D. Mackim)	Vi rej
CVE 34907-3	The Holy City (Stephen Adams)	Vi rej (12")
CVE 34908-2	Les Rameaux {The Palms} (m: J. Faure)	Vi 68762(12")
BVE 34909-2	Mor {Mother} (O. Hralbye)	Vi 78651
	orch d Rosario Bourdon	Camden, NJ February 18, 1926

BVE 34906-4	Det Var Kun En Drøm {It Was But A Dream} (D. Mackim)	Vi 78651
CVE 34907-5	The Holy City (Stephan Adams)	Vi 68762(12")
	orch d Bruno Reibold	Camden, NJ March 4, 1926

BVE 35431-3	Ved Rundarne {The Wanderer's Return} (E. Grieg, op. 33 no. 9) Vi rej
BVE 35432-2	Norge Midnatsolens Land {Norway} (Fred Fischer)	Vi 79081
	as before	Camden, NJ April 27, 1926

BVE 36825-1	Julesang {Cantique De Noel} (Adolphe Adam)	Vi 78978
BVE 36826-2	Sans Til Juletræ Et (E. Grieg, op. 61 no. 2)	Vi 78978
	orch d Nathaniel Shilkret	NY October 14, 1926

BVE 36776-2	Du Var Et Sangvals (M.B. Landstad-Reidar Thommesen)	Vi 79142
BVE 36777-2	Høststemning {Autumn Mood} (Th. Knutsen-Reidar Thommesen)	Vi 79081
BVE 36778-1	Sov, Min Prinsesse {Sleep, My Princess} (w: Ewald Sundberg, m: Fenger Gron, op. 8)	Vi 79142
	orch d Bruno Reibold	Camden, NJ November 26, 1926

BVE 37398-3	Magnis-Sang (Marius Loaritz-Ulvested, op. 34 no. 1)	Vi 80598
BVE 37399-3	Kvedo-Sang For Blakken (E. Grieg, op. 61 no. 5)	Vi 80598
	as before	Camden, NJ February 7, 1927

BVE 36778-3	Sov, Min Prinsesse {Sleep, My Princess} (w: Ewald Sundberg, m: Fenger Gron, op. 8)	Vi rej
BVE 37829-3	Majsang (G.A. Lembcke)	Vi rej
BVE 37830-2	Sølvert {The Silver} (T. Lammers-Gibbson)	Vi rej
	orch d Leroy Shield	Camden, NJ February 18, 1927

33.41. Maud Wilson *soprano*

B 23094-2	Efteraar (P.E. Lange-Muller, op. 61)	Vi 72889
B 23095-2	Vidste Du Vei (Halfdan Kjerulf)[1]	Vi rej
B 23096-3	Sporven (Catharinus Elling, op. 52)	Vi rej
	orch d Rosario Bourdon	NY July 28, 1919

B 23100-3	Alverden Skal Synge {The Whole World Shall Sing}	
	(Agathe Backer-Grondahl, op. 31)	Vi rej
B 23101-3	Gyngevise {Swing Song} (Eyvind Alnæs, op. 1 no. 4)¹	Vi rej
B 23102-2	Nytaarsmorgen {New Years Morning}	
	(Theodore Casparl-Nikolai Lindtner)¹	Vi rej
	orch d Rosario Bourdon or ¹Joseph Pasternack	NY July 30, 1919

B 23095-4	Vidste Du Vei (Halfdan Kjerulf)	Vi 72889
B 23096-5	Sporven (Catharinus Elling, op. 52)	Vi rej
B 23100-4	Alverden Skal Synge {The Whole World Shall Sing}	
	(Agathe Backer-Grondahl, op. 31)	Vi rej
B 23102-4	Nytaarsmorgen {New Year's Morning}	
	(Theodore Casparl-Nikolai Lindtner)	Vi rej
	orch d Nathaniel Shilkret	NY August 14, 1919

33.42. Carsten Th. Woll *tenor (b. 1885)*

| | Mit Hjerte Og Min Lyre (Halfdan Kjerulf) | Vi trial |
| | Fred Bachman-p | NY October 7, 1913 |

B 13914-1	Nytaarssalme {New Year's Hymn} (N.F.S. Grundtvig)	Vi 65597
B 13915-1	Den Store, Hvide Flok (Edvard Grieg)	Vi 65687
B 13916-1	Syng Mig Hjæm (Bj. Bjørnson-Edmund Neupert, op. 26)	Vi 65598
B 13917-1	Ingalill {Little Inga} (L. Rosenfeld)	Vi 65599
B 13918-1	Mit Hjerte Og Min Lyre (Halfdan Kjerulf)	Vi 65599
B 13919-1	Mor (Hvalbye)	Vi rej
B 13920-1	Endnu Et Streif (A.B. Grondahl, op. 70)	Vi 65601
B 13921-1	Da Barnet Sov Ind (Halfdan Kjerulf)	Vi 65601
B 13922-1	Venetiansk Serenade (Johan Svendsen, op. 24 no. 3)	Vi 65686
B 13923-1	Ja, Vi Elsker Dette Landet-National Song (w: Bj. Bjørnson,	
	m: R. Nordraak)	Vi 65598
B 13924-1	Solefaldssang, from "Svein Urad" (Ole Olsen)	Vi 65686
B 13925-1	Til Min Gyldenlak (H. Wergeland-Emil Frija)	Vi 65688
B 13926-1	Julsang (Adolphe Adam)	Vi 65597
B 13927-1	Hun Er Sød, Hun Er Blød (Halfdan Kjerulf)	Vi 65689
	as before	NY October 8, 1913

B 13915-2	Den Store, Hvide Flok (Edvard Grieg)	Vi rej
B 13919-2	Mor (Hvalbye)	Vi rej
B 13923-2	Ja, Vi Elsker Dette Landet-National Song (w: Bj. Bjørnson,	
	m: R. Nordraak)	Vi rej
B 13928-1	Nørkken (Halfdan Kjerulf)	Vi rej
B 13929-1	Eg Veit Ei Liti Gjenta (Catharinus Elling)	Vi 65689
B 13930-1	Danebrogssang (Johan Halvorsen)	Vi rej
B 13931-1	Majnat {A May Night} (Christian Sinding)	Vi 65600
B 13932-1	Sæterjentens Søndag (Ole Bull)	Vi 65688
B 13933-1	En Svane {A Swan} (w: H. Jusen-Edvard Grieg)	Vi 65600
B 13940-1	Kirken, Den Er Et Gammelt Hus; Fred Til Bod-Hymns	Vi 65687
B 13941-1	Med Dina Blaa Øgon (Fritz Arlberg)	Vi rej
	as before	NY October 9, 1913

46549-1	Mor {Mother} (O. Hvalbye)	Co E2539
46550-1	Aa Kjøre Vatten Aa Kjøre Ve {Come Fetch The Water And Haul the Wood}	Co E2491
46551-1	Den Norske Fisker {The Norse Fisherman} (Grieg)	Co E2493
46552-1	Du Gamle Mor {My Dear Old Mother} (Grieg)	Co E2491
46553-1	Aagots Fjeldsang (A. Thrane)	Co E2493
46554-1	Paal Paa Haugen {Paul On The Hillside}	Co E2540
46555-1	Millom Bakkar Og Berg {Among Hills And Brooks}	Co E2539
46556-1	Kjerringa Med Staven {The Old Woman On Crutches}	Co E2540
46557-1	Eg Gjætte Tulla	Co E2591
46558-1	Astri, Mi Astri	Co E2590
46559-1	Kan Du Glemme Gamle Norge {Old Norway} (Chr. Danning)	Co E2539
46571-1	Blandt Alle Lande {Among All Countries} (B.M. Hausen)	Co E2538
46572-1	Ja, Vi Elsker Dette Landet (Nordraak-Bjørnson)	Co E2492
46573-1	Tænk Naar En Gang	Co E3046
46574-1	Sønner Af Norge (C. Blom)	Co E2492
46575-1	Mens Nordhavet Bruser {Norway's Flag Song} (L.M. Ibsen)	Co E2538
46577-1	Eg Ser Deg Ut For Gluggjin	Co E2590
46578-1	Og Ræven Laa Under Birkerod	Co E2591
46579-1	Naar Fjordene Blaaner (A. Paulsen)	Co E2589
46580-1	Os Har Gjort Paa Gjerast Skulde	Co E3046

orch   Chicago   August 1915

B 20225-3   Norge, Mit Norge {Norway My Norway} (w: Theodore Caspari,
                m: Alfred Paulsen)   Vi rej
B 20226-2   Med En Primula Veris (w: John Paulsen, m: Grieg)   Vi rej
B 20227-2   Vuggesang Om Julekvelden (w: Albert, m: F. Melius Christiansen)
                                                               Vi rej
King's Orchestra d Rosario Bourdon   NY   July 17, 1917

B 20236-2   Dei Vil Alted Klaga Og Kyla (w: Ivor Aasen)   Vi rej
B 20237-1   Se Norges Blomsterdal (w: A. Aabel)   Vi 72987
B 20238-2   Astri Mi Astri   Vi 73129
B 20241-2   Gud Signe Norigs Land   Vi rej
as before   NY   July 19, 1917

B 20246-2   I Himmelen I Himmelen (w: Laurentius Laurenti,
                m: Gammel Nork Folketone)   Vi 69751
B 20247-2   Blandt Alle Lande I Ost Og Vest   Vi rej
B 20248-2   Ved Rundarne (w: A.O. Vinje, m: E. Grieg)   Vi rej
B 20249-2   Jeg Reiste En Deilig Sommerkveld (w: John Paulsen, m: Grieg) Vi rej
King's Orchestra   NY   July 24, 1917

B 20227-4   Vuggesang Om Julekvelden (w: Albert, m: F. Melius Christiansen)
                                                              Vi 69663
B 20253-1   Jeg Er Saa Glad Hver Julekveld   Vi 69663
King's Orchestra d Rosario Bourdon   NY   July 26, 1917

B 20262-2   Deilig Er Jorden {Fair Is The Earth} (w: B.S. Ingemann, 1789)
                                                              Vi 69751
Edward T. King-org   NY   July 30, 1917

B 20265-2   Her Kommer Dine Arme Smaa (H.A. Brovson-J.A.P. Scultz,
                arr John Dahle)
                                                               Vi rej

2641

B 20266-1   Kjarringa Mæ Staven; En Liden Gut I Fra Tistedaln   Vi 73129
             King's Orchestra d Rosario Bourdon   NY July 31, 1917

B 20225-5   Norge, Mit Norge {Norway, My Norway} (w: Theodore Caspari,
                 m: Alfred Paulsen)   Vi 69625
B 20287-2   Killebukken (Björnson-Nordraak); Blaamand   Vi 73028
             as before   NY August 7, 1917

B 20241-3   Gud Signe Norigs Land   Vi 69625
B 20249-4   Jeg Reiste En Deilig Sommerkveld (w: John Paulsen, m: Grieg) Vi rej
B 20267-1   Lille Haakons Vuggesang {Cradle Song} (Grieg)   Vi 72987
B 20275-2   Nokken (Welhaven-Halfdan Kjerulf)   Vi rej
B 20276-2   Mor {Mother} (m: O. Hvalbye)   Vi rej
B 20277-3   Vaagn Af Din Slummer (P. Heise)   Vi rej
             as before   NY August 8, 1917

B 20275-4   Nokken (Welhaven-Halfdan Kjerulf)   Vi rej
B 20276-4   Mor {Mother} (m: O. Hvalbye)   Vi 73028
B 20277-6   Vaagn Af Din Slummer (P. Heise)   Vi rej
             as before   NY August 9, 1917

84821-1   Sæterjentens Søndag (Ole Bull)   Co E4183
84824-   Det Er Saa Yindigt At Folges Ad   Co E7111
84829-   Østerdalsmarschen   Co E4269
84830-2-6   Den Store, Hvide Flok (E. Grieg)   Co E4364
84831-   Ola Glomstulen   Co E4240
84832-1   Glade Jul, Dejlige Jul-Christmas Song   Co E4364
84838-2   Roselil   Co E4150
84840-1-2   Brudefærden I Hardanger   Co E4150
84842-1   Eg Elsker Dei Voggande Tonar   Co E4183
84843-2   Serenade "Naar Ved Nat"   Co E4151
84846-1-2   Sov, Min Prinsesse   Co E4151
84847-   God Morgen   Co E4269
84848-   Laurdagskvell   Co E4240
             Der Stod Sig Et Slag Udi Kjøgebugt   Co E4182
             Hellig Olaf   Co E4182
             Kirken, Den Er Et Gammelt Hus (Lindemann)   Co E4239
             Vor Gud Han Er Saa Fast En Borg   Co E4239
             Lille Madit   Co E4414
             Du Er Min Sol   Co E4414
             orch   NY ca September 1918

6658   Paal Paa Hougje {Paul On The Hillside}   Ed 78010, 9240(4 min)
6659   Eg Ser Deg Ut Før Gluggjin {I See Your Shadow Yonder}; En Liten Gut
                 {A Little Lad}   Ed 78009
             orch   NY March 10, 1919

6663   Aa Kjøre Vatten Aa Kjøre Ve {Come Haul The Water And Haul The Wood};
                 Kjerringa Med Staven {Here Comes Sally On Crutches}
                                                         Ed 78009, 9246(4 min)
6664   Astri! Mi Astri! {Homage To Sweden} (Helge Sandberg)
                                                         Ed 78010, 9245(4 min)
             orch   NY March 12, 1919

6671   Sæterjentens Sondag {The Chalet Girl's Sunday} (Reissiger-Ole Bull)
                                                  Ed 78013, 9243(4 min)
         orch   NY March 17, 1919

6675   Gamle Norge {Song Of Norway} (Kristian Nilsson)
                                                  Ed 78012, 9247(4 min)
6676   Den Store Hvide Flok {The Vast Unnumbered Throng} (Grieg)   Ed 78013
         orch   NY March 19, 1919

6693   Vor Gud Han Er Saa Fast En Borg {A Mighty Fortress Is Our God}
                 (Martin Luther, 1529)   Ed 78012, 9241(4 min)
         orch   NY March 28, 1919

6702   Ja Vi Elsker Dette Landet {Yes, We Love With Fond Devotion}
                 (w: Björnsterne Björnson, m: Rikard Nordraak)
                                              Ed 78011, 9244(4 min)
         orch   NY   April 2, 1919

6708   Ola Glomstulen, Hjemreise Fra Sætren {Home From The Mountain}
                                                Ed 78017, 9242(4 min)
         orch   NY   April 7, 1919

6755   Sommersol Til Sidste Stund {Silver Threads Among The Gold}
                 (H.P. Danks)   Ed 78011, 9252(4 min)
         orch   NY   April 30, 1919

B 22948-3   A Mighty Fortress Is Our God (Martin Luther, 1529) [in English]
                                                            Vi rej
B 22949-2   Now Thank We All Our God (M. Rhinhart-Johann Cruger, 1648)
                 [in English]   Vi rej
                 Nathaniel Shilkret-org   NY   July 1, 1919

B 22954-3   How Blessed Is The Little Flock (N.J. Holm-Ludv. M. Lindeman)
                 [in English]   Vi rej
B 22955-3   Built On the Rock The Church (N.F. Grundtvig-Ludv. M. Lindeman)
                 [in English]   Vi rej
                 as before   NY   July 3, 1919

B 22948-4   A Mighty Fortress Is Our God (Martin Luther, 1529) [in English]
                                                         Vi 72744
B 22949-2   Now Thank We All Our God (M. Rhinhart-Johann Cruger, 1648)
                 [in English]   Vi 72744
                 as before   NY   July 11, 1919

85914-	Smyg Mig Hjem[1] [2]	Co E7371
85916-	Kjølstad "Je Tjente Pas Kjolstad Ifjor"	Co E7111
85921-	Gylden Sol[1] [2]	Co E7371
85922-2	Aften Er Stille	Co E7159
85923-	Syng Kun I Din Ungdoms Vaar	Co E4619
85924-	Sidste Reis[1] [2]	Co E4917
85925-	Brumbasken I Bumba-Killebukken	Co E4619
89526-	Vi Vil Os Et Land[1] [2]	Co E4917
89527-2	Jeg Synger Julekvad-Christmas Song[2] [3]	Co E4797
89528-	Beautiful Saviour, King Of Creation[1] [2]	Co E7286

85930-1	Hvor Salig Er Den Lille Flok-Christmas Song[2] [3]	Co E4797
85931-	Barndomsminne Fraa Nordland (Thomas-Blix)	Co E7029
85932-	Bor Jeg Paa Det Høje Fjeld	Co E7029
85933-2	Venetiansk Serenade	Co E7159
85934-	In Heaven Above[1] [3]	Co E4682
85935-2	Fred Til Bod For Bittert Savn[1] [3]	Co E4798
85936-	Jesus Jesus, Only Jesus[1] [3]	Co E4682
85937-	Sorgen Og Glæden De Vandre Tilhobe[1] [3]	Co E7439
85938-	Den Signede Dag[1] [3]	Co E4798
85939-	Give Praise To God Our King[1] [2]	Co E7286
85940-	Katten Og Killingen; Veslegutten Oppe Bakken[2]	Co E7439

orch, or [1]vln, [2]p, [3]org   NY February 1920

7315	The Sturdy Norseman (Gretry)	Ed 80551
7316	Norway, My Norway (Alfred Paulsen); Little Mountain Maid	
	(P.S. Lange-Müller)	Ed 80551

orch   NY April 23, 1920

7318	The Old Mother (E. Grieg, op. 33 no. 7); First Violet (E. Grieg,	
	op. 26 no. 4)	Ed 80552
7319	One More Glimpse Of The Sun (Agathe Backer-Grondahl, op. 70); Light	
	Of The World (Oscar Arnefeldt)	Ed 80552

Robert Gayler-p   NY April 26, 1920

7379	Vuggesang Om Julekvælden (F. Melius Christiansen)	Ed 78020

orch   NY June 2, 1920

7396	Jeg Langter Mot Sol Og Sommer {I Long Towards Sun And Summer}	
	(w: Robert Loennecken, m: Rudolph Møller)	
		Ed 78015, 9251(4 min)

orch   NY June 9, 1920

7416	Ingalill (Leopold Rosenfeld)	Ed 78014, 9248(4 min)

orch   NY June 21, 1920

7428	Majnat {May Night} (w: Vilhelm Knag, m: Christian Sinding)	
		Ed 78014, 9250(4 min)

orch   NY June 28, 1920

7433	Jeg Reiste En Deilig Sommerkvæld	
	{I Walked Abroad One Lovely Summer Night}; Veste Gutten Uppi	
	Backen {Little Boy On The Hill}	Ed 78017
7434	Bor Jeg Paa Det Hoie Fjeld {Dwell On The Lofty Mount}	
	(w: Johan Nordahl Brun)	Ed 78016, 9249(4 min)

orch   NY July 6, 1920

7438	Millom Bakkar Og Berg Utmed Havet	
	{'Mong The Rocks By The North Sea's Blue Waters}	Ed 78016
7439	Sövnen {Slumber} (w: Björn, m: H. Kjerulf)	Ed 78015

Robert Gayler-p   NY July 7, 1920

7466	If With All Your Hearts [in English]	Ed 80584
7467	Carry Me Back To Old Virginny [in English]	Ed 80585

NY July 30, 1920

7470	Mother Machree [in English]	Ed 80585
7471	Lass With The Delicate Air [in English]	Ed 80584
		NY August 2, 1920

9633/4	Paal Paa Haugen	Vo 14422
9644	Herre Konge, Blio Her! (Heise)	Vo 14596
9648/9	Du Gamle Mor (Grieg)	Vo 14422
9658	Jeg Saa Ham Som Barn	Vo 14628
9660	Amdagen	Vo 14628
9662/3/4	Vuggesang Om Julekvelden (Christiansen)	Vo 14440
9665/6	Jeg Er Saa Glad Hver Julekveld	Vo 14440
9667	To Brune Oine {Med On Primula Veris} (Grieg)	Vo 14596
	Last Night	Vo 14423
	The Sturdy Norseman	Vo 14423
		NY ca August 1922

8673	Du Gamla, Du Fria [in Swedish]	Ge 5353
8674-A	Kan Du Glemme Gamle	Ge 5354
8675-A	Millom Bakkar Aa Berg	Ge 5354
8676	Fogeles Visa [in Swedish]	Ge 5353
	orch	NY December 19, 1923

9303	Min Hjerte Og Min Lyre {My Heart And Lute} (H. Kjerulf)	Ed 78018
9304	Fågelns Visa {The Bird's Song} (W. Th. Söderberg) [in Swedish]	
		Ed 78021
	John F. Burckhardt-p	NY December 24, 1923

9305	Taaren {The Tear}	Ed 78018
9306	Svärmeri {Dreams} (Fritz Arlberg) [in Swedish]	Ed 78019
9307	I For Gjætt'e Gjeitinn {The Shepherd's Lament}	Ed 78020
9308	Om Dagen Vid Mitt Arbete {In My Thoughts} [in Swedish]	Ed 78019
	orch	NY December 26, 1923

	Sæterjentens Søndag (O. Bull)	Ok 25023
	Kan Du Glemme...{Gamle Norge}	Ok 25023
	Dei Vil Altid Klage	Ok 25024
	Budeiens Vise	Ok 25024
	Paal Paa Haugen	Ok 25025
	Frierrasen	Ok 25025
	orch	NY ca 1923

	Jens Tollerists Klagesang	Co 17000-F
	Gigsgutten	Co 17000-F
		NY 1923-4

B 29175-3	Norske Steve {Norwegian Steve}	Vi 77302
B 29176-2	Vær Snil Mod Mor {Be Kind To Mother}	
	(Rev. K. Solberg-J. Rode-Jacobsen)	Vi rej
B 29177-1	Peter Tordenskjold	Vi rej
B 29178-2	Navnebytte-Vise {Naa Bytter Vi Lidt Navn} {Change Of Names}	
	(Carsten Woll)	Vi 77302
	orch d Leroy Shield	NY January 3, 1924

Den Store Hvide Flok (Grieg)	Br 40092
Gamle Norge	Br 40092
Naar Fjordene Blaaner	Br 40093
Ola Glomstulen	Br 40093
Fogelns Visa	Br 40094
Astri Mi Astri	Br 40094
Kirken Den Er Et Gammelt Hus (Grundtvig)	Br 40095
Fred Til Bod Hymn	Br 40095
	NY ca 1924

SECTION 34. SCANDINAVIAN

34.1. Fritz Aase-Hugo Johnson *accordion duet*

Dallrande Blad; Roald Amundsen | Vi trial
NY March 14, 1917

B 19466-1	Roald Amundsen-March	
B 19467-2	Puddefjorden-Waltz	Vi rej
B 19468-1	Min Tös-Schottische	Vi 69465
B 19469-3	Mazurka No. 1 (Hugo Johnson)	Vi 69410
B 19470-2	Kristiania-Valsen (Hugo Johnson)	Vi 69465, HMV X461
		Vi 69465, HMV X461
		NY April 11, 1917

B 19466-3	Roald Amundsen-March	
B 20113-2	Sommarkväll-Vals (Oscar Merikanto)	Vi rej
	Kesäilta Vals	Vi 69602
B 20114-1	Finnjorka-Chottis	Vi 69652
	Vengierka-Schottische	Vi 69602, 69652
B 20115-1	På Baltiskan {On The Baltic}-Vals (David Hellstrom)	Vi 73738
B 20116-3	Dragonpolka	Vi 73476
		Vi rej
		NY June 13, 1917

Vi 69652 is a Finnish issue; Vi 73738 is Lithuanian.

34.2. Ottar Agre *accordion (b. 1896)*

This artist's name is also spelled AKRE.

B 27251-1	Norsk Militär Marsch (S. Jevanaker)	Vi 73723
B 27252-1	Møllerguttens Søn {The Miller's Son}-Mazurka (T. Torgeirsen)	
		Vi 73723
		NY December 21, 1922

B 29911-1	Hammarsforsens Brus	
B 29912-2	Klokke Polka	Vi 77518
B 29913-1	Hambo Mazurka	Vi 77518
	vla, p	Vi rej
		NY April 21, 1924

Ottar Agree's Quintette

W 106603-2	Sailor's Waltz (G. Stählberg)	Co 12038-F
	Rauha Myrskyssä-Valssi	Co 3025-F, 16135
W 106604-2	My Little Friend-Schottische (Schwente)	Co 12047-F

	Min Lilla Vän-Schottis	Co 22034-F
W 106605-2	Wesoły Parobek-Polka	Co 18133-F
	Alle Småpigers-Polka	Co 22034-F
W 106606-2	Santa Claus Polka (S. Jevnäker)	Co 12038-F
	Na Opavě-Polka	Co 92-F
	Joulupukin Polkka	Co 3025-F, 16135
	Polka Zabawa	Co 18133-F
	Julenissens Polka	Co 22033-F
	own and another-2 acn, unk vln, xyl, g	NY April 1926

Co 92-F as COLUMBIA HUDEBNI KVINTET, 3025-F and 16135 as COLUMBIA SOITTO KVINTETTI, 12047-F as COLUMBIA QUINTETTE, 18133-F as INSTRUMENTOWY KWARTET "WARSZAWA", 22033-F as COLUMBIA NYHETSKVINTETTEN

34.3. Eric Berg   *accordion*

Kring Granen	Vi trial
Miller-vln	NY September 19, 1921

Berg And Johnson

B 25685-2	Kring Granen {Around The Christmas Tree}-Mazurka	Vi 73146
	Aplink Kalēdu Eglaite	Vi 73268
	Na Travinku-Mazurka	Vi 73814
B 25686-1	Efter Balen {After The Ball Is Over}	Vi 73146
	Balu Pasigaibus-Valcas	Vi 73268
	Do Wuja Starca	Vi 73814
	Mendoza-vln	NY October 31, 1921

Vi 73268 is a Lithuanian release; Vi 73814 is Polish.

34.4. Columbia Scandinavian Orchestra

44461-	Klackjärnspolska	Co E3197
44463-	Hambo-Polska	Co E3197
	d William Oscar	NY ca December 1916

Some copies of Co E3197 as COLUMBIA ORCHESTRA

58681-1	Nya Kväsarvalsen (A. Englund)	Co E3641
58682-1	Hjärterövalsen (Hellström)	Co E3641
58683-2	Kungl. Kronobergs Regementes Paradmarsch	Co E3642
58684-2	Svenska Arméns Tapto	Co E3642
58685-2	Godt Hymor-Schottisch (Wm. Oscar)	Co E3698
	d William Oscar	NY ca October 1917

58723-1	Brudefärden I Hardanger {A Wedding In Hardanger}	Co E3681
58725-1	Norsk Potpourri	Co E3681
58726-1	Bland Fjällen¹	Co E3682
58784-1	Stockholms-Schottisch (Wm. Oscar)	Co E3698
	d William Oscar, ¹Benjamin Klatzkin-c	NY ca November 1917

58814-1	Friarevalsen	Co E3778
58815-1	I Alla Fulla Fall (That's The Way It Goes)-Waltz	Co E3779
58816-2	Ack Elvira-Polka	Co E3779
58817-1	Oriental Dans	Co E3778
	d William Oscar	NY ca November 1917

84087-	Maskerad Polka	Co E4484
84088-1	Bergs Klockan-Polka Mazurka	Co E4004
84090-1	Del Mūsu̱ Jaunimo-Polka	Co E4796
84091-1	Skridskoåker Valsen	Co E4004
	Skaters Waltz	Co E4253
84092-	Štášny Hoši V Horach-Valčik	Co E3924
84093-2	Ack Värmeland, Du Sköna	Co E4005
	Nevinný Valčik	Co E4549
	as before	NY February 1918

Co E3924 (Bohemian) as ČESKÁ KAPELA, E4253 as COLUMBIA INTERNATIONAL BAND, E4549 (Bohemian) as COLUMBIA KAPELA, E4796 (Lithuanian) as COLUMBIJOS BENAS. Co E4005 has also been reported with matrix 58941-1.

84280-2	Hell Dig-Marsch	Co E4003
84281-	Kungl. Göta Lifgardes-Parad Marsch	Co E4003
	as before	NY April 1918

85383-1	Solnedgång I Sverige	Co E4483
85384-1	Eko Från Skandinavien	Co E4483
		NY November 1919

34.5. Hans Erichsen *accordion (1890-1973)*

Hans & Henry Erichsen

39215-1	Höstdröm-Mazurka	Co E2000, Banjar BR-1840(33)
	Gudri-Mazurka	Co E2706
39216-1	Spansk Dans	Co E2000
	Hiszpański Taniec	Co E2598
39217-1	Numedalernes Bataljons Marsch	Co E1694
39218-1	Borghild Rheinlander	Co E1694
	Kariškas Maršas	Co E2582
39219-1	Columbia Polka	Co E1695
	Zemaičiu̱ Polka	Co E2706
	own, Henry Erichsen (1895-1977)-2 acn	NY February 5, 1914

39220-1	Ny Fiskarvals	Co E1695
	Žuvininku̱-Valcas	Co E2580
	Nowy Walc Rybaków	Co E2769
39221-1	Jemtlandsvalsen	Co E1696
39222-2	Prairieliljan	Co E1696
39223-1	Wiener Krostpolka	Co E1697
	Gražioji Polka	Co E2581
39224-1	Svensk Rheinlander	Co E1697
39225-1	Variable-Mazurka	Co E1698

	Zmienna-Mazurka		Co E2597
39226-1	Kristiania Waltz {Kristiania 1914}		Co E1698
	Walc 1914 Roku		Co E2598
39227-1	Aages Waltz		Co E1699, C3722
39228-1	Berliner Polka		Co E1699, C3722
39229-1	Tyroler Galop		Co E1700, E2597
39230-1	Frykdal Polka		Co E1700, E2597
	Pavasario Rytas-Polka		Co E2581
	Wiosenny Poranek-Polka		Co E2769
	Šalies Grožybė		Co E2580
	Kalnų Aukštumose-Valcas		Co E2582
	as before		NY February 1, 1914

Co E2597, E2598 and E2769 are Polish releases; E2580, E2581, E2582 and E2706 are uncredited Lithuanian releases.

Hans Erichsen-Harry Syvertson

	Strile-Waltz		Vi trial
	Harry Syvertson-2d acn		NY July 13, 1920

B 24237-1	Skynd Dig-Reinlander	Vi 72891, HMV X1283
B 24238-1	Strile-Vals	Vi 72980, HMV X1408
	Žuvininkų {Fisherman's}-Valcas	Vi 77758
B 24239-1	Farmerliv-Reinlander (Hans Erichsen)	Vi 72801, HMV X1406
B 24240-1	Thyra-Vals (Hans Erichsen)	Vi rej
B 24241-1	Kadet-Polka (O. Berg)	Vi 72823
B 24242-1	Min Nye-Mazurka (Hans Erichsen)	Vi 72823
B 24243-1	Paa Kampen-Vals	Vi 72891, HMV X1283
B 24244-2	Tuna-Vals (Rydberg)	Vi rej
	as before	NY August 5, 1920

Hans Erichsen

B 24246-2	St. Hans-Vals (Hans Erichsen)'	Vi 72980, HMV X1408
	Vidurvasario {Midsummer}-Valcas	Vi 77758
		NY August 5, 1920

Vi 77758 is a Lithuanian issue.

34.6. Erickson And Anderson *accordion duet*

GE 12879-A	U-Båts {U-Boat}-Valsen	Ge 6230, Sil 5113, 8282, Supertone 9102
GE 12880-A	Klack {Heel}-Polka	Ge 6229, Sil 4098, 5115, 8282, Supertone 9102
		St. Paul June 27, 1927

34.7. Erikson Brothers *instrumental*

	Fjäderholmen	Co 22012-F
	Aina-Hambo	Co 22012-F
		NY 1925

34.8. Frank Brothers *accordion duet*

89977-1	Den Gula Paviljongen	
89979-2	Fjällbruden-Vals	Co 22007-F
		Co 22007-F
		NY May 1924

34.9. Arvid Franzen *accordion*

Franzen Och Berg

86808-2	Bökeviks Valsen	
86809-2	Kinnekulle-Schottisch	Co E7409
86810-1	Midsommarnatts Dröm	Co E7038, 7638
86811-3	Västgöta Sväng	Co E7107
86849-3	Lördags Valsen	Co E7038, 7638
86850-1	Kronobergs Regementes Paradmarsch	Co E7107
	Eric Berg-2d acn	Co E7409
		NY ca December 1920

B 25490-2	Sjömanskärlek {A Sailor's Love}-Vals	Vi rej
B 25491-2	Lundby-Vals	Vi 73128
B 25492-2	På Klack {On Heel}-Schottis (Alex. Prince)	Vi rej
B 25493-2	Norrlandsjentan-Mazurka	Vi rej
	as before	NY September 8, 1921

B 25490-5	Sjömanskärlek {A Sailor's Love}-Vals	Vi rej
B 25492-5	På Klack {On Heel}-Schottis (Alex. Prince)	Vi 73175
B 25493-4	Norrlandsjentan-Mazurka	Vi 73128
	as before	NY September 21, 1921

B 25490-7	Sjömanskärlek {A Sailor's Love}-Vals	Vi 73224
B 25811-2	Friare Valsen	Vi rej
B 25812-3	Livet I Finnskogarna {Life In The Woods Of Finland}-Vals	Vi 73175
	as before	NY November 21, 1921

Arvid Franzen-Charles Hillgren

B 25872-1	Till Nordpolen {To The North Pole}-Polka	Vi 73197
	own acn, Nathaniel Shilkret-cl	NY December 16, 1921

Arvid Franzen-Einar Holt

B 30193-3	Scandia Waltz (E. Holt)	Vi 77607
B 30194-2	The Heart Cabin-Waltz	Vi 77675
B 30195-2	Leap Year Hambo	Vi 77675
B 30196-3	Little Frieda And I (L. Brandstrup-L. Bonnard)	Vi 77607
	Einar Holt-2d acn, unk vln, p	NY June 16, 1924

BVE 33267-2	Carolina-Hambo (Anselm Johansson, op. 42)	Vi 78361
BVE 33268-2	Över Atlanten {Across The Atlantic} Vals (Einar Holt)	Vi 78361
BVE 33269-1	Ta Mej Hem {Take Me Home}-Schottis (Arvid Anderson)	
		Vi 78450, V-20080, 26-0021
BVE 33270-1	Inga Lill {Little Inga}-Hambo (Einar Bjorke)	Vi 78307

BVE 33271-1 Wooden Shoe-Polka (Axel Dahlquist)   Vi 78307
BVE 33272-2 Solskensvalser {Sunshine Waltzes} (J. Golden-G. Robbins)
                                                         Vi 78450, V-20080, 26-0021
        Einar Holt-2d acn   Camden, NJ September 11, 1925

W 105912-1 På Höganloft-Hambo   Co 22024-F, 7861
W 105913-1 Turallera-Vals   Co 22024-F, 7861
W 105914-2 Lätta Brisar-Vals   Co 22025-F
W 105915-2 Skärgårds Hambo   Co 22025-F
        as before   NY September 1925

BVE 35560-1 Botilda-Sjömansvals {Sailor's Waltz} (Ragnar Fred Stange)
                                                         Vi 78832, V-20081, 26-0022
BVE 35561-1 Midsummer Schottische {Janka No. 2 and No. 3}   Vi 78832
BVE 35562-1 Hälsa Dem Där Hemma {Greetings To Those At Home}-Vals
                 (Elith Worsing)   Vi 78926
BVE 35563-3 Innerst I Hjärtat Jag Alltid Har Burit Dej {Deepest In The Heart}
                 (Herman Cassell)   Vi 78926, Bb B-2726
        as before   NY July 1, 1926

W 108929-2 Bjurängshambo (P. Lindberg)   Co 22077-F
W 108930-2 Ett Sjömansbrev-Vals (Einar Westling)   Co 22077-F
W 108931-2 Styrmansvalsen   Co 22071-F, X13360
W 108932-2 Fåglarna Vid Bäcken-Schottis (Rob. Stulz)   Co 22071-F, X13360
        as before   NY March 1928

Franzen-Holt Quartet

BVE 40241-1 Flygar Valsen   Vi 80394
BVE 40242-2 På Skutö Brygga-Valsen¹   Vi rej
BVE 40242-3 På Skutö Brygga-Valsen¹   Vi 80214
BVE 40243-2 Jag Är Ute När Gumman Min Är Inne-Fox Trot¹ ² Vi 80214
BVE 40244-2 Rysk Dans {Rustic Dance}-Schottische¹ ²   Vi 80394
        Einar Holt-2d acn, unk vln, ¹xyl, ²traps   NY September 27, 1927

Franzen-Gadde Kvartet

W 109952-2 Sommarsol-Waltz (Berta Önnerberg)   Co 22095-F
W 109953-   Bonn-12an-Hambo (Einar Björke)   Co 22087-F
W 109955-2 S.O.S. Valsen (Sandberg)   Co 22087-F
                                                    NY November 1928

Franzen-Gadde Kvintet

W 110388-   Livet I Granhede-Hambo (Ragnar Sundquist)   Co 22099-F, DI24
W 110389-2 Seglarflickan-Waltz (Ralph Andry)   Co 22099-F
W 110390-1 Sjömansvalsen (Eric Wide)   Co 22093-F
W 110391-2 Polkan Går (Ryberg-Nymar)   Co 22095-F
W 110392-1 Dans I Lägret-Schottisch (Spelman Från Lerberg) Co 22093-F, DI24
                                                    NY February 1929

Franzen-Freeman Quartet

BS 071577-1	Bevä-rings {Draft}-Schottis (A. Franzen)	Std
BS 071578-1	Grann Kalas {Neighbour's Party}-Schottis (A. Franzen)	Std T-2052
BS 071579-1	Lilla Dottan {Little Girlies}-Hambo (A. Franzen)	Std T-2045
BS 071580-1	Krake Mala {Crow}-Jazzen Schottis (A. Franzen)	Std T-2077
BS 071581-1	Värmlands-Polka	Std T-2077
BS 071582-1	All-Svensk Vals Potpurri (A. Franzen)	Std T-2052
BS 071583-1	Ålandstöser-Schottis (A. Franzen)	Std
BS 071584-1	Dansa Medan Du Ar Ung {Dance While You Are Young}-Schottis	
	(A. Franzen)	Std T-2079

own, Harold Freeman-2 acn, S.A. Williams-el g, J. Genauso-sbs

NY October 22, 1941

34.10. Harold Och Hildur Freeman's Dragspel Orkester

BS 073641-1	Nordiska Nätter {Northern Lights} {Jerry The Seal}-Schottish	
	(M. Fryberg)	Vi V-20121, 26-0052
BS 073642-1	Skridsko {Ice Skaters} {Swinemunde}-Hambo (M. Fryberg)	
		Vi V-20119, 26-0050
BS 073643-1	Dans På Viking-Schottish (Harold Freeman)	Vi V-20118, 26-0049
BS 073644-1	Höga Klackar {High Heels}-Schottish (Hildur Freeman)	
		Vi V-20119, 26-0050
BS 073645-1	Hangö-Schottish (M. Fryberg)	Vi V-20122, 26-0053
BS 073646-1	Slumrande Rosor {Sleeping Roses} {In Hamburg Bei Nacht}-Waltz	
	(M. Fryberg)	Vi V-20120, 26-0051
BS 073647-1	Vilda Skogar {Wild Woods} {Varnamo}-Schottish (Harold Freeman)	
		Vi V-20120, 26-0051
BS 073648-1	Dans Vid Klarälven {Dance By The Clear Stream}-Polka	
	(Harold Freeman)	Vi V-20118, 26-0049

Harold Freeman, Harold M. Kirchstein, H. Burgeson-3 acn, Pawlo
Zamulenko-sbs   NY March 24, 1942

34.11. Hagstead's Orchestra

W 107179-3	Gripsholmsschottisch	Co 22046-F
W 107180-1	Hemlandstoner-Potpuri	Co 22046-F
		NY October 1926

34.12. R. Hannell & E. Gylling *accordion duet*

W 107009-2	Wimmerby Mazurka	Co 22045-F, 7872
W 107010-2	Sverige Är Bäst Ändå-Vals	Co 22045-F, 7872
W 107011-2	Te Dans Med Ölandstösera-Polka	Co 22036-F
W 107012-3	Varje Liten Tanke-Vals	Co 22036-F
		Chicago July 1926

34.13. Kurt Henning *accordion*

Kurt Henning And Sam Carlsson

89177-1	Den Farliga Månen-Vals	Co E9028
89178-1	Det Tycker Nästan Alla	Co E9056
89179-1	Kullernas Vals	Co E9056
89180-2	Flickan Med Kortklippt Hår-Fox Trot	Co E9028
	Sam Carlsson-2d acn	NY April 1923

Henning Och Frank

S 72331-B	Släckta Fyrar-Vals	Ok 19104
S 72332-A	Ping-Pong-Hambo	Ok 19105
S 72333-A	Ska Vi Inte Ta' Å Jazza-Fox Trot	Ok 19104
	Im Hotel Zur Grünen Wiese-Fox Trot	Od 10313
S 72334-A	Lilla Frida Och Jag-Fox Trot	Ok 19105
	Eleine Frieda-Fox Trot	Od 10313
	Frank-2d acn	NY February 23, 1924

S 72463-A	Avestaforsens Brus-Vals	Ok 19114
S 72464-A	Stockholm Hambo	Ok 19114
	as before	NY April 1924

Kurt Henning Trio

W 107064-2	Sommargille {At The Picnic}-Vals (J. Anderson)	Co 22039-F
W 107065-2	Lilla Lola Lo {Lula Lu}-Fox Trot (Clayton)	Co 22039-F
W 107066-2	I Vinternatten {In A Winter Night}-Vals (John Blom)	Co 22042-F, 7870
W 107067-1	Dansbacillen-Fox Trot (Harold De Bozi)	Co 22042-F, 7870
		NY August 1926

34.14. Einar Holt *accordion (ca 1900-1977)*

105048-	Avestaforsens Brus-Vals	Co 22008-F, 7625
105049-1	Undan Med Gubbarna-Vals	Co 22008-F, 7625
	Släckta Fyrar-Vals	Co 22009-F
	Jazz Gossen-Fox Trot	Co 22009-F
		NY ca July 1, 1924

Eddie Holt Og Harold Ekeland

W 113832-2	Hankø-Valsen (Kristian Haugen-Gunnar Kristoffersen)¹ [in Norwegian]	
		Co 22176-F
W 113833-2	Mazurka Kokett-Hambo (Eddie Holt)	Co 22176-F, GN235
W 113834-2	Duryea Polka (Eddie Holt)	Co 22177-F, GN235
W 113835-1	Holttempo-Polka (Eddie Holt)	Co 22180-F, GN237
W 113844-2	Rosspiggen-Schottische (E. Olzen)	Co 22180-F, GN237
W 113845-1	Radio Lyttervalsen (Chr. Hartmann-Arne Svendsen)	Co 22177-F
	own, Harold Ekeland (b. 1907)-2 acn, ¹Magnhild Fjeldheim-vo	
		NY ca January 1934

34: Scandinavian

34.15. J. Jacobson Och Henry Magnuson *accordion duet*

84029-1	Kirta {Harvest Feast}-Polka	Co E3886
84030-2	Gök {Cuckoo}-Valsen (Jonasson)	Co E3886
84031-1	Tjosan {T Jason}-Hambo	Co E3930
84032-1	Hemlands Toner-Schottische	Co E3930
84034-1	Dala Polka	Co E4130
84037-1	Nya Dragspelsvalsen	Co E4130
84038-1	Nya Kostervalsen	Co E4157
		NY ca February 1918

Some copies of Co E3886 as ACCORDION DUET with titles in English only; other copies spell the second artist's name as MAGNUSSA; some copies of Co E3930 as HANDKLAVERDUETT

34.16. Eddy Jahrl *accordion (1901-1977)*

E. Jahrl

W 106539-2	En Sjömansvals	Co 22031-F
	Merimiesvalssi	Co DI59
W 106540-2	Skymnings Tankar-Polka	Co 22031-F
	Hämärä Polkka {Thoughts At Twilight} (E. Jahrl)	Co 3030-F, 16139
	Ilta Hämärässä-Polkka	Co DI59
	acn solo	NY March 1926

Jahrl Nyhetskvintetten

W 106997-2	Gökvalsen	Co 22038-F, 7723, GN63
	Kukačka-Valčik	Co 92-F
	Käki-Valssi	Co 3043-F, 13353
	Cuckoo Waltz	Co 12059-F, RZ G9336
	Kuku-Walc	Co 18177-F
	Kukavica-Valček	Co 25051-F
W 106998-2	Livet I Finnskogarna-Vals	Co 22038-F, 7784, GN63
	Kevät Suomen Metsissä-Valssi	Co 3043-F, Sävel SÄLP 662(33)
W 106999-1	Vals Ombord	Co 22041-F, GN124
	Valssi Laivan Kannella	Co DI57
W 107100-2	Jubileumsschottis	Co 22050-F, 7633
	Warszawska Polka	Co 18177-F
	Vzajemnost-Sotis	Co 25051-F
W 107101-2	Inga-Vals	Co 22044-F, 7815, GN62
W 107102-2	När Mor Var Ung-Vals	Co 22044-F, 7815, GN62
	Young Ladies-Waltz	Co 12055-F
W 107103-1	Vals Allra Bäst	Co 22041-F, 7869
	Parhain Valssi	Co DI57
W 107104-2	Greetings From Home	Co 12045-F
	Koti	Co 16003
W 107105-1	Echo-Mazurka	Co 12045-F
	Kaiku-Masurkka	Co 16003
W 107106-2	Avestaforsens Brus-Vals	Co 22050-F, 7633, GN219

2655

The Queen Of The Waves-Waltz   Co 12047-F
own acn, unk vln, fl, xyl/bells, g   NY July 1926

Co 92-F and 25051-F as COLUMBIA HUDEBNI KVINTET, 3043-F and Sävel SÅLP 662 as COLUMBIAN SOITTO KVINTETTI, 12047-F, 12055-F and 12059-F as COLUMBIA QUINTETTE, 18177-F as INSTRUMENTOWY KWARTET "WARSZAWA"

E. Jahrl

W 107125-	Donaus Vågor (Ivanovici)	Co 22051-F, 7631
	Tonavan Aallot-Valssi	Co 3033-F, 16141
W 107126-2	Över Vågorna (Rosas)	Co 22051-F, 7631
	Yli Aaltojen-Valssi	Co 3033-F, 16141
	acn solo	NY September 1926

E. Jahrl Trio

W 107175-1	Låt Oss Vara Glada-Polka	Co 22058-F
	Šefcovská Polka	Co 84-F
	Bodimo Veseli-Polka	Co 25054-F
W 107176-2	Walle Wille Wall-Vals	Co 22047-F, 7873
W 107177-2	Zigenare-Polka	Co 22047-F, 7873
W 107178-2	Helge Åns Stränder-Vals	Co 22058-F
	Na Adriatski Břehu-Valčík	Co 84-F
	Na Jadranski Obali-Valček	Co 25054-F
	own acn, others unk	NY October 1926

Co 84-F as NÁSTROJOVÉ TRIO, 25054-F as KRANJSKI INSTRUMENTAL TRIO

Columbia Nyhetskvintetten

W 107610-2	Hälsa Dem Därhemma (E. Worsing)'	Co 26048-F
W 107611-1	Alla Jäntor Ä' Lika (E. Rolf)'	Co 26048-F
W 107612-2	Lilla Frida Och Jag-Fox Trot (Leon Bonnard)	Co 22053-F
W 107613-	Carolina-Hambo (Anselm Johansson) Co 22053-F, 12055-F, DI198, GN124	
	own acn, unk vln, fl, g, xyl/dm, 'chorus	NY January 1927

Co 12055-F as COLUMBIA QUINTETTE, GN124 as E. JAHRL NYHETSKVINTETT

E. Jahrl Nyhetskvintett

W 108188-2	Vårglädje-Hambo (Formanowski)	Co 22060-F, 7879
W 108189-	Skörde-Fest-Polka	Co 22059-F, 7723
	Harvest Fest	Co 12059-F, RZ G9336
W 108190-2	Hammarforsens Brus-Vals	Co 22059-F, 7784, GN219
W 108191-1	Hem Till Justina-Vals (G. Lundberg)	Co 22060-F, 7879
		NY June 1927

Co 12059-F as COLUMBIA QUINTETTE

E. Jahrl

W 108241-1	Barrikaadeille-Marssi {Ikävä Synnyinseudulle}	Co 3057-F, 16160
W 108242-2	Sorretun Elämä-Vals (H.J. Reinikainen)	Co 3057-F, 16160
	acn solo	NY August 1927

E. Jahrls Nyhetskvintett

W 108263-2	Docklisa-Fox Trot	Co 22061-F, 16207
	The Happy Girl {Püppchen Liese}-Fox Trot	Co 12064-F
W 108264-2	Gud Vet Vem Som Kysser Dig Nu-Vals (J.E. Howard)	Co 22063-F
	I Wonder Who's Kissing Her Now {Tausend Küsse}-Waltz	Co 12064-F
W 108265-1	Bättre Och Bättre Dag För Dag-Fox Trot (Mark Strong)	Co 22063-F
W 108266-2	Granbacka Valsen (H. Marcussen)	Co 22061-F
		NY August 1927

Co 12064-F as COLUMBIA QUINTETTE

Jahrl Instrumental Quintet

BVE 40146-1	Promenade Polka	Vi 80395
BVE 40147-1	Var Barmhjärtig-Waltz	Vi 80395
BVE 40148-1	Min Egen Lilla Sommarvisa {My Own Little Summer Tune}-Hambo	
		Vi 80648, V-20088, 26-0028, Bb B-2728
BVE 40149-2	Efter Balen {After The Ball} (C.K. Harris)	
		Vi 80648, V-20088, 26-0028
	own acn, unk vln, fl/sax, xyl/dm, g	NY October 5, 1927

E. Jahrl Nyhetskvintett

W 108583-3	Minnen Ur Finlands Dalar-Hambo	Co 22066-F, 7796
	In The Valleys Of Finland-Mazurka	Co 12070-F
W 108584-1	Kostervalsen (Hellström)	Co 22066-F, 7769
	On Board-Waltz	Co 12070-F, 38003-F
	Kostervalssi	Co 3068-F, 7801
W 108585-1	Spelmansvalsen	Co 22067-F, 7797
W 108586-1	Friarevalsen	Co 22067-F, 7797
	own acn, others unk	NY November 1927

Eddy Jahrl's Kvintett

This group is identified as CHRIS TAULOW'S SWEDISH ORCHESTRA in the CBS files.

W 400106-A	Konvaljens Afsked-Waltz (Otto Lindwall)	Ok 19233
	Lelija-Valcas	Ok 26060
W 400107-A	Roslags Låt-Schottish (N. Stenberg)	Ok 19233
	Žvirblelis-Šocas	Ok 26060
	Glueck Auf!-Schottisch	Ok 10485
W 400108-A	Om Lördag-Hambo (E. Bjorke)	Ok 19237
W 400109-B	Hjärterö-Valsen	Ok 19237

Schneegloeckschen-Waltzer   Ok 10485
own acn, unk vln, fl, xyl/dm, g   NY February 28, 1928

Ok 10495 as SCHWEDISCHES TANZORCHESTER, 26060 as ŠOKIU ORKESTRA

Jahrl Instrumental Quintet

BVE 43683-2	Styrmans (Mate's)-Vals Vi 81202, 81532, V-20075, 26-0017, 18120	
	Marynarz Walc	Vi 81203
BVE 43684-2	Bohuslänska Sjömans Valsen (Sailors Waltz From Bohuslan)	
	Vi 81509, V-20077, 26-0018, Bb B-2727	
BVE 43685-2	Skogens Blomster (Forest Flower)-Schottis (Albert)	
	Vi 81509, V-20077, 26-0018, Bb B-2727, Banjar BR-1840(33)	
BVE 43686-2	Balen I Karlstad (The Ball In Karlstadt)-Schottis	
	Vi 81201, 81532, V-20075, 26-0017, 18120	
	Wesołe Czasy	Vi 81203, V-16532
BVE 43687-2	Livet I Finnskogarna (Life In The Finnish Woods)-Vals	
	Vi 81456, V-20076, Bb B-2734	
	Na Breg-Valček	Vi 81204
	own acn, unk vln, sax, g, traps	NY April 30, 1928

Vi 81203 and V-16532 (Polish) as INSTRUMENTOWY KWINTET "WARSZAWA", 81456 as INTERNATIONAL OCTETTE, 81204 (Slovenian) as VICTOR HUDEBNI KVINTET, 18120 (Canadian) as INSTRUMENTAL QUINTET

E. Jahrl Nyhetskvintett

W 109413-3	Signe-Vals	Co 22076-F
W 109414-1	Ann-Maries Första Bal-Vals	Co 22074-F, 16207
	Ann-Marie's First Ball-Waltz	Co 12085-F
W 109415-2	Flygare-Valsen (Winter-Sylvain)	Co 22074-F, 16207
	Airplane Waltz	Co 12085-F
W 109416-2	Nyårs-Hambo (Sven Runö)	Co 22076-F
	own acn, others unk	NY June 1928
	Sol Ute, Sol Inne-Vals	Co 22080-F
	Horgalåten Från Hambo	Co 22080-F, GN16
		NY 1928

E. Jahrls Nyhetskvintett

W 109614-1	Sunlight Waltz	Co 12089-F, 38003-F
	Päivänpaiste-Valssi	Co 3089-F, 16168
	To Fos Tou Iliou-Waltz	Co 7041-F
W 109615-1	A Morning In Autumn	Co 12089-F
	Syysaamuna-Masurkka	Co 3089-F, 16168
	Fthinoporini Proia-Mazoryka	Co 7041-F
W 109616-1	Vintergatan-Vals (J. Sylvain)	Co 22083-F
	The Milky Way-Waltz	Co 12110-F
W 109617-1	Potpourri Över Svenska Julpolskor	Co 22082-F, 22146-F
	own acn, others (inluding sg) unk	NY August 1928

Co 3089-F and 16168 as JAHRLIN UUSI KVINTETTI, 7041-F as COLUMBIA NOVELTY QUINTETTE, 12089-F, 12110-F and 38003-F as E. JAHRL'S NOVELTY QUINTETTE

W 109724-1   I Sjunde Himlen-Vals (G. Enders)   Co 22083-F
W 109725-2   Vind För Våg (Lindberg-Stevens)'   Co 26085-F
W 109726-2   Uti Ljusa Sommarnatt-Schottis (Sandell-Pehrson)'   Co 26085-F
W 109727-2   Potpourri Över Svenska Gånglåtar   Co 22082, 22147-F, 16210
              own acn, unk vln, bj, g, bbs, 'G. Lundqvist-vo   NY September 1928

W 110067-2   Lundby-Valsen   Co 22088-F, 3102-F, 16118
                Medley Waltz   Co 12097-F
W 110068-2   Lördagsnatt-Schottisch (S.C. Westbye)'   Co 26087-F
W 110069-1   Lördagsnatt-Schottisch (S.C. Westbye)   Co 22089-F
              own acn, unk tp, vln, xyl/bells, g, bbs, 'Axel Larson, R.
              Brändlund-vo   NY November 1928

Co 12097-F as E. JAHRL'S NOVELTY QUINTETTE

W 110100-   Du-Vals (G. Enders)'
W 110101-1   Du-Vals (G. Enders)   Co 26087-F
W 110102-2   Alte Kameraden {Old Comrades}-Marsch   Co 22089-F
                                                      Co 22088-F, 12097-F, 16118
                Vanhat Toverit   Co 3102-F
              as before   NY December 1928

Co 3102-F as JAHRLIN UUSI KVINTETTI, 12097-F as E. JAHRL'S NOVELTY QUINTET

W 110368-1   En Skärgårdstös-Waltz (Sven Runö)   Co 22098-F
W 110369-2   Beværings-Hambo (Sven Runö)   Co 22094-F, DI25
                Sotilaan Tanssi   Co 3113-F, 16227
                Military Dance   Co 12104-F, 16232
W 110370-1   Mustalainen-Waltz (Igor Borganoff)   Co 22094-F
                The Gypsy Waltz   Co 12104-F, 16232
                Mustalaisen Valssi   Co 3113-F, 16227
W 110371-1   På Skansen   Co 22098-F, DI25
                                                                       NY February 1929

Co 3113-F and 16227 as JAHRLIN UUSI KVINTETTI, 12104-F and 16232 as E. JAHRL'S
NOVELTY QUINTETTE

Jahrl Quintette

BVE 50938-2   Min Lilla Putte {My Little Darling}-Polka (Jean Gilbert)
                                               Vi V-20005, V-10, 25-0004, 26-0001
BVE 50939-2   Brud {Bride}-Valsen (Goran Svenning)   Vi V-20009, 26-0005
BVE 50940-1   Hemlands Toner {Tunes From Home}-Schottische   Vi V-20005, V-10,
                             25-0004, 26-0001, Bb B-2728, Banjar BR-1840(33)
BVE 50941-2   Nya Dragspels {New Accordion}-Valsen   Vi V-20009, 26-0005
              own acn, unk vln, fl, xyl, g, tuba   NY March 14, 1929

W 110576-2   Två Unga Hjärtan-To Unge Hjerter
                 {Kronprins Olavs Och Princessan Märthas Vals} (Georg Enders)
                                                                                    Co 22096-F
W 110577-2   Törs Inte Du, Så Törs Inte Ja'-Schottische, ur Södra Teaterns
                 Nyårsrevy 1929, "Det Ligger I Indien" (Helan)   Co 22096-F

Joll' Et Uskalla Sinä, Niin En Uskalla Minä-Schottische

		Co 3145-F, DI63
W 110578-2	Värmlands-Hambo (N. Melander)	Co 22106-F
	Uudenmaan-Masurkka	Co 3145-F
W 110579-2	Hembygdsminnen-Waltz (transcription of "Säterjentens Söndag")	Co 22106-F
	(Sigurd Hanmel)	NY May 1929

Co 3145-F as JAHRLIN UUSI KVINTETTI

E. Jahrls Kvintett

W 111010-2	Styrmans Valsen (Marcusson)	Co 22104-F, DI117, GN97, GN892
	The Steerman's Waltz	Co 12121-F
	Marynarz Walc	Co 18349-F
	Perämiehen Valssi	Co DI98
W 111013-2	Brud-Valsen (Göran Svenning)	Co 22107-F, DI195, GN16
W 111014-2	Te' Dans Mä Karlstatösera-Waltz (Erik Uppström)	Co 22104-F, DI117
	The Ball In Karlstad-Waltz	Co 12121-F
	Wesołe Czasy-Walc	Co 18349-F
	Naantalin Aurinko-Sottiisi	Co DI98
	Karlstadtreinlander	Co GN97
W 111015-2	Nya Dragspelsvalsen	Co 22107-F, DI194
		NY August 1929

Co 12121-F as E. JAHRL'S NOVELTY QUINTETTE, 18349-F as ORKIESTRA WARSZAWSKA

W 111128-2	Helgdagskväll-Waltz (Einar Westling)	Co 22112-F, DI194
W 111129-1	Lilla Dottan-Hambo (Sten Anderson)	Co 22112-F, DI194
W 111130-	När Bröllopsklockor Ringa-Waltz (Bert Carsten)	Co 22103-F
W 111131-2	Vi Ska' Segla Hela Livet Samman (Walter Harrison)	Co 22103-F
		NY September 1929

Co 22103-F as JAHRL'S ORCHESTRA

E. Jahrl's Dansorkester

W 111936-2	Säg Det I Toner-Waltz (J. Sylvain)	Co 22115-F
W 111937-2	Linnea-Schottisch (Edwin Jahrl)	Co 22115-F
W 111938-3	Adriana-Polka	Co 22121-F, DI177
W 111939-3	Emigrantvalsen	Co 22121-F, DI177
	own acn, unk vln, 2 sax, bbs	NY ca April 1930

Jahrls Orkester

W 112167-	När Näckrosen Blommar-Waltz (Sven Du Reitz)	Co 22129-F
W 112168-	Stein Song-March (E.A. Fenstad)[1]	Co 26117-F
W 112170-1	Motboksägarnas Egen Vals (Wehle-Cassel)[1]	Co 26117-F
W 112171-2	Valborgsmässo-Hambo (Knut Johan)	Co 22129-F
	[1]Jack Wick-vo	NY June 1930

Jahrls Dansorkester

W 112506-2	Kärlekens Blomma-Vals (Edwin Zoë)	Co 22133-F
W 112507-3	Jag Skänker Er Violer-Vals (Alexander Yrneh)	Co 22137-F
W 112508-2	Släck Alla Ljus Och Ställ Dörren På Glant (Frank Talboth)	Co 22137-F
	Lauantaijazzi-Fox Trot	Co DI214
W 112509-1	Totalisator-Jazzen-Vals (Karl Wehle)	Co 22133-F
		NY November 1930

Jahrl's Novelty Quintette

W 112937-2	For You, from "Two Hearts In 3/4 Time"	Co 12146-F
	Sinäkin-Fox Trot	Co DI250
W 112938-1	Two Hearts In Waltz Time-Waltz (Robert Stolz)	Co 12146-F
	Kaksi Sydäntä Valssin Tahdissa-Valssi	Co DI250
		NY April 1931

Co DI250 as JAHRLIN UUSI KVINTETTI

Jahrl's Nyhetskvintett

W 112999-2	Svenska Ringdanser-Potpourri	Co 22146-F
W 113000- (W 130410)	Folklåtar-Potpourri	Co 22147-F
		NY ca June 1931

Jahrl & Lager

W 113173-1	Dansen Går På Frösön-Waltz (Sven Landahl)	Co 22151-F
W 113174-1	Julbal På Landet-Schottis	Co 22151-F
W 113175-	Målarhio {Alla Målares Vals} (Henrik Witt)	Co 22156-F
W 113176- (W 130569)	Backes Polka (E. Jahrl)	Co 22156-F
	John Lager-2d acn	NY September 1931

Jahrl's Trio

W 113359-1	Sjömansfröjd-Waltz (Brunnkvist & Co.)	Co 22159-F
	Sailor's Joy-Waltz	Co 12180-F, RZ G21475
W 113360-1	Kyss-Valsen (Eric Julander)	Co 22174-F
W 113361-1	Lottas Hambo (Eric Friberg)	Co 22174-F
W 113362-1	Hej Pojkar-Schottische	Co 22159-F
	Always Happy!	Co 12180-F, RZ G21475
	own acn, unk vln, g	NY February 1932

Co 12180-F as INSTRUMENTAL TRIO, RZ G21475 as REGAL INSTRUMENTAL TRIO

Jahrl's Orkester

W 113437-1	Vasa Ordens Invignings; Paradmarsch (Axel W.E. Austin)	Co 22161-F
W 113438-1	Amerikas Söner Och Döttrar Av Sverige	Co 22161-F
W 113439-1	Östan Om Månen Och Västan Om Solen-Waltz (Jules Sylvain)	
		Co 22164-F, DI268
W 113440-1	Bondstugan-Schottische	Co 22164-F, DI268
W 113441-1	Rorsmannens Sång-Waltz (Henry Freeman)	Co 22181-F

W 113442-1   På Slåtterkalas-Hambo (Klang Johan)   Co 22181-F, GN236
NY March 1932

Co 22161-F as E. JAHRL'S MILITÄR BAND, GN236 as JAHRLS NYHETTSKVINTETT

Jahrl's Instrumental Kvartett

W 113560-   Nu Är Det Lördag Igen-Vals (Gunnar Johanssom)
                                    Co 22178-F, Banjar BR-1840(33)
W 113561-1   En Vårdrill-Hambo (Tom Wilson)   Co 22168-F
W 113562-1   Ölandstöser-Schottische (Otto Hultner)
                          Co 22178-F, GN236, Banjar BR-1840(33)
W 113563-1   Alla Glada Gårdsmusikanters Vals (Gosta Stevens)   Co 22168-F
NY June 1932

Co GN236 as JAHRLS NYHETSKVINTETT

Jahrl-Stein Orchestra

BS 83331-1   Midsommarnatt {Midsummer Night}-Vals (Bert Carsten)
                                        Vi V-24087, 26-1005
          Keskikesän Yö-Valssi   Vi V-4146, 26-6001
BS 83332-1   Vårens Rop {Call Of Spring}-Waltz (Wm. E. Stein) Vi V-24089, 26-1007
          Kevät Kutsuu-Valssi   Vi V-4148
BS 83333-1   Tivoli-Hambo (O. Baza) Vi V-24085, V-4144, V-4169, 26-1003, 26-6014
BS 83334-   Gubben Och Gumman-Schottis (arr Wm. E. Stein)   Vi V-24089, 26-1007
          Ukko Ja Akka-Sotiisi   Vi V-4148
BS 83335-1   After Bröllopet {After The Wedding}-Schottis (arr Wm. E. Stein)
                                        Vi V-24085, 26-1003
          Häitten Jälkeen-Sotiisi   Vi V-4144, V-4169, 26-6014
BS 83336-1   Här Är Inget Vilohem {This Is No Resting Place}-Polka
                                        Vi V-24085, 26-1005
          Miksi Lepäät-Polkka   Vi V-4146, 26-6001
          own acn, unk vln, sax, p   NY June 21, 1934

From this point, the artist spells his last name JARL.

Jarl Trio

BS 028363-1R   Dragspelslåt-Schottische (Jean Clæsson)   Vi V-20083, 26-0025
BS 028364-1R   Spel Opp-Schottische (Otto Hultner)   Vi V-20083, 26-0025
BS 028365-1R   Morfars-Vals   Vi V-20084, 26-0024
BS 028366-1R   En Dragspelslåt-Hambo (C. Wickman)   Vi V-20087, 26-0027
BS 028367-1R   I Friveckan-Schottische (F. Sandstrom)   Vi V-20084, 26-0024
BS 028368-1R   Gammal-Polka   Vi V-20087, 26-0027
          own acn, unk xyl, g   NY November 3, 1938

Jarl-Franzen Quartette

BS 041730-1   En Dala Hambo {A Hambo From Dala}   Vi V-20090, 26-0029
BS 041731-1   Hipp Hopp {Hop-Skip}-Hambo   Vi V-20092, 26-0031
BS 041732-1   Dans På Landsvägen {Dance On The Country Road}-Schottische
                                        Vi V-20094, 26-0032
BS 041733-1   Halvan Går {Second Drink}-Polka   Vi V-20094, 26-0032

```
                  We Snie-Polka                              Vi V-16532, 25-9114
BS 041734-1  Dans På M.S. Kungsholm {Dance Aboard The Kungsholm}-Schottische
                                                             Vi V-20091, 26-0030
BS 041735-1  Klackar I Taket {With Heels On The Ceiling}-Schottische
                                                             Vi V-20092, 26-0031
BS 041736-1  Grasshopporna {Grasshopper}-Polka              Vi V-20091, 26-0030
             Z Konca Swiata {From The End Of The World}-Polka
                                                             Vi V-16496, 25-9103
BS 014737-1  Klarinett Polka Vi V-20090, V-186, V-6428, 25-0047, 25-4074, 26-0029
             Dziaduniu {Grandpop}-Polka                     Vi V-16496, 25-9103
             Arvid Franzen-2d acn, unk g, sbs               NY  October 10, 1939
```

Vi V-16496, V-16532, 25-9103 and 25-9114 as ORKIESTRA HARMONISTÓW, V-186 and 25-0047 as VICTOR ACCORDION BAND

```
BS 047947-1  Upp I Luften {Up In The Air}-Schottische       Vi V-20099, 26-0034
BS 047948-1  Tokiga Kalles {Crazy Kalles}-Polka             Vi V-20099, 26-0034
BS 047949-1  Björneborgarnes-March                              Vi V-20098
BS 047950-1  Finska Rytteriets-March                            Vi V-20098
             as before                                      NY  March 13, 1940

BS 053683-1  Friska Takter {Snappy Rhythm}-Polka (Karl Pehrman)
                                                             Vi V-20104, 26-0038
BS 056384-1  Stampa Takten Pojkar-Schottische (Karl Pehrman) Vi V-20105, 26-0039
BS 056385-1  En Sväng På Bryggan {Dancing On The Dock}-Hambo (Karl Pehrman)
                                                             Vi V-20104, 26-0038
BS 056386-1  Expo Vals (Karl Pehrman)                       Vi V-20105, 26-0039
             as before                                      NY  October 4, 1940
```

34.17. Bob Johnson & Einar Erickson *(Bob & Erik); instrumental*

```
W 110708-1   New Sweden-Vals (Bob Johnson)                          Co 22110-F
W 110709-2   Sällinge-Hambo (Einar Erickson)                        Co 22110-F
W 110710-2   En Bondvals                                            Co 22097-F
W 110711-1   Ljusen-Hambo                                           Co 22097-F
                                                             NY  May 1929
```

34.18. Hugo Johnson *accordion*

```
             Jämtlandsvals                                          Vi trial
                                                             NY  October 18, 1915
```

Hugo Johnson-Matti Söderlund

```
B 21123-2    Var Barmhjärtig-Russian Waltz (Bakaleinikow)           Vi 69922
B 21124-2    På Fäbovallen-Schottische (I. Söderblum)               Vi 69922
B 21125-2    Norrskenet-Mazurka (F. Holmberg)                       Vi rej
             Matti Söderlund-2d acn                         NY  November 28, 1917

B 21757-3    Dallrande Blad {Trembling Leaves}-Waltz (G. Holmberg)  Vi rej
B 21758-2    Dragon-Polka                                           Vi rej
B 21759-2    Bergsklockan-Schottische (Kinkel)                      Vi rej
```

B 21760-2   Rospiggen-Polka (Osterman)   Vi rej
              as before   NY April 10, 1918

Herr Och Fru Hugo Johnson

          Dallrande Blad; Norrlands Polka   Vi trial
                                          NY December 26, 1918

B 22708-2   Norrlands Polka (I. Soderblom)   Vi rej
B 22709-2   Dallrande Blad {Trembling Leaves}-Waltz (G. Holmberg)   Vi 73029
B 22710-2   Bergsklockan-Schottische (G. Kinkel)   Vi rej
B 22711-2   Konvaljens Avsked {The Lily-Of-The-Valley's Farewell}-Waltz
              (Lindblad)   Vi 73029
              Nina Johnson-2d acn   NY March 12, 1919

Nina Och Hugo Johnson

86966-2   John Johnson's Wedding-Komisk Sång¹   Co E7132
86967-   Pelle I Flakabrask   Co E7377
86968-   Frykdaldans No. 2   Co E7377
86969-2   Wilhelmina-Poka   Co E7132
86970-2   Blinda Kalles Vals   Co E7255
              as before, ¹Hugo Johnson-vo   NY January 1921

H. Johnson

87018-2   Medley Of Folksongs   Co E7167
87019-2   Summernight Waltz   Co E7167
              acn solos   NY January 1921

Nina Och Hugo Johnson

87021-   På Klavere   Co E7169
87022-2   På Isen-Polka   Co E7255
87023-   Bergsklockan   Co E7169
              Nina Johnson-2d acn   NY January 1921

87283-2   Dallrande Blad-Vals (Holmberg)   Co E7440
87284-1   Norrlands Polka (Söderberg)   Co E7440
87285-1   Jämtlandsvals   Co E7833
              as before   NY ca April 1921

Hugo Johnson

9961   Hambo; Fjällnäs Polska; Dalpolska-Hemlandstoner {Homeland Tunes}
                                                Ed rej
9962   Kristiania Valsen   Ed rej
9963   Finska Valsen {Finnish Waltz} (D. Hellström)   Ed rej
                                        NY January 23, 1925

9961   Hambo; Fjällnäs Polska; Dalpolska-Hemlandstoner {Homeland Tunes}
                                           Ed 59013
9962   Kristiania Valsen   Ed 59012
9963   Finska Valsen {Finnish Waltz} (D. Hellström)   Ed 59012

9983	Lockaren {The Call}-Vals (C. Mathisen)	Ed 59013
9984	Fiskarvals Från Bohuslän {The Fisherman's Waltz} (D. Hellström)	
9985	Kostervalsen {Koster Island Waltz} (D. Hellström)	Ed 59014
		Ed 59014
		NY January 30, 1925

10943	Släckta Fyrar-Vals (Fred Winter)	Ed rej
10944	Flickan Med Kortklippt Hår-Fox Trot (Ernst Rolf)	Ed rej
		NY April 27, 1926

10943	Släckta Fyrar-Vals (Fred Winter)	Ed 59015
10944	Flickan Med Kortklippt Hår-Fox Trot (Ernst Rolf)	Ed 59015
10953	Margit Vals (R. Berger)	Ed 59016
10954	Gula Paviljongen-Fox Trot (John Redland)	Ed 59016
		NY April 30, 1926

34.19. Fred Johnzen *accordion*

W 112810-2	Oslo-Valsen (Hugo Johnson)	
W 112811-2	Bonn Jazz-Schottische (Hjalmer Pitterson)	Co 22138-F
W 112812-2	Livet I Finnskogarna-Vals (Karl Karlson)	Co 22142-F
W 112813-2	Minnen Från Kusten-Schottische	Co 22142-F
		Co 22138-F
		NY February 1931

34.20. John Lager *accordion*

Lager & Olson

43560-1	Lockarenvalsen-Norsk Bondvals {Norwegian Peasant Waltz}	
	Šuhajko Moj-Valčik	Co E2863, 7634
43561-3	Kostervalsen	Co E3592
43562-1	Rostofsky Polka (Rostofsky)	Co E2833
	Slaviček-Polka	Co E2833
43563-1	Lundbyvalsen (Johnson)	Co E3591
43564-1	En Liten Skälm (Dizzsso)	Co E2863
43565-2	Finska Valsen (Hellström)	Co E2775
43566-2	Skogens Blomster (Albert)	Co E2776
43567-1	Bond Valsen (Prince)	Co E2776
	Primer Vals De Aldeano	Co E2777
	Sedlacký-Valčik	Co C3604
43568-1	Brud Valsen (Pinnet)	Co E3591
	Svadobný Valčik	Co E2775
43569-1	Min Lilla Putte-Vals (Hellström)	Co E3592
43774-1	Uppsala Minne Valsen	Co E2777
	Eric Olson-2d acn	Co E3193
		NY late 1915

Co E3591 and E3592 (Slovak) as HARMONIKOVÉ DUETT

John Lager-Eric Olson

	Koster Valsen as before		Vi trial NY July 24, 1916
B 18478-2	Kyss Vals (Kiss Waltz)		Vi 69079
B 18479-2	Balen I Karlstad {The Ball In Karlstad}-Schottische		Vi 69133
B 18480-2	Hjärterö Vals		Vi 69079
B 18481-1	Styrmansvals	Vi 69133,	Banjar BR-1840(33)
	as before		NY October 3, 1916

44540-1	Luna Polka (Kiren)	Co E3145, C3606
44541-2	Hopp Hopp-Polka-Mazurka	Co E3339
44542-2	Midsommar Valsen (Hellström)	Co E3194
	En Pleno Verano-Vals	Co C3630
44543-4	Nya Bondvalsen (Pinet)	Co E3255
	Segundo Vals Del Aldeano	Co C3607
44544-1	Haga Schottisch (Backman)	Co E3193, 7635
44545-1	Fiskarvals Från Bohuslän	Co E3194
44546-2	Wäddövalsen	Co E3339
44547-2	Bavarian Waltz (Hellström)	Co E3145, C3606
44548-3	Lilla Kärestan Min-Vals	Co E3255
	Mi Noviecita-Vals	Co C3607
	as before	NY ca January 1917

	Vida Triste-Vals	Co C3604
	El Templo De Los Pastores-Polka	Co C3608
	Arriba Y Abajo-Vals	Co C3608
		NY 1917

These three Spanish titles are almost certainly drawn from the above session.

58469-1	Prairieliljan	Co E4407
	Ant Šešupes Kranto	Co E3626
58470-1	Styrmansvalsen	Co E3643
58471-1	Hesselby Steppen (Kul)	Co E3587
58472-1	Hjärterö Valsen (Hellström)	Co E3587
	Na Plesu-Valček	Co E3742
58473-2	Min Tös-Schottisch (Otto Hultner)	Co E3588
	Kur Upelis Teka-Polka	Co E3624
	Vesela Poskočnica-Polka	Co E3741
58475-2	Nya Fiskarvalsen (Hellström)	Co E3588
	Lilijos Žiedas-Valčas	Co E3626
58476-1	Bal Med Värmlandstöserna {Dance With The Farmland Girls}	Co E3644
	Bailando Con Mi Muchacha Campesina	Co C3892
	Sienapiute-Polka Mazurka	Co E3624
58477-1	Kyssvalsen {Kiss Waltz}	Co E3644
	Besos-Vals	Co C3537, C3892
58478-1	Balen På Bakgården	Co E3643
	Bailando Con Mi Campesina	Co C3537
	as before	NY August 1917

Co E3624 and E3626 (Lithuanian) and E3741 (Slovenian) are uncredited.

84154-1	Södermanlands Reg. Parad Marsch	Co E3887, 7636
84155-2	Nya Kostervalsen	Co E3887, 7636
84157-1	Stockholms Valsen	Co E4044, 7637
84158-2	Gräshoppornas Polka	Co E4044, 7637
84159-1	Borghild Schottisch	Co E4079
84160-2	Nya Kristiania Valsen	Co E4079
84161-1	Kring Granen-Hambo	Co E3931
84162-1	Rosens Valsen	Co E3931
	as before	NY ca March 1918

84947-1	Karlskoga Valsen	Co E4247
84949-2	Jul På Landet	Co E4407
84951-2	Hoppsan Hejsan Hambo	Co E4200
84961-3	Amburgo Mazurka	Co E4347
84962-2	Hala Trallen	Co E4247
84963-1	Silver Månen-Schotisch	Co E4347
84965-3	Skandinavsk Mazurka	Co E4764
84966-	Kuba Jurek-Mazur	Co E4198
	På Herdarnes Bal-Polka	Co E4214
	Upp Och Ned-Polka	Co E4214
		NY ca October 1918

Co E4198 (Polish) is uncredited. Co E4350, Jäähyväiset (Finnish), is an accordion
duet which may be from this session.

85081-2	Fastmans Valsen	Co E4764
	Mergele Tu Manc Miela-Valcas	Co E4647
85082-	Sjömansvalsen	Co E4484
	as before	NY 1918-9

Co E4647 (Lithuanian) is uncredited.

John Lager And Eric Olson

B 22752-2	Dans På Logen {Dance In The Barn}-Valsen (Widequist)	Vi 72432
B 22753-2	Bökeviks Valsen (Nystrom)	Vi 72954
B 22754-2	Frykdals Dans-Schottische	Vi rej
B 22755-3	Kungl. Kronobergarnas	
	{The Royal Kronoberger's Parade March}-Paradmarsch	Vi 73540
	as before	NY April 29, 1919

B 22754-3	Frykdals Dans-Schottische	Vi 72432
	as before	NY July 15, 1919

B 23267-2	Schottis Från Axvala {Schottisch From Training Camp}	Vi 72583
B 23268-2	Pottpuri Af Mitt Svärmeri, Och Svenska Gossar (arr Evert)	Vi rej
B 23269-2	Arholma-Valsen	Vi rej
B 23270-2	Donau Vågornas {Waves Of The Danube}-Valsen (J. Ivanovici)	Vi 72721
	Donauwellen	Vi 72779, 73118
	Dunojas Vilnys	Vi 73056
	Dunavski Valovi-Valcer	Vi 73119
	Donaugolven Wals	Vi 73283
	Fale Dunaju {Na Falach Dunaju}	Vi 73392

B 23271-1   Malmö-Valsen (Hellstrom)   Vi 72583
              as before   NY September 22, 1919

Vi 72779 is a Jewish release; 73056 is Lithuanian, 73118 is German, 73119 is
Croatian, 73283 is Dutch, and 73392 is Polish. None of these are pseudonymous.

B 23359-2   Trondhjem {Jämtlands}-Valsen {Landscape Valse} (Speljonte) Vi 72543
B 23360-2   Hejsan-Hambo {Let's Go-Polka} (Ocke)   Vi 73197
              as before   NY November 25, 1919

              Mammy O'Mine   Vi trial
              as before   NY November 29, 1919

B 23268-3   Pottpuri Af Mitt Svärmeri, Och Svenska Gossar (arr Evert)   Vi 72543
B 23269-4   Arholma-Valsen   Vi rej
B 23364-2   Dala {Landscape}-Hambo (Janson)   Vi 72721
B 23365-2   Fiammetta-Polka (Becucci)   Vi rej
              as before   NY December 1, 1919

B 23891-1   En Sommarkväll {A Summer Night}-Vals (Widgust)   Vi 73001
B 23892-2   I Alla Fulla Fall {Anyhow}-Vals (Englund)   Vi 72954
B 23893-2   Bevärings {Soldiers}-Polka (Krix)   Vi rej
B 23894-2   Infanteri Marsch (Halger)   Vi rej
              as before   NY April 9, 1920

B 23365-   Fiammetta-Polka (Becucci)   Vi rej
B 23899-2   Rysk Dans-Mazurka   Vi 72771, HMV X1115
B 24000-2   Jänta Å Menskera-Folkdanser   Vi 73001
B 24001-2   Feste Floreali {Sans Fakon}-Polka   Vi 72726
              as before   NY April 16, 1920

B 24045-1   Agevole {Dröm}-Vals   Vi 72726
B 24046-2   Pas De Quatre-Schottische   Vi rej
B 24047-2   Gärdo {På Byaran}-Hambo   Vi 73114
              as before   NY May 10, 1920

B 23893-4   Bevärings {Soldiers}-Polka (Krix)   Vi 72771, HMV X1115
B 24046-3   Pas De Quatre-Schottische   Vi 72929
B 24074-2   Konvaljens Afsked-Vals   Vi rej
              as before   NY May 28, 1920

B 23269-5   Arholma-Valsen   Vi 72929
B 23365-7   Fiammetta-Polka (Becucci)   Vi rej
              as before   NY June 28, 1920

John Lager-Arvid Franzen

B 26939-2   Gyllene Medelvägen {The Golden Midway}-Vals (Tomeson)   Vi 77076
B 26940-2   Memories Of The Coast {En Skärgårds Låt}-Shottische   Vi 73545
B 26941-1   Mora-Hambo   Vi 73545
B 26942-1   Friare Valsen {The Suitor's Waltz} {Proposing Waltz}   Vi 73540
              Arvid Franzen-2d acn   NY October 9, 1922

B 27181-3	O Susanna-Rheinländer (Wilhelm Hinsch)'	Vi 73663
B 27182-1	Midsummer Night's Dream {Midsomarnatts Dröm}-Vals	Vi rej
	as before, 'Nathaniel Shilkret-p	NY November 24, 1922

B 27436-2	The Smålands Waltz	Vi 73720, Banjar BR-1840(33)
B 27437-2	The Saturday Waltz {Lördags Valsen}	Vi 73720
B 27438-1	High Air {Hög Luft}-Polka	Vi 73756
	own, Arvid Franzen-2 acn, Lew Shilkret-p	NY January 29, 1923

B 27182-2	Midsummer Night's Dream {Midsomarnatts Dröm}-Vals	Vi 73756
B 27464-2	Sverige {Sweden}-Shottis	Vi rej
B 27465-1	Fjällbruden {The Mountain Bride}-Vals	Vi 77076
	as before	NY February 8, 1923

B 28062-3	Brage Gillo-Mazurka	Vi 73924
B 28063-1	Bakaby Valsen	Vi 73924
	as before	NY June 11, 1923

B 27464-3	Sverige {Sweden}-Shottis	Vi rej
B 29105-3	Grasshopper {Gräshopps}-Polka	Vi 77272
B 29106-1	Seven O'Clock {Klockan 7}-Vals (Ansheim Johansson)	Vi 77272
	own, Arvid Franzen-2 acn, M. Posner-vln, Lew Shilkret-p	NY December 5, 1923

89575-1	Grabo Valsen	Co 22004-F
89578-3	Bröllops Polkan	Co 22004-F
		NY December 1923

	En Gång Till	Co 22006-F
	Permissions Valsen	Co 22006-F
	Fjällbruden	Co 22007-F
	Den Gula Paviliongen	Co 22007-F
		NY 1923-4

John Lager-Hans Larsen

B 30603-2	Margit {Margaret}-Vals	Vi 78017
B 30604-3	Koster-Valsen (David Hellström)	Vi 77661
B 30605-1	Swagger {Kväsar}-Vals (Arthur Hogstedt); Fireside {Spiskroks}-Vals	
	(Kal Dompan)	Vi 77661
B 30606-1	Knoll Och Tott {Katzenjammer Kids}-Schottis	Vi 78017
	own, Hans Larsen-2 acn, Lou Raderman-vln, Lew Shilkret-p	NY July 21, 1924

John Lager-Arvid Franzen

B 27464-4	Sverige {Sweden}-Schottish (D. Lunkan)	Vi 78119
B 32013-3	Från Frisco Till Cap {From Frisco To Cape}-Vals	Vi 77993
B 32014-3	Valbo-Hambo (John Petterson)	Vi 78119
B 32015-2	Midsommarnattens Sista Vals {Midsummer Night's Last Waltz}	Vi 77993
	Arvid Franzen-2d acn	NY February 25, 1925

105489-	Då Skulle Morsan Vara Mä	Co 22016-F
105490-	Under Paris Broar	Co 22016-F

	Skepp Som Mötas	Co 22015-F
	Kom Till Göteborg	Co 22015-F
	as before	NY ca February 1925

W 105674-1	Bonn Jazz (Wahlberg)	Co 22018-F, 7624
W 105675-2	Kulkurin Masurkka (Herman Sjöblom)	Co 3011-F, 16125
W 105676-2	En Stjärnenatt (Einar Westling)	Co 22018-F, 7624
W 105677-1	Vapaa Venäjä March (W.N. Kostakowsky)	Co 3011-F, 16125
	as before	NY June 1925

John Lager-Edwin Jahrl

W 106120-2	Hemma Ensam-Hambo	Co 22027-F, 7620
W 106121-1	Salta Tåren-Vals	Co 22027-F, 7620
	Devojački-Valcer	Co 1019-F
	Magdalena-Walc	Co 18107-F
W 106122-1	En Morgon I Skogen-Vals	Co 22028-F
	Na Hospodarstvo-Lendler	Co 25048-F
	Aamu Metsässä-Valssi	Co DI56
W 106123-2	Hammarby Polka	Co 22028-F
	Barbara-Polka	Co 18107-F
	Na Kranjskih Gor-Polka	Co 25048-F
	Hammarkylän Polkka	Co DI56
	own, Eddy Jahrl-2 acn, unk bj	NY December 1925

Co 1019-F and 18107-F as HARMONIKA DUET, 25048-F as JAHRLOVI TRIO

BVE 34787-3	Klarinett-Mazurka Hambo (E. Falsten)	Vi 78698
BVE 34788-2	Lilla Vännen På Glittrande Våg	
	{My Little Friend On The Glittering Waves}-Valse	
		Vi 78747, V-20082, 26-0023
BVE 34789-3	Malajen {Malay}-Schottis (Karl Namdeman)	Vi 78747, V-20082, 26-0023
BVE 34790-2	Min Hembygdmelodi {Melodies From Home}-Vals	Vi 78698
	acn duet	Camden, NJ April 19, 1926

Lager & Olson

BVE 36672-1	Jubileums-Schottish (Svenson)	Vi 79088, V-20081, 26-0022
BVE 36673-1	Bonn Tolva {A Hayseed's Card Game} (Karlson)	Vi 79041
BVE 36674-1	Dans På Hågenloft {Dancing In The Loft} (Ekman)	
		Vi 79088, V-20086, 26-0026
BVE 36678-1	Du Vet' Et {You Know It}-Polka (Ekman)	Vi 79041
	Eric Olson-2d acn	Camden, NJ November 10, 1926

Lager Och Franzen

W 107336-2	Sjömans Fröjd-Vals (E. Ekman)	Co 22049-F, 7875
W 107337-2	Flygmaskins Polka	Co 22048-F
W 107338-2	Läppsnuvan-Hambo	Co 22048-F, RZ MR255
W 107339-2	En Sväng På Däck-Vals (I. Rixon)	Co 22049-F, 7875
	Arvid Franzen-2d acn	NY November 1926

Lager, Olzen & Co.

W 107686-2	Böljornas Drottning-Vals (B.L. Klemi)	Co 22054-F, 7782
	Aallotar Valssi	Co 3047-F, 16153
W 107687-2	Den Gamla Sekretären-Vals	Co 22055-F, 7783
W 107688-2	Solstrålarna-Polka	Co 22055-F, 7783, Banjar BR-1840(33)
W 107689-2	Skärgårdsflickan-Mazurka (E. Felenius)	Co 22054-F, 7782
	Skargardin Tyttö	Co 3047-F, 16153
		NY March 1927

Lager & Olson Quartet

BVE 39679-3	Koster Valsen (David Hellström)	
		Vi 80073, V-20067, 26-0013, Bb B-2725
BVE 39680-3	Hönshus {In The Chicken Coop}-Polka	
		Vi 80073, V-20067, 26-0013, Bb B-2725
BVE 39681-1	Kväsar Valsen; Spiskroks Valsen (A. Högstedt-Kal Dompan)	Vi 80145
BVE 39682-1	Dala Hama	Vi 80145
	own, Eric Olson-2 acn, unk vln, cl	NY June 20, 1927

34.21. Henry Magnuson And Einar Holt   *accordion duet*

	Repasz March; Kornblixten Waltz	Vi trial
		Camden, NJ October 29, 1919

Magnuson Och Holt

86099-3	På Begäran-Hambo	Co E4765
		NY March 1920
86252-2	Horn Kroks Valsen	Co E4765
		NY May 1920
89382-1	Lilla Greta-Schottisch	Co 22001-F
89383-1	Dans På L'On-Vals	Co 22001-F
89384-1	Södergrabbarnas Hambo	Co 22000-F
89385-2	Ölandstöser-Schottish	Co 22000-F
		NY August 1923

34.22. Birger Nordström   *accordion*

84309-2	Konvaljens Afsked	Co E4080
84310-1	På Baltiskan-Vals	Co E4129
84311-	Intermezzo-One Step	Co E4620
84312-1	Vinåkersdans-Mazurka	Co E4129
84313-1	Amerikansk Patrull {American Patrol}	Co E3945
84314-1	Lapp Nisse's Polska	Co E4080
		NY April 1918

34.23. N.Y. Kulturell Kapell *band*

W 112367-1	Amandus-Sjömansvals (Helge Lindberg)	Co 22131-F
W 112368-2	Jungman Janssons Polka (Sven Runö)	Co 22131-F
W 112369-2	Solviksminnen-Waltz (David Oriell)	Co 22125-F
W 112370-2	Midsommar-Dansen-Schottische	Co 22125-F
		NY October 1930

34.24. Friis Olsen Scandinavians *instrumental*

BS 060794-1 Den Vackra Flickans Dans {The Pretty Girl Dances}-Schottis
            (A.F. Olsen)   Vi V-20108, 26-0042
BS 060795-1 Hilda Och Tilda {Hilda And Tilda}-Hambo (A.F. Olsen)   Vi V-20109
BS 060796-1 Fest I Gatan {Festival In The Street}-Polka (A.F. Olsen) Vi V-20109
BS 060797-1 Ska Han Lefva? Ja Man Ska!-Polka (A.F. Olsen)   Vi V-20108, 26-0042
      vln, acn, p, sbs   NY March 3, 1941

BS 066426-1 Gamla Bellman {Old Bellman}-Polka (A.F. Olsen) Vi V-20110, 26-0043
BS 066427-1 Trip Trap Träsko {Wick Wack Wooden Shoe}-Hambo (A. Olsen)
                                   Vi V-20111, 26-0044
BS 066428-1 Göteborg-Schottisch (J. Anderson [Bier])   Vi V-20111, 26-0044
BS 066429-1 Smörgåsbord-Schottisch (J. Anderson [Bier])   Vi V-20110, 26-0043
      as before   NY June 27, 1941

34.25. Eric Olson *accordion*

Eric Olson-Ottar Agre

BVE 33247-1 Trip Trap Polka (S. Jevnaker)   Vi 78405, V-20066
BVE 33248-3 Hal Topseil, Min Pige {Heave Topsail, My Girl}-Vals
            (M.B. Landstad-Reidar Thommesen)   Vi 78405, V-20066
BVE 33249-2 Dans Paa Plattinger {Down On The Platform}-Schottische (Ottar Agre)
                                      Vi 78552
BVE 33250-3 Philippine-Mazurka (Ottar Agre)   Vi 78552
      own, Ottar Agre-2 acn   Camden, NJ August 25, 1925

Olson-Holt Quartet

BVE 37646-3 Sjömansfröjd {Sailor's Joy}-Vals (Ekman)   Vi 79205
BVE 37647-2 Oslo-Waltz (Einar Holt)   Vi 79275, Bb B-2739
BVE 37648-2 Stockholms-Hambo {Hambo From Stockholm} (Johannson)   Vi 79205
BVE 37649-2 Fjord {Nya Bonnjazzen}-Schottische   Vi 79275, Bb B-2739
      own, Einar Holt-2 acn, unk c, bj   Camden, NJ January 20, 1927

34.26. William Oscar *violin*

58727-1   Sæterjentens Söndag   Co E3682
       Columbia Scandinavian Orchestra   NY November 1917

William Oscar's Orkester

B 21815-1	Hipp Och Hopp-Hambo Från Nordland (arr William Oscar)	Vi 72219
B 21816-1	Svenska Folkets Kläm-Waltz (arr William Oscar)	Vi 72219
B 21817-1	Norske Valsen-Vals Potpourri (arr William Oscar)	Vi 72221
B 21818-2	Aarhus Tappenstreg-March (C.C. Moller, arr William Oscar)	Vi 72221
	2 vln, 2 c, fl, cl, tb, tuba, bells	NY May 2, 1918

William Oscar

84369-	Solskrikjan (Laxdal)	Co E4005
	Columbia Scandinavian Orchestra	NY May 1918

B 21852-2	Värmlandsvisan	Vi 72522
B 21853-1	Vuggevise (Emil Hartmann)	Vi 72522
	orch d Nathaniel Shilkret	NY May 16, 1918

85129-2	Vöggulied (Bjarnason)	Co E4538
	orch	NY April 1919

85227-1	Humoreske (Sveinbjörnsson)	Co E4386
85228-2	Lugn Hvilar Sjön; Polka Capriccio	Co E4386
	p	NY ca May 1919

William Oscar's Instrumental Trio

86492-2	Två Fryksdals-Valser	Co E4926
86493-1	Delsbo Valsen	Co E4926
86494-2	Te' Dans Me' Smålandstöser'a	Co E4843
	A To Łobusz, Jakich Mało	Co E7245
86495-2	Karlskoga Valsen	Co E4843
86496-	Bond-Vals (Th. Pinet)	Co E7130
86497-	Kadrilj Från Öland	Co E7130
	own and another-2 vln, unk p	NY August 1920

Co E7245 (Polish) as INSTRUMENTAL TRIO

William Oscar's Military Band

59976-2	Kungl Upplands Infanteriregementes Marsch (A. Bergström)	
		Co 65000-F(12")
59977-2	Gamla Minnen (Wm. Oscar)	Co 65000-F(12")
59978-1	Nytt Och Gammalt-Valspotpourri	Co 65001-F(12")
59979-2	Lindblads Sånger-Marsch Potpourri	Co 65001-F(12")
		NY ca June 1925

William Oscar

W 105705-2	Norrländingens Hemlängtan (H. Broman)	Co 22019-F
W 105706-2	Solveigs Sang (E. Grieg)	Co 22023-F
W 105707-2	Säterjentens Söndag (Ole Bull)	Co 22023-F

W 105708-1   Värmlandsvisan   Co 22019-F
                                                              NY July 1925

Co 22023-F as WILLIAM OSCAR INSTRUMENTAL QUARTET

34.27. Royal Scandinavian Orchestra

                  Swedish Waltz-Pt. 1   Pe 11194
                  Swedish Waltz-Pt. 2   Pe 11194
                                                              NY 1924

34.28. Royal Vikings *instrumental*

BS 058691-1   Viking Schottische (John Muth, Jr.)   Vi V-20106, 26-0040
BS 058692-1   Min Hemland {My Homeland}-Hambo (John Muth, Jr.) Vi V-20107, 26-0041
BS 058693-1   Friska {Snappy}-Polka (John Muth, Jr.)   Vi V-20106, 26-0040
BS 058694-1   Gladje Musikanter {Merry Musicians}-Polka (John Muth, Jr.)
                                                            Vi V-20107, 26-0041
              acn, sax, sbs   NY January 3, 1941

BS 067876-1   Nordenland {Northland}-Hambo (John Muth, Jr.)¹ Vi V-20114, 26-0058
BS 067877-1   Sving {Swing}-Hambo (John Muth, Jr.)¹   Vi V-20112, 26-0045
BS 067878-1   Harmoni Schottis (John Muth, Jr.)¹   Vi V-20113, 26-0046
BS 067879-1   Rytmiska Melodi-Rheinlander (John Muth, Jr.)¹ Vi V-20114, 26-0058
BS 067880-1   I Gamle Wien {In Old Vienna}-Vals (John Muth, Jr.)
                                                            Vi V-20115, 26-0047
                  Im Alten Wien   Vi V-6510
BS 067881-1   Kastellvals {Castle Waltz}-Sjömansvals (John Muth, Jr.)
                                                            Vi V-20112, 26-0045
                  Luftschlösser Walzer   Vi V-6514
BS 067882-1   Vårdshussång {Tavern Song}-Polka   Vi V-20113, 26-0046
                  In Der Wirtschaft-Polka   Vi V-6514
BS 067883-1   Skynda {Hurry Up}-Polka (John Muth, Jr.)   Vi V-20115, 26-0047
                  Eile Mit Weile-Polka   Vi V-6510
              John Muth, Jr.-acn, William Muth-cl, A. Olsen-p, ¹Stefan Gula-sbs
                                                            NY September 18, 1941

Vi V-6510 and V-6514 as GEBRÜDER MUTH MIT SCHRAMMELN BEGLEITUNG

34.29. Herman Sandby *violoncello*

43991-2   Roselil   Co E3181
43993-2   Sæterjentens Søndag   Co E3181
              orch   NY May 1916

59424-1   Necken Spelar På Böljan Blå {Necken Plays On The Blue Wave}
                                                            Co E5135(12")
59426-2   Ack Värmeland, Du Sköna   Co E5135(12")
              Brude Marsch {Norwegian Bridal March}   Co E3047
              Elferhöj {Elf Hill}   Co E3047
              Afton Sång {Evening Song}   Co E3476

2674

```
            Adagio                                              Co E3476
            orch                                                NY  1916
```

34.30. Scandinavian Bell Ringers *instrumental*

```
969-1       Ring The Bells Of Heaven {Ring I Himmelens Klockor}
                                                        SBR 123, Wallin's 123
970-2       Home Sweet Home {Hem Ljuva Hem}             SBR 123, Wallin's 123
971-1       Evening Chimes {Afton Klockor}              SBR 122, Wallin's 122
972-2       Pleasant Dreams {I Ljuva Drömmar}           SBR 122, Wallin's 122
                                                        Chicago  mid-1920s
```

Scandinavian Bell Ringers (Temple Carillon Players) (200 Bells)

```
BVE 42947-2    Ring I Himlens Klockor {Ring The Bells Of Heaven} (Roth)  Vi V-20003
BVE 42948-2    Rose Dreams (Stasny)                                      Vi V-20001
BVE 42949-2    Gånglåt Från Helsingland {Footsteps From Helsingland}     Vi V-20001
CVE 42950-2    Love's Way-Waltz (L. King)                                Vi 59096(12")
BVE 42951-2    Beautiful Star Of Heaven (Drumheller)                     Vi V-20003
CVE 42952-2    Meditation (G.S. Morrison, op. 90)                        Vi 59096(12")
          5 men playing carillon of 200 bells, d G. Ringchrist
                                            Camden, NJ  September 13, 1928
```

Vi 59096 as TEMPLE CARILLON PLAYERS (Scandinavian Bell Ringers)

34.31. Scandinavian Concert Trio *instrumental*

```
B 23829-3      Aftenstemning {Evening Mood} (Halfdan Kjerulf); Halling-Dance; I
                  Ensomme Stunde {In Lonesome Moments} (Ole Bull)        Vi 73688
               Peter Eisenberg-vln, William Feder-vc, Nathaniel Shilkret-p/org, unk
               cel, bells                                        NY  March 8, 1920
```

34.32. John Strom And How *violin, accordion*

```
GE 12816-A     Swedish Love Waltz                           Ge 6229, 20294
GE 12821-A     My Favorite Schottisch                     Ge 6246, Sil 4098
GE 12850-A     Swedish Hart Waltz                         Ge 6193, Sil 4097
GE 12869       Skansen Waltz           Ge 6231, 20294, Sil 5115, 8278, Supertone 9099
GE 12870       Waltz By The River                           Ge 6231, 20293
GE 12871-A     Jampland's Mazurka                                     Ge 6230
GE 12872-A     Grasshopper Polka          Ge 6207, Sil 5115, 8278, Supertone 9099
                                                        St. Paul  June 1927
```

34.33. Ragnar Sundquist *accordion (1892-1951)*

Ragnar Sundquist And Eric Berg

```
B 21619-2      Bagni Di Lucca-March
B 21620-2      Clarinett Polska                                       Vi rej
B 21621-2      Hejsan-Hambo                                           Vi rej
                                                                   Vi 72988
```

B 21622-2	Sotar Valsen	Vi rej
B 21623-1	Finska Valsen	Vi 72329
B 21624-1	På Logen-Mazurka	Vi 72762
B 21625-2	Uppsala Minnen-Schottische	Vi 72052
	Eric Berg-2d acn	Camden, NJ March 20, 1918
B 21626-1	Eskilstuna Hambo	Vi 72329
B 21627-2	Svensk Gardes {Swedish Guard}-March	Vi rej
B 21628-1	Messommarsvalsen	Vi 72052
B 21629-2	Franke's Polka	Vi 72175
B 21630-1	Bil-Bol-Waltz	Vi 72851
B 21631-2	Jubelbal På Landet-Schottische	Vi 72115
B 21632-2	Dala Trallen-Polka	Vi rej
	as before	Camden, NJ March 21, 1918
B 21619-4	Bagni Di Lucca-March	Vi 72510
B 21620-4	Clarinett Polska	Vi rej
B 21632-4	Trallen Polka	Vi rej
B 21707-2	Livliga Minnen {Amburgo}-Mazurka	Vi rej
	as before	NY March 27, 1918
B 21622-5	Sotar Valsen	Vi rej
B 21627-4	Svensk Gardes {Swedish Guard}-March	Vi rej
B 21707-3	Livliga Minnen {Amburgo}-Mazurka	Vi rej
B 21715-1	Alra Käraste Min-Waltz	Vi 72115
	as before	NY March 29, 1918
B 21765-1	Hemlängtan-Mazurka	Vi 72851
B 21766-2	Picnic I Det Gröna-Mazurka	Vi 72228
B 21767-2	I Vinternatt-Waltz	Vi rej
B 21768-2	Aicha-Intermezzo	Vi rej
	as before	NY April 15, 1918
B 21620-6	Clarinett Polska	Vi 72762
B 21622-6	Sotar Valsen	Vi 72175
B 21767-4	I Vinternatt-Waltz	Vi rej
B 21768-3	Aicha-Intermezzo	Vi 72510
	as before	NY July 15, 1918
B 21627-6	Svensk Gardes {Swedish Guard}-March	Vi 72988
B 21632-7	Dala Trallen-Polka	Vi 72373
B 21707-5	Livliga Minnen {Amburgo}-Mazurka	Vi 72373
B 21767-6	I Vinternatt-Waltz	Vi 72228
	as before	NY July 18, 1918

Ragnar Sundquist-Arvid Franzen

	Lirans Vals	Vi trial
	Arvid Franzen-2d acn	NY July 1, 1919
B 23212-3	Lirans Vals	Vi rej
B 23213-2	I Alla Fulla Fall-Vals	Vi rej
B 23214-3	Rallar Oscars Favorit-Polka	Vi rej
	as before	NY August 14, 1919

B 23222-1	Väddö Valsen	Vi 72676
B 23223-2	Vackra Kalles Schottische {Handsome Charley's Schottische}	Vi 72634
B 23224-2	Morsans Valsen	Vi rej
B 23225-1	Hipp Hopp {Hippety-Hop}-Mazurka	Vi 73224
	as before	NY August 22, 1919

B 23224-4	Morsans Valsen	Vi 73049
B 23226-1	Dans På Landsvägen-Schottisch	Vi 72676
B 23227-2	Sommar Drömmar {Summer Dreams}-Vals	Vi 72634
B 23228-1	Hemlandstoner Polka	Vi 72919
B 23229-2	Haga Valsen	Vi 73049
	as before	NY August 28, 1919

B 23212-4	Lirans-Vals	Vi 72919
B 23213-4	I Alla Fulla Fall-Vals	Vi rej
B 23214-5	Rallar Oscars Favorit-Polka	Vi rej
B 23279-3	Svensk Folk Melodi-Mazurka (Viland)	Vi rej
	as before	NY September 29, 1919

Ragnar Sundquist-Eric Olson

B 28569-2	The Girl With Bobbed Hair {Flickan Med Kortklippt Hår} {En Tös Med Kortklippt Hår}-Fox Trot	Vi 77144
B 28570-2	The Dangerous Moon {Den Farliga Månen}-Waltz	Vi 77144
B 28571-3	In The Yellow Pavilion {I Den Gula Paviljongen}-Fox Trot (J. Redland)	Vi 77209
B 28572-2	The Darkened Lighthouses {Släckta Fyrar}-Waltz (P. Fries)	Vi 77209
	Eric Olson-2d acn	NY September 18, 1923

B 30673-2	My Country Sweetheart {Mitt Söderfjäs}-Hambo (Ansel Johansson)	Vi 77792
B 30674-2	The Roar Of The Avesta Rapids {Avestaforsens Brus}-Waltz (Karl Karlsson Jularbo)[1]	Vi 77792
B 30675-3	Scandinavian Medley Polka (arr Ragnar Sundquist-Eric Olson)[2]	Vi 77700
B 30676-1	Sailor's Life {Sjömansliv}-Waltz (Max Keller)	Vi 77700
	own, Eric Olson-2 acn, Joe Green-[1]bells/[2]xyl, unk vln, p	NY August 26, 1924

Sundquist & Olsen

105143-1	Från Frisco Till Cap	Co 22010-F
105146-2	Gamla Folkmelodier	Co 22010-F
	Jazz Flickan	Co 22011-F
	Gamla Folklåtar	Co 22011-F
	Eric Olson-2d acn	NY September 1924

B 31722-3	Inga-Valse (Sven Runö, op. 20)	Vi rej
B 31723-3	Skepp Som Mötas {Ships That Meet}-Valse (Fred Winter)	Vi rej
B 31724-2	Det Tycker Nästan Alla-Popourri: Oh Douglas (Dufri Dimois-William Rowers)	Vi rej
B 31725-3	På Fjäderholmen {On Feather Island}-Hambo	Vi rej
	as before	NY January 16, 1925

B 31722-6	Inga-Valse (Sven Runö, op. 20)	Vi 77933
B 31723-5	Skepp Som Mötas {Ships That Meet}-Valse (Fred Winter)	Vi 77933
B 31725-4	Det Tycker Nästan Alla-Popourri; Oh Douglas	
	(Dufri Dimois-William Rowers)	Vi 78059
B 31794-	Vildkatten {The Wildcats}-Fox Trot (Jacobson)	Vi 78059
	as before	NY February 2, 1925

BVE 33233-3	Solrosen {Sunflower}-Schottische (Eysholdt)	
		Vi 78506, V-20065, 26-0012
BVE 33234-1	Det Var En Solskens Dag {A Sunny Day}-Waltz (Thommesen)	
		Vi 78506, V-20065, 26-0012
BVE 33235-1	Kirta Polka	Vi 78267
BVE 33236-1	Latta Brisar {Light Breezes}-Waltz	Vi 78267
BVE 33237-2	Det Tycker Nästan Alla-Fox Trot Potpourri	Vi rej
	as before	Camden, NJ August 19, 1925

BVE 35941-1	Älv Dansen {Dance Of The Fairies}-Vals (Karlsen)	Vi 78888
BVE 35942-3	Jag Vill Ha En Liten Tös Med Långa Flätar-Fox Trot (R. Nelson)	
		Vi rej
BVE 35943-2	Rospiggen-Schottische (Ragnar Sundquist) Vi 78888, V-20086, 26-0026	
BVE 35944-2	Klackjärns {Iron-Shod Boot}-Polka (Erikson)	Vi 78973
BVE 35945-2	Österåkers Vals (Eric Olson)	Vi 78973
BVE 35946-1	Dalbo Drillen-Hambo (Smen)	Vi 79140
	as before	NY July 27, 1926

| BVE 36032-3 | Spå Valsen | Vi 79140 |
| | as before | NY August 10, 1926 |

W 107068-2	Siljans Vågor-Vals (Karlson)	Co 22043-F, 7871
	Na Adriatske Bregu-Valček	Co 25052-F
W 107069-2	Boden-Vals	Co 22040-F, 7868
W 107070-3	Karusell Schottis (Anderson)	Co 22043-F, 7871
W 107071-2	Lump Lenas-Polka	Co 22040-F, 7868
	Na Veseljesvadbe-Polka	Co 25052-F
		NY August 1926

Co 25052-F as KRANJSKI HARMONIKA DUET

34.34. Harry Syvertson *accordion*

| B 24245-2 | Permesions-Vals | Vi 72801, HMV X1408 |
| | | NY August 5, 1920 |

34.35. Arthur E. Uhe *violin*

| | Etude De Concert | Vi trial |
| | | NY December 31, 1918 |

B 22378-1	Sæterjentens Søndag {The Chalet Girl's Sunday} (Ole Bull)	Vi 72356
B 22379-2	Solvejgs Sang (E. Grieg)	Vi rej
	Nathaniel Shilkret-org, unk chimes	NY February 21, 1919

B 23825-2   I Rosens Doft {When Roses Grow} (Prince Gustaf)   Vi 72798
             vc, p   NY   March 4, 1920

B 23826-3   Till Österland Vill Jag Fara {Now Far, Far Eastward I'll Hie}
                 (arr Gustav Hagg)   Vi 72798
             Nathaniel Shilkret-p   NY   March 5, 1920

B 26019-2   Astri, Mi Astri   Vi rej
             vla, cel, org, d Nathaniel Shilkret   NY   January 9, 1922

B 27283-3   Norrländingens Hemlängtan {The Northlander's Longing For Home}
                 (Hanna Brooman, arr Nathaniel Shilkret)   Vi 73688
             Nathaniel Shilkret-p, unk cel   NY   January 3, 1923

B 28202-3   Iceland (transcribed by Nathaniel Shilkret)   Vi 78220
             Nathaniel Shilkret-cel, Leroy Shield-p   NY   June 20, 1923

B 30287-4   The Little Boy From Tistedalen {En Liten Gut I Fra Tistedalen}
                 (arr Nathaniel Shilkret)   Vi 77606
B 30288-2   O Wermland, Thou Lovely {Ack Värmeland, Du Sköna}
                 (Gustav Hagg-Nathaniel Shilkret)'   Vi 77606
             International Quartet: vc, harp, p, bells, or 'vc, p
                                                       Camden, NJ June 17, 1924

BVE 35754-3 Spinn, Spinn (arr Nathaniel Shilkret)   Vi 78899
BVE 35755-3 Alt Lægger For Din Fot Jed Ned {At Thy Feet I Lay All} (H. Kjerulf,
                 arr Nathaniel Shilkret)   Vi rej
             Joe Green-vibrharp/bells, unk vln, fl, vc, p   NY   July 9, 1926

BVE 22378-5 Sæterjentens Søndag {The Chalet Girls Sunday} (Ole Bull)   Vi rej
             Bruno Reibold-vc, J.M. Coopersmith-org   Camden, NJ October 23, 1929

34.36. Viking Accordion Band

N 19423-   Prsi, Prsi {Rain, Rain}-Polka   Ch 16722, 45016, De 5927
N 19424-   Muziky, Muziky-Polka (Kmoch)   Ch 16738, 45013
N 19425-   Livet I Finnskogarna-Waltz (Karlsson Jularbo)   Ch 16738, 45013
N 19426-   Bak Bak Smallan Puttlroch Fraser {Motor Boat Waltz}
                                                    Ch 16722, 45016, De 5927
             Nestor Sybilrud-tp, Verne Perry-cl/sax, Roy Simonson-acn, Fritzjof
             "Fritz" Rygh-p, L.A. "Skipper" Berg (b. 1905)-bj, Ralph "Beans"
             Dillon-bbs, Floyd "Wimpy" Wright-dm/cel   Richmond, IN December 12,
                                                                            1933

C 740-C   Skål, Skål, Skål (Louis Noiret)   Ba 33277, Vo 15970
C 741-A   Vienna Forever-March
                         Ba 33277, Cq 9661, Me M13244, Vo 15970, Co 12507-F
C 742-B   Little Dancer-Schottische (Edward Trafficante)
                         Ba 33306, Cq 9661, Me M13297, Pe 16055, Vo 15971
C 743-B   Barbara-Polka   Ba 33306, Me M13273, Pe 16055, Vo 15971, Co 12566-F
C 744-   Mayflower Polka Ba 33370, Cq 9362, Me M13337, Vo 15973, Co 12507-F

C 745-   The Prune Song (arr Karel Echtner)
                                Ba 33370, Cq 9362, Me M13337, Vo 15973
            as before   Chicago October 22, 1934

C 746-   The Jolly German-Waltz (Ascher-Mahl)   Ba 33369, Me M13336, Vo 15972
C 747-   Joe The Dandy-Polka (arr Frank Tryner) Ba 33369, Me M13336, Vo 15972
C 748-A   Norska-Waltz (A.V. Landstrom)
                          Ba 33276, Me M13243, Pe 16040, Vo 15969, Co 12566-F
C 749-B   Bonn Jazz; I Går Så Var Den Din; Min Besta Sjömans Bit-La Crosse
                   Schottische Medley   Ba 33276, Me M13243, Pe 16040, Vo 15969
C 750-B   Our Mike-Polka (Karel Echtner)   Ba 33307, Me M13274
C 751-B   Our Katie-Polka   Ba 33307, Me M13274
            as before   Chicago October 23, 1934

C 1037-A   Bezejmenna-Polka (Karel Echtner)
                          Ba 6-01-08, Me 6-01-08, Or 6-01-08, Pe 6-01-08
C 1038-A   Zvadla Růže {Faded Rose}-Waltz (Fred J. Divisek)
                          Ba 6-01-08, Me 6-01-08, Or 6-01-08, Pe 6-01-08
C 1039-A   Hubička {The Kiss}-Polka (Karel Echtner)
                          Ba 6-07-06, Me 6-07-06, Or 6-07-06, Pe 6-07-06
C 1040-A   Muziky-Muziky (Fr. Kmoch)
                          Ba 6-07-06, Me 6-07-06, Or 6-07-06, Pe 6-07-06
C 1041-A   Skaters Waltz (Eddie Wendland-Waldteufel)   Vo 15974, Co 12483-F,
                   Cq 9347, Ba 35-10-09, Me 35-10-09, Or 35-10-09, Pe 35-10-09
C 1042-A   The Jolly Coppersmith-Polka (Karel Echtner)   Vo 15974, Co 12483-F,
                   Cq 9347, Ba 35-10-09, Me 35-10-09, Or 35-10-09, Pe 35-10-09
            Nestor Sybilrud-tp, Cecil Turner, Verne Perry-cl/sax, Roy
            Simonson-acn, Fritzjof "Fritz" Rygh-p, L.A. "Skipper" Berg-bj, Ralph
            "Beans" Dillon-bbs, Floyd "Wimpy" Wright-dm/cel
                                            Chicago June 28, 1935

C 1043-A   Das Bienenhaus {The Bee Hive}-Two Step
                          Ba 5-11-07, Me 5-11-07, Or 5-11-07, Pe 5-11-07
C 1044-A   Deutschland Medley (arr Cecil Turner-Albert Lee)
                          Ba 5-11-07, Me 5-11-07, Or 5-11-07, Pe 5-11-07
C 1045-A   Helsa Dem Där Hemma-Waltz
                          Ba 5-12-07, Me 5-12-07, Or 5-12-07, Pe 5-12-07
C 1046-A   Young Widow Polka (arr Adolf Svec)
                          Ba 6-03-17, Me 6-03-17, Or 6-03-17, Pe 6-03-17
C 1047-A   Seamen's Waltz (David Hellström)
                          Ba 6-03-17, Me 6-03-17, Or 6-03-17, Pe 6-03-17
C 1048-A   Hopeless-Polka   Ba 5-12-07, Me 5-12-07, Or 5-12-07, Pe 5-12-07
            as before   Chicago June 29, 1935

C 1571-1   Jolly Crowd {Čupr Chasa}-Polka (A.J. Tesinský)
                          Ba 7-02-19, Me 7-02-19, Or 7-02-19, Pe 7-02-19
C 1572-2   Mossrosen; En Gamel-Moss Rose Schottisch Medley
                          Ba 7-06-10, Me 7-06-10, Or 7-06-10, Pe 7-06-10
C 1573-2   Two Canaries-Polka   Ba 7-03-04, Me 7-03-04, Or 7-03-04, Or 7-03-04
C 1574-2   Jungfrau-Rheinlander {Schottische} (Cecil Turner)
                          Ba 7-05-06, Me 7-05-06, Or 7-05-06, Pe 7-05-06
C 1575-2   Midsummer's Waltz {Messommers Valsen}
                          Ba 7-06-10, Me 7-06-10, Or 7-06-10, Pe 7-06-10

C 1576-1   The Jolly Tinsmith {Der Pfannenflicker}-Polka
                        Ba 7-04-16, Me 7-04-16, Or 7-04-16, Pe 7-04-16
C 1577-1   Beer Waltz Medley   Ba 7-05-06, Me 7-05-06, Or 7-05-06, Pe 7-05-06
C 1578-1   Fisherman's Holiday-Schottisch
                        Ba 7-03-04, Me 7-03-04, Or 7-03-04, Pe 7-03-04
            Nestor Sybilrud-tp, Cecil Turner, Paul Donnelly-cl/sax, Roy
            Simonson-acn, Fritzjof "Fritz" Rygh-p, L.A. "Skipper" Berg-bj, Ralph
            "Beans" Dillon-bbs, Floyd "Wimpy" Wright-dm/cel
                                            Chicago October 19, 1936

C 1584-1   Tom Cat {Já Mám Doma Kocoura}-Polka
                        Ba 7-02-19, Me 7-02-19, Or 7-02-19, Pe 7-02-19
C 1585-2   Theroux Schottisch-German Rheinlander
                        Ba 7-04-16, Me 7-04-16, Or 7-04-16, Pe 7-04-16
C 1586-1   Tinker {Dráteník}-Polka (arr Louis Vitak)
                        Ba 7-03-13, Me 7-03-13, Or 7-03-13, Pe 7-03-13
C 1587-1   Wanderer {Tulak}-Polka (arr Louis Vitak)
                        Ba 7-03-13, Me 7-03-13, Or 7-03-13, Pe 7-03-13
            as before   Chicago October 20, 1936

93833-A   I Love To Dance Polka (J. Vejvoda, arr Andrew Grill) De 4417, 45098
93834-A   Oslo Waltz (Sigurd Lindström)   De 4417, 45098
93835-A   Chimney Sweeper Polka (Fr. Poupě)   De 4332, 45064
93836-A   Chicken Polka (arr Andrew Grill)   De 4171, 45039
93837-A   Prune Dumpling Polka   De 4171, 45039
93838-A   New Fisherman's {Ny Fiskar}-Waltz (David Hellström) De 4332, 45064
            Nestor Sybilrud-tp, Cecil Turner, Paul Pierson-cl/sax, Lawrence
            Malmberg-acn, Russsell Olson-p, L.A. "Skipper" Berg-bj, Gale Hunn-bbs,
            Floyd "Wimpy" Wright-dm/cel   Chicago November 24, 1941

34.37. Vikings Trio *instrumental*

87435-2   På Isen Vals (R. Scheringson)   Co E7362
87436-1   Vid Forsen (R. Scheringson)   Co E7362
87437-   Saturday Waltz   Co E7251
87438-   Hipp Hopp   Co E7251
            vln, p, bj   NY May 1921

SECTION 35. SWEDISH

35.1. Anna Greta Adamsen *vocal*

Öfver Böljorna De Blå (Bandereau)   USE 21576(4 min)
Kärlekens Besvärligheter (Lugström)   USE 21577(4 min)
                                            NY   ca 1912

35.2. Folke Andersson *tenor (b. 1892)*

BVE 38691-1	En Hälsning Till Lindbergh {O Du Gamla, O Du Fria}	
	{A Greeting To Lindbergh}	Vi 79423
BVE 38692-2	Där Björkarna Susa {Where The Birches Sigh} (Oskar Merikanto)	
		Vi 79423
BVE 38693-2	Hej Dunkom	Vi 80064
BVE 38694-2	Visa I Folkton (Peterson-Berger)	Vi 80064
	vln, vc, p	Chicago June 14, 1927

4678-	Jag Undrar Hur De Gamla Har Det Nu	Wallin's 126
4679-	Hå Hå Ja Ja De Fleckera	Wallin's 126
4695-	O Hur Stilla	Wallin's 125
4696-	I Herrens Helgedom	Wallin's 125
		Chicago ca June 1927

35.3. Albert Arveschoug *baritone*

Martha: Portervisan (Flotow)   Ed 18836(2 min)
Edison Symphony Orchestra   NY March 22, 1905

Bland Fjellen (Heland)   Ed 18848(2 min)
as before   NY May 5, 1905

35.4. Arvid Asplund *tenor*

Mandom, Mod Och Morske Män   Ed 18829(2 min)
Sångaren På Vandring (Naumann)   Ed 18832(2 min)
Drick Ur Ditt Glas (Bellman)   Ed 18833(2 min)
Se Movitz, Hvi Står Du Och Gråter (Bellman)   Ed 18835(2 min)
Längtan (Genser)   Ed 18837(2 min)
Du Är Min Ro (Collan)   Ed 18838(2 min)
Rhenvinets Lof (Peters)   Ed 18839(2 min)
Fåfäng Önskan (Collan)   Ed 18841(2 min)
Soldatgossen (Pacius)   Ed 18843(2 min)

	Du Gamla, Du Friska	Ed 18844(2 min)
	Trubadurens Dödssång (Fogelberg)	Ed 18845(2 min)
	Spinn, Spinn	Ed 18847(2 min)
	Som I Ungdomens År (Durand)	Ed 18849(2 min)
	Wermlands Polska	Ed 18850(2 min)
	Rose Marie (Collan)	Ed 18851(2 min)
	Edison Symphony Orchestra	NY November 28, December 23, 1904, February 17, 1905

Arvid Asplund–Albert Arveschoug

	Här Är Gudagodt Att Vara (Wennerberg)	Ed 18830(2 min)
	Nattmarschen I St. Eriks Gränd	Ed 18842(2 min)
	as before	NY March 20, 1905

Arvid Asplund

	Ack! I Arkadien–Ur Gluntarne	Ed 9400(4 min), 9425(4 min)
	Norrländingens Hemlängtan (Hanna Brooman)	
		Ed 9401(4 min), 9426(4 min)
	Klara Stjärna (H. Wetterlind)	Ed 20549(2 min)
	Min Lilla Vrå Bland Bergen	Ed 20550(2 min)
	Soldatvisa (Aug. Söderman)	Ed 20551(2 min)
	orch	NY February 24, April 13, April 15, 1910

	Kossackvisa	USE 5784(2 min)
	Rhenvinets Lof	USE 5785(2 min)
	Du Gamla, Du Fria	USE 5786(2 min)
	Förbjuden Musik	USE 21572(4 min)
	Vin Kärlek Och Sång (Wine, Women And Song)	USE 21573(4 min)
	Kung Heimer Och Aslog	USE 21574(4 min)
	Fåfäng Önskan	USE 21578(4 min)
	Sångaren På Vandring	USE 21579(4 min)
	Fly Fogel (Hariman) [in Danish]	USE 22000(4 min)
		NY 1911-2

36445-1	Soldatgossen	Co rej (12")
36446-1	Förbjuden Musik	Co rej (12")
38254-1	Trubaduren's Dödssång	Co rej
38255-1	Sångaren På Vandring	Co rej
38256-1	Kossackvisa	Co E1241
38257-1	Fåfäng Önskan	Co E1240
	orch	NY September 12, 1912

38271-1	Jul Sång-Pt. 1	Co E1052
38272-1	Jul Sång-Pt. 2	Co E1052
	org	NY September 13, 1912

38278-1	Du Gamla, Du Fria	Co E1241
38279-1	Mandom, Mod Och Morske Man	Co E1240
	p	NY September 17, 1912

35.5. Carl Barcklind *vocal, accordion*

W 108984-	Hur Ska' Kvinnfolk Ta's?	
W 108985-2	Amanda	Co 26076-F, 16060
W 108990-2	En Sorglustig Visa Om Kärlek	Co 26076-F, 16060
W 108991-1	Bonddrängens Klaga	Co 26072-F, 13430
W 108992-1	Luffarbaronen: Opp Och Hoppa!¹	Co 26072-F, 13430
	¹with Hilma Barcklind	Co 26074-F
		NY ca March 31, 1928

35.6. Hilma Barcklind *soprano*

W 108993-1	Ann-Maries Första Bal	Co 26074-F
		NY ca March 31, 1928

35.7. Anna Bejbom And Selma Linde

36447-1	Bröllops-Marsch, from "Et Bondbröllop" (August Södermann)	
38270-1	O, Hur Underskön Är Ej Vårens Tid!	Co E5023(12")
		Co rej
		NY September 13, 1912

35.8. Bergslagsmor (Lydia Hedberg) *soprano*

87752-1	Landsvägs Trall	Co E7412, Caprice CAP2011(33)
87753-1	Han Å Ho	Co E7412
87754-1	En Visa Om Kärlekens Besvärlighet (A. Engström)	Co E7442
87755-1	En Vårvisa (J. Lambert)	Co E7442
	orch	NY September 1921

B 26348-2	Tandvärken {Toothache}	Vi 73421, Caprice CAP2011(33)
B 26349-1	Lilla Jonson {Little Johnson} (w: Bergslagsmor, m: P. Nyman)	
		Vi 73421
	orch d Nathaniel Shilkret, extra voices by orch and Mr. Hedberg	
		NY May 10, 1922

B 26351-1	Avmagringen {Reducing Weight}	Vi 73477
	orch d Nathaniel Shilkret	NY May 12, 1922

B 32665-2	En Kar Ska' Jag Ha' Mej {I Want A Man} (Ragnar Akerblom)	Vi 78120
B 32666-1	Lappflickan	Vi 78241
B 32667-2	Bonnjazz {Hick Jazz} (Skansek Lasse-G.R. Wahlberg)	Vi 78120
B 32668-2	Jag Såg Mot Aster	Vi 78241
	vln, cl, acn, p, d Leroy Shield	NY May 26, 1925

35.9. Oscar Bergström *bass*

43859-1	Storstugans Marsch	
43860-1	Visan Om Hemmet	Co E2933
43861-1	Den Käraste Sagan (Körling)	Co E2879
		Co E2933

43862-1	Undan Ur Vägen (Bellman)	Co E2880
43863-1	Hör Pukor Och Trumpeter (Bellman)	Co E2880
43864-1	Källan Sprang Ur Jordens Barm (Lagerkrantz)	Co E2879
43865-1	Skördemannen (Fogelberg)	Co E2934
43866-	Var Barmhärtig	Co E3423
43870-2	Sverige Är Mitt Allt På Jorden (Helenius)	Co E2934
43871-	Dalkarlsång (Lindblad)	Co E3006
43872-	Kung Karl, Den Unge Hjälte (Westermark)	Co E3006
	orch	NY 1916

35.10. Olle, Jussi Och Gösta Björling *vocal*

85780-1	O, Hur Stilla	Co E4768
85781-1	I Himmelen	Co E4691
85782-1	Guds Rena Lamm Oskyldig (Decius)	Co E4691
85798-2	Sommarglädje'	Co E4547
85799-1-2	Barndomshemmet'	Co E4547
85800-1-2	Psalm No. 4	Co E4768
	org, or 'vln, p	NY ca November 1919

Co E4547 as JUVENILE TRIO; these are the childhood recordings of the Metropolitan
Opera tenor Jussi Björling (1911-1960). (Gösta Bjorling, 1912-1957)

35.11. Clifford Bloom *tenor*

W 106752-2	Bergsblomman (V. Groom)	Co 26034-F
W 106753-2	Min Lilla Vrå Bland Bergen (J.A. Wadman)	Co 26034-F
	orch	NY May 1926

W 106773-2	Den Heliga Staden {The Holy City} (S. Adams)	Co 26041-F
W 106774-2	Hur Ljuvt Det Är Att Komma (E. Baker)	Co 26041-F
		NY May 1926

35.12. Harry Brandelius *vocal*

BS 065746-1	Har Du Varit Me' Om De' Nån Gång	
	{Have You Ever Done Anything Like It} (Gus Brandelius)	
		Vi V-24175
BS 065747-1	Det Var Bal {It Was A Ball}-Valsen (Tor Benner)	Vi V-24175
BS 065748-1	De'r For Dig Mit Hjerte Slår Gamle Norge	
	{It's For You My Heart Is Beating Old Norway} (Alf Hartmann)	
	[in Norwegian]	Vi V-15068
BS 065749-1	Gamle Norge {Jeg Og Prammen} {Me And The Barge} (Arne Svendsen)	
	[in Norwegian]	Vi V-15068
	tp, sax, acn, Hammond org	NY May 22, 1941

35.13. Anna Brandt *vocal*

B 17772-1	Rida Ranka (August Ekenberg)	Vi rej
B 17773-2	Irmelin Rose (Wilh. Peterson-Berger, op. 3 no. 3)	Vi rej
	King's Orchestra	NY June 1, 1916

B 17772-2	Rida Ranka (August Ekenberg)	Vi rej
B 17773-3	Irmelin Rose (Wilh. Peterson-Berger, op. 3 no. 3)	Vi rej
	as before	NY July 20, 1916

35.14. Brooklyn Svenska Mans Kvartetten *vocal*

B 20709-2　Framåt Kristi Stridsmän {Onward Christian Soldiers} (w: Gould,
　　　　　　　m: A. Sullivan)'　　　　　　　　　　　　　　　　Vi rej
B 20710-2　Närmare Gud Till Dig {Nearer My God To Thee}'　　Vi 69754
B 20711-1　Stridsbön {Battle Prayer} (O. Lindblad-C.V.A. Strandberg)　Vi rej
W. Stenberg-1st ten, A. Lindquist-2d ten, Eric Norgren-1st bs, C.
Lundberg-2d bs, 'Edward T. King-org　　　　　NY September 26, 1917

B 20901-1　Stå Upp, Stå Upp För Jesus (Webb)'　　　　　　Vi 69754
B 20902-2　Tonerna (Lagerkrants)　　　　　　　　　　　　Vi rej
as before, 'Edward T. King-org　　　　　　　NY October 19, 1917

B 20709-4　Framåt Kristi Stridsmän {Onward Christian Soldiers} (w: Gould,
　　　　　　　m: A. Sullivan)'　　　　　　　　　　　　　　Vi 69892
B 20711-2　Stridsbön {Battle Prayer} (O. Lindblad-C.V.A. Strandberg)　Vi 72101
B 20961-3　Verka Ty Natten Kommer {Work, For The Night Is Coming}
　　　　　　　(Lowell Mason)　　　　　　　　　　　　　　Vi 69937
B 20962-2　Hållen Fastet Tills Jag Kommer {Hold The Fort} (P.T. Bliss)'
　　　　　　　　　　　　　　　　　　　　　　　　　　　　Vi 69937
B 20963-2　Säker I Jesu Armar {Safe In The Arms Of Jesus} (W.H. Doane)'
　　　　　　　　　　　　　　　　　　　　　　　　　　　　Vi 69892
　　　　　as before, 'Edward T. King-org　　　NY November 12, 1917

B 21729-1　Jag Lyfter Mina Händer {I Lift My Eyes}　　　Vi 72850
B 21730-2　Skymningsbönen {Evening Prayer} (Robert Schumann)　Vi rej
B 21731-1　Bida Hos Mig {Abide With Me}　　　　　　　　Vi 72850
B 21732-1　Var Är Min Son I Kväll {Where Is My Boy Tonight}　Vi 72482
singers unidentified, Edward T. King-org　　　NY April 3, 1918

B 21731-3　Bida Hos Mig {Abide With Me}　　　　　　　Vi rej
B 21839-2　Han Mig Gömmer {He Hideth Me} (McGranahan)　Vi 72482
B 21840-2　Helsning Till Hemlandet {Greeting To Homeland}　Vi 72101
as before　　　　　　　　　　　　　　　　NY May 8, 1918

B 22073-2　Hvar Stund Jag Dig Behöfver {I Need Thee Every Hour}　Vi rej
B 22074-2　Nästan En Kristen {Almost Persuaded} (P.P. Bliss)　Vi rej
B 22075-2　Möts Vi Då? {Shall We Meet Beyond The River?}　Vi rej
B 22076-1　Rum Invid Korset {Room At The Cross}　　　　Vi rej
as before　　　　　　　　　　　　　　　　NY July 26, 1918

35.15. Grace Eklund Carlson *vocal*

Bland Fjellen   Vi trial
Edward T. King-p   NY November 17, 1916

B 19082-1   Bland Fjellen   Vi 69323
B 19084-1   Hemlandet {Home Sweet Home}'   Vi 69323
             King's Orchestra, 'with Florence Eklund Reims   NY February 15, 1917

B 19267-2   Lärkan (F.V. Heland)   Vi 69366
B 19268-2   Höstvisa (A.M. Myrberg)'   Vi rej
B 19269-2   Lugn Hvilar Sjön (Heinrich Pfeil)'   Vi rej
             King's Orchestra d Rosario Bourdon, 'with Florence Eklund Reims
                                                         NY March 13, 1917

Grace E. Carlson-Florence E. Reims

B 19268-4   Höstvisa (A.M. Myrberg)'   Vi 69521
B 19269-5   Lugn Hvilar Sjön (Heinrich Pfeil)   Vi 69521
B 19496-2   Farväl!; Aftonstämning (A.M. Myrberg)   Vi 69668
             King's Orchestra   NY April 18, 1917

B 20785-2   Hvilken Vän Vi Ha I Jesus {What A Friend We Have In Jesus}
                (A. Bonar-C.C. Converse)   Vi 69787
B 20786-3   Klippa Du Som Brast För Mig {Rock Of Ages}
                (A.M. Toplady-Thomas Hastings)   Vi 69787
B 20787-1   Led Milda Ljus {Lead Kindly Light} (J.H. Newman-J.B. Dykes) Vi 72271
             Edward T. King-org   NY October 17, 1917

B 20958-1   Göken {Ku Ku} {The Coo Coo} (J. Blomquist)   Vi 73069
B 20959-2   En Söndagsmorgon {Sunday Morning} (Mendelssohn)   Vi 72558
B 20960-2   Vid Nattetid {Wanderer's Night Song} (Ant. Rubinstein) Vi 72358
             King's Orchestra   NY November 9, 1917

B 21377-2   Ach Ett Land Mera Skönt Än En Dag (Jos. P. Webster)   Vi rej
B 21378-3   Längse'n {Long Long Ago} (Thos. H. Bayley, arr G. Rosey) Vi 72261
             as before, d Nathaniel Shilkret   NY January 24, 1918

Grace Eklund Carlson

B 21377-3   Ach Ett Land Mera Skönt Än En Dag (Jos. P. Webster)' Vi 72271
B 21571-2   O Hur Underskön Är Ej Vårens Tid (Franz Abt)'   Vi rej
B 21574-2   Sommarnatten (O.D. Lindvall)   Vi rej
             as before, 'with Florence Eklund Reims   NY March 12, 1918

B 21828-1   I Modersfamnen {In Mother's Arms} (Joel Blomqvist)'   Vi 78171
B 21829-2   Aftonstjernan {The Evening Star} (A.M. Myrberg); Fjärran Toner
                (A.M. Myrberg)   Vi 72358
B 21830-2   Om Hösten {In The Fall} (Joel Blomquist)   Vi rej
B 21831-2   Våren {The Spring} (Joel Blomquist)   Vi 73069
             orch d Nathaniel Shilkret, 'with Florence Eklund Reims
                                                         NY May 7, 1918

B 21574-3   Sommarnatten (O.D. Lindvall)   Vi 72558
B 21895-1   Hvar Jag Går {Wherever I Go}-Sacred Song   Vi 78171
             as before   NY June 7, 1918

B 25865-2   Barndomshemmet {My Childhood Home} (w: Karl Ewert, m: P. Wurck)'
                                                                  Vi 73179
B 25866-2   Silvertrådar {Silver Threads Among The Gold}
             (Eben E. Rexford-H.P. Danks)   Vi 73179
             as before, 'with Florence Eklund Reims   NY December 12, 1921

35.16. Fred Carlsten *tenor*

             Afsked Från Hemmet   Vi trial
             Nathaniel Shilkret-p   NY July 26, 1918

             En Solnedgång I Eklundshofsskogen   Vi trial
             as before   NY April 19, 1926

Fred Carlsten-Hugo Olsen

BVE 36805-2 En Solnedgång I Eklundshofsskogen (Gunnar Wennerberg)   Vi 79141
BVE 36806-2 Uppsala Är Bäst (Gunnar Wennerberg)   Vi 79282
BVE 36807-1 Vid Brasan På Magisterns Kammare, Efter En Stor Middagsbjudning
             (Gunnar Wennerberg)   Vi 79282
BVE 36808-2 Huruledes Månen Interesserar Sig För Glunten Och Magistern
             (Gunnar Wennerberg)   Vi 79141
             Lew Shilkret-p   NY October 11, 1926

Fred Carlsten

W 107947-2   Dalaminnen-Vals (Max Formanowski)   Co 26053-F, 7687
W 107948-1   I Vårens Ljusa Nätter-Vals (E. Westling)   Co 26053-F, 7687
W 107949-2   Torparglädje-Bondvals (Klang-Johan)   Co 26054-F
W 107950-2   Grythyttepojken-Bondvals   Co 26054-F
             Fyra Glada Gossar   NY May 1927

W 108641-2   Från Frisco Till Kap-Sjömansvals (Ernst Rolf)   Co 26069-F
W 108645-2   På Skutö Brygga-Skärgårdsvals (E. Westling)   Co 26068-F
W 108646-2   Längtan Till Värmland (Arvid Hammarström)   Co 26068-F
W 108647-2   Jungman Janssons Polka (Sven Rüno)   Co 26069-F
                                                              NY January 1928

W 109571-1   En Böljedans-Vals {K.S.S.S. Valsen} (Landin-Grandin-Winter)
                                                                  Co 26086-F
W 109572-2   Det Var Dans Bort I Vägen (Lambert-Froding)   Co 26082-F
W 109573-2   Jag Sjunger Och Dansar-Eriks Sång, from "Värmlänningarna"
             (Randal-Dahlgren)   Co 26082-F
W 109574-2   På Väg Opp-Sjömansvalsen (A. Olners)   Co 26086-F
             orch d William Oscar   NY August 1928

W 109694-2   Halleluja, Ja' Ä' Koling {Hallelujah, I'm A Bum}
             (Joe Mac-Fred Carlsten)   Co 26079-F

W 109695-2   Kolingens Visa {The Bum Song} (H. McClintock-Fred Carlsten)
                                                                  Co 26079-F
             acn, bj   NY September 1928

W 109711-   Min Ängel {Angela Mia} (Erno Rapee-Fred Carlsten)   Co 26080-F
W 109714-2   Syrénernas Tid {Jeannine, I Dream Of Lilac Time}
                 (L. Wolfe Gilbert-Fred Carlsten)   Co 26080-F
             orch   NY September 1928

BVE 47551-1   Mitt Barndomshem {My Childhood Home} (Karl Wekle-Ernest Rolf)
                                                                  Vi V-24000
BVE 47552-1   Fäbodvalsen {Cowbarn Waltz} (N.G. Granath)   Vi V-24000
BVE 47553-2   Sista Man På Skansen {The Last Man On Fort Skansen}
                 (Valdenar Dalquist-Fred Winter)   Vi V-24003
BVE 47554-1   Anna Du Kan Väl Stanna {Anna, I Wish You Would Stay}
                 (Valdemar Dalquist-Jules Sylvain)   Vi V-24003
             vln, fl, acn, g, traps, d Alfredo Cibelli   NY September 24, 1928

35.17. Chicago Premier Kvartett *vocal*

997   Mitt Hemlands Dal (Pfeil)   Wallin's 101
998   Sång Fåglarne (Lindblad)   Wallin's 101
             John Chellman, Henry Corsell, N.W. Anthony, H.J. Ebeson-vo
                                                            Chicago ca 1923

35.18. Chicago Swedish Glee Club *male chorus*

BVE 35053-2   Morgon {Morning} (Eklöf)   Vi 78641
BVE 35054-2   Jan Hinerk   Vi 78641
             d H. William Nordin   Chicago March 11, 1926

BVE 35069-2   Hör Oss, Svea {Hear Us Sweden} (Gunnar Wennerberg)   Vi 78835
BVE 35070-3   Vandringssång {Wanderer's Song} (Kerling); Bröllopsvisa
                 {Wedding Song} (Enderberg)   Vi 78835, X-16176
             as before   Chicago May 27, 1926

35.19. Aimee Clayton-Jones *contralto*

B 27192-3   Vårvindar Friska, Leka Och Hviska {Spring Breezes Crisp}
                 (arr Gustaf Hagg)   Vi rej
B 27193-1   I Rosens Doft {Where Roses Grow} (Prince Gustaf)   Vi rej
             orch d Nathaniel Shilkret   NY November 29, 1922

35.20. Henry Corsell *tenor*

5096   Mor Lilla Mor   Wallin's 103
5097   Månstrålar Klara (Tanti)   Wallin's 103
                                                       Chicago early 1920s

2690

548   Du Gamla Du Fria   Wallin's 113
                   Svensk-Amerikanska Sångar Förbundet, d Joseph M. Wahlton
                                                                    Chicago ca June 1924

W 106299-2   Morgon (Eklöv)   Co 26026-F
W 106300-1   Du Bleu Blott En Dröm (Lundmark)   Co 26026-F
              orch   Chicago February 1926

W 107624-1   Vid Siljan Är Mitt Hem (Eklund-Miller)   Co 26050-F
W 107625-1   Näcken Han Spelar På Böljan Blå   Co 26051-F
W 107626-2   Varje Liten Tanke-Sångvals (R. Thommesen)   Co 26051-F
W 107627-3   Bor Du Hemma Hos Din Mamma? (J. Sylvain)   Co 26050-F
                                                                    NY February 1927

W 109169-1   Hälsa Dem Därhemma (E. Norsing)   Co 26070-F
W 109170-2   En Stjärnenatt (E. Westling)   Co 26070-F
W 109171-2   Norrländingens Hemlängtan (H. Brooman)   Co 26071-F
W 109172-2   Avsked Från Hemmet   Co 26071-F
                                                                    NY April 1928

W 109538-1   Skönhetsfläcken-Fox Trot (Hugo Frey)   Co 26077-F
W 109539-2   Nyckelhålet-Vals (Helge Lindberg)   Co 26077-F
              Eric Olson-acn   NY July 1928

W 113920-2   Se Farfar Dansar Gammal-Vals (Tom Andy-Elsie Paul)   Co 26199-F
W 113921-2   Flickan På Ingarö Strand-Vals (Einar Björke-S.O. Sandberg)
                                                                        Co 26199-F
W 113922-2   Håll Takten Spelemen, För Nu Dansar Jag!
                  (Jules Sylvain-Gösta Stevens)   Co 26200-F
W 113923-2   Å Jänta Å Ja'-Hambo   Co 26200-F
              Jahrl's Instrumental Trio   NY ca August 1934

35.21. Magda E. Dahl *soprano*

              Fågelns Visa (Söderberg)   Ed 18831(2 min)
              Edison Symphony Orchestra   NY April 17, 1905

35.22. Eric Dahlström *spoken*

105283-1   Tätning Af En Båt   Co 26012-F
105284-1   Nationale Ekonomi   Co 26012-F
                                                                    NY ca December 1924

35.23. Oscar Danielson's Orkester

W 111346-3   Norsk Bond-Vals (A.V. Landström)   Co 22116-F, DI193
W 111347-2   Landsplågan-Vals (H. Lindberg)   Co 22116-F, DI193
W 111348-2   Är Det Nån Som Sett Maria? (H. Lindberg)¹   Co 26105-F
W 111349-2   Floda-Hambo¹   Co 26105-F
W 111350-2   Lillan Ska' Sova' (Jules Sylvain)²   Co 26108-F
W 111351-   Vad Tallarna Viska I Nordanland (Sven Rüno)²   Co 26108-F

                                                                                    2691

W 111352-1   Ah, Amalia²   Co 26104-F
W 111353-2   Strö Lite' Rosor På Den Väg Vi Vandrar (Helan)²   Co 26104-F
              'Ernst Svedelius, Jr., ²Oscar Danielson-vo   Chicago December 1929

W 112064-2   På Begäran-Hambo   Co 22120-F, DI193
W 112065-1   Hälsning Till Hemmet-Waltz   Co 22118-F
W 112066-1   Fusyjama-Fox Trot (H. Lindberg)   Co 22118-F, DI256
W 112067-2   I Går Så Var Den Din (H. Lindberg)   Co 22120-F
W 112068-1   En Kärleksnatt I Barcelona-Fox Trot (H. Lindberg)'   Co 26139-F
W 112069-2   Skål, Skål, Skål!-Vals'   Co 26111-F
W 112070- (W 194987) Edit, Ä De' Ledit?-Fox Trot (H. Dardanell-Dick Fryman)'
                                               Co 26139-F
W 112071-2   Säg Lilla Emma, När Är Du Hemma? (Helan)'   Co 26111-F
              'Oscar Danielson-vo   Chicago May 1930

Co 22118-F and 22120-F as OSCAR DANIELSON'S DANSORKESTER, DI256 as COLUMBIA TANSSIORKESTERI

35.24. Florence Ecklund Reims *soprano*

              Neckens Polska   Vi trial
              Our Land'   Vi trial
              Edward T. King-p, 'with Grace Eklund Carlson   NY November 17, 1916

B 19083-2   Necken (words adapted by Miss S.E. Throop)   Vi 69366
               King's Orchestra   NY February 15, 1917

B 19714-1   Längtan {Longing} (Herm. Satherberg-August Soderman)   Vi 69668
              as before   NY April 26, 1917

B 21379-2   En Liten Fågel   Vi 72261
              as before, d Nathaniel Shilkret   NY January 24, 1918

B 21575-2   Hemlängtan {Longing For Home} (Prince Gustaf, arr C.F. Hansen)
                                               Vi 78192
              as before   NY March 12, 1918

35.25. Alfred Edström's Orchestra

BVE 41358-2   Den Lustige Kopparslagaren (C. Peter)   Vi 80414
BVE 41359-1   Bor Du Hemma Hos Din Mamma?   Vi 80414
BVE 41360-2   En Stärnenatt {A Starry Night} (Ejnar Westling)'   Vi 80480
BVE 41361-1   Efter Balen {After The Ball} (Charles K. Harris)   Vi 80480
              2 c, 3 sax, acn, tb, bj, tuba, traps, 'vo   Chicago December 9, 1927

35.26. Einar Ekberg *vocal*

170028-2   Löftena Kunna Ej Svika (Lewis Pethrus)   Co 65-P
170029-2   Det Ljusnar Nu   Co 65-P
         Robert Hood Bowers-p   NY ca February 13, 1925

35.27. Adolph Elmblad *vocal*

Herdegossen	Ed 12105(2 min)
Fågelns Visa	Ed 12106(2 min)
Rose Marie	Ed 12107(2 min)
Vaggvisa	Ed 12108(2 min)
Necken	Ed 12109(2 min)
Man Tro? Jo Jo	Ed 12110(2 min)
Nara	Ed 12202(2 min)
	NY 1900-1

35.28. Oscar Engstrand *baritone*

W 108314-2	Det Är Solsken (J.A. Hultmans Solskensång no. 5)	Co 26063-F
W 108315-2	Du Gamla, Du Fria (Wilb. Stenhammar)	Co 26060-F
W 108316-2	Hem, Ljuva Hem {Home Sweet Home} (J. Howard Payne)	Co 26060-F
W 108317-2	Vid Besök I Barndomshemmet (J.A. Hultmans Solskensång, no. 31)	
		Co 26063-F
		NY September 1927

35.29. Selma Erickson *vocal*

BVE 33619-3	Är Det Ödsligt Och Mörkt Och Kallt? {Hvad Fattas Dig} {The Light Of The World}¹	Vi rej
BVE 33620-3	Kommer Du Ej Snart (Lina Sandell)	Vi rej
BVE 33621-3	Vak Upp (Lina Sandell-Oscar Ahnefeldt)	Vi rej
	vln, cl, vc, org, d Leroy Shield, or ¹p Camden, NJ November 19, 1925	

BVE 33619-5	Är Det Ödsligt Och Mörkt Och Kallt? {Hvad Fattas Dig} {The Light Of The World}	Vi 78436
BVE 33620-6	Kommer Du Ej Snart (Lina Sandell)	Vi 78436
	vln, cl, vc, harp, org, d Rosario Bourdon	
	Camden, NJ November 27, 1925	

35.30. Faith Gospel Male Quartette

GE 12841-A	Glad Såsom Fågeln {Happy As A Bird}	Ge rej
GE 12881-A	Löftena Kunna Ej Svika {His Promises Cannot Fail}	Ge rej
GE 12882-A	Tell Mother I'll Be There [in English]	Ge rej
	p	St. Paul June 1927

35.31. Gustav Fonandern *tenor (1880-1960)*

87085-	Kicki-One Step	
87086-	Bökeviks Valsen	Co E7109
87087-1-2	Midsommartrall	Co E7109
87088-2	Dolly	Co E7131
	orch	Co E7131
		NY February 1921

B 24934-1	Tio Små Negerpojkar {Ten Pickaninnies} (Gustav Fonandern)	Vi 72955
B 24935-1	Karlson Och Jungfrun {Carlson And The Maiden}	Vi 72955
B 24936-2	Mosters Gitarr {My Aunt's Guitar} (Gustav Fonandern)	Vi 73477
	orch d Nathaniel Shilkret	NY February 11, 1921

B 25098-1	Gubben Och St. Per {The Old Man And St. Peter}	Vi 73212
B 25099-2	Jag Är Kommen Bak I Världen Te A Tjäna; Där Är Flickan I Världen	
		Vi 73047
B 25400-2	Månen Han Skiner {The Moon Is Shining}	Vi 73212
B 25401-2	Flickan Gångar Sig Till Brunnen	Vi 73047
	acn	NY May 19, 1921

87449-1	Skön Cisilia	Co E7292
87450-1-2	En Sorglustig Visa	Co E7292
87451-2	Lotta	Co E7336
87452-2	Frieriet I Hölasset	Co E7336
	acn	NY ca May 1921

B 26934-2	Karl, Alfred Och Eleonor {Carl-Alfred And Eleonor}	Vi 73658
B 26935-2	Turalleri-Turallera {Tra-la-la} (w: Anna Myrberg)	Vi 73658
	orch d Nathaniel Shilkret	NY October 6, 1922

89236-2	Från Engeland Te Skottland-Gammal Skepparvisa	Co E9057
89237-1	Flickan Från Havana	Co E9057, 26119-F
89238-2	Min Lilla Sommarvisa	Co E9029
89239-1	Pågar Å Gräbbor	Co E9029
	acn	NY ca June 1923

B 28799-3	Lördagsvalsen {Saturday Waltz} (Svarta Masken-Anselm Johanson)	
		Vi 78015
B 28900-2	Baklandets Vackra Maja {Pretty May Of The Backwoods Country}	
	(Arvid Horne-Hanna Hagborn)	Vi 78015
	orch d Nathaniel Shilkret	NY October 31, 1923

7088	Jazz-Gossen	Wallin's 106
7089	Lilla Frida Och Jag	Wallin's 106
	p	Chicago early 1920s

8021	Kärlek Och Handklaver	Wallin's 108
8022	Flickan Med Kortklippt Hår {En Liten Tös Med Kortklippt Hår}	
		Wallin's 108
8023	Sjömans Vals	Wallin's 112
8024	Kristin-Vals	Wallin's 112
	Anderson, Edström-2 acn	Chicago mid-1920s

BVE 33678-2	O De Ska Bli Skönt Att Komma Hem Igen (Karl Ewert-John Burke)	
		Vi 78555
BVE 33679-3	Johansens Födelsedag {Johansen's Birthday} (Klang-Johan)	Vi 78555
BVE 33680-2	En Trovärdig Sjömansvals (w: Martin)	Vi 78655
BVE 33681-3	Den Sköna Helen {Beautiful Helen}-Sailor's Song	Vi 78655
	Eddy Jahrl-acn	NY January 22, 1926

| W 106280-2 | Din Mun Svarar Nej, Nej (Jos. H. Santley) | Co 26024-F |
| W 106281-1 | Jag Går Åt Mitt Håll (Vincent Youmans) | Co 26024-F |

W 106282-2	Du Gamle Måne (Kai Norman)	Co 26025-F
W 106283-2	Här Dansar Fridolin (Fritz Loewe)	Co 26025-F
		NY ca February 1926

W 106696-2	Fångens Sång	Co 26032-F, 7604
W 106697-1	Den Gamle Zigenaren	Co 26032-F, 7604
	orch	NY April 1926

W 107495-1	Syréndoft-Sångvals (Nanné)	Co 26049-F, 7649
W 107496-2	Som I Ungdomens År (E. Durand)	Co 26047-F, 7648
W 107497-2	Konvaljens Afsked (O. Lindvall)	Co 26047-F, 7648
W 107498-1	Kärlek, Vin Och Sång	Co 26049-F, 7649
		NY December 1926

35.32. A.J. Freeman *tenor*

646	Hemlängtan[1]	Autograph unnumbered
647	Längtan Till Fosterjorden	Autograph unnumbered
	Säg Har Du Fannit Vila?[1]	Autograph unnumbered
	Vad Gor Det Val?	Autograph unnumbered
	vc, p, [1]with Esther Freeman Holmer	Chicago 1925

35.33. Fyra Glada Gossar *instrumental quartet*

105317-	Skånska Valsen	Co 22013-F
105320-	Skepp Som Mötas	Co 22013-F
	På Fjäderholmen	Co 22014-F
	Inga	Co 22014-F
		NY ca April 1925

W 105788-2	En Sjöman Så Glittrande Glad	Co 22022-F
W 105789-2	Hipp Å Hopp Hambo	Co 22022-F
		NY November 1925

W 106541-2	När Jag Kommer Igen-Vals	Co 26030-F
W 106542-2	Min Hembygds Melodi (Einar Westling)	Co 26027-F
W 106543-2	Grönköpingssocietens Vals (Klang-Johan)	Co 26027-F
W 106544-2	En Jazz Uppå Handklaveret	Co 26030-F
		NY March 1926

De Glada Gossarna

W 106969-1	Ingen Kan Kyssa Som Du (C. Ekberg)	Co 26036-F
W 106970-1	O, Du Lilla Ti-Pi-Ti-Pi (E. Westling)	Co 26039-F
W 106971-1	Fagerövalsen (E. Rolf)	Co 26039-F
W 106972-3	Spå Valsen (J. Sylvain)	Co 26036-F
	orch, whistling	NY July 1926

Fyra Glada Gossar

W 107359-2	U-Båtsvalsen (F. Winter)	Co 26045-F
W 107360-1	Varför Ler Du Aldrig Mot Mej (Brink)	Co 26045-F

W 107361-1	Sjömansliv (Ejnar Westling)	Co 26044-F, 7632
W 107362-2	Lapplandsvalsen (Jules Sylvain)	Co 26044-F, 7632
	orch	NY November 1926

W 109128-1	Kväsar-Valsen	Co 22072-F, 13361
W 109129-2	Klackjärns-Polka	Co 22072-F, 13361
W 109130-1	Hollands Vals	Co 22075-F
W 109131-2	Flickan I Gröna Skogen-Schottis	Co 22075-F
	tp, acn, tb, bbs, percussion	NY March 1928

35.34. Oscar W. Green *baritone*

	David's 117de Psalm	Co 26001-F
	Öppna Ditt Hjärta För Herren	Co 26001-F
	Låt Mig Få Höra Om Jesus	Co 26002-F
	Jag Såg En Ros	Co 26002-F
		Chicago(?) 1923

719	Ofta Min Tanke (E.W. Greene)	Special unnumbered
	p	Chicago ca 1925

821	O Kunde Jag Förtalja (Bilhorn) [no vo]	Special unnumbered
	p solo, unk vln, vc	Chicago ca 1925

Label note: Rodeheaver Record Co.

W 108114-2	Aftonklockan	Co 26057-F
W 108115-1	Visa I Mark Och Skog	Co 26057-F
W 108116-2	Tro Dig Igenom	Co 26058-F
W 108117-1	En Skara Stor Och Strålande	Co 26058-F
		Chicago July 1927

35.35. William Gustafson *bass (1887-1931)*

	Armorer's Song [in English]	Vi trial
	Neckens Polska	Vi trial
	Edward T. King-p	NY September 26, 1916

B 19201-1	Ur Svenska Hjärtans Djup En Gång-National Song (Otto Lindblad)	
		Vi 69367
B 19202-2	Källan (The Spring) (W. Lagerkrantz)	Vi 69367
	King's Orchestra	NY February 20, 1917

B 19992-2	Mandom, Mod Och Morske Män (Manhood, Might And Men As Well)	
	(arr Gustav Hägg)	Vi 69681
B 19993-2	I Himlar Sjungen (Creation Hymn) (Beethoven)	Vi 69681
	as before	NY June 8, 1917

B 22090-2	Gör Mig Stilla-Hymn (Almfelt)	Vi 73110
B 22091-2	Kring Källan-Hymn (F. Engelke)	Vi 73110
	Edward T. King-org	NY August 29, 1918

7011-A   Scipio: Hear Me, Ye Winds And Waves (Handel) [in English] Ed 77(33)
                orch
                                                              NY November 17, 1919

35.36. Hans Hagman *baritone*

BVE 45335-2 Hjalmar Och Hulda
                                                                          Vi rej
BVE 45336-1 En Sjöman Älskar Hafvets Våg {A Sailor Loves The Ocean's Wave}
                                                                          Vi rej
             vln, acn, p, g   Chicago June 9, 1928

35.37. Carl Halgren *baritone*

268-1   Säg Det I Toner {Say It With Music} (Jules Sylvain)   RS unnumbered
269-1   Då Reser Jag Med Klara Till Sahara {I'll Take Klara Till Sahara}
             (Tom Wilson)   RS unnumbered
             Sven Eric-p   NY late 1920s

W 112939-2   Efter Vinter Kommer Vår-Valse Romance, ftmp "Charlotte Löwensköld"
             (w: Karl Ewert, m: Jules Sylvain)   Co 26149-F
W 112940-2   För Hennes Skull-Vals Romance, ftmp "För Hennes Skull"
             (w: Gosta Stevens, m: Jules Sylvain)   Co 26149-F
             orch d Eddy Jahrl   NY April 1931

W 113001-   Vårkänslor-Vals (Einar Björke-Sten Hage)   Co 26155-F
W 113003-   När Ringarna Växlas Om Våren-Vals, ftmp "Brokiga Blad"
             (Sylvain-Dalquist)   Co 26155-F
             as before   NY June 1931

35.38. C.F. Hanson *vocal*

A 985-1   Anders, Ta Mej {Andrew Take Me}   Vi 985(7")
M 3600-1   Anders, Ta Mej {Andrew Take Me}   Mon 3600
A 986-1   Min Vän {My Friend}; Glädjens Blomster {A Perfect Day} Vi 986(7")
                                                              NY October 8, 1901

35.39. Lillian Hanson Gray *vocal*

A 975-1   Mandom, Mod Och Morske Män (w: Dybeck)   Vi 975(7")
M 3594-1   Mandom, Mod Och Morske Män (w: Dybeck)   Mon 3594
A 976-1   Necken {Neptune}   Vi 976(7")
M 3595-1   Necken {Neptune}; Stromkarlen   Mon 3595
A 977-1   Fjorton Är {When At Seventeen} (w: Dannstrom)   Vi 977(7")
                                                              NY October 7, 1901

M 3596-1   Fjorton Är {When At Seventeen} (w: Dannstrom)   Mon 3596
A 978-1   Spinn Spinn Dottern Min   Vi 978(7")
M 3597-1   Spinn Spinn Dottern Min   Mon 3597
A 979-1   Det Är Så Underliga Ställen   Vi 979(7")
M 3598-1   Det Är Så Underliga Ställen   Mon 3598
A 980-1   Life's Lesson [in English]   Vi rej (7")

M 3599-1   Daddy   Mon 3599
                                                           NY October 8, 1901

35.40. Gustaf Holmquist *baritone*

B 20946-1   Guds Barns Trygghet   Vi 72061
B 20947-2   Min Klippa (m: Jost Blomquist)   Vi 72061
B 20948-2   Och Hör Du Unga Dora (arr Gustaf Hägg)   Vi 69869
B 20949-1   Hur Ljuft Det Är Att Komma (Isidor Dannström)   Vi rej
             King's Orchestra   NY November 5, 1917

B 20952-3   Norrlänningens Hemlängtan (Hanna Brooman)   Vi rej
B 20953-1   Du Är Min Ro (E.W. Olson-Karl Collan)   Vi 72523
B 20954-2   Signalen Ljuder Och Grafven Bjuder (J. Dannström)   Vi 69867
             as before   NY November 7, 1917

B 20949-2   Hur Ljuft Det Är Att Komma (Isidor Dannström)   Vi 72523
B 21065-2   Fåfäng Önskan (Karl Collan)   Vi 73755
B 21070-1   Jag Är Ung (Ivar Hallstrom); Tänker Du Att Jag Förlorad Är Vi 69869
B 21071-3   Kung Heimer Och Aslog (Aug. Söderman)   Vi 69867
             as before   NY November 8, 1917

B 25272-2   Skärkarlen {The Coast Islander} (H. Saitherberg-J.A.S. Svanson)
                                                                    Vi 73330
B 25273-2   Aftonsång {Evening Song} (Joh. Nybom-Alfred Berg)   Vi 73013
B 25274-2   Grindpojken {The Toll-Gate Boy} (G.R. Nyblom)   Vi rej
B 25292-1   Norrlänningens Hemlängtan {The Northlander's Longing For Home}
                 (E. Sehlstedt-Hanna Brooman)   Vi 73013
B 25293-2   Skördemannen {The Reaper} (J. Fogelberg)   Vi 73147
B 25794-3   Stilla Nott {Silent Night} (Gruber)   Vi 77043
             orch d Nathaniel Shilkret   Camden, NJ May 9, 1921

B 25274-3   Grindpojken {The Toll-Gate Boy} (G.R. Nyblom)   Vi 73330
B 25298-2   Den Älskades Namn {The Beloved's Name} (Franz Abt)   Vi 73755
B 25299-2   Ack, Vermeland, Du Sköna {O, Vermeland, Thou Beautiful} Vi 73147
             as before   Camden, NJ May 11, 1921

35.41. Hugo Hultén *baritone*

39276-1   Folkvisans Ton   Co E1762
39277-1   Östersjön (Konung Oscar II)   Co E1762
39278-1   Alls Ingen Flicka Lastar Ja   Co E1763
39279-1   Vårvindar Friska, Leka Och Hviska; Längtan Till Landet Co E1763
39280-1   Kofvan, from "Förgylda Lergöken"   Co E1764
           orch   NY March 13, 1914

36903-   Trollflöjten   Co E5050(12")
           orch   NY probably March 13, 1914

44483-1   Lilla Tjäll {"Hydda Lill, Tyst Och Still"}-Serenade   Co E3261
44484-2   Konvaljens Afsked (Lindvall))   Co E3196

44485-2	Tess Lördan (Rielman)	Co E3196
	orch	NY ca January 1917

44700-2	Vandringssång {"Vi Vandra Genom Skogen En Högsommardag"} (Körling)	Co E3261
	orch	NY ca March 1917

58549-1	Amerika	Co E3597
58550-1	Den Stjärnströdda Fana {The Star Spangled Banner} (F.S. Key)	
	orch	Cc E3597
		NY ca September 1917

35.42. George G. Hultgren *tenor*

BVE 36293-2	Hvite Syrener (Eillis-Engdahl)	Vi 79029
BVE 36294-3	Aftonstämning (Aug. Körling)	Vi 79029
BVE 36295-2	Vid Siljan Är Mitt Hem (arr Eklund Miller)	Vi 79087
BVE 36296-2	Nu Julens Ängel Viskar Sakta (w: A. Bjorklund, m: Pfeil)	Vi 78956
	orch	Webster Hotel, Chicago September 23, 1926

BVE 36297-2	Jag Vet En Hamn (Soderberg)	Vi 79087
BVE 36298-2	Julen Är Inne (N. Frykman-Th. Soderberg)	Vi 78956
BVE 36299-2	That's Why I Love Him (Scott Lawrence) [in English]	Vi 79155
BVE 36400-1	I'm A Pilgrim (Shindler-Ahnfelt) [in English]	Vi 79155
	fl, vc, org, chimes	Webster Hotel, Chicago September 24, 1926

BVE 45308-2	Hälsa Dem Där Hemma {Greet Those That Are At Home} (Elith Worsing)	
		Vi 81529
BVE 45309-2	Syrendoft {Fragrance Of Lilacs} (Hanne)	Vi 81347
BVE 45310-2	Mor, Lilla Mor {Mother, Little Mother} (Ellen Hejkorn)	Vi 81529
BVE 45311-2	Alprosen {Rose Of The Alps}	Vi 81347
	vln, p, g	Chicago June 6, 1928

BVE 48779-2	Lyssnar Du Till Mig I Kväll, Lilla Mor {Are You Listening In, Little Mother} (Igor Borganoff)	Vi V-24006
BVE 48780-2	I Barndomens Ängder {In Childhood Lanes} (Jules Sylvain)	Vi V-24007
BVE 48781-2	Vackra Vita Flingor {Beautiful White Snowflakes} (George Enders)	
		Vi V-24007
BVE 48782-2	När Lindarna Blomma {When The Linden Trees Are Blooming} (S. Sune)	
		Vi V-24006
	vln, vc, p	Chicago January 15, 1929

35.43. Johannes Alfred Hultman *vocal (1861-1942)*

33079-1	Han Är Likadan I Dag (J.A. Hultman)	Co
33157-1	Det Brister Er Sträng (J.A. Hultman)	Co
33161-1	Säg Har Du I Dag Ej En Blomma (J.A. Hultman)	Co
33162-1	Med Glädje Jag Sjunger (J.A. Hultman)	Co
33163-1	Min Hembygd (J.A. Hultman)	Co
33164-5	O, Sköne Vär (J.A. Hultman)	Co
33165-1	O, Att Jag Kunde	Co
33166-	Stridssång I Harmageddon	Co

33169-	Du Lill Fågel (Joel Blomquist)	Co
33170-1-2	Vi En Pilgrimsskapa Glad (A.L. Skoog)	Co
33171-1	Redeemed (J.B. Towner) [in English]	Co
33172-1	Jag Sjunger Ändå (J.A. Hultman)	Co
33173-1	May There Be Many Stars (J.A. Hultman) [in English]	Co
33174-1	När Hela Jorden Sover (J.A. Hultman)	Co
p		NY ca 1914

61873-	Jag Älskar Norden (J.A. Hultman)	Co
61874-1	Till Kristi Kors	Co
61875-	title untraced	Co
61876-1	Låt Oss Sprida Solsken (J.A. Hultman)	Co
61877-1	Tak, O Gud For Vad Som Varit (J.A. Hultman)	Co rej
61878-3	Mitt Barndomshem (J.A. Hultman)	Co
61879-	Längtan Till Fosterjorden (J.A. Hultman)	Co
p		NY September 19, 1917

61880-1	Liten Fågel Högt I Linden (J.A. Hultman)	Co
61881-	title untraced	Co
61882-	title untraced	Co
61883-1	Släpp Nu Litet Solsken In (J.A. Hultman)	Co
61884-	title untraced	Co
61885-1	Glöm Aldrig Bort De Kära (J.A. Hultman)	Co
61886-	title untraced	Co
61887-	title untraced	Co
61888-1	Mer Än Millionär (J.A. Hultman)	Co
p		NY September 21, 1917

61890-3	Jag Stod På Den Öde Stranden	Co
61891-	Jubla Min Aude (J.A. Hultman)	Co
p		NY September 22, 1917

61877-2	Tak, O Gud For Vad Som Varit (J.A. Hultman)	Co
p		NY October 4, 1917

91026-	Gud Ske Lov Min Sjal Ar Fralst (J.A. Hultman)	Co
91027-	Till Lustgarden Kom Jag (J.A. Hultman)	Co
91030-1	Ett Hem Om Än Så Ringa (J.A. Hultman)	Co
91031-2	Var Är Ditt Hem? (J.A. Hultman)	Co
91348-1	På Bryggan Jag Stod Vid Midnatt (Lindsey)	Co
91352-1	Invid Porten, Hjärtats Stängda Port (J.A. Hultman)	Co
p		NY late 1910s

Label note: "Specially made for J.A. Hultman & Son Co., Worcester, Mass." The records have no catalog numbers and are coupled as follows: 33079/33174, 33157/33161, 33162/33163, 33164/33165, 33166/33169, 33170/33172, 33171/33173, 61873/61879, 61874/61890, 61876/61880, 61877/61891, 61878/61885, 61883/61888, 91026/91027, 91030/91031, 91348/91352.

35.44. I.O.G.T. Double Quartette, Worcester, Mass. *vocal*

W 170332-2	Vandringslust {Wanderlust} (Stubbe)	Co 119-P
W 170333-1	Mitt Hemlands Dal {The Valley Of My Homeland} (Dfeil)	Co 119-P

W 170334-2	Frieripolka {Courting Polka}	Co 120-P
W 170335-2	Aftenröster {Evening Voices} (Borg)	Co 120-P

NY October 20, 1928

35.45. Chas. Johanson *tenor*

BVE 45304-1	Vintergatan {Milky Way} (Jules Sylvain)	Vi 81326
BVE 45305-1	Mors Porträtt {Mother's Portrait} (Ejnar Westling)	Vi 81326
BVE 45306-2	Midsommarnatts Drömmen {Midsummer Night's Dream}	Vi 81699
BVE 45092-1	Jungfru Under Lind {Maiden Under The Linden} (Wilh. Peterson-Berger)	Vi 81699

vln, acn, vc, p, d Leroy Shield   Chicago June 5, 1928

35.46. Rev. Gustav Johnson *spoken*

Pastor Gustav F. Johnston

C 31196-2	Jul Glädje {Christmas Joy} {Kristi Andra Tillkommelse} {Return Of The Lord}-Sermon; I Midnattstimmens Tysta Stund {It Came Upon A Midnight Clear} (R.S. Willis)	Vi 68709(12")
C 31197-1	Jul Glädje {Christmas Joy} {Midnattsljuset Från Himmelen} {Midnight Light From Heaven}-Sermon (Rev. Johnston); Bethlehem Stjärna (A.L. Skogg)	Vi 68709(12")

sermons, with George G. Hultgren-ten solo, Edward T. King-org, H.W. Gage-chimes   Minneapolis November 20, 1924

Rev. Gustav F. Johnson

B 31198-2	Herren Kommer {The Coming Of The Lord}-Pt. 1	Vi 77823
B 31199-2	Herren Kommer {The Coming Of The Lord}-Pt. 2	Vi 77823

spoken   Minneapolis November 20, 1924

Pastor Gustaf F. Johnson

BVE 35613-3	God's Way Of Salvation-Pt. 1 [in English]	Vi 78759
BVE 35614-1	God's Way Of Salvation-Pt. 2 [in English]	Vi 78759
BVE 35615-1	Kristuslös Kristendom {A Christless Christianity}-Pt. 1	Vi 78848
BVE 35616-2	Kristuslös Kristendom {A Christless Christianity}-Pt. 2	Vi 78848

spoken   NY May 19, 1926

35.47. Ted Johnson And His Scandinavian Orchestra

C 1635-	Svenska Valsen	Vo 15947, Nordvest TJ4318(33)
C 1636-1	Johan På Snippen-Schottisch	Vo 15958, Nordvest TJ4318(33)
C 1637-1	Hesselby Steppen-Polka	Vo 15958
C 1638-2	På Begäran {By Request}-Mazurka	Vo rej
C 1639-1	Nikolina (arr Karl S. Johnson)	Vo 15947, Nordvest TJ4318(33), LC LBC-11(33)
C 1640-2	Bor Du Hemma Hos Din Mamma? {Home And Mother}-Two Step	Vo rej
C 1641-	Styrmans Valsen {Pilot's Waltz} (arr E. Olzen)	Vo 15959, Co 12435-F, Nordvest TJ4318(33)

2701

C 1642-	Kalle Pe {Carl's Polka}	Vo 15952, Cq 9612, Nordvest TJ4318(33)
C 1643-	Triplett Schottisch	Vo 15952, Cq 9612, Nordvest TJ4318(33)
C 1644-2	Nya Dragspels {Accordion}-Valsen	Vo rej
C 1645-2	Dallbackatrallen-Polka	Vo rej
C 1646-	Grönland Rheinlander-Schottisch	
		Vo 15959, Co 12455-F, Nordvest TJ4318(33)

Ted Johnson-vln/'vo, Orville E. Lindhelm-acn, Flo Seidel-p, Howard
Dellwo-sbs, Bill Hesselgrave-dm/vibraharp　　　　NY　October 29, 1936

35.48.　Svan Jonson　*vocal*

W 109532-2	De' Va' En Gång En Gubbe	Co 26078-F
W 109533-2	Svan Jonsons Amerikabrev	Co 26078-F
		NY　July 1928

35.49.　Ebba Kjempe-Kjellgren　*soprano*

7065	Flickan I Skogen	Wallin's 105
7066	Släckta Fyrar	Wallin's 105
	Elsa Frick-p	NY　ca 1921

35.50.　Kungl. Svenska Flottans Musikkår　*band*

W 106547-2	Kungl. Flottans Defilardmarsch (Teike)	Co 26028-F
W 106548-2	Kungl. Södermanlands Regt. Marsch	Co 22032-F
W 106549-2	Nya Bonnjazzen (Rolf)	Co 26033-F
W 106550-	En Sommarvals (Vidquist)	Co 26033-F
W 106551-2	Sverige (W. Stenhammar)	Co 26028-F
W 106552-1	Wasaduken (Ragnar Althén)	Co 22032-F
W 106553-1	Bellmansmelodier-Pt. 1	Co 26029-F
W 106554-2	Bellmansmelodier-Pt. 2	Co 26029-F
W 106555-2	Dans På Logen (Widquist)	Co 22037-F
		NY　March 1926

35.51.　H.F. Larson　*tenor*

745	Jesus Gör Mig Nojd Och Stilla-Alpmelodi (w: Lagerstrom)	Rainbow 300
750	Om Dagen Vid Mitt	Rainbow 300
	Vill Du Möta Hos Jesus	Rainbow 301
	Jesus Kallar (Crosby-Stebbins)	Rainbow 301
	orch	Winona Lake, MN　1922-3

35.52.　Teddy Larson　*tenor*

W 105689-2	Släckta Fyrar	Co 26015-F
W 105693-2	Skepp Som Mötas	Co 26015-F
W 105694-2	Skördemannen	Co 26016-F
W 105695-	Stilla Natt-Christmas Song	Co 26017-F
W 105696-2	Den Heliga Julnatten-Christmas Song	Co 26017-F

W 105697-1	Folkvisa	Co 26016-F
	orch	NY June 1925

W 106083-1	Älskling På Vägen	Co 26022-F
W 106084-1	Det Blåser Upp En Sunna Vind (Einar Björke)	Co 26023-F
W 106085-	Lördags Valsen	Co 26020-F
W 106086-1	Jag Vill Ha En Litentös Med (Långa Flätor) (Rudolph Nelson)	
		Co 26023-F
W 106087-2	Höstens Violiner (Jules Sylvain)	Co 26022-F
W 106088-	Min Egen Lilla Mor	Co 26020-F
W 106089-1	Tonerna	Co 26021-F
W 106090-2	Inga Lill	Co 26021-F
	orch	NY November 1925

W 106611-2	Soldatgossen (F. Pacius)	Co 26031-F
W 106612-2	Kung Erik	Co 26031-F
W 106613-1	Sverige Är Bäst Ändå (Helge Lindberg)	Co 26037-F
W 106614-2	Med Det Gjorde Mamma När Mamma Var Flicka (Ellis Olson)	Co 26037-F
		NY April 1926

35.53. **Ingeborg Laudon** *soprano*

This singer's name is given as INGELONG LAUDON in the Columbia files.

38810-2	Greta Och Lasse	Co
38811-1	Greta Lill	Co rej
	p	NY April 24, 1913

38819-2	Höstmanöver	Co
38820-1	Eva	Co rej
38822-2	Kärlek På Italienska Och Svenska	Co E1594
38823-1	Bohuslänska Sjömansvalsen	Co rej
	orch	NY April 29, 1913

38823-2	Bohuslänska Sjömansvalsen	Co E1594
	p	NY June 18, 1913

38911-1	Ny Fiskar Vals	Co
38912-2	Akta Dej För Mej	Co
		NY June 19, 1913

35.54. **Bert Leman** *vocal*

BVE 42396-2	Josefin Med Symaskin (Josephine With The Sewing Machine)	
	(Bert Leman)	Vi 81334
BVE 42397-2	Jumpa (To Jump) (Bert Leman)	Vi 81334
BVE 42398-1	Då Ska Morsan Vara Me' (Mother Will Be With Us Then) (John Redland)[1]	
		Vi 81440
BVE 42399-2	Kärleken (Love) (Bert Leman)	Vi V-24001
BVE 45300-1	Sörmanlands Beväringa (Sodermanlands Military Training)	
	(Bert Leman)[1] [2]	Vi 81440

BVE 45301-1   Gånglåt Från Munga {Beväringetrall} {Promenade Song From Munga}
              (w: Bert Leman)¹ ²   Vi V-24016
              vln, acn, ¹p, ²traps   Chicago June 4, 1928

BVE 45302-2   Syrvorkeri {Fireworks} (E. Norlander)   Vi V-24001
BVE 45303-2   Så Är Den Da'n Förstörd {This Day Is Also Spoiled} (Bert Leman)
                                                                  Vi V-24016
              vln, acn   Chicago June 5, 1928

35.55. Lydia Lindgren *soprano*

              Tag Omod Kiausen   Vi trial
              Pendant Le Bal [in French]   Vi trial
              Edward T. King-p   NY May 19, 1916

B 18475-2   Glädjens Blomster {Flowers Of Joy} (arr Gustav Hägg)   Vi 69096
B 18476-2   När Jag Blef Sjutton År {When I Was Seventeen}   Vi rej
B 18477-2   Jag Ser Uppå Dina Ogön {If I See Your Eyes} (arr Gustav Hägg)
                                                                  Vi 69096
              King's Orchestra   NY October 3, 1916

B 18492-1   Allt Under Himmelens Fäste {In Heaven's Vault Above Me}   Vi 69144
B 18493-2   Vårvindar Friska Leka Och Hviska {Spring Breezes Crisp}
              (Julia Nyberg, arr Gustav Hägg)   Vi rej
B 18494-1   Synnöves Sang (Bjornson-Kjerulf) [in Norwegian]   Vi 69109
              as before   NY October 6, 1916

B 18622-2   Solveigs Sang, from "Peer Gynt" (Grieg) [in Norwegian]   Vi 69109
B 18623-2   Du Har Sörjit Nu Igen {Dear One, Thou Hast Wept Once More}   Vi rej
              as before   NY October 20, 1916

B 18476-5   När Jag Blef Sjutton År {When I Was Seventeen}   Vi rej
B 18631-1   Mor Britta (W. Peterson-Berger)   Vi 69144
B 18632-3   Svärmeri {Fond Fancy} (F. Arlberg)   Vi rej
              as before   NY October 24, 1916

B 18476-7   När Jag Blef Sjutton År {When I Was Seventeen}   Vi rej
B 18493-4   Vårvindar Friska Leka Och Hviska {Spring Breezes Crisp}
              (Julia Nyberg, arr Gustav Hägg)   Vi rej
B 18623-5   Du Har Sörjit Nu Igen {Dear One, Thou Hast Wept Once More}   Vi rej
B 18632-5   Svärmeri {Fond Fancy} (F. Arlberg)   Vi 69619
              as before   NY November 24, 1916

B 18695-3   Herdegossen (J.A. Berg)   Vi rej
              as before   NY November 27, 1916

B 18493-6   Vårvindar Friska Leka Och Hviska {Spring Breezes Crisp}
              (Julia Nyberg, arr Gustav Hägg)   Vi rej
B 18695-5   Herdegossen (J.A. Berg)   Vi rej
              as before   NY December 18, 1916

B 19050-1   Månn Tro? Jo, Jo {Ah, Why? Ay, Ay!} (A.F. Lindblad)   Vi 69619
              as before   NY January 17, 1917

B 18476-10	När Jag Blef Sjutton År {When I Was Seventeen}		Vi 69478
B 19931-2	Klara Stjärnor Med De Ögon Snälla {Little Stars,		
	Whose Bright Eyes Shine Above Me}		Vi rej
B 19932-2	Som Stjärnan Uppå Himmelen Så Klar {The Stars Above Me}		Vi 69478
	as before, d Rosario Bourdon	NY	May 22, 1917

35.56. Sam Ljungkvist *tenor*

| | Vuggesang [in Norwegian]; Aflonstämning | | Vi trial |
| | | NY | July 3, 1916 |

B 18279-2	Sten Sture (Wilhelm Svedbom)		Vi 69027
B 18280-2	Näckens Polska		Vi rej
B 18281-2	Kristallen Den Fina		Vi rej
B 18282-1	Natthimmelen (E.G. Geijer)		Vi 69027
	King's Orchestra	NY	August 29, 1916

B 18446-1	Spelmansvisa {The Fiddler} (A. Karlfeldt-I. Wideen)		Vi 69132
B 18447-1	Lyft Mig {Lift Me} (Felix Körling-E. Lundberg)		Vi 69172
	as before	NY	September 21, 1916

B 18465-2	Sommarkärlek {Summer Love} (Sigurd V. Koch)		Vi 69172
B 18466-1	Skogen Sofver (Hugo Alfven)		Vi rej
B 18467-2	Sverige (W. Stenhammar)		Vi rej
B 18468-2	Jeg Giver Mit Digt Til Våren (Emil Sjögren) [in Norwegian]		Vi rej
	as before	NY	September 27, 1916

44430-2	"Tallarnes Barr Och Björkarnas Blad"-Serenad (I. Widéen)		Co E3058
44431-2	Det Var Dans Bort I Vägen (H. Lambert)		Co E3058
44432-1	Sverige (W. Stenhammar)		Co E3059
44433-1	Hemlängtan-"Helga Minne, Dig Jag Beder" (J.A. Josephson)		Co E3059
	orch	NY	ca September 1916

B 18281-3	Kristallen Den Fina		Vi 69361
B 18465-4	Sommarkärlek {Summer Love} (Sigurd V. Koch)		Vi rej
B 18466-2	Skogen Sofver (Hugo Alfven)		Vi rej
B 18467-4	Sverige (W. Stenhammar)		Vi rej
	King's Orchestra	NY	November 24, 1916

B 18465-6	Sommarkärlek {Summer Love} (Sigurd V. Koch)		Vi rej
B 18467-7	Sverige (W. Stenhammar)		Vi 69361
	as before	NY	February 27, 1917

4574-	Vårvindar Friska		Em 18001
4575-1-2	Förgäfves Uppå Stigen {In Vain Upon The Pathway}		Em 18002
4577-2	Å Jänta Å Ja {The Maiden And I}		Em 18002
	Jag Sjunger Och Dansar		Em 18001
	orch	NY	ca November 1919

35.57. Elda Lund *vocal*

B 22082-2	Psalm CXXXVII	Vi rej
B 22083-1	Jag Är En Gäst Och Främling	Vi 72179
	Edward T. King-org	NY August 2, 1918

B 22082-3	Psalm CXXXVII	Vi 72179
	Nathaniel Shilkret-org	NY August 15, 1918

B 23230-3	Flyg Som En Fogel {Flee As A Bird}	Vi 72928
B 23231-3	Om Dagen Vid Mitt Arbete {When In The Daytime Working}; Rosor Och	
	Violer {Roses And Violets}	Vi rej
B 23233-1	Herre, Mitt Hjärta {My Heart Longs For Thee, O Lord} (Carl Sjögren);	
	Fardil Ej Ditt Ansigte För Mig {Lord,	
	Hide Not Thy Face From Me}'	Vi 72928

King's Orchestra d Nathaniel Shilkret, or 'Nathaniel Shilkret-org

NY September 8, 1919

35.58. Oscar A. Lundberg *baritone*

B 17779-2	Min Hemlandsdal (Louis Liebe)	Vi 67947
B 17780-1	Äktenskapsfrågan	Vi 67947
	King.'s Orchestra	NY June 1, 1916

B 18460-2	I Villande Skog	Vi rej
B 18461-2	Per Svinaherde	Vi 69289
	as before	NY September 26, 1916

B 18460-4	I Villande Skog	Vi 69289
	as before	NY November 15, 1916

61754-	test recording	Co
		NY July 6, 1917

58677-1	Necken Spelar På Böljan Blå	Co E3640
58678-1	Kristallen Den Fina	Co E3639
58679-1	Fjärilen Vingad Syns På Haga (Bellman)	Co E3640
58680-1	Min Lilla Vrå Bland Bergen	Co E3639
	orch	NY September 1917

88880-	Är Jesus När? (L. Lincoln Hall)	Co E7824
88881-	Af Himlens Höjd {Psalm No. 63}	Co E7824
		NY November 1922

89425-1	Julotta I Kyrkan-Pt. 1	Co 26000-F, 7699
89426-1	Julotta I Kyrkan-Pt. 2	Co 26000-F, 7699
	Påskgudstjänst-Pt. 1	Co 26003-F
	Påskgudstjänst-Pt. 2	Co 26003-F
	predikan av Carl G. Westerdahl	NY September 1923

	Den Glade Trumpetaren	Co 26004-F

Äktenskapsfrågan   Co 26004-F
                                                        NY   1923-4

89702-1   Midsommar   Co 26010-F
89703-2   Hembygden   Co 26010-F
            acn   NY   January 1924

35.59. Gustave Lundh *tenor*

85079-2   Barndomshemmet   Co E4289, 26114-F
85080-   På Roines Strand (Linsen)   Co E4387
            orch   NY   ca June 1919

85303-   Rosen I December   Co E4387
            orch   NY   ca July 1919

35.60. Joseph Lycell *baritone*

B 25621-2   Jag Är Främling   Vi 73196
B 25622-2   Vid Jesu Hjärta   Vi 73196
            Nathaniel Shilkret-org, unk vln   NY   September 27, 1921

B 26386-2   Tonerna (O.L. Sjöberg)   Vi 77208
            orch d Ted Levy   NY   August 18, 1922

B 26908-3   När Juldagsmorgon Glimmar {When Christmas Morn Is Gleaming} Vi 73518
B 26909-3   Det Är En Ros Utsprungen {There Is A Rose Blooming}   Vi 73518
            fl, vln, vc, org, traps, d Nathaniel Shilkret   NY   September 29, 1922

B 28303-2   Se Natten Flyr   Vi 77043
            Leroy Shield-org, orch d Nathaniel Shilkret   NY   July 20, 1923

B 28733-2   Den Farliga Månen (Reidar Thomessen)   Vi 77208
            orch d Nathaniel Shilkret   NY   October 12, 1923

B 29016-3   Barndomshemmet {My Childhood Home} (Karl Ewert-P. Wurk)   Vi 77245
B 29017-3   Sångarens Epilog {A Singer's Epilogue}, taken from "In The Gloaming"
              (w: Erik Bergquist)   Vi 77245
            orch d Leroy Shield   Camden, NJ November 20, 1923

B 28998-3   Det Är Guds Ord {God's Word} (Ahnefeldt)   Vi 77311
B 28999-3   Vår Store Gud {Our Great God} (N. Frykmen) Vi 77311
            Leroy Shield-org, unk vln, chimes   NY   December 3, 1923

The composer of matrix B 28998 is given as "I.A.P. Schultz" in the Victor files.

B 29672-3   Bida Blott! {Only Wait}   Vi 77646
B 29673-3   Frälst Af Nåd {Saved By Grace}   Vi 77646
            orch d Leroy Shield   Camden, NJ March 17, 1924

B 29796-3   Bed Dig Igenom   Vi rej
B 29797-2   De Komma {They Are Coming} (Thor Harris-Russell De Koven) Vi 77516

B 29798-2   Tro Dig Igenom {Let Faith Carry You Through} (N.J. Russell) Vi 77516
              vln, fl, p, org, d Leroy Shield   NY April 15, 1924

B 30712-3   O Du Saliga, O Du Heliga {O Thou Blessed, O Thou Holy}-Christmas
                  Song   Vi 77698
B 30713-2   Till Bethlehem {To Bethlehem}-Christmas Hymn   Vi 77698
              orch d Leroy Shield   Camden, NJ August 20, 1924

B 31350-3   Sarons Blomma {Rose Of Sharon} (Eric Bergquist)   Vi 77881
B 31351-2   Sök Ej Kristus Bland De Döda (P.B. Bliss)   Vi 77881
              orch d Charles Prince   Camden, NJ November 24, 1924

PBVE 158-2   Om Jag Ägde Allt, Men Icke Jesus {If I Had All, But Not Jesus}
                  (Anna Olander)   Vi 78768
PBVE 159-2   Guds Källa {The Fountain Of The Lord}   Vi 78768
PBVE 160-2   Ej Silver Ej Guld {Nor Silver Nor Gold} (Towner)   Vi 78881
PBVE 161-2   Löftena Kunna Ej Svika {The Promises Shall Never Fail} (Levi Petrus)
                                                                        Vi 78881
PBVE 162-3   Ballad Ur Gustaf Vasas Saga {Ballad From Gustaf Of Vasas Saga}
                  (Hallen)   Vi rej
              Leroy Shield-org   Oakland, CA April 16, 1926

PBVE 163-2 (43293) Är Det Sant Att Jesus Min Broder? {Is It True,
                  That Jesus Is My Brother?} {Under Öfver Under}
                  {Wonder Over Wonder} (Lina Sandell)   Vi 80675
PBVE 164-2 (43292) En Dag I Sänder {Faith Day By Day} (D. Ahnfelt)   Vi 80675
PBVE 165-3   Vår Gud Är Oss En Väldig Borg {A Mighty Fortress Is Our God}
                                                                        Vi 78941
PBVE 166-2   Jesu Kristi Dag {Day Of Jesus Christ}   Vi 78941
              as before   Oakland, CA April 17, 1926

35.61. Lyran, New York, Och Gleeklubben, Brooklyn *male chorus*

W 106912-2   Hälsning Till Hemlandet (Kromer)   Co 26035-F
W 106913-1   Fansång (Wennerberg)   Co 26040-F
W 106914-2   Vårsång (Prins Gustaf)   Co 26038-F
W 106917-1   Kinkan-Halvan (K. Sylvan-Wennerberg)   Co 26038-F
W 106918-1   Stridsbön (Lindblad)   Co 26040-F
W 106919-1   Sveriges Flagga-Dalkarlsång (Alfvén-Lindblad)   Co 26035-F
              d Karl Sylvan   NY July 1926

35.62. The Lyric Quartet *vocal*

BS 99888-1   My Homeland; Spring; Buxom Lassies; Neptune (arr Stella Marek
                  Cushing, from "Music Highways And Byways," pub. Silver Burdett
                  Company) {Trips Abroad-Sweden}   Vi 25382
              d Gustav V. Lindgren   NY March 17, 1936

35.63. William Mattison *tenor*

Någon Bjuder	Ber 2975(7")
Den Sköna Adlaida	Ber 2976(7")
Suppeen {Georgie}	Ber 2977(7")
Hej Dunka	Ber 2978(7")
Malin	Ber 2979(7")
Asnoria	Ber 2980(7")
Karl August {The Whistling Coon}	Ber 2981(7")
p	NY May 28, 1898

35.64. Joel Mossberg *baritone*

B 3503-1	Min Älskades Namn {Ich Hab' Ihren Namen Geschrieben} (Abt)	Vi 3404, 63382
B 3504-1	Flickorna I Nerike (Lars Bondessons Variété Kupletter)	Vi 3417, 63388
B 3505-1	Grythyttepågen (Lars Bondessons Variété Kupletter)	Vi 3418, 63389
B 3506-1	Stor-Olas Maja-Bondvisa	Vi 3424, 63392
B 3507-1	Liss Olof Larsons Stockholmsresa-Bondvisa	Vi 3425, 63392
B 3508-1	Fotografering (Lars Bondessons Variété Kupletter)	Vi 3419, 63389
E 3509-1	Djurkuplett (Lars Bondessons Variété Kupletter)	Vi 3403(8")
B 3510-1	Ett Förfluget Ord (Lars Bondessons Variété Kupletter)	Vi 3420, 63390
p		NY July 10, 1906

B 3513-1	Trollhättan (Lindblad)	Vi 3405, 63382
B 3514-1	Martha: Porter Visa (Flotow)	Vi 3406, 63383
B 3515-1	Soldatgossen (Pacius)	Vi 3407, 63384
B 3516-1	Per Svinaherde (Lars Bondessons Variété Kupletter)	Vi 3413, 63386
B 3517-1	Till Svenska Fosterjorden {Du Gamla, Du Fria}	Vi 3414, 63387
B 3518-1	Neckens Polska	Vi 3415, 63387
B 3519-1	I Djupa Källarhvalfvet {Im Tieffer Kellars} (Fischer)	Vi rej
B 3520-1	Pompa (Lars Bondessons Variété Kupletten)	Vi 3421, 63390
B 3521-1	Stenkuplett (Lars Bondessons Variété Kupletten)	Vi 3422, 63391
B 3522-1	Kväsarvalsen-Bondvisa	Vi 3423, 63391
B 3523-1	Fogels Visa	Vi rej
p		NY July 11, 1906

B 3519-2	I Djupa Källarhvalfvet {Im Tieffer Kellars} (Fischer)	Vi 3408, 63384
E 3525-1	Och, Hör Du Unga Dora	Vi 3402(8")
E 3526-1	Min Lilla Vrå Bland Bergen (Wadman)	Vi 3400(8")
E 3527-1	Necken Han Spelar På Böljan Blå	Vi 3401(8")
B 3528-1	Ljungby Horn (Frieberg)	Vi 3410, 63385
B 3529-1	I Rosens Doft (Prins Gustaf)	Vi 3411, 63385
B 3530-1	Värmlandsvisan	Vi 3416, 63388
B 3531-1	Drick Ur Ditt Glas (Bellman)	Vi 3412, 63386
		NY July 12, 1906

43818-1	Hvad Det Är Skönt Ändå (Wennerberg)'	Co E2876
43819-	Gluntens Vigilans (Wennerberg)'	Co E2834
43821-1	Visst Va Vi Lite Mosiga; Gluntens Misstag (Wennerberg)'	Co E2876
43822-1	Nattmarschen I Sanct Eriks Gränd (Wennerberg)'	Co E2834

43823-2	Ljungby Horn (Frieberg)	Co E2835
43824-1	Trollhättan (Lindblad)	Co E2878
43825-1	Norrländingens Hemlängtan (Brooman))	Co E2878
43826-2	Till Österland Vill Jag Fara	Co E3008
43827-1	Lugn Hvilar Sjön (Pfeil)	Co E2835
43828-1	Vårt Land (Pacius)	Co E2877, 26125-F
43829-1	Härlig Är Kvällen (Ekström)	Co E3008
43830-3	Du Gamla, Du Fria-National Song (R. Dybeck)	Co E2531
43831-1	O, Helga Natt-Julsång	Co E2961, 26116-F
43832-1	Dufvan {La Paloma} (Yradier)	Co E2932
43833-1	I Gröna Palmers Skrud (Faure)	Co E3159
	orch, 'Oscar Bergström-bs	NY ca April 1916
43850-1	Sof I Ro (Mohring)	Co E3160
43853-1	Var Hälsad Sköna Morgonstund {Psalm 55}	Co E2961, 26116-F
43854-1	Hosianna Davids Son	Co E3159
43855-1	Närmare, Gud, Till Dig	Co E3160
43858-2	Björneborgarnes-Marsch	Co E2877, 26125-F
	orch	NY April 1916
44020-1	Vi Gå Öfver Daggstänkta Berg (Thuman)	Co E2932
	orch	NY May 1916
44054-	Sångarfanan (Freiberg)	Co E3007
44055-2	Engelbrektsmarschen-National Song (Blanche)	Co E2931
44056-	Magisterns Misslyckade Serenad (Wennerberg)'	Co E2929
44057-2	Bror, Jag Är Ledsen (Wennerberg)'	Co E2930
44058-	Upsala Är Bäst (Wennerberg)'	Co E2929
44059-1	Hulda Skymning (Wennerberg)'	Co E2930
44062-	Per Svinaherde	Co E3007
44063-1	En Glad Trall (Scholander)	Co E3355
	Den Röda Näsan	Co E3009
	Skratta, Mina Barn Och Vara Glada (Bellman)	Co E3009
	orch or 'p, with Hugo Hulten-bs	NY ca June 1916
5032	Kung Carl XII (w: E. Tegner, 1782-1846, m: O. Westermark, 1799-1850)	
		Ed 78005, 9450(4 min)
5033	Neckens Polska (A.A. Afzelius, 1785-1871)	Ed 78001, 9451(4 min)
5034	Å Jänta Å Ja (P.A. Dahlgren, 1816-1895)	Ed 78002, 9452(4 min)
5035	Vårvindar Friska, Leka Och Hviska; Och Flickan Hon Går I Dansen	
		Ed 78004, 9461(4 min)
	orch	NY October 2, 1916
5036	Hör Oss, Svea! (Gunnar Wennerberg, 1817-1901)	Ed 78002, 9453(4 min)
5037	Min Lilla Vrå Bland Bergen (w: J.A. Wadman, 1777-1837, m: J.	
	Sandstrom, 1824-1880)	Ed 78005, 9448(4 min)
5038	På Roines Strand (arr Collan)	Ed 78001, 9449(4 min)
	orch	NY October 3, 1916
5040	Soldatgossen (F. Pacius)	Ed 78006, 9454(4 min)
5041	Vi Ska' Ställa Te En Roliger Dans; Tänker Du Att Jag Förlorad Är?;	
	Aspåkers Polska (W. Peterson Berger)	Ed 78021, 9462(4 min)

5042	Finska Rytteriets {Finnish Cavalry} Marsch (Z. Topelius, 1818-1898,	
	arr Emil Carson)	Ed 78006, 9455(4 min)
	orch	NY October 4, 1916

5045   Hyllning Till Sverige; Du Gamla, Du Fria, Du Fjällhöga Nord
               {Song Of The North}   Ed 78003, 9459(4 min)
5046   Mandom, Mod Och Morske Män; Längtan Till Landet (O. Lindblad,
               1809-1864)   Ed 78004, 9460(4 min)
5047   Fågelns Visa {The Birds' Song} (w: Z. Topelius, 1818-1898, m: Th
               Söderberg, 1845-)   Ed 78007, 9456(4 min)
5048   Ack, Värmeland, Du Sköna (A. Fryxell, 1795-1881)
                                        Ed 78003, 9457(4 min)
5049   Tre Trallande Jäntor (w: Gustaf Fröding, 1860-1911,
              m: Felix Körling)   Ed 78007, 9458(4 min)
          orch   NY October 5, 1916

44465-2	Marseljäsen-Socialist Song (De L'Isle)	Co E3161
44470-2	Arbetets Söner-Socialist Song	Co E3161
	orch	NY October 1916
	Finska Rytteriets Marsch	Co E3423
		NY 1916
85034-2	Mor Britta	Co E4289, 26114-F
85035-	Sång Efter Skördeanden	Co E4927
85038-	Psalm 84-Easter Song	Co E4927
	Svensk Folkvisa No. 4	Co E4432
	Beväings Visa	Co E4432
	orch	NY ca March 1919
	Så Kom Du	Vi trial
	Nathaniel Shilkret-p	NY February 19, 1920

35.65. H. William Nordin *baritone*

BVE 34574-3 Om Gud Så Kläder Gräset {If God So Clothes The Grass} (J. Bischoff)
                                                           Vi 78640
BVE 34575-2 Min Lilla Vrå Bland Bergen {My Home Midst Hills And Valleys}
               (J. Sandstrom)   Vi rej
          orch d Leroy Shield   Chicago March 2, 1926

BVE 35047-2 Mor, Lilla Mor   Vi rej
BVE 35048-2 Där Björkorna Susa {Where The Birch Trees Rustle}
               (Viktor Lund-Oskar Merikanto, op. 1)   Vi 78640
          as before   Chicago March 11, 1926

35.66. Eric Norgren *bass*

39206-1	Afsked Från Hemmet {Bort Till Fjärran Land I Soder}	Co E1702
39207-1	Lifdrabanten Och Kung Erik	Co E1702
39208-1	Jätten	Co E1703
39209-1	Svärmeri	Co E1703

39210-1	Folkvisans Ton	Co rej
39211-1	Hur Ljuft Det Är Att Komma	Co E1704
	p	NY February 4, 1914

35.67. Norrlands Trion (Northland Trio) *vocal*

B 26243-2	På Roines Strand (Z. Topelius-K. Collan)	Vi 73279
B 26244-2	Tess Lörda'n {Till Saturday}	Vi 73279
B 26245-2	Under Rönn Och Syren (Herman Palm)	Vi rej
B 26246-1	Vall Sång {Shepherd Song}	Vi 78351
	Rose Burgeson-sop, Signe Martensen-alt, Mary Peterson-mezzo sop, unk vln, fl, p	NY March 15, 1922

B 27138-2	Mor, Lilla Mor {Mother, Little Mother} (Ellen Heijkern)	Vi 73623
B 27139-1	Konvaljens Afsked {Goodbye, Lillies Of The Valley} (Otto Lindwall)	Vi 73851
B 27140-1	Spinn, Spinn Sång {Spinning Song} (Hugo Jungst)	Vi 73623
B 27141-2	Fågelns Visa {The Bird Song}	Vi 78192
B 27142-1	Tula Vall¹	Vi rej
	as before, or 'unaccompanied	NY November 10, 1922

BVE 35377-3	Norrländingens Hemlängtan	Vi rej
BVE 35378-3	Hymn Till Stjärnorna	Vi rej
BVE 35379-2	Där Björkarna Susa	Vi rej
BVE 35380-2	Näckrosen	Vi rej
	Rose Burgeson-sop, Signe Martensen-alt, Mary Peterson-mezzo sop, unk vln, fl, vc, p, d Nathaniel Shilkret	NY May 7, 1926

35.68. North Star Singers Of Bridgeport

BS 036603-1	Tes Lordan (Richeau)	Vi V-24125, 26-1027
BS 036604-1	Vårt Land (J.L. Runeberg)	Vi V-24126, 26-1028
BS 036605-1	Spinn, Spinn (Jungst)	Vi V-24126, 26-1028
BS 036606-1	Du Gamla Du Fria (Dybeck-Laurin)	Vi V-24125, 26-1027
BS 036607-1	Näckrosen (E. Geibel)	Vi V-24127
BS 036608-1	Till Mitt Hem (Kremer)	Vi V-24127
	17 voices, p	NY April 22, 1939

35.69. Gösta Nyström *vocal*

B 29471-2	Den Gula Paviljongen (Emil Norlander-John Redland)	Vi 77433
B 29472-1	Klocka, Ring, Fred (Sophus Anderson)	Vi 77801
	orch d Leroy Shield	Camden, NJ February 14, 1924

B 29925-2	Månstrålar Klara-Serenad (Tantis)	Vi 77801
	as before	NY April 22, 1924

89897-2	Barndomshemmet	Co 26006-F
	acn	NY April 1924

89946-2   Skaffa Mig En Liten Våning {Give Me A Little Cozy Corner} Co 26006-F
                 as before   NY ca May 1924

                 Och Hennes Ögon   Co 26005-F
                 Mit Svärmeri   Co 26005-F
                                                                          NY   1924

35.70. Knut Öhrström *tenor*

9039   Carmela {Ibland Blommor Och Grönskande Lundar}   Wallin's 114
9040   Ingalill   Wallin's 114
9064   Stjarnor I Kronan   Wallin's 115
9065   Jag Är En Pilgrim   Wallin's 115
85201-B (11010-2) Hembygden   Wallin's 119
85202-B (11011-2) Längtan Till Sverige   Wallin's 120
85203-B (11012-2) Zigenarvisa   Wallin's 119
85204-B (11013-2) Ack, Värmeland Du Sköna   Wallin's 120
                 Serenad   Wallin's 121
                 Hälsa Dem Därhemma   Wallin's 121
                 Harry T. Carlson-p   Chicago mid 1920s

35.71. Olle I Gråthult *spoken*

88715-   Olas Sorger (Lars Bonderson)   Co E7748
88716-   Stora Fötter   Co E7748
                                                                          NY   July 1922

88944-1   Matts Månsons Afskedsbref   Co E7904
88946-1   Skottårsdagen   Co E7904
                                                                          NY December 1922

                 Bohusläns Folksong   Co 26009-F
                 En Envis Jänta   Co 26009-F
                                                                          NY ca 1923

The following artist may well be the same as the foregoing; the word "Strathult"
has no meaning in Swedish.

35.72. Olle I Strathult *vocal*

88910-1   Bröllop I Hagellela   Co 26011-F
88911-2   Pasasher Frau   Co 26011-F
                                                                          NY December 1922

35.73. Elis Olson-Ellis *tenor*

B 11158-1   I Denna Fula Stad, I Detta Ruskiga Land-Kuplett, ur "Stockholmsluft"
                 (Emil Norlander)   Vi 67082
                 Fred Bachman-p   NY November 1, 1911

B 11159-1	Soldatens Flammor Ur Skådespelet, from "Fanrik Ståls Sägner"	
	(Elis Olson-Ellis)	Vi 63575
B 11160-1	Äktenskapsfrågan (w: Fröding, m: Elis Olson-Ellis)	Vi 63562
B 11161-1	Röda Hafvet-Kuplett (w: Carl Cederstrom, m: Elis Olson-Ellis)	
		Vi 63575
B 11162-1	Alls Ingen Flicka Lastar Ja'7-Gammal Folkvisa	Vi 63577
B 11163-1	Humöret-Kuplett (w: August Westling)	Vi 63560
B 11164-1	Ja' E' En Stackars Bonnadräng-Bondvisa (Englund)	Vi 63576
B 11165-1	Att Vara Full I Tusa' E' En Tvungen-Bondvisa (Englund)	Vi 63576
B 11166-1	Skogsrån (w: Fröding-Olson-Ellis)	Vi 63562
B 11167-1	Ack Visste Du Blot (w: August Westling)	Vi 63562
B 11168-1	Lifvets Saga (w: August Westling)	Vi 63577
B 11169-1	Akta Dej För Mej (w: Gustavus, m: Elis Olson-Ellis)	Vi 63561
B 11173-1	Rosen I December (w: Ernest Arendorff, m: Elis Olson-Ellis)	Vi 63561
C 11174-1	Vårtan-Skånsk Ballad (Elis Olson-Ellis)	Vi 68329(12")
C 11175-1	Det Gjorde Mamma När Mamma Var Flicka (w: Gustavus,	
	m: Elis Olson-Ellis)	Vi rej (12")
B 11176-1	Lycklige John, ur "Gubben I Rehnberget" (w: Emil Norlander)	Vi 67082
B 11177-1	Sten Stensson Stéen (1 Ackt 8 Scen) (John Wigfors)'	Vi 63646
B 11178-1	Sten Stensson Stéen (1 Ackt 14 Scen) (John Wigfors)'	Vi 63645
C 11179-1	Sten Stensson Stéen (1 Ackt 3 Scen) (John Wigfors)'	Vi 68328(12")
C 11180-1	Sten Stensson Stéen (1 Ackt 15 Scen) (John Wigfors)'	Vi 68328(12")
	as before, or 'spoken with Ebba Olson-Ellis	NY November 2, 1911

B 11163-2	Humöret-Kuplett (w: August Westling)	Vi rej
B 11169-2	Akta Dej För Mej (w: Gustavus, m: Elis Olson-Ellis)	Vi rej
C 11175-2	Det Gjorde Mamma När Mamma Var Flicka (w: Gustavus,	
	m: Elis Olson-Ellis)	Vi 68329(12")
B 11176-2	Lycklige John, ur "Gubben I Rehnberget" (w: Emil Nordlander)	Vi rej
B 11183-1	Orpheus I Underjorden; Rysk Mazurka'	Vi rej
B 11184-1	Svenska Bondlåtar'	Vi rej
	Fred Bachman-p, or 'hca solos	NY November 3, 1911

35.74. Hugo Olsson *tenor*

Min Hemlands Dal	Co 26013-F
Aftonsång	Co 26013-F
Ålandsflickan	Co 26014-F
Gamla Minnen	Co 26014-F
	NY 1925

35.75. Evangelist A.B. Ost *vocal*

Där Jesus Är, Är Himmelen (C.J. Butler-J.M. Black)	
	Special unnumbered
p	Chicago early 1920s

Label note: Rodeheaver Record Company, Chicago. The above is coupled with a selection by ENOCH B. SWANSON, q.v.

35.76. Arvid Paulson *spoken (Skådspelare)*

38502-1	Ja Ä Grisarnas Far! {The Farmer And The Pigs}	Co E1239
38503-1	A Tragedy Of Life	Co
38504-1	Letter From Miss Melinda Pears To Her Friend In Sweden	Co
38505-1	En Visa Om Kärlekens Besvärlighet {A Story Of The Troubles Of Love}	
		Co E1239
	spoken	NY December 16, 1912

35.77. Esther Pearson *soprano*

87299-2	Fågelns Visa	Co E7168
87300-1	I Villande Skogen	Co E7168
87301-	Kors Och Krona (P.N. Stenhammer)	Co E7291
87302-	Vägen (C.J.O. Laurin)	Co E7291
	orch	NY April 1921

35.78. Hjalmar Peterson (Olle I Skratthult) *vocal (1886-1960)*

	Fastmon Min Johann-Recitation	Vi trial
		NY March 6, 1914

43766-1	Den Lustige Kopparslagaren (Peters)	Co E2806
43767-1	Svensk Potpourri (18 Svenska Sångar)	Co E2806
43768-1	Hjärterö Valsen (Hellström)	Co E2807
43769-1	Flickorna I Nerike (Bondeson)	Co E2807
	p	NY ca March 1916

58068-	Luffare Valsen	Co E3424
58069-2	Spiskroksvalsen	Co E3425
58070-2	Calle Gla Mä Sola (H. Lambert)	Co E3495, 26113-F
58071-1	Malmö Valsen; På Baltiskan (Hellström)¹	Co E3426, 26115-F
58072-1	Min Sångröst Den Kan Ej Betalas Med Guld¹	
		Co E3426, 26115-F, Caprice CAP2011(33)
58073-2	Svensk Potpourri	Co E2806, 26130-F
58074-1	Flickorna I Nerike (Bondeson)	Co E2807, 26120-F
58075-1	Hjärterö Valsen (Hellström)	Co E2807, 26120-F
58076-1	Den Lustige Kopparslagaren (Peters)	Co E2806, 26130-F
58077-1	Fotograferinga	Co E3425
58078-	Ä Du Mä På Dä (w: G. Fröding)	Co E3424
58079-1	Nikolina	Co E3494, 26103-F
58080-1	Flickan Med Paraply't (August Bondeson)	Co E3495, 26113-F
58081-2	Sven Svenssons Sven (T. Wich)	Co E3494, 26103-F
	orch, ¹with Olga Lindgren	NY ca March 1917

Co E2806 and E2807 are remakes from Peterson's first session; some labels accordingly indicate piano accompaniment despite the orchestra's presence.

B 29115-2	Storbonnernas Vals {Prosperous Farmer's Waltz} (Gunnar Ekerot)	
		Vi 77271
B 29116-3	Nikolina	Vi 77284

```
B 29117-2    Finska Valsen {The Finnish Waltz} (H. Wahlort)              Vi 77271
B 29118-1    Kopperslagaren {Jolly Coppersmith}                          Vi 77284
             orch d Nathaniel Shilkret                          NY   December 7, 1923

5011         Det Var Et Gäng En Gubbe                              Wallin's 102
5012         Storbönnernas Vals                                   Wallin's 102
             Harry Swanson-p                                   Chicago  mid 1920s

BVE 37151-1  Friare Valsen                      Vi 79109, Caprice CAP2011(33)
BVE 37152-2  Beväringsvisa {Josserhorseevaringa}                       Vi 79109
BVE 37153-2  I Värmeland En Fager Kvinna Bodde                         Vi 79156
BVE 37154-2  Frykdalsdansen {"Ut Pa Landsväjen"}                       Vi 79156
BVE 37155-2  I Värmeland Där Ä Dä Så Gutt Gutt              Vi 79278, Bb B-2729
BVE 37156-2  Flickan På Bellmansro                         Vi 79278, Bb B-2732
             c, vln, fl, cl, p, tuba, traps, d Nathaniel Shilkret
                                                           NY   December 18, 1926
```

Olle I Skratthult's Luffare Kapell

```
BVE 38317-1  U-Båts {U Boat} {Submarine}-Valsen (Fred Winter)   Vi 79321, 20677,
                              V-20070, 26-0014, 443-0001(45), Bb B-2737
             Vedenalais Valssi                                        Vi 80142
             Sous-Marin-Valse                                         Vi 150000
             Na Wysokych Gorach-Walc                                  Vi V-16449
BVE 38318-1  Pask Liljan {The Easter Lily}-Schottische (O. Hagstedt)
                              Vi 79427, V-24098, 26-1012, Bb B-2738
             Pääsiäis Lilja-Sottiisi                                  Vi 80143
BVE 38319-3  Från Frisco Till Cap {From Frisco To Cape Cod}-Vals Vi 79231, 20677,
                              V-20070, 26-0014, 443-0001(45), Bb B-2737
             Friskosta Cape Cod'iin-Valssi                            Vi 80142
             De Frisco Au Cap Cod                                     Vi 150000
BVE 38320-1  Hesselby Steppen-Two Step
                              Vi 79427, 80143, V-24098, 26-1012, Bb B-2738
BVE 38321-2  Inga Lill-Hambo (Einar Björke)          Vi 80066, V-24134, 26-1031
             Inga Pieni-Masurkaa                                      Vi 80171
BVE 38322-1  Jubileum-Schottische  Vi 80066, V-24134, 26-1031, Banjar BR-1840(33)
             Juhla-Sottiisi                                           Vi 80171
             Benny Posner-vln, Carson J. Robison-g, Joe Green-xyl, traps, unk p,
             bj, no vo                                        NY   April 1, 1927
```

Vi 20677 as PETERSON'S HOBO ORCHESTRA, 80142, 80143 and 80171 (Finnish) as HJALMAR
PETERSON'IN JÄTKÄ ORKESTERI, 150000 (Canadian) as PETERSON ET SON ORCHESTRE,
V-16449 as ORKIESTRA WIEJSKA, V-20070 and 443-0001 as HJALMAR PETERSON'S ORCHESTRA

Olle I Skratthult

```
BVE 38423-2  Jazz På Landet {Bonn Jazz}                    Vi 79428, Bb B-2729
BVE 38424-2  Fest Hos Gustafson's                          Vi 79320, Bb B-2732
BVE 38425-2  Malajen                                                  Vi 79428
BVE 38426-1  När Morsan Fyller Femtio År                              Vi 79320
             own vo, acc as before                         NY   April 2, 1927
```

Olle I Skratthult's Luffare Kapell

BVE 45312-2   Sista Man På Skansen {The Last Man On Skansen} (Fred Winter)
                                                      Vi 81415
BVE 45313-2   En Böljedans {A Wave Dance}-Waltz (Landin-Granath-Fred Winter)
                                                      Vi 81415
BVE 45314-2   Lördagsvalsen {Saturday Waltz} (Svarta Masken-Anselm Johansen)
                            Vi 81531, V-20078, 26-0019, Banjar BR-1840(33)
BVE 45315-2   Kalle {Carl P.}-Polka   Vi 81697
BVE 45316-1   Kinne Kulle {The Hill Of Kinne}-Schottische
                                      Vi 81531, V-20078, 26-0019
BVE 45317-2   Lill Karin-Hambo Mazurka (Olaf Gudmunsson)   Vi 81697
        vln, acn, p, g, no vo   Chicago June 6, 1928

Olle I Skratthult

BVE 45329-2   Motorcykeln {The Motorcycle} {Skånska Lasse}   Vi 81333, Bb B-2732
BVE 45330-2   Medel För Kalla Ben {Cure For Cold Legs} (Lars Bondeson)   Vi 81333
BVE 45331-1   Ja' Glick Mig Ut En Sommardag {I Went Out One Summer Day} Vi 81530
BVE 45332-2   Alunda-Visan {Alunda Song} (A.A. Afzelius)   Vi 81530
BVE 45333-2   Avsked {The Farewell}; Hur Sorjli A Inte Livets Skiften[1] Vi V-24002
BVE 45334-2   Min Sång Röst Den Kan Ej Betalas Med Guld
                {My Voice Can't Be Paid With Gold}[2]   Vi V-24002
        own vo, unk vln, acn, p, g, [1]acn omitted, [2]with Ruth O. Peterson
                                       Chicago June 9, 1928

Olle I Skratthults Luffare Kapell

BVE 55663-2   När Brollopsklockorna Ringa {When Wedding Bells Are Ringing}-Waltz
                (w: Olof Sandberg, m: Bert Carsten)
                                    Vi V-20015, V-20062, 26-0010
BVE 55664-1   Minnen Från Västern {Memories From The West}-Polka
                                    Vi V-20015, V-20062, 26-0010
        Na Zdrowie-Polka   Vi V-16449
BVE 55665-1   Friar Hambo-Mazurka (w: Jekyll, m: Ralph Audry) Vi V-20036, 26-0008
BVE 55666-1R Vi Skall Segla Livet Samman-Waltz (Gosta Stevens-Walther Harrison)
                                          Vi V-20036, 26-0008
BVE 55667-2   Min Lilla Vän {My Little Friend}-Schottis (Schwente)
                                          Vi V-20022, 26-0007
BVE 55668-1   Gråt Inte Anne Marie {Do Not Cry, Anne Marie}-Waltz
        (Ernst Rolf-Alf Peters)   Vi V-20022, 26-0007
        Arvid Franzen-acn, unk vln, sax, p, g, sbs, no vo NY August 30, 1929

Vi V-16449 as ORKIESTRA WIEJSKA

Olle I Skratthult (Hjalmar Peterson)

BVE 57343-2   Målare Visa {The Painters Song}   Vi V-24028
BVE 57344-2   Jag Ha Aldrig Haft Så Roligt I Mitt Syndiga Liv
                {I Have Never Had So Much Fun In My Sinful Life}   Vi V-24028
        Arvid Franzen-acn, unk p   Chicago October 30, 1929

BVE 57401-2   Hjalmar Och Hulda   Vi V-24061

BVE 57402-1   Nikolina
    Vi V-24031, 26-1002, Bb B-2733, Banjar BR-1840(33), Caprice CAP2011(33)
BVE 57403-1   Tattare Emma {Gypsy Emma}   Vi V-24061
BVE 57404-1   Polkangår {The Polka Is On}   Vi V-24031, 26-1002, Bb B-2733
    H. Swanson-vln, Arvid Franzen-acn, H. Jalen-p
                   Chicago   November 7, 1929

35.79. Iver Peterson *accordion*

BVE 36577-3   Dala Hambo-Schottische   Vi rej
BVE 36578-3   Duluth {Högsby}-Valsen   Vi rej
BVE 36579-3   Kalmar Valsen   Vi 80065
     Kalmari Valssi   Vi 80170
BVE 36580-3   Niagara Falls-Polka   Vi rej
                  NY   November 2, 1926

BVE 36577-6   Dala Hambo-Schottische   Vi 80065
     Taalaanmaan Hambo   Vi 80170
BVE 36578-6   Duluth {Högsby}-Valsen   Vi 79325, Bb B-2736
BVE 36580-6   Niagara Falls-Polka   Vi 79325, Bb B-2736
                  NY   January 12, 1927

Vi 80170 is a Finnish release.

W 108731-2 (W 194410) Siljan Vals (Iver Peterson)   Co 22108-F
W 108732-2 (W 194411) Karlskoga-Hambo   Co 22108-F
                  NY   January 1928

35.80. Ruth O. Peterson *soprano*

BVE 45318-1   Min Framtidsdag {My Future} (N. Frykman) Vi 81416, V-24084
BVE 45319-1   Guds Löften Hålla {God's Promises Stand} (Joh. Holmstrand)
                  Vi 81416, V-24084
    vln, g, p   Chicago   June 7, 1928

BVE 48785-2   Under Hans Vingar {Under His Wings} (N.L. Ridderhoff) Vi V-24011
BVE 48786-2   Morgon Mellan Fjällen {Morning Between The Mountains} Vi V-24011
    Leroy Shield-p   Chicago   January 15, 1929

35.81. Willie Sandberg *spoken*

58243-2   Hur Jäntorna Ska' Tas (D. Stjerne)   Co E3497
58245-1   Mina Funderingar I Äktenskap'n (A. Killian)   Co E3497
     En Moder   Co E3697
     Vintergatan   Co E3697
                  NY   April 1917

35.82. Torkel F. Scholander *vocal*

B 10634-1	Der Meilinstein (E. Binder-Scholander) [in German]	Vi
B 10635-1	Vårvisa (Jeremias Tröstlösa-Scholander)	Vi 63361
B 10636-1	Tattare Emma (Jeremias Tröstlösa-Scholander)	Vi 63357
B 10637-1	Fredmans Epistel No. 16 {Till The Birfilare På Then Konungstiga Djurgården Klinger Väl Uppå Oboë} (Bellman)	Vi 63429
B 10638-1	Den Utestängde Äktemannen (Sehlstedt-Scholander)	Vi 63428
B 10639-1	Fästmansköpet (Dahlgren-Scholander)	Vi 63358
B 10640-1	Kannibalvisa	Vi 63357
B 10641-1	Jäntblig (Fröding-Scholander)	Vi 63358
B 10642-1	Fredmans Epistel No. 69 {Till The Innebyggare På Gröna Lund} (Bellman)	Vi 63361
B 10643-1	Fredmans Sång No. 35 {Om Gubben Noak} (Bellman)	Vi 63430
	lute	NY June 30, 1911

B 10644-1	Visa På Förstugukvisten (Sehlstedt-Scholander)	Vi 63430
B 10645-1	Farväll En Sorgens Ton Ifrån Amerika (Froding)'	Vi 63359
B 10646-1	Jon Blund (Scholander)'	Vi 63359
B 10647-1	Frieriet {The Proposal} (Johan Jolin)	Vi 63360
B 10648-1	Vårmorgon Vid Hafvet (Scholander-Sehlstedt)	Vi 63428
B 10649-1	Gå På Dompen (Fröding-Sehlstedt)	Vi 63360
	lute or 'unaccompanied	NY July 1, 1911

B 10671-1	Visan Om Drängen Som Spelte På Klaver	Vi 63429
	lute	NY July 24, 1911

35.83. John A. Scott *tenor*

BVE 45231-1	När Morgonen Kommer (A.L. Long)	Vi 81328
BVE 45232-1	Han Kommer, Vår Jesus (J.D. Blomquist)	Vi 81698
BVE 45233-2	Det Saliga Landet	Vi 81328
BVR 45234-1	Luljan Uti Dalen (C.W. Fry)	Vi 81698
	Charles O'Connell-org	Camden, NJ June 4, 1928

BVE 50638-1	Hvar Jag I Kogar, Berg Och Dalar {Whither I Wander In Woods, Hills And Dales}	Vi V-24019
BVE 50639-1	En Little Tid {A Little While}	Vi V-24015
BVE 50640-2	De Nittionio {The Ninety And Nine} (Ira D. Sankey)	Vi V-24015
BVE 50641-2	Skallquedet Smaltas? {Should The Gold Be Melted?}	Vi V-24019
	as before	Camden, NJ March 22, 1929

35.84. Marie Sidenius Zendt *vocal*

B 23378-2	Hvad Jag Har Lofvat (arr Gustav Hägg)	Vi rej
	King's Orchestra d Nathaniel Shilkret	NY November 14, 1919

B 23477-3	I Villande Skogen {All In The Dim Forest} (m: Andreas Randel, arr G. Hägg); Titania (Wilhelm Peterson Berger, op. 17 no. 3)	Vi rej
B 23478-2	Vaggvisa {Cradle Song} (W. Th. Soderberg)	Vi rej

B 23479-2   Vår Och Kärlek {Spring And Love} (Herman Berens)   Vi rej
             orch d Rosario Bourdon   NY November 28, 1920

B 23477-5   I Villande Skogen {All In The Dim Forest} (m: Andreas Randel,
             arr G. Hägg); Titania (Wilhelm Peterson Berger, op. 17 no. 3)
                                                                        Vi rej
B 23478-4   Vaggvisa {Cradle Song} (W. Th. Soderberg)   Vi rej
B 23479-5   Vår Och Kärlek {Spring And Love} (Herman Berens)   Vi rej
             orch d Rosario Bourdon   NY January 22, 1920

             My Saviour First Of All   Vi trial
             Nathaniel Shilkret-p   NY March 18, 1920

B 23477-7   I Villande Skogen {All In The Dim Forest} (m: Andreas Randel, arr G.
             Hägg); Titania (Wilhelm Peterson Berger, op. 17 no. 3) Vi rej
B 23479-8   Vår Och Kärlek {Spring And Love} (Herman Berens)   Vi rej
B 23778-2   Hvad Jag Har Lofvat Det Skall Jag Hålla (Hägg)   Vi rej
             orch d Rosario Bourdon   NY March 22, 1920

B 23477-10   I Villande Skogen {All In The Dim Forest} (m: Andreas Randel,
             arr G. Hägg); Titania (Wilhelm Peterson Berger, op. 17 no. 3)
                                                                      Vi 73795
B 23778-4   Hvad Jag Har Lofvat Det Skall Jag Hålla (Hägg)   Vi 73795
B 27713-2   När Jag Blev Sjutton År {When I Was Seventeen}
             (Folkvisa sjungen af Christine Nilsson)   Vi rej
             orch d Nathaniel Shilkret   Camden, NJ March 27, 1923

B 27713-3   När Jag Blev Sjutton År {When I Was Seventeen}
             (Folkvisa sjungen af Christine Nilson)   Vi 73850
B 27814-1   Fågelns Visa {Song Of The Bird} (W. Tho. Söderberg)   Vi 73850
             as before   NY April 9, 1923

35.85. Charles Sjökvist *baritone*

4614-2   Min Moder {Mother Machree}   Em 18004
4616-2   Vikingens Farväl   Em 18004
                                                    NY ca November 1919

Calle Sjöquist

85466-2   Skragge Polkan   Co E4488
85467-2   Storbönnernas Vals   Co E4488
85468-1   Lilla Lisa   Co E4546
85469-1   Allmogevals   Co E4546
85470-1   Dans Visa   Co E4690
85471-1   Sjömans-Låt   Co E4690
             Manicurist Visa   Co E4627
             Fia-Tragikomisk Kärleksvisa   Co E4627
             orch   NY 1920

Co E4488 as CHARLES SEAQUIST

86388-1-2	Akta Dej För Mej	Co E4847
86392-1	Ack Giv Ett Tecken Julianna	Co E7039
86393-1	Logelåt	Co E7039
86394-1	På Gästgivaregården	Co E4847
	orch	NY ca July 1920

	Min Första Flamma	Co E7108
	Flickörna Förr Och Nu	Co E7108
	Silfverstrött Är Re'n Mitt Hår	Co E7254
	En Liten Blå Förgät Mig Ej	Co E7254
	Soldatens Flammor	Co E7337
	Kärlekens Mystær	Co E7337
	Det Raka Min Näsa Förbi	Co E7376
	Kring Majstången	Co E7376
	Livets Tunga Stig	Co E7413
	Om Nå'n Bjuder	Co E7413
		NY 1921-2

35.86. Fabian Skrållbom *(John Nordéen); vocal*

Skrållbom

W 107630-1	Hopp Sunta Li A Lua-Comic Song	Co 26052-F, 16217
W 107631-1	Tjolanta Å Ja'-Comic Song	Co 26052-F, 16217
		NY February 1927

Fabian Skrållbom

W 108320-2	The Gröt Nordisk Race-Comic Monologue	Co 26067-F, 16216
W 108321-2	Alkoholet-Comic Monologue	Co 26067-F, 16216
W 108322-2	Hästhandlar-Pelle-Comic Song	Co 26064-F
W 108323-1	Lovisas Gröna Kjol-Comic Song	Co 26064-F
		NY September 1927

35.87. Agnes Staberg-Hall *soprano*

| 38210-1 | Skjutsgossen På Heewägen | Co E1051 |
| | orch | NY August 16, 1912 |

38211-1	Mot Kveld	Co
38212-1	Det Är Så Underliga Ställen	Co E1051
	orch	NY August 20, 1912

36430-1	Rida, Rida Ranka	Co E5024(12")
36431-1	Inga Lill	Co E5024(12")
	Solveigs Sång (Grieg)	Co E5022(12")
		NY August 1912

36547-	Mor Britta	Co E5035(12")
38613-1	Sotargossen {The Chimney Sweep}	Co E1592
38614-2	Liten Fågel	Co E1387
	orch	NY February 5, 1913

38724-1	Norrländingens Hemlängtan	Co E1387
38725-1	Om Dagen Vid Mitt Arbete	Co E1386
38726-1	Ack Värmeland, Du Sköna	Co E1388
38727-1-2	Den Store Hvide Flok	Co E1390, E2301
	orch	NY March 25, 1913

38739-1	Aftonstämning	Co rej
38740-1-2	Norwegian Echo Song	Co E1389
38741-1	Irmelin Rose (Peterson-Berger)	Co E2300
38742-2	Longt I Fjärran Hörs Eko Svara	Co E1388
	orch	NY March 27, 1913

38814-1	Aftonstämning	Co E1592
38815-2	Agnes	Co E2301
38816-1	Saeterjentens Söndag	Co E1389
38817-1	Dansk Folkvisa	Co E1390
	Det Var En Lördag Aften	Co E2300
38818-1	I Rosens Doft	Co
	orch	NY April 25, 1913

38821-1	Fjorton År	Co E1386
	orch	NY April 29, 1913

36711-2	Jul Sång	Co E5035(12")
	orch	NY April 1913

35.88. Birger Stenberg *tenor*

61755-	test recording	Co
		NY July 6, 1917

58937-1	Balen På Bakgården (E. Nordlander)	Co E3791
58938-	Ack Elvira (Frage Bergowist)	Co E3791
58939-	I Alla Fulla Fall (Ernst Rolf)	Co E3792
58940-	Stackars Ohlsson (Ernst Rolf)	Co E3792
	orch	NY ca October 1917

B 22032-2	Stjernor I Kronan Så Skön (J.R. Sweeney)	Vi 72202
B 22033-2	Låten Barnen Få Komma Till Mig (John A. West)	Vi 72202
	orch d Nathaniel Shilkret	NY June 21, 1918

84493-1	Ny Fiskarvals (Hellström)	Co E4022
84494-1	Luffare Valsen (Nordlander)	Co E4022
84495-1	Det Står Ett Ljus I Österland	Co E4928
	orch	NY June 1918

84991-	Kvinnlig Polis	Co E7040, 7639
84992-1	Andres De Wahl	Co E4769
84993-2	Ett Hem	Co E4928
85077-	Irmelin Rose	Co E4349
85078-	Sångaren På Vandring	Co E4349
	orch	NY ca March 1919

```
85648-1      Styrmansvalsen                             Co E4487, 7639
85649-1-2    Bobby                                           Co E4487
85650-       Vaxholms Flickan                                Co E7040
85651-       Det Gamle Stockholm                             Co E4626
85652-       Min Mamma                                       Co E4626
             orch                                    NY  November 1919

86165-       Par Om Par                                      Co E4848
86166-       Munkbro Fruns Kuplett                           Co E4848
86168-1      Älskling Jag Är Gammal Vorden                   Co E4769
             orch                                       NY  April 1920

B 24575-2    Rose-Marie (Topelius-Collan)                     Vi 72957
B 24576-2    Sjung För Mig (August Söderman)                  Vi 72957
             as before                              NY  November 19, 1920
```

35.89. Marie Sundelius *soprano*

```
43813-1      Bland Fjällen (Von Heland)                      Co E2836
43814-1      Hvad Jag Har Lofvat Det Skall Jag Hå            Co E2836
             orch                                     NY  ca April 1916
```

35.90. Ernst Svedelius Jr. *vocal*

```
W 111416-2   Den Vackraste Visan I Världen (Georg Enders)    Co 26106-F
W 111417-1   Minns Du... Waltz (Erik W. Bergman)             Co 26122-F
W 111418-2   Där Blåklinten Lyser I Vaggande Råg (Ahlin Ernfrid)  Co 26106-F
W 111419-2   En Kärleksnatt I Barcelona-Fox Trot (Helge Lindberg)  Co 26122-F
             orch                                    NY  December 1929
```

35.91. Svensk Amerikanska Sångarförbundet *chorus*

```
549          Hör Oss Svea                               Wallin's 113
             d Ernest Francke                   Chicago  mid-1920s
```

35.92. Svenska Glee Klubben I Brooklyn (Swedish Glee Club Of Brooklyn)

```
39157-1      Ur Bond Bröllopet                               Co rej
39158-1      Hör Oss, Svea                                   Co E1701
39159-1      Nattlig Song                                    Co rej
39160-1      Brumbasken I Bumba                              Co E1701
                                                NY  December 23, 1913

45765-1      Ångbåtsång (O. Lindblad)                        Co E2440
45766-1      Vårt Land (Josephson)                           Co E2440
45767-1      Vårsång (Prince Gustaf)                         Co E2439
45768-1      Hvila Vid Denna Källa (Bellman)                 Co E2439
             p                                       NY  June 14, 1915
```

Konsertvals	Co E5070(12")
Kör I Vind-Polka	Co E5070(12")
	NY 1915

35.93. Svenska Manskvartetten *male quartet*

W 105922-1	Ur Svenska Hjärtans Djup (O. Lindglad)	Co 26018-F
W 105923-1	Sätt Maskinen I Gång (O. Lindglad)	Co 26018-F
W 105924-1	Svanehvit {Integer Vitae}	Co 26019-F
W 105925-1	Tonerna	Co 26019-F
		NY October 1925

35.94. Svenska National Kören De Svenske *chorus*

W 108050-2	Jag Går I Tusen Tankar	Co 26059-F, 16081
W 108051-2	Spinn, Spinn	Co 26056-F, 7688
W 108052-2	Säv, Säv Susa'	Co 26059-F, 16081
W 108053-1	Nu Komma De Svenske! (Sven Körling)	Co 26055-F
W 108054-2	Å Jänta Å Ja'	Co 26056-F, 7688
W 108055-2	Sveriges Flagga (Hugo Alfvén)	Co 26055-F
	d Emil Carelius, 'John Johanson-bar solo	Chicago(?) June 1927

Co 26055-F as SÅNGSÄLLSKAPET DE SVENSKE (The Singing Vikings)

35.95. Svenska Sjömans Orkestern

BVE 48783-1	Emigrant-Valsen (W. Berner)'	Vi V-24008, 26-1001
BVE 48784-2	Lördags Natt {Saturday Night}-Schottis (Sigurd C. Westbye)	
		Vi V-20012, 26-0006
BVE 48787-2	Vackra Nels {Handsome Nels}-Hambo (Nels Dahglren)	
		Vi V-20012, 26-0006
BVE 48788-2	Öckerö-Valsen (Lon Gog)	Vi V-20008, 26-0004
	vln, acn, p, g, traps, 'group vo	Chicago January 15, 1929
BVE 48789-2	Minnenas Melodi {Memory's Melody}-Vals (Einar Westling)	Vi V-20019
BVE 48790-2	Det Står Skrivet Uti Stjärnorna {Written In The Stars}-Fox Trot	
	(Jules Sylvain)	Vi V-20019
BVE 48791-2	Brustna Strängar {Broken Strings}-Vals (Berta Onnerberg)	Vi V-20011
BVE 48792-2	Vintergatan {Starry Skies}-Vals (Jules Sylvain)	Vi V-20011
BVE 48793-2	Långa Sven {Tall Sven}-Schottis	Vi V-20008, 26-0004
BVE 48794-2	En Liten Flicka Med Resegrammofon	
	{A Little Girl With A Portable Victrola}-Hambo (Ejnar Björke)	
		Vi V-20027
BVE 48795-2	Den "Riala" Jazzen (Helge Lindberg)	Vi V-20027
BVE 48796-1	När Fyrarna Tändas {When The Lighthouses Are Bright}-Vals	
	(Fred Winter)	Vi V-24008, 26-1001
	vln, acn, p, g, traps	Chicago January 16, 1929

35.96. Enoch B. Swanson *vocal*

815   Tro Dig Igenom   Special unnumbered
           vln, p   Chicago mid-1920s

Label note: Rodeheaver Record Company, Chicago. The above is coupled with a selection by EVANGELIST A.B. OST, q.v.

35.97. Swedish Ladies Trio *vocal*

Hälsning Från; Norrländingens   Vi trial
Elsa Söderstam-1st sop, Miss M. Sinn-2d sop, Miss S. Mortensen-alto,
Edward T. King-p   NY June 7, 1918

Sångarvalsen; Kostervalsen   Vi trial
singers as before, Nathaniel Shilkret-p   NY June 13, 1918

84473-	Kostervalsen	Co E4081
84474-	Hälsning Från Sverige	Co E4082
84475-1	Vall Sång	Co E4128
84476-1	Brudefärden I Hardangar (Kjerulf)	Co E4128
84482-	I Rosens Doft	Co E4082
84483-1	Sång Vals	Co E4105
84484-1	Köss Valsen	Co E4105
84485-	Bohus Rillen	Co E4081
84486-	Gulla Lilla	Co E4023
84487-	Waxholms Valsen	Co E4002
84488-	Till Mitt Hem	Co E4023
84489-	Fyra Små Grisar	Co E4002
	orch	NY ca June 1918

35.98. Swedish Male Quartet *vocal*

B 18270-2   Närmare Gud Till Dig {Nearer My God To Thee}
                 (Lowell F. Mason-Sarah F. Adams)   Vi rej
B 18271-2   Bön {Prayer} (F. Fleming)   Vi rej
B 18272-2   Fram, I Kristi Strids-män {Onward Christian Soldiers}
                 (S.B. Gould-Arthur Sullivan)   Vi rej
Birger Stenberg, Gustav Erickson, Emil Sorenson, Oscar Sundberg-vo,
Edward T. King-org   NY November 23, 1916

B 18272-3   Fram, I Kristi Strids-män {Onward Christian Soldiers}
                 (S.B. Gould-Arthur Sullivan)   Vi rej
          as before   NY November 23, 1916

35.99. Swedish Quartet *vocal*

A 965-	Vårt Land (Josephsen)	Vi rej (7")
M 3583-1	Vårt Land (Josephsen)	Mon 3583
A 966-	Stina Polka (Wallin)	Vi rej (7")

M 3584-	Stina Polka (Wallin)	Mon 3584
A 967-	Under Rönn Och Syren (Toppelius-Palm)	Vi rej (7")
M 3585-	Under Rönn Och Syren (Toppelius-Palm)	Mon 3585
A 968-1	Skarne Basson Og Rosen {The Beetle And The Rose} (Veit)	Vi 968(7")
M 3586-	Skarne Basson Og Rosen {The Beetle And The Rose} (Veit)	Mon 3586
A 969-2	Vårsång {Spring Song} (Prince Gustaf)	Vi rej (7")
M 3587-	Vårsång {Spring Song} (Prince Gustaf)	Mon 3587
A 970-1	Brudefærden I Hardanger {Bridal Tour Of Hardanger} (Kjerulf)	
		Vi 970(7")
M 3588-	Brudefærden I Hardanger {Bridal Tour Of Hardanger} (Kjerulf)	
		Mon 3588

NY October 7, 1901

A 970-2	Brudefærden I Hardanger {Bridal Tour Of Hardanger} (Kjerulf)	
		Vi rej (7")
A 971-1	Feltvakten {The Sentinel} (Kreutzer)	Vi 971(7")
M 3589-	Feltvakten {The Sentinel} (Kreutzer)	Mon 3589
A 972-1	Käraste Broder {Jolly Brothers} (Bellman)	Vi 972(7")
M 3590-	Käraste Broder {Jolly Brothers} (Bellman)	Mon 3590
A 973-1	Brumbasken I Bumba (Grieg)	Vi 973(7")
M 3591-1	Brumbasken I Bumba (Grieg)	Mon 3591
A 974-1	Stridsbön {Battle Prayer} (Lindblad)	Vi 974(7")
M 3592-	Stridsbön {Battle Prayer} (Lindblad)	Mon 3592

NY October 8, 1901

1178-	Sång Till Glädjen	Co 1178
	Sång Till Glädjen	Co 32114(2 min)
1179-2	Brudefærden	Co 1179
	Brudefærden	Co 32115(2 min)
1180-	Herdens Söndags Sång	Co 1180
	Herdens Söndags Sång	Co 32116(2 min)
1181-	Aftonhelsning	Co 1181
	Aftonhelsning	Co 32117(2 min)
1182-	Ulla Min Ulla	Co 1182
	Ulla Min Ulla	Co 32118(2 min)

NY ca 1903

All the above Columbia discs were recorded in 7" and 10" versions.

14623-	test recording	Co

NY January 16, 1909

35.100. Constance Thane *instrumental*

GE 12831-A	Ute På Landsvägen-Barn Dance	Ge rej
GE 12832-A	Harmonika Visa-Polska	Ge rej

St. Paul June 8, 1927

35.101. The Three Vikings *instrumental*

W 81318-B	Musik Polka	Ok 19222
W 81319-A	Triplet-Schottisch	Ok 19223

```
W 81320-B    Ny Fiskar-Vals                                      Ok 19222
W 81321-A    Bess-Hambo                                          Ok 19223
W 81322-B    William Polka                                       Ok 19224
W 81323-A    Lundby Valsen                                       Ok 19224
             d Ray Lindstroem              Minneapolis  September 7, 1927
```

35.102. Greta Torpadie Och Sam Ljungquist *vocal*

```
87811-1    Dina Blå Ögon Ha Talat Till Vågen (C.J. Lewerth)      Co E7461
87812-1    Sjung! (F. Karling)                                   Co E7441
87813-1    I Rosens Doft (Prince Gustav)                         Co E7441
87814-2    Respolska                                             Co E7461
           orch                                    NY  ca November 1921
```

35.103. Unknown Vocal

```
           Herdegossen                                  Co 30300(2 min)
           Nära                                         Co 30301(2 min)
           Fågelns Visa                                 Co 30302(2 min)
           Vaggvisa                                     Co 30303(2 min)
           Rose Marie                                   Co 30304(2 min)
           p                                            NY  ca 1901
```

35.104. Mary Valeer *vocal*

```
AFS 2418A2&B1  Nicolina                                              LC
AFS 2418B2     Nu Är Det Sommar Och Sol                              LC
                                          Bessemer, MI  October 7, 1938
```

35.105. Aage Wang-Holm *vocal*

```
           Vaagn Af Din Slummer [in Danish]                     Vi trial
           Du Gamla, Du Fria                                    Vi trial
           p                                     NY  September 16, 1915
```

```
B 17248-2    Hell Dig Du Höga Nord {Hail Northland High All Hail} (B. Crussell,
             1775-1838)                                         Vi 67907
B 17249-2    Fågelns Visa {The Bird's Song}; Dår Sjöng En Fågel På Lindekvist
             (W.T. Soderberg, b. 1845)                          Vi 67794
B 17250-2    Kung Karl XII (O. Westermark, 1799-1850)           Vi rej
B 17251-1    Min Lilla Vrå Bland Bergen {My Home Midst Hills And Valleys}
             (J. Sandstrom, 1824-1880)                          Vi 67794
B 17252-2    Till Österland Vill Jag Fara {Now Far Eastward I'll Hie Me}
             (arr Gustav Hägg)                                  Vi rej
             King's Orchestra                        NY  March 3, 1916
```

```
B 17250-3    Kung Karl XII (O. Westmark, 1799-1850)             Vi 67907
B 17252-3    Till Österland Vill Jag Fara {Now Far Eastward I'll Hie Me}
             (arr Gustav Hägg)                                  Vi rej
B 17621-1    Sångaren På Vandring (T.W. Naumann)                Vi rej
```

B 17622-1	Lifdrabanten Och Kung Erik (Otto Linblad)	Vi 67963
B 17623-1	Björkens Visa (G. Raab)	Vi rej
	as before	NY May 5, 1916

B 17252-4	Till Österland Vill Jag Fara (Now Far Eastward I'll Hie Me)	
	(arr Gustav Hägg)	Vi rej
B 17662-2	Rose Marie (Karl Collan)	Vi rej
	as before	NY May 11, 1916

B 17252-5	Till Österland Vill Jag Fara (Now Far Eastward I'll Hie Me)	
	(arr Gustav Hägg)	Vi 67963
B 17621-3	Sångaren På Vandring (T.W. Naumann)	Vi 67908
B 17623-3	Björkens Visa (G. Raab)	Vi rej
B 17732-3	Hvarför Skall Man Tvinga Mig Att Sjunga; Här Ar Gudagodt Att Vara	
		Vi 67908
B 17737-2	Kärlek Vin Och Sång	Vi rej
	as before	NY May 25, 1916

B 21186-2	Ved Jägerhuset (F.P.E. Hartmann) [in Danish]	Vi rej
B 21187-2	Gurre (H. Rung) [in Danish]	Vi rej
	as before, d Nathaniel Shilkret	NY December 18, 1917

CVE 33148-3	Det Er Saa Yndigt At Følges Ad (It Is Beautiful To Be Together)	
	(Weyse); Kjærlighed Fra Gud (Love From God) (Johnke); Jert Hus	
	Skal I Bygge (Thou Shall Build Thy Throne) (Hartman)'	
	[in Danish]	Vi rej (12")
BVE 33151-3	Hist Hvor Vegen Slaar En Bugt (Begauer); Den Lille Ole Med	
	(Jacobsen); Flyv Fugl Flyv (Hartman) [in Danish]	Vi 78304
BVE 33152-3	Kongernes Konge (Hornemann)' [in Danish]	Vi 78304
CVE 33153-3	Ved Fremmed Kyst; Midsommervise Af Der Var Engang; Ved Öresunds	
	Kyst' [in Danish]	Vi 68718(12")
	orch d Nathaniel Shilkret, with 'A. Peterson-sop, Mrs. E. Von	
	Holstein-alt, J. Haae-Zink-bar	Camden, NJ August 6, 1925

CVE 33148-5	Det Er Saa Yndigt At Følges Ad (It Is Beautiful To Be Together)	
	(Weyse); Kjærlighed Fra Gud (Love From God) (Johnke); Jert Hus	
	Skal I Bygge (Thou Shall Build Thy Throne) (Hartman)	
	[in Danish]	Vi 68718(12")
	A. Peterson-sop, Mrs. E. Von Holstein-alt, J. Haae-Zink-bar, orch d	
	Leroy Shield	Camden, NJ September 16, 1925

35.106. N.O. Welander *baritone*

5205-1	Du Gamla, Du Friua; Här Är Guda-Godt Att Vara	Electra unnumbered
5209-1	Så Kom Du (Lönnerblad)	Electra unnumbered
	Mrs. N.O. Welander-p	Chicago 1920s

35.107. Chas. G. Widdén *vocal*

38806-1	Lyckliga Jim-Komisk Sång	Co E1421
38807-1	A' Så' Rulla Vi På Kuttingen	Co E1421
38808-1	Sockerdricka	Co E1422

| 38809-1 | Comme Il Faut | Co E1422 |
| | p | NY April 24, 1913 |

38812-1	Farväll Och Skogsrån (Fröding)	Co E1420
38813-1	Bergslagstroll (Fröding)	Co E1420
	spoken, unk p	NY April 25, 1913

3445	Bergslagstroll På Bygderå {Spook In The Forest} (Gustav Fröding)'	
		Ed 50223, 59004
3446	Sockerdricka {Soft Stuff}-Kuplett	Ed 50223, 59005
3447	Å Så Rulla Vi På Kuttingen-Kuplett (Axel Engdahl)	Ed 50204, 59004
3448	Våran Bal-Parodi (m: Irving Berlin)	Ed 50204, 59005
	orch, or 'spoken	NY November 21, 1914

Ed 50223 was never released.

39621-1	Ny Fiskarvals	Co E2131
39622-1	Fleckera	Co E2162
39623-1	En Drängvisa	Co E2162
39624-1	Koster-Valsen (Hellström)	Co E2130
39625-1	Pansarbåtsvisan	Co E2130
39626-1	Bohuslänska Sjömansvalsen	Co E2131
	orch	NY November 23, 1914

45722-1	Våran Bal {Everybody's Doing It} (w: Calle Sjökvist, m: I. Berlin)	
		Co E2441
45723-1	Mister Johnsons Klagan {Don't Take Me Home}	Co E2441
45724-1	Kärlek Och Geografi-Visa Om Sveriges Städer	Co E2612
45725-2	Jäntblig (G. Fröding)	Co E2442
45726-1	Clara (M. Flagstad)	Co E2612
45727-1	Tänk Om Sankte Per Det Visste (M. Flagstad)'	Co E2611
45728-1	Putte, Du Är Min Ögonsten (Puppchen)'	Co E2611
45729-1	Styrmansvalsen'	Co E2613, 26124-F
	orch, or 'acn	NY June 1, 1915

45733-1	Brudvalsen (w: Göran Svenning)	Co E2443
45734-1	Kom Adolfina; Friare Valsen	Co E2613, 26124-F
45735-1	Släkta Är Värst'	Co E2443, 26129-F
45736-1	Fleckeras Vals-Finska Valsen	Co E2442
	orch, with Eric Berg, or 'spoken	NY June 2, 1915

B 17322-1	Sockerdricka	Vi 67959
B 17324-2	Koster Valsen (David Hellström)	Vi 67958
B 17325-2	Bohuslänska Sjömansvalsen (David Hellström)	Vi 67961
B 17326-1	Fiskar-Vals Från Bohuslän (David Hellström)	Vi 69077
B 17327-1	En Drängvisa (Gunnar Pedersen)	Vi 67960
B 17328-1	Sjömansvisa	Vi 67957
B 17329-1	Tandvärk	Vi 67957
	King's Orchestra	NY March 17, 1916

B 17369-1	Jänteras Frierefäl (Gustaf Fröding)	Vi 67960
B 17370-1	Ä Du Mä På Dä (Gustaf Fröding)	Vi 67959
B 17371-2	Soldatgossen-Parodi	Vi 67961

B 17372-1   I Bönhuset (Gustaf Fröding); Herre I Sitt Hus (Gösta)   Vi 67958
             spoken   NY   March 27, 1916

B 17873-1   Bondvalsen (Theo. Pinet)   Vi 69268
B 17874-1   Beväringsvals (Hellström)   Vi 69131
B 17875-1   Kössvalsen (Svenning)   Vi 69017
B 17876-1   Messommers Vals (Hellström)   Vi 69017
B 17877-1   Kärestan Min (Hellström)   Vi 69131
             John Lager, Eric Olson-2 acn   NY   June 16, 1916

B 18464-2   Kvinnsvisan   Vi 69077
             King's Orchestra   NY   September 26, 1916

B 19033-2   Hjärterövalsen (David Hellström)[1]   Vi 69269
B 19034-2   "Olle Ve Quarnas" Järnvägsresa   Vi 69379
B 19035-1   "Olle Ve Quarnas" Turkish Bad (Charles Widdén)   Vi 69269
B 19036-2   Hund På Katt (Charles Widdén)[2]   Vi 69268
             spoken, or [1]King's Orchestra, [2]Edward T. King-p   NY   January 10, 1917

58102-2   Fiskarvals Från Bohuslän (David Hellström)   Co E3496
58103-1   Man Och Öfverman   Co E3598
58104-1   En Tusen Konstnär (B. Grant)   Co E3496
58105-1   Midsommarvalsen (David Hellström)   Co E3599
58106-   Kvinnsvisan (Amerikansk Melody, w: O. Hemberg)   Co E3427
58107-2   Lilla Kärestan Min (David Hellström)   Co E3598
58108-1   Järnvägsresan (C.G. Widdén)   Co E3599
58109-   Gå På Dompen (w: G. Fröding)   Co E3427
             orch   NY   ca March 1917

B 19405-2   Nya Kostervalsen {På Koster} (David Hellström)   Vi 69379
B 19406-2   Beata-Waltz Song (arr Sam Goodness)   Vi rej
             King's Orchestra   NY   March 22, 1917

B 19933-2   Bobby (G. Steen Jensen)   Vi 69475
B 19934-2   Sångvals {Song Waltz} (David Hellström-Goran Svening)   Vi 69475
             as before   NY   May 23, 1917

B 19957-1   Peterson At The Turkish Bath {Peterson I Turkiska Badet}
                  [in English]   Vi 69565
B 19958-2   Peterson's Brother In Law {Petersons Svåger} (Charles Widdén)
                  [in English]   Vi 69565
             spoken   NY   May 26, 1917

B 19406-3   Beata-Waltz Song (arr Sam Goodness)   Vi 69788
B 20270-1   Agata (Sven Nyblom Sterny)   Vi rej
             King's Orchestra d Rosario Bourdon   NY   July 31, 1917

B 20270-3   Agata (Sven Nyblom Sterny)   Vi 69632
B 20291-1   Arholma Valsen   Vi 69632
             King's Orchestra   NY   August 8, 1917

B 20782-2   Jäntblig (Björn Haliden)   Vi 69718
B 20783-3   Hafver Ni Sett Karlson {Has Anyone Seen Karlson?}   Vi 72318

B 20784-1   En Bondsväng {A Country Dance} (Adolf Englund)   Vi 72318
             as before   NY October 17, 1917

B 21194-1   Spiskroks Valsen   Vi 69954
B 21194-2   Slåtterölet   Vi 69954
             as before, d Nathaniel Shilkret   NY December 20, 1917

B 21395-2   Comme Il Faut (E. Wallmark)   Vi rej
B 21396-1   Kalle (w: Karl Ewert, m: Rudolph Nelson)   Vi 73934
B 21397-2   Skördedans (m: Albert Gille)   Vi 72770
             as before   NY January 31, 1918

B 21525-2   Fleckera (Adolph Englund)   Vi 72770
B 21526-2   Kalle Mä Klavere {Charlie And His Accordion} (Adolph Englund)
                                                                        Vi 72140
             King's Orchestra d Nathaniel Shilkret   NY February 19, 1918

B 21843-2   Stockholms Valsen {The Stockholm Waltz} (Scholander-Wilhelm Hansen)
                                                                        Vi rej
B 21844-2   Finska Valsen (Ernst Rolf-H. Wahlrot)   Vi rej
B 21845-2   I Det Soliga Blå (Coran Svenning-David Hellström)   Vi rej
             orch d Nathaniel Shilkret   NY May 9, 1918

B 21843-3   Stockholms Valsen {The Stockholm Waltz} (Scholander-Wilhelm Hansen)
                                                                        Vi 72140
B 21844-4   Finska Valsen (Ernst Rolf-H. Wahlrot)   Vi 72661
B 21845-3   I Det Soliga Blå (Göran Svenning-David Hellström)   Vi 72918
B 22022-2   Fallera   Vi 72661
B 22023-1   Luffare Valsen (Emil Nordlander)   Vi 73284
             as before   NY June 20, 1918

B 23391-2   Höganäs-Johan (Charles Widdén)   Vi 72511
B 23392-2   Dumt Folk (Froding)   Vi rej
B 23393-1   På Tal Om Dyre Tider (Charles Widdén)   Vi 72675
B 23394-1   Gå På Dompen (Froding)   Vi 72675
             spoken   NY March 1, 1919

B 22745-3   Sjösjukan {Sea Sickness} (Charles Widdén)   Vi 72511
B 22746-2   Peterson Vid Telefonen {Peterson Calls Up}-Swedish Dialect
                 (Charles Widdén)   Vi 72719
             spoken   NY April 17, 1919

B 22835-2   Brollops Valsen (David Hellström)   Vi 72374
B 22836-1   Nödbroms Visan   Vi 72829
B 22837-1   Stackars Olson (Emil Norlander)   Vi 72829
B 22838-2   Landsvägstrall (David Hellström)   Vi 72374
             orch d Rosario Bourdon   NY May 6, 1919

B 23332-3   Olle Ve Kvarna I Amerika (Charles Widdén)   Vi 72719
             spoken   NY November 11, 1919

B 23474-2   Genom Sotat Glas   Vi 72979
B 23475-1   Mi Lilla Adolfin (Helfrid Lambert)   Vi 72557

| B 23476-2 | Skragge-Polka | Vi 72557 |
| | orch d Rosario Bourdon | NY November 17, 1919 |

B 23965-2	I Alla Fulla Fall (E. Rolf-A. Englund)	Vi rej
B 23966-1	Vi Gå Över Daggstänkta Berg (O. Thunman)	Vi 72918
B 23967-1	Allmogevals (A. Ewald)	Vi 72979
B 23968-2	Det Vet Man Aldrig (John Colden-Melville Gideon)	Vi rej
	as before	NY April 23, 1920

B 24547-2	Diktarelott (Oscar Stjerne)	Vi 72906
B 24548-2	Ett Un' Lit Folk (Oscar Stjerne)	Vi 72906
B 24549-2	Sågspån Å Korf (Charles Widdén)	Vi 78746
B 24550-2	När Kumla-Erik Tjente Ve Artillerit (Charles Widdén)	Vi rej
	spoken	NY October 23, 1920

B 25023-2	Bergslagstroll (Gustav Fröding)	Vi 73000
B 25024-1	Släkta Mi {Släkta Är Värst?} (Gustav Fröding)	Vi 73000
	spoken	NY April 4, 1921

B 25426-1	Sven Svensons Sven	Vi 73048
B 25427-2	Nikolina	Vi 73048
	orch d Nathaniel Shilkret	NY June 6, 1921

B 25354-2	Lars Å Mas På Amerika (Charles Widdén)	Vi 73934
B 25356-2	Bonden Och Värvaren	Vi rej
	as before	NY June 20, 1921

| B 25356-4 | Bonden Och Värvaren | Vi rej |
| | as before | NY July 14, 1921 |

B 25665-1	Tre Trallande Jäntor {Three Singing Lassies}	
	(Gustaf Froding-Korling)	Vi 73284
	as before	NY October 24, 1921

| B 25684-2 | Patterson På Semester | Vi rej |
| | spoken | NY October 29, 1921 |

B 26325-2	Skratt {Laughter}	Vi 73335
B 26326-2	Sven Dufva (J.L. Runeberg)-Pt. 1	Vi 73820
B 26327-2	Sven Dufva (J.L. Runeberg)-Pt. 2	Vi 73820
	Nathaniel Shilkret-p	NY April 29, 1922

B 26912-2	Julotta {Christmas Morn} (Charles Widdén)	Vi 73519
B 26913-2	Lutfisk {The Yule Fish} (Charles Widdén)	Vi 73519
	spoken	NY September 30, 1922

B 26983-2	Shampinjoner {Mushrooms} (Froding)	Vi 73546
B 26984-2	Vad Som Hände Mej I Går {What Happened Yesterday}'	Vi 73546
	spoken, 'Nathaniel Shilkret-p	NY October 21, 1922

B 27452-2	Jazz-Gossen {Jazz Boy} {En Lille Rystedans} (w: Karl Gerhard,	
	m: Lars Bondeson)	Vi 73728
	orch d Nathaniel Shilkret	NY February 5, 1923

B 28504-2   Dag Efter Dag (Ernest Rolf)   Vi 78746
             orch d Leroy Shield   NY August 24, 1923

B 28587-1   Olle Ve Kvarnas Om Base Ball (Charles Widdén)   Vi 77149
B 28588-2   Olle Ve Kvarnas Tokerier (Charles Widdén)   Vi 77149
             spoken   NY September 24, 1923

105032-2   Skåningen I Amerika   Co 26008-F
105033-1   Peterson Om Baseball   Co 26008-F
             Bröllops Valsen   Co 26007-F
             Mitt Land Mitt Hem Och Min...   Co 26007-F
             acn   NY June 1924

PART 8

ENGLISH LANGUAGE

SECTION 36. IRISH

36.1. Michael Ahern *baritone*

W 143516-2   When It's Springtime In Killarney, I'll Come Back To You
                    (Dan J. Sullivan)   Co 33159-F, Vo 84006
W 143517-3   Wearin' Of the Green   Co 33159-F, Vo 84006
          orch   NY February 23 or 24, 1927

W 143604-2   Be Sure And Kiss The Blarney Stone   Co 33181-F, Vo 84077
W 143605-2   The Foggy Dew   Co 33181-F, Vo 84077
W 143606-1   The Low Back'd Car   Co 33213-F
          orch   NY   March 7, 1927

W 108311-1   Old Ireland Shall Be Free   Co 33225-F, RZ G20261
W 108312-1   The Fields O' Ballyclare   Co 33225-F, RZ G20261
W 108313-1   Carrigdhoun   Co 33213-F
          orch   NY   September 1927

W 109381-2   All Erin Is Calling Mavourneen   Co 33346-F
W 109388-3   Paddy Duffy's Cart   Co 33346-F
                                                        NY   June 1928

W 110634-2   Farewell But Whenever You Welcome The Hour   Co 33418-F, RZ MR249
W 110635-2   Three Leaves of Shamrock   Co 33433-F, RZ MR1988
W 110636-2   Rose of Killarney   Co 33392-F, Vo 84094, RZ MR1988
W 110640-2   A Handful of Earth From My Mother's Grave
                                         Co 33392-F, Vo 84094, RZ IZ742
W 110641-2   Asthore   Co 33433-F, RZ IZ742
                                                        NY   April 1929

              Ireland Is Ireland To Me   Co 33218-F
              Dear Little Shamrock   Co 33218-F
              Avourneen   Co 33278-F
              Take A Look At Molly   Co 33278-F
              Molly O   Co 33315-F
              Irish Names   Co 33315-F
              You'd Better Ask Me   Co 33418-F, RZ MR249
                                                        NY   1927-9

36.2. Josephine Beirne *soprano*

Josephine Beirne And George Sweetnam

39096-A-B	My Bonny Irish Lass	De 12031, F5421, W4036, Rex U266
39097-B	The Dear Little Girl Next Door	De 12026, F5662, W4038, Rex U267
39098-A	A Mother's Love Is A Blessing	De 12031, F5421, W4036, Rex U266
39099-A	My Heart Is Tonight In Texas	De 12026
	vln, p	NY November 24, 1934

The second singer's name is spelled SWEATNAM on De 12026.

Josephine Beirne

39566-A	Absent (J.W. Metcalf-Catherine Young Glen)	De 12047
39568-A	My Bonnie Irish Boy (Jerry Donovan)	De 12054, F5664, W4151, Rex U509
39571-A	The Faithful Sailor Boy (Jerry Donovan)¹	
		De 12055, F5662, W4038, Rex U267
	vln, acn, ¹with George Sweetnam	NY June 1, 1935

Josephine Beirne And George Sweetnam

61391-A	The Maid of Malabar	De 12092, W4141, Rex U568
61392-	There's Somebody Waiting For Me	De 12075, W4140, Rex U567
61393-A	I'll Forgive But I'll Never Forget	De rej
61394-	The Maid Of Erin's Isle	De 12074, F6355, W4130, Rex U241
	vln, p	NY November 8, 1936

61408-	Far Away In Australia	De 12075, W4021, Rex U572
61409-	The Boys From The County Armagh	De 12079, F6355, W4130, Rex U241
61410-	My Mother and My Sweetheart	De 12074, W4140, Rex U567
61411-	An Irish Rebel's Grave	De 12079, W4141, Rex U568
	vln, g	NY November 13, 1936

Josephine Beirne

62197-A	The Old Rustic Bridge By The Mill	De rej
62198-A	I'll Forgive But I'll Never Forget¹	De 12092, W4021, Rex U572
62199-	Bonnie Banks of Loch Lomond	De 12091, W4674
62200-	In The Shade Of The Old Apple Tree	
	(Harry H. Williams-Egbert Van Alstyne)	De 12091
62201-A	An Irish Farewell	De 12156, W4177, Rex U221
	vln, ten sax, p, ¹with George Sweetnam	NY May 14, 1937

63567-A	Lay My Head Beneath A Rose (G. Falkenstein-W. Madison)	De rej
63568-A	The Old Rustic Bridge By The Mill	De 12156
63569-A	Smilin' Through (Arthur A. Penn)	De rej
63570-A	My Father's Servant Boy (Brian O'Higgins)	De W4281, Rex U625
63571-A	Erin Is My Home¹	De 12149, W4279, Rex U623
63572-A	Barney Come Home¹	De 12149, W4279, Rex U623
	vln, acn, p, ¹with Tim Donovan	NY April 7, 1938

Josephine Beirne And Tim Donovan

64242-	Mary On The Silvery Tide	De 12227, W4381, Rex U645
64243-	The Groves Of Cloghereen	De 12227, W4861
64244-	Boucaileen Dhoun	De W4381, Rex U645
64245-	What Will You Do Love?	De 12244, W4309, Rex U634
64246-	The Green Mossy Banks Of The Lee	De 12244, W4309, Rex U634
	Paddy Killoran Trio	NY June 28, 1938

Josephine Beirne

65827-	Bring Back My Barney To Me	De 12212, W4489, Rex U671
65828-	Farewell Dear Erin'	De 12212, W4489, Rex U671
65830-	My Bonnie Boy In Blue	De 12237, W4674
65832-	The Woodlands Of Loughlynn'	De 12237, W4488, Rex U670
	orch d Patrick Killoran, 'with Tim Donovan	NY June 15, 1939

36.3. Martin Beirne *bagpipes*

Martin Beirne And His Irish Blackbirds Orchestra

CO 20222-1	The Merry Harriers; Old Maids Of Galway-Reels	Co 33556-F, Vo 84059
CO 20226-2	Boys From County Cork; Darling Girl From Clare-Barn Dances	
		Co 33558-F, Vo 84061, RZ IZ657
CO 20227-2	A Glass In The Morning; Road To Killadeer-Jigs	
		Co 33560-F, Vo 84063, RZ IZ730
CO 20228-2	The Road To The Isles-Highland Fling	Co 33559-F, Vo 84062
CO 20229-1	The Ballinamore Lass-Polka	Co 33561-F, Vo 84064, RZ IZ730
CO 20230-1	Hughie Cavanaugh's Favorite; Rising Sun-Reels	Co 33562-F, Vo 84106
CO 20232-2	Kilkenny For Me; Boys Of Wexford-Marches	
		Co 33557-F, Vo 84060, RZ IZ657
CO 20233-2	The Boys From French Park; Jackson's Rambles-Jigs	
		Co 33562-F, Vo 84106
CO 20234-1	The Grand Spy-Reel'	Co 33558-F, Vo 84061, RZ IZ639

probably: own bagpipes, John Mulvihill-vln, John Griffin or James Darcy-fl, William McElligott-acn, Alex Brown-p, or 'bagpipe solo, Alex Brown-p   NY November 10, 1936

22461-1	Thady Regan-Barn Dances	Vo 84182
22462-1	Lucy Campbell; Mamma's Pet-Reels'	Vo 84182
22463-1	The Lark In The Morning; Paudeen O'Rafferty-Jigs'	Vo 84185
22464-1	Walls Of Limerick; Girl I Left Behind Me	Vo 84184
22465-1	Love Will You Marry Me; Oh Johnnie When You Die	Vo 84183
22466-1	Comin' Thru The Rye; Skibbereen	Vo 84183
	orchestra or 'bagpipe solo, unk p, sbs	NY February 24, 1938

22492-1	Bonnie Mary Of Argyle-Waltz'	Vo 84185
22493-	Wheel Of Fortune; The Varsouviana	Vo 84184
	tp, 2-3 sax, tb, p, sbs, dm, 'Alice Dorain-vo	
		NY probably March 2, 1938

36.4. Bowen's Irish Orchestra

```
W 108080-1    Galway Girl; Stokestown Reel                             Co 33445-F
W 108081-2    Lass Of Slievenamon; Behind The Bush In The Garden       Co 33445-F
              possibly: Patrick Doran-fl, William McCormick, Joe Owens-2 vln, Joseph
              Sullivan or Dennis Flynn-bagpipes, Mike Hart-p      Chicago  July 1927
```

36.5. Colin J. Boyd *violin (1891-1975)*

```
W 113393-1    The Flowers Of May-Jig                          Co 33514-F, CB 1(33)
W 113394-1    The Little Burnt Potato-Jig                     Co 33506-F, CB 1(33)
W 113395-1    Tarbolton Lodge-Reel                            Co 33506-F, CB 1(33)
W 113396-1    Paddy On The Turnpike; Fisherman's Home-Reels
                                          Co 33520-F, RZ IZ213, MR938, CB 1(33)
W 113397-1    Sterling Castle-Schottische                     Co 33514-F, CB 1(33)
W 113398-2    Casey's Pig-Schottische
                                 Co 33520-F, IFB314, RZ IZ213, MR938, CB 1(33)
          p                                              NY   ca February 1932
```

36.6. John Burke *tenor*

```
              Molly Brannigan                                            Pm 33075
                                                                   NY   1920


              Wrap The Green Flag 'Round Me, Boys   Arto 3063, Bell S63, Globe L63
              God Made Ireland A Nation             Arto 3063, Bell S63, Globe L63
              Lt. Ridgely's 69th Regiment Band                       NY   1921
```

36.7. Tom Burke *tenor*

```
80044-3       If You'll Remember Me                                     Co rej
                                                       NY   October 25, 1921

80044-6       If You'll Remember Me                                     Co rej
80102-3       Little Town In The Ould County Down                       Co rej
                                                       NY   December 15, 1921

W 140913-2    Kathleen Mavourneen (Crouch)          Co 463-D, 33007-F, Vo 84066
W 140914-2    Killarney (Balfe)                     Co 463-D, 33007-F, Vo 84066
              orch                                    NY   September 8, 1925

W 141250-2    The Snowy Breasted Pearl (Stephen Edward De Vese,
                   arr Joseph Robinson)                                  Co 536-D
W 141251-2    I'm Sitting By The Stile, Mary {Song Of The Irish Immigrant}
                   (Barker)                                              Co 536-D
              George Stehl-vln, Robert Hood Bowers-p, unk vc   NY   November 6, 1925
```

Other Burke Columbia records are either of domestic popular material or recorded
abroad.

36.8.   Michael Carney *bagpipes (ca 1860-1938)*

W 110372-2	The Peeler's Jacket; The Duke Of Leinster-Reels'	Co 33350-F
W 110373-2	Pol Ha' Penny Hornpipe; Fisher's Hornpipe'	Co 33350-F
W 110374-2	The Geese In The Bog-Jig	Co 33336-F
W 110375-1	The Jolly Tinker-Reel	Co 33336-F
	'with James Morrison-vln	NY February 1929

36.9.   James D. Casey *vocal*

W 107082-2	Shule, Shule, Agre	Co 33112-F
W 107083-1	Pat Malloy And The Ass	Co 33114-F, RZ IZ250, MR1383
W 107084-1	Dhrimen Dhown Dheelish	Co 33112-F
W 107085-2	The Irish Volunteer	Co 33114-F, RZ IZ250, MR1383
	Dan Sullivan-p	NY August 1926

36.10.   Michael J. Cashin *violin*

BVE 46403-1	The Kerry Reel; Shannon Shores	
		Vi 21594, HMV B3271, MS 45001(33), Sh 33001(33)
BVE 46404-1	Ginger's Favorite; Bogs Of Allen-Jigs	
		Vi 21594, HMV B3271, FW 8821(33)
BVE 46405-1	Touhey's Favorite; Lamb On The Mountain-Reels	Vi V-29037
BVE 46406-1	Heather And Sedge; Trip To Erin-Jigs	Vi 21718
BVE 46407-1	Lord Leitrim's Downfall; Hod-Carrier's Reel	Vi V-29037
BVE 46408-1	Drowsy Maggie; Scotch Mary-Reels	Vi 21718
	Tom Doyle-fl, unk p	Chicago July 13, 1928

36.11.   Cashin, Cawley And Ford

W 111326-2	Coming From Reilly's Party-Sketch	Co 33388-F, RZ IZ146, MR131
W 111327-2	Silver Tip; Frog In The Well Co 33400-F, Vo 84152, RZ IZ146, MR131	
W 111328-2	Mountain Lark; Wheels Of The World	
		Co 33400-F, Vo 84152, RZ IZ147, MR132
W 111329-2	Bashful Bachelor; Sunshine-Hornpipes Co 33388-F, RZ IZ147, MR132	
	Francis Cashin, Tom Cawley (1905-1945)-2 vln, Ford-p	
		Chicago December 1929

36.12.   Patrick J. Cawley *violin*

W 110664-2	The Traveler-Reel	Co 33383-F
W 110665-1	Memories Of Dublin-Hornpipe	Co 33383-F
	p	NY ca May 1, 1929

36.13.   James Claffy *violin*

W 143525-3	Laughing Molly	Co 33151-F
W 143526-1	Kerry Man's Rambles; Mountain Dew-Reels	Co 33151-F

W 143527-1	Bonnie Kate	Co 33212-F
W 143528-2	Shannon Bells; Irish Wedding-Jigs	Co 33239-F
W 143529-2	Paddy Whack; Boys Of Wexford	Co 33212-F
W 143530-2	The Roving Piper-Reel	Co 33239-F
	p	NY February 24, 1927

W 108621-1	Flowers Of Edinboro-Hornpipe	Co 37007-F
W 108622-2	Blue Bells Of Scotland-Jig	Co 37008-F
W 108623-1	Roy's Wife; Who Wadna Fecht For Charlie; We Saw Johnny	
	Coming-Highland Schottisches	Co 37008-F
W 108624-1	Fenton's Hornpipe	Co 37012-F
W 108625-1	Roger's Hornpipe	Co 37012-F
W 108626-2	Lord MacDonald's Reel	Co 37007-F
	The Laddie With His Pladdie; The Lord Of Cockpen-Highland Flings	
		Co 37018-F
	Gang Awa To Yon Toon-Reel	Co 37018-F
	p	NY January 1928

W 110339-3	The Coulin (Tho' The Last Glimpse Of Erin)	Co 33326-F
W 110340-2	The Blackbird	Co 33430-F
W 110341-1	John O'Dwyer Of The Glen	Co 33333-F
W 110342-1	Remember The Glories Of Brian The Brave	Co 33333-F
W 110343-2	Sauntree-Lullaby	Co 33326-F
W 110347-1	The Banks Of The Suir	Co 33398-F, RZ IZ192, MR692
	The Morning Of Life	Co 33339-F
	Savourneen Dheelish	Co 33339-F
	The Old Shady Bohereen	Co 33376-F
	Ned Of The Hill	Co 33376-F
	Robert Hood Bowers-p	NY February 1929

At least one of the last six titles was re-recorded in November 1929; its matrix
number is W 110344-4.

36.14. Patrick J. Clancy *violin*

	Medley Of Reels	Vi trial
	Arthur P. Kenna-p	NY August 9, 1918

B 23234-2	Sporting Paddy; Mile From Galway; Limerick Lassies-Reels	Vi rej
B 23235-2	Little House Under The Hill; Kitty Bahan; The Lark In The	
	Morning-Jigs	Vi rej
B 23236-2	Mason's Apron; McCormack's Reel; My Love Is In America-Reels	Vi rej
B 23237-2	Tattered Jack Walsh; Dublin Jig; The Rover-Jigs	Vi rej
	as before	NY September 9, 1919

B 23235-4	Little House Under The Hill; Kitty Bahan; The Lark In The	
	Morning-Jigs	Vi rej
B 23236-5	Mason's Apron; McCormack's Reel; My Love Is In America-Reels	Vi rej
B 23237-4	Tattered Jack Walsh; Dublin Jig; The Rover-Dublin Jig Medley	
		Vi 18639
	as before	NY October 7, 1919

```
            Dublin Reel; Coming Through The Fields-Reels              untraced
            Jimmy Egan's Favorite-Jigs                               untraced
            The New Policeman; My Love Is In America-Reels           untraced
            The Bridle                                               untraced
                                                                  NY  1920s
```

The above were probably made for New Republic.

36.15.   James Clark *violin*

```
W 109722-    Mother's Delight-Reel                                    Co rej
                                                            NY  September 1928
```

```
W 109722-3   Mother's Delight-Reel                       Co 33309-F, Ok 21078
W 109825-1   The Old Thatched House-Hornpipe             Co 33309-F, Ok 21078
        p                                                   NY  October 1928
```

Jim Clark

```
CO 18423-1   Pretty Peggy Ann-Reels          Co 33546-F, Vo 84176, RZ IZ801
CO 18425-1   Dowd's Favorite-Reels                     Co 33547-F, Vo 84177
            Frank Quinn's Duo: Frank Quinn-vln, Eileen White-p
                                                    NY  December 21, 1935
```

Only one violin can be heard on matrix CO 18423.

36.16.   Michael Coleman *violin (1891-1945)*

```
549-2        Frost Is All Over-Jigs                   Shannon 2503, Metro 142
550-2        Reidy Johnson's Reels                    Shannon 2503, Metro 141
            John Muller-p                                        NY  ca 1920
```

Metro 141 and 142 are coupled.

```
7366         Shaskeen; Bag Of Potatoes-Reels                        Vo 14201
            as before                                       NY  ca April 1921
```

```
7518         Jackson's Morning Brush; The Rambling Pitchfork-Jigs
                                            Vo 14492, Intrepid unnumbered(33)
7519         Murray's Fancy-Hornpipe                   Vo 14201, IRC 3327(33)
7521         O'Dowd's Favorite Reel Medley              Vo 14541, Sil 3058
            as before                                         NY  ca May 1921
```

```
87795-1      Paddy Ryan's Dream-Reels                               Co E7470
87796-1      The Monaghan-Jig                                       Co E7470
87797-1      Farewell To Ireland-Reels                              Co E7396
87798-2      Harvest Home-Hornpipe                                  Co E7396
        p                                                 NY  October 1921
```

```
            Apples In Winter-Jigs                                   NR 1120
            Rakish Paddy-Reels                                      NR 1120
            Larry O'Gaff-Jigs                                       NR 1121
```

```
                The Sailor On The Rock-Reels                              NR 1121
                John Muller-p                                    NY   early 1922
```

It has been suggested that New Republic 1120 and 1121 are viola solos.

```
8752          Shaskeen; Bag Of Potatoes-Reels     Vo 14201, Intrepid unnumbered(33)
8754/5        O'Dowd's Favorite Reel Medley                              Vo 14541
8756          Humorous Of Ennistymon-Jigs                                Vo 14322
              Humors Of Ennistymon                                     IRC 3327(33)
8759          The Boys At The Lough-Reels                  Vo 14322, Beltona 79
              Boys Of The Lough; Devils Of Dublin-Reels              IRC 3327(33)
              p                                                NY  ca April 1922
```

Matrix 8759 was reissued on a 45 rpm disc, 45-5020, with no label name; Beltona 79
(English) as DENNIS MOLLOY

```
S 70820-D     The Pigeon On The Gate-Reels                     Ok 4703, Pa E3093
S 70821-D     McDermott's Hornpipe (McDermott)         Ok 4703, Pa E3093, RZ IZ762
              p                                            NY   July-August 1922
```

```
711-A-2       The "Real Blackthorn Stick"-Reel                           NR 2310
              Blackthorn Stick; Green Groves Of Erin-Reels
                                                      Intrepid unnumbered(33)
711-B-1       Killarney Wonder-Schottische                  NR 2310, IRC 3327(33)
718-B-1       Kerry Reel-Reels                                           NR 2327
              The Kerry Reel; Perthshire Hunt        Sh 33002(33), IRC 3327(33)
721-B-1       Jackson's Jigs¹               NR 2327, IRC 3327(33), Sh 33002(33)
744-A-2       Prohibition Reel¹ ²                                        NR 2330
744-B-1       Up Sligo-Jigs¹                    NR 2330, Intrepid unnumbered(33)
749-A-2       Sunny Banks-Reels³                                         NR 2333
749-B-2       The Lark On The Strand-Jigs³                               NR 2333
              The Crooked Road To Dublin-Reels                               NR
              Casey's Polka                                                   NR
              Arthur P. Kenna or ¹Ed Geoghegan-p, ²Thomas Gannon-vln, ³Michael
              Walsh-fl                                          NY   early 1920s
```

```
N 105039-     Wellington's Reels    Pat 021098, Pe 11171, Cameo 9113, Lincoln 3140,
                                       Ro 915, OBDW 39068, Intrepid unnumbered(33)
N 105040-     Dougherty's Jigs     Pat 021098, Pe 11171, OBDW 39068, Sh 33002(33)
              as before                                    NY  ca December 1923
```

Cameo 9113, Lincoln 3140 and Ro 915 as DANIEL KELLER

```
W 105838-1    Humors Of Bally Connoll; Captain Rock-Reels¹    Co 33069-F, Vo 84189
W 105839-2    Heights Of Alma; All The Way To Sligo-Polkas¹
                                                    Co 33068-F, Sh 33006(33)
W 105840-2    Jackson's Reel         Co 33069-F, 33520-F, Vo 84189, Sh 33002(33)
W 105841-2    Fox Hunter Jig    Co 33068-F, Intrepid unnumbered(33), Sh 33006(33)
              p, ¹Tom J. Morrison-fl                        NY   September 1925
```

```
GEX 377-A     The Grey Goose-Jig                                            OBDW
GEX 378-A     The Leitrim Ladies; The Fair Of Ballinsloe                    OBDW
              p                                           NY   December 8, 1926
```

```
BVE 37841-2   The Stage; The Western-Hornpipes          Vi 79284, IRC 3327(33)
BVE 37842-2   The Morning Dew-Reels                      Vi 79322, HMV B3401
              The Morning Dew; The Woman Of The House-Reels
                                             Sh 33006(33), IRC 3327(33)
BVE 37843-1   Tell Her I Am-Jigs                         Vi 79322, HMV B3401
              Dougherty's; Tell Her I Am-Jigs
                                    Sh 33006(33), Intrepid unnumbered(33)
BVE 37844-2   The Kerryman's Daughter; Bird In The Tree-Reels Vi 79284, Bb B-4975,
                          MW M-8634, Yv K-506, Sh 33002(33), IRC 3327(33)
              Edward Lee-p                          Camden, NJ March 4, 1927

E 22165/6     Farrel Gara's Medley Reels                           Br rej
E 22167/8     James Gannon's Barn Dances                           Br rej
E 22170       Black Haired Lass-Reels'                      Br 68003, 4969
E 22171/2     Miss Ramsey's Highland Fling'                 Br 68003, 4969
              Stirling Castle; Miss Ramsey's-Highland Flings    Sh 33002(33)
              Ed Geoghegan-p, 'Packie Dolan-2d vln         NY March 30, 1927
```

Br 68003 and 4969 as MICHAEL COLEMAN TRIO; the latter is a Canadian issue.

```
E 22367/8     Kerrigan's Fancy-Jig'                                Br 68002
E 22369/70    Lord McDonald's Reels'                               Br 68002
              McDonald Medley                                  Sh 33002(33)
E 22371       James Gannon's Barn Dances           Br 68004, B165-L, 6080
E 22372       Farrel Gara's Medley Reels
                          Br 68004, B103-L, 6080, Intrepid unnumbered(33)
              Ed Geoghegan-p, 'possibly Paddy Finlay-pic   NY April 13, 1927
```

Br 68002 as MICHAEL COLEMAN TRIO; Br B103-L and B165-L are part of a "Mood
Accompaniment Library" series and are uncredited. Br 6080 is a Canadian issue.

```
W 107904-2    Tom Ward's Downfall; Reel Of Mullinavat-Reels
              Co 33178-F, 33520-F, Vo 84124, Sh 33006(33), Intrepid unnumbered(33)
W 107905-2    The Royal Blackbird            Co 33178-F, 33507-F, Vo 84124
              The Blackbird-Set Dance    Sh 33006(33), Intrepid unnumbered(33)
              Herbert G. Henry-p                              NY  May 1927

W 107925-1    The Duke Of Leinster And His Wife-Reels    Co 33179-F, 33523-F,
                          Vo 84008, RZ G9187, IZ136, Sh 33006(33)
W 107926-2    The Royal Stack Of Barley
                          Co 33179-F, 33523-F, Vo 84008, RZ G9187, IZ136
              Packie Dolan-2d vln, unk p                     NY  May 1927

BVE 39293-2   Tommy Hill's Favorite-Hornpipe    Vi 20850, Intrepid unnumbered(33)
BVE 39294-1   The Frieze Britches-Jig                             Vi 20850
BVE 39295-2   Trim The Velvet-Reel      Vi 20916, Bb B-4931, MW M-8947, Yv K-509
BVE 39295-    Trim The Velvet-Reel                            Sh 33002(33)
BVE 39296-1   Tobin's Fancy-Jig                                   Vi 20916
              Tobin's Jigs                                    Sh 33002(33)
              Ed Geoghegan-p                        NY  June 27, 1927

W 108603-2    Green Fields Of America; Swallow's Tail-Reels
                          Co 33246-F, Vo 84019, Sh 33002(33)
W 108604-2    Liverpool; O'Neill's-Hornpipes    Co 33246-F, Vo 84019, IRC 3327(33)
```

W 108605-2   Lord McDonald's Reel   Co 33237-F, 33507-F, Vo 84129, FW FP18(33),
                                  FW6818(33), Sh 33006(33), Intrepid unnumbered(33)
W 108606-2   The Grey Goose-Jig Co 33237-F, Vo 84129, Sh 33002(33), IRC 3327(33)
        as before   NY December 1927

Matrix W 108604 was also issued on a 45 disc, 45-5020, with no label name.

W 110796-2   Doctor Gilbert's Reel; Queen Of May
                             Co 33375-F, Sh 33006(33), IRC 3327(33)
W 110797-2   Mrs. Kenney's Barn Dance   Co 33375-F, RZ G20719, Sh 33006(33)
        Herbert G. Henry-p   NY May 1929

38978-A   Bonnie Kate; Jennie's Chickens-Reels De 12015, F5424, F18066, W4087,
                         Rex U274, AH 95(33), CRL 57464(33), Sh 33006(33)
38979-A   The Wandering Minstrel; Fasten The Leg On Her; Coleman's Cross-Jigs
                De 12015, F5424, W4087, Rex U274, AH 95(33), CRL 57464(33)
        Michael (Whitey) Andrews-g   NY November 9, 1934

39112-A   Stack Of Barley Medley   De 12036, F5425, W4070, Rex U275,
                        CRL 57464(33), AH 95(33), MS 45001(33), Sh 33001(33)
39113-A   Tar Bolton; Longford Collector; The Sailor's Bonnet-Reels De 12036,
                    F5425, W4070, Rex U275, MS 45001(33), Sh 33001(33)
39114-A   The Men Of The West; Mrs. Kenny-Waltzes   De 12037, F5426, W4053,
                                 Rex U276, AH 95(33), CRL 57464(33)
39115-A   Lord Gordon's Reel   De 12037, F5426, W4053, Rex U276, AH 95(33),
                                  CRL 57464(33), Sh 33002(33)
        as before   NY November 28, 1934

39634-A   The Banks-Barn Dances   De 12056, F5667, W4007, Rex U207, AH 56(33),
                                           CRL 57369(33)
39635-A   Murphy's Hornpipe   De 12057, F5666, W4024, Rex U278, AH 56(33),
                                           CRL 57369(33)
39636-A   Cherish Ladies-Jig   De 12057, F5665, W4040, Rex U277, AH 56(33),
                                           CRL 57369(33)
39637-A   Crowley's Reels   De 12056, F5667, W4007, Rex U207, AH 56(33),
                                           CRL 57369(33)
39638-A   Lucy Campbell-Reel   De 12046, F5665, W4040, Rex U277, AH 56(33),
                                           CRL 57369(33)
39639-A   Job Of Journey Work-Long Reel   De 12046, F5666, W4024, Rex U278
        Eileen O'Shea-p   NY June 15, 1935

61303-A   Miss McLoud's Reel; Philip O'Beirne's Delight-Reels De 12085, F6220,
                            W4118, Rex U562, AH 56(33), CRL 57369(33)
61304-A   Tell Her I Am; Richard Brennan's Favorite-Jigs   De 12085, F6218,
                            W4119, Rex U560, AH 56(33), CRL 57369(33)
61305-A   The Wind That Shakes The Barley; The Lady On The Island-Reels
                  De 12067, F6217, W4054, Rex U245, AH 56(33), CRL 57369(33)
61306-A   The Kid On The Mountain-Jig   De 12067, F6220, W4118, Rex U562,
                                       AH 56(33), CRL 57369(33)
61307-A   The Liffey Banks; The Shaskeen-Reels   De 12080, F6217, W4054,
                                  Rex U245, AH 56(33), CRL 57369(33)
61308-A   Paddy Clancey's Jig; Trip To The Cottage-Jigs   De 12076, F6219,
                          W4144, Rex U561, AH 56(33), CRL 57369(33)

```
61309-A      High Level; McCormack's-Hornpipes  De 12076, F6219, W4144, Rex U561,
                                                AH 95(33), CRL 57464(33)
61310-A      O'Rourk's Reel; Wild Irishman-Reels
                                         De 12080, F6218, W4119, Rex U560, CRL 57369(33)
             Kathleen Brennan-p                                    NY  October 3, 1936
```

De 12036, 12067 and 12085 are in album 205.

```
             The Derry Hornpipe {Londonderry Hornpipe}            Shanachie 33006(33)
             The Girls Of Bainbridge; Cherish Ladies-Jigs               Shanachie rej
             Malloy's Favorite {Molloy's Favorite}-Reel           Shanachie 33006(33)
             The High Level Hornpipe                              Shanachie 33006(33)
             unaccompanied                                                NY  ca 1940
```

36.17. Barney Conlon *violin (1899-1946)*

Fireman Barney Conlon And Fireman John McKenna

```
694-2        Arigna's Green Vale-Jigs
700-1        Over The Lakes-Reels                                          NR 2300
701-1        Judy Callahan-Jigs                                           NR 2300
             John McKenna-pic, John Muller-p            NR 2301, JMc unnumbered (C)
                                                             NY  early 1920s
```

Fireman Barney Conlon

```
704-1        Miss Shaw's Highland Shottisches
             John Muller-p                                                 NR 2301
                                                             NY  early 1920s
```

Fire Patrolman Barney Conlon

```
712-D-1      Peter Toughey's Favorite
             Arthur P. Kenna-p                                             NR 2302
                                                             NY  early 1920s
```

Fireman Barney Conlon

```
743-A-1      Flowers Of Red Hill-Reels                                     NR 2329
743-B-1      Hearty Boys Of Ballymote; On The Coach Road To Sligo-Jigs    NR 2329
             Ed Geoghegan-p                                      NY  early 1920s
```

36.18. Mary Ellen Conlon *accordion*

```
8539-B       Rory O'More-Jig                                              Ge 5270
8540-A       Miss Ramsey-Schottische                                      Ge 5270
             p                                             NY  September 28, 1923
```

36.19. Peter James Conlon *accordion*

```
61945-1      test recording                                                   Co
                                                          NY  November 2, 1917
```

58984-2	The Humors Of The Whiskey-Jig	Co E3896, 33033-F
58985-2	Rose In The Garden-Reel	Co E3876, 33032-F
58986-1	Keel Row-Schottisch	Co E3876, 33032-F
58987-2	Saddle The Pony-Jig	Co E3987, 33034-F
58988-2	The Wind That Shakes The Barley	
	(The Wine That Shakes The Barley)-Reel	Co E3896, 33033-F
	p	NY November 1917
84058-1	The Mill Stone Grinder	Co E3987, 33034-F
		NY ca December 1917
14107	Paddy On The Turnpike-Reel	Lyric 4806
14108-2	The Black Thornstick-Jig	Lyric 4806
	p	NY 1920-1
S 7704-B	Harvest Home; Galway Bay-Hornpipes	Ok 4264, Pa E3176
S 7723-B	The Scholar-Reel	Ok 4264, Pa E3176, RZ MR3223
	p	NY January 1921
S 7887-B	Gurren's Castle; Money Musk-Highland Schottisches	
		Ok 4321, Apex 4321, Pa E3177
S 7888-A	The Heathery Breeze-Reel	Ok 4321, Apex 4321, Pa E3177
S 7889-A	Hennessey's Hornpipe	Ok 4322, Apex 4322, Pa E3178
S 7890-B	Paddy O'Rafferty's Jig	Ok 4323, Apex 4323, Pa E3179
S 7891-A	Gordon's Reel	Ok 4323, Apex 4323, Pa E3179
S 7892-B	Happy To Meet And Sorry To Part-Jig	Ok 4322, Apex 4322, Pa E3178
	Joseph J. Garry-p	NY ca April 1921
7670-A	Stack Of Barley	Ge 4797, Con 3036
7671	McBan's Reel	Ge 4797, Con 3036
	John Muller-p	NY October 16, 1921
S 70342-A	Stack Of Barley-Long Dance	Ok 4518, Pa A2248, E3025
S 70343-A	Cameronian Reel	Ok 21005, Pa E3026
S 70344-A	Kitty's Ramble-Jig	Ok 21006, Pa E3027
S 70345-C	Irishman's Blackthorn-Reel	Ok 21006, Pa E3027
S 70346-A	Barn Dance	Ok 21005, 45030, Pa E3026
S 70347-A	The Irish Washerwoman-Jig	Ok rej
	Nelly Meany-p	NY December 1, 1921
S 70347-B	The Irish Washerwoman-Jig	Ok 4518, Pa A2248, E3025
	as before	NY December 19, 1921
8653	Baxter's Jig	Ge 5340, Starr 9521
8654	The Way's To The Racket-Reels	Ge 5340, Starr 9521
8655	Medley Of Slip Jigs	Ge 5343, Apex 399, Starr 9506
8656	The Lark In The Morning-Jig	Ge 5343, Apex 399, Starr 9506
	R.J. Robson-p	NY December 10, 1923
8899	The Banks Of Ireland; The Ships Are Sailing-Reels'	
		Ge 5477, OBDW 39027
8900	The Plains Of Boyle	Ge 5478

| 8901 | The Salt Hill Pipes' | Ge 5478 |

8901 The Salt Hill Pipes'   Ge 5478
        Tom J. Morrison-fl, Miss McGoldrick-p, 'T. Higgins-vln
                                                    NY May 26, 1924

138-1   Sherren's Reel   Gaelic 1012
146-   Tom Ennis Jigs   Gaelic 1014
        Joseph J. Garry-p   NY 1920s

W 109680-3 The Banks Of Newfoundland-Jig   Co 33285-F, Vo 84134
W 109681-1 The College Grove; The Flaggon Reel   Co 33285-F, Vo 84134
W 109682-2 The Lark In The Morning; Clancy's Jig   Co 33307-F
W 109683-2 The Flax In Bloom; The Bag Of Potatoes-Reels   Co 33307-F
        p   NY September 1928

W 110096-2 The Broken Pledge; Kitty In The Lane-Reels   Co 33349-F
W 110098-1 The Irish Girl; Green Fields Of America-Jigs [actually reels]
                                                            Co 33349-F
        Manning's Jig; The Country Jig   Co 33322-F
        The Tuam Reel; The Salamanca Reel   Co 33322-F
        p, bj   NY January 1929

Conlon And Morrison

W 110109-2 The Tap Room; The Moving Bogs-Reels
                Co 33318-F, Vo 84140, RZ IZ196, MR696, Sh 33004(33)
W 110110-2 Old Man Dillon; The Rose In The Heather-Jigs
                Co 33318-F, Vo 84140, RZ IZ196, MR696, Sh 33004(33)
        James Morrison-vln, unk p   NY January 1929

Peter J. Conlon

W 110435-3 The Fiddler's Delight-Reels   Co 33435-F, Vo 84157
W 110436-1 Contentment Is Wealth-Jigs   Co 33435-F, Vo 84157
        p   NY March 1929

36.20. Frank J. Corbett *vocal*

        Killarney   Ok 4507
        Kathleen Mavourneen   Ok 4507
                                                    NY ca 1921

36.21. County Mayo Boys *instrumental*

W 113165-1 Oft In The Stilly Night-Fox Trot   Co 33492-F
W 113166-1 Maid Of Sweet Brown Knowe; Ballyjamesduff-One Step
                                            Co 33492-F, RZ G21346
W 113167-2 Boys Of Wexford; Eileen Alannah   Co 33488-F
W 113168- O'Donnell Aboo   Co 33488-F, RZ G21346
        vln, acn, p, bj   NY September 1931

36.22. Rev. James R. Cox, A.M., Ph.D. *vocal*

W 112040-1	Jesus, Jesus, Come To Me	Co 33414-F, Vo 84155
W 112041-1	The Unknown Soldier	Co 33414-F, Vo 84155
		NY ca April 1930

36.23. Curran, Fitzpatrick And O'Rourke *instrumental*

9468-A	Leitrim; Kiss The Bride-Reels	Ge 5717, OBDW 39033
9469	Merry Old Woman; Irishmen's Hearts For The Ladies-Jigs	
		Ge 5717, OBDW 39033
	Michael Curran and another-2 vln, unk fl, p	NY April 17, 1925

9588-A	The Beauties Of Ireland-Reels¹	Ge 5742
9589-A	The Sunny South-Hornpipe¹	Ge 5742
9590-A	Sporting Paddy; In The Merry Days Of Easter	Ge rej
9591-A	The Morrill Jig; Haste To The Wedding	Ge rej
	Michael Curran and another-2 vln, Elizabeth A. Doyle-p, unk fl, ¹unk	
	vln, fl omitted	NY June 15, 1925

One or both of the above may be as FITZPATRICK, CURRAN AND O'ROURKE.

36.24. James Darcy *flute*

CO 20223-1	The Barmaid; The Milliner's Daughter-Reels	Co 33557-F, Vo 84060
	John Mulvihill-vln	NY November 10, 1936

36.25. Dean And Mack *vocal, instrumental*

8915-A	Believe Me If All Those Endearing Young Charms; O'Brien's Favorite;	
	The Boys Of Kilkenny	Ge 5487
8916-A	Last Rose Of Summer; Reel Of Bogie	Ge 5487
	Dean Newton-ten, Hughie J. Mack-bagpipes, Frank O'Neal-p	
		NY June 9, 1924

36.26. Packie Dolan *(James P. Dolan); violin*

W 175296-1	test recording	Co
		NY February 14, 1927

E 22182/3	Miss Morrow's Fancy; Kitty In The Lane	Br rej
E 22184/5	Walsh's Jigs	Br rej
E 22186/7	Tynan's Polkas¹	Br rej
E 22188/9	The White Leaf-Reels¹	Br rej
	Ed Geoghegan-p, ¹Michael Gray-fife	NY March 30, 1927

W 107828-2	McFadden Reels	Co 33185-F
W 107829-1	The Fair Of Drumlish-Jig	Co 33185-F
	p	NY April 1927

Packie Dolan's Melody Boys

BVE 45100-2	Mother Malone[1] [3] [4]	Vi 21541
BVE 45101-1	Mullin's Fancy-Reel[3]	Vi 21484, MS 45001(33), Sh 33001(33)
BVE 45102-2	Lasses Of Donnibrook-Highland Fling[2]	Vi 21484, MS 45001(33), Sh 33001(33)
BVE 45103-1	Fitzmaurice's Flight-Reel	Vi 21442
BVE 45104-1	The Cork-Hornpipe	Vi rej
BVE 45105-1	The Grove-Hornpipe	Vi 21442, Yv K-504
BVE 45106-1	The Cavan Lassies-Jig[2]	Vi 21541, Yv K-512, LC LBC-4(33)

own vln/'vo, unk [2]whistle, bones, [3]p, [4]dancing   NY May 3, 1928

BVE 46981-2	Steampacket Reel; Flogging Reel[2] [3]	Vi 21679, HMV B3397
BVE 46982-2	First Of May Hornpipe[2] [3]	Vi 21679, Yv K-514, HMV B3397, FW 8821(33)
BVE 46983-2	Royal Charley-Old Time Set Tune[2]	Vi V-29006, HMV B3389
BVE 46984-2	The Windy Gap-Reel[2] [3]	Vi V-29006, HMV B3389
BVE 46985-1	The Lady Of The House-Reel	Vi V-29005
BVE 46986-2	One, Two, Three[1]	Vi V-29005

own vln/'vo, unk p, [2]fl, [3]tambourine   NY September 5, 1928

Packie Dolan And His Boys

BVE 48591-2	The Irish Girl; The Blue Breeches-Reels[3]	Vi V-29059
BVE 48592-1	Kilkenny Reel[3]	Vi V-29025
BVE 48593-2	A Drink In The Morn[1] [3]	Vi V-29034
BVE 48594-2	Erin's Green Shore[1] [3]	Vi V-29025, 26-7511, Bb B-4902, MW M-8619
BVE 48595-1	The Ships Are Sailing-Reel[2]	Vi V-29059, Yv K-508
BVE 48596-2	Killarney Wonder[3]	Vi V-29034

own vln/'vo, unk [2]tin whistle, [3]p   NY January 22, 1929

36.27. Harry Donnelly *instrumental*

7503-2	Harry Donnelly's Dublin Hornpipe	Ba 7023, Cq 7205, Re 8490

Geoghegan's Emerald Trio: Ed Geoghegan-p, unk vln, pic

NY September 9, 1927

The trio constitutes the entire ensemble, and it is not clear which instrument is meant to be the soloist.

36.28. Thomas Donohue *tenor*

In The Land Where The Green Shamrock Grows	Ok 40016
Smile Through Your Tears	Ok 40016

NY ca 1923

36.29. Tim Donovan *tenor*

63573-A	My Wild Irish Boy[1]	De 12157, W4280, Rex U624
63574-A	The Exile Of Cork	De 12157, W4280, Rex U624

vln, cl, p, [1]acn

NY April 7, 1938

```
65829-        The Furze Bush Hedge In Bloom                      De 12242, W4861
65831-        The Star Of Donegal                      De 12242, W4488, Rex U670
              orch d Patrick Killoran                           NY   June 15, 1939
```

36.30. Patrick Doran *flute*

```
12073-A       Hard Road To Travel-Reel                                   Ge 5617
12074-A       Happy To Meet And Sorry To Part-Jig (arr Chief O'Neill)    Ge 5634
12075         Captain Coughlin's Hornpipe (Doran)                        Ge 5604
12076-A       Bowen's Favorite Jig (Doran)                               Ge 5604
12077-A       The Duke Of Leinster                                       Ge rej
              Kathleen Kearney-p               Richmond, IN  November 7, 1924

12078         Morning Star Reel (O'Neill)                                Ge 5634
12079         The Maid On The Green-Jig                                  Ge 5617
12080         Miss McLeod's Reel                                         Ge rej
                                               Richmond, IN  November 9, 1924
```

Patrick Doran, Tom Cawley And Frances Malone

```
W 107004-1    Sweeney's Favorite Reel                       Co 33110-F, RZ G8941
W 107005-2    The Moving Bogs Of Powelsboro-Jig             Co 33110-F, RZ G8941
W 107006-2    The Drumshambo Jig                                        Co 33144-F
W 107007-2    The Gatehouse Maid-Reel                                   Co 33182-F
W 107008-2    The Castle Bar Lassies-Jig                                Co 33182-F
              Patrick Doran-fl, Tom Cawley-vln, Frances Malone-p  Chicago  July 1926

W 107094-1    Miss Forkan's Fancy-Reel                                  Co 33144-F
              as before                                     Chicago  August 1926
```

Patrick Doran, Joe Owens, Dennis Flynn And Mike Hart

```
W 108084-2    Tom Henry's Favorite; Pete Brown's Fancy-Reels           Co 33238-F
W 108085-1    Off She Goes; Valleys Are Blooming-Jigs                  Co 33238-F
              own fl, Joe Owens-vln, Dennis Flynn-bagpipes, Mike Hart-p
                                                             Chicago  July 1927
```

Patrick Doran, Joseph Sullivan And Joe Owens

```
W 108089-1    Follow Me Around The Garden; The Lark In The Meadow-Jigs  Co 33202-F
              own fl, Joe Owens-vln, Joseph Sullivan-bagpipes, probaly Mike Hart-p
                                                             Chicago  July 1927
```

36.31. Dinny Doyle *vocal*

```
BVE 48155-2   Let Mr. McGuire Sit Down¹                              Vi V-29016
BVE 48156-1   Tommy Murphy Was A Soldier Boy                         Vi V-29016
              Dan Sullivan-p, ¹own hca              NY  November 13, 1928
```

36.32. Dublin Concert Orchestra

W 143205-2	Echoes Of Ireland-Pt. 1	Co 33135-F, RZ IZ237, MR1370
W 143206-1	Echoes Of Ireland-Pt. 2	Co 33135-F, RZ IZ237, MR1370
		NY December 21, 1926

36.33. Dublin Orchestra

W 107762-2	Danny Boy; Come Back To Erin	Co 33214-F, Vo 84126
W 107763-2	Believe Me If All Those Endearing Young Charms; Wearin' Of The Green	
		Co 33214-F, Vo 84126
		NY April 1927

36.34. Jim Dwyer *tenor*

62812-A	My Heart Is At Home In Old Ireland	De 12141, W4243
62813-A	Tipperary Far Away	De 12128, W4239, Rex U607
62814-A	The Irish Brigade	De 12128, W4239, Rex U607
62815-A	Christmas Eve In London	De 12141

Paddy Killoran Trio: Patrick Killoran-vln, unk ten sax, acn
NY November 26, 1937

63329-A	The Old Homestead (Thomas B. Shaw-Patrick McCormack, adapted to "Terence's Farewell")	De 12142
63330-A	In A Cottage By The Twilight	De 12142, W4261, Rex U611
63333-A	The Devil And The Bailiff (Cathal MacGarvey)	De 12150, Rex U616
63334-A	The Kildare Exile (Thomas B. Shaw-Patrick McCormack, adapted from "Teddy O'Neale")	De 12150, W4261, Rex U617

orch
NY February 22, 1938

64305-A	Father Murphy Of Boolavogue	De 12182, W4328
64306-A	The Foggy Dew (1916 Easter version)	De 12182, W4328, Rex U640
64307-A	United Ireland	De 12172, W4380, Rex U640
64308-	The Yankee Boy	De 12184, W4380, Rex U644
64311-A	The Brave Volunteers (arr Meakin)'	De 12172, W4308, Rex U617
64312-	Just A Rose In Old Killarney (Frank Swain)	De 12184

Paddy Killoran Trio: Patrick Killoran-vln, Jim McGinn-p/'acn, unk ten sax
NY July 12, 1938

65868-A	Dermot Astore	De 12215, W4677
65869-A	An Irish Song From An Irish Heart-Waltz Song (Stevens-Scott)	
		De 12215
65870-A	Ireland The Land Of My Birth (Henry Jackson-Gerald Scott)	De 12224
65871-A	The Girl I Knew In Old Killarney (Scott-Parsons)	De 12224, Rex U644
65872-	When I Dream Of Old Erin I'm Dreaming Of You	De 12232, Rex U673
65873-	The Donovans	De 12232, W4677

Patrick Killoran-vln, unk acn, ten sax, p
NY June 22, 1939

36.35.   James Early And John Mc Fadden   *instrumental*

The Kildare Fancy-Hornpipe	Skylark SK1002(C)
Lord Mayo {Version Of Lord Mayo}-Air	Skylark SK1002(C)
John McFadden-violin, James Early-bagpipes	Chicago early 1900s

The above are taken from privately recorded cylinders and are attributed to
PATRICK TOUHEY on the cassette. Early is known to have been born in 1848.

36.36.   James Egan   *tenor*

165-A	When It's Moonlight In Mayo	Ge 5490, OBDW 39006
166-A	Irish Serenade	Ge
		NY ca February 2, 1922
	Exile's Lament	NR 2323
	My Old Home Town In Ireland	NR 2323
		NY early 1920s
8911-A	Sligo {Just To Hear My Mother Sing}	Ge 5490, OBDW 39006
	Dick Barry-p	NY June 1924
W 143523-1	The Old Rustic Bridge By The Mill	Co 33150-F
W 143524-1	That's An Irish Lullaby	Co 33150-F
		NY February 24, 1927
W 109030-	I Loved You Better Than You Knew	Co rej
W 109180-2	Sligo {Just To Hear My Mother Sing}	Co 33354-F, RZ MR1989
W 109182-3	'Twas Only An Irishman's Dream	Co 33284-F
	orch	NY April 1928
W 109356-2	Al Smith	Co 33259-F
W 109357-1	Little Annie Rooney	Co 33259-F, RZ G20346
W 109358-2	The Daughter Of Rosie O'Grady	Co 33354-F, RZ MR1989
		NY May 1928
W 109030-4	I Loved You Better Than You Knew	Co 33284-F
	orch	NY June 1928
	Irish Eyes Of Love	Co 33305-F
	My Old Home Town In Ireland	Co 33305-F
		NY ca 1929
W 112165-	Amber Tresses Tied In Blue	Co rej
W 112166-	A Brown Bird Singing	Co rej
		NY June 1930
W 112165-4	Amber Tresses Tied In Blue	Co 33452-F
W 112166-4	A Brown Bird Singing	Co 33452-F, RZ G21286
		NY 1930

36.37. Tom Ennis *bagpipes (1889-1931)*

<pre>
                 Last Rose Of Summer; Hornpipe; Jig; Reel   Vi trial
                                                      NY February 28, 1917

B 19563-1   Believe Me If All Those Endearing Young Charms (Thos. Moore);
               Killarney (Balfe); The Last Rose Of Summer (Thos. Moore)'
                                                                  Vi 18286
B 19563-2   Believe Me If All Those Endearing Young Charms (Thos. Moore);
               Killarney (Balfe); The Last Rose Of Summer (Thos. Moore)
                                                                    Vi rej
B 19564-1   The Three Little Drummers; The Connachtman's Rambles; The Joy Of My
               Life; Nancy Hynes-Jigs'   Vi 18286, MS 45001(33), Sh 33001(33)
B 19564-2   The Three Little Drummers; The Connachtman's Rambles; The Joy Of My
               Life; Nancy Hynes-Jigs   Vi rej
B 19565-1   Murphy's Hornpipe; Londonderry Clog; McNamara Hornpipe-Hornpipe
               Medley No. 3'   Vi rej
B 19565-2   Murphy's Hornpipe; Londonderry Clog; McNamara Hornpipe-Hornpipe
               Medley No. 3   Vi 18366
B 19566-1   The Maid That Left The County; Drowsy Maggie; Around The World For
               Sport-Reel Medley No. 6   Vi 18366
          'Ted Levy-p   NY April 17, 1917

B 20638-2   Trim The Velvet; Lord Gordon's Reel; Limestone Rock-Reels   Vi rej
B 20639-1   The Cook In The Kitchen; The Gold Ring; Hanafin's Jig-Jigs   Vi rej
                                                      NY August 23, 1917

T 67735-   Irish Jigs Medley   Pat 20402
T 67736-   Irish Reels Medley   Pat 20402
                                                          NY ca May 1919

T 68445-   The Maid In The Meadow; The Frieze Breeches; Pay The Reckoning-Jigs
                              Pat 20550, 021090, Pe 11162, Sil 1270
T 68446-   The Swallow's Tail; The Maid Behind The Bar; The Fermoy Lasses-Reels
         Pat 20550, 021090, Pe 11162, Cameo 9115, Lincoln 3142, Operaphone 51139, Ro 917,
                                                                   Sil 1270
           p   NY ca March 1920

Operaphone 51139 is uncredited.

8-146   Cherish The Ladies-Jigs   Emerald 4008
8-147-B   Blackbird-Long Dance   Emerald 4008
                                                         NY early 1920s

C 652-2   Little Judy Reels   Cardinal 2028
C 653-   Cook In The Kitchen-Jigs   Cardinal 2028
C 654-2   Trim The Velvet-Reels   Cardinal 2029
C 655-2   Humors Of Bandon-Long Dance   Cardinal 2029
             John Muller-p   NY March 1921

41763-1   Walsh Favorite; Butcher's March-Jigs   Em 10394, Medallion 8303
41764-1-2   Eileen Curran; Five Mile Chase-Reels   Em 10394, Symphonola 4334
                                                          NY April 1921
</pre>

```
S 7970-B      Frieze Breeches-Jig   Ok 4383, Apex 4383, Pa E3023, Topic 12T390(33)
S 7971-A      Kildare Fancy-Hornpipe              Ok 4383, Apex 4383, Pa E3023
              Kildare Fancy; Stack Of Wheat                  Topic 12T390(33)
          John Muller-p                                   NY  ca June 1921


O 8213-B      Dear Irish Boy          Od Od20077, Ok 4490, Starr 16005, Pa E3024
O 8214-B      The Coulin              Od Od20077, Ok 4490, Starr 16005, Pa E3024
              as before                                     NY  ca 1921
```

Tom Ennis, Jas. Morrison And John Muller

```
              Job of Journey Work-Long Dance or Hornpipe             untraced
              Kerryman's Rambles; Cook In The Kitchen                untraced
                                                        NY  early 1920s
```

The above was probably issued on New Republic.

```
9086          New Steamboat; Bucks Of Oranmore; Gardner's Daughter-Reels
                                              Vo 14354, Topic 12T390(33)
9088          Paddy In London; Butcher's March; Sligo Bay-Jigs
                                              Vo 14354, Topic 12T390(33)
          James Morrison-vln, John Muller-p           NY  ca May 1922
```

Ennis, Morrison And Muller

```
80403-2       The Blackbird-Long Dance                          Co rej
80404-3       The Bag Of Potatoes; Temple House Reel; Pigeon On The Gate-Reels
                                                                 Co rej
              as before                             NY  June 14, 1922


80403-4       The Blackbird-Long Dance           Co A3679, 33042-F, Vo 84110
80404-6       The Bag Of Potatoes; Temple House Reel; Pigeon On The Gate-Reels
                                    Co A3679, 33042-F, VT 7029-V, Vo 84110
              Bag Of Spuds; Temple House Reel; Pigeon On The Gate
                                                       Topic 12T390(33)
              as before                             NY  July 27, 1922
```

Tom Ennis And John Garridy

```
8104-A        Irish Polka                    Ge 5003, OBDW 39025, Starr 9318
8105          Miss Thornton's; The Merry Blacksmith; The Bush In Bloom-Reels
                                             Ge 5003, OBDW 39025, Starr 9318
          John Gerrity-vln, Paddy Muldoon-p          NY  November 14, 1922
```

Ennis, Morrison And Muller

```
80681-1       Job Of Journey Work-Long Dance   Co A3773, 33021-F, Topic 12T390(33)
80682-1       Maid On The Green; Trip To The Cottage; Wedding Trip-Jigs
                                             Co A3773, 33021-F
          James Morrison-vln, John Muller-p          NY  November 21, 1922
```

Tom Ennis

```
8182-A      Mamma's Pet; My Love Is On The Ocean-Reels¹      Ge 5054, OBDW 39024
8183        Cook In The Kitchen-Jig¹ ²                                    Ge 5054
8184        Miss McLeod's Reel; Rakish Paddy²      Ge 5040, OBDW 39039, Starr 9364
8185        Connaughtman's Rambles; Frost Is All Over²
                                                   Ge 5040, OBDW 39039, Starr 9364
            John Muller-p, ¹Redie Johnson-acn, ²Tom Quigley-vln
                                                          NY   January 23, 1923
```

Tunes are listed in reverse order on both sides of Gennett 5040.

Ennis, Morrison And Muller

```
80828-3     The Humors Of Bandon                          Co A3836, 33046-F
80829-3     Maid Behind The Bar; Trim The Velvet
                                          Co A3836, 33046-F, Topic 12T390(33)
80830-3     Kid On The Mountain-Hop Jig                               Co rej
80831-3     Londonderry Hornpipe          Co 35-D, 33043-F, RZ G8237, IZ111
            James Morrison-vln, John Muller-p             NY February 2, 1923

80945-3     The Black Rogue; Saddle The Pony-Jigs
                            Co 35-D, 33043-F, RZ G8237, IZ111, Topic 12T390(33)
            as before                                     NY April 10, 1923

11193/4/5   Lime Stone Rock-Reels                                   Vo 14588
            Lime Stone Rock; Hayden's Favourite          Topic 12T390(33)
11196/7/8   Kid On The Mountain-Hop Jig                             Vo 14588
            as before                                     NY  ca April 1923
```

Tom Ennis

```
8550        Cherish The Ladies-Jig          Ge 5283, OBDW 39020, Starr 9479
8551        Trim The Velvet; Maid Behind The Bar-Reels
                                            Ge 5283, OBDW 39020, Starr 9479
            Harry Race-p                              NY October 8, 1923

K2-1        Sarsfield's Jig; The Rakes Of Clonmel            Keltic 1001
            p                                               NY ca 1923

BVE 43387-1 Ragan's Jig; Trip To The Cottage-Jigs                 Vi rej
BVE 43388-1 Miss Thornton's Reel; Star Of Munster-Reels           Vi rej
            John Gerrity-vln, Ed Geoghegan-p          NY  March 21, 1928

BVE 43939-2 Trip To The Cottage-Jig    Vi 21444, Aurora 36-110, Topic 12T390(33)
BVE 43940-2 Dublin Reel                          Vi 21444, Aurora 36-110
BVE 43941-2 Miss Casey-Jig                                      Vi 21542
BVE 43942-2 Wexford Reel                                        Vi 21542
            Ed Geoghegan-p                            NY  May 2, 1928

W 111233-3  Roy's Wife-Fling            Co 33394-F, RZ G20755, IZ148, MR133
W 111235-1  Trim The Velvet            Co 33421-F, RZ IZ148, MR133
W 111279-2  Rickett's Hornpipe; Dr. Carroll's Hornpipe
                                       Co 33421-F, RZ IZ149, MR134
```

```
W 111280-1    Ragan's Jig; Nora Greena-Jigs    Co 33394-F, RZ G20755, IZ149, MR134
              p                                         NY  November 1929
```

36.38. The Erin Boys Orchestra

```
W 143500-2    The Irish Counties-Fox Trot-Pt. 1                  Co 33149-F
W 143501-2    The Irish Counties-Fox Trot-Pt. 2                  Co 33149-F
                                                    NY  February 21, 1927
```

36.39. Erin's Isle Ballroom Orchestra

```
W 112850-1    Come Back To Erin                     Co 33471-F, Vo 84162
W 112851-2    Rose In The Garden; Rose Of Tralee; Terence's Farewell
                                                    Co 33475-F, RZ G21171
W 112852-2    Dark Eyed Lassie; Caledonian Hunt     Co 33471-F, Vo 84162
W 112853-2    Believe Me If All Those Endearing Young Charms; Mullingar Races
                                                    Co 33475-F, RZ G21171
                                                            NY  March 1931
```

36.40. Billy Fagan *tenor*

```
S 73895-B     Kilkenny                              Ok 21030, Pa E3218
S 73896-A     Down Deep In An Irishman's Heart (Brennan-McHugh)        Ok 21030
              Jimmy McHugh-p                                 NY  January 1926
```

36.41. John Fahey *violin*

```
62099-A       Paddy Ryan's Dream; The Milliner's Daughter-Reels
                                                    De 12129, W4180, Rex U210
62100-A       Off To The Hunt; The Butcher's March-Jigs¹ De 12129, W4180, Rex U210
              Johnny Connors-p, ¹Joe Fahey-bj               NY  April 4, 1937
```

36.42. Jack Feeney *tenor*

The Columbia files state that this is a pseudonym for JOHN GRIFFIN.

```
1583-3        That's How I Spell I-R-E-L-A-N-D (McConnell-Downey-Sanford)
                                                    Cr 3262, Ho 23046, Vars 7002
1584-1        Sweet Inniscara                       Cr 3262, Ho 23046, Vars 7051
              orch                                          NY  December 29, 1931
```

Varsity 7051 as GREEN'S DUBLIN BAND

```
1656-2        The Rose Of Tralee (Spencer-Glover)        Cr 3295, Ho 23048
1657-1        I'll Take You Home Again, Kathleen (Thomas B. Westendorf)
                                                    Cr 3295, Ho 23048
              vln, p                                        NY  March 2, 1932
```

```
1738-2      Far Away In Australia'                               Cr 3342
1739-2      Bard Of Armagh                            Cr 3343, Vars 7007
1740-2      The Snowy Breasted Pearl                  Cr 3343, Vars 7007
1741-1      The Irish Emigrant                        Cr 3342, Vars 8008
            Jim McGinn-p, 'unk vln, Bridie Feeney-vo      NY  May 31, 1932

39007-A     A Shawl Of Galway Grey (Joseph Stanley-Patrick Hogan)
                                                       De 12038, Rex U604
39008-A     When It's Moonlight In Mayo               De 12038, Rex U306
39009-A     That Old Irish Mother Of Mine (Harry Von Tilzer-William Jerome)
                                                       De 12014, Rex U604
39010-A     Molly Brannigan'                              De 12014
            orch or 'Helen Merchant-p              NY  November 12, 1934

CO 20224-1  The Shamrock, The Shannon And You (John Grffin) Co 33559-F, Vo 84062
CO 20225-2  Where Wicklow Looks Down On The Sea-Waltz (John Griffin)
                                                    Co 33561-F, Vo 84064
            Martin Beirne And His Irish Blackbirds Orchestra: probably Martin
            Beirne-bagpipes, John Mulvihill-vln, John Griffin-fl, William
            McElligott-acn, Alex Brown-p              NY  November 10, 1936
```

John (Jack) Feeney

```
62304-A     The Green Bushes               De 12122, W4422, Rex U652
62305-A     The Song My Mother Used To Sing De 12110, W4190, Rex U205
62306-A     The Connemara Shore                   De 12115, W4283
62307-A     There's An Echo Of Old Ireland Everywhere
              (Sanford Osborne-Jack Feeney) De 12115, W4189, Rex U204
62308-A     She Moved Thru The Fair               De 12121
62309-A     The Dawning Of The Day           De 12121, W4679
62310-A     The Tan Yard Side            De 12111, W4189, Rex U204
62311-A     Open The Door Softly, Kitty My Love   De 12110, W4858
62312-A     Teddy O'Neale               De 12111, W4190, Rex U205
62313-A     On The Banks Of My Own Lovely Lee     De 12122, W4283
            Helen Merchant-p                  NY  June 23, 1937
```

De 12014, 12038, 12111 and 12138 are in album A-517.

```
62844-A     The Gartan Mother's Lullaby            De 12139
62845-A     The Fanaid Grove                       De 12143
62846-A     Marie My Girl (George Aitken-John Keegan Casey)   De 12130
62847-A     I Cannot Sing The Old Songs (Claribel)  De 12143
62848-A     Sweet Genevieve (Henry Tucker-George Cooper)  De 12130, W4679
62849-A     In An Old Fashioned Town (W.H. Squire-Ada Leonora Harris) De 12139
62850-A     Bless This House (May H. Brahe-Helen Taylor)
                                           De 12185, W4422, Rex U652
62851-      The Silent Hour {Blessed Hour Of Prayer}
              (Charles Wakefield Cadman-Helen Boardman Knox)  De 12185
            vln, acn, p                   NY  December 2, 1937
```

De 12014, 12038, 12111 and 12139 are in album A-517.

```
64174-A     Ballymoney (Sean O'Hara)               De 12177
```

64175-A	At The End Of Cobblestone Road (Thomas Burke-Carlo Sanders)	
		De 12177, W4858
64176-A	A Handful Of Earth (From My Dear Mother's Grave) (Joseph Murphy)	
		De 12170, W4310, Rex U635
64177-A	My Home In The County Mayo (Alma Sanders-Monte Carlo)	
		De 12190, W4383, Rex U647
64178-A	My Irish Home (Frank)	De 12170, W4310, Rex U635
64179-A	One Clear Summer Morning, Near Blue Avonree	
		De 12190, W4383, Rex U647
	orch	NY June 21, 1938

36.43. John Finnegan *tenor*

This artist recorded classical material and Irish songs for Edison, Empire, Indestructible, New Republic, Victor and probably other companies.

36.44. Frank Fitzpatrick *accordion*

9366-A	The Peeler And The Goat¹	Ge 5700, 3023
9367-A	The Leitrim Jig	Ge 5700, 3023
	¹with lilting	NY February 25, 1925

36.45. Michael J. Fitzpatrick *vocal*

This artist is one of the Fitzpatrick Brothers, q.v.

9569	You're Just Like Your Mother (A Beautiful Rose) (M.J. Fitzpatrick)	
		Ge 5748
	p	NY May 28, 1925

| BVE 37136-1 | An Armful Of Cats (M.J. Fitzpatrick) | Vi 79106 |
| | Matty Levine-p | NY   December 15, 1926 |

| BVE 38165-2 | McFadden's Flats (M.J. Fitzpatrick) | Vi 79303 |
| | Joe Linder-p | NY   March 14, 1927 |

36.46. Patrick Fitzpatrick *bagpipes (b. 1860)*

| 5270 | The Kilfenora; The Flower Of The Flock; The Floggan-Reels   Ed 51692 |
| | NY   January 8, 1917 |

| 5286 | Comedy Maid; Rakes Of Kildare; Miss Daly's Jig Ed 50615, 5270(4 min) |
| | NY   January 13, 1917 |

| | Irish Jigs | Vi trial |
| | | NY   February 26, 1917 |

47409-2	Three Drops Of Brandy-Reel	Co A2309, Sil 3168
47410-2	Donnybrook Fair-Jig	Co A2309, 33019-F, Sil 3168
		NY March 9, 1917

```
                  Irish Reels                                      Em 7236(7")
                  Irish Jigs                                       Em 7236(7")
                                                                   NY   1917

6094-1-1510       Louden's Bonnie Woods And Braes                  Lyric 4117
6095-1-1511       Comedy Maid-Jig                                  Lyric 4117
                                                                   NY   ca 1919
```

36.47. Fitzpatrick Brothers *vocal*

```
9383              Corned Beef And Cabbage (Michael J. Fitzpatrick)    Ge 5703, 3020
9384              McFadden's Goat (Michael J. Fitzpatrick)           Ge 5703, 3020
         p                                                       NY   March 4, 1925

9568-A            The Chimes Of Trinity                               Ge rej
         p                                                       NY   May 28, 1925

W 105802-2        Fiddler At The Wedding                              Co 33006-F
W 105803-3        Mike Clancy's Hack                                  Co 33006-F
         vln, p                                                  NY   ca July 1925

BVE 37137-1       Abraham Riley (Fitzpatrick Brothers)                Vi 79132
BVE 37138-2       The Piper At The Christening (Fitzpatrick Brothers)
                                                                Vi 79106, HMV B2566
BVE 37139-2       Corned Beef And Cabbage (Fitzpatrick Brothers)      Vi 79132
                  Matty Levine-p                                NY   December 17, 1926

BVE 38163-2       Pretty Lady Bug (Fitzpatrick Brothers)              Vi 79287
BVE 38164-2       Patrick Mind The Baby                               Vi 79303
BVE 38166-2       The Mulligan Guards (Fitzpatrick Brothers)     Vi 20760, Yv K-527
BVE 38167-2       Mr. And Mrs. Malone                                 Vi 79287
                  Joe Linder-p                                  NY   March 14, 1927

BVE 43544-1       The Market On A Saturday Night (Harrigan-Hart)      Vi 21482
BVE 43545-2       Sidewalks Of New York'                               Vi 21377
BVE 43546-1       Mr. Dooley's Geese (Harrigan-Hart)                  Vi 21482
BVE 43547-2       Never Take The Horseshoe From The Door              Vi 21377
                  Joe Green-traps, unk vln, fl, p, 'xyl         NY   April 9, 1928

                  The Bowery Grenadiers                              Co 33250-F
                  Land League Band                                  Co 33250-F
                                                                NY   ca 1928
```

36.48. Flanagan Brothers *vocal, instrumental*

Both Flanagans sing and play several instruments on the following recordings, though it is not always clear who is singing or playing which instrument. Joe Flanagan usually plays accordion and Michael plays guitar or banjo. There are no vocals on their pre-1926 recordings. Others that follow are vocals except as indicated.

	An' Corowath-Hornpipes	NR 1107
	Red Haired Boy	NR 1107
	By The Sea-Waltz	NR 1108
	Irish Republican Airs-One Step	NR 1108
	acn, 2 bj	NY 1921

80839-1	The Morning Star; The Collier's Reel	Co 95-D, 33044-F
80840-1	Bonnie Scotland; Johnny, Will You Marry Me; Keel Row-Highland Flings	
		Co A3849, 33051-F
80841-2	The Red Haired Boy; The Lady On The Island-Reels	Co A3849, 33051-F
80842-2	Frieze Breeches; The Cook In The Kitchen; Lannigan's Ball-Jigs	
		Co 95-D, 33044-F
	acn, g, bj	NY February 10, 1923

42362-1	Irish Barn Dance	Em 10612, Sil 2648
42363-1	The Maid Is Not Twenty Yet	Em 10612, Sil 2648
		NY March 1923

Sil 2648 was issued pseudonymously, but what name was used is not clear.

8347-A	Down The Meadows; The Rambler's Jig	OBDW 39022, Starr 9422
8348-A	The Hearty Bucks Of Cranmore-Reel	OBDW 39022, Starr 9406
8349-A	Irish Boy-One Step	Ge 5169, Starr 9406, Topic 12T365(33)
8350-A	The Rights Of Man; Hennessey's Hornpipe	
		Ge 5169, OBDW 39023, Starr 9422
	acn, g, bj	NY April 30, 1923

11464/5	Rakes Of Clonmel; Sarsfield's Jig-Jigs	Vo 14638
11468/9	Cavan Reel; Gardener's Daughter-Reels	Vo 14638
	acn, bj, harp-guitar	NY ca May 1923

The tunes on each side of the above are played in reverse order.

8448-B	Jenny Picking Cockles; Drowsy Maggie-Reels	
		Ge 5206, OBDW 39026, Starr 9420
8449-A	The Maid On The Green; The Frost Is All Over-Jigs	
		Ge 5206, OBDW 39026, Starr 9420
8450-B	The Gaelic Barn Dance	Ge 5205, Starr 9451
8451	Holly And Ivy-Reels	Ge 5205, Starr 9451
	as before	NY July 7, 1923

12202/3/4	Rakes Of Kildare; Irish Washerwoman-Jigs	Vo 14704, Sil 3060
12205/6/7	Green Mountain Reel; The Teetotaler Reel	Vo 14704, Sil 3060
	as before	NY September 1923

```
12988/9/90    Biddy Daly's Jiggs                                    Vo 14804, Sil 3059
12991/2       The Maid That Left The County; More Power To Your Elbow-Reels
                                                                     Vo 14804, Sil 3059
              as before                                              NY  April 1924

W 106666-2    Boys At The Lough; The Shaskeen; The Honeymoon-Reels¹ [no vo]
                                                     Co 33103-F, RZ G20718
W 106667-1    Kerry Mill's Barn Dance² [no vo] Co 33096-F, IFB248, RZ G8935, IZ115
W 106668-1    Fun At Hogan's-Comic Sketch² ³             Co 33103-F, RZ G8937, IZ117
W 106669-2    Flanagan At The Racket-Comic Sketch       Co 33096-F, RZ G8936, IZ116
              ¹bj duet, ²acn, bj, ³g                                 NY  April 1926

BVE 36861-1   The Night Pat Murphy Died  Vi 79010, Bb B-4963, MW M-8633, Yv K-539,
                                                     HMV B2566, Zon 5157, RZ T5157
BVE 36862-1   The Heart Of Man-Barn Dance² ³ [no vo]                 Vi 79011
BVE 36863-3   Irish Delight¹   Vi 79010, Bb B-4963, MW M-8633, Zon 5157, RZ T5157,
                                                     Topic 12T365(33)
BVE 36864-1   Reconciliation-Reel¹ ² [no vo]                         Vi 79011
              ¹acn, ²bj, ³g, Charles Bender-p              NY  October 25, 1926

BVE 36468-2   Paddy In London-Jig [no vo]   Vi 79096, 20-3265, 26-7504, Bb B-4975,
                                            MW M-8634, Yv K-506, K-540, Topic 12T365(33)
BVE 36469-2   The Widow McCarty¹                          Vi 79014, HMV B2899
BVE 36470-2   The Flanagans At Dinty Moore's                         Vi 79014
              acn, bj, p, or ¹p, g             Camden, NJ  November 17, 1926

W 107369-3    Johnny Williams Hornpipe [no vo]                       Co 33125-F
              Jimmy William's Hornpipe                      RZ G8936, IZ116
W 107370-2    The Geese In The Bog-Jig (with set calls 4th figure)
                                Co 33126-F, IFB248, Vo 84075, RZ G8935, IZ115
W 107371-2    The Flanagans Chase The Banshee¹        Co 33126-F, IFB305, Vo 84075,
                                                     RZ G9384, G20673, IZ140
W 107372-2    In An Irishman's Shanty                  Co 33125-F, RZ G8937, IZ117
              acn, bj, ¹hca, jews-harp, kazoo                    NY  November 1926

6890-2        The Hat Me Father Wore                   Ba 2138, Do 0165, Or 814, Re 8194,
                                                     OBDW 39075, Apex 8570, Starr 10229
6891-2        Highland Flings Medley                   Ba 2138, Do 0165, Or 815, Re 8194,
                                          OBDW 39075, Apex 8571, Do 21246, Starr 10230
6906-2        Irish Fair Day    Ba 2140, Do 0169, Or 815, Pe unnumbered, Re 8237,
                                                     OBDW 39074, Apex 8570, Starr 10229
6907-2-3      Green Meadows Reel Ba 2140, Do 0169, Or 814, Pe unnumbered, Re 8237,
                                          OBDW 39074, Apex 8571, Do 21246, Starr 10230
              acn, bj, p, Mattie Haskins-vo                    NY  ca November 1926
```

The Perfect unnumbered sides are coupled. Oriole 814 and 815 as COUNTY CORK TRIO;
Starr 10229 as MATTIE HASKINS. The Apex and Starr issues and Domino 21246 are
Canadian.

```
BVE 37082-3   The Blackbird-Exhibition Hornpipe [no vo]        Vi 79127, Bb B-4919,
                    MW M-8626, Yv K-514, Vi 20-3265, 26-7504, Topic 12T365(33)
BVE 37083-2   Buttermilk Mary-Jigs [no vo]                             Vi 79198
```

BVE 37084-2   Reviewing St. Patrick's Day Parade
                    {The Flanagans At The Parade On St. Patrick's Day}
                    (Flanagan Bros.)   Vi 79127, Bb B-4976, Yv K-529, HMV B2899
BVE 37085-3   The Irishman, The Englishman And The Scotchman   Vi 79198
               acn, bj, longpipe, p   Camden, NJ December 28, 1926

W 143252-3   An' Corowath; Stack Of Wheat-Hornpipes [no vo]
                    Co 33136-F, Vo 84187, RZ G9186, IZ135, Topic 12T365(33)
W 143253-4   The Flanagans Visit Killarney Co 33136-F, Vo 84187, RZ G9186, IZ135
              acn, bj   NY January 1927

W 143627-   The Stack O' Barley   Co rej
W 143628-2   Sprig O'Shillelagh-Polka [no vo]
                    Co 33156-F, RZ G9185, G20719, IZ134, Topic 12T365(33)
W 143629-2   A Quiet Night At Flanagans'   Co 33156-F, RZ G9185, IZ134
W 143630-2   Erin Go' Bragh-Comic Sketch   Co 33157-F, Vo 84005
             acn, bj/'g   NY March 23, 1927

W 143627-7   The Stack O' Barley' [no vo]   Co 33157-F, Vo 84005
W 107951-2   Flanagan's Naturalization Troubles²   Co 33180-F, Vo 84076
W 107954-1   Tickling The Keys-Clogs' [no vo]   Co 33187-F
W 107961-2   Mick From Tralee³   Co 33187-F
W 107962-2   A Bunch Of Forget-Me-Nots-Waltzes' [no vo]   Co 33200-F, Ok 21049
W 107963-2   Kilgannon's Dream-Jigs' [no vo]   Co 33180-F, Vo 84076
             'acn, bj, ²talking with acn, ³vo duet with acn, bj/g   NY June 1927

W 108175-2   Cod Liver Oil'   Co 33195-F, IFB306, Vo 84010, RZ G9473, IZ143
W 108177-3   The Auld Blackthorn Reel [no vo]   Co 33195-F, 33513-F, IFB306,
                                     Vo 84010, RZ G9473, IZ143, Topic 12T365(33)
             acn, bj, Charles Bender-p, 'unk vln, cl   NY June 1927

W 108482-2   Irish Washerwoman Medley-Jig Set [no vo]
                    Co 33227-F, Vo 84127, RZ G20262
W 108483-1   Leitrim Thrush-Reel [no vo]   Co 33222-F, RZ IZ240, MR1373,
                                     FL 9010(33), FW FP18(33), FW6818(33)
W 108484-1   The Old School Master-Reel [no vo]
                    Co 33227-F, Vo 84127, RZ G20262, Topic 12T365(33)
W 108485-2   On The Road To The Fair' [no vo]   Co 33222-F, RZ G22376, IZ241,
                                     MR1374, FL 9010(33), FW FP18(33), FW6818(33)
             Il Passatempo-Danza Caratteristico   Co 14347-F
             Gaidžio Polka   Co 16093-F
             Polka "Kogucik"   Co 18248-F
             acn, bj, p, or 'jews-harp, g   NY November 1927

Co 14347-F as TROMBA DEI ZINGARI, 16093-F as LIAUDIES ORKESTRA, 18248-F as WESOŁA
DWÓJKA.

             Flanagans At St. Patrick's Parade   Co 33230-F
             Ireland's 32   Co 33230-F
                                                                     NY ca 1927

W 108671-2   Just Like Home-Jazz Set [no vo]   Co 33255-F
W 108672-2   The Sidewalks Of New York {East Side, West Side} (Charles B. Lawlor)
                    Co 33233-F, Vo 84016, Cq 9742, RZ G20281

W 108673-2   Sweet Rosie O'Grady (Maude Nugent)
                              Co 33233-F, Vo 84016, Cq 9742, RZ G20281
W 108674-3   The I.R.A.'   Co 33243-F, Vo 84017
              acn, p, bj, or 'md, g   NY January 1928

W 108695-2   The Banty Legged Mule
                      Co 33249-F, Vo 84082, RZ IZ240, MR1373, Topic 12T365(33)
W 108696-2   Sarsfield Lilt-Jig   Co 33249-F, Vo 84082, RZ G22376, IZ241, MR1374
W 108697-2   McGonagle Taste-Hornpipe [no vo]   Co 33295-F, Vo 84086, RZ G20503,
                                                          G20563, IZ278, MR1741
W 108717-2   Old Irish Barn Dance [no vo]   Co 33271-F, IFB310, RZ IZ183, MR683
W 108718-2   Shaskeen Reel [no vo]   Co 33243-F, 33513-F, Vo 84017
              acn, bj   NY January 1928

W 108789-2   My Irish Molly-O
                      Co 33271-F, RZ G20569, IZ278, MR1741, Topic 12T365(33)
W 108790-3   The Girl I Left Behind Me
                      Co 33295-F, Vo 84086, RZ G21154, IZ160, MR276
W 108791-3   Around The Old Turf Fire' [no vo]   Co 33255-F, LC LBC-4(33)
              'hca, jews-harp   NY February 1928

W 109360-2   You Can't Keep A Good Man Down   Co 33263-F
W 109361-2   Bells Of Athenry-Hornpipe' [no vo]   Co 33263-F
W 109362-1   Kelly's House Party-Comic Scene   Co 33265-F, Vo 84131, RZ G20569
W 109363-2   Highland Schottische [no vo]   Co 33265-F, Vo 84131
              'tiple, g   NY ca May 1928

W 109587-1   Brian O'Lynn   Co 33286-F, Vo 84085, RZ IZ188, MR688
W 109588-1   The Pretty Maid Milking Her Cow   Co 33300-F, RZ IZ188, MR688
              vln, cl, p   NY August 1928

W 109589-2   Over The Waves-Waltz [no vo]
                      Co 33286-F, Vo 84085, RZ G20453, IZ155, MR245
W 109590-1   Chicken Reel; Turkey In The Straw; Arkansas Traveler-Reels [no vo]
                      Co 33300-F, 12092-F, RZ G20503, G20563, IZ182, MR682
              acn, bj, unk vln, cl, p   NY August 1928

Co 12092-F as COLUMBIA INSTRUMENTAL TRIO

W 109648-   Hallelujah! I'm A Bum   Co 33279-F
W 109649-2   The Bum Song   Co 33279-F
W 109650-3   Three O'Clock In The Morning-Waltz [no vo]
                              Co 33302-F, Vo 84137, RZ G20453
                              NY September 1928

W 109723-4   Tom Steel Medley-Reels [no vo]
                      Co 33302-F, Vo 84137, RZ IZ302, MR1807
                      NY October 1928

W 110196-   Let Ye All Be Irish Tonight (W.J. McKenna)   Co rej
W 110197-   The Beggarman Song   Co rej
W 110198-   The Wanderer Medley-Jigs [no vo]   Co rej
                              NY December 1928

W 110196-4   Let Ye All Be Irish Tonight (W.J. McKenna)   Co 33323-F, 33506-F,
                                          Vo 84027, RZ G9382, G20672, IZ138
              vln, cl, p   NY January 1929

W 110197-5   The Beggarman Song (The Auld Rigadoo)   Co 33323-F, Vo 84027,
                                          RZ G9382, G20672, IZ138, Topic 12T365(33)
W 110198-4   The Wanderer Medley-Jigs [no vo] Co 33338-F, RZ G21382, IZ156, MR246
W 110301-2   Universal Reel Medley [no vo]   Co 33338-F, RZ G21395, IZ175, MR471
W 110325-1   A Gay Caballero   Co 33320-F, Vo 84087, RZ G9383, IZ139
W 110326-2   The Little Black Mustache
                                          Co 33320-F, Vo 84087, RZ G9383, G20738, IZ139
              acn, bj, p   NY January 1929

W 110350-3   The Rights Of Man-Exhibition Hornpipe [no vo]
                            Co 33329-F, 33512-F, Vo 84088, RZ IZ182, MR682
W 110351-1   Old Time Waltz Medley [no vo] Co 33329-F, 33512-F, IFB305, Vo 84088,
                                          RZ G9384, G20673, IZ140, Topic 12T365(33)
              acn, bj, p   NY February 1929

W 110429-3 (W 194089) Finnegan's Ball   Co 33351-F, RZ G20659, IZ156, MR246
W 110430-3   The Tipperary Christening   Co 33332-F, RZ IZ155, MR245
W 110431-3   Hartigan's Pride-Jig [no vo]   Co 33351-F, RZ G20659, IZ168, MR389
W 110432-3   Paddy Ryan's Dream-Reel [no vo]
                            Co 33332-F, RZ G21395, IZ175, MR471, Topic 12T365(33)
              acn, bj   NY March 1929

W 110491-   Delaney's Donkey   Co rej
W 110492-1   Bonnie Scotland; Johnny, Will You Marry Me?; The Keel Row-Highland
                 Flings [no vo]   Co 33345-F, IFB310, RZ G20629, IZ183, MR683,
                                                              Topic 12T365(33)
                                                              NY March 1929

W 110491-3   Delaney's Donkey   Co 33345-F, RZ IZ168, MR389
                                                              NY April 1929

W 110739-2   The Coach Road To Sligo; Hearty Boys Of Ballymote-Jigs [no vo]
                                          Co 33352-F, Vo 84144, RZ G20630
W 110740-2   Cavan Reel; More Power To Your Elbow-Reels [no vo]
                                          Co 33352-F, Vo 84144, RZ G20630
W 110741-2   Flower Of Edinburgh; Soldier's Joy [no vo]
                                          Co 33359-F, Vo 84090, RZ G21219
                                                              NY June 1929

W 111004-2   Humors Of Bandon Medley [no vo]   Co 33359-F, Vo 84090, RZ G21219
W 111006-1   Bright Star Of Munster-Reel [no vo]   Co 33373-F, RZ G21241
              acn, bj   NY August 1929

Matrix W 111006 was also assigned to a selection by the Krestyanskyj Orkestr (Co
20189-F), according to the Columbia files.

              Twilight In Athlone-Hornpipe [no vo]   Co 33369-F
                                                              NY ca 1929

W 111215-   Up The Hill Of Down-Highland Fling [no vo]   Co rej
W 111216-2   Sullivan's Troubles   Co 33380-F, Vo 84149
             acn, bj, p   NY   October 1929

W 111215-4   Up The Hill Of Down-Highland Fling [no vo]
                          Co 33402-F, Vo 84095, RZ G21382, MR158
             as before   NY   November 1929

W 111240-4   The New Irish Barn Dance [no vo]
                      Co 33380-F, Vo 84149, RZ G20737, Topic 12T365(33)
W 111241-6   International Echoes [no vo]   Co 33397-F, RZ IZ150, MR136
             as before   NY   late 1929

W 194730   Kelly's Cow Has Got No Tail
                      Co 33402-F, Vo 84095, RZ G21154, IZ160, MR276
             vln, fl, p   NY   ca December 1929

W 111480-2   The Tunes We Like To Play On Paddy's Day [no vo]
                                          Co 33397-F, RZ IZ150, MR136
             acn, bj   NY   January 1930

W 111691-2   In Our Back Yard   Co 33411-F, RZ G20900, MR158
                                                         NY   February 1930

W 112293-2   Flanagan The Lodger   Co 33446-F, 33506-F, Vo 84040
W 112294-2   Fogarty's Christmas Cake   Co 33437-F, RZ IZ579, MR1984
W 112295-1   Galway Farewell Clog [no vo]   Co 33446-F, Vo 84040, RZ G22161
             The Garden Of Daisies [no vo]   Co 33437-F
                                                     NY   ca September 1930

W 112545-2   Out On The Ocean Medley [no vo]   Co 33460-F, RZ G22160
W 112546-1   The Moving Bogs Medley-Reels [no vo]   Co 33453-F
W 112547-2   Darkey's Dream-Fox Trot [no vo]   Co 33450-F, RZ G22161
W 112550-2   The Grand Hotel In Castlebar¹   Co 33453-F, RZ G22159
W 112551-1   The Bologna Song¹   Co 33450-F, RZ G22159
             Irish Fair Day   Co 33460-F
             acn, p, bj, or ¹vln, cl, p   NY   ca November 1930

W 112710-2   Maloney Puts His Name Above The Door   Co 33463-F, Vo 84160
             vln, cl, p   NY   December 1930

W 112724-2   Haley's Double Header [no vo]   Co 33473-F, RZ G22160
                                                         NY   January 1931

W 130280   Irish Boy March¹ [no vo]   Co 33463-F, Vo 84160
             The Contrary Reel [no vo]   Co 33469-F
             Lannigan's Ball   Co 33469-F
             The Old Boreen   Co 33473-F
             ¹acn, p, bj   NY   December 1930-January 1931

36.49.   Joe Flanagan *vocal, accordion (ca 1890-ca 1937)*

J. Flanigan

105622-2	Gather The Blossoms-Jigs [no vo]	Co 33000-F
105623-1	The Parnell Waltz [no vo]	Co 33000-F
105624-1	My Aunt Jane; The Rakes Of Mallow-Polkas [no vo]	
		Co 33002-F, RZ G8530, Topic 12T365(12")
105625-1	Manchester; Fisher-Hornpipes [no vo]	Co 33002-F, RZ G8530
	Charles Bender-p	NY ca April 1925

Joe Flanagan

N 106084-	The Star Of Munster-Reel [no vo]	Pat 021150, Pe 11223, P418
N 106085-	The Smash-Jig [no vo]	Pat 021150, Pe 11223, P418
	p	NY July 1925

Pe P418 is an English issue.

W 105834-	Dublin Lassies Medley-Reels [no vo]	Co rej
W 105835-	Mickey The Mauler; Tobin's Jig [no vo]	Co rej
		NY September 1925

W 105834-4	Dublin Lassies Medley-Reels [no vo]	Co 33067-F, RZ G22377, MR1384
W 105835-5	Mickey The Mauler; Tobin's Jig [no vo]	Co 33073-F
W 105920-1	Tatter Jack Welsh-Jigs[1]	Co 33067-F, RZ G22377, MR1384
W 105921-1	Scotch Mary Medley-Reels [no vo]	Co 33073-F
	p, [1]vln	NY ca October 1, 1925

Titles are listed in reverse order on matrix W 105835.

N 106461-	The Lime Stone Road-Reel [no vo]	Pat 021161, Pe 11234, Cameo 9115,
		Lincoln 3142, Ro 917, OBDW 39067
N 106462-	Ennis' Favorite Hornpipe [no vo]	Pat 021161, Pe 11234, OBDW 39067
	p	NY November 1925

Cameo 9115, Lincoln 3142 and Ro 917 as TOM RYAN

W 108176-2	Barney Come Home	Co 33200-F, Ok 21049
	vo, unk vln, cl, p	NY June 1927
	Kitty Wells	Co 33369-F
		NY ca 1929
	Little Bridget Flynn	Co 33411-F, RZ IZ302, MR1807
		NY ca January 1930

W 113706-4	The Half Crown Song	Co 33528-F, Vo 84168, RZ IZ222, MR1107
W 113708-4	Sunshine; Off To California-Hornpipes[1] [no vo]	
		Co 33528-F, Vo 84168, RZ IZ222, MR1107
	Michael (Whitey) Andrews (1902-1961)-g, or [1]unk bj, bj-uke NY 1933	

36.50. Michael Flanagan *vocal, banjo*

BVE 36467-2   Avourneen (E. Cecilia Fitzpatrick-Wilton King)   Vi 79096
              vo, Charles Bender-p   Camden, NJ November 16, 1926

W 111005-1   Tickling The Strings [no vo]   Co 33373-F, RZ G20718
                                                        NY August 1929

36.51. Arthur Flynn *tenor*

64416-B   Blarney (Paul Ambrose-Stephen Chalmers)   De rej
              orch   NY August 3, 1938

64418-   I'm Only Just Foolin' (Mana-Zucca-Herman A. Heydt)   De 12251
64419-   I'll Be Straying Back To Ireland (Some Fine Day) (J. Will
                  Callahan-Gerald Griffin-Gerald W. Sullivan)   De 12191
64420-   When I Dream Of Killarney And You (Harry Scanlon-Gene Calhoun)
                                                                     De 12191
64421-   Down Limerick Way (George H. Cartlan)   De 12245
64422-   The Skies Of Auld Kilkenny (Cornelia Ayer Paine-Maud Luise Gardiner)
                                                                     De 12245
              orch   NY August 4, 1938

36.52. Barney Flynn *vocal*

              I'll Not Work A Minute Overtime   Co 33436-F
              There'll Be Murder There Tonight   Co 33436-F
              Growler   Co 33462-F
              O'Houlihan   Co 33462-F
                                                          NY ca 1930

36.53. Bert Flynn *violin*

S 71351-B   The Blackbird   Ok 4840, Pa E3180
          p   NY March 1923

36.54. John Fogarty *vocal*

38966-A   The Old Refrain (Alice Mettullath, arr Fritz Kreisler)   De 12013
38970-A   Roses Of Picardy (Haydn Wood-Fred E. Weatherly)   De 434, 12013
38971-A   The Rose Of Tralee (Charles W. Glover-C. Mordaunt Spencer) De 12012
38972-A-B   Molly O (William J. Scanlan)   De 12012, Rex U603
36973-A   Ireland, My Sireland (Victor Herbert-Henry Blossom)   De 12040
38974-A   When You And I Were Young, Maggie (J.A. Butterfield)
                                    De 434, 12040, W4135, Rex U310
              orch   NY November 8, 1934

39011-A   Flow Gently Sweet Afton (J.E. Spilman-Robert Burns)
                                                     De 14000, Rex U603

```
39012-A      Mary Of Argyle (Charles Jeffreys)                    De 14000, Rex U310
             orch                                                 NY  November 12, 1934
```

36.55. Four Irish Masters

A contingent from the Grey Gull label's house band recorded Irish dance medleys under this name in the late 1920s.

36.56. The Four Provinces *instrumental*

```
13598/9      McGettigan's; Miss Ramsey; The Keel Row-Highland Schottische
                                                                          Vo 14875
13600/1      Leather Away; The Rattling Boys Of Paddy's Land-Polkas       Vo 14875
             John McCormick-vln, Edward Lee-p, unk pic              NY  August 1924

13955/6      Katie Connor; Colleen Rue; Foggy Dew; Moll Room             Vo 14931
13958        The First Of May; Molly MacAlpine; Slieve Gorm-Hornpipes    Vo 14931
13959/60     Kitty's Wedding; Ships Are Sailing; Scholar-Reels           Vo 14943
             as before                                             NY  November 1924

9519         Braes Of Mar; Tie The Bonnet; Coming From The Races-Highland
                     Strathspey                               Ge 5731, OBDW 39034
9520-A       Kilsheelan Bridge; Petticoat Lane; Killy Begs-Jigs          Ge 5730
9521         Irish Barn Dance                               Ge 5731, OBDW 39034
9522-A       Clune-Hornpipe                                               Ge 5730
             John McCormick-vln, Edward Lee-p, unk fl          NY  May 11, 1925

9780-A       The Ten Penny Bit; McAvoy's Favorite; Hinchy's Jig-Jigs     Ge 5746
             John McCormick-vln, Edward Lee-p, unk pic     NY  October 19, 1925
```

Four Provinces Orchestra

```
BVE 36194-3  Katie Connor; Hillside; Jackets Green; Colleen Dhas         Vi rej
BVE 36195-2  Little Stack Of Barley; Sand's Hornpipe         Vi 79008, HMV B2559
BVE 36196-1  The Fairy Reel; Sheehan's Reel                  Vi 79009, HMV B2559
BVE 36197-1  The Seven Step; Shoe The Donkey                 Vi 79009, HMV B2931
             Edward Lee-p, unk vln, fl, bj, dulcimer (or piano-dulcimer)
                                                          NY  September 20, 1926

BVE 36194-5-6 Katie Connor; Hillside; Jackets Green; Colleen Dhas
                      Vi 79008, Bb B-4958, MW M-8631, Yv K-519, HMV B2931
BVE 36465-1  Sandy Buchanan Highland Strathspey                          Vi 79090
BVE 36466-2  The Job Of Journeywork; The Blackbird-Long Hornpipes
                                                         Vi 79090, Yv K-516
             Edward Lee-p, unk 2 vln, pic, p, bj     Camden, NJ  November 16, 1926
```

Yv K-516 and K-519 as SHAMROCK ORCHESTRA

```
GEX 417-A    The Red Haired Boy; The Flowers Of Edinburgh-Reels          OBDW
GEX 418-A    The Friendly Visit; The Manchester Hornpipes                OBDW
GEX 419-A    Old Woman Wrapped In A Blanket; The Jolly Corkonian-Jigs    OBDW
GEX 420-A    Paddy The Fowler; Rolling In The Rye Grass                  OBDW
```

GEX 421-A	Tow Row Row; Boys Of Clontarre; Down By The Irish Sea	OBDW
GEX 422-A	Some Say The Devil's Dead; Maggie Cameron	OBDW
	John Kennedy-vln, John Cali-bj, others unk NY late December 1926	

W 109102-2	Pride Of Clyde: Marquis Of Huntley; Skin-A-Ma-Rink-Highland Flings	
	Co 33258-F, Vo 84022	
W 109103-2	The Stone Outside Dan Murphy's Door-Waltz	
	Co 33258-F, Vo 84022, RZ G20346, Topic 12T367(33)	
W 109105-1	Pride Of Leinster: Hole In The Wall; Dublin Jig	
	Co 33264-F, Vo 84083, RZ IZ184, MR684	
W 109106-2	The Pride Of Ulster: Maggie Pickens; Cameron's Wife	
	Co 33262-F, RZ IZ184, MR684	
W 109108-3	Pride Of Connacht: Drowsy Maggie; Claddagh Reel	Co 33282-F
W 109109-2	Pride Of Donegal: If Ever I Go; Rogaire	Co 33282-F
	John McCormick or John Kennedy-vln, Sam Moore-acn, Edward Lee-p, unk	
	pic, bj, John McGettigan-vo	NY March 1928

W 110135-2	The First Of May-Hornpipe	Co 33328-F, Vo 84142
W 110136-1	Katie Connor	Co 33328-F, Vo 84142
W 110138-1	The Merry Blacksmith; The Lightning Flash-Reels	
	Co 33344-F, RZ G20629	
W 110141-2	Leather Away With The Wattle O'-Polka	
	Co 33324-F, Vo 84028, RZ G20912, IZ342	
W 110142-2	Rolling In The Rye Grass	Co 33364-F, RZ IZ185, RZ MR685
	vln, pic, p, bj	NY December 1928

W 111246-1	The Drummer Boy-Highland Fling Co 33379-F, Vo 84031, RZ IZ185, MR685	
W 111248-2	Johnny Cope	Co 33404-F, Vo 84153
W 111252-1	Sunshine-Hornpipe	Co 33389-F, Vo 84150
	vln, p, bj	NY November 1929

W 112119-2	Tibbie Inglis; Lady Mary Ramsay-Highland Flings	Co 33419-F
W 112120-1	Highland Bonnets-Highland Fling	Co 33432-F
W 112123-2	The Tartan Prince	Co 33428-F
W 112125-2	Teddy O'Neill-Waltz	Co 33456-F, Vo 84043, RZ G21071
	Limerick Races	Co 33420-F
	vln, pic, p, bj	NY ca May 1930

36.57. Michael Gaffney *banjo (1896-1972)*

38957-A	The Night Cap; Mysteries Of Knock-Jigs	
	De 12041, F5430, W4074, Rex U311	
	Della McMahon-p	NY November 6, 1934

36.58. Patrick J. Gaffney *violin*

	Medley Of Reels	Vi trial
		NY October 18, 1922

S 71117-B	Mulligar Races-Reel	Ok 21011, Pa E3029, RZ MR3224
S 71118-C	Jolly Corkonian-Jigs	Ok 21011, Pa E3029, RZ MR3225
	John Muller-p	NY ca December 20, 1922

```
S 71404-B     Paddy On The Turnpike                             Ok 21013, Pa E3030
S 71405-B     McAllister's Fling; The Girl I Left Behind-Plain Quadrille
                                                                Ok 4840, Pa E3180
S 71407-A     Hide And Seek; The Top Of Cork Road-Jigs          Ok 21013, Pa E3030
              p                                              NY  ca April 10, 1923

S 72113-B     Maid Behind The Bar-Reel                          Ok 21018, Pa E3052
S 72115-B     Paddy Ryan's Dream-Reel                           Ok 21018, Pa E3052
              Susan Peters-p                                    NY  December 1923

S 72770-A     Jim Haley's Favorite-Reel                         Ok 21023, Pa E3095
S 72771-A     Sweep's Horn Pipe                                 Ok 21023, Pa E3095
S 72772-A     Willie Walsh's Jig                                Ok 21024, Pa E3096
S 72774-A     Saddle The Pony-Jig                               Ok 21025, Pa E3097
S 72775-A     Fermoyle Lassie-Reel                              Ok 21025, Pa E3097
S 72778-A     Leinster Reel                                     Ok 21024, Pa E3096
              as before                                      NY  August 20, 1924

140127-2      The Southern Shore-Hornpipe         Co 289-D, 33056-F, Harmony 5114-H
140128-2      My Love Is A Lassy-Quadrille        Co 289-D, 33056-F, Harmony 5114-H
140129-2      Maggie In The Woods-Polka           Co 251-D, 33058-F, Harmony 5102-H
140130-2      The Girl I Left Behind Me-Quadrille
                                                  Co 251-D, 33058-F, Harmony 5102-H
140131-       Wilson Clog                                                    Co rej
              as before                                       NY  November 8, 1924


Harmony 5102-H and 5114-H as MICHAEL MAHAFFEY

140472-1      Green Grows The Rushes Oh                         Co 350-D, 33057-F
140473-1      Jerry Daly's Hornpipe                             Co 350-D, 33057-F
140474-       Fairy House Races                                            Co rej
              as before                                        NY  March 27, 1925
```

36.59. Michael Gallagher *bagpipes (ca 1890-1972)*

```
8850-A        Moran's Hornpipe; The Plains Of Boyle; Leitrim Fancy
                                            Ge 5451, OBDW 39021, Starr 9567
8851-A        Lucy Campbell; The Cup Of Tea-Reels  Ge 5451, OBDW 39021, Starr 9567
              Arthur P. Kenna-p                             NY  April 19, 1924

657-1         Garden Of Daisies-Long Dance                       Shamrock 1235
658-1         Collier's; Salamanca-Reels                         Shamrock 1235
                                                               NY  1920s
```

36.60. Thomas Gannon *violin*

```
BVE 37665-2   The Achonry Lassies; Lady Gardner's Troops-Reels          Vi 20712
BVE 37666-2   Kip's Favorite; Blackbird-Reels                           Vi rej
BVE 37667-2   Shoreham; Conley's Favorite-Hornpipes                     Vi 20712
BVE 37668-1   Morning Star; Welcome Me Home-Waltzes                     Vi rej
              Herbert G. Henry-p               Camden, NJ  February 8, 1927
```

36.61. Ed Geoghegan *piano*

This artist's last name is sometimes spelled Gagan.

Ed Geoghegan And His Orchestra

BVE 38474-2	Paddy The Dandy; The Bells Of Shandon; The Far Down Jig-Jigs	
		Vi 20711
BVE 38475-1	Mullinavat; Ballina Trooper-Reels	Vi 20711
BVE 38476-2	The Flowers Of Adrigole; Showman's Fancy-Hornpipes	Vi 79345
BVE 38477-1	Sterling Castle-Highland Schottische	Vi 79345
	Ed Geoghegan-p, unk vln, cl, traps	NY April 20, 1927

BVE 39944-2	Sweeney's Party-Jigs (arr Ed Geoghegan)	Vi rej
BVE 39945-3	Drops Of Brandy-Slip Jig (arr Ed Geoghegan)	
		Vi 20887, Zon 5065, RZ T5065
BVE 39946-2	Casey The Tinker-Hornpipe (arr Ed Geoghegan)	Vi 21004
BVE 39947-2	The Milliner's Daughter-Reel	Vi 20887, Zon 5065, RZ T5065
	as before	NY August 8, 1927

BVE 39944-4	Sweeney's Party-Jigs (arr Ed Geoghegan)	Vi 21004
BVE 40256-2	Highland Schottische	Vi 21088, Aurora 36-112
BVE 40257-1	The Banks Of The Shannon-Hornpipe	Vi 21088, Aurora 36-112
BVE 40258-1	Stackin' The Hay-Sketch¹	Vi rej
	as before, ¹Jack Murphy-talking	NY September 29, 1927

Ed Gagan And His Orchestra

2354-A-B	Irish Jigs And Reels-Series No. 1	GG 4016, Radiex 4016
2355-C	Irish Jigs And Reels-Series No. 2	GG 4016, Radiex 4016
	Ed Geoghegan-p, unk vln, pic, acn	NY ca 1927

In 1923, The GUARDS' BAND recorded these titles (matrices 1831-A/1832-A), which were released with the same catalog numbers.

Eddie Geoghegan

BVE 43673-2	Has Sorrow Thy Young Days Shaded; Believe Me If All Those Endearing	
	Young Charms	Vi 21483
BVE 43674-1	Erin, Remember The Days Of Old; Molly Box	Vi 21483
	p solos	NY April 26, 1928

36.62. John Gerrity *violin*

86732-1	Gerrity Reel	Co E7084, 33029-F
86733-1	Night Cap-Jig	Co E7084, 33029-F
86734-1	The Bush In Bloom	Co E4977, 33028-F
86735-2	Welcome To Cork	Co E4977, 33028-F
	p	NY October 1920

36.63. Hugh Gillespie *violin*

62190-A	Master Crowley's Reels	De 12105, W4187, Rex U217, Topic 12T364(33)
62191-A	The Irish Mazurka	De 12105, W4186, Rex U216, Topic 12T364(33)
62192-A	The Mullinger Lee; The Star Of Munster-Reels	
		De 12112, W4186, Rex U216
62193-A	McCormick's Hornpipe	De 12112, W4187, Rex U217
	Mark Callahan-g	NY May 10, 1937

63974-A	Jenny's Welcome To Charlie-Reel In Four Parts	
		De 12164, W4295, Rex U630, Topic 12T364(33)
63975-A	Master Crowley's Favorites-Jigs	
		De 12164, W4312, Rex U637, Topic 12T364(33)
63976-A	Dowd's Favorite-Reel In Three Parts	
		De 12171, W4295, Rex U630, Topic 12T364(33)
63977-A	Versevanna-Long Dance	De 12171, Topic 12T364(33)
63978-A	Farewell To Leitrim; Tom Steele-Reels	
		De 12186, W4382, Rex U637, Topic 12T364(33)
63979-A	McKenna's Farewell-Hornpipes	De 12186, Topic 12T364(33)
63980-A-B	Paddy Finley's Fancy; Joe O'Connell's Dream-Reels	
		De 12192, W4312, Topic 12T364(33)
63981-A	Finnea Lassies; Gurren's Castle-Highland Flings	
		De 12192, W4382, Rex U646, Topic 12T364(33)
	Jack McKenna-g	NY June 14, 1938

65895-A	The Girl That Broke My Heart; Dick Cosgroves Reel	
		De 12213, W4688, Topic 12T364(33)
65896-A	The Pigeon On The Gate; The Lady Of The House-Reels	De 12225, W4688
65897-A	Dowd's Number Nine; Jackson's-Reels	
		De 12229, W4862, Topic 12T364(33)
65898-A	The Donegal Traveler; Miss Montgomery-Reels	
		De 12233, W4689, Topic 12T364(33)
65899-A	Contentment Is Wealth; Finley's Jig-Jigs	
		De 12213, W4689, Topic 12T364(33)
65900-A	Jackson's Favorite; Kips-Jigs	De 12229, W4862, Topic 12T364(33)
65901-A	Mountain Stream; Parker's Fancy-Hornpipes	
		De 12225, W4538, Rex U646, Topic 12T364(33)
65902-A	The Stage; The Rights Of Man-Hornpipes	De 12233, W4538, Rex U677
	as before	NY June 27, 1939

36.64. Michael A. Glynn *flute*

W 110489-2	Kitty's Wedding	Co 33441-F, Vo 84096
W 110490-2	Ulster Reel	Co 33441-F, Vo 84096
		NY April 1929

W 113251-1	Heathery Breeze; Castle Ray Fancy-Reels	Co 33494-F
W 113254-1	The Red Haired Boy; The Stack Of Barley-Hornpipes	Co 33494-F
	Dublin Fancy; Green Castle	Co 33508-F
	House On The Hill; Owen Moore's Favorite-Jigs	Co 33508-F
		NY ca December 1931

36.65. Gray Brothers *instrumental*

W 109781-2	The Teetotalers Fancy-Reel	Co 33298-F
W 109782-2	The Caven Fancy; The Irish Favorite-Polkas	Co 33298-F
	2 fl, p	NY October 1928

36.66. Gerald Griffin *tenor*

S 70168-B   It's Only A Step From Killarney To Heaven
                  (Gerald Griffin-H. Kahn-T. Lyman)   Ok 4472, Pa X3008
                                                             NY September 1921

O 8205-B   Irish Eyes Of Love, from "The Heart Of Paddy Whack"
                  (J.E. Killalea-E.R. Ball)   Od Od20069, Ok 21007
O 8207-C   Ireland Is Ireland To Me, from "Killarney"
                  (F. O'Hara-J. Keirn Brennan-E.R. Ball)
                                         Od Od20069, Ok 4537, 21007, Pa X3008
          orch   NY 1921

42182-2   Saint Patrick's Day (M.J. Barry)   Ba 2076
                                                     NY ca February 11, 1922

S 70847-C   Kate Kearney (Fay-Oliver)   Ok 21012, Pa X3059
                                                             NY ca August 1922

S 71227-C   Saint Patrick's Day (M.J. Barry)   Ok 21012, Pa X3059
                                                             NY ca March 1923

S 71636-B   The Bard Of Armagh   Ok 4895, Pa X3009
                                                             NY July 1923

              Soldiers Of Erin   Ok 4379
              When The Harp That Once Through Tara's Halls Rings Again With
                  Freedom's Glory   Ok 4419, Pa X3058
              In The Valley Near Slievenamon   Ok 4419, Pa X3058
              Macushla   Ok 4433, Pa X3000
              Come Back To Erin   Ok 4433, Pa X3000
              My Wild Irish Rose   Ok 4621, Pa X3001
              The Low Back'd Car   Ok 4621, Pa X3001
              The Coulin   Ok 4635, Pa X3002
              The Risin' Of The Moon   Ok 4635, Pa X3002
              The Lass From County Mayo   Ok 4699, Pa X3004
              Sweet Inniscara   Ok 4699, Pa X3004
              Mother In Ireland   Ok 4782, Pa X3003
              That's What Ireland Means To Me   Ok 4782, Pa X3003
              Where The River Shannon Flows   Ok 4790, Pa X3009
              Believe Me If All Those Endearing Young Charms   Ok 4831, Pa X3005
              My Snowy Breasted Pearl   Ok 4831, Pa X3005
              Dublin Bay   Ok 4854, Pa X3006
              The Pretty Girl Milking Her Cow   Ok 4854, Pa X3006
              Molly Bawn   Ok 4874, Pa X3007
              A Puff O' Me Pipe And A Song   Ok 4874, Pa X3007

	My Gal Sal	Ok 4891
	A Welcome On The Mat¹	Ok 4974
	I'll Be Straying Back To Ireland¹	Ok 4974
	Just A Bit Of Irish Lace	Ok 4910, Pa X3010
	River Shannon Moon	Ok 4910, Pa X3010
	Fairy Tales Of Ireland	Ok 40171, Pa X3083
	Ireland Is Heaven To Me	Ok 40171, Pa X3083
	That's How The Shannon Flows	Ok 40194, Pa X3082
	What An Irishman Means By "Machree"	Ok 40194, Pa X3082
	¹Justin Ring-p	NY 1921-4

S 72926-B	My Sweet Killarney Rose	
	(Gerald Griffin-Bartley Costello-Roy Barton)¹	
		Ok 40224, Pa X3084
S 72929-B	A Window In Old Athlone (Harold Robe-Terence Brady)¹	
		Ok 40224, Pa X3084
S 72930-B	The Singer Was Irish {It Was Christmas Eve In London}	
	(C.W. Murphy-Harry Castling)	Ok 40273, Pa X3085
S 72931-B	When They Ask You What Your Name Is (Harry Castling-Fred Godfrey)	
		Ok 40273, Pa X3085
	Just Day Dreams	Ok 40225, Pa X3247
	Shamrock Leaves	Ok 40225, Pa X3247
	orch or ¹Justin Ring Trio: vln, vla, p	NY October 1924

10-112-A	Molly Bawn¹	Emerald 3002
10-121-A	Ireland Is Ireland To Me	Emerald 3002
	orch, or ¹vln, vc, p	NY 1920s

TO 1592	Mother; Molly Brannigan	Co test
		NY ca January 1936

36.67. John Griffin *(The Fifth Avenue Bus Man); vocal, flute*

8960-A	My Mary Jane-Reel	Ge 5495, OBDW 39040
8961-A	Apples For Ladies; Maid Of The Mill-Jigs	Ge 5495, OBDW 39040
	Paddy Muldoon-p	NY June 15, 1924

9031-A	The Girl I Left Behind Me	Ge 5526, OBDW 39041
9032-A	The Gap Of Dunlow; The Three Lakes [no vo]	Ge 5526, OBDW 39041
	as before	NY August 15, 1924

9165-A	All The Way To Galway-Polka	Ge 5619, OBDW 39042
9166-A	By Moonlight On The Water-Reel [no vo]	Ge 5619, OBDW 39042
		NY November 1924

9407-A	The Lass From Mullingar-Reel	Ge 5701, 3028, OBDW 39044
9408	Castlebar Boys-Reels [no vo]	Ge 5701, 3028, OBDW 39044
	p	NY March 17, 1925

BVE 36679-2	Finnegan The Tailor	Vi 20761
BVE 36680-2	At Twilight On The Bridge-Reel	Vi rej
BVE 36681-2	Why She Couldn't Drink Her Tea-Reel	Vi 79015

```
BVE 36682-2   Kitty's Favorite-Polka                                      Vi 79015
              Lew Shilkret-p                           Camden, NJ  November 11, 1926

W 175230-     test recording                                                    Co
                                                       NY  December 3, 1926

BVE 37370-1   Oh Dear Me                                                   Vi 79262
BVE 37371-2   The Old Bog Oak Ring                                        Vi 79262
              Lew Shilkret-p                           Camden, NJ  January 21, 1927

W 143392-2    The Real Old Mountain Dew    Co 33145-F, IFB304, Vo 84002, RZ G9188,
                                                            IZ137, FL 9010(33)
W 143393-2    My Beauty Of Limerick        Co 33145-F, IFB304, Vo 84002, RZ G9188
              p                                        NY  February 3, 1927

W 107826-2    Peggy Malone                                              Co 33173-F
W 107827-2    The Widow McGee                                           Co 33173-F
                                                       NY  April 1927

BVE 36680-4   At Twilight On The Bridge-Reel [no vo]                     Vi 20761
              Jack Shilkret-p                          Camden, NJ  June 13, 1927

W 108370-3    The Old Side Car              Co 33220-F, RZ IZ304, MR1809
W 108371-2    My Kerry Colleen                                          Co 33290-F
W 108372-1    The Old Country Party                                     Co 33206-F
W 108373-1    Oh, Where Is Kathleen                                     Co 33206-F
              p                                        NY  October 1927

W 108510-2    The Old Irish Jig                                         Co 33290-F
W 108511-2    Three Little Leaves Of Irish Green  Co 33220-F, RZ IZ242, MR1375
              p                                        NY  November 1927

W 108765-2    The Land Where The Shamrocks Grow                         Co 33231-F
W 108766-2    St. Patrick's Day                                         Co 33231-F
              p                                        NY  February 1928

              Jolly Boatman                            Co 33245-F, Ok 21060
              He Loved His Jenny Dearly                 Co 33245-F, Ok 21060
                                                       NY  1928

W 109240-2    The Irish Clock Maker         Co 33268-F, RZ IZ280, MR1743
W 109241-2    The Pride Of Mayo             Co 33268-F, RZ IZ242, MR1375
                                                       NY  April 1928

W 109471-3    Come Back Paddy Reilly, To Ballyjamesduff      Co 33270-F, Vo 84132
W 109472-1    My Auld Skillara Hat                           Co 33270-F, Vo 84132
              p                                        NY  July 1928

W 109700-2    Barney McCoy                                              Co 33337-F
W 109701-1    The Green Hills Of Drumore                                Co 33337-F
              p                                        NY  September 1928

W 110166-1    This Bunch Of Shamrocks From My Mother Dear       Co 33317-F
W 110167-1    The Green Above The Red           Co 33317-F, RZ G9386, IZ142
```

```
W 110168-1    The Lass From Mullingar {The Old Torn Petticoat}
                                                    Co 33356-F, RZ IZ243, MR1376
              p                                         NY   ca December 1928

W 110656-1    Kathleen Asthore                      Co 33361-F, RZ IZ243, MR1376
W 110657-2    The Boy From County Clare             Co 33361-F, RZ IZ290, MR1795
W 110659-4    Pretty Molly Brannigan                              Co 33356-F
              p                                         NY   ca April 1929

W 110931-1    Nellie Ray                            Co 33391-F, RZ IZ304, MR1809
W 110932-2    Meself And Martin Tracy   Co 33391-F, RZ IZ280, MR1743, FL 9010(33)
              When You And I Were Young, Mary                     Co 33382-F
              My Heart It Is In Leitrim                Co 33382-F, RZ MR1743
                                                        NY   July 1929

W 111187-1    The Flag Of Sinn Fein                 Co 33413-F, RZ MR1795
W 111189-2    The Mac's And The O's                              Co 33423-F
W 111190-2    Molly Muldoon                                      Co 33423-F
                                                        NY   October 1929

W 111664-2    The Wife Of The Bold Tenant Farmer
                                        Co 33406-F, RZ IZ300, MR162, MR1805
W 111665-2    My Rose From Killarney       Co 33406-F, RZ IZ300, MR1805
W 111666-2    The Cow That Ate The Piper    Co 33413-F, RZ IZ154, MR162
              p                                         NY   February 1930

W 112285-2    Dear Old Granuale                                  Co 33440-F
W 112286-2    Kitty Farrell                                      Co 33440-F
                                                        NY   September 1930

W 112393-1    Asthore Thig Gin Thu                               Co 33474-F
W 112394-1    Bold Tipperary Boy                                 Co 33474-F
              p                                         NY   October 1930

W 112549-2    The Autumn Leaves Are Falling    Co 33523-F, RZ IZ297, MR1802
                                                        NY   ca November 1930

W 113143-1    The Little Harvest Rose                            Co 33491-F
W 113144-2    The Fair Haired Lass                               Co 33491-F
              p                                         NY   September 1931

W 113317-1    The Widow Malone                                   Co 33519-F
W 113318-1    The Jolly Plow Boy            Co 33519-F, RZ IZ206, MR927
              p                                         NY   ca January 1932

W 113546-1    Here's To The Hills Of Ireland                     Co 33518-F
W 113547-1    My Sweetheart When I Was A Boy                     Co 33518-F
                                                        NY   June 1932

              Bright Emerald Isle Of The Sea                     Co 33447-F
              How I Met With Malloy                              Co 33447-F
              In Limerick Once More                              Co 33457-F
              In The May More Dew                                Co 33457-F
              Hills Of Knock Na Shee                             Co 33478-F
```

```
           It's The One Word "Mother"                              Co 33478-F
           Boatman From Clonmel                                    Co 33484-F
           How The Old Shannon Flows                               Co 33484-F
           The Maid Of Listowel Town                               Co 33503-F
           My Colleen Dhas Machree                                 Co 33503-F
           My Darling Molly Flynn              Co 33523-F, RZ IZ300, MR1805
                                                               NY  1930-2
```

36.68. Larry Griffin *vocal*

```
BVE 47760-1   My Old Dudeen                                        Vi V-29002
BVE 47761-2   Off To Ireland                                       Vi V-29002
BVE 47762-1   The Boys From Home-Dialogue And Song¹ ²      Vi V-29001, Yv K-539
BVE 47763-1   Little Johnny Dugan-Dialogue And Song¹               Vi V-29001
              Dan Sullivan-p, ¹with Dinny Doyle-vo/²hca (The Boys From Home)
                                                         NY  October 17, 1928

BVE 48151-1   My Dad's Dinner Pail                                 Vi V-29015
BVE 48152-2   Molly I Can't Say You're Honest                      Vi V-29033
BVE 48153-2   The Buck Billy Goat                                  Vi V-29015
BVE 48154-2   The Irish Christening                                Vi V-29033
BVE 48157-2   Down Went McGinty¹                                   Vi V-29013
BVE 48158-2   The Man That Stole My Luncheon¹                      Vi V-29013
              as before                               NY  November 13, 1928

BVE 50746-2   She's One Of The Good Old Kind (Dan Sullivan)        Vi V-29072
              Dan Sullivan-p                            NY  March 12, 1929

BVE 53864-2   An Irishman's Lament (L. Griffin)¹                   Vi V-29066
BVE 53865-2   Eileen Aroon                                         Vi V-29051
BVE 53866-2   John O'Dwyer Of The Glen (arr Dan Sullivan)          Vi V-29051
BVE 53867-1   Off To Philadelphia¹                                 Vi V-29066
              as before, ¹George Tapley-acn            NY  June 24, 1929
```

36.69. George Halpin *violin*

```
              The Maid On The Green                                   untraced
              The Hare's Foot                                         untraced
                                                       NY  early 1920s

9055-A        Johnny, I Hardly Knew You-Jig                          Ge 5536
9056-A        The Heart Of The Loaf-Jig                              Ge 5536
              Dennis Marion-p                          NY  August 25, 1924

9151          The Fun At The Fair-Jig                      Ge 5582, Starr 9624
9152-A        Drowsy Maggie-Reel                           Ge 5582, Starr 9624
              as before                               NY  October 27, 1924

W 80433-B     The Lass Of Barramore-Reel                  Ok 21035, Pa E3569
W 80434-B     The Frost On The Heather-Jig                Ok 21035, Pa E3569
W 80435-A     Miss Ramsay's Fling                                     Ok rej
```

W 80436-A   Connie The Soldier-Jig   Ok rej
                 James Flood-p   NY February 17, 1927

Philippe Varlet has supplied standard tune titles for matrices W 80435 and W 80436; the latter tune appears again below on matrix W 108788.

Halpin & Stanford

              Maid Of Ballintra-Reel   Co 33216-F
              Thrush On The Hedge-Jig   Co 33216-F
                                                   NY ca 1927

George Halpin

W 108787-2   Miss Thornton's Reel   Co 33281-F
W 108788-2   The Sprigs Of Stradone   Co 33281-F
              p   NY February 1928

36.70. Connie Hanafin *accordion*

BVE 48496-2 Kildare Fancy-Hornpipe   Vi V-29028, HMV B3620
BVE 48497-1 Johnnie Thro The Glen-Reel   Vi V-29028, HMV B3620
              Dan Sullivan-p   NY November 18, 1928

36.71. Michael C. Hanafin *violin (1880-1970)*

W 107080-1 Kilderry Hornpipe   Co 33113-F
W 107081-2 Lord Gordon's Reel   Co 33113-F, Topic 12T366(33)
              Dan Sullivan-p   NY August 1926

W 142529-3 Miss McLeod's Reel; Greenfields Of Rossbeigh   Co 33115-F
W 142530-3 The Irish Washerwoman; Tatter Jack Welsh   Co 33115-F
              as before   NY August 13, 1926

W 107778-1 Dan Sullivan's Favorite-Hornpipe
                            Co 33183-F, 33508-F, Vo 84125, Topic 12T366(33)
W 107779-2 Billy Hanafin's Reel {The Bird In The Tree}
                                     Co 33162-F, Topic 12T366(33)
W 107780-2 Bantry Bay-Hornpipe   Co 33199-F
W 107781-2 Jockey Thro' The Fair   Co 33190-F
W 107796-1 The Blue Ribbon Polka'   Co 33207-F
              Groves Hornpipe'   Co 33163-F, Topic 12T366(33)
              Dan Sullivan-p, 'Daniel P. Moroney-whistle   NY April 1927

BVE 48488-2 The King Of The Fairies-Long Dance'   Vi V-29022
BVE 48489-1 Rodney's Glory-Long Dance'   Vi V-29032, HMV B3403
BVE 48490-2 Miners Of Wicklow; Kennedy's Jig-Jigs'   Vi V-29022
BVE 48491-1 Bantry Bay Hornipe'
                         Vi V-29032, MW M-8624, HMV B3403, Topic 12T366(33)
BVE 48494-2 Bandon Jig   Vi V-29064, Bb B-4916, MW M-8624, HMV B3621

BVE 48495-1   Boys Of Milltown-Reel   Vi V-29064, HMV B3621
              Dan Sullivan-p 'Connie Hanafin-acn   NY December 18, 1928

Vi V-29022, V-29032, MW M-8624, HMV B3403 and Topic 12T366 as THE HANAFINS

36.72. Thomas Barry Hannom *baritone*

Thomas Hannom

              The Old Fenian Gun   OBDW 1000
              Kevin Barry   OBDW 1000
                                                       NY early 1920s

label note: Dedicated to all the Fenians, living or dead. No label name is
actually given, and this pairing may be derived from the following.

8730-A   The Old Fenian Gun (O'Neill)   Ge 5387, OBDW 39003
8731-A   Kevin Barry (Cogley)   Ge 5387, OBDW 39003
              orch   NY January 28, 1924

8775-A   Kelly The Boy From Killarn (McCall-Cogley)   Ge 5403
8776-A   The West's Awake (Davis)   Ge 5404
              orch   NY March 3, 1924

8783-A   The Smashing Of The Van (dedicated to Allen, Larkin and O'Brien, the
                       Manchester martyrs)   Ge 5403
8784-A   Vengeance (dedicated to the men of Easter Week)   Ge 5404
8785-A   Kevin Barry (Cogley)   Ge 5387
              orch   NY March 7, 1924

8963-A   The Boys Of Wexford (Joyce)   Ge 5468
8964-A   O'Donnell Aboo-Clan Connell War Song (McCaun)   Ge 5468
8965   Ireland, Boys, Hurrah! (Sullivan)   Ge rej
              orch   NY May 2, 1924

9271-A   The Minstrel Boy (Moore)   Ge rej
9272   The Ould Plaid Shawl (Fahy)   Ge 5651
9273   Off To Philadelphia (Stanford)   Ge 5651
              orch   NY January 9, 1925

Thomas Barry Hannom

BVE 45505-2   The Irish Emigrant-Pt. 1: Danny's Letter   Vi 21481
BVE 45506-1   The Irish Emigrant-Pt. 2: Danny's Return   Vi 21481
BVE 45507-1   The Irish Emigrant-Pt. 3: Danny Says   Vi rej
BVE 45508-2   The Irish Emigrant-Pt. 4   Vi rej
              vln, acn   NY May 22, 1928

36.73. Domenic Hannon *violin, vocal*

Lannigan's Ball		untraced
Showman's Fancy-Hornpipe		untraced
		NY 1920s

The above was probably released on New Republic.

36.74. Pat Harrington *vocal*

65170-A	Dear Old Donegal {Shake Hands With Your Uncle Mike} {Back To Dear Old Donegal}	
	De 2410, 18786, W4433, Rex U653, CRL 57367(33)	
65171-A	Tread On The Tail Of Me Coat De 2411, 18787, 25050, W4459, Rex U661, CRL 57367(33)	
65172-A	Finnegan's Ball (Otto Bannell) De 2412, 18788, 25050, W4449, Rex U659, CRL 57367(33)	
65173-A	McSorley's Two Beautiful Twins De 2412, 18788, 25051, W4449, Rex U659, CRL 57367(33)	
65174-A	Paddy McGinty's Goat (R.P. Weston-Bert Lee) De 2410, 18786, W4433, Rex U653, CRL 57367(33)	
65175-A	Irish Jubilee (Chas. Lawlor) De 2411, 18787, 25050, W4459, Rex U661, CRL 57367(33)	
	orch	NY March 14, 1939

De 2410-12 are in album 44; 18786-88 are in album A-430.

69031-A	When The One You Love Loves You	De 3828
69032-A	Montmartre Rose	De 3828
69033-	You're In Love With Everyone	De 3779
69034-	Just A Girl That Men Forget	De 3779
	orch	NY April 21, 1941

36.75. Catherine Harte And George Sweetnam *vocal*

65373-A	Hold Your Head Up Patsy McCann	De 12238, W4458, Rex U660
65375-A	The Sailor's Sweetheart	De 12219, W4593, Rex U680
65377-A	Molly Bawn And Brian Oge (Cathal Garvey)'	De 12203, W4458, Rex U660
	orch d Patrick Killoran or 'Harry Horlick	NY April 10, 1939

36.76. Mattie Haskins *tenor*

BVE 36943-1	Mary Clary	Vi 79044
BVE 36944-1	Nora McNamara	Vi 79044
	Ed Geoghegan-p	NY November 18, 1926

BVE 37510-2	The Irish Jaunting Car	Vi 79159
BVE 37511-3	Killarney, My Home O'er The Sea	Vi 79159
	as before	NY January 4, 1927

```
GEX 579-A    Courtafurteen                                            Ge 6110
GEX 580-A    Irish Market Day'                                        Ge 6110
             Geoghegan's Emerald Trio: Ed Geoghegan-p, others unk, 'with John
             Murphy                                           NY  April 17, 1927


E 22799/800/01 Paddy Murphy's Barn Dance'                            Br 68000
E 22802/3    Riley's House Racket'                                   Br 68000
E 22804/5    I Left Ireland And Mother                              Br 68001
E 22806/7    Captain Barry                                          Br 68001
             vln, p, 'bagpipes                                 NY  April 30, 1927


Br 68000 as MATTIE HASKINS AND THE EMERALD TRIO


BVE 39260-1  Fun At The Fair (Mattie Haskins)                       Vi 20762
BVE 39261-1  O'Brien's Wedding                                      Vi 20762
             vln, acn, p                                      NY  June 15, 1927


7501-1-2     My Irish Home {Hogan Leaves Ireland}      Ba 2170, Do 0197, Or 1142
7502-1       Soldier's Song-Irish National Anthem           Ba 7022, Do 0197
7504-        Maloney's Christening'                          Ba 2170, Re 8492
             Geoghegan's Emerald Trio, 'with Mary Haskins   NY  September 9, 1927


7725-2       Shall My Soul Pass Through Ireland?       Ba 7024, Or 1142, Re 8491
7726-        The Felons Of Our Land                    Ba 7022, Or 1143, Re 8491
             orch d Jim McGrath                            NY  January 11, 1928


Or 1142 and 1143 as PAT O'BRIEN


BVE 43621-2  Mary Carnet From Killarney                              Vi 21379
BVE 43622-1  An Old Irish Cot                                        Vi 21378
BVE 43623-1  O'Reilly, The Fisherman                                 Vi 21379
BVE 43624-1  Lord Lurgan's Great Greyhound                           Vi 21378
             vln, cl, p                                       NY  April 9, 1928
```

Matthew Haskins

```
8433-2       Farewell My Native Irish Home (Haskins-Gagan)           SS 1935
8434-1       I Will If You Will (Haskins-Gagan)           Domino 0273, SS 1936
8435-2       Turf Man From Ardee (Haskins-Gagan)          Domino 0273, SS 1936
8436-1       Bold Robert Emmet (Haskins-Gagan)                       SS 1935
             vln, md, p, d Jim McGrath                     NY  January 3, 1929
```

Mattie Haskins

```
W 111179-2   When Ireland Belongs To The Irish Again Co 33372-F, RZ IZ291, MR1796
W 111180-2   My Home In Donegal                      Co 33387-F, RZ IZ582, MR1987
W 111181-2   I Won't Hear Old Ireland Run Down       Co 33387-F, RZ IZ582, MR1987
W 111182-2   Daughter Of Daniel O'Connell            Co 33372-F, RZ IZ282, MR1745
                                                          NY  October 1929


W 111622-2   Good-by Johnny Dear                              Co 33430-F
W 111623-2   A Lonely Little Cabin                    Co 33416-F, RZ IZ541
W 111624-2   A Miner's Dream Of Ireland               Co 33416-F, RZ IZ541
                                                          NY  January 1930
```

W 111180-4   My Home In Donegal   Co rej
                                                                   NY   March 1930

36.77. Edward Healy *tenor*

W 114005-1   I Know Where I'm Goin' (Herbert Hughes) Co 33537-F, RZ IZ303, MR1808
W 114006-1   The Ninepenny Fidil (Herbert Hughes)   Co 33537-F, RZ IZ303, MR1808
              James Morrison's Instrumental Trio: James Morrison-vln, unk p, bj
                                                              NY   January 21, 1935

36.78. Jack Healy *tenor*

62816-   Homeland   De 12140, W4243
62817-   Red River Valley; Put On Your Old Grey Bonnet
                  (Percy Wenrich-Sammy Murphy)   De 12140
              Paddy Killoran Trio: Patrick Killoran, Patrick Sweeney-2 vln, unk acn,
              p   NY   November 26, 1937

63331-   The Donegal Sailor (Lawrence Vincent)   De 12144, Rex U616
63332-   Old Ireland Far Over The Sea (John Fash-H.C. Gillespie) De 12144
              orch   NY   February 22, 1938

64247-A   Ireland Over All   De 12178, W4308, Rex U633
64248-A   Travelling   De 12178
              Paddy Killoran Trio: Patrick Killoran-vln, unk acn   NY   June 28, 1938

65833-   Kitty McCreagh-Waltz Song (Meredith-Scott)   De 12216, W4676
65834-   The Dear Ould Dart (Ben Gordon-Frank Hughes)   De 12216, W4676
              orch d Paddy Killoran   NY   June 15, 1939

65867-   In Dreams I Go To Sligo   De 12251
              as before   NY   June 22, 1939

36.79. Edward Herborn *accordion*

Edward Herborn And James Wheeler

47022-1   The Maid Behind The Bar-Reel   Co A2147, Consolidated A2147
47023-2   The Rambler's Jig   Co A2147, Consolidated A2147
                                                          NY   September 15, 1916

47242-2   The Mouse In The Cupboard-Jig   Co A2182, 33050-F
47243-1   Miss Dalton's Reel   Co A2182, 33050-F
              James Wheeler-bj   NY   December 18, 1916

47280-1   The Stack Of Barley   Co A2217, 33052-F, Vo 84113
47281-1   The Rocky Road To Dublin   Co A2217, 33052-F, Vo 84113
              as before   NY   January 9, 1917

Eddie Herborn

S 72147-A	Tattered Jack Welsh; Double Head-Jigs		Ok 21020, Pa E3054
S 72148-A	Rackety Jack; The Ha' Penny-Reels		Ok 21021, Pa E3055
S 72149-A	Uncle Tom's Best-Medley Of Straight Jigs		Ok 21019, Pa E3053
S 72150-A	The Morning Fair-Hornpipe		Ok 21019, Pa E3053
S 72153-A	O'Byrne's Favorite Jig		Ok 21021, Pa E3055
S 72154-A	Exhibition Reel		Ok 21020, Pa E3054
	Joe Kennedy's Jig		Ok 21022, Pa E3056
	Steeplechase Reel		Ok 21022, Pa E3056
	Thomas Bolger-p		NY December 7, 1923

36.80. James A. Hughes *tenor*

9472	The Bells Of Shandon (Rev. Francis Mahoney-J.J. Daly)[1]	
		Ge 5716, OBDW 39011
9475	The Meeting Of The Waters (Thos. Moore)	Ge 5716, OBDW 39011
	vln, p, 'bells	NY April 21, 1925

W 110718-2	My Little Colleen	Co 33368-F, Vo 84147
W 110719-2	The Green Hills Of Ireland	Co 33368-F, Vo 84147
	orch	NY May 1929

36.81. Hyde Brothers *accordion duet*

W 175446-1	test recording	Co
		NY August 3, 1927

W 108905-1	The Blind Fiddlers-Reel	
		Co 33251-F, 33502-F, Vo 84021, FW FP18(33), FW6818(33)
W 108906-2	Back O' The Haggart-Jig	Co 33251-F, 33502-F, Vo 84021
		NY ca March 1928

36.82. Innisfail Irish Orchestra

W 111696-2	Happy To Meet, Sorry To Part	Co 33403-F
W 111697-2	Medley Of Two Steps	Co 33403-F, RZ G20912, IZ187, MR687
W 111699-1	Medley Of Waltzes	Co 33415-F, RZ G20912, MR687
	Innisfail Special-Fox Trot	Co 33415-F
	vln, acn, p, bj	NY February 1930

36.83. Irish-American Male Quartette *vocal*

W 109783-2	Holy God, We Praise Thy Name	Co 33292-F, RZ G20430
W 109784-2	See! Amid The Winter Snow	Co 33292-F, RZ G20430
W 109785-2	Faith Of Our Fathers	Co 33291-F, RZ G20431
W 109786-3	Ave Maria	Co 33291-F, RZ G20431
	org	NY October 1928

36.84. Irish Big Four *instrumental*

W 112951-2	Salamanca; The Slasher-Reels	Co 33479-F
W 112952-2	Cuckoo's Nest; Down The Meadows-Reels	Co 33479-F
W 112955-2	Scholar Medley-Reels	Co 33481-F
W 112956-2	By Heck-Barn Dance	Co 33481-F
	The Bartender; Teetotler-Reels	Co 33480-F
	Buttermilk Mary Medley-Jigs	Co 33480-F
	fl, acn, p, bj	NY ca May 1931

36.85. Irish Male Chorus

W 108881-2	Hail! Glorious Apostle	Co 33240-F
W 108882-2	Hymn To The Holy Name (William Cardinal O'Connell)	Co 33240-F
	p	NY February 1928

36.86. Irish Pipers' Band Of Boston *instrumental*

BVE 38827-2	Maggie In The Woods {Dick Brickley's Favorite}-Polka (Set-3rd Figure)	Vi 20721, Yv K-520
BVE 38828-1	Father O'Flynn-Jig (Set-2nd Figure)	Vi 20720, Bb B-4995, MW M-8637, Yv K-502
BVE 38829-1	Connaught Man's Rambles-Polka (i.e. jig) (Set-1st Figure)	Vi 20720, Bb B-4995, MW M-8637, Yv K-502
BVE 38830-1	Bonnie Jockey Bright And Gay-Polka (Set-4th Figure)	Vi 20721
BVE 38831-2	Hops And Malt-Reel (Set-5th Figure)	Vi 20722
BVE 38832-2	O'Connell's Reel {O'Connell Twomey's Favorite}	Vi 20722
	2 vln, acn, p	NY May 24, 1927

36.87. Mrs. Redie Johnston *accordion*

8552-A	Scotchman Over The Border; Wards Jig-Jigs	Ge 5284
8553	Redie Johnston's Reels	Ge 5284
	Harry Race-p	NY October 8, 1923

36.88. Patrick Jordan *baritone*

| O 8160-B | God Save Ireland | Od Od20049, Ok 21003, Pa E3061 |
| | orch | NY ca 1921 |

36.89. Eleanor Kane *piano*

| C 90450-A | Morning Dew; Travelers; Shark's Favorite-Reels | De 12068 |
| | | Chicago November 15, 1935 |

36.90. John Kelvin *tenor*

2060-1   Little Town In The Ould County Down (Pascoe-Carlo-Sanders)
                                               Cr 3487, Vars 8007
2061-1   That Old Irish Mother Of Mine (Jerome-Von Tilzer) Cr 3487, Vars 8007
     p   NY April 28, 1933

36.91. William A. Kennedy *tenor*

8506   Dear Little Shamrock (Cherry)   Ed 51038, 4687(4 min)
      orch   NY June 26, 1922

80742-2   Little Town In The Ould County Down (Carlo-Sanders)
                                             Co A3796, 33014-F
80743-2   In The Valley Near Slievenamon (Sullivan)   Co A3796, 33014-F
      orch   NY December 20, 1922

80797-2   Mother In Ireland (Griffen-Kahn-Lyman)   Co A3847, 33023-F
80798-4   Just A Bit Of Irish Lace (L. and A. Solman)   Co A3847, 33023-F
      orch   NY January 17, 1923

80977-   The Lass From County Mayo (Browne)   Co rej
80978-   My Wild Irish Rose (Olcott)   Co rej
      orch   NY June 20, 1923

80977-11 The Lass From County Mayo (Browne) Co A3962, 33015-F, Vo 84107
80978-   My Wild Irish Rose (Olcott)   Co rej
      orch   NY July 20, 1923

80978-9   My Wild Irish Rose (Olcott)   Co A3962, 33015-F, Vo 84107
      orch   NY July 31, 1923

81207-4   When Clouds Have Vanished And Skies Are Blue   Co rej
81208-4   Kiss Me With Your Eyes   Co rej
      orch   NY September 11, 1923

81454-5   Irish Moon, from "Shamrock" (Hess-Santly)   Co rej
      orch   NY January 5, 1924

81489-5   In The Land Where The Green Shamrock Grows (Von Tilzer)   Co rej
      orch   NY January 17, 1924

81580-4   When Shall I Again See Ireland? (Victor Herbert-Henry Blossom)
                                             Co rej
      orch   NY February 2, 1924

81454-7   Irish Moon, from "Shamrock" (Hess-Santly)   Co 85-D, 33041-F
81489-7   In The Land Where The Green Shamrock Grows (Von Tilzer)
                                             Co 85-D, 33041-F
      orch   NY February 9, 1924

```
81580-5     When Shall I Again See Ireland? (Victor Herbert-Henry Blossom)
                                                    Co 253-D, 33060-F
81581-4     My Irish Song Of Songs (Daniel J. Sullivan-Alfred Dubin)
                                                    Co 253-D, 33060-F
            orch                                    NY  February 21, 1924

81689-3     The Harp That Once Through Tara's Halls (arr N. Clifford Page)
                                                    Harmony 2-H
81690-3     In Dublin's Fair City (arr N. Clifford Page)    Harmony 2-H
            orch                                    NY  April 15, 1924

81798-3     The Old Refrain (Fritz Kreisler)                Co 172-D
81799-3     I Hear You Calling Me (Charles Marshall)        Co 172-D
            orch                                    NY  May 29, 1924

81863-1     Won't You Come Back To Mother Machree (Roland A. Ball)
                                                    Co 184-D, 33059-F
81864-3     Sadie O'Brady (B. Lindemann-D. Gregory-B. Schafer)  Co 184-D
            orch                                    NY  July 7, 1924

W 140577-2  Shamrock Leaves (Arthur-Robe)                   Co 421-D
W 140578-2  A Window In Old Athlone (Brady-Robe)            Co 421-D
            George Stehl-vln, R. Stehl-vc, Robert Hood Bowers-p    NY  May 2, 1925

W 140592-3  Th' Breath Of An Irish Smile (Bowers-De Witt)   Co 448-D
W 140593-2  On The Road To Bal-Na-Pogue (Geo. J. Trinkaus)  Co 448-D
            orch                                    NY  May 8, 1925

W 140775-1  The Bard Of Armagh                              Co 589-D
W 140776-3  Would God I Were The Tender Apple Blossom        Co 589-D
            Walter Biedermann-vln, C. Hahn-vc, Robert Hood Bowers-p
                                                    NY  July 17, 1925

W 141452-1  When Irish Eyes Are Smiling (Ball-Olcott)
                         Co 1003-D, 33167-F, Vo 84123, RZ G20187
W 141453-2  'Tis An Irish Girl I Love And She's Just Like You, from "Macushla"
                    (Ernest R. Ball)                Co 1645-D, RZ G20455
            Robert Hood Bowers-p                    NY  January 4, 1926

W 141455-3  Sweet Inniscarra (Chauncey Olcott)              Co 987-D
W 141456-2  I Love The Name Of Mary (Ball-Olcott)
                         Co 1003-D, 33167-F, Vo 84123, RZ G20187
            orch                                    NY  January 6, 1926

W 141990-3  The Old Fashioned Mother (Chauncey Olcott)   Co 1645-D, RZ G20455
W 141991-3  Molly O!, from "Mavourneen" (Wm. J. Scanlan)    Co 987-D
            orch                                    NY  April 21, 1926

W 142114-4  Kathleen Aroon, from "The Isle O' Dreams" (Ball-Olcott-Weslyn)
                                                    Co 1690-D, Re G9387
W 142115-2  The Click Of Her Little Brogans, from "The Ragged Robin"
                    (Ball-Brennan)                  Co 1690-D, Re G9387
            orch                                    NY  April 30, 1926
```

```
W 142156-3   She's The Daughter Of Mother Machree (Ball-Nenarb)
                                        Co 663-D, 33097-F, RZ G20329
W 142157-3   Dear Old Fashioned Irish Songs My Mother Sang To Me (Ball-Nenarb)
                                        Co 663-D, 33097-F, RZ G20329
             Robert Hood Bowers-p                        NY  May 6, 1926

W 142396-2   In The Valley Near Slievenamon (Daniel J. Sullivan)
                                             Co 742-D, RZ G20157
W 142397-3   Little Town In The Ould County Down (Carlo-Sanders-Pascoe)
                                             Co 742-D, RZ G20157
W 142398-1   My Wild Irish Rose (Chauncey Olcott)    Co 743-D, RZ G20095
W 142399-1   The Lass From County Mayo (Raymond A. Browne)  Co 743-D, RZ G20095
      orch                                      NY  July 15, 1926

W 142699-3   That Tumble Down Shack In Athlone (Carlo-Sanders-Pascoe)
                                             Co 1233-D, RZ G20214
W 142700-3   The Minstrel Boy                 Co 1232-D, RZ G20215
W 142701-1   Little Mother Of Mine (Burleigh) Co 1233-D, RZ G20214
W 142702-3   The Harp That Once Thro' Tara's Halls   Co 1232-D, RZ G20215
      orch                                 NY  September 29, 1926

W 142750-2   That Tumble Down Shack In Athlone (Carlo-Sanders-Pascoe)   Co rej
             Fred Landau-vln, Robert Hood Bowers-p   NY  October 7, 1926

W 146353-2   Oft In The Stilly Night (Thomas Moore)        RZ IZ177, MR473
W 146354-2   At The End Of An Irish Moonbeam (w: Phil Ponce, m: Ernie Golden)
                                        Co 2083-D, RZ G20347, IZ177, MR473
W 146355-4   Has Sorrow Thy Young Days Shaded? (Thomas Moore)      RZ G20233
             vln, vc, p                            NY  May 28, 1928

W 146362-2   The Girl I'll Call My Sweetheart Must Look Like You
                         (Olcott-Sullivan)                RZ G20347
W 146363-3   Bells Of Killarney (w: Joseph M. White, m: George J. Trinkaus)
                                                          RZ G20348
W 146364-3   The Shamrock, The Shannon And You (Daniel J. Sullivan)  RZ G20348
                                                   NY  May 29, 1928

W 146445-1   Maureen Mavourneen (w: Joseph M. White, m: Geo. J. Trinkaus)
                                             Co 2083-D, RZ G20233
             vln, vc, p                            NY  June 14, 1928

BVE 45663-1  John Mitchell                                Vi 21540
BVE 45664-1  My Dark Rosaleen (arr Needham)               Vi 21540
BVE 45665-2  The Snowy Breasted Pearl   Vi V-29041, 26-7511, Bb B-4918, MW M-8625
BVE 45666-2  It Is A Charming Girl I Love, from "The Lily Of Killarney"   Vi rej
             orch d Alfredo Cibelli                NY  June 28, 1928

BVE 46927-2  The Dear Little Shamrock {The Shamrock Of Ireland}
                         (Andrew Cherry-W. Jackson)       Vi 21662
BVE 46928-1  Killarney (Edmund Falconer-M.W. Balfe)       Vi V-29007
BVE 46929-2  Genevieve (Cooper-Adams)                     Vi 21662
BVE 46930-2  The Thirty-Two Counties                      Vi V-29007
             as before                         NY  August 22, 1928
```

BVE 45666-3   It Is A Charming Girl I Love, from "The Lily Of Killarney"
                   (Jules Benedict)   Vi V-29041
              as before   NY May 14, 1929

BVE 53649-1   The Valley Lay Smiling Before Me (Thomas Moore)   Vi V-29058
BVE 53650-1   Let Erin Remember The Days Of Old (Thomas Moore)   Vi V-29058
BVE 53651-1   The Wearing Of The Green   Vi V-29071
BVE 53652-2   Tri Colored Ribbon   Vi V-29071
              as before   NY May 21, 1929

39256-A   O Mary Dear (John McCormack, arr Edwin Schneider) De 12032, Rex U389
39257-A   Moonlight In Killarney (J.J. Gallagher)   De 12032, Rex U387
39258-A   Bless This House (May H. Brahe-Helen Taylor)   De 364, 12033
39259-A   O Lord Most Holy (Panis Angelicus) (César Franck)   De 364, 12033
39260-A   St. Patrick's Day (M.J. Barry, arr Shane O'Kelley)'
                                                              De 12034, Rex U389
39261-B   Miss Kitty O'Toole (Daniel Bros.)'   De 12034, Rex U387
              orch d Justin Ring or 'p   NY January 17, 1935

62223-   Paddy, ftmp "Paddy The Next Best Thing"
                   (L.E. De Francesco-Lester O'Keefe)   De 12101
62224-   A Little Dash Of Dublin, ftmp "Peg Of Old Drury"
                   (Maurice Sigler-Al Goodheart-Al Hoffman)   De 12101
62225-A   The Bard Of Armagh   De 12109
62226-A   That's How I Spell I-R-E-L-A-N-D
                   (George B. McDonnell-Morton Downey-Dick Safford) De 12123
62227-A   A Little Bit Of Heaven (Shure They Call It Ireland)
                   (Ernest R. Ball-J. Keirn Brennan)   De 12123
62228-A   The Meeting Of The Waters (Thomas Moore)   De 12109
              George A. Henninger-p   NY May 26, 1937

36.92. Shaun Kildare *Dublin's Famous Bass-Baritone*

              The I.R.A.'s Answer To The Black And Tans   NR 1109
              The Boys Of '98   NR 1109
              Lieut. Ridgely's 69th Regt. Orchestra   NY 1921

36.93. Patrick Killoran *violin (1904-1965)*

Patrick Killoran & His Pride Of Erin Orchestra

1279-2   Stack O' Barley   Cr 3126, Ho 23043, Vars 7019, JD 3606, NW 264(33)
1280-2   Primrose Vale; The Rambler-Jigs
                                 Cr 3126, Ho 23043, Vars 7019, JD 3606
              own, Patrick Sweeney-2 vln, Edmund Tucker-p, unk acn
                                                        NY April-May 1931

Joe Davis 3606 as BARN DANCE BOYS or PAT KILLORAN AND HIS ORCHESTRA

Patrick Killoran And Patrick Sweeney

```
1281-2        Mullinger Races; The Boys On The Hilltop-Reels     Cr 3127, Ho 23044,
                    Me 93021, Vars 7022, JD 2834, Sterling 26169, Sh 33003(33)
1282-2        Gannon's Favorite-Hornpipes
                    Cr 3127, Ho 23044, Vars 7021, Me 93022, Sterling 26169
1283-2        Farrell Gara; Silver Spire-Reels     Cr 3128, Ho 23045, Vars 7022,
                    Me 93021, LC LBC-4(33), Sh 33003(33)
1284-2        McDermott's; Memories Of Sligo-Barn Dances     Cr 3128, Ho 23045,
                    Vars 7021, JD 2834, Me 93022, Sh 33003(33)
          own, Patrick Sweeney-2 vln, Edmund Tucker-p        NY  April-May 1931
```

Joe Davis 2834 as BARN DANCE BOYS, Varsity 7021 and 7022 as PATRICK KILLORAN AND
HIS PRIDE OF ERIN ORCHESTRA

Melotone 93021 and 93022 and Sterling 26169 are Canadian issues.

Patrick Killoran & His Pride Of Erin Orchestra

```
1580-1        Ballina Lass; Sligo Maid-Reels
                    Cr 3263, Ho 23047, MW M-1054, Vars 7001, FL 9010(33)
1581-3        Donegal Lassies; Stirling Castle-Highland Flings
                    Cr 3263, Ho 23047, MW M-1054, Vars 7001
          as before, unk acn added                NY  December 29, 1931
```

MW M-1054 as IRISH BARN DANCE BAND, Varsity 7001 as IRISH BARN DANCE BOYS

```
1652-3        Green Meadows; Lady Of The House-Reels
                    Cr 3296, MW M-1059, Vars 7008, JD 3600
1653-1        Cherish The Ladies-Jig     Cr 3296, MW M-1059, Vars 7008, JD 3600
1654-1        Morning Dew; Colleen Bawn-Reels     Cr 3297, Vars 7009, JD 3601
1655-1        Apples In Winter; Rose Of Lough Gill-Jigs
                    Cr 3297, Vars 7009, JD 3601
          own, Patrick Sweeney-2 vln, probably Edmund Tucker-p, unk acn, ten
          sax, bj                                  NY  March 3, 1932
```

MW M-1059 as IRISH BARN DANCE BAND, Varsity 7008, 7009, JD 3600 and 3601 as IRISH
BARN DANCE BOYS

Patty Killoran And Patty Sweeney

```
1736-1        A Surely; The Steeplechase-Reels     Cr 3344, Sh 33003(33)
              Surely; The Steeplechase-Reels                 Vars 7006
              Steeplechase-Reels                             MW M-1058
1737-3        Bat Henry's Favorite; Chaffpool Post-Barn Dances        Cr 3344
              Henry's Favorite; Chaffpool-Barn Dances     MW M-1058, Vars 7006
          own, Patrick Sweeney-2 vln, Edmund Tucker-p     NY  May 31, 1932
```

MW M-1058 as IRISH BARN DANCE BAND, Varsity 7006 as IRISH BARN DANCE BOYS

Paddy Killoran And His "Pride Of Erin" Orchestra

```
38891-A       The Girls Of Brainbridge-Jig          De 12000, F5355, Rex U392
38892-A       Dublin Lassies-Reel                   De 12000, F5355, Rex U392
```

```
38893-A      Johnson's Barn Dance              De 12001, F5356, W4333, Rex U393
38894-A      The Fair Maids Of Cavan-Highland Fling
                                               De 12001, F5356, W4333, Rex U393
38897-A      Kitty Malloy's Favorite; Bonnie Annie-Polkas
                                               De 12003, F5369, W4075, Rex U394
38898-A      Galway Bay-Hornpipe               De 12003, F5369, W4075, Rex U394
38899-A      Sweeps; Heirloom-Hornpipes                               De 12004
38900-A      Jerry Donovan's Favorite-Jig                             De 12004
             own, Patrick Sweeney-2 vln, Jack Healy-fl/sax, Eileen O'Shea-p, James
             Ryan-bj/g, probably William McElligott-acn      NY  October 27, 1934
```

Paddy Killoran

```
38901-A      Tansey's Favorite; Heathery Breezes-Reels'
                              De 12005, F5357, W4104, Rex U396, Sh 33003(33)
38902-A      The Scotchman Over The Border; The Tenpenny Bit-Jigs'
                              De 12005, F5357, W4104, Rex U396
             vln solos, Eileen O'Shea-p                      NY  October 27, 1934

61395-A      Sligo Maids Lament; Malloy's Favorite-Reels
                              De 12077, W4067, Rex U243, Sh 33003(33)
61396-A      The Geese In The Bog-Jig
                              De 12077, F6357, W4003, Rex U574, Sh 33003(33)
             vln solos, Michael (Whitey) Andrews-g           NY  November 8, 1936

61407-A      Jolly Tinker; Pretty Girls Of Mayo-Reels
                              De 12081, F6357, W4003, Rex U574, Sh 33003(33)
61412-A      The Lucky Penny; Coach Road To Sligo-Jigs
                              De 12081, F6269, W4052, Rex U569, Sh 33003(33)
61413-A      Roaring Mary; Maid Of Castlebar-Reels
                              De 12090, F6269, W4052, Rex U569, Sh 33003(33)
61414-A      The Harvest Home; The Londonderry-Hornpipes
                              De 12090, W4067, Rex U243, Sh 33003(33)
             as before                                       NY  November 13, 1936

62130-A      The Maid Of Mt. Kisco; The Hunter's Purse-Reels
                              De 12095, W4182, Rex U212, Sh 33003(33)
62131-A      Leitrim Jig; Guertin Boys-Jigs       De 12095, W4181, Rex U211
             vln solos, Jim McGinn-p                         NY  April 10, 1937

62202-A      Memories Of Ballymote; Gurkin Cross-Polkas De 12103, W4182, Rex U212
62203-A      Paddy On The Turnpike; Colliers-Reels      De 12103, W4181, Rex U211
             as before                                       NY  May 12, 1937
```

Paddy Killoran's Irish-American Serenaders

```
62243-A      A Little Dash Of Dublin-Fox Trot, ftmp "Peg Of Old Drury"
                (Maurice Sigler-Al Goodheart-Al Hoffman)'              De 12116
62244-A      My Little Colleen-Waltz'                                  De 12113
62245-A      The River Shannon; Tumble Down Shack In Athlone-Fox Trots
                              De 12113, W4184, Rex U214
62246-A      Norah The Pride Of Kildare-Waltz'               De 12114, W4183
62247-A      Paddy, ftmp "Paddy The Next Best Thing"
                (L.E. De Francesco-Lester O'Keefe)'          De 12114, Rex U213
```

```
62248-A      Come Back Paddy Reilly To Ballyjames Duff-Waltz¹          De 12124
62249-A      O'Donnell Abu; Kelly The Boy From Killan; The Minstrel Boy; The Harp
                 That Once-Marches                   De 12124, W4183, Rex U213
62250-A      Teddy O'Neil; Galway Bay-Waltzes                  De 12116, W4184
       own vln, unk 3 sax, acn, p, sbs, dm, ¹Jack Healy-vo  NY  June 10, 1937
```

Killoran's Irish Entertainers

```
62551-A      Ireland Is Ireland To Me                   De 12132, W4335, Rex U588
62552-A      The Cottage With The Horseshoe O'er The Door¹
                                                 De 12125, W4335, Rex U588
62553-A      Fair Sligo Thee I Now Must Leave¹          De 12125, W4244, Rex U612
62554-A      Take This Message To My Mother             De 12117, W4334, Rex U587
62555-A      Drowsy Maggie; Toss The Feathers-Reels²                   De 12138
62556-A      The Gold Ring; Haste To The Wedding-Jigs²                  De rej
62557-A      The Glorious Old Round Towers Of Ireland   De 12117, W4244, Rex U612
62558-A      The Maid From Donegal                      De 12132, W4334, Rex U587
       Jim Dwyer or ¹Jack Healy-vo, or ²vln solos, unk p  NY  August 19, 1937
```

De 12138 as PADDY KILLORAN

Paddy Killoran

```
62789-A      The Gold Ring; Haste To The Wedding-Jigs   De 12145, W4465, Rex U667
62790-A      Down The Broon; The Gatehouse Maid-Reels   De 12145, W4465, Rex U667
62791-A      Maguire's Fiddle; O'Donnell's Hornpipe-Hornpipes       De 12138, W4690
       vln solos, unk p                           NY  November 18, 1937
```

Paddy Killoran And Paddy Sweeney

```
62818-A      Humors Of Lisadell; Sweeney's Dream-Reels
                                         De 12131, W4691, Sh 33003(33)
62819-A      Decca Polka; Jim Ryan's Fancy-Polkas            De 12131, W4691
       vln duets, unk p                           NY  November 26, 1937
```

Paddy Killoran

```
63335-A      Dwyer's Favorite; The Star Of Monster-Reels              De 12158
63336-A      If There Wasn't Any Woman On The World-Barn Dances¹      De 12158
       p, ¹melodeon                               NY  February 22, 1938
```

Killoran's Irish-American Serenaders

```
63821-       In County Clare-Fox Trot                                 De 12162
63822-       Old Fashioned Mother Of Mine-Waltz (Marvin Smolev-Dean T. Wilton)
                                                                      De 12162
63823-A      I'll Go Back To The Old Place And Mother Machree!-Fox Trot
                 (William A. Kelly)                                   De 12173
63824-A      Sweet Are The Flowers That Bloom In Dear Kerry-Waltz     De 12173
63825-A      Savourneen Dheelish-Fox Trot                             De 12181
63826-A      The Lass From The County Mayo-Waltz (Raymond A. Browne)   De 12181
63827-A      Slievenamon-Waltz                                        De 12187
```

63828-A   A Little Bunch Of Shamrocks (I Am Holding In My Hand)-Fox Trot
             (Harry Von Tilzer-William Jerome-Andrew B. Sterling)   De 12187
      Jack Healy-vo   NY   May 19, 1938

Paddy Killoran

64309-A   The Boys Of Ballysodare; Bat Henry's Favorite-Reels
                                     De 12179, Rex U638
         The Boys Of Ball Isodarte; Att Henry's Favorite-Reels   De W4313
64310-A   The Humors Of Ballinafad; McPaddin's Favorite-Jigs
                                De 12179, W4313, Rex U638
      vln solos, Jim McGinn-p   NY   July 12, 1938

65261-A   The Mason's Apron; Langton's Favorite-Reels   De 12201
65262-A   The Enchanted Lady; The Holy Land-Reels   De 12201, W4690
      as before   NY   March 23, 1939

65519-A   Farrell Gara; The Silver Spire-Reels   De 12204
65520-A   Shannon's Favorite; Highland Bonnet-Highland Flings   De 12204
      vln solos, unk p   NY   May 1, 1939

65874-A   McGovern's Favorite; Tom Ward's Downfall-Reels
                               De 12220, Sh 33003(33)
65875-A   Cherish The Ladies-Jig   De 12220
      as before   NY   June 22, 1939

36.94.   John J. Kimmel   *accordion (1866-1942)*

3494   American Polka   Zon 6060(9")
3497   Irish Jigs And Reels-Medley   Zon P6006(7")
3498   Irish Jigs And Reels-Medley   Zon C6006(9")
        Bedelia-With Variations (Theodore F. Morse)   Zon P5996, Ox 5996(7")
        Bedelia-With Variations (Theodore F. Morse)   Zon C5996(9")
        Irish Reels Medley   Zon 6047(9")
        Straight Jig Medley   Zon 6071(9")
        Yankee Doodle Boy-With Variations (George M. Cohan)   Zon 6168(9")
        Suwannee River (Foster)   Zon 6177(9")
4953   American Clog   Zon 212, 5058
        Yankee Doodle Dandy (George M. Cohan)   Zon 234, 5333, Ox 234
        Otto Kost-p   NY   1904-5

John Kimmble

        American Cake Walk (Edward De Veau)   Ed 9341(2 min)
        Medley Of Reels   Ed 9389(2 min)
        as before   NY   May 8, 1906

Ed 9389 includes "Union Reel" and "Teetotaler's Reel."

        Kimmble March   Ed 9581(2 min)
        Medley Of Straight Jigs   Ed 9665(2 min)
        American Polka   Ed 9761(2 min)
        as before   NY   February 7, 1907

John J. Kimmel

B 4784-1	Irish Boy March (J.J. Kimmel)	
		Vi 5237, 16747, 62565, Leader LED2060(33)
B 4785-1-2	Medley Of Popular Reels, Including Buck And Wing Dance	
		Vi 5307, 16421, 16948, FW RF112(33)
B 4786-1	Kitty's Wedding; Kimmel's; The Black Rogue; The Top Of Cork	
	Road-Jigs (arr J.J. Kimmel)	Vi 5238, 16406, FW RF112(33)
E 4786-1	Medley Of Irish Jigs (arr J.J. Kimmel)	Vi 5238(8")
B 4787-1-2	Medley Of Straight Jigs	Vi 5254, 16534, FW RF112(33)
p		NY August 10, 1907

"Union Reel" is included on matrix B 4785.

7593	American Polka	Zon 761, 5333
7594	Suwannee River; Annie Laurie-Straight Jigs	Zon 843, 5332, Ox 843
7595	Irish Jig Medley	Zon 750, 5058
7596	Irish Jigs And Reels Medley	Zon 783, 5059, Ox 783
7597	Marche De Concert	Zon 7026, 4026, Ox 7026(12")
7598	Cakewalk	Zon 861, 5059, Ox 861
	Schottische Medley	Zon 911, 5332, Ox 5332-B
	Otto Kost-p	NY 1907

B 6014-1-2	American Cakewalk (J.J. Kimmel)	Vi 5438, FW RF112(33)
B 6015-2	Minor March (Kost)	Vi 16028, 62552, FW RF112(33)
B 6016-1	American Polka (J.J. Kimmel)	Vi 5417, 16408, 62546
E 6016-2	American Polka (J.J. Kimmel)	Vi 5417(8")
B 6017-1	Floggan Reel; Union Reel; Green Fields Of America;	
	Teetotalers-Medley Of Reels No. 2 (arr J.J. Kimmel)	
		Vi 5468, 16171, 63010
E 6017-1	Medley Of Reels No. 2 (arr J.J. Kimmel)	Vi 5468(8")
p		NY March 6, 1908

John Kimmble

Medley Of Irish Jigs	Ed 9881(2 min)
Schottische Medley	Ed 9943(2 min)
Popular Straight Jigs	Ed 9975(2 min)
Otto Kost-p	NY May 13, 1908

The Miner March	Ed 10071(2 min)
Fans' March	Ed 10172(2 min)
Medley Of Irish Reels	Ed 10284(2 min)
as before	NY September 29, 1908

John J. Kimmel

B 6512-2	The Fans March (J.J. Kimmel)	Vi rej
B 6513-1-3	Indian Intermezzo (Kus)	Vi 16129, 63010
B 6514-1-2	Medley Of German Waltzes (arr J.J. Kimmel)	Vi 16127

```
B 6515-2      Tipperary (Helf)                                       Vi rej
         p                                            NY   October 6, 1908
```

Matrices B 6513-3 and B 6514-2 were intended for Canadian release.

```
B 6840-2      Medley Of Hornpipes (arr J.J. Kimmel)        Vi 16317, 62537
B 6841-1      Barn Dance (Kost)                                       Vi rej
B 6842-1      Medley Of German Polkas (arr J.J. Kimmel)               Vi rej
B 6843-1      Medley Of Clogs (arr J.J. Kimmel)    Vi 16438, Leader LED2060(33)
C 6843-1      Medley Of Clogs (arr J.J. Kimmel)               Vi rej (12")
              probably Otto Kost-p                     NY   March 2, 1909

8954          Medley Of German Waltzes         Zon 1201, 5331, Ox 5331-A
8955          Tipperary-March                     Zon 5184, Ox 5184-A
8956          Medley Of Irish Reels No. 3         Zon 5473, Ox 5473-B
8957          Straight Jig Medley No. 2           Zon 5473, Ox 5473-A
              The Irish Boy-March                       Zon 1189, 5331
              The Fan-March (Otto Kost)           Zon 5184, Ox 5184-B
              The Indian Intermezzo               Zon 5615, Ox 5615-A
              Scotch Pipes                        Zon 5615, Ox 5615-B
              Librato Polka                             Zon 4023(12")
              as before                                      NY   1909
```

Zon 5000 issues are double-side; others are single-side, as are all Oxford issues, despite their use of -A and -B designations from the originals! Zon and Ox 5615 may have been recorded in 1910.

```
              Kimmel March (J.J. Kimmel)                  Ind 769(2 min)
              Medley Of Jigs                              Ind 784(2 min)
              Medley Of Straight Jigs                     Ind 805(2 min)
              Medley Buck And Reel                        Ind 813(2 min)
              Medley Of Straight Jigs No. 2               Ind 836(2 min)
              Medley Of Schottisches                      Ind 895(2 min)
              Medley Of Reels No. 2                       Ind 946(2 min)
              Minor March (J.J. Kimmel)                   Ind 969(2 min)
              Medley Of German Waltzes (arr Otto Kost)    Ind 995(2 min)
              New Tipperary March (Helf)                 Ind 1014(2 min)
              Fan's March (Otto Kost)                    Ind 1065(2 min)
              Indian Intermezzo (J. Kost)                Ind 1090(2 min)
              Medley Of Hornpipes                        Ind 1266(2 min)
              Medley Of German Polkas (Kohl)             Ind 1327(2 min)
              Medley Of Buck Dances (Johnson)            Ind 1367(2 min)
              as before                                    NY   1908-10
```

John Kimmble

```
              International March; Fan's March            Ed 504(4 min)
              Buck Dance Medley               Ed 553(4 min), 2384(4 min)
              German Waltz Medley                       Ed 10417(2 min)
                                                  NY   May 27, 1910


              Elite March (Edgar De Veau)                 Ed 927(4 min)
              New Tipperary March                       Ed 10525(2 min)
                                                  NY   October 29, 1910
```

John J. Kimmel

72-Z	Scotch Sword Dance (J.J. Kimmel)	Ind 3088(4 min)
73	Kimmel Medley (J.J. Kimmel)	Ind 3073(4 min)
	March Of National Airs (J.J. Kimmel)	Ind 3067(4 min)
		NY 1910

The selections on Ind 3067 and 3088 occupy only half of each cylinder. The remainder of each are by Charles D'Almaine and Vess L. Ossman respectively.

	Dill Pickles (Charles L. Johnson)	USE 364(2 min)
365-1	Medley Of Reels	USE 365(2 min)
	Medley Of Irish Reels	USE 417(2 min)
	Samland March	USE 418(2 min)
	Irish Songs Medley	USE 1185(4 min)
	Irish Jigs Medley	USE 1339(4 min)
	p	NY 1911-2

B 16351-3	Cuckoo's Nest; Mason's Apron-Irish Reel Medley No. 3
	Vi 17849, Leader LED2060(33)
B 16352-1	Salamango; Off Key-Irish Reel Medley No. 4
	Vi 17849, Leader LED2060(33)
B 16353-3	Irish Mixture-Jigs
B 16354-2	Go To It (Ed. De Veau)
	Ed. De Veau-p

Vi rej (16353-3), Vi rej (16354-2) NY August 13, 1915

46261-3	Mason's Apron; Cuckoo's Nest-Reels	Co A1917, 33026-F, Vo 84109
46262-2	Connaught Men's Ramble-Jigs	Co A1917, 33026-F, Vo 84109
46263-2	Rights Of Man; Liverpool; Fisher's Hornpipe-Hornpipes	
		Co A1977, Leader LED2060(33)
46264-3	Fall In Line	Co rej
	p	NY December 11, 1915

Some copies of Co A1977 erroneously list "Sailor's Hornpipe" as the final title.

	Along The Line (Kimmel)
	Joe Linder-p

Empire 3301, Rex 5301 NY 1915-6

46491-1	Haste To The Wedding; Larry O'Gaff; The Smash-Jigs
	Co A2036, VT 7028-V
46492-1-2	Stack Of Barley; Blackberry Blossoms; Green Fields Of America-Reels
	Co A1977
46493-1-2	International Echoes (Joe Linder)
	Co A2094, FW RF112(33)
	as before

NY March 11, 1916

46822-1	Bonnie Kate; Swallow Tail; Star Of Munster-Reels (arr Joe Linder)
	Co A2036, 33040-F, VT 7028-V
46823-2	Flogan Reel; Cup Of Tea-Reels (arr Joe Linder)
	Co A2094
46824-3	Geese In The Bog; Colairne; Trip To The Cottage-Jigs
	Co A2283, 33019-F, FW RF112(33)
	as before

NY June 2, 1916

```
B 16353-4    Irish Mixture-Jigs                                          Vi rej
B 18242-2    Bonnie Kate; Swallow's Tail; Star Of Munster-Reels          Vi rej
B 18243-2    Stack Of Barley; Blackberry Blossom; Green Fields Of America-Reels
                                                                         Vi rej
B 18244-2    Floggan Reel; Cup Of Tea-Reels                             Vi rej
B 18245-2    The Rights Of Man; Liverpool; Fisher's-Hornpipes           Vi rej
             as before                                    NY  August 1, 1916

B 18242-4    Bonnie Kate; Swallow's Tail; Star Of Munster-Reels          Vi rej
B 18267-2    Haste To The Wedding; Larry O'Gaff-Jigs                     Vi rej
B 18268-2    Geese In The Bog; Colairne; Trip To The Cottage-Jigs       Vi rej
B 18269-2    International Echoes (arr J. Linder)                        Vi rej
             as before                                    NY  August 8, 1916

B 16353-6    The Three Little Drummers; Connaught Man's Ramble; Sweet Biddy Daly;
                Devlin's Favorite {Medley Of Irish Jigs No. 2}
                {An Irish Mixture}                                    Vi 18207
B 18242-6    Bonnie Kate; Swallow's Tail; Star Of Munster
                {Medley Of Irish Reels No. 8}    Vi 18998, Leader LED2060(33)
B 18243-3    Stack Of Barley; Blackberry Blossoms; Green Fields Of America-Reels
                                                Vi 18193, Leader LED2060(33)
B 18244-3    Floggan Reel; Cup Of Tea {Medley Of Irish Reels No. 5}
                                                Vi 18207, Leader LED2060(33)
B 18245-4    The Rights Of Man; Liverpool; Fisher's-Hornpipes           Vi rej
B 18267-5    Haste To The Wedding; Larry O'Gaff-Jigs                    Vi rej
B 18268-3    Geese In The Bog; Colairne; Trip To The Cottage-Jigs       Vi 18193
B 18269-4    International Echoes (arr J. Linder)                        Vi rej
             as before                                    NY  October 30, 1916

332          Haste To The Wedding; The Coralaine-Jigs              Pq 70(7½")
335          Floggan Reel; Cup Of Tea-Reels                       Pq 70(7½")
             International Echoes (Kimmel)                         Pq 115(7½")
             Swallow's Tail; Green Fields Of America-Reels         Pq 115(7½")
                                                           NY   ca 1917

6043         Kimmel March                             Ed 50604, 3493(4 min)
6044         Bonnie Kate; Swallow Tail; Green Fields Of America-Reels
                                                      Ed 50604, 3577(4 min)
6045         Connaught Man; To The Ladies; The Rattler-Jigs  Ed 50692, 3521(4 min)
6045-B       Three Little Drummers; Connaughtman's Ramble; To The Ladies;
                Devlin's Favourite                        Leader LED2060(33)
             as before                                    NY  March 4, 1918

B 22941-3    Irish Freedom-March                                        Vi rej
B 22942-1    My Partner's Fancy; Top Of The Morning-Reels              Vi 19271
B 22943-2    Haley's Favorite-Jigs                  Vi 18727, Leader LED2060(33)
             Nathaniel Shilkret-p                        NY  June 25, 1919

4568-1-2     Haste To The Wedding; Larry O'Gaff; Trip To The Cottage-Jigs
       Em 1099, Ba 2083, Bell 1143, Clover 1701, Do 0136, NML 1088, Puritan 9125,
                                                                   Re 9431
```

4569-2   Bonnie Kate; Green Fields Of America-Reels
                         Em 1099, Ba 2083, Do 0136, NML 1088, Puritan 9125
                                                  NY ca October 1919

Most issues titled simply "Medley Of Irish Jigs" and "Medley Of Irish Reels." NML
1088 as EDWARD KELLY; other issues may also be pseudonymous.

4657-4   Rakes Of Kildare; To The Ladies; Devlin's Dream-Jigs   Em 10144,
                         10592, Ba 2085, Clover 1700, Medallion 8165, Re 988
4658-2-4   The Blackbird; Rights Of Man-Hornpipes   Em 10144, 10592, Do 0127,
                         Medallion 8165, Or 330, Re 987, OBDW 39053, FW RF112(33)
           p   NY ca November 1919

Re 987, 988 and OBDW 39053 as EDWARD McCONNELL, Or 330 as GILBERT (or GEORGE)
McKENNA

7115   Haste To The Wedding; Larry O'Gaff; Corlaine-Jigs
                                                  Ed 50653, 4194(4 min)
7115-A   Haste To The Wedding; Larry O'Gaff; Colairne   Leader LED2060(33)
7116   Oh Gee!; Maid Of Kildare-Reels   Ed 50870, 3895(4 min), FW RF112(33)
7117   Haley's Fancy-Jigs   Ed 4076(4 min)
7118   Homeward March   Ed 50674, 4111(4 min), FW RF112(33)
           Joe Linder-p   NY January 17, 1920

4670-2   The Bartender Reel   Em 10190, Do 0127, Ba 2086, Or 331, Re 987,
                                                  Sil 2646
4871-1-2   To The Ladies; Connaught Man's Ramble; The Runner-Jigs   Em 10190,
                         Ba 2085, Medallion 8303, OBDW 39053, Re 988, Sil 2646
           p   NY ca February 1920

Ba 2085, 2086, Re 987, 988 and OBDW 39053 as EDWARD McCONNELL, Sil 2646 as FRED
DONNER, Or 331 as GILBERT (or GEORGE) McKENNA.

46823-3   Flogan Reel; Cup Of Tea-Reels   Co A2094
46824-4   Geese In The Bog; Colairne; Trip To The Cottage   Co A2283
79068-1-2   Bryant's Favorite; Birds In The Tree-Hornpipes   Co A2951
79069-1   Rakes Of Kildare; Devlin's Favorite-Jigs
                                             Co A2951, Leader LED2060(33)
79069-2   Rakes Of Kildare; Devlin's Favorite-Jigs   Co A2951
79070-2   Blackbird Medley   Co rej
79073-   Molly Maguire; Salamanca   Co rej
           Joe Linder-p   NY March 6, 1920

46263-4   Rights Of Man; Liverpool; Sailor's Hornpipe-Hornpipes   Co A1977
46491-2   Haste To The Wedding; Larry O'Gaff; The Smash-Jigs
                                             Co A2036, 33040-F, VT 7028-V
           p   NY March 26, 1920

79191-3   Pat's In His Glory; Contentment Is Wealth   Co rej
79192-2   Paddy's Farwell To America; The Coming Of Barney   Co rej
           p   NY May 21, 1920

                Patsey's Farewell To America; Contentment And Love   Vi trial
           p, bj   NY July 6, 1920

	Stack O' Barley	Arto 3020, Bell S20, Globe L20
	Geese In The Bog	Arto 3020, Bell S20, Globe L20
		NY 1920

760	Medley Of Irish Jigs	Federal 5095, Resona 75095, Sil 2095
772	Medley Of Irish Reels	Federal 5095, Resona 75095, Sil 2095
		NY 1921-2

It is not certain that Resona 75095 was actually issued.

8567	Stack O' Barley; Blackberry Blossom; Green Fields Of America-Reels
	Ed 51041, 4688(4 min)
8568	Contentment Is Wealth; Father Jack Walsh-Jigs
	Ed 51041, Leader LED2060(33)
	Joe Linder-p	NY August 8, 1922

Leader LED2060 uses matrix 8568-C.

N 70102-	Coo Coo's Nest; Mason's Apron-Reels	Pat 10663, 021038, Pe 11143
N 70103-	Byant's Favorite-Hornpipes	Pat 10580, 020956, Pe 11112, OBDW 39056
	Bryant's Favorite	Cameo 9113, Lincoln 3140, Ro 915, Sil 1262
	Bryant's Favourite; Birds In The Tree-Hornpipes Leader LED2060(33)
N 70104-	Devlin's Fancy	Pat 11142, 021115, GP 18549
N 70105-	Stack Of Barley-Hornpipes	Pat 10580, 020956, Pe 11112, OBDW 39056,
		Sil 1262, VH 17
N 70106-	Haste To The Wedding; Larry O'Gaff	
		Pat 10663, 021038, Pe 11143, VH 17
	p	NY ca March 1923

Cameo 9113, Lincoln 3140 and Ro 915 as JOHN STANLEY, Grand Pree 18549 (Australian)
as JOHN CASANI, Vox Humana VH17 (Australian) as JOHN CRAIG

Fred Donner

1-2438	Medley Of Hornpipes	Federal 5377, Resona 75377, Sil 2377
	Medley Of Jigs And Reels No. 2	Federal 5377, Resona 75377, Sil 2377
		NY ca January 1924

it is not certain that Resona 75377 was actually issued.

John J. Kimmel

BVE 43974-2	Bryant's Favorite-Hornpipe	Vi 21596
BVE 43975-2	Irish Boy-March	Vi 21441
	Chłopiec Z Irlandyi-Marsz	Vi 81332
BVE 43976-2	Fitzmaurice Polka	Vi 21441, FW RF112(33)
	Polka Z Krojczyna	Vi 81332
BVE 43977-2	Haste To The Wedding-Jig	Vi 21596, Bb B-4976, Yv K-505
	Andrew Fiedler-g	NY May 14, 1928

Vi 81332 (Polish) as JAN KIMELSKI

18968	Bryant's Favorite-Hornpipe	Ed 52488
18969	Fitzmaurice's Polka	Ed 52488
	as before	NY December 27, 1928

A note for this session states that John Kimmel was featured on a weekly radio broadcast, "Main Street Sketches", on WOR in New York City.

18982	Floggan Reel	Ed 52499
18983	Trip To The Cottage-Jig	Ed 52499, Leader LED2060(33)
	as before	NY January 3, 1929

Leader LED2060 uses matrix 18983-B.

Folkways RF112 includes two titles which Kimmel recorded several times, "New Tipperary March" and "Indian Intermezzo;" which versions were used is not clear.

36.95. Hugh Lally, Walter Lally, Ed. Geoghegan *instrumental*

748-A-1	Roll Her In The Mountain-Reels	NR 2336
748-B-1	The Widower Well Married-Jigs	NR 2336
	Hugh Lally-acn, Walter Lally-bj, Ed Geoghegan-p	NY early 1920s

36.96. John A. Leahy *violin*

W 109094-1	Toss The Feather-Reel	Co 33248-F
W 109095-1	Leahy's Barn Dance	Co 33248-F
	p	NY ca March 1928

36.97. Joseph Lee *baritone*

9523-A	An Old Irish Hill In The Morning	Ge rej
9524	The Tanyard Side	Ge 5747, OBDW 39014
	Edward Lee-p	NY May 11, 1925

| 9779-A | Out And Make Way For The Fenian Men | Ge 5747, OBDW 39014 |
| | as before | NY October 19, 1925 |

A file note attached to matrix 9779-A states: voice punk.

BVE 36463-1	Tipperary Hills	Vi 79105
BVE 36464-2	The Men Of The West	Vi 79105
BVE 36598-2	The West's Asleep	Vi 79154
BVE 36599-2	An Old Irish Hill In The Morning (w: Fahy)	Vi 79154
	as before	Camden, NJ November 17, 1926

36.98. Patrick Lynch *accordion*

9808	High Level; Royal Belfast-Hornpipes {Gypsy Medley}	Ed 51460
9809	Donnybrook Fair; Paddy's Favorite; Slasher's-Jigs	Ed 51460
		NY October 27, 1924

S 73854-B	Green Mountain Bogs; Light Of The Moon-Old Country Dances	
		Ok 21031, Pa E3250
S 73856-B	Bonnie Kate; Miss McLeods Reel-Clogging Reels	Ok 21031, Pa E3250
	The High Level-Hornpipe	Ok 21028, Pa E3249
	In The Valley Near Slievenamon; Danny Boy	Ok 21028, Pa E3249
		NY December 1925

36.99. Joseph Maguire *tenor*

62783-A	The Braes Of Strablane (Ellen Maguire)	De 12133, W4246, Rex U614
62784-	Tatterin' Pat O'Hara (M. Gilsenan)	De 12134, W4238, Rex U606
62785-A	By Lurgan Stream (J. Tunney)	De 12136, W4282, Rex U626
62786-A	Lovely Lough Erne (Joseph Maguire)	De 12136, W4237, Rex U605
62787-	Next Monday Morning (Ellen Maguire)	De 12134, W4238, Rex U606
62788-A	The Pride Of Glencoe (arr Father Peter Conefrey)	
		De 12133, W4237, Rex U605

Killoran Trio: Patrick Killoran-vln, unk alt sax, acn
NY November 18, 1937

63147-A	General Owen Roe (Joseph Maguire)	De 12137, W4262, Rex U618
63148-A	The Country Girl (Joseph Maguire)	De 12137, Rex U643
63149-	McNamara From Mayo (Joseph Maguire)	De 12146, W4245, Rex U613
63150-	Down By The Nut Bushes (Joseph Maguire)	De 12146, W4282, Rex U626
63151-A	The County Tyrone (Joseph Maguire)	De 12147, W4246, Rex U614
63152-A	By Kells Water (Joseph Maguire)	De 12147, Rex U643
63153-A	My Father's Cabin (Joseph Maguire)	De 12151, W4245, Rex U613
63154-A	The Rose Of Ardee (Joseph Maguire)	De 12151, W4262, Rex U618
63155-A	The Rakes Of Paddy Roe (Joseph Maguire)	De 12160, W4247, Rex U615
63156-A	The Star Of Drum {County Monaghan} (Joseph Maguire)	
		De 12160, Rex U615

Paddy Killoran's Quartet: Patrick Killoran-vln, unk alt sax, acn, p
NY January 13, 1938

63996-A	The Wicklow Mountain High	De 12168, W4306, Rex U631
63997-A	My Charming Jenny Shea (Joseph Maguire)	De 12163, W4292, Rex U627
63998-A	The Whistler From Bawn (Joseph Maguire)	De 12163, W4292, Rex U627
63999-	My Irish Laboring Boy (Joseph Maguire)	De 12180, W4460, Rex U662
64200-A	The Boy From Ballytore (Anna Meakin)	De 12188, W4329, Rex U641
64201-A	The Milestone (Anna Meakin)	De 12188, W4329, Rex U641
64202-A	My Mary O (Joseph Maguire)	De 12180, W4306, Rex U631
	orch	NY June 15, 1938

| 64417-A | Corrigan {The Irish Airman} (Joseph Maguire) | De 12168 |
| | tp, vln, cl, p | NY August 4, 1938 |

65253-A	Kate From Ballinamore	De 12199, W4460, Rex U662
65254-A	I Know A Church Crowned With Ivy	De 12199, W4508, Rex U674
65255-A	My Willy O (arr Father Peter Conefrey)	De 12205, W4508, Rex U674
65256-A	The Blackbird Of Sweet Avondale (arr Father Peter Conefrey)	
		De 12205, W4755
65257-	An Irishman's Toast	De 12214, W4436, Rex U656
65258-	Happy Days Gone By	De 12214, W4448, Rex U658

```
65259-A    The Dublin Brigade                        De 12230, W4436, Rex U656
65260-A    Round The Lovely Banks Of Boyne           De 12230, W4448, Rex U658
           Paddy Killoran's Orchestra: Patrick Killoran-vln, probably Jim
           McGinn-p, unk alt sax, acn                NY  March 23, 1939


67825-     An Irish Greeting (Joseph Maguire)            De 12239, W4755
67826-     'Round Our Old Cottage Home In Old Ireland    De 12239, W4756
67827-A    Soldiers Of Old Ireland {On The Run} (Joseph Maguire)
                                                         De 12243, W4756
67828-A    At The Foot Of Rooskey Hill                       De 12243
           Paddy Killoran's Orchestra                   NY  May 27, 1940
```

36.100. Danny Malone *vocal*

```
39106-A    There's A Cottage By The Shannon
               (Alice Sanders-Monte Carlo-Jack Scholl)
                                                  De 12043, W4132, Rex U439
39107-A  . I'll Take You Home Again, Kathleen (Thomas P. Westendorf)
                                                  De 12052, W4132, Rex U439
39108-A    In The Valley Near Slievenamon (Daniel J. Sullivan)
                                                  De 12043, W4103, Rex U440
39109-A    The Low Back'd Car; Cruiskeen Lawn      De 12025, W4103, Rex U440
39110-B    Cockles And Mussels (arr Herbert Hughes)  De 12025, W4099, Rex U441
39111-B    All That I Want Is In Ireland {All That I Had And All That I Have
               And All That I Want Is In Ireland} (Evans Lloyd-Jeff Branen)
                                                  De 12052, W4099, Rex U441
           orch                                   NY  November 27, 1934
```

Some copies of De 12025 substitute matrix 39106 for 39110.

36.101. Charles Massinger *vocal*

```
BVE 37637-2   Ireland, I Love You, Macushla Machree (Raymond A. Browne)
                                                     Vi 79184, HMV B2898
BVE 37638-3   Little Town In The Ould County Down
                 (Richard W. Pascoe-Monte Carlo-Alma M. Sanders)      Vi rej
              orch d Bruno Reibold            Camden, NJ  January 19, 1927


BVE 37638-4   Little Town In The Ould County Down
                 (Richard W. Pascoe-Monte Carlo-Alma M. Sanders)      Vi 79263
BVE 37656-3   The Birth Of The Shamrock (Jamie Kelly-Wm. Cahill)
                                                     Vi 79184, HMV B2567
BVE 37657-3   A Shawl Of Galway Grey (Pat Hogan-Jos. Stanley)         Vi 79263
              orch d Leroy Shield             Camden, NJ  January 31, 1927


BVE 38015-3   My Dark Rosaleen (James Clarence Mangan-Alicia Adelaide Needham)
                                                                      Vi rej
              orch d Bruno Reibold            Camden, NJ  April 28, 1927
```

36.102. James C. McAuliffe *bagpipes*

Minstrel Boy	Ed 7229(2 min)
Miss McCloud's Reel	Ed 7230(2 min)
Donnybrook Fair	Ed 7231(2 min)
Stack Of Barley	Ed 7232(2 min)
	NY 1899
Paddy On The Turnpike	Ed 7504(2 min)
Pigeon On The Gate	Ed 7653(2 min)
	NY 1900
Blackbird	Ed 7712(2 min)
Maid Of The Beach	Ed 7713(2 min)
Dirge Of The Carlin	Ed 7714(2 min)
O'Donnell Aboo	Ed 7715(2 min)
Coulin	Ed 7716(2 min)
Rights Of Man	Ed 7717(2 min)
Red Haired Man's Wife	Ed 7718(2 min)
Pretty Girl Milking Her Cow	Ed 7719(2 min)
	NY 1900-1
Cock Of The North	Co 31600(2 min)
Highland Laddie-Military March	Co 31601(2 min)
Campbells Are Coming	Co 31602(2 min)
	NY 1901
Miss McCloud's Reel	Ed 8184(2 min)
	NY 1902
Minstrel Boy	Ed 8487(2 min)
	NY 1903

This artist recorded again for Edison on March 16 and 18, 1909, possibly to remake some earlier titles. Three were remade in Canada, ca 1903: Pretty Maid Milking Her Cow (12880), Paddy On The Turnpike (12881) and Donnybrook Fair (12882).

36.103. James McCarthy *violin*

9486	Pay The Girl Her Fourpence-Reels	Ge 5718
9487	Medley Of Irish Jigs	Ge 5718
9488	Shanahan's Hornpipe; Howke's Hornpipe	Ge 5725
9489	The Broken Pledge; Kit Shea's Reel	Ge 5725
	Paddy Muldoon-p	NY April 24, 1925

36.104. Pat McCarthy *baritone*

63486-A	Off To Philadelphia (Battison Haynes-Stephen Temple)	De 12165
63487-A	A Breath Of Old Ireland And You (Joseph A. Burke-Sam Downing)	
		De 12174
63488-	Along The Rocky Road To Dublin (Bert Grant-Joe Young)	De 12193

```
63489-      Sailing (Godfrey Marks)                                    De 12193
63490-A     My Galway Rose (Walter Scanlan-George A. Kershaw)    De 12165, W4860
63491-A     On The Green Hills Of Donegal (Joseph J. Gallagher)        De 12174
63492-A     My Mother's Rosary (Joseph J. Gallagher)            De 12152, W4860
63493-A     Smile Again, Kathleen Mavourneen (Owen Murphy-William Jerome)
                                                                       De 12152
            cl, acn, p                                     NY  March 24, 1938
```

36.105. McConnell's Four Leaf Shamrock Orchestra

```
B 30514-1   Dublin Jig; Geese In The Bog; Connaughtman's Rambles-Jigs   Vi 19446
B 30515-1   The Old Torn Petticoat; Off To Dublin; The Boys Of Lough-Reels
                                                                        Vi 19446
            Adam McConnell-vln, unk pic, p           Camden, NJ  July 11, 1924

B 30514-3   Dublin Jig; Geese In The Bog; Connaughtman's Rambles-Jigs   Vi rej
B 30515-3   The Old Torn Petticoat; Off To Dublin; The Boys Of Lough-Reels
                                                                        Vi rej
            Adam McConnell-vln, Thos. Maloney-bagpipes, John McNulty-pic, Jos.
            Dolan-p                              Camden, NJ  August 13, 1924

B 31121-1   Babes In The Woods; Moore's Favorite-Polkas                 Vi 19539
B 31122-1   Humors Of Cappa; Green Grows The Rushes; Ewe Fling-Highlands
                                                                        Vi 19539
            c, 2 vln, pic, bagpipes, p, traps       NY  October 25, 1924
```

36.106. John McCormick *violin*

```
13961/2     Reidy Johnson Reels; Bright Star Of Munster             Vo 14943
            Edward Lee-p                             NY  November 1924

9781-A      The Buncaana Reel                                       Ge 5746
            as before                               NY  October 19, 1925
```

36.107. Frank McCowie *vocal*

```
            The Women Are Worse Than The Men                    Co 33344-F
                                                   NY  ca January 1928
```

36.108. Bill McCune And His Orchestra

```
M 868-      "Gone Again" Corrigan-Fox Trot                          Vo 4281
M 869-2     Mother In Ireland-Waltz (Griffin-Kahn-Lyman)            Vo 4669
M 870-      Along The Rocky Road To Dublin-Fox Trot                 Vo 4281
M 871-1     You'll Have To Pass Through Ireland
                  (When You're On Your Way To Heaven)-Fox Trot (Griffin-Silver)
                                                                    Vo 4669
            Gerald Griffin-vo                       NY  July 28, 1938
```

36.109.   Charles McDonough   *violin*

759-B	Rights Of Man-Hornpipe	Cameo 463, Lincoln 2148
760-B	Kitty's Wedding-Reel	Cameo 463, Lincoln 2148
	Josephine Donohue-p	NY December 1923
W 80364-A	The Green Groves Of Erin	Ok 21034
W 80365-A	Liverpool Hornpipe	Ok 21034, RZ IZ762
	Gus Scharff-p	NY January 31, 1927

36.110.   William McElligott   *vocal, accordion*

38895-A	Washington Hornpipe [no vo]	De 12002, W4191, Rex U208
38896-A	Jackson Polka [no vo]	De 12002, W4191, Rex U208
	Eileen O'Shea-p	NY October 27, 1934
CO 20221-1	The Dublin; Concert-Hornpipes [no vo]	Co 33556-F, Vo 84059
CO 20231-1	Bridge Of Athlone-Reel [no vo]	Co 33560-F, Vo 84063
	Alex Brown-p	NY November 10, 1936
63591-	Cod Liver Oil	De 12200, W4311, Rex U636
63592-	Patrick Sheehan	De 12175, W4294, Rex U629
63593-A	The Mountjoy Hotel	De 12166, W4278, Rex U622
63594-	It's An Irishman In Paris	De 12200, W4278, Rex U622
63595-	Paddies Evermore	De 12175, W4294, Rex U629
63596-A	The Next Market Day	De 12166, W4311, Rex U636
	g	NY April 12, 1938
64841-	Soldiers Of 22	De 12221, W4421, Rex U651
64842-	Ireland Shall Be Free	De 12194, W4421, Rex U651
64843-	Sprig Of Shillelah	De 12206, Rex U664
64844-	There's A Heart In Old Ireland	De 12206, Rex U664
64845-	Queenstown Harbor	De 12194, W4313, Rex U655
64846-	St. Patrick Was A Gentleman	De 12221, W4313, Rex U655
	g	NY December 30, 1938

36.111.   Liam McGairdainn   *bass*

They Knew Not My Heart	Co 33327-F
While Gazing On The Moon's Light	Co 33327-F
	NY ca 1928

36.112.   John McGettigan   *tenor, violin (1882-1965)*

John McGettigan's Orchestra

The Waterford; Fisherman's Widow; Larry O'Gaff [no vo]	Vi trial
First Of May; Slievenamon; Friendly Visit [no vo]	Vi trial
	NY November 28, 1922

Three Leaf Shamrock Orchestra

BVE 37411-2   Katie Connor; The Irishman's Toast; Nellie Gray; The Old Foggy Dew
                                                                      Vi rej
            probably: Edward V. Reavy-vln, Michael Crowley-p, Joseph Conroy-bj
                                              Camden, NJ January 11, 1927

John McGettigan

BVE 43484-2   Rare Ould Irish Whiskey   Vi V-29019, 26-7501, Bb B-4917, MW M-8944,
                                              RZ MR1614, Topic 12T367(33)
BVE 43485-3   Fitzmaurice, The Dublin Flier {The Irish German Fliers}
                  (m: Edward V. Reavy)   Vi 21380
BVE 43486-2   Mary Malone   Vi 21380, Bb B-4930
            Killarney Trio: Michael Crowley-p, Joseph Conroy-bj
                                              Camden, NJ April 25, 1928

No violin is present, despite a file note to the contrary.

BVE 48293-2   McManus And Kehoe   Vi V-29024
BVE 48294-2   Me Husband's Flannel Shirt   Vi V-29024, 26-7502, Bb B-4917,
                      MW M-8944, Yv K-501, RZ MR1382, Topic 12T367(33)
BVE 48295-2   The Boys From The County Mayo
                  Vi V-29019, Bb B-4901, MW M-8618, Yv K-536, RZ MR1617
            own vo/vln, unk fl, p   NY January 17, 1929

John McGettigan And His All-Irish Orchestra

BVE 55938-1   The Hills Of Donegal
                  Vi V-29062, Bb B-4901, MW M-8618, Yv K-533, RZ MR1617
BVE 55939-2   County Galway And Norah McShane
                  Vi V-29062, Bb B-4502, MW M-8938, Yv K-533
BVE 55940-2   Cutting The Corn In Creeslough Today
                  Vi V-29061, Bb B-4502, MW M-8938, Topic 12T367(33)
BVE 55941-2   My Grey Haired Irish Mother
                  (dedicated to the Irish National Foresters) (John McGettigan)
                                              Vi V-29061, Yv K-534
            own vo, Mac Barrett-vln, Joe Maher-g, Michael Crowley-p, McIntyre-bj
                                              Camden, NJ September 26, 1929

John McGettigan's Three Leaf Shamrock Orchestra

BVE 64047-1   I'm Proud Of The Irish Now {Don't Be Ashamed Of The Shamrock Green}'
                                                                  Vi V-29077
BVE 64048-1   Rambling Irishman'
                  Vi V-29078, Bb B-4900, MW M-8617, RZ MR1381, Topic 12T367(33)
BVE 64049-1   The Irish Soldier Boy'
                  Vi V-29076, Bb B-4900, MW M-8617, Yv K-534, RZ MR1381
BVE 64050-1   Highland Schottische Medley   Vi V-29076, Topic 12T367(33)
BVE 64051-1   The Three Little Drummers; The Geese In The Bog
                  {McGettigan's Jig Medley}   Vi V-29077, Topic 12T367(33)
BVE 64052-1   McGettigan's New Katie Connor Medley   Vi V-29078
            Frank Meehan, Joseph O'Neill-2 vln, Al Duffy-p, John Daugherty-bj,
              'own vo   Camden, NJ November 6, 1930

John McGettigan And His Irish Orchestra (Or McGettigan's Irish Minstrels)

BS 78466-1	Mulroy Bay-Pt. 1	Bb B-4913, RZ MR1801
BS 78467-1	Mulroy Bay-Pt. 2	Bb B-4913, RZ MR1801
BS 78468-1	The Roving Galway Boy	Bb B-4914, MW M-8943, RZ MR1618
BS 78469-1	Norah-Pt. 1	Bb B-4921, RZ MR1740
BS 78470-1	Norah-Pt. 2	Bb B-4921, RZ MR1740
BS 78471-1	Londonderry On The Banks Of The Foyle	Bb B-4981
BS 78472-1	Shoe The Donkey Dance¹	Bb B-4982, Topic 12T367(33)
BS 78473-1	Katie Connor¹	Bb B-4981
BS 78474-1	Miss Monahan; The Haymaker-Reels¹	Bb B-4914, MW M-8943, RZ MR1618
BS 78475-1	Sinn Fein Amain-Patriotic Song	Bb B-4982, Vi 26-7510

own vo, unk vln, vc, p, or ¹own and another-2 vln, Dan Marquette-acn,
unk vc, p   Camden, NJ December 23, 1933

John McGettigan

38994-A	Colleen Dhas	De 12051, F5396, W4025, Rex U436
38995-	The Road To Creslough	De 12009, F5395, W4084, Rex U254
38996-A-B	Lovely Old Finntown	De 12051, F5395, W4084, Rex U254
38998-A	McCarthy	De 12009, F5414, W4201, Rex U255
38999-	Terry My Blue Eyed Irish Boy	De 12010, F5414, W4201, Rex U255
39000-A	Buacaill Ruad	De 12039, F5394, W4041, Rex U253
39001-A	Deep Sheephaven Bay-Pt. 1	De 12048, F5415, W4008, Rex U437
39002-A	Deep Sheephaven Bay-Pt. 2	De 12048, F5415, W4008, Rex U437
39003-A	Norah McGee	De 12039, F5396, W4025, Rex U436
39004-A	White, Yellow And Green	De 12010, F5394, W4041, Rex U253

McGettigan's Irish Minstrels: 2(?) vln, vc, p   NY November 12, 1934

John McGettigan's Irish Minstrels

BS 0372-1	Jackets Green¹	Bb B-4997, MW M-8639, Vi 26-7508, RZ MR2365
BS 0373-1	Fisher's Hornpipe; Higgins' Hornpipe	
		Bb B-4996, MW M-8638, RZ MR2288, Topic 12T367(33)
BS 0374-1	Martha, The Flower Of Sweet Strabane¹	
		Bb B-4996, MW M-8638, RZ MR2287, Topic 12T367(33)
BS 0375-1	Salamanca; Blackthorn-Reels	Bb B-4998, Vi 26-7510
BS 0376-1	The Little Three Leaf Shamrock From Glenore¹	
		Bb B-4500, MW M-8616, RZ MR2366
BS 0377-1	Medley Of Highlands	
		Bb B-4500, MW M-8616, Vi 26-7503, 26-7526, 43-7526(45)
BS 0378-1	The Hills Of Glenswilly¹	Bb B-4998, RZ MR2366
BS 0379-1	Kitty's Wedding; Sweet Biddy Daly-Jigs	
		Bb B-4997, MW M-8639, Vi 26-7512
BS 0380-1	Sailing Away From Ireland¹	Bb B-4501, RZ MR2365
BS 0381-1	The Star Of Donegal¹	
		Bb B-4999, MW M-8640, Vi 26-7508, RZ MR2287, Topic 12T367(33)
BS 0382-1	Medley Of Katie Connors	Bb B-4501
BS 0383-1	Maggie In The Woods; The Spanish Ladies; All The Way To	
	Galway-Polkas	
		Bb B-4999, MW M-8640, Vi 26-7512, RZ MR2288, Topic 12T367(33)

own vln, Dan Marquette-acn, Jimmy McDade-g, unk p, or ¹own vo, unk
vln, p   NY September 14, 1936

John McGettigan

```
61457-A   The Night Of The Big Wind         De 12082, F6310, W4066, Rex U570
61458-    The Turfman From Ardee   De 12082, F6253, Rex U242, Topic 12T367(33)
61459-B   The Irish Jaunting Car             De 12083, F6310, W4066, Rex U570
61460-    My Mother's Last Goodbye                De 12083, F6253, Rex U242
61461-A   The Little Old Thatched Cabin On The Hill
                                            De 12086, F6311, W4081, Rex U232
61462-A   The Green Fields Of Dromore        De 12086, F6311, W4081, Rex U232
          vln, acn, g                                 NY  December 7, 1936
```

John McGettigan's Irish Minstrels

```
BS 06507-1   The Bold Fenian Men (John McGettigan)'
                                          Bb B-4503, MW M-8939, RZ MR2581
BS 06508-1   The Tar Road To Sligo; Saddle The Pony {Old Time Medley Of Jigs}
                                          Bb B-4503, MW M-8939
BS 06509-1   Where The Three Leaf Shamrocks Grow'    Bb B-4504, MW M-8940
             Three-Leaf Shamrock Shore                   RZ MR2562
BS 06510-1   Medley Of Hornpipes                    Bb B-4504, MW M-8940
BS 06511-1   The Maid Of The Moorlough Shore'
                                   Bb B-4509, RZ MR2562, Topic 12T367(33)
BS 06512-1   The Mullingar Races; Sligo Maid-Reels  Bb B-4509, Topic 12T367(33)
BS 06513-1   The Fenian Gun'                        Bb B-4505, MW M-8941
BS 06514-1   Medley Of Highlands                    Bb B-4505, MW M-8941
BS 06515-1   Lovely Molly'    Bb B-4510, Vi 26-7509, RZ MR2581, Topic 12T367(33)
BS 06516-1   The Blackbird; The Job Of Journey Work      Bb B-4510, Vi 26-7509
             own vln/'vo, Alfred Baldassari-vln, Dan Marquette-acn, George Tracy-p,
             Jimmy McDade-g                              NY  March 22, 1937
```

```
BS 024000-1   The Dying Rebel'                       Bb B-4506, MW M-8942
BS 024001-1   Irelands 32'               Bb B-4506, MW M-8942, Co IFB372
BS 024002-1   The Banks Of Kilrea'                            Bb B-4508
BS 024003-1   Where The Shamrocks Still Grow'                 Bb B-4508
BS 024004-1   Erin's Lovely Lee'             Bb B-4507, Topic 12T367(33)
BS 024005-1   My Darling Asleep; The Maid On The Green-Jigs
                                          Bb B-4507, Topic 12T367(33)
BS 024006-1   Medley Of Highlands No. 1                           Bb
BS 024007-1   Medley Of Reels                              Co IFB372
BS 024008-1   Medley Of Highlands No. 2                           Bb
BS 024009-1   Medley Of Reels                                     Bb
              own vln/'vo, Dan Marquette-acn, Jimmy McDade-g, unk p
                                                  NY  March 24, 1938
```

John McGettigan

```
65506-    The Fanad Mare'                    De 12207, W4537, Rex U676
65507-    The Home I Left Behind             De 12207, W4486, Rex U668
65508-A   Johnston's Motor Car               De 12218, W4506, Rex U672
65509-A   The Hillside Way Up In The Corner  De 12218, W4562, Rex U678
65510-A   Sweet Leenane By The Sea           De 12226, W4486, Rex U668
65511-A   Ballard Strand                     De 12226, W4506, Rex U672
65512-    Erin's Flag                        De 12235, W4562, Rex U678
```

```
65513-         Sweet Donegal                           De 12235, W4537, Rex U676
               Patrick Killoran-vln, unk alt sax, p, 'tp      NY  May 1, 1939
```

36.113. Peter McGettrick *Boy Emmet; spoken*

```
               Robt. Emmet's Speech From The Dock                    NR 1103
                                                                     NY   1921
```

36.114. Bernard McGovern And Thomas O'Brien *instrumental*

```
BVE 40366-2   Kick Out The Scrub; Jackson's Chogue-Jigs             Vi 21319
BVE 40367-2   Humors Of Macken; Toss The Feathers-Reels             Vi 21319
BVE 40368-2   Maids Among The Heather; Green Groves Of Erin-Reels     Vi rej
BVE 40369-2   Last Night's Fun                                        Vi rej
               Bernard McGovern-fl, Thomas O'Brien-vln   Camden, NJ  January 13, 1928
```

36.115. Pat McGovern *flute*

```
C 90438-A     Leitrim's Fancy; Dunphy's Hornpipe                  De 12059
               Eleanor Kane-p                        Chicago  November 11, 1935

C 90490-A     The Jockey To The Fair-Long Dance    De 12062, F5887, W4437, Rex U497
               Johnny McGreevy, Jim Donnelly-2 vln, Eleanor Kane-p, Pat
               Richardson-dm                         Chicago  November 29, 1935
```

36.116. Jim McGrath's Orchestra

```
7723-2        Varsovienna'          Ba 7024, Cq 7205, Or 1144, Re 8490, SS 1934
7724-         Rights Of Man-Hornpipe       Ba 7023, Or 1144, Re 8492, SS 1934
               vln, cl, p, 'Mattie Haskins-vo          NY  January 11, 1928
```

Cq 7205 as KELLY'S DUBLIN ORCHESTRA, Or 1144 as COUNTY COURT MERRY MAKERS (7723)
and THOMAS McQUIRE'S ORCHESTRA (7724)

36.117. Johnny McGreevy *violin (b. 1919)*

Johnny McGrevy

```
C 90452-A     The Bank Of Ireland; Cavan Lassies-Reels       De 12059, Rex U395
               Pat McGovern-fl, Eleanor Kane-p         Chicago  November 15, 1935

C 90487-A     Slievenamon; Dublin-Hornpipes                       De 12062
               Eleanor Kane-p                          Chicago  November 29, 1935
```

36.118. Madeleine McGuigan *violin*

Among this classical violinist's recordings for Edison (1919, 1921) and Gaelic (early 1920s) are some sentimental Irish titles. She also recorded as Madeleine McGuigan Sokoloff.

36.119. James McInerney *violin*

K1-1	The Cavan Reel; The Star Of Munster-Reels		Keltic 1001
	p		NY ca 1923
	Dublin; Leitrim-Hornpipes		untraced
	Brethney; Miss Peasle's-Reels		untraced
			NY ca 1923

The above were probably issued on New Republic.

36.120. McIntyre's Irish Orchestra

303-1	Stack Of Barley	
	Ba 2040, Re 9432, Bwy 8033, OBDW 39050, Triangle 9088	
304-1	Highland Fling	Ba 2040, Re 9432, OBDW 39050
	Highland Schottische	Bwy 8033, Triangle 9088
		NY early 1920s

Bwy 8033 as McINTYRE'S IRISH VOLUNTEERS, Triangle 9088 as McINTYRE'S IRISH VOLUNTEER ORCHESTRA

36.121. John McKenna *flute (1880-1947)*

713-1	Roscommon Reels	NR 2302
	Arthur P. Kenna-p	NY early 1920s
	The Leprechaun's Favorite-Jig	NR
	The Rollicking Irishman-Reel	NR
	The Duke of Leinster-Reel	NR
	The Cork Fancy-Jig	NR
		NY 1920s

The above are in an E. O'Byrne Dewitt & Sons catalog for 1925-6 and probably were issued on New Republic.

Fireman John McKenna

9085-A	The Lady Of The House-Reels	Ge 5549, OBDW 39028, JMc unnumbered (C)
9086-A	Fire Away You Devil You-Jig	Ge 5549, OBDW 39028
	own pic, Paddy Muldoon-p	NY September 19, 1924
9282	Reels Of Mullingate'	Ge 5686, OBDW 39030
9283	Foggy Dew'	Ge 5686, OBDW 39030

```
9284            The Sailor On The Rock; The Corry Boys-Reels²
                              Ge 5649, OBDW 39043, JMc unnumbered (C)
9285            The Buck From The Mountain; McPartlin's Style-Hornpipes
                              Ge 5649, OBDW 39043
            own fl/²lilting, Paddy Muldoon-p, 'Michael Gaffney-banjo mandolin
                                          NY   January 19, 1925

9774            Early Breakfast; Scotch Mary-Reels       Ge 5749, OBDW 39038
9775-A          Humors Of Ballinafad; Around The Bench Of Rushes-Jigs
                                           Ge 5749, OBDW 39038
            own fl, Michael Gaffney-banjo mandolin, Paddy Muldoon-p
                                          NY   October 9, 1925
```

McKenna And Gaffney

```
W 106091-1    Parnell's Reel                            Co 33076-F
W 106094-1    Dillion Jigs                              Co 33076-F
              Maids Of Galway-Reel                      Co 33075-F
              Roland's Return-Jigs                      Co 33075-F
              as before                        NY  November 1925
```

McKenna plays tin-whistle on "Roland's Return."

John McKenna

```
W 109141-2    Down The Meadow; House On A Hill      Co 33254-F, Ok 21075
W 109142-2    Gallant Boys Of Tipperary; Three Little Drummers
                                          Co 33254-F, Ok 21075
W 109143-1    Back In The Garden; Flowers Of Red Mill-Reels
                              Co 33274-F, JMc unnumbered (C)
W 109144-2    Clancy's Dream; Leitrim Town-Jigs    Co 33274-F, JMc unnumbered (C)
         p                                    NY   March 1928
```

John McKenna And James Morrison

```
W 109740-2    My Love Is But A Lassie; The Dark Girl Dressed In Blue-Polkas
                      Co 33296-F, Vo 84136, Sh 33004(33), JMc unnumbered (C)
W 109741-2    The Highland Skip; The Sailor's Bonnet-Reels
                          Co 33342-F, Vo 84089, JMc unnumbered (C)
W 109742-2    Thady Regan; Trippin' On The Mountain-Polkas
                          Co 33342-F, Vo 84089, JMc unnumbered (C)
W 109743-1    Gardner's Favorite; Streams In The Valley-Reels
                      Co 33296-F, Vo 84136, FL 9010(33), JMc unnumbered (C)
            own fl, James Morrison-vln, unk p      NY   September 1928

W 110352-2    The Boy In The Gap; Miss Hogan's Reel     Co 33357-F, Vo 84146
W 110353-2    The Mouse In The Cupboard; Gallagh An Airgid; Hag With Money-Jigs
                                          Co 33357-F, Vo 84146
W 110354-2    The Tailor's Thimble; The Red Haired Lass-Reels
                  Co 33393-F, Vo 84151, NW 264(33), Sh 33004(33), JMc unnumbered (C)
              as before                       NY   February 1929
```

John McKenna

W 112552-2	Colonel Frazer	Co 33470-F, Vo 84044, JMc unnumbered (C)
W 112553-2	Kid On The Mountain	Co 33470-F, Vo 84044
p		NY ca December 1930

38953-A	Up And Away; Merry Girl-Polkas'	De 12042, F5429, W4233, Rex U318,
		FW 8821(33), JMc unnumbered (C)
38954-A	Colonel Roger's Favorite; Happy Days Of Youth-Reels'	
		De 12011, F5428, W4091, Rex U317, JMc unnumbered (C)
38955-A	Dever The Dancer; Connie, The Soldier-Jigs'	
		De 12011, F5429, W4233, Rex U318, JMc unnumbered (C)
38956-A	The Ballroom Favorite-Barn Dance Medley'	
		De 12042, F5428, W4091, Rex U317, JMc unnumbered (C)
38958-A	Lucky In Love; The Bloom Of Youth-Reels	
		De 12041, F5430, W4074, Rex U311, JMc unnumbered (C)
	Della McMahon-p, 'Michael Gaffney-bj	NY November 6, 1934

36.122. Jimmie McLaughlin *bagpipe*

8691-A	Judy Hynes; Sullivan's Jig-Jigs	Ge 5356
8692-A	Road To Galway; Jenny Bang The Weaver-Reels	Ge 5356
	Federic D. Wood-p	NY January 5, 1924

36.123. Manus P. McLaughlin *violin*

W 109998-2	The Union And The Belvidere-Hornpipe	Co 33319-F
W 109999-1	The Sailor Sat On The Shore-Reel	Co 33319-F
W 110000-1	Molly From Longford-Reel	Co 33347-F
W 110001-1	The Fair Hills Of Donegal; Little Peggy's Jig	Co 33347-F
p		NY November 1928

36.124. Rose McLoughlin *accordion*

B 21531-2	Moore's Hen's Nest; Swallow's Tail; Mamma's Pet; Carry Me Down To	
	Charlie's-Reels	Vi rej
B 21532-2	The Maid Is Not Twenty; The Mouse In The Cupboard; The Blue Eyed	
	Girl-Jigs	Vi rej
B 21533-2	Ballaulough Thrasher; Granny's Best; Lord Gordon-Reels	Vi rej
B 21534-2	Roscommon Girl; Frieze Breeches-Jigs	Vi rej
		NY February 20, 1918

36.125. Dominic McNally *vocal*

W 113500-1	Darling Machree (D. McNally)	Co 33510-F
W 113501-1	The Sunshine Sailed Away From Killarney	Co 33510-F
	cym (dulcimer)	NY April 1932

36.126. Walter McNally *baritone*

W 143677-	The West's Awake	Co rej
		NY March 17, 1927

W 107858-2	Love Thee Dearest	Co 33175-F, RZ G9177, IZ126
W 107859-2	The Croppy Boy (Malone, arr Johnson)	
		Co 33166-F, IFB303, RZ G9178, IZ127
W 107860-2	The Men Of The West (Rooney, arr Johnson)	
		Co 33166-F, IFB303, RZ G9178, IZ127
	orch	NY May 1927

W 108282-1	A Nation Once Again	Co 33197-F, Vo 84012
W 108283-1-2	The Soldier's Song	Co 33197-F, Vo 84012
	chorus, orch	NY July 1927

W 108296-2	Open The Door Softly; Kitty, Will You Marry Me? Co 33217-F, RZ G9177	
W 108297-1	Kathleen Mavourneen	Co 33217-F, RZ G9177, IZ126
		NY ca August 1927

W 108336-1	The Minstrel Boy (Moore-Wekerlin)	Co 33280-F
W 108337-1	The Exile's Return (Needham-Locke)	Co 33280-F
		NY September 1927

W 108577-2	The Irishman	Co 33228-F, RZ G20263
W 108580-2	Come To The Fair	Co 33228-F, RZ G20263
	orch	NY December 1927

W 143677-4	The West's Awake¹	Co 33175-F, RZ G9179, IZ128
	God Save Ireland	Co 33204-F
	The Donovans	Co 33204-F
	¹p	NY 1927

36.127. P.J. McNamara *piccolo*

125	The Blackbird	Gaelic 1023
751-B-2	Walls Of Limerick-Polkas	NR 2341
	p	NY early 1920s

The reverse of New Republic 2341, by FRANK QUINN, is credited to McNamara.

P.J. McNamara Trio

9438/9	Riley's Hornpipe; Rights Of Man; Red Haired Boy	Vo 14420
9440/1	Stack Of Barley Medley	Vo 14420
	own pic, unk vln, p	NY July 1922

12418/9/20	The Blackbird-Set Piece Hornpipe	Vo 14730
12421/2/3	The Jockey At The Fair-Set Piece Jig	Vo 14730
	as before	NY December 1923

McNamara's Emerald Orchestra

8852-A	Blarney Roses; Irish Counties; Foggy Dew-Two Steps	
		Ge 5455, Starr 9568
8853-A	Boys Of Kilkenny; Tanyard Side-One Steps	Ge 5455, Starr 9568
8854-A	The Garden Of Daisies	Ge 5456
8855-A	The Sally Grove; The Black Swan; The Tallow Boys	Ge 5456
	own pic, unk vln, p, dm	NY May 1, 1924

P.J. McNamara Trio

13379/80	Garryowen-Jigs (Irish Set-2nd Figure)	Vo 14845
13381/2	Kincora-Reels (Irish Set-1st Figure)	Vo 14845
	own pic, unk vln, p	NY ca July 1924

9159	Stack Of Barley Medley	Ge 5583
9160	Limerick; Cork-Hornpipes	Ge 5583
9161-A	The Cowlin; The Lament-Ancient Irish Classic's	Ge rej
9162	The Boys Of The West; The Snowy Breasted Pearl-Waltzes	
		Ge 5702, 3027, OBDW 39031
	as before	NY October 1924

File note next to matrix 9161-A: "By God that apostrophe wasn't my idea; musically and mechanically bad!"

525/6/7W	Collection Of Irish Reels	Vo 15120
528/9/30/1W	Collection Of Irish Jigs	Vo 15120
	as before	NY March 11, 1925

9409-A	The Coulin; The Irish Exile; Lament For Ireland-Ancient Irish	
	Classics	Ge 5702, 3026, OBDW 39031
9410	The Dingle Puck Goat-Jig	Ge 5704, 3026, OBDW 39032
9411	My Love Is On The Ocean; Bonnie Kate-Reels	Ge 5704, 3027, OBDW 39032
	as before	NY March 19, 1925

105596-2	Road To Galway; Farewell To Whiskey {Bridge Of Athlone}-Polkas	
		Co 33001-F
105597-1	Kerrigan's Jig; Mouse In The Cupboard-Jigs	Co 33001-F
	as before	NY April 1925

851/2W	Green Groves Of Erin-Reel	Vo 15059
853/4W	Love Will You Marry Me; Green Grow The Rushes O	Vo 15059
		NY June 15, 1925

P.J. McNamara

W 106115-2	Walls Of Limerick	Co 33074-F
W 106116-2	Boys From The Hill-Reel	Co 33074-F
	p	NY November 1925

S 73899-B	The Irish Emigrant[1]	Ok 21032, Pa E3252
S 73900-B	My Wild Irish Rose (Olcott)[1]	Ok 21032, Pa E3252
S 73901-B	The Peeler And The Goat	Ok 21029, Pa E3251

```
S 73902-B      Judy's Reel                                    Ok 21029, Pa E3251
               own pic or 'fl, unk p, 'vln                      NY  January 1926
```

Ok 21032 as P.J. MCNAMARA TRIO

```
9966           The Kerry Hornpipe                                      Ge 5751
9967           Brian Boru-Jig                                          Ge 5751
               own pic, unk vln, p                             NY  February 1926
```

```
9999           The Hills Of Clare-Hornpipes                            Ge 5754
X1             The Castle Street-Jig                                   Ge 5754
               as before                                   NY  February 23, 1926
```

The last matrix number is the beginning of a new series which Gennett used for its
New York studio products through 1932.

P.J. McNamara Quartet

```
BVE 36336-1    Tipperary Hills; Cup Of Tay-Jigs                       Vi 79000
BVE 36337-1    Come In Out Of The Wet-Polka                           Vi 79000
               own pic, Murty Phillips-p, unk c, vln     NY  September 21, 1926
```

P.J. McNamara

```
BVE 36338-1    The Horse And Jockey-Reel                              Vi 79001
BVE 36339-2    The Shannon Breeze-Hornpipe                            Vi 79001
               Murty Phillips-p                          NY  September 21, 1926
```

P.J. McNamara's Quartet

```
BVE 38400-2    Cashel Set; Geese In The Bog-Jigs            Vi 79324, HMV B2888
BVE 38401-2    Morning Star; Judy's Reel                    Vi 79324, HMV B2888
BVE 38402-2    Gabbetts Grove-Polka                                   Vi 20713
BVE 38403-2    Devil's Bit-Hornpipe                                   Vi 20713
               own fl, unk c, vln, p                        NY  March 23, 1927
```

36.128. Margaret McNiff Locke *accordion*

Margaret McNiff Locke's Instrumental Trio

```
W 112161-2     Brown's Hornpipe                  Co 33426-F, LC LBC-4(33)
W 112162-2     Keel Row-Highland Fling                          Co 33426-F
W 112163-2     The Clare Reel                                   Co 33431-F
W 112164-2     The Mason's Apron                                Co 33431-F
               own acn, Joseph Tansey-vln, E. Colclough-bj     NY  June 1930
```

Margaret McNiff, J. Tansey, E. Colclough

```
W 113537-1     West Hornpipe                           Co 33525-F, Vo 84166
W 113539-1     Bonnie Ann-Reel                         Co 33525-F, Vo 84166
W 113540-1     Cullen House Reel                       Co 33521-F, RZ IZ213
W 113541-1     Trippin' Up Stairs-Jig                  Co 33521-F, RZ IZ213
               Kate of Kenmare                                 Co 33511-F
```

                    Miss Gayton's Hornpipe   Co 33511-F
                    as before   NY May 1932

Mrs. And Miss Mc Niff-Locke

BS 81001-1   The Frost Is All Over-Jig (arr Margaret McNiff-Locke)
                                                          Bb B-4922, MW M-8945
BS 81002-1   Terry's Ramble-Reel (arr Margaret McNiff-Locke) Bb B-4922, MW M-8945
BS 81003-1   Killmore Fancy-Reel (arr Margaret McNiff-Locke) Bb B-4928, MW M-8946
BS 81004-1   Fallon's Delight-Reel (arr Margaret McNiff-Locke)
                                                          Bb B-4928, MW M-8946
              own acn, Miss McNiff Locke-bj   NY December 27, 1933

36.129. Eileen And Peter McNulty And Their Orchestra

66610-A   Eileen O'Dair {The Sweetest Colleen At The Fair}-Fox Trot
              (w: Claude Garreau-David A. Boyd, m: Claude Reese)   De 2963
66611-A   I'm Living The Life O'Reilly-Fox Trot (w: Claude Garreau,
              m: Claude Reese)   De 2963
           with vo   NY September 19, 1939

36.130. Gene McNulty *tenor (1917-1988)*

63618-A   Two Little Orphans
63619-A   The Blind Girl   De 12159, W4857
63620-A   Lightning Express   De 12159
63621-A   The Ship That Never Returned   De 12202
63622-A   I Wish I Had Someone To Love   De 12202, W4680
63623-A   The Innocent Prisoner   De 12167, W4857
           g   De 12167, W4680
                                                     NY April 19, 1938

De 12167 as WILLIAM McELLIGOTT; this artist was better known as comedian Dennis
Day.

36.131. The McNulty Family *vocal, instrumental*

Records by this popular group feature vocals and step-dancing by Eileen and/or
Peter McNulty, with acn, p, g, bj or smaller combinations thereof; a violin is
occasionally added. The accordion player is probably Ma McNulty.

61397-A   The Stone Outside Dan Murphy's Door-Waltz Clog With Tap Dance
                                             De 12072, W4020, Rex U234
61398-A   Polly O' The Automat-Comic Song With Tap Dance (Mrs. Ann McNulty)
                                             De 12073
61399-A   The Half Door-Song With Tap Dance (Shaun O'Nolan)
                                             De 12072, W4020, Rex U234
61400-A   Mother's Silver Curl-Song With Tap Dance (Shaun O'Nolan)
                                             De 12073, F6267, W4002, Rex U244
61401-A   Master McGraw-Sketch   De 12071
61402-A   The Hills Of Donegal
                                 De 12071, F6267, W4002, Rex U244
                                             NY November 10, 1936

```
61977-A    The Boys Of The County Cork    De 12087, 9-12087(45), W4051, Rex U577
61978-A    Moriarity, The Happy Cop                      De 12088, W4856
61979-A    I'm Sighing Tonight For Killarney And You  De 12089, W4051, Rex U577
61980-A    The Old House Far Away                 De 12088, W4035, Rex U235
61981-A    McNulty's Irish Show Boat-Sketch
                   De 12087, 9-12087(45), W4420, Rex U650, CRL 57368(33)
61982-A    Back To Donegal          De 12089, W4035, Rex U650, CRL 57464(33)
                                                  NY  February 18, 1937

62229-A    Song Of The 32 Counties    De 12107, 9-12107(45), W4170, Rex U201
62230-A    Ireland, Boys, Hurrah!              De 12099, W4170, Rex U201
62231-A    Moon Behind The Hill                De 12108, W4171, Rex U202
62232-A    Star Of The County Down             De 12108, W4172, Rex U203
62233-A    A Mother's Lament          De 12107, 9-12107(45), W4172, Rex U203
62234-A    Highland Mary                             De 12100, W4856
62235-A    Let Mr. McGuire Sit Down             De 12100, W4171, Rex U202
62236-A    The Rollicking Skipper-Jig [no vo]   De 12099, W4178, Rex U231
                                                  NY  May 27, 1937

62503-A    Come In Out Of The Rain Barney McShane    De 12126, W4464, Rex U666
62504-A    Over The Hills And Far Away-Fling [no vo] De 12126, W4227, Rex U240
62505-A    I'd Sing Like A Thrush                 De 12127, Rex U238
             Little Bridget Flynn                       De W4240
62506-A    Irish Greens And Bacon                     De 12127
62507-A    When Rafferty Brought The Rumba To The Town Of Aughnacloy
                                            De 12118, W4226, Rex U239
62508-A    The Galway Rogue      De 12118, 12271, W4240, Rex U238, U608
62509-A    Slippin' The Jig-Jig [no vo]         De 12119, W4227, Rex U240
62510-A    I Don't Care If I Do                 De 12119, W4226, Rex U239
                                                  NY  August 6, 1937

63610-A    Barney Brannigan                     De 12155, W4274, Rex U619
63611-A    Erin's Green Shore    De 12155, W4293, Rex U628, CRL 57464(33)
63612-A    The Dawning Of The Morning           De 12154, W4274, Rex U619
63613-A    The Maid Of The Sweet Brown Knowe    De 12148, W4307, Rex U632
63614-A    We'll Take You Back To Ireland
                   De 12148, W4277, Rex U621, CRL 57464(33)
63615-A    Walker Walked Away                   De 12176, W4594, Rex U681
63616-A    Waltz Me Around Again, Willie (Shields-Cobb)
                                            De 12176, W4594, Rex U681
63617-A    Shall My Soul Pass Through Old Ireland    De 12154, W4276, Rex U620
                                                  NY  April 15, 1938

63894-A    Let Ye All Be Irish Tonight          De 12169, W4327, Rex U639
63895-A    The Real Old Mountain Dew    De 12161, 9-12161(45), W4378, Rex U642
63896-A    The Old Potato Cake                  De 12169, W4307, Rex U632
63897-A    Kerry Long Ago                       De 12189, W4277, Rex U621
63898-A    Grandfather Brian                         De 12189, W4378
             Grandfather's Briar                        Rex U642
63899-A    My Beauty Of Limerick        De 12161, 9-12161(45), W4276, Rex U620
63900-A    The River Moy                        De 12183, W4293, Rex U628
                                                  NY  June 1, 1938
```

```
64585-A      Haste To The Wedding (P.J. McCall)
                     De 12195, 9-12195(45), W4394, Rex U648, CRL 57368(33)
64586-A      Knock At My Window Tonight, Love        De 12198, W4405, Rex U649
64587-A      O Son Remember My Love Today            De 12196, W4563, Rex U679
64588-A      Christmas In Exile                      De 12183, W4327, Rex U639
64589-A      Biddy Donahue                           De 12197, W4405, Rex U649
64590-A      If You Ever Go Over                     De 12196, W4394, Rex U648
64591-A      Mother Malone               De 12195, 9-12195(45), W4420, Rex U650
                                                 NY  October 21, 1938
```

De 12195 is in album A-518.

```
65328-A      I Ne'er Loved Another, But You-Waltz Song  De 12217, W4447, Rex U657
65329-A      They Sailed Away From Dublin Bay        De 12208, W4434, Rex U654
65330-A      The Little House Under The Hill (Francis A. Fahy)
                                                     De 12208, W4463, Rex U665
65331-A      The Thief Of The World (Francis A. Fahy)  De 12198, W4536, Rex U675
65332-A      Good Bye Johnny Dear                    De 12197, W4434, Rex U654
65333-A      McDonnell's Old Tin Roof (W.J. Scanlon)  De 12209, W4447, Rex U657
                                                 NY  April 4, 1939

65533-A      Denny McCall                            De 12210, W4463, Rex U665
65534-A      I Don't Work For A Living               De 12222, W4464, Rex U565
65535-A      The Kellys                              De 12209, W4487, Rex U669
65536-A      Dunloe Fair                             De 12210, W4487, Rex U669
65537-A      John Mitchell                           De 12217, W4563, Rex U679
65538-A      Amber Tresses Tied In Blue              De 12222, W4536, Rex U675
                                                 NY  May 4, 1939

67449-A      O'Bryan Has No Place To Go                De 12236, 9-12236(45)
             O'Bryan Had No Place To Go                De W4645, Rex U684
67450-A      In Old Ballymoe            De 12240, 9-12240(45), W4672, Rex U685
67451-A      At The Close Of An Irish Day (Anne McNulty)
                                  De 12241, W4645, Rex U684, CRL 57368(33)
67452-B      There's A Sweetheart Waiting For You    De 12241, W4672, Rex U685
67453-A      Kelly The Boy From Killan  De 12236, 9-12236(45), W4644, Rex U683
67454-A      The Groves Of Kilteevan    De 12240, 9-12240(45), W4644, Rex U683
                                                 NY  April 2, 1940

68465-A      Tipperary Daisy              De 12247, W4871, CRL 57464(33)
68466-A      The Golden Jubilee                       De 12246, W4872
68467-A      Shamus O'Brien                           De 12247, W4872
68468-A      Daisy Bell                               De 12246, W4874
68469-A      The Rose Of Aranmore    De 12252, 9-12252(45), W4871, CRL 57368(33)
68470-A      The Limerick Races      De 12252, 9-12252(45), W4873, CRL 57368(33)
                                                 NY  December 9, 1940

69320-A      A Mother's Love            De 12254, 9-12254(45), W4874
69321-A      I Have A Bonnet Trimmed With Blue; Maggie In The Woods-Polkas
                [no vo]                                  De 12253
69322-A      The Flowery Dell; Miss Drury's Reel [no vo]         De 12255
69323-A      Chasing The Chicken; Maid On The Green-Jigs [no vo]  De 12255
69324-A      Miss Fogarty's Christmas Cake
                        De 12254, 9-12254(45), W4873, CRL 57368(33)
```

```
69325-A      Rolling Rocks Of Glan; River Meadow Reel-Reels [no vo]      De 12253
                                                              NY   June 6, 1941

70868-A      Susie O'Malley (Anne McNulty)                              De 12256
70869-A      Molly Bawn                                                 De 12257
70870-A      Far Away In Australia                       De 12256, CRL 57368(33)
70871-A      Mickey Hickey's Band (Kearney)                             De 12257
70872-A      Garryowen; Three Little Drummers-Jigs [no vo]              De 12258
70873-A      Rattigan's Fancy; Blackberry Blossom-Reels [no vo]         De 12258
                                                              NY   June 11, 1942
```

De 12252, 12254 and 12256 are in album A-518.

36.132. Lily Meagher *soprano*

```
W 143674-2   A Letter From Mary Of Mourne                           Co 33165-F
             orch                                          NY   March 17, 1927
```


36.133. Edward Meehan *flute (1900-1940)*

Edward Meehan's Rosaleen Orchestra

```
W 113700-2   Ballyneety; The Piper's Delight-Polkas                  Co 33530-F
W 113701-2   The Honeymoon; The Cora Dhun               Co 33527-F, Vo 84167
W 113702-2   Streams Of Pol-A-Phooka-Reels                          Co 33530-F
W 113703-1   The Scotsman Over The Border               Co 33527-F, Vo 84167
             own fl, Albert Curley-p, others unk                    NY   1933
```

Eddie Meehan And John McKenna

```
62176-A      Tripping To The Well; The Kiss Behind The Door-Polkas
                              De 12104, W4188, Rex U206, JMc unnumbered (C)
62177-A      The Sandlark; Lawson's Favorite-Hornpipes                 De 12104
62178-A      Bridie Morley's Reels                                     De 12096
62179-A      Cook In the Kitchen; Mist On The Meadows-Jigs
                              De 12096, W4188, Rex U206, JMc unnumbered (C)
62180-A      The Maid Behind The Bar-Reel'          De 12120, W4185, Rex U215
62181-A      The Newport Lass; The Hag With The Money-Jigs'
                                             De 12120, W4185, Rex U215
             own, John McKenna-2 fl, F. Fallon-p, 'L. Redican-vln   NY May 5, 1937
```

De 12120 as EDDIE MEEHAN'S ROSALEEN QUARTET, De W4185 and Rex U215 as ROSALEEN QUARTET

36.134. Daniel P. Moroney *whistle*

```
             Trip To The Cottage                                    Co 33172-F
             Harvest Home Hornpipe                                  Co 33236-F
                                                          NY   April 1927
```

36.135. Agnes Morris *soprano*

W 110185-1	Irish Lullaby	Co 33314-F
W 110186-2	Teddy O'Neale	Co 33314-F
		NY December 1928

36.136. James Morrison *violin (1893-1947)*

	Gardiner's Favorite-Reels	NR 1106
	The Provincial-Hornpipes	NR 1106, Sh 33004(33)
	John Muller-p	NY 1921
S 70939-B-C	The Girl That Broke My Heart; The Galway Reel-Reels	
		Ok 21009, Pa E3057, Topic 12T390(33)
S 70940-C	The Mist On The Meadow; The Castlebar Races-Jigs Ok 21009, Pa E3057	
	John Muller-p	NY October 18, 1922
8592-A	Bonnie Kate; Miss Lyons' Fancy; The Haymaker-Reels	
		Ge 5304, OBDW 39015, Starr 9490, Sh 33004(33)
8593	Apples In Winter; Friars Breeches-Jigs	
		Ge 5304, OBDW 39015, Starr 9490
	Arthur P. Kenna-p	NY November 3, 1923
8833-A	The Holly Bush; Captain Kelley; The Moving Bogs-Reels	
		Ge 5446, Starr 9545, Sh 33004(33)
8834-A	The Highland Bonnet-Schottische	Ge 5445, Starr 9569
8835-A	The High Level; Garibaldi-Hornpipe	Ge 5446, Starr 9569
8836-A	Kitty's Wedding; The Rambler-Jigs Ge 5445, Starr 9545, Sh 33004(33)	
	Jack Eldridge-p	NY April 17, 1924
HS 32	Monaghan's Reel; Pigeon On The Gate	Gaelic 502
HS 33	Jackson's Morning Brush; Over The Boulder	Gaelic 502
		NY early 1920s
W 106429-2	The Return Of Spring; The Mountain Pathway-Polkas	
		Co 33088-F, RZ G8939, IZ119, Topic 12T390(33)
W 106430-2	The Glen of Aherlow; Master McGraw-Waltzes	
		Co 33088-F, RZ G6121, G8939, IZ119
W 106431-2	The Lark In The Morning; Wandering Minstrel-Jigs	
		Co 33108-F, RZ G8940
W 106432-2	The Flax In Bloom; The Millstone; The Dairy Maid's Reel	
		Co 33108-F, RZ G8940
	Claire Reardon-p	NY March 1926
W 109330-1	If We Hadn't Any Women In The World {The Bereffoy}-Barn Dance	
		Co 33267-F
W 109331-2	Roderick; Merry Makers-Schottisches	Co 33267-F
W 109332-1	Noon Day Feast; Rambles With Rory-Jigs Co 33277-F, Vo 84133	
W 109333-2	Fisherman's Lilt; Colonel Frazer; New Tobacco-Reels	
		Co 33277-F, Vo 84133, Sh 33004(33)
	Charles Wilkens-bj, unk p	NY May 1928

W 110355-1   The Plains Of Boyle; Lawson's-Hornpipes
                                    Co 33393-F, Vo 84151, Sh 33004(33)
           p   NY February 1929

James Morrison And His Orchestra

W 111466-1   Farmer's Daughter; Little Brown Jug; The Girl I Left Behind Me'
                                    Co 33427-F, Vo 84156, RZ G21241
W 111467-2   Rambles Through Ireland-Pt. 1'   Co 33396-F, Vo 84035, RZ MR137
W 111468-2   Rambles Through Ireland-Pt. 2'   Co 33396-F, Vo 84035, RZ MR137
W 111469-1   Money Musk; Jenny Will You Marry Me?; Keel Row
                                    Co 33427-F, Vo 84156, Topic 12T390(33)
           own vln, unk acn, p, bj, 'Neal Smith-vo   NY December 1929

James Morrison

W 111471-2   Dunphy's Hornpipe; Flower Of Ballymote-Hornpipes
                                    Co 33422-F, Vo 84036, Sh 33004(33)
           p   NY December 1929

W 111626-2   The Wheels Of The World; Rakish Paddy-Reels
                          Co 33422-F, Vo 84036, MS 45001(33), Sh 33001(33)
           p   NY January 1930

The tunes on matrix W 111626 are played in reverse order.

James Morrison And His Orchestra

W 113267-1   The Dawning Of The Day; The Old Rustic Bridge By The Mill; The Flag
                  Of Freedom   Co 33505-F, RZ G21418
W 113268-3   Henry The VIII; My Wild Irish Rose; Sweet Inniscara
                                    Co 33499-F, Vo 84101, RZ G21418
W 113269-1   The Ship That Ne'er Returned; Kelly The Boy From Killan; Bridgeen
                  Bawn Asthore   Co 33499-F, Vo 84101, RZ G21419
              When You And I Were Young, Maggie; Little Mud Wall Cabin; Let Erin
                  Remember   Co 33505-F, RZ G21419
           with vo   NY December 1931

James Morrison

W 114007-2   Thomond Bridge; Souvenir   Co 33534-F, Vo 84053, RZ MR1804
W 114008-2   The Happy Birdie; The Blue Bell-Polkas   Co 33536-F, Vo 84054,
                                    RZ G22539, IZ298, MR1803, Sh 33004(33)
W 114009-2   Miss Langford's Reel; The Milestone At The Garden-Reels
                                    Co 33538-F, Vo 84172, RZ G22590, IZ820
W 114010-2   Strike The Gay Harp; The Legacy-Jigs
                                    Co 33538-F, Vo 84172, RZ G22590, IZ820
W 114011-2   Curlew Hills; Peach Blossoms-Barndances   Co 33536-F, Vo 84054,
                                    RZ G22539, IZ298, MR1803, Topic 12T390(33)
W 114012-2   The Skylark; Maud Miller-Reels
                                    Co 33534-F, Vo 84053, RZ IZ299, MR1804
           p, bj   NY January 21, 1935

James Morrison's Instrumental Quartet

CO 18029-1   The Bed Of Roses-Flings   Co 33544-F, Vo 84104, RZ IZ587, MR1995
CO 18032-1   The Flower Of Spring-Hornpipes
                                    Co 33540-F, Vo 84173, RZ G22667, IZ586, MR1994
              Tailor's Twist; The Flower Of Spring   Topic 12T390(33)
CO 18033-1   Farewell To Ireland-Reels   Co 33544-F, Vo 84173, RZ IZ586, MR1994
              Farewell To Ireland; Miss Monaghan   Topic 12T390(33)
              own vln, Thomas Carmody-acn, unk p, bj   NY August 10, 1935

James Morrison's Instrumental Trio

CO 18030-1   Granuale-Barn Dance   Co 33542-F, Vo 84174, RZ IZ768
CO 18031-1   Flee As A Bird   Co 33542-F, Vo 84174, RZ IZ638
              own and another-2 vln, unk p   NY August 10, 1935

James Morrison

CO 18034-1   The Irish Girl; The Musical Priest; Lord Wellington-Reels
                      Co 33540-F, Vo 84173, RZ G22667, IZ587, MR1995, Sh 33004(33)
              p   NY August 10, 1935

James Morrison's Instrumental Quartet

CO 18567-1   Wreck Of The '99; The Old Pine Tree; Golden Slippers-Waltzes[1] [2]
                                          Co 33548-F, Vo 84057, RZ IZ765
CO 18568-1   When Irish Eyes Are Smiling-Waltzes[2] Co 33548-F, Vo 84057, RZ IZ806
CO 18569-1   Cup Of Tea; Peter Street-Reels[1] Co 33551-F, Vo 84179, RZ IZ766
CO 18570-1   Showman's Fancy; The Sand Lark-Hornpipes[1]
                                          Co 33549-F, Vo 84058, RZ IZ766
CO 18571-1   The Turnpike; Dublin Reel; Miss Thornton-Reels
                                          Co 33549-F, Vo 84058, RZ IZ638
CO 18572-1   Maurice Carmody's Favorite-Jigs   Co 33551-F, Vo 84179, RZ IZ767
              own vln, Tom Banks-p, unk g, [1]Thomas Carmody-acn, [2]unk bj
                                                    NY January 24, 1936

Matrices CO 18569 and CO 18570 as JAMES MORRISON'S TRIO, CO 18571 and CO 18572 as
JAMES MORRISON

CO 19016-1   The Magic Slipper; The Little Diamond-Polkas[1]
                                          Co 33553-F, Vo 84181, RZ IZ767
CO 19017-1   The Festival; Queen Anne's-Flings[1] [2] Co 33555-F, Vo 84148, RZ IZ802
CO 19018-1   The Golden Wreath; The Quarrelsome Piper-Hornpipes[1] [2]
                                          Co 33555-F, Vo 84148, RZ IZ802
CO 19019-1   Belle Of The Ball; Hayes' Favorite-Barn Dances[1] [2]
                                          Co 33554-F, Vo 84105, RZ IZ768
CO 19020-2   Adieu To Innisfail; Believe Me If All Those Endearing Young Charms[2]
                                          Co 33554-F, Vo 84105, RZ IZ806

CO 19021-1   McFadden's; Blackberry Blossom; Tom And Moss' Fancy-Reels
                        Co 33553-F, Vo 84181, RZ IZ765, Sh 33004(33)
              own vln, Tom Banks-p, Martin Christi-g, 'Thomas Carmody-acn, ²2d vln
                                                      NY April 14, 1936

Matrix CO 19017 as JAMES MORRISON'S QUINTET, CO 19021 as JAMES MORRISON

36.137. Thomas Joseph Morrison *flute*

Tom Morrison

8898-A   Tenpenny Bit-Jigs   Ge 5477, OBDW 39027
              Miss McGoldrick-p   NY May 26, 1924

746-A-1   Rising Sun; Limerick Lassies-Reels   NR 2334
746-B-1   Maggie In The Woods-Polkas   NR 2332
747-A-1   The Indian On The Rock; Maids Of Fair Hill-Reels   NR 2332
747-B-1   My Old Clay Pipe; The Cow With One Horn-Jigs   NR 2334
              Ed Geoghegan-p   NY early 1920s

GEX 374-A   Three Merry Sisters; The Star Of Kilkenny-Reels'   OBDW
GEX 375   Clamping The Turf; The Hills Of Connemara-Jigs'   OBDW
GEX 376-A   The Jolly Tinker; The Ballinrobe-Reels   OBDW
GEX 379   The Piper's Back Stitch   OBDW
              p, 'Michael Coleman-vln   NY December 8, 1926

Tom Morrison And John Reynolds

W 108271-1   Dunmore Lassies; Manchester Reel; Castlebar Traveler-Reels
                        Co 33210-F, 33501-F, 37380, Vo 84015, FW 8821(33)
W 108272-2   Sweet Flowers Of Milltown; The Boys From Knock-Schottische
                        Co 33210-F, 33501-F, 37380, Vo 84015
              own fl, John Reynolds-tam   NY September 1927

W 108925-2   Maggie In The Woods-Polka   Co 33260-F
W 108926-2   Indian On The Rock; The Jolly Plowboy; The Fox Chase-Reels
                                                                  Co 33260-F
W 108927-2   Roscommon Reel   Co 33247-F, 33503-F, Vo 84020
W 108928-1   The London Clog-Hornpipe   Co 33247-F, 33503-F, Vo 84020
              as before, Ed Gagan (Geoghegan)-p   NY March 1928

W 109736-2   The Connaught Reel; The Shepherd's Daughter-Reels
                                                  Co 33293-F, Vo 84135
W 109737-2   The Cow That Ate The Blanket-Jig'   Co 33293-F, Vo 84135
W 109738-3   Kregg's Pipes; The Boys From Mayo-Reels Co 33308-F, Vo 84023
W 109739-2   The Little Green Cottage-Polka   Co 33308-F, Vo 84023
              as before, but 'Reynolds omitted   NY September 1928

W 110962-1   The Rattling Rover; The Westport Reel   Co 33434-F, Vo 84037
W 110963-2   The Pretty Girls From The West-Jigs   Co 33434-F, Vo 84037
W 110964-1   The Holy Land; The Star Of Kilkenny-Reels Co 33370-F, Vo 84091
W 110965-1   The Boys From Galway-Polka   Co 33370-F, Vo 84091
              p   NY July 1929

36.138. W.J. Mullaly *concertina (1884-1959)*

W 106415-1	Jackson's Thought-Jig	Co 33086-F, RZ G8938, IZ118
W 106416-1	Lady Carbury; The Races Of Athlone-Reels	Co 33086-F, RZ G8938, IZ118

Ed Geoghegan-p   NY March 1926

BVE 37017-1	The Green Groves Of Erin; The Ivy Leaf-Reels	
		Vi 79097, HMV B2556, IM383
BVE 37018-1	Drumraney Lass; Jug Of Brown Ale-Jigs	Vi 79097
BVE 37019-2	Within A Mile Of Dublin; West Meath Hunt-Reels	
		Vi 79199, HMV B2887, IM390
BVE 37020-1	Humors Of Mullinger; Jackson's Wife-Jigs	Vi 79199

Edward Lee-p   Camden, NJ November 22, 1926

BVE 38935-2	Little House Under The Hill-Jig	Vi 20814
BVE 38936-2	Tory Island Reel	Vi 20814
BVE 38937-3	Miss Monroe's Jig	Vi 20763
BVE 38938-1	Salamanca; Peter Street-Reels	Vi 20763

as before   Camden, NJ June 6, 1927

36.139. James J. Mullan *baritone*

BVE 38063-2	Barney McShane	Vi rej
BVE 38064-3	If You're Irish Come Into The Parlor	Vi rej

Edward Lee-p   Camden, NJ June 10, 1927

James Mullan (High Chief Ranger, USA Irish National Foresters)

W 109104-2	Arrah, Come In Out Of The Rain, Barney McShane
	Co 33262-F, RZ IZ205, MR926
W 109107-1	If You're Irish¹ Co 33264-F, IFB313, RZ IZ195, MR695, Vo 84083

Four Provinces Orchestra: John Kennedy or John McCormick-vln, Sam
Moore-acn, Edward Lee-p, unk bj, ¹2d male vo   NY March 1928

W 110137-2	I Don't Care If I Do Co 33364-F, IFB313, RZ G20713, IZ195, MR695
W 110139-1	I Don't Work For A Living (Edward Lee-James J. Mullan)¹
	Co 33324-F, Vo 84028, RZ MR23

Four Provinces Orchestra: vln, p, bj, ¹2d male vo   NY December 1928

RZ G20713 as FOUR PROVINCES ORCHESTRA

W 111247-2	Fish And Chips	Co 33379-F, Vo 84031, RZ IZ350, MR343
W 111249-2	Jim Whelahan's Automobile	Co 33420-F, RZ IZ223, MR1108
W 111250-3	Murphy	Co 33404-F, Vo 84153, RZ IZ350, MR343
W 111253-2	The Rocky Road To Dublin	Co 33389-F, Vo 84150, RZ G20738

as before   NY November 1929

Jim Mullan

W 112121-1-3	When Will We Have Prohibition	Co 33419-F, RZ IZ203, MR924
W 112122-1	The Wee Duck	Co 33428-F, RZ IZ205, MR926

```
W 112124-3    Hippity Hop                       Co 33432-F, RZ IZ224, MR1109
W 112126-1    Typical Tipperary      Co 33456-F, Vo 84043, RZ IZ224, MR1109
              as before                                        NY  May 1930
```

James Mullan (The Singing Insurance Man)

```
W 113341-1    In The Garden Where The Praties Grow
                                     Co 33507-F, Vo 84048, RZ IZ203, MR924
W 113342-1    Drumcolliher           Co 33513-F, Vo 84049, RZ IZ301, MR1806
W 113343-1    Jimmy The Fiddler      Co 33504-F, Vo 84163, RZ IZ223, MR1108
W 113344-1    Song Of The Thirty-Two Counties          Co 33513-F, Vo 84049
W 113345-1    The Limerick Races     Co 33504-F, Vo 84163, RZ IZ204, MR925
W 113346-1    Let Mr. Maguire Sit Down   Co 33507-F, Vo 84048, RZ IZ204, MR925
              as before                                   NY  January 1932
```

36.140. E. Mullaney-P. Stack *instrumental*

```
BVE 36225-1   Harvest Home-Hornpipe                     Vi 79002, Yv K-518
BVE 36226-1   Maid In A Cherry Tree-Reel    Vi 79003, MS 45001(33), Sh 33001(33)
BVE 36227-2   Four Courts Of Dublin-Reel                Vi 79012, Yv K-518
BVE 36228-1   Mullaney Favorite; Ladies' Pantalettes-Reels         Vi 79012
BVE 36229-1   Chicago Reel                                         Vi 79002
BVE 36230-1   Rambling Pitchfork-Jig         Vi 79003, FW FP18(33), FW6818(33)
              Edward Mullaney (ca 1885-1971)-bagpipes, Patrick Stack-vln
                               Webster Hotel, Chicago  September 13, 1926
```

Folkways FP18 and FW6818 as E. MULLANEY-P.STARCK

36.141. Martin Mullin *violin*

```
W 107798-1    Irish Mary-Reel                                   Co 33224-F
              Johnny Knocked Over His Uncle                     Co 33164-F
              Dan Sullivan-p                              NY  April 1927
```

36.142. Frank Murphy *accordion*

```
BVE 41533-1   Eel In The Sink                          Vi 21318, HMV B3402
BVE 41534-2   Mayo Hornpipe                            Vi 21318, HMV B3402
              Ed Geoghegan-p                      NY  January 10, 1928

BVE 43998-2   Cuckoo's Nest-Reel                                  Vi 21480
BVE 43999-1   Rakes Of Clonmell-Jig    Vi V-29008, Bb B-4993, MW M-8635, HMV B3395
BVE 45500-1   Mason's Apron-Reel                 Vi V-29008, HMV B3395
BVE 45501-1   Sterling Castle-Fling                              Vi 21480
              as before                          NY  May 21, 1928
```

36.143. Jack Murphy *vocal, accordion*

```
BVE 40216-2   Widow Magee                                        Vi 20975
BVE 40217-1   I Was Driving My Cart To Ould Castle Fair          Vi 21001
```

```
BVE 40218-2    Her Golden Hair Was Hanging Down Her Back-Barn Dance [no vo]  Vi rej
BVE 40219-1    Sweet Maids Of Caven; Saddle The Pony-Jigs [no vo]          Vi 20975
            Ed Geoghegan-p                                 NY  September 16, 1927

BVE 40218-3    Her Golden Hair Was Hanging Down Her Back-Barn Dance [no vo]
                                                                         Vi 21001
BVE 38593-2    Little Judy's Reel [no vo]                                   Vi rej
BVE 38594-2    Mary On The Peach Tree-Jig [no vo]                      Vi V-29073
BVE 38595-2    Out For The Water; The Kettle To Boil                     Vi 21317
BVE 38596-2    Shake Hands With Your Uncle, Mike Me Boy (Jack Murphy)    Vi 21087
BVE 38597-2    Outside Casey's Cabin (Jack Murphy, arr Ed Geoghegan)     Vi 21317
BVE 38598-2    The Village Blacksmith (Jack Murphy, arr Ed Geoghegan)    Vi 21087
BVE 38599-2    The Irish Rover (Jack Murphy)                             Vi 21014
BVE 39855-2    The Courting Of Nan O'Shea (Jack Murphy)                  Vi 21014
            as before                            Camden, NJ  September 27, 1927

BVE 38593-3    Little Judy's Reel [no vo]                              Vi V-29073
BVE 41128-2    Paddy Be Aisy                                             Vi 21158
BVE 41129-1    Kelly's Old Gray Mare                                     Vi 21158
BVE 41130-2    The Limerick Wedding (Jack Murphy)                        Vi 21177
BVE 41131-2    Haste To The Wedding¹                                     Vi 21177
            as before, ¹John Carroll, Pat Delaney-2 hca   NY  November 30, 1927
```

36.144. James Murphy *accordion*

```
86117-1        Maid Of Athlone-Jig                              Co E4792, 33030-F
86118-1        Maid Behind The Bar-Reel                                  Co E4792
86119-1        Salamanca                                 Co E4830, 33031-F, 14163
86122-1        Shaskeen                                  Co E4830, 33031-F, 14163
            p                                                    NY  March 1920
```

36.145. New York Street Band

```
            The Festival Polka                                        Co 33515-F
            Sidewalks Of New York                                     Co 33515-F
                                                                     NY  1932
```

36.146. Neil Nolan *banjo*

```
BVE 47758-1    Boys Of The Lough; Teetotalers-Reels        Vi V-29000, HMV B3396
BVE 47759-1    Floggin' Reel; Miss McCloud's Reel                    Vi V-29000
            Dan Sullivan-p                                  NY  October 17, 1928

BVE 50740-2    Speed The Plough; Soldier's Joy-Reels                 Vi V-29039
BVE 50741-1    Miller's Reel; Duffy The Dancer-Reels  Vi V-29039, Topic 12T366(33)
            as before                                       NY  March 11, 1929

BVE 53683-2    Arkansaw Traveler-Country Dance                       Vi V-29052
BVE 53684-2    Mullingar Races; Wexford Lassies            Vi V-29052, HMV B3396
BVE 53685-2    Tomorrow Morning; Smoky Chimney-Hornpipes¹            Vi V-29057
            as before, ¹Murty Rabbett-fl                     NY  May 28, 1929
```

```
BVE 55633-2   Nolan's Favorite Reels                              Vi V-29068
BVE 55634-2   The Dancing Master-Jig                              Vi V-29068
              Dan Sullivan-p                              NY  July 26, 1929
```

36.147. Sean Nolan *violin*

Sean Nolan's Dublin Orchestra

```
BVE 35782-1   Repeal Of Union; The Gallbally Farmer; The Wedding-Jigs
                                        Vi 79005, V-153, HMV B2553
BVE 35783-2   The Green Castle; The Derry; The Liverpool-Hornpipes
                                        Vi 79005, 0155, V-153, HMV B2553
              own vln, unk pic, acn, p                  NY  July 19, 1926
```

Vi 0155 was distributed for theater use.

Sean Nolan

```
BVE 35784-2   The Coolin                                            Vi rej
                                                         NY  July 19, 1926
```

```
BVE 35599-1   Stack Of Barley {Little Stack}; Rights Of Man-Highland Flings
                                Vi 79004, Bb B-4958, MW M-8631, HMV B2887, IM390
              Lew Shilkret-p                             NY  July 22, 1926
```

```
BVE 36015-4   Teddy O'Neale; The Pretty Girl Milking Her Cow-Old Irish Airs Vi rej
BVE 36016-3   Barney's Favorite; Swallow's Tail; Blackberry Blossom-Reels  Vi rej
              as before                                  NY  August 2, 1926
```

```
BVE 36015-7   Teddy O'Neale; The Pretty Girl Milking Her Cow-Old Irish Airs Vi rej
BVE 36016-5   Barney's Favorite; Swallow's Tail; Blackberry Blossom-Reels
                                        Vi 79004, HMV B2556, IM383
              as before                                  NY  August 10, 1926
```

All issues of matrix BVE 36016 show titles for matrix BVE 36015.

Sean Nolan's Dublin Orchestra

```
BVE 37754-2   The Showman's Fancy; Vinegar Hill; The Boys Of Bluehill-Hornpipes'
                                        Vi 79219, HMV B2885
BVE 37755-2   The Shaskeen Reel; The Hawthorn Bush; The Galway Reel-Reels'
                                        Vi 79219, HMV B2885
BVE 37756-1   The Bantry Hunt; Glengariffs Pride; The Pet Of The Pipers-Jigs
                                        Vi 79264, HMV B2886
BVE 37757-2   The Leinster Echo; The Honeysuckle; The Star Hornpipe-Hornpipes
                                        Vi 79264, HMV B2886
              own vln, unk p, 'pic, acn                 NY  February 9, 1927
```

Vi 79264 and HMV B2886 as SEAN NOLAN

```
BVE 39241-2   Thomond Bridge; Standing Abbey-Hornpipes              Vi 20764
BVE 39242-2   The Crazy Fiddler; The New Fiddle-Hornpipes           Vi 20764
```

```
BVE 39243-2   Larry Coggan; Saddle The Pony; Jackson's Morning-Jigs        Vi 20815
BVE 39244-1   The Avonmore; Green Gate; Honeymoon-Reels                    Vi 20815
              own vln, unk pic, acn, p, bj                   NY  June 13, 1927


BVE 40593-1   The Kinnegad Slashers; The Ticknock Jig; The Unknown-Jigs
                                                             Vi 21157, HMV B3232
BVE 40594-2   Sheehan's Reel; The Soldier's Joy; The Peeler's Jacket-Reels
                                                             Vi 21181, HMV B3390
BVE 40595-2   The Morehampton Hornpipes; Twenty One Mount Shannon; Martin's
                   Favorite-Hornpipes                        Vi 21181, HMV B3390
BVE 40596-1   The Pledge; Maids Of Tulla; The Moon Coin-Reels  Vi 21157, HMV B3232
              own vln, unk pic, acn, p                 NY  November 18, 1927


BVE 45107-1   When The Kettle Boils Over; Haste To The Wedding-Jigs
                                                             Vi 21660, HMV B3391
BVE 45108-1   Bonnie Kate-Reel Vi 21544, Bb B-4931, MW M-8947, Yv K-504, HMV B3392
BVE 45109-2   Donnal's Favorite-Hornpipe                     Vi 21660, HMV B3391
BVE 45110-2   The Humors Of Bandon-Set Dance                 Vi 21544, HMV B3392
BVE 45111-2   The Washerwoman-Jig             Vi 21479, Bb B-4956, MW M-8629
BVE 45112-2   St. Patrick's Day-Jig                          Vi 21479, Yv K-529
              own vln, unk pic, acn, p                    NY  May 4, 1928
```

36.148. John Oakley *bass*

```
W 175236-1    test recording                                              Co
                                                       NY  December 7, 1926


W 107832-2    O'Donnell Aboo                                         Co 33174-F
W 107833-2    Father O'Flynn                                         Co 33174-F
                                                         NY   April 1927


W 107990-1    Bantry Bay                                   Co 33188-F, Ok 21047
W 107991-2    Bold Jack Donohue                            Co 33188-F, Ok 21047
                                                          NY   June 1927


W 108448-1    Kevin Barry                                  Co 33244-F, Vo 84018
W 108449-3    The Queen Of Connemara                                Co 33288-F
              orch                                         NY   October 1927


W 108670-2    Wrap The Green Flag 'Round Me, Boys          Co 33244-F, Vo 84018
                                                          NY   January 1928


W 109028-1    The Heart Bow'd Down (M.W. Balfe)                      Co 33266-F
              orch                                         NY   March 1928


W 109138-2    My Dark Rosaleen (Alicia A. Needham)                   Co 33266-F
              orch                                         NY   April 1928


W 109597-3    The Winding Banks Of Erne                              Co 33288-F
              orch                                         NY   August 1928


              Well, The Irish And The Germans Got Together          Co 33253-F
              They Landed Over Here                                 Co 33253-F
```

```
                Kelly, The Boy From Killan                         Co 33306-F
                The Shan Van Vocht                                 Co 33306-F
                Away In Athlone                          Co 33358-F, Ok 21080
                My Galway Girl                           Co 33358-F, Ok 21080
                                                              NY    1928-9
```

36.149. Donnell O'Brien *vocal*

```
BVE 37876-2   The Mountains O' Mourne (Percy French, arr Houston Collison)  Vi rej
BVE 37877-2   Eileen Oge (Percy French, arr Houston Collison)                Vi rej
              orch d Bruno Reibold                    Camden, NJ  March 30, 1927

BVE 37876-3   The Mountains O' Mourne (Percy French, arr Houston Collison)
                                                          Vi 79323, Bb B-4930
BVE 37877-5   Eileen Oge (Percy French, arr Houston Collison)         Vi 79323
              as before                              Camden, NJ  April 14, 1927

BVE 39220-3   Too Ra Loo Ra Loo Ral, That's An Irish Lullaby (J.R. Shannon)
                                                                      Vi 20816
BVE 39221-2   The Little Irish Girl (Edward Teschemacher-Hermann Lohr)  Vi 20816
              2 vln, vc, p, d Leonard Joy                      NY  June 6, 1927

BVE 49217-2   O'Laughlin (Carson Robison)                            Vi V-29010
BVE 49218-2   The Heroes Of The Vestris (Carson Robison)             Vi V-29010
              orch d Leonard Joy                        NY  December 1, 1928
```

36.150. George O'Brien *tenor*

```
W 106754-2    The Meeting Of The Waters          Co 33100-F, RZ IZ247, MR1380
W 106755-1    The Valley Lay Smiling Before Me   Co 33100-F, RZ IZ247, MR1380
W 106756-1    'Tis The Last Rose Of Summer             Co 33102-F, Vo 84118
              orch                                            NY  May 1926

W 106869-1    The Harp That Once Thro' Tara's Halls    Co 33102-F, Vo 84118
W 106870-2    Believe Me If All Those Endearing Young Charms     Co 33124-F
W 106871-3    Kilkenny                                           Co 33124-F
              orch                                            NY  June 1926

W 107327-1    It Is A Charming Girl I Love, from "The Lily Of Killarney"
                 (Sir Julius Benedict)                           Co 33142-F
W 107328-1    Eily Mavourneen, from "The Lily Of Killarney" (Sir Julius Benedict)
                                                                 Co 33142-F
W 107329-1    Let Erin Remember The Days Of Old (arr N. Clifford Page)
                                                    Co 33127-F, RZ G8945, IZ124
W 107330-1    The Gap In The Hedge                                Co 33127-F
              orch                                         NY  November 1926

BVE 36790-2   Skibbereen {County Tyrone}        Vi 79065, HMV B2558, IM384
BVE 36791-2   The Darlin' Girl From Clare (Percy French)
                                             Vi 79064, Bb B-4977, Yv K-503
BVE 36792-2   The Blarney Roses (w: A. Melville, m: Flint)
                             Vi 79065, Bb B-4977, Yv K-517, HMV B2558, IM384
```

BVE 36793-3 The Hills Of Donegal (P.J. O'Reilly-Wilfrid Sanderson)   Vi 79064
             orch d Rosario Bourdon   Camden, NJ December 3, 1926

W 107830-2   That Old Irish Mother Of Mine   Co 33186-F, Vo 84009
W 107831-1   A Shawl From Galway   Co 33186-F, Vo 84009
             vln, cl, p, sbs   NY April 1927

W 107992-2   The Moon Has Raised Her Lamp Above'   Co 33208-F
W 108173-1   Killarney, My Home O'er The Sea   Co 33194-F, Vo 84079, Cq 9561
W 108174-2   Come Back To Erin   Co 33194-F, Vo 84079
             orch, 'with John Oakley   NY June 1927

George O'Brien And John Oakley

W 108447-3   When Thro' Life Unblest We Rove   Co 33208-F
             orch   NY ca October 1927

George O'Brien

W 108668-1   For Killarney And You   Co 33232-F
W 108669-2   Green Isle Of Erin   Co 33232-F
                                                        NY January 1928

W 109136-2   Marguerite (White)   Co 33275-F
W 109137-1   The Song That Reached My Heart (Jordon)   Co 33275-F
                                                        NY March 1928

W 109799-1   Rose Machree   Co 33378-F
W 109800-1   Sweet Little Peggy O'Shea   Co 33378-F
             orch   NY October 1928

             Casey, The Fiddler   Co 33203-F
             Rory O'Moore   Co 33203-F
             They Call It Old Ireland   Co 33294-F, RZ G20568
             There's A Mother Back In Ireland Waits For Me Co 33294-F, RZ G20568
             Ireland   Co 33325-F
             Mavourneen Roamin'   Co 33325-F
                                                        NY 1927-9

W 110327-2   Maggie Murphy's Home   Co 33384-F, Vo 84093
W 110328-2   Macushla Machree   Co 33331-F, RZ MR161
W 110329-2   Colleen O'Mine   Co 33331-F, RZ MR161
                                                        NY January 1929

W 110393-2   My Dad's Dinner Pail   Co 33384-F, Vo 84093
                                                        NY February 1929

W 110731-2   I'm Sure There Must Be A Heaven   Co 33398-F
                                                        NY May 1929

36.151. Jerry O'Brien *accordion*

W 110043-2	Little Judy-Reel	Co 33367-F, Vo 84029, RZ G20454
W 110064-2	The Kildare Fancy-Hornpipe	Co 33312-F, Vo 84026, RZ IZ192, MR692
	p	NY November 1928

36.152. Joe O'Callahan *tenor*

W 105814-2	The Cruiskeen Lawn	Co 33005-F
W 105815-2	The Irish Exile	Co 33005-F
	orch	NY August 1925
	Molly O'Shea	Co 33087-F
	The Rocky Road To Dublin (Isn't Rocky Any More)	Co 33087-F
		NY 1926

36.153. Doreen O'Dare *vocal*

39117-A	That Old Wooden Rocker (Crumit)	De 12044, Rex U465
	acn, cel	NY November 14, 1934

De 12044 shows matrix number 39017 in the wax.

39126-A	Great Grandma	De 12022
39127-A	Granny's Old Armchair (Frank Crumit)'	De 12022, Rex U465
39128-A	My Mother's Old Red Shawl	De 12044
	vln, acn, 'p	NY November 16, 1934

36.154. Felix O'Day *tenor*

7794-A	Dear Little Shamrock (Cherry)	Ge 4847
7795-A	The Pretty Girl Milking Her Cow	Ge 4847
	orch	NY March 10, 1922
7818	Father O'Flynn (Graves)	Ge 4865
7819	Molly Brannigan	Ge 4865
	orch	NY March 30, 1922

36.155. Seamus O'Doherty *tenor*

9492	Haste To The Weddin'	Ge 5724, OBDW 39012
9493-A	The Maid O' The Sweet Brown Knowe	Ge 5724, OBDW 39012
	Josephine Smith-p	NY April 29, 1925
W 105871-2	The Rose Of Tralee (Charles W. Glover)	Co 33065-F, 3923, Vo 84068
W 105872-2	The Old Bog Road (M.K. O'Farrelley)	Co 33065-F, 4032, Vo 84068
W 105873-2	Miss Kitty O'Toole	Co 33066-F, 4032
W 105882-2	Kitty Of Colairne	Co 33066-F, 3923
	orch	NY September 1925

W 106256-1   Emmet's Farewell To His Love (arr Josephine Smith)
                                    Co 33079-F, RZ G9176, IZ125
W 106257-1   Pearse To Ireland (arr Josephine Smith)
                                    Co 33095-F, Vo 84072, RZ IZ190, MR690
W 106258-1   The Cuckoo's Call (arr Josephine Smith) Co 33079-F, RZ G9176, IZ125
W 106259-4   Skibbereen (arr Josephine Smith)   Co 33098-F, Vo 84073
          orch   NY   January 1926

W 106580-2   The Leprehann (arr Josephine Smith)   Co 33098-F
              The Leprechaun   Vo 84073
W 106581-2   Danny Boy (Londonderry Air) Co 33095-F, Vo 84072, Cq 9560, RZ MR690
          orch   NY   April 1926

W 106878-2   The Maid Of The Sweet Brown Knowe (arr Josephine Smith)
                                    Co 33101-F, Vo 84117, RZ G8945, IZ124
W 106879-2   Jug Of Punch (arr Josephine Smith)   Co 33109-F
W 106880-1   The Blarney Roses (D. Frame Flint)   Co 33109-F
W 106881-3   The Ould Plaid Shawl   Co 33101-F, Vo 84117
          orch   NY   June 1926

W 107255-2   Una Waun   Co 33116-F
W 107256-2   Eileen Aroon   Co 33116-F
          Josephine Smith-p   NY   November 1926

W 143194-2   Molly Bawn (Samuel Lover)   Co 33143-F
W 143195-1   Bells Of Shandon   Co 33137-F, Vo 84001, RZ IZ1076, MR3345
W 143196-1   The Mountains O' Mourne   Co 33137-F, 33165-F, Vo 84001
W 143197-2   Norah, The Pride Of Kildare (J. Parry)   Co 33143-F
          orch   NY   ca December 17, 1926

W 143318-3   Drumin Donn Dilis   Co 33158-F
W 143319-2   Sal Og Ruad   Co 33158-F
          Josephine Smith-p   NY   January 19, 1927

W 143652-1   Nellie, Me Love And Me   Co 33196-F, Vo 84011
W 143653-2   I'll Take You Home Again, Kathleen   Co 33169-F, Vo 84007, Cq 9561
W 143654-3   Molly Brannigan   Co 33169-F, Vo 84007
          orch   NY   March 4, 1927

W 108185-1   When It's Moonlight In Mayo   Co 33196-F, Vo 84011
W 108186-1   The Hills Of Donegal (Sanderson)
                          Co 33209-F, IFB320, Vo 84014, RZ IZ244, MR1377
W 108187-2   The Tri-Colored Ribbon (arr Josephine Smith)
                          Co 33209-F, Vo 84014, RZ IZ246, MR1379
          orch   NY   June 1927

W 108355-2   I'll Be With You When The Roses Bloom Again
                          Co 33205-F, Vo 84013, RZ IZ279, MR1742
W 108356-2   The Darlin' Girl From Clare   Co 33219-F, Vo 84080
W 108357-2   I Left Ireland And Mother Because We Were Poor
                          Co 33205-F, IFB320, RZ G22362, IZ244, MR1377
W 108358-1   The Glen Of Aherlow   Co 33219-F, Vo 84080
          orch   NY   September 1927

```
W 108763-2   The Pride Of Tipperary         Co 33252-F, RZ G20343, IZ273, MR1616
W 108764-1   The Stutterin' Lovers          Co 33252-F, RZ G20343, IZ279, MR1742
             Josephine Smith-p                              NY  February 1928

W 108901-1   Shall My Soul Pass Through Ireland
                                   Co 33241-F, Vo 84081, RZ G22362, IZ246, MR1379
W 108902-1   Ned O'The Hill            Co 33241-F, Vo 84081, RZ IZ245, MR1378
W 108903-1   Just A Rose In Old Killarney      Co 33257-F, Vo 84130, RZ G20345
W 108904-2   A Little Bunch Of Shamrocks       Co 33257-F, Vo 84130, RZ G20345
             vln, fl, cl, p, bbs                              NY  March 1928

W 109390-2   John Mitchell (arr Josephine Smith)                     Co 33273-F
                                                              NY  June 1928

W 109465-2   She Lived Beside The Anner (arr Josephine Smith)        Co 33273-F
                                                              NY  July 1928

W 109801-1   Limerick Is Beautiful               Co 33377-F, RZ IZ245, MR1378
                                                              NY  October 1928

             The Next Market Day; The Ballymore Ballad              Co 33289-F
             By The Short Cut To The Rosses                         Co 33289-F
                                                              NY  ca 1928

W 110117-1   My Irish Home Sweet Home    Co 33313-F, Vo 84138, RZ IZ153, MR160
W 110118-2   Mother In Ireland           Co 33313-F, Vo 84138, RZ IZ153, MR160
                                                              NY  December 1928

W 110720-2   Let Me Carry Your Cross For Ireland       Co 33360-F, RZ IZ542
W 110721-2   Colleen Oge Asthore                 Co 33377-F, RZ IZ245, MR1378
                                                              NY  May 1929

W 110926-2   Going Home To Ireland                     Co 33360-F, RZ MR1986
                                                              NY  ca July 1929

W 111065-    When The Fields Are White With Daisies I'll Return        Co rej
W 111066-2   In A Little Town Near By            Co 33407-F, RZ IZ189, MR689
                                                              NY  September 1929

W 111065-5   When The Fields Are White With Daisies I'll Return
                                                   Co 33399-F, RZ G20692
W 111217-2   Barbara Allen                       Co 33412-F, RZ IZ158, MR248
W 111218-2   I Saw From The Beach                Co 33407-F, RZ IZ158, MR248
W 111219-2   The Blackbird             Co 33407-F, RZ G20692, IZ189, MR689
             vln, vc, p                                      NY  October 1929

W 111398-1   The Boys Of Wexford[1]  Co 33386-F, IFB309, Vo 84033, 84188, RZ IZ181,
                                                              MR129, MR634
W 111399-3   The Legion Of The Rear Guard {The Song Of The Republic}-Rallying
                  Song[1]     Co 33386-F, IFB309, Vo 84033, 84188, RZ MR129, MR634
             The Song Of The Legion Of The Rear Guard (J. O'Sheehan)    RZ IZ181
W 111400-1   Hail! Glorious Saint Patrick[2]         Co 33395-F, RZ IZ145, MR130
```

```
W 111401-2    The Shrine At The Miracle Grave (Reilly-Duffy)
                                    Co 33395-F, RZ IZ145, MR130
              Josephine Smith-p, ¹Irish Volunteers-chorus, ²2d male vo
                                         NY  December 1929


              The Moon Behind The Hill              Co 33340-F
              The Connemara Shore                   Co 33340-F
              Dhreenaun Dhown                       Co 33399-F
                                                    NY   1929


W 112093-1    Ireland, Mother Ireland    Co 33429-F, RZ IZ580, MR1985
W 112094-2    For The Green              Co 33429-F, RZ IZ580, MR1985
W 112095-2    Because I Love You So       Co 33424-F, RZ MR1986
W 112096-2    My Heart's In Ireland Still    Co 33424-F, RZ IZ542
                                              NY  May 1930


W 112338-2    Take Me Back To Old Erin Again      Co 33439-F, Vo 84039
W 112340-3    Eileen Alannah                      Co 33439-F, Vo 84039
              The Jackets Green                            Co 33442-F
              Old Donegal                                 Co 33442-F
          orch                              NY  September 1930
```

36.156. Joseph D. O'Donnell *spoken*

```
BVE 40727-2   O'Hoolihan's Wake (J. O'Donnell)-Pt. 1¹       Vi 21095
BVE 40728-2   O'Hoolihan's Wake (J. O'Donnell)-Pt. 2        Vi 21095
BVE 40729-2   O'Hoolihan's Wake (J. O'Donnell)-Pt. 3        Vi 21096
BVE 40730-1   O'Hoolihan's Wake (J. O'Donnell)-Pt. 4¹       Vi 21096
BVE 40731-1   Mike Sherbalya (J. O'Donnell)-Pt. 1¹          Vi rej
BVE 40732-1   Mike Sherbalya (J. O'Donnell)-Pt. 2²          Vi rej
              ¹Basil Fomeen-acn          Camden, NJ  November 21, 1927


BVE 41238-2   Says Mike (Joseph D. O'Donnell)-Pt. 1         Vi 21162
BVE 41239-1   Says Mike (Joseph D. O'Donnell)-Pt. 2         Vi 21162
BVE 41240-2   Says Mike (Joseph D. O'Donnell)-Pt. 3         Vi rej
BVE 41241-2   Says Mike (Joseph D. O'Donnell)-Pt. 4         Vi rej
BVE 41242-1   The League Of Laughs (Joseph D. O'Donnell)-Pt. 1   Vi 21161
BVE 41243-1   The League Of Laughs (Joseph D. O'Donnell)-Pt. 2   Vi 21161
                                         Camden, NJ  December 19, 1927
```

Vi 21162 as MIKE SHERBALYA

Joseph O'Donnell And Nancy Van

```
BVE 45113-2   Expectin' A Son (Joseph O'Donnell)-Pt. 1      Vi 21446
BVE 45114-1   Expectin' A Son (Joseph O'Donnell)-Pt. 2      Vi 21446
BVE 45115-2   The Ould Gent And The Flapper (Joseph O'Donnell)-Pt. 1   Vi 21721
BVE 45116-2   The Ould Gent And The Flapper (Joseph O'Donnell)-Pt. 2   Vi 21721
BVE 45117-2   Ballyhootch (Joseph O'Donnell)-Pt. 1          Vi 21592
BVE 45118-2   Ballyhootch (Joseph O'Donnell)-Pt. 2          Vi 21592
              Nancy Van-talking/p               NY  May 7, 1928
```

Joseph O'Donnell And Betty Singer

BVE 48311-1	The Irish Jubilee (James Thornton-Chas. Lawler)-Pt. 1	Vi rej
BVE 48312-1	The Irish Jubilee (James Thornton-Chas. Lawler)-Pt. 2	Vi rej
BVE 48313-1	The Irish Wedding (Dan Maguinness, arr William Gooch)-Pt. 1	
		Vi V-29070
BVE 48314-1	The Irish Wedding (Dan Maguinness, arr William Gooch)-Pt. 2	
		Vi V-29070
BVE 48315-2	Abe Cohen's River Shannon	Vi V-29026
BVE 48316-2	Tim McCarthy's Daughter	Vi V-29026
	p, bj	NY January 28, 1929

36.157. Thomas O'Dowd *baritone*

1-2-3	The Orange, White And Green {The Song Of Erin's Flag}	
	(Thomas O'Dowd)	Pm unnumbered
2-1-3	Up! De Valera (Thomas O'Dowd)	Pm unnumbered
3-1	Let Him Rest In Sweet Erin (With Emmett And Tone) (O'Dowd)	
		Pm unnumbered
4-2	The Wearing Of The Green-New Version (O'Dowd)	Pm unnumbered
	orch	NY 1922

Matrices 1 and 2 are coupled, as are 3 and 4, which have "Famous Songs of Irish Freedom" in place of the label name.

	Michael Collins Rosary (Thomas O'Dowd)	O'Dowd 111
	Irish Battle Cry Of Freedom (Thomas O'Dowd)	O'Dowd 112
	p	NY ca 1922

Label note: Famous Songs of Irish Freedom (This Record Made Exclusively for Thomas O'Dowd, New York). O'Dowd 111 and 112 are coupled.

	De Valera, You're The Man (Thomas O'Dowd)	O'Dowd 900
	1922 Wearing Of The Green (Thomas O'Dowd)	O'Dowd 900
	p	NY 1922
	The Valley Lay Smiling Before Me	O'Dowd 902
	If It Wouldn't Do For Sam 'Twould Never Do For Pat (O'Dowd)	
		O'Dowd 902
	Richard Bernard-p	NY ca 1922

36.158. Shaun O'Farrell *tenor*

169-A	The Irish Volunteer	Ge
170-A	The Darlin' Girl From Clare	Ge
		NY ca March 2, 1922
734-	Three Colored Ribbon	NR 2324
734-	Skibbereen	NR 2324
	Bridget Flynn	NR 2325
	Phil The Fluter's Ball	NR 2325
		NY early 1920s

```
8799-A        The Star Of County Down                        Ge 5434, OBDW 39004
8800-A        The Darling Girl From Clare        Ge 5469, OBDW 39005, Starr 9540
              orch                                             NY  March 19, 1924

8811-A        When Shall The Day Dawn In Erin (Hogan)        Ge 5434, OBDW 39004
8812-A        Blarney Roses                      Ge 5469, OBDW 39005, Starr 9540
              orch                                             NY  April 1, 1924

9333-A        When They Ask You What Your Name Is (Casting-Godfrey)
                                                             Ge 5666, OBDW 39008
9334-A        Kate Muldoon (The Old Boreen) (Stewart)        Ge 5666, OBDW 39008
              Jimmie O'Brien-p                             NY  February 10, 1925

BVE 41404-2   The Irish Volunteer (Shaun O'Farrell)                     Vi 21178
BVE 41405-2   Mary You're Contrary (Shaun O'Farrell)                    Vi 21178
              2 vln, fl, vc, p, bbs, dm, d Bruno Reibold
                                                  Camden, NJ  December 9, 1927
```

36.159. Emmet O'Hara *vocal*

Some issues may be as EMMET O'MARA

```
S 71584-A     Eileen Allana                                              Ok 4895
              The Wearin' Of The Green                      Ok 4790, Pa E3061
                                                              NY  ca May 1923
```

36.160. Cathol O'Hare *baritone*

```
O 8162-A      Who Fears To Speak Of Easter Week                        Ok 21004
                                                               NY  ca 1921
```

36.161. Michael Gus O'Keefe *bass*

```
W 110733-2    Pride Of Petravore                                      Co 33363-F
W 110734-2    Off To Philadelphia                                     Co 33363-F
              orch                                             NY  May 1929

W 111067-2    The Felons Of Our Land                                  Co 33409-F
              Felons Of The Land                                       RZ IZ633
W 111068-2    Savourneen Deelish          Co 33409-F, RZ IZ301, MR1806
                                                       NY  September 1929
```

36.162. Thomas O'Kelly *baritone*

```
301-1         Foggy Dew (Iascaire)          Ba 2034, Metro 100, Pm 33089
302-1         God Save Ireland               Ba 2034, Pm 33089, Re 9433
```

```
                    God's Ireland                                   Metro 100
                McIntyre's Irish Orchestra                      NY   early 1920s
```

Metro label note: This record made expressly for Tom Ennis-New York

36.163. Liam O'Kennedy *tenor*

```
                    In The Wee Little Home I Love            Ok 4365, Pa E3060
                    When Irish Eyes Are Smiling              Ok 4365, Pa E3060
                    Molly Brannigan                          Ok 4379, Pa E3013
                    Held Fast In A Baby's Hands                       Ok 4388
                                                              NY   1921
```

```
S 70733-B       Sinn Fein Awahn (Brian O'Higgins-McCaun)            Ok 21008
                orch                                           NY   July 1922
```


36.164. Chauncey Olcott *tenor* *(1865-1938)*

```
B 2985-1        My Wild Irish Rose (Olcott)                             Vi rej
B 2986-1        My Beautiful Irish Maid (Olcott)                        Vi rej
                orch                                      NY   January 5, 1906
```

```
38656-2         When Irish Eyes Are Smiling (Ball-Olcott)
                        Co A1310, 33011-F, CoR 2310, Re G6267, G6863
38657-1         My Wild Irish Rose (Olcott)          Co A1308, CoR 2310, Re G6267
38658-1         Sweet Inniscara (Olcott)      Co A1309, 33022-F, CoR 2311, Re G6268
                orch                                     NY   February 25, 1913
```

```
38659-1         Molly O (Scanlon)       Co A1309, 33022-F, CoR 2311, Re G6268
38660-1         Mother Machree (Olcott-Ball)                   Co A1337, 33024-F
                orch                                     NY   February 26, 1913
```

```
38662-1-2       My Beautiful Irish Maid (Olcott)      Co A1337, CoR 2313, Re G6270
38663-1         I Used To Believe In Fairies (George Spink)
                                        Co A1308, CoR 2312, Re G6269
38664-1         I Love The Name Of Mary (Ball-Olcott)  Co A1310, CoR 2312, Re G6269
                orch                                     NY   February 27, 1913
```

```
38913-          Where The River Shannon Flows                            Co rej
38914-          Isle Of Dreams                                           Co rej
38915-          In The Garden Of My Heart                                Co rej
                orch                                        NY   June 20, 1913
```

```
38968-1         Too-Ra-Loo-Ra-Loo-Ral {That's An Irish Lullaby} (J.R. Shannon)
                                                                      Co A1410
38969-1         Peggy Darlin' (K. Stewart)                            Co A1411
38970-1         My Little Dudeen (Ball)                               Co A1411
38974-          I Never Met Before A Girl Like You                      Co rej
                orch                                        NY   July 30, 1913
```

```
38983-1         Dream Girl Of Mine (Cass Freeborn)                    Co A1410
                orch                                        NY   August 2, 1913
```

79320-2-3	That's How The Shannon Flows, from "Macushla" (Ball)	
		Co A3525, 33012-F
79321-2	'Tis An Irish Girl I Love And She's Just Like You, from "Macushla"	
	(Ball)	Co A2988, 33018-F
79323-2	Macushla Asthore {Pulse Of My Heart}, from "Macushla" (Ball)	
		Co A2988, 33018-F
79324-2	I'll Miss You, Old Ireland, God Bless You, Good-Bye, from "Macushla"	
	(Ball)	Co A3525, 33012-F
	orch	NY June 29-30, 1920

36.165. Dennis O'Leary *vocal*

39023-A	The Letter Edged In Black (Hattie Nevada)	De 435, 12023
39024-A	In The Baggage Coach Ahead (Gussie L. Davis)	De 435, 12023
39025-A	The Little Lost Child (Jos. W. Stern-Edw. B. Marks)	De rej
	vln, acn	NY November 18, 1934

36.166. O'Leary's Irish Minstrels *instrumental*

W 107261-1	I've Got A Bonnet Trimmed With Blue; Come Upstairs And We'll Have A	
	Night Of It-Polkas	Co 33139-F
W 107262-1	The Grenadiers; The Colleen Bawn-Polkas	
		Co 33130-F, IFB300, Vo 84122, RZ G8932, IZ112
W 107263-1	Paddy's Land; Soldier's Joy	Co 33120-F
W 107264-1	Louden's Braes So Bonnie; Money Musk; Green Grow The Rushes	
	Oh!-Highland Flings	Co 33147-F
W 107265-1	Weel Made The Keel Row; Johnny Won't You Marry Me-Highland Flings	
		Co 33132-F, RZ G8932, G20737
W 107266-2	Connaughtman's Rambles; Father O'Flynn-Jigs	Co 33130-F, Vo 84122
W 107267-2	The Rakes Of Kildare; A Trip To The Cottage-Jigs	Co 33119-F
W 107268-2	Larry O'Gaff; Strop The Razor-Jigs	Co 33120-F
W 107269-1	Maid On The Green; Three Little Drummers-Jigs	Co 33146-F
W 107270-2	Jackson's Morning Brush-Jig	Co 33119-F
W 107271-1	Old Man Dillon; Walls Of Liscara-Jigs	Co 33146-F
W 107272-2	The Campbells Are Coming; Garry Owen-Jigs	
		Co 33140-F, RZ G9184, IZ133
W 107273-2	Come, Haste To The Wedding; When The Kettle Boils Over-Jigs	
		Co 33131-F, RZ IZ113
W 107274-2	The Favorite Jig; The Mouse In The Cupboard-Jigs	
		Co 33131-F, RZ G8933
W 107275-3	The New Stack Of Barley; Flowers Of Edinboro-Hornpipe Schottisches	
		Co 33122-F, Vo 84121
W 107276-1	The Rights Of Man; The Green Castle-Hornpipe Schottisches	
		Co 33132-F, RZ G8933
W 107277-1	Minstrel's Favorite; The Londonderry-Hornpipe Schottisches	
		Co 33147-F
W 107278-1	The Liverpool; Rickets-Hornpipe Schottisches	Co 33122-F, Vo 84121
W 107279-1	Swallowtail; O'Connells-Reels (5th Figure, Dance Set No. 1)	
		Co 33121-F, Vo 84120
W 107280-2	The Wind That Shakes The Barley; Bonnie Kate-Reels	Co 33139-F
W 107281-2	The Teetotalers-Reel	
		Co 33129-F, RZ G8934, IZ114

```
W 107282-2    The Girl I Left Behind Me; The White Cockade-Reels
                                    Co 33140-F, RZ G9184, IZ133
W 107283-1    Rolling On The Rye Grass-Reel                     Co 33141-F
W 107284-1    God Save Ireland; The Wearing Of The Green-Marches
                                    Co 33148-F, 33500-F, Vo 84003
W 107285-2    O'Donnell Aboo; The Boys Of Wexford-Marches
                                    Co 33148-F, 33500-F, Vo 84003
W 107286-3    Danny Boy-Waltz                                   Co 33141-F
W 107287-3    In The Valley Near Slievenamon-Waltz    Co 33129-F, RZ G8934, IZ114
W 107288-2    Bold Jack Donahue; When Irish Eyes Are Smiling-Waltzes
                                                 Co 33121-F, Vo 84120
                                                 NY  November 1926


W 110039-2    Turkey In The Straw-Reel (5th Figure, Dance Set No. 2)
                           Co 33312-F, Vo 84026, RZ G20454, IZ186, MR686
W 110040-2    The Irish Rover-Jig (2nd Figure, Dance Set No. 2)
                           Co 33310-F, 33504-F, Vo 84024, RZ IZ297, MR1802
W 110041-2    Jack McGrale's Jig (4th Figure, Dance Set No. 2)       Co 33311-F,
                           33505-F, 37378, Vo 84025, RZ IZ186, MR686
W 110042-1    The Devil's Dream-Reel          Co 33410-F, Vo 84154, RZ IZ152, MR159
W 110044-2    My Wild Irish Rose-Waltz¹    Co 33353-F, Vo 84145, RZ G20628, MR1993
W 110045-1    The Blackbird-Long Dance                  Co 33455-F, Vo 84042
W 110046-2    The Red Haired Boy-Hornpipe    Co 33410-F, Vo 84154, RZ IZ152, MR159
W 110047-2    Black Rogue-Jig (1st Figure, Dance Set No. 3)  Co 33365-F, RZ MR1992
W 110048-1    Drowsy Maggie-Reel (5th Figure, Dance Set No. 3)
                                                 Co 33367-F, Vo 84029
W 110049-1    Fair Colleen-Jig (2nd Figure, Dance Set No. 3) Co 33365-F, RZ MR1993
W 110061-2    The Rakes of Mallow-Polka (3rd Figure, Dance Set No. 2)  Co 33311-F,
                           33505-F, 37378, IFB308, Vo 84025, RZ G21384, IZ176, MR472
W 110065-2    The Pigeon On The Gate-Reel  Co 33353-F, Vo 84145, RZ G20628, MR1992
W 110066-1    Paddy In London-Jig (1st Figure, Dance Set No. 2)       Co 33310-F,
                           33504-F, IFB308, Vo 84024, RZ G21384, IZ176, MR472
              Maggie In The Woods (3rd Figure, Dance Set No. 3)       Co 33366-F
              Miss Casey's Jig (4th Figure, Dance Set No. 3)          Co 33366-F
              ¹Johnny Riley-vo                              NY  November 1928
```

36.167. Myles O'Malley *tin whistle*

```
61251-A       Off To California-Hornpipe          De 12065, F6221, W4158, Rex U563
61252-A       Connaught Man's Ramble; Haste To The Wedding-Jigs
                                    De 12065, F6221, W4158, Rex U563
61253-A       Sweeps-Hornpipe                     De 12066, F6352, W4163, Rex U571
61254-A       The Swallow's Tail; The Heather Breeze-Reels
                                    De 12066, F6352, W4163, Rex U571
              Eileen White-p                      NY  September 2, 1936

62093-A       Shannon Bells; The Joy Of My Life-Jigs
                                    De 12106, F6421, W4126, Rex U583
62094-A       The Kildare Fancy; The Boys Of Blue Hill-Hornpipes
                                    De 12106, W4179, Rex U222
62095-A       The Morning Star; The Ships Are Sailing-Reels          De 12135
62096-A       We'll Dance The Keil-Row; Johnny Will You Marry Me?-Highlands
                                    De 12097, F6421, W4126, Rex U583
```

```
62097-A     Quarrelsome Piper; Harvest Home-Hornpipes'
                                        De 12098, F6422, W4127, Rex U584
62098-A     Four Hand Reel; The Ivy Leaf-Reels'     De 12098, W4179, Rex U222
62101-A     The Londonderry Hornpipe                    De 12097, W4178
62102-A     Off She Goes; Fire On The Mountain-Jigs
                                        De 12135, F6422, W4127, Rex U584
            alt sax, p, bj, dm, or 'Johnny Connors-p      NY  April 4, 1937

De 12066, 12098, 12106 and 12135 are in album A-516.
```

36.168. Shaun O'Mally *tenor*

```
O 8161-A     The Felons For Our Land                           Ok 21004
             orch                                          NY  ca 1921
```

36.169. George O'Miller *tenor*

```
W 108088-2   Old Man Shea                                      Co 33202-F
             probably Mike Hart-p                      Chicago  July 1927
```

36.170. James O'Neill *tenor*

```
O 8150-A     When Irish Eyes Are Smiling                       Ok 21001
O 8157-C     The Foggy Dew (New Version)      Od Od20043, Ok 21001, Pa E3016
O 8197-B     Willy Reilly And His Coleen Bawn  Od Od20065, Ok 21002, Pa E3017
             orch                                           NY  1921

             The Darling Girl From Clare                      O'Dowd 901
             Let My Epitaph Be Written (The Song Of Robert Emmet)   O'Dowd 901
                                                            NY  1922
```

36.171. Selena O'Neill *violin*

```
BVE 45349-2  The Bantry Hornpipe                               Vi 21526
BVE 45350-1  Thanksgiving                                      Vi 21661
BVE 45351-2  The Swaggering Jig; Give Us A Drink Of Water-Jigs    Vi 21526
BVE 45352-1  The Job Of Journey Work; The Blackbird-Long Dances
                                            Vi V-29009, HMV B3230
BVE 45353-1  Miss Johnson-Reel; Sheehan's Reel   Vi V-29009, HMV B3230
             Leroy Shield-p                     Chicago  June 12, 1928

BVE 46440-1  Whitney's Fancy; Tim O'Neill's Hornpipe-Hornpipes    Vi 21661
BVE 46441-1  The Cuckoo's Nest; The Flowers Of Edinburgh-Hornpipes    Vi
BVE 46442-1  The Humors Of Bantry; The Bridal Jig-Jigs            Vi
             as before                          Chicago  July 19, 1928
```

36.172. Shaun O'Nolan *(Wicklow Piper); tenor, bagpipes*

W 106099-1	Going To Mass Last Sunday; Bold Jack Donohue	
		Co 33072-F, Vo 84070, RZ G9182, IZ131
W 106101-1	The Fisherman's Widow; The Walls Of Liscara-Jigs	Co 33070-F
W 106103-2	The Gilda Ray; Shake It Up Shanahan	Co 33070-F
W 106104-2	Magpies' Nest¹	Co 33071-F, Vo 84069
W 106105-1	Back To Donegal²	Co 33072-F, Vo 84070, RZ G9182, IZ131
W 106106-1	The Kelleys¹	Co 33071-F, Vo 84069
	The Cuckoo's Nest; The Tailor's Thimble-Reels	Co 33081-F
	Believe Me; Last Rose Of Summer	Co 33081-F
	Gilda Ray Hornpipe	Co 33085-F
	The Fisherman's Widow-Jig	Co 33085-F
	bagpipes, unk p, or ¹vo, unk vln, cl, p, dm, or ²vo, unk cl/alt sax,	
	p, dm	NY November 1925

Some of the above may have been remade in April 1926.

W 106371-1	Sargeant Early's Jig	Co 33091-F
W 106372-1	Tailor's Thimble Reel	Co 33091-F
	bagpipe solos	NY February 1926

All subsequent issues are vocal solos without bagpipes.

W 106373-3	Kerry Long Ago (Shaun O'Nolan)	
		Co 33092-F, IFB302, Vo 84071, RZ G8943, IZ122
W 106374-2	Dan McCann (Shaun O'Nolan)	
		Co 33092-F, IFB301, Vo 84071, RZ G8942, IZ121
W 106375-2	The Boys Of The County Cork (Shaun O'Nolan)	
		Co 33099-F, IFB301, Vo 84074, RZ G8942, IZ121
W 106376-1	Mrs. Gillhooley	Co 33099-F, IFB302, Vo 84074, RZ G8943, IZ122
W 106377-3	Ceide Meile Faltue {One Hundred Thousand Welcomes} (Shaun O'Nolan)	
		Co 33104-F, RZ G9179, IZ128
W 106378-1	Nell Flaherty's Drake	Co 33104-F
	p	NY February 1926

W 107214-1	Mary O'Leary	Co 33176-F
W 107215-2	The Bandon Blarney Stone	Co 33123-F
W 107217-2	Mora Thasha	Co 33133-F, RZ G8944, IZ123
W 107218-2	Moriarity	Co 33133-F, RZ G8944, IZ123
W 107219-1	Close The Half Door	Co 33123-F
	vln, cl, p	NY October 1926

W 143577-1	The Maid Of Kensale	Co 33152-F
W 143578-3	My Love Nell	Co 33160-F
W 143579-1	The Man That Struck O'Hara	Co 33153-F
	as before	NY March 3, 1927

W 143586-	Little Mickey Flanagan	Co 33168-F, RZ G9181, IZ130
W 143587-1	Paddy Kane	Co 33160-F
W 143588-1	Donovan's Jubilee	Co 33168-F, RZ G9181
W 143589-1	Phil The Fluter's Ball	Co 33153-F
	as before	NY March 4, 1927

```
W 143595-1    Dawn On The Irish Coast-Recitation                          Co 33152-F
W 143596-2    Mahoney's Fenian Cat-Recitation                             Co 33176-F
              spoken                                             NY  March 4, 1927


W 108011-2    The Star Of The County Down    Co 33189-F, Vo 84078, RZ G9180, IZ129
W 108012-1-2  Ireland                                                     Co 33191-F
W 108013-2    The Shamrock                                                Co 33191-F
W 108014-1    The Donegal Widow              Co 33189-F, Vo 84078, RZ G9180, IZ129
W 108015-2    The Shan Van Vough                                          Co 33201-F
W 108016-1    The Fenian Gun                                              Co 33201-F
              vln, cl, p                                           NY  June 1927


W 108431-1    Johnny, I Hardly Knew You                                   Co 33211-F
W 108433-1    Lantry Larry                                   Co 33235-F, RZ IZ633
W 108436-2    The Enniskillen Dragoon                                     Co 33211-F
W 108437-2    My Rose Of Killarney                          Co 33226-F, RZ MR1385
W 108438-2    My Galway Colleen                                           Co 33235-F
W 108439-1    United Ireland                       Co 33226-F, RZ IZ252, MR1385
              Ceoch O'Leary                                               Co 33221-F
              Irish Fiddler                                               Co 33221-F
                                                               NY  October 1927


              Little Old Dudeen                                           Co 33261-F
              The Piper                                                   Co 33261-F
                                                                     NY  1927-8


W 109151-2    The Green Bushes                                            Co 33256-F
W 109153-1    Herself And Meself                    Co 33276-F, RZ IZ167, MR388
W 109154-2    The Man From Mullingar       Co 33287-F, Ok 21064, RZ IZ167, MR388
W 109155-1    Didar A Macarny                       Co 33297-F, RZ IZ174, MR470
W 109156-2    The Simple Aumathawn                  Co 33297-F, RZ IZ174, MR470
W 109157-2    How Do You Do                                               Co 33256-F
W 109158-2    Nora Bawn Asthore            Co 33287-F, Ok 21064, RZ IZ545, MR327
W 109160-2    The Shaughraun                        Co 33276-F, RZ IZ157, MR247
              vln, cl, p                                          NY  April 1928


W 109864-2    When The Praties Are Dug              Co 33304-F, RZ IZ159, MR266
W 109867-1    Cullinatreen                          Co 33301-F, RZ IZ545, MR327
W 109868-1    Andy Callaghan's Lunch                Co 33301-F, RZ IZ159, MR266
W 109869-2    Cork Beside The Lee                   Co 33304-F, RZ IZ157, MR247
              as before                                       NY  November 1928


W 111161-2    Mother's Silver Curls                          Co 33371-F, Vo 84030
W 111162-1    Yes You Did                                    Co 33371-F, Vo 84030
W 111163-2    Rosy O'Magrory            Co 33390-F, Vo 84034, RZ IZ579, MR1984
W 111164-3    I Took Her Under Me Arm                        Co 33390-F, Vo 84034
                                                               NY  October 1929


W 112904-2    Up Kerry                                                    Co 33476-F
W 112905-2    Jerry, Go And Oil That Car                                  Co 33476-F
              p                                                    NY  June 1931
```

```
W 112949-2    Ballinasloe                     Co 33483-F, Vo 84046, RZ IZ1085, MR3360
W 112950-1    Side Of The Road                Co 33483-F, Vo 84046, RZ IZ1085, MR3360
              vln, cl, p                                              NY  ca June 1931

              Going To Mass Last Sunday                                   Co 33425-F
              Says I To Julia                                             Co 33425-F
              An Anti-Irishman                                            Co 33444-F
              Mother Malone                                               Co 33444-F
              Furze Bush Hedge In Ireland                                 Co 33487-F
              My County Leitrim Queen                                     Co 33487-F
                                                                        NY  1930-1
```

36.173. Mike O'Shea *cornet*

```
              Killarney                                                Gaelic 1023
              p                                                     NY  early 1920s
```

36.174. Cornelius O'Sullivan *tenor*

```
BVE 37191-1   I'm A Man You Don't Meet Every Day            Vi 79126, HMV B2567
BVE 37192-1   Molly Bawn                                            Vi 79200
BVE 37193-1   St. Patrick's Day                                     Vi 79126
BVE 37194-2   I've Nothing Else To Do                               Vi 79200
              Lew Shilkret-p                               NY  December 30, 1926

BVE 38411-2   Ould Ireland You're My Darlin'                       Vi 79346
BVE 38412-3   The Fair Headed Boy (Bouchal Na Gruiaga Brabuie) Vi 79346, HMV B2898
              Ed Geoghegan-p                                 NY  March 28, 1927

BVE 40233-2   Molly Aroon (J.H. Wadsworth)                         Vi rej
BVE 40234-2   Ballyhooley (Robert Martin)                          Vi rej
              vln, fl, vc, p, d Leonard Joy                NY  September 26, 1927

BVE 40233-4   Molly Aroon (J.H. Wadsworth)                         Vi rej
BVE 40234-4   Ballyhooley (Robert Martin)                          Vi rej
              as before                                     NY  November 1, 1927
```

36.175. Emmett O'Toole *tenor*

```
O 8167-B      The Harp That Once Thro' Tara's Halls (Moore)
                                         Od Od20049, Ok 21003, Pa E3016
O 8192-B      In The Valley Of Slievenamon (D.J. Sullivan)           Od Od20065
O 8193-B      Danny Boy (Fred E. Weatherly)     Od Od20066, Ok 21002, Pa E3017
              orch                                                  NY  1921

S 7977-A-B    Wrap The Green Flag Round Me, Boys (Kevin O'Reilly-Joseph Crafts)
                                                                    Ok 21008
              orch                                           NY  ca June 1921

8201-B        Killarney (Balfe)                              Ge 5068, Starr 9352
```

8202-A	The Foggy Dew	Ge 5068, OBDW 39001, Starr 9352
	orch	NY February 5, 1923

8433-A	A Shawl Of Galway Grey (Hogan-Stanley)	
		Ge 5214, OBDW 39002, Apex 417, Starr 9429
	orch	NY July 2, 1923

8460-A	Laddie Buck Of Mine	Ge 5214, OBDW 39002, Apex 417, Starr 9429
	orch	NY July 1923

9355	All That I Want Is In Ireland (Jeff Brannen)	
		Ge 5695, 3014, OBDW 39009
9356-A	Bold Robert Emmet	Ge 5695, 3016, OBDW 39009
9357	Bold Jack Donohue	Ge 5712, 3014, OBDW 39010
9358	The Jackets Green	Ge 5712, 3016, OBDW 39010
	Parnell McKelvery-p	NY February 19, 1925

9952	The Croppy Boy (Malone)	Ge 5752, OBDW 39001
9953-A	All Praise To Saint Patrick {St. Patrick's Day} (Barry)	Ge 5752
	Tovian Trio: vln, vc, p	NY January 1926

BVE 37671-3	My Own Dear Galway Bay	Vi 79215, Bb B-4962
BVE 37672-1	Oh Sweet Are The Flowers That Bloom In Dear Kerry, from "Mavourneen"	
	(w: Bartley Campbell, m: Wm. J. Scanlan)	Vi 79215, Yv K-538
	orch d Leroy Shield	Camden, NJ February 9, 1927

BVE 38860-2	Bold Jack Donohue	Vi rej
BVE 38861-1	Teddy O'Neal	Vi 20849
BVE 38862-2	They Sail'd Away From Dublin Bay	Vi 20849
BVE 38863-2	Off To Philadelphia In The Mornin'	Vi rej
	vln, vc, p, d Leonard Joy	NY June 3, 1927

36.176. Philadelphia Police Band

The King Clown-Reel	Ok 4618
Up The Street March	Ok 4618
	NY ca 1922

36.177. George Potter *baritone*

46815-2	Inghin An Phalaitinigh Shule Agrah {The Palatine's Daughter}	
		Co A2093
46816-2	Caitheamh An Ghlais {Wearing Of The Green}	Co A2093
46817-	The Fair Of Windy Gap	Co
46818-	Druimfhionn Donn Dilis {Drimeen Dhun Deelish}-A Jacobite Ballad	Co
	orch	NY June 8, 1916

47268-3	Molly Branigan	Co A2216
47269-2	O'Donnell Aboo-Irish War Song	Co A2216
	orch	NY January 5, 1917

```
47446-         The Foggy Dew                                                      Co
47447-         In Dublin's Fair City                                              Co
                                                                NY  March 30, 1917

S 7990-B       Shule A Grah {Walk My Love}                            NF unnumbered
S 7991-A       An Spalpeen Fanach {The Rover}                         NF unnumbered
               vln, harp                                         NY  ca June 1921
```

The above were both single-side issues and a coupling.

36.178. Frank Quinn *vocal, accordion, violin*

Frank Quinn recorded alone and with various ensembles. Details for each matrix
are not uniformly available.

Francis Quinn

```
79831-2        Sailor's Hornpipe            Co A3566, 33118-F, RZ IZ1077, MR3346
79832-2        Miss McLeod's Reel; Blackberry Blossoms        Co A3566, 33118-F
79833-         Trip It Up The Stairs                                   Co A3567
79834-1        Heathery Breeze                                         Co A3567
               acn, John Muller-p                              NY  May 9, 1921
```

Patrolman Frank Quinn

```
8303           The Cherry Blossom-Jig                                 Vo 14280
8304           The Swallow's Tail-Reel                                Vo 14280
               as before                                       NY  December 1921
```

Frank Quinn

```
N 69877-       Casey At The Party             Pat 020882, Pe 11094, OBDW 39055
N 69878-       Bowl Of Coffee-Reel            Pat 020882, Pe 11094, OBDW 39055
               acn/talking, unk p                      NY  ca September 1922

S 71030-A      Bonnie Annie-Reel                            Ok 21010, Pa E3028
S 71031-B      Drowsy Maggie-Reel                           Ok 21010, Pa E3028
               acn, unk p                                   NY  November 1922
```

Patrolman Frank Quinn

```
10315          The Union Reel                                         Vo 14492
10317/8        The Basket Of Shamrocks-Jig               Vo 14541, Sil 3058
               acn, unk p                                   NY  December 1922
```

Francis Quinn

```
80843-2        The Longford Jig                             Co A3894, 33048-F
80844-3        The Virginia Reel         Co A3894, 33048-F, VT 7029-V
               acn, John Muller-p                       NY  February 7, 1923
```

Frank Quinn

8223-A	Margaret Collins Reel	Ge 5072, OBDW 39045, Apex 423, Starr 9358
8224-A	Quinn's Irish Polka	Ge 5072, OBDW 39045, Apex 423, Starr 9358
	as before	NY February 15, 1923

8232-B	The Connaught Man's Rambles-Jig	Ge 5074, OBDW 39046
8233-A	The Varsouvianna	Ge 5074, OBDW 39046
	as before	NY February 20, 1923

| | The Young Teetotaler; Dick Sheridan's Reel; Behind The Bush In The Garden; Cook In The Kitchen | Vi trial |
| | acn, unk p | NY April 16, 1923 |

8689-A	The Cat In The Corner-Jig	Ge 5355, OBDW 39017, Starr 9530
8690	The New Found Out Reel[1]	Ge 5355, OBDW 39017, Starr 9530
	acn/[1]vo, Arthur P. Kenna-p	NY December 28, 1923

8749-A-B	The Four Courts-Reel	Ge 5396, Starr 9525
	The Court-Reel	OBDW 39018
	acn/vo	NY February 4, 1924

| 8764, -A | Green Grows The Rushes | Ge 5396, OBDW 39018, Starr 9525 |
| | vln/vo, Ed Geoghegan-p | NY February 16, 1924 |

8837-	My Irish Jaunting Car[1]	Ge 5442, OBDW 39037, Starr 9544
8838-	The Grand Old Dame-Reel	Ge 5442, OBDW 39037, Starr 9544
	acn or [1]cl/vo, Ed Geoghegan-p	NY April 17, 1924

| 751-A-1 | The Peeler And His Goat | NR 2341 |
| | vo/vln, unk p | NY early 1920s |

New Republic 2341 as P.J. McNAMARA

81773-3	Kate From The County Down[1] [2]	Co rej
81774-2	Miss Wallace's Reel[2]	Co 137-D, 33055-F
81775-2	Haste To The Wedding-Jig[1] [3]	Co 137-D, 33055-F
81776-3	Love Will You Marry Me-Schottische[1] [2]	Co rej
	[1]vo/[2]vln/[3]acn, Arthur P. Kenna-p	NY May 12, 1924

B 30349-2	The Frog In The Well-Jig[1]	Vi 19540
B 30350-2	The Young Teetotler-Reel[2]	Vi 19540
B 30351-3	Get This[1]	Vi rej
B 30352-2	The Peeler And His Goat	Vi rej
	[1]vln, [2]acn, Ed Geoghegan-p	NY July 3, 1924

13776/7/8	Dublin Hornpipe	Vo 14899
13779/80/1	Rakes Of Drumlish	Vo 14899
	acn solos, Ed Geoghegan-p	NY September 1924

9103-A	Pop! Goes The Weasel[1]	Ge 5567, OBDW 39029, Starr 9599
9104	The Flogging Reel	Ge 5567, OBDW 39029, Starr 9599
	vln/[1]vo, Ed Geoghegan-p	NY October 1, 1924

Patrolman Quinn

N 105706-	Molly On The Shore-Jig	Pat 021131, Pe 11204, OBDW 39057
N 105707-	Up In The Loft-Reel[1]	Pat 021131, Pe 11204, OBDW 39057
	vln or [1]acn/vo, unk p	NY ca December 1924

Frank Quinn

S 73054-C	Father O'Flynn	Ok 21026, Pa E3098
S 73055-B	Get This	Ok 21026, Pa E3098
	vln/vo, Ed Geoghegan-p	NY ca December 29, 1924

136-	Trim The Velvet	Gaelic 1014
147-	Scholar's Jig	Gaelic 1012
	acn solos, unk p	NY ca 1924

9280-A	Molly In The Woods	Ge 5656, OBDW 39007
9281-A	Old Skib	Ge 5656, OBDW 39007
	Ed Geoghegan-p	NY January 15, 1925

9335,-A	Doran's Ass[1]	Ge 5667, OBDW 39016
9336,-A	St. Patrick's Day	Ge 5667, OBDW 39016
	vln/[1]vo, Ed Geoghegan-p	NY February 10, 1925

S 73195-B	Pop Goes The Weasel	Ok 21027, 45030, Pa E3181
S 73196-B	Katy Jones Reel	Ok 21027, Pa E3181
	vo/vln, unk p	NY ca March 1, 1925

9602-A	Love Will You Marry Me-Schottische (Quinn)[1]	Ge 5741, OBDW 39036
9603-A	The New Stack Of Barley (Quinn)	Ge 5741, OBDW 39036
9604	Innisfail-Jig (Quinn)	Ge 5740, OBDW 39035
9605	My New Shoes-Varsouvianna (Quinn)[1]	Ge 5740, OBDW 39035
	vln/[1]vo, unk p	NY June 18, 1925

W 105764-2	The Leg Of The Duck-Jig	Co 33004-F, Vo 84065
W 105765-1	The Home Brew-Hornpipe	Co 33003-F
W 105766-1	The Enneskillen Dragoon[1]	Co 33003-F
W 106767-1	A Morning In July[1]	Co 33004-F, Vo 84065
	as before	NY ca July 1925

W 105916-1	The Peeler And The Goat[1] [2]	Co 33063-F
W 105917-2	The Old Bog Hole[1] [2]	Co 33064-F
W 105918-1	Murphy's Wife[1] [2] [4]	Co 33064-F
W 105919-2	The Old Tea Kettle-Reel[3]	Co 33063-F
	[1]vo/[2]vln/[3]acn, [4]Kathleen (Kitty) Hand-laughing, unk p	
		NY October 1, 1925

W 106212-2	The Ballinamuck Jig[3]	Co 33077-F, Vo 84114
W 106213-2	Twelve Stone Two[1] [3]	Co 33080-F, FL 9010(33)
W 106214-1	McKeon's Reel[2]	Co 33080-F
W 106215-3	The Tan Yard Side[1] [2]	Co 33077-F, Vo 84114, FL 9010(33)
	[1]vo/[2]vln/[3]acn	NY January 1926

```
W 106252-2   The Birth Of St. Patrick                                    Co 33078-F
W 106253-2   Kelly's Dream-Recitation¹                                   Co 33078-F
             vo/acn or ¹spoken                                   NY  January 1926

BVE 35771-3  Rafferty's Reel²                      Vi 79006, Bb B-4957, MW M-8630
BVE 35772-1  The Shan Van Vough¹ ²                                       Vi 79007
BVE 35773-2  Ireland Boys Hurrah¹ ²                                      Vi 79007
BVE 35774-1  The Emerald Medley {Medley Of Old Irish Airs}²              Vi 79134
BVE 35775-1  Eddie Dunn's Favorite Reel³                                 Vi rej
BVE 35775-2  Eddie Dunn's Favorite Reel³ ⁴                      Vi 79134, HMV B2557
BVE 35776-1  The Wise Maid-Jig³                                          Vi rej
BVE 35776-2  The Wise Maid-Jig³ ⁴       Vi 79006, Bb B-4957, HMV B2557, MW M-8630
             ¹vo/²vln/³acn, Ed Geoghegan-p, or ⁴Geoghegan omitted
                                                           NY  July 15, 1926

BVE 36850-2  The Westport Chorus¹            Vi 79133, Bb B-4960, FL 9010(33)
BVE 36851-2  Paddy McGinty's Goat           Vi 79013, 26-7502, Bb B-4959
BVE 36852-2  Billy O'Rourke                           Vi 79133, Bb B-4960
BVE 36853-2  Patrick Sheehan          Vi 79013, 26-7502, Bb B-4959, MW M-8632
             vo/vln, Ed Geoghegan-p or ¹P. Crowley-acn    NY  October 21, 1926

W 107343-2   Paddy McGinty's Goat                          Co 33117-F, FL 9010(33)
W 107344-2   If You Are Irish Come Into The Parlor                       Co 33117-F
W 107346-3   Do You Want Your Old Lobby Washed Down                      Co 33128-F
             vo/vln, Ed Geoghegan-p                            NY  November 1926

W 107345-2   The Rocks Of Bawn                                           Co 33128-F
             vln, unk acn                                      NY  November 1926

W 143352-2   McSorley's Twins                     Co 33138-F, RZ G9183, IZ132
W 143353-3   Goodbye Mike, Goodbye Pat            Co 33138-F, RZ G9183, IZ132
             vo/vln, unk p                                     NY  January 1927

W 143664-1   Willy Reilly And His Dear Colleen Bawn                      Co 33161-F
             vo/vln, Ed Geoghegan-p                         NY  March 16, 1927

W 143668-1   Phil The Fluter                                             Co 33170-F
W 143669-1   The Hat My Father Wore                                      Co 33155-F
W 143671-2   Kate Muldoon                                                Co 33170-F
W 143672-2   The Old Swallow Reel [no vo]                                Co 33155-F
             vln/vo, Ed Geoghegan-p                         NY  March 17, 1927

W 143670-1   The Cherry Blossom-Jig                        Co 33161-F, FL 9010(33)
             acn solo, unk percussion                      NY  March 17, 1927

W 108156-1   John McCaffrey's Favorite Reel                              Co 33193-F
             vln solo, Ed Geoghegan-p                          NY  June 1927

W 108158-1   Sailing Home-Fox Trot                                       Co 33299-F
             vo/acn, Joe Maguire-vo/vln, unk woodblocks        NY  June 1927

W 108496-1   The Kerry Polka              Co 33234-F, Vo 84128, RZ G21417
W 108497-2   The Varsouviana            Co 33234-F, Vo 84128, RZ G21417
             own acn, Joe Maguire-vln, unk percussion      NY  December 1927
```

W 108498-1	Cadden's Fancy-Jig Set	Co 33223-F
W 108499-1	Donovan's Reel-Reel Set	Co 33223-F
	own, Joe Maguire-2 vln	NY December 1927

W 108599-2	The Cluckin' Hen And Duck	Co 33229-F
	vo/vln, Joe Maguire-2d vln, Ed Geoghegan-p	NY December 1927

W 108600-2	Oh Mind Your Eye	Co 33242-F
W 108601-1	The Mist On The Mountain-Jig²	Co 33229-F
W 108602-1	The Hare In Corn¹	Co 33242-F
	vo or ¹acn, or ²own, Joe Maguire-2 vln, Ed Geoghegan-p	
		NY December 1927

	Frank Quinn In His New Car	Co 33193-F
		NY 1927

W 109473-1	No One To Welcome Me Home¹	Co 33272-F, Vo 84084, RZ MR3361
W 109474-2	Green Grow The Rushes Oh	Co 33272-F, Vo 84084
W 109475-2	Jersey Lightning	Co 33283-F, FL 9010(33)
W 109476-2	Pat O'Hara	Co 33283-F
	vo, ¹Ed Geoghegan-p	NY July 1928

W 109777-1	The Connaught Man's Ramble-Jig²	Co 33316-F, Vo 84139
W 109778-1	The Belfast Spider-Reel² ³	Co 33299-F
W 109779-1	So There You Are¹	Co 33303-F, RZ IZ161, MR305
W 109780-2	Bold Jack Donohue¹	Co 33303-F, RZ IZ161, MR305
	¹vo/vln or ²acn solo, Ed Geoghegan-p, ³unk dm	NY October 1928

W 110154-1	The Temple House Reel¹	Co 33321-F, Vo 84141, RZ G9385
W 110155-2	My Irish Molly-O	Co 33316-F, Vo 84139, RZ G9386, IZ142
	vo/vln or ¹vln solo, unk p	NY December 1928

W 110275-1	The Plains Of Boyle-Hornpipe	Co 33330-F
	acn, unk woodblocks	NY January 1929

W 110311-1	The Water Street Polka³	Co 33374-F, Vo 84092
W 110312-1	Patrick's Day Parade¹	Co 33321-F, Vo 84141, RZ G9385, IZ141
W 110314-2	The Wicklow Mountains High²	Co 33330-F
	¹vo/acn, ²vo/vln or ³vln solo, Ed Geoghegan-p	NY January 1929

	Molly O'Morgan¹	Co 33341-F
	The Tenpenny Bit-Jig²	Co 33341-F
	The Cup Of Tea-Reel²	Co 33348-F
	The Rocky Road To Dublin-Fling³	Co 33348-F
	Molly Durkin¹	Co 33355-F
	Halfpenny Reel	Co 33355-F
	They Wouldn't Do It Now¹	Co 33362-F
	Paddy Doyle¹	Co 33362-F
	¹vo, ²vln, ³acn	NY 1929

W 111123-2	Kilkenny Races-Sketch	Co 33374-F, Vo 84092
	acn solo, unk p, bj, spoken	NY September 1929

```
W 111134-2    The Lassie From Donegal-Waltz              Co 33381-F, Vo 84032
              vo/acn, unk p                              NY  September 1929

W 111135-2    The Home I Left Behind                     Co 33381-F, Vo 84032
              vo/vln, unk p                              NY  September 1929

W 111136-1    The Irish Girl-Highland Fling       Co 33417-F, RZ IZ191, MR691
              acn solo, unk p, bj                        NY  September 1929

W 111628-2    Jack Welch-Jig¹ [no vo]                              Co 33405-F
W 111629-1    Heathery Breeze; The Moving Bogs-Reels¹ [no vo] Co 33417-F, RZ MR163
W 111630-1    Jim O'Shea                                 Co 33401-F, RZ MR135
W 111631-1    Doherty The Senator¹                Co 33408-F, RZ IZ191, MR691
              vo/vln, unk p or ¹acn, Eddie Dunn, Jr.-bj, unk p    NY  January 1930

W 111645-2    Mary's Favorite-Reel                                Co 33405-F
W 111646-2    Behind The Garden Gate-Reel                         Co 33461-F
W 111647-1    Londonderry Hornpipe                       Co 33408-F, RZ MR163
              vln solos, unk p                           NY  January 1930
```

Frank Quinn And Nan Fitzpatrick

```
W 112312-2    Daisy Bell          Co 33438-F, IFB317, Vo 84038, RZ IZ226, MR1111
W 112313-1    I'll Forgive But I'll Never Forget
                                  Co 33438-F, IFB317, Vo 84038, RZ IZ226, MR1111
W 112314-1    One Night I Came Home To My Kitty
                                  Co 33443-F, Vo 84097, RZ IZ1071, MR3334
W 112315-1    Going To The Fair                          Co 33443-F, Vo 84097
              vo duets, own vln, unk p                   NY  September 1930
```

Frank Quinn

```
W 112537-1    The Rambling Irishman                      Co 33461-F, Vo 84159
W 112539-1    Tony And The Cop-Sketch-Pt. 1¹             Co 33449-F, Vo 84041
W 112540-2    The Court Scene-Sketch-Pt. 2¹              Co 33449-F, Vo 84041
              vo or ¹spoken                              NY  ca November 1930

W 113025-2    My Bonnie Boy In Blue¹        Co 33477-F, Vo 84045, RZ MR3361
W 113027-2    Connamora Dan                              Co 33477-F, Vo 84045
              Connemara Dan                              RZ IZ1076, MR3345
W 113028-1    I'm A Happy Boy From Ireland Co 33489-F, Vo 84098, RZ IZ1071, MR3334
              vo/vln, unk p, bj, ¹with Nan Fitzpatrick    NY  June 1931

W 113138-1    An Irish Farewell                          Co 33493-F, Vo 84100
W 113139-1    Barney McCoy²         Co 33490-F, Vo 84099, RZ IZ1070, MR3333
W 113140-1    I Wish I Was Single Again    Co 33493-F, Vo 84100, RZ IZ1086, MR3362
W 113141-1    Mary Brown¹                                Co 33490-F, Vo 84099
W 113142-1    My Mother And My Sweetheart²               Co 33489-F, Vo 84098
              vo, vln or ¹acn, unk p, bj, ²with Nan Fitzpatrick   NY  September 1931

              Irish Waltz Medley¹ ²                               Co 33401-F
              Sullivan Will Be There¹                             Co 33454-F
              Falling Leaves³                                     Co 33454-F
              Evening Star-Reel³                                  Co 33482-F
```

O'Brien Has No Place To Go[1]   Co 33482-F
[1]vo/[2]vln/[3]instrumental duets with Eddie Dunn, Jr.-bj   NY   1930-1

Frank Quinn And Nan Fitzpatrick

W 113308-1   The Campbells Are Coming   Co 33502-F
W 113309-1   God Save Ireland   Co 33502-F
W 113310-1   My Blackbird Of Sweet Avondale
                             Co 33498-F, Vo 84047, RZ IZ1070, MR3333
W 113311-2   Far Away In Australia   Co 33498-F, Vo 84047
              vo duets, own vln, unk p   NY   January 1932

Frank Quinn

              The Turfman   Co 33512-F
              Barney O'Hare   Co 33512-F
              Phelim Brady   Co 33516-F
              Dan Murphy   Co 33516-F
                                                                  NY   1932

W 113644-2   The Green Hills Of Erin   Co 33522-F, Vo 84165, RZ IZ291, MR1745
W 113645-2   The Cottage Home In Old Ireland
                             Co 33522-F, Vo 84165, RZ IZ282, MR1796
W 113646-2   The Men Of The West   Co 33526-F, Vo 84051, RZ IZ207, MR928
W 113647-2   The Humor Is On Me Now   Co 33526-F, Vo 84051, RZ IZ207, MR928
              vo/acn   NY   ca October 1932

W 113802-2   The Mail Car Driver   Co 33531-F, Vo 84170, RZ MR1207
W 113803-2   Bring Back My Barney To Me[1]   Co 33532-F, Vo 84171, RZ IZ232, MR1206
W 113804-2   The Fair Of Mullingar-Reel And Fling[2]
                             Co 33532-F, Vo 84171, RZ IZ232, MR1206
W 113805-2   The Shamrock From Drumore[1]   Co 33531-F, Vo 84170, RZ MR1207
              vo/acn, [1]with Betty Conaty, or [2]acn-bj duet   NY   1933-4

Frank Quinn And Jim Clark "Smiles And Tears Of Erin" Orchestra

W 113979-1   Mike Carney's Fancy-Reel[1]   Co 33545-F, Vo 84056
                 Irish Dance No. 1[1]   RZ IZ801
W 113980-2   Jennie Is Welcome Home To Charlie-Reel   Co 33539-F, Vo 84055
W 113981-2   The Bunch Of Rushes-Reel   Co 33541-F, Vo 84103
W 113982-1   Master Rogers-Reel Medley[1]   Co 33533-F, Vo 84052
W 113983-1   The Bells Of Tipperary-Reel Medley   Co 33533-F, Vo 84052
W 113984-2   The Bridge Of Athlone-Reel Medley   Co 33543-F, Vo 84175
              own acn or [1]vln, James Clark-vln, unk fl, p, percussion
                                                    NY   November 30, 1934

Co 33543-F, 33545-F and RZ IZ801 as FRANK QUINN'S IRISH ORCHESTRA

Frank Quinn With Frank, Jr.

W 114013-1   Two Big Feet-Song Sketch[1]   Co 33535-F, Vo 84102, RZ IZ299
W 114014-   The Blind Harper-Song Sketch   Co 33535-F, Vo 84102
              vo/acn, [1]Grace-vo   NY   January 1935

Frank Quinn

CO 17928-1	The Mantle So Green	Co 33539-F, Vo 84055, RZ IZ583, MR1991
CO 17929-1	The Bobby On The Post	Co 33543-F, Vo 84175, RZ IZ1086, MR3362
CO 17930-1	Patsy McCann	Co 33545-F, Vo 84056, RZ IZ583, MR1991
CO 17931-1	The Tinker And His Budget	Co 33541-F, Vo 84103
	vo/acn	NY August 2, 1935

CO 18424-1	John Mitchell-Ballad[1] [2]	Co 33546-F, Vo 84176
CO 18426-1	Pat And Mike[1]	Co 33547-F, Vo 84177
CO 18427-1	Seaman's Hornpipe	Co 33550-F, Vo 84178, RZ MR3346
	vln/[1]vo, James Clark-vln, Eileen White-p, [2]one vln omitted	
		NY December 21, 1935

Matrix CO 18427 as FRANK QUINN'S IRISH DUET

Frank Quinn-Eddy Dunne

CO 18722-1	50 Years Ago[1] [2] [4]	Co 33550-F, Vo 84178, RZ IZ731
CO 18723-1	The Boys Of Wexford[1] [2] [4]	Co 33552-F, Vo 84180
CO 18724-	The Fighting Men-Reel[3]	Co 33552-F, Vo 84180
	[1]vo, [2]vln, [3]acn, Eddie Dunn, Jr.,-bj/[4]vo, unk p NY February 25, 1936	

36.179. Louis E. Quinn *instrumental*

Louis E. Quinn And His Shamrock Minstrels

14464-1	Stack Of Barley; The Friendly Visit-Hornpipes	Ba 32952, Me M12895,
		Or 2831, Pe 11357, Ro 2204, De W5079
14465-1	Gannon's Favorite-Barn Dances	Ba 32952, Me M12895, Or 2831,
		Pe 11357, Ro 2204, De W5079
14466-1	Reddy Johnson; Miss Monaghan-Reels	Ba 32951, Me M12894, Or 2830,
		Pe 11356, Ro 2203, De W5196
14467-1	Johnston's Hornpipe Ba 32951, Me M12894, Or 2830, Pe 11356, Ro 2203,	
		De W5196
14468-1	The Harp That Once Through Tara's Halls; The Green Flag; The Wearing	
	Of The Green-Marches Ba 32953, Me M12896, Or 2832, Pe 11358,	
		Ro 2205, De W5182
	Louis E. Quinn, James O'Beirne (1911-1980)-2 vln, Patrick Lynch-acn,	
	unk p, g	NY December 15, 1933

Louis E. Quinn-James O'Beirne

14469-1	High Level-Clog Hornpipes	Ba 32953, Me M12896, Or 2832, Pe 11358,
		Ro 2205, De W5182
	own 2 vln, unk p	NY December 15, 1933

36.180. Peter Quinn *concertina*

80271-A	Johnny, Won't You Marry Me-Highland Fling	Ok rej
80272-A	The Leg Of The Duck-Jig	Ok rej
		NY December 29, 1926

36.181. Thomas L. Quinn *tenor*

BVE 39245-3	In The Valley Near Slievenamon	Vi 20765
BVE 39246-1	The Meeting Of The Waters	Vi 20765
	vln, fl, vc, p, d Leonard Joy	NY June 13, 1927

BVE 41522-2	The Little Red Lark Of The Mountains (Alfred Perceval Graves)	
		Vi 21717
	2 vln, sax, p, vc, d Leonard Joy	NY January 5, 1928

BVE 43618-3	Shall My Soul Pass Through Old Ireland?¹	
		Vi 21445, Bb B-4929, MW M-8628, Yv K-535
BVE 43619-2	The Rose Of Tralee (Charles W. Glover)	Vi 21717
BVE 43620-2	The Old Bog Road (M.K. O'Farrelley)	
		Vi 21445, Bb B-4929, MW M-8628, Yv K-515
	Leonard Joy-p/dm, Joe Green-traps, unk 2 vln, fl, vc, ¹Lew Shilkret-org	NY April 6, 1928

Tom Quinn

W 110319-2	The Bowld Sojer Boy	Co 33455-F, Vo 84042
W 110320-1	The Coulin (Tho' The Last Glimpse Of Erin)	Co 33334-F, Vo 84143
W 110321-1	The Bells Of St. Mary's (A. Emmett Adams)	
		Co 33334-F, Vo 84143, Cq 9560
	orch	NY January 1929

36.182. William Quinn *accordion, vocal*

Wm. Quinn And His Dublin Orchestra

W 113426-1	The Disappointed Couple	Co 33517-F, Vo 84164
W 113428-1	Sweet Biddie Daly	Co 33517-F, Vo 84164
W 113429-1	Moonlight In Mayo-Waltzes	Co 33524-F, Vo 84050, RZ IZ208, MR929
	own acn, unk vln, p	NY March 1932

W 113508-1	Toss The Feathers; The Duke Of Leinster-Reels	
		Co 33524-F, Vo 84050, RZ IZ208, MR929
	acn solo (despite credit to the orchestra)	NY April 1932

William Quinn

	Mrs. Mulligan	Co 33509-F
	Medley Of Hornpipes¹	Co 33509-F
	vo or ¹acn solo	NY 1932

William Quinn & His Dublin Orchestra

1855-1	Quinn's Irish Barn Dance Medley	
		Cr 3400, MW M-1055, Vars 7003, THat 1006
1856-1	Money Musk; Green Grow The Rushes O; Keel Row-Highland Schottische	
		Cr 3400, Vars 7051

```
1860-1      Rakes of Mallow; Maggie In The Wood-Polka Set Tunes¹
                                                      Cr 3402, Vars 7004
1861-1      Stack Medley, including Dublin Breakdown¹  Cr 3402, Vars 7004
1862-1      The Frost Is All Over; Father O'Flynn      Cr 3403, Vars 7020
            own acn, unk p, bj, ¹vln               NY  September 21, 1932
```

MW M-1055 as IRISH BARN DANCE BAND, Varsity 7051 as GREEN'S DUBLIN BAND, Top Hat
1006 as DUBLIN IRISH ORCHESTRA

```
1857-1      Beautiful High Level Hornpipe Medley   Cr 3401, MW M-1055, Vars 7003
1858-2      Floggin Reel; The Pride Of Poulaphouca¹
                                              Cr 3401, MW M-1060, Vars 8009
1859-1      Leitrim Thrush; Blackberry Blossoms       Cr 3403, Vars 7020
            as before                            NY  September 22, 1932
```

MW M-1055 and M-1060 as IRISH BARN DANCE BAND

William Quinn

```
1885-1      Rights Of Man-Exhibition Hornpipe         Cr 3417, Vars 7005
            Exhibition                                      MW M-1057
1886-1      The Swallow's Tail               Cr 3417, MW M-1057, Vars 7005
            acn solos                                 NY  November 1932

C 2124-     Hornpipe Medley {McDermotts}           MW M-1060, Vars 8009
            own acn, unk p, bj                     NY  June-July 1933
```

MW M-1057 and M-1060 as IRISH BARN DANCE BAND

Quinn's Irish Orchestra

```
TO 1357     Moonlight In Mayo                                 Co test
TO 1358     A Visit In Londonderry                            Co test
                                                 NY  November 27, 1933
```

36.183. **Murty Rabbett** *vocal, flute*

```
BVE 48492-1  Dublin Reel; Tipperary Lassies-Reels¹ [no vo]      Vi V-29020
BVE 48493-2  Girl In Blue; Kerry Polka-Polkas [no vo]           Vi V-29020
             Dan Sullivan-p, ¹Jim O'Brien-tam       NY  December 18, 1928

BVE 50742-2  The Donkey                                         Vi V-29036
             Dan Sullivan-p                         NY  March 11, 1929

BVE 50743-1  Molly Durkin                           Vi V-29036, Yv K-522
             as before                              NY  March 12, 1929

BVE 53675-1  The Tail Of My Coat                                Vi V-29043
             Dan Sullivan-p, unk acn, bj            NY  May 27, 1929
```

BVE 53682-1   The Shirt I Left Behind Me
        Vi V-29043, Bb B-4920, MW M-8627, RZ MR1382
    Dan Sullivan's Shamrock Band: Dan Sullivan-p, unk acn, bj, traps
                NY May 28, 1929

BVE 55629-2   Pat O'Hara   Vi V-29055
BVE 55630-2   Coming In   Vi V-29055
    vo/pic, with Dan Sullivan's Shamrock Band: George Tapley-acn, Dan
    Sullivan-p, Neil Nolan-bj, unk traps   NY July 26, 1929

36.184. Edward V. Reavy *violin (1897-1988)*

BVE 43482-2   Donegal Hornpipe; The Cliff Hornpipe¹   Vi 21593, HMV B3400
BVE 43483-1   The Boys At The Lough; Tom Clark's Fancy Reel   Vi 21593, Bb B-4956,
        MW M-8629, Yv K-505, HMV B3400, Rounder 6008(33)
    Michael Crowley-p, ¹Joseph Conroy-bj   Camden, NJ April 25, 1928

Matrix BVE 43482 as THE KILLARNEY TRIO

36.185. Larry Reilly *vocal*

65690-A   Dawn On The Irish Coast-Dramatic Impression (John Locke)-Pt. 1
                   De 12211
65691-A   Dawn On The Irish Coast-Dramatic Impression (John Locke)-Pt. 2
                   De 12211
65692-   Those Were The Days, Forty Years Ago (Larry Reilly)   De 12223
65693-   McGinty; Och I Dunno {An Irish Girl's Lament} (Percy French)
                   De 12223
65694-   Shanahan's Ould Shebeen {An Liaigh}-Reverie-Pt. 1   De 12228
65695-   Shanahan's Ould Shebeen {An Liaigh}-Reverie-Pt. 2   De 12228
65696-   The Racing Of Finn McCool (Theresa Brayton)-Pt. 1   De 12234
65697-   The Racing Of Finn McCool (Theresa Brayton)-Pt. 2   De 12234
    Alfred Stobbi Stoner-p   NY May 31, 1939

36.186. Lt. Ridgely's 69th Regiment Band

620-   Tenth Regiment March (Hall)   Pm 33062, Puritan 9062
621-2   Sixty-Ninth Regiment March (arr Lt. Ridgely)   Ba 2031, GG 4041,
    Globe 4041, Madison 14041, Pm 33063, Puritan 9063, Radiex 4041
622-   National Emblem March (Bagley)   GG 4041, Globe 4041, Madison 14041,
          Pm 33062, Puritan 9062, Radiex 4041
623-2   Rainbow March (Maurice, arr Lt. Ridgely)
          Ba 2031, Pm 33063, Puritan 9063
                NY ca June 1920

    Garry Owen; The Low Back'd Car; Top O' Cork Road; St. Patrick's Day;
      Bay Pipes-Reels   Arto 3064, Bell S64, Globe L64
                  NY 1921

Vi 79169 and one side of Bb B-4961 are also credited to Ridgely, though both are
actually by the Victor house band, directed by Nathaniel Shilkret.

36.187. Pat Roche's Harp And Shamrock Band (Irish Village, Chicago Century Of Progress)

C 9584-A   The Boys Of Blue Hill; The Stack O' Wheat-Hornpipes'   De 12007,
                       F5427, F18064, W4085, Rex U494, FW 8821(33)
C 9585-A   Molly Durkin; Doran's Favorite-Polkas
                           De 12007, F5888, W4138, Rex U498
C 9586-A   Green Mountain; Longford Maid-Reels De 12008, F5427, W4085, Rex U494
C 9587-A   The Blackbird-Reel'   De 12008, F5888, W4138, Rex U498
     Jim Donnelly, Johnny McGreevy-2 vln, Pat McGovern-fl, Pakey Walsh-acn,
     Eleanor Kane-p, Pat Richardson-dm, 'Pat Roche-tap dancing
                             Chicago October 25, 1934

C 90439-A   The Humors Of Bandon-Long Dance   De 12060, F5886, W4196, Rex U496
C 90440-A   The Garden Of Daisies-Long Dance'
                     De 12058, F5885, F18014, W4350, Rex U495
     Tom Richardson, 'Pat Roche-step dancing   Chicago November 11, 1935

C 90449-A   The Job Of Journey Work-Long Dance'   De 12061
C 90451-A   The Rocky Road To Dublin-Slip Jig   De 12058, F5887, W4437
     'Agnes Cavanaugh-step dancing   Chicago November 15, 1935

C 90488-A   St. Patrick's Day-Long Dance'
                     De 12061, F5885, F18014, W4350, Rex U495
C 90489-A   Babes In The Woods; The Little Green Cottage-Polkas
                          De 12060, F5886, W4196, Rex U496
     'Hanna O'Brien-step dancing   Chicago November 29, 1935

36.188. William Ryan *tenor*

W 143666-2   Macushla   Co 33154-F, Vo 84004, Cq 9599
W 143667-2   Mother Machree   Co 33154-F, Vo 84004, Cq 9599
            orch   NY March 16, 1927

36.189. K. Scanlon *violin*

148021-   Turkey In De Straw   Harmony rej
148022-   The Arkansas Traveler   Harmony rej
148023-2   Bonnie Kate; Swallow's Tail; Molly Brannigan-Reels   Harmony 867-H
148024-2   Father O'Flynn; Irish Washerwoman; Haste To The Wedding-Jigs
                                   Harmony 867-H
     Mel Bernard-p   NY March 5, 1929

36.190. Patrick J. Scanlon *accordion*

77154-2   Father O'Flynn; Haste To The Wedding-Jigs   Co A2837, 33039-F
77155-2   Liverpool; O'Neil's Favorite-Hornpipes   Co A2902, 33045-F
         p   NY June 15, 1917

77156-1	Swallow Tail; Green Fields Of America-Reels	Co A2902
77156-2	Swallow Tail; Green Fields Of America-Reels	Co A2902, 33045-F
77157-2	Keel-Row; Money Musk-Highland Flings	Co A2837, 33039-F
	p	NY June 16, 1917

5775	The Green Fields Of America; Teetotalers; Swallows Tail-Reels	
		Ed 50500, 3467(4 min)
5776	Kitty's Wedding; Donnybrook Fair; The Top Of Cork Road-Jigs	
		Ed 51692, 3361(4 min)
	Dennis L. Smith-p	NY September 10, 1917

41021	The Green Fields Of America; Teetotalers; Swallows Tail-Reels	
		Meteor 1209, Arto 3024, Bell S24, Globe L24
41022	Kitty's Wedding; Donnybrook Fair; The Top Of Cork Road-Jigs	
		Meteor 1209, Arto 3024, Bell S24, Globe L24
	p	NY ca 1919

Meteor 1209 as PATRICK J. SCANLAN'S BAND

36.191. Shamrock Trio *instrumental*

N 105355-	The Humors Of Ennistymon-Jig	Pat 021122, Pe 11195, OBDW 39066
N 105356-	The Girl That Broke My Heart-Reel	Pat 021122, Pe 11195, OBDW 39066
	vln, acn, p	NY ca June 4, 1924

36.192. John Shaughnessy *tenor*

8875-A	Norah, My Own	Ge 5481, Starr 9555
8876-A	That Was A Perfect Dream	Ge 5481, Starr 9555
		NY May 1924

8924-A	Sometime {I'll Hear Your Sweet Voice Calling} (Lockwood-Lockwood)	
		Ge 5493, Apex 394, Starr 9570
8925-A	Take A Look At Molly (Lockwood-Lockwood)	
		Ge 5493, Apex 394, Starr 9570
	orch	NY June 1924

9134-A	Athlone (Chapman-O'Connor)	Ge 5578
9135-A	Down By The Sally Gardens (Yeats)	Ge 5748
9136-A	If I Were King Of Ireland (Graves)	Ge 5578
	orch	NY October 17, 1924

9578-B	Let Me Call You Sweetheart	Ge 3092
9579-A	Sweet Bunch Of Daisies	Ge 3092
	orch	NY June 15, 1925

9782	Where The Sunset Turns The Ocean's Blue To Gold (Buckner-Petrie)	
		Ge 3169
9783-A	Will You Love Me In December As You Do In May (Walker-Ball)	Ge 3168
9784-A	I Wonder How The Old Folks Are At Home (Lambert-Vandersloot)	Ge 3169
	orch	NY October 20, 1925

36.193. John Sheridan *vocal, flute*

BVE 43342-2	Miss McCleod's Reel [no vo]	Vi 21320
BVE 43343-1	The Virginia Jig [no vo]	Vi 21316
BVE 43344-1	Killarney; Believe Me If All Those Endearing Young Charms [no vo]	
		Vi V-29017
BVE 43345-1	The Maid That Left The County-Reel [no vo]	Vi 21316
BVE 43346-1	The Londonderry; The Cork-Hornpipes [no vo]	Vi 21320, Yv K-516
BVE 43347-1	The Jackets Green	Vi V-29017, Yv K-536
	Lew Shilkret-p	NY March 12, 1928

BVE 43961-1	Come Back Paddy Reilly To Bally James Duff	Vi 21443, 26-7501,
		Bb B-4902, MW M-8619, Yv K-532, RZ MR1744
BVE 43962-1	My Auld Skillara Hat	
		Vi 21443, Bb B-4915, MW M-8623, Yv K-532, RZ MR1744
BVE 43978-1	The Flowers Of Edinburgh-Reel [no vo]	Vi 21543
BVE 43979-2	Murphy's Hornpipe [no vo]	Vi 21543
	as before	NY May 14, 1928

A file note accompanying matrix BVE 43978 states that Sheridan uses a "smaller flute", probably a piccolo.

BVE 47517-2	The Boyne Hunt-Reel [no vo]	Vi 21720
BVE 47518-2	The Maid Behind The Bar-Reel[1] [no vo]	Vi V-29004,
	The Maid Behind The Barrel-Reel	HMV B3398
BVE 47519-2	The Sack Of Potatoes-Jig[1] [no vo]	Vi 21720, Bb B-4961
BVE 47520-2	The Frost Is All Over-Jig[1] [no vo]	Vi V-29004, HMV B3398
BVE 47521-1	The Sergeant And Pat[2]	Vi V-29072
	p, bj, [1]2d bj, [2]p only	NY September 17, 1928

John Sheridan And His Boys

The following are all instrumental.

BVE 49938-2	The Cup Of Punch-Jig	Vi V-29027, HMV B3617
BVE 49939-2	The Ship In Full Sail-Reel	Vi V-29027, HMV B3617
BVE 49940-2	Miss Monahan-Reel	Vi V-29063
BVE 49941-2	Bradley's Favorite-Hornpipe	Vi V-29063
	own pic, unk acn, p, bj	NY February 11, 1929

BVE 53698-1	The Keel Row; Money Musk-Highland Flings	Vi V-29049, Yv K-530
BVE 53699-1	Soldier's Joy-Polka	Vi V-29049, Yv K-530
BVE 53800-1	The Star Of Munster-Reel	Vi V-29075
BVE 53801-1	The Heathery Breeze-Reel	Vi V-29075
	own fl, Alfredo Cibelli-bj, unk acn, p	NY June 3, 1929

36.194. Robert G. Slattery *tenor*

W 113247-2	That Dear Little Cottage And Mother Machree	Co 33495-F
W 113248-	That's How I Spell Ireland	Co 33495-F
	The Bells Of Killarney	Co 33500-F

Has Sorrow Thy Young Days Shaded   Co 33500-F
                                                 NY December 1931

36.195. Jimmy Smith *harmonica*

BVE 35254-2   Mountain Blues {Smith And Holden Blues} (Smith-Holden)   Vi 20020
BVE 35255-3   Old Kentucky Home; Old Black Joe; Swanee River-Southern Melody Soft
                 Shoe Dance   Vi 20020
              Harry Holden-g   NY March 31, 1926

BVE 36001-4   Abie's Irish Blues   Vi V-29056
BVE 36002-3   Medley Of Reels, Major And Minor   Vi V-29056
              Frank Banta-p   NY July 26, 1926

BVE 36055-4   When Down South Morgan Plays The Mouth Organ   Vi rej
              Clarence Gaskill-p   NY August 20, 1926

36.196. Neal Smith *tenor*

              The Cabin With Roses At The Door   Co 33385-F
              My Dear Irish Home   Co 33385-F
                                                           NY   ca 1929

36.197. Phillip Storm

19145-2   Eileen Alannah   Co rej
              orch   NY December 2, 1910

36.198. Dan Sullivan *piano*

Sullivan's Shamrock Band

W 106344-1   Miss Monaghan; The Peeler's Jacket-Reels   Co 33083-F
W 106345-1   When The Kettle Boils Over; Donnybrook Fair-Jigs
                                                    Co 33084-F, Vo 84115
W 106346-1   My Love Is But A Lassie; Lass O'Gowrie-Polkas   Co 33082-F
W 106347-1   Garryowen-March   Co 33094-F
W 106348-2   Fairy Dance; Five Mile Chase-Reels   Co 33094-F
W 106349-2   Johnnie In The Glen; O'Connell's Reel-Reels   Co 33084-F, Vo 84115
W 106350-2   Jackson's Fancy; Apples In Winter-Jigs   Co 33093-F
W 106351-2   Colliers Reel; Miss Thornton's Reel   Co 33082-F
W 106352-2   Rory O'More; Bridal Jig-Jigs   Co 33083-F
W 106353-1   The Morning Star; Rakish Paddy-Reels   Co 33093-F
W 106354-1   Rickett's Hornpipe; College Hornpipe   Co 33105-F
W 106355-1   Top O'Cork Road; Gallant Tipperary Boys Co 33106-F, RZ IZ269, MR1612
W 106356-1   Brian Boru's March   Co 33089-F, 33527-F, Vo 84116
W 106357-2   Mary Jane; Black Haired Lass-Reels   Co 33111-F
W 106358-2   Neeley's March   Co 33111-F
W 106359-1   Londonderry Hornpipe   Co 33105-F, Topic 12T366(33)
W 106360-1   Boil The Kettle Early   Co 33134-F, RZ G8931, Topic 12T366(33)

```
W 106361-1    Ships A' Sailing                           Co 33134-F, RZ G8931
W 106362-2    Tenpenny Bit; Maid On The Green    Co 33106-F, RZ IZ269, MR1612
W 106363-2    The Blackbird             Co 33089-F, 33527-F, Vo 84116
              own p, Michael C. Hanafin, Thomas Ryan-2 vln, Daniel J.
              Murphy-bagpipes, Daniel P. Moroney-whistle        NY  February 1926
```

Dan Sullivan

```
W 106364-2    Pretty Maid Milking Her Cow; Star Of Munster        Co 33107-F
W 106365-1    Nano's Favorites                                    Co 33107-F
W 106366-2    The Wearing Of The Green                            Co 33090-F
W 106367-2    The Irish On Parade                                 Co 33090-F
              p solos                                      NY  February 1926
```

Sullivan's Shamrock Band

```
W 107764-2    Haste To The Wedding-Jig        Co 33183-F, 33508-F, Vo 84125
W 107765-1    My Love Is In America-Reel                         Co 33199-F
W 107766-1    Green Groves Of Erin-Reel                          Co 33190-F
W 107767-1    Heathery Breeze-Reel            Co 33215-F, RZ IZ239, MR1372
W 107768-1-2  Boys Of Ballanahinch-Reel      Co 33269-F, RZ IZ238, MR1371
W 107770-2    The Milliner's Daughter-Reel                       Co 33184-F
W 107775-2    Into The Room I Want You-Reel       Co 33198-F, FL 9010(33)
W 107776-2    Tie The Ribbon-Reel                                Co 33171-F
W 107777-2    The Suit of Corduroy-Jig                           Co 33224-F
W 107785-2    Top Of The Malt-Jig                                Co 33171-F
W 107786-     The Rabbit Catcher-Jig         Co 33162-F, Topic 12T366(33)
W 107787-1    The Mouse In The Cupboard-Jig  Co 33215-F, RZ IZ239, MR1372
W 107788-1    Biddy Of Sligo-Jig             Co 33269-F, RZ IZ238, MR1371
W 107789-1    Lanigan's Ball-Jig             Co 33198-F, Topic 12T366(33)
W 107791-1    Going To Donnybrook-Jig                            Co 33207-F
W 107792-1    Fire In The Mountain-Jig                           Co 33184-F
W 107799-1    Hawke's Hornpipe                                   Co 33164-F
              The Kid On The Mountain-Slip Jig                   Co 33163-F
              The Cat That Ate The Candle                        Co 33172-F
              Rakes Of Clonmel                                   Co 33177-F
              Kildare Fancy                                      Co 33177-F
              Jackson's Bottle Of Brandy                         Co 33236-F
              own p, Michael C. Hanafin, Martin Mullin-2 vln, Daniel P.
              Moroney-whistle, Owen Frain-fl, Dominic J. Doyle-bagpipes
                                                         NY  April 1927
```

Dan Sullivan's Shamrock Band

```
BVE 47752-1   Connaught Man's Rambles; A Trip To The Cottage-Jigs
                                          Vi V-29012, HMV B3610, IM407
BVE 47753-1   Blackberry Blossom; Bonnie Kate-Reels
                              Vi V-29003, HMV B3393, IM401, Topic 12T366(33)
BVE 47754-1   Green Grow The Rushes O' Vi V-29003, Bb B-4905, MW M-8622, Yv K-523,
                                          HMV B3393, IM401, Topic 12T366(33)
BVE 47755-1   The Humors Of Bantry; Maid On The Green-Jigs        Vi V-29011
BVE 47756-1   O'Connell's Reel; The Morning Star-Reel Vi V-29012, HMV B3610, IM407
```

```
BVE 47757-1    Rickett's Hornpipe; The Little Stack Of Barley-Hornpipe
                                                Vi V-29011, Yv K-526
               own p, Murty Rabbett-fl, Neil Nolan-bj, unk hca, 'lilting
                                                NY  October 17, 1928


BVE 48472-2    The Boys Of Wexford; God Save Ireland-Marches  Vi V-29014, HMV B3613
BVE 48473-1    Jackson's Morning Brush-Jig                     Vi V-29023
BVE 48474-1    The Fisherman's Widow; The Black Rogue-Jigs            Vi
BVE 48475-2    Carwailte Hornpipe                              Vi V-29021
BVE 48476-2    The Girl I Left Behind Me; Rakes Of Mallow-Marches
                                                Vi V-29014, HMV B3613
BVE 48477-1    Gordon's Reel                    Vi V-29030, HMV B3611
BVE 48478-1    Wilson's Clog; Fisher's Hornpipe-Hornpipes            Vi rej
BVE 48479-2    Tattered Jack Welch; Sweet Biddy Daly-Jigs
                                    Vi V-29054, Yv K-507, HMV B3608
BVE 48480-1    Paddy's Land; White Cockade-Polkas      Vi V-29021, Yv K-511
BVE 48481-2    Over The Moor To Maggie; Coming Through The Fields-Reels      Vi
BVE 48482-2    Paddy Ryan's Dream; Star Of Munster-Reels
                                    Vi V-29060, Yv K-507, HMV B3607
               own p, Michael C. Hanafin and another-2 vln, Murty Rabbett-pic, Connie
               Hanafin-acn, Neil Nolan-bj, Jim O'Brien-tam    NY  December 17, 1928


BVE 48483-2    Kilderry Hornpipe; Murphy's Hornpipe    Vi V-29054, HMV B3608
BVE 48484-2    Merry Old Widow; Donnybrook Fair-Jigs   Vi V-29030, HMV B3611
BVE 48485-2    Old Man Dillon; Walls Of Liscara-Jigs   Vi V-29060, HMV B3607
BVE 48486-1    Rights Of Man; Flowers Of Edinburgh-Hornpipes         Vi rej
BVE 48487-2    Drowsy Maggie; Pigeon On The Gate-Reels   Vi V-29023, Yv K-519
               as before                        NY  December 18, 1928


BVE 48478-4    Wilson's Clog; Fisher's Hornpipe-Hornpipes   Vi V-29031, Yv K-509
BVE 50734-1    The Leg Of The Duck; Roarin' Kate-Jigs    Vi V-29031, HMV B3394
BVE 50735-2    Bold Jack Donohue; Aileen Alanna-Waltz Set
                                    Vi V-29035, HMV B3231, IM392
BVE 50736-2    Maid Of The Sweet Brown Knowe; Believe Me If All Those Endearing
                    Young Charms-Waltz Set  Vi V-29035, Yv K-524, HMV B3231, IM392
BVE 50737-2    Rights Of Man; Boys Of The Scarf-Hornpipes            Vi V-29040
BVE 50738-1    Molly Put The Kettle On; The Bright Dawn Of Day-Reels
                                    Vi V-29040, HMV B3394
BVE 50739-1    Kathleen My Dear; Gypsy Hornpipe-Hornpipes   Vi V-29074, Yv K-511
               own p, probably: Murty Rabbett-pic, George Tapley-acn, Neil Nolan-bj
                                                NY  March 11, 1929


BVE 50744-1    Listen To The Mocking Bird¹         Vi V-29029, MW M-8636, RZ G23180
BVE 50745-1    Shamus O'Brien¹  Vi V-29045, 26-7507, Bb B-4918, MW M-8625, Yv K-528
BVE 50747-1    The Rambler From Clare¹               Vi V-29045, Yv K-524
BVE 50748-2    From Galway To Dublin {Sightseeing Tour}¹   Vi V-29029, 26-7503,
                    26-7526, 43-7526(45), Bb B-4994, MW M-8636, Yv K-510,
                                                RZ G23180
BVE 50749-2    Johnny Will You Marry Me²  Vi V-29038, Bb B-4905, MW M-8622, Yv K-523
BVE 50750-1    Johnny And His Fiddle O²                         Vi V-29038
BVE 50751-2    Pop Goes The Weasel²             Vi V-29074, Yv K-511
               as before, unk traps, ¹Larry Griffin, ²Murty Rabbett-vo
                                                NY  March 12, 1929
```

BVE 55625-1 Tobin's Favorite; My First Night In America-Jigs   Vi V-29069
BVE 55626-2 Fasten The Leg On Her; The Banks Of Lough Gonna-Jigs   Vi rej
BVE 55627-2 John Connor's Hornpipe; Whistling Mike-Hornpipes   Vi rej
BVE 55628-1 Sailor's Jacket; Old Maids Of Galway-Reels   Vi V-29069, Yv K-508
       as before   NY May 26, 1929

BVE 53667-1 My Galway Girl'   Vi V-29044, Yv K-522
BVE 53668-2 I'm Leaving Tipperary'   Vi V-29042, 26-7507, Bb B-4919, MW M-8626,
                                      Yv K-537, Topic 12T366(33)
BVE 53669-2 Johnny, I Hardly Knew Ye'   Vi V-29042
BVE 53670-2 Fare You Well, Sweet Irish Town'
                Vi V-29044, Bb B-4920, MW M-8627, Yv K-537, RZ MR1614
BVE 53671-1 My Darling Asleep; Yesterday Morning {Irish Dance Set,
           Figure 1}-Jigs   Vi V-29046, Bb B-4903, MW M-8620, Yv K-520,
                                        HMV B3233, IM394
BVE 53672-2 Sporting Nell; Drogheda Bay {Irish Dance Set, Figure 2}-Reels
       Vi V-29046, Bb B-4903, MW M-8620, HMV B3233, IM394, Topic 12T366(33)
BVE 53673-2 From Cork To Dublin'   Vi V-29047
BVE 53674-2 Irish Whoopee   Vi V-29057
       as before, 'Larry Griffin-vo   NY May 27, 1929

BVE 53676-1 Sailor On The Rock; Dan Sullivan's Favorite {Irish Dance Set,
           Figure 3}-Hornpipes   Vi V-29053, Bb B-4904, MW M-8621,
                                Yv K-531, HMV B3609, IM406
BVE 53677-1 Paddy Whack; Saddle The Pony {Irish Dance Set, Figure 4}-Jigs
           Vi V-29053, Bb B-4904, MW M-8621, Yv K-531, HMV B3609, IM406
BVE 53678-2 Irish Dance Set, Figure 5-Reels   Vi rej
BVE 53679-1 The Humors Of Whiskey; Maurice Gudgeon-Jigs   Vi V-29047
BVE 53680-1 The Silver Slipper; Jerry Daly's Hornpipe-Hornpipes
                        Vi V-29067, Yv K-507, Topic 12T366(33)
BVE 53681-1 Allister McAllister; Abbey Fale Lasses-Reels   Vi V-29067, Yv K-526
       as before   NY May 28, 1929

Vi V-29047 shows "Maurice Gudgeon" as composer.

B 39069-A   Londonderry Hornpipe   De 12016, F5410, W4210, Rex U504
B 39070-A   An Irishman's Gift To The Ladies; Tatter Jack Welch-Jigs
                           De 12016, F5410, W4210, Rex U504
B 39071-A   All The Way To Galway; The Rakes Of Mallow-Polkas
                           De 12017, W4045, Rex U505
B 39072-A   The Boyne Hunt; The Shaskeen Reel-Reels   De 12017, W4045, Rex U505
B 39073-A   Stanton's Hornpipe; The Little Stack Of Wheat-Hornpipes
                         De 12018, F5409, W4193, Rex U503
B 39074-A-B Johnny Will You Marry Me?'
                De 12018, F5409, W4193, Rex U503, Topic 12T366(33)
B 39075-A   The Peeler's Jacket; Rakish Paddy-Reels
                         De 12049, F5413, W4012, Rex U507
B 39076-A   The Favorite Jig; Humors Of Ballyfannia-Jigs
                         De 12049, F5413, W4012, Rex U507
B 39077-A   Green Grow The Rushes O''   De 12045, F5412, W4029, Rex U506
B 39078-A   The Leg Of The Duck; Fire In The Mountain-Jigs
                         De 12045, F5412, W4029, Rex U506
       'Murty Rabbett-vo   Boston November 18, 1934

36.199. John Sullivan *vocal*

A Song Of "Royalty" (John Martin)   JM 6000
The "Ku Klux Klan" And The "Black And Tan" (John Martin)   JM 6000
p   NY   early 1920s

36.200. Joseph Sullivan And Wm. McCormick *bagpipes, violin*

W 108082-1   The Merry Blacksmith; Fair Athenry-Reels   Co 33192-F
W 108083-1   Tuohy's Favorite-Hornpipe   Co 33192-F
               May Rodney-p   Chicago   July 1927

36.201. Sweeney Brothers *instrumental*

BVE 39198-2   Mary At School; Miss Kerney's Reel-Reels
                                            Vi 21005, Zon 5833, RZ T5833
BVE 39199-1   Ballashanon Boys; Rollican Boys-Jigs   Vi 21005, Zon 5833, RZ T5833
BVE 40108-2   Lonford Lassies; Swallow's Tail-Reels' Vi 21006, Zon 5136, RZ T5136
BVE 40109-1   Sweeney's Favorite; Limerick Boys-Jigs' Vi 21006, Zon 5136, RZ T5136
               John Sweeney-vln, Francis Sweeney-p, 'unk g, traps
                                                       NY   September 21, 1927

Vi 21006 as EMERALD QUARTET

Emerald Quartet

BVE 41100-2   Tartan Plaid; Long Hills Of Donegal-Reels   Vi 21160
BVE 41101-2   Sweeney's Jig; Dancing Gaels-Jigs   Vi 21160
BVE 41102-2   Sligo Boys; Limerick Rover-Reels   Vi 21180, HMV B3399
BVE 41103-2   Sons Of Erin; Joe's Favorite-Jigs   Vi 21180, HMV B3399
               John Sweeney-vln, Francis Sweeney-p, unk g, traps
                                                       NY   November 22, 1927

36.202. Patrick Sweeney *violin (1894-1974)*

Paddy Sweeney

38903-A   George White's Favorite; The Lass Of Carracastle-Reels
                                            De 12006, F5358, W4092, Rex U508
38904-A   Fitzpatrick's Favorite-Jig'   De 12006, F5358, W4092, Rex U508
               Eileen O'Shea-p, 'William (Billy) McElligott-acn NY October 27, 1934

62820-A   Concert Reel; Custom Gap-Reels   De 12153
62821-A   Rogers Jig; Village Jig   De 12153
               p   NY   November 26, 1937

36.203. George Sweetnam *tenor*

39567-A	Someone Thinks Of You Tonight (Write Home To Dear Old Mother)	
	(George Sweetnam)	De 12055, W4150, Rex U226
39569-A	My Own Dear Galway Bay (Jerry Donovan)	De 12047, W4150, Rex U226
39570-A	Erin Graw Machree (Jerry Donovan) De 12054, F5664, W4151, Rex U509	
	vln, acn	NY June 1, 1935

62124-A	The Hills Of Knock-Na-Shee	De 12093, W4175, Rex U219
62125-A	The Wild Hazel Glen	De 12093, W4176, Rex U220
62126-A	The Bold Fenian Man	De 12094, W4177, Rex U221
62127-A	There'll Be No One To Welcome Me Home	De 12094, W4281, Rex U625
62128-A	Kevin Barry	De 12102, W4176, Rex U220
62129-	She Lived Beside The Anner	De rej
	Paddy Killoran Trio: Patrick Killoran-vln, unk ten sax, p	
		NY April 10, 1937

62196-A	She Lived Beside The Anner	De 12102, W4175, Rex U219
	as before	NY May 14, 1937

65371-A	The Grave Of Peter Crowley	De 12203, W4593, Rex U680
65372-	Paddy Kane	De 12231, W4461, Rex U663
65374-A	Paudrig Oge Machree	De 12219, W4675
65376-	Asthore Machree When You're Far Away	De 12231, W4461, Rex U663
65378-A	Dear Old Skibbereen	De 12238, W4675
	orch d Patrick Killoran	NY April 10, 1939

36.204. James Swift *violin (ca 1872-1933)*

W 110356-2	Hough's Favorite; What Ails You-Reels	
	Co 33459-F, MS 45001(33), Sh 33001(33)	
W 110357-2	Saddle The Pony; Go To The Dance And Shake Yourself-Jigs Co 33459-F	
	O'Connell's Welcome-Jig	Co 33335-F
	Life On The Ocean-Reel	Co 33335-F
	p	NY February 1929

36.205. Joseph Tansey *violin*

BVE 37165-2	St. Patrick's Night; Cruiskeen-Reels	Vi 79115
BVE 37166-2	Slievenamon; The Merrymaker's Club-Jigs (O'Connellan-J. O'Neill)	
		Vi 79201
BVE 37167-1	Summer In Ireland; The Maid In The Dawn-Reels	Vi 79201
BVE 37168-1	The Rose In The Garden; Autumn Leaves-Jigs	Vi 79115
	Lew Shilkret-p	NY December 22, 1926

Titles for these medleys given in the Victor files are at some variance from the above:

BVE 37165	St. Patrick's Night; The Maid In The Dawn-Reels
BVE 37166	Slievenamon; Merrymaker's Club-Hornpipes
BVE 37167	The Summer Of Love; Pleasures Of Romance-Reels

BVE 37168   The Rose In The Garden; Cruiskeen-Jigs

It is probable that label titles are the correct ones, though the tunes on matrix
BVE 37166 are actually hornpipes.

36.206. George Tapley *accordion*

BVE 53860-1	Saratoga Hornpipe	Vi V-29065, Yv K-512
BVE 53861-2	The Chorus Jig	Vi V-29065
BVE 53862-2	O'Donnell Aboo; Let Erin Remember The Days Of Old-Patriotic Marches	
		Vi V-29050
BVE 53863-1	Garry Owen-March	Vi V-29050
	Dan Sullivan-p	NY June 24, 1929

BVE 55631-2	McElligot's Fancy; Billy Taylor's Fancy-Hornpipes	Vi rej
BVE 55632-2	East At Glangart; The Maid At The Well-Double Jigs	Vi rej
	as before	NY July 26, 1929

36.207. Patrick J. Touhey *bagpipes (1865-1923)*

This artist recorded material on home-made cylinders beginning in 1901. These
were distributed via newspaper advertisements and other means; copies survive both
in America and Ireland. Two published cassettes include nearly all existing
titles:

Barney The Piper {My Former Wife}-Jig	Skylark SK1002(C)
The Beauty Spot-Reel	Skylark SK1002(C)
Blame Not The Bard-Air	
Bonny Kate-Reel	Skylark SK1002(C)
The Boyne Hunt-Reel	Skylark SK1002(C)
The Boys Of The Loch-Reel	Skylark SK1002(C)
Brian The Brave-Air	NPU 001(C)
Molly McAlpin-March	Skylark SK1002(C)
The Cabin On The Hill {The Maid That Dare Not Tell}-Reel	
	Skylark SK1002(C)
The Collier's Reel	
Colonel Frazer-Reel	NPU 001(C), Skylark SK1002(C)
Delaney's Frolics-Reel	
The Duke Of Leinster-Reel	Skylark SK1002(C)
The Duke Of Leinster's Wife {The Ladies' Pantalettes}-Reel	
	Skylark SK1002(C)
Fasten The Leg In Her-Jig	NPU 001(C)
Peadar Clancy's Jig	Skylark SK1002(C)
The Fermoy Lasses-Reel	Skylark SK1002(C)
The Garden Of Daisies-Set Dance	Skylark SK1002(C)
Garryowen-March	NPU 001(C)
The Geese In The Bog-Jig	Skylark SK1002(C)
Gusty's Frolics-Jig	NPU 001(C)
Halligan's Fancy-Reel	NPU 001(C)
The Kerryman's Daughter-Reel	Skylark SK1002(C)
Harvest Home-Hornpipe	NPU 001(C)
The Humours Of Ennistymon-Jig	NPU 001(C), Skylark SK1002(C)

```
          The Humours Of Glin-Jig; The Maid Behind The Bar-Reel     NPU 001(C)
            The Sligo Rambler-Jig; untitled reels (sic)       Skylark SK1002(C)
          The Humours Of Whiskey-Slip Jig                     Skylark SK1002(C)
          I Won't Be A Nun-March                              Skylark SK1002(C)
          The Irish Washerwoman-Jig                                 NPU 001(C)
            The Irish Washwoman-Jig                           Skylark SK1002(C)
          Jackson's Morning Brush-Jig          NPU 001(C), Skylark SK1002(C)
          Jenny Dang The Weaver-Reel
          The Kildare Fancy-Hornpipe           NPU 001(C), Skylark SK1002(C)
          Killarney-Air (Balfe)                                    NPU 001(C)
            The Lakes Of Killarney-March                      Skylark SK1002(C)
          Molly From Longford-Reel
          The Morning Star-Reel                NPU 001(C), Skylark SK1002(C)
          The Munster Gimlet-Jig                                   NPU 001(C)
          Kitty Come Down To Limerick {The Munster Gimlet}-Slip Jig
                                                              Skylark SK1002(C)
          Pol Ha' Penny Hornpipe; The Swallow's Tail-Reel
                                               NPU 001(C), Skylark SK1002(C)
          A Pretty Girl Milking Her Cow-Air                   Skylark SK1002(C)
          The Rakes Of Clonmel-Jig; Toss The Feathers-Reel         NPU 001(C)
            Tobin's Jig; Toss The Feathers-Reel              Skylark SK1002(C)
          The Rocky Road-Jig¹                                 Skylark SK1002(C)
          The Shaskeen Reel                    NPU 001(C), Skylark SK1002(C)
          The Sword In Hand-Reel                                   NPU 001(C)
            Around The World For Sport-Reel                   Skylark SK1002(C)
          Tell Her I Am-Jig²                                  Skylark SK1002(C)
          The Three Little Drummers-Jig; The Ivy Leaf-Reel   Skylark SK1002(C)
          Touch Me If You Dare {Honeymoon Reel}-Reel         Skylark SK1002(C)
          The Wicklow Miners {The Miners Of Wicklow}-Jig     Skylark SK1002(C)
        ¹untitled in cassette notes, ²programmed twice on cassette
                                            Boston-Chicago-New York   1900s


          Hornpipe; Jig; Reel                                        Vi trial
                                              NY   September 20, 1919

B 23333-3    Stack Of Barley; Fancy Fair; London Dairy-Hornpipes     Vi rej
                                              NY   November 12, 1919

B 23333-4    Stack Of Barley; Fancy Fair; London Dairy-Hornpipes     Vi rej
B 23334-2    The Maid On The Green; Jackson's Jig; A Drink Of Water-Jigs
                       Vi 19271, MS 45001(33), Sh 33001(33), NPU 001(C)
             Out On The Ocean; Jackson's Bottle Of Brandy; Give Us A Drink Of
                  Water                                     Skylark SK1002(C)
B 23335-2    Drowsy Maggie; Scotch Mary; Flogging Reel-Reels
                 Vi 18639, FW P504(33), FW4504(33), NPU 001(C), Skylark SK1002(C)
             Drowsy Maggie                                        FW FE4525(33)
B 23336-1    Steam Packet; Morning Star; Miss McCleod-Reels
                 Vi 18727, MS 45001(33), Sh 33001(33), NPU 001(C), Skylark SK1002(C)
             On A Sunday Morning; Bold John Donohue                 Vi trial
                                              NY   November 14, 1919


Folkways FE4525 uses only the first part of matrix B 23335.
```

36.208. Edmund Tucker *Irish war pipes*

192	The Connaughtman's Rambles; Paddy Whack-Jigs	Gaelic 1018
193	Miss McLeod's Reel	Gaelic 1018
		NY early 1920s

36.209. Michael Tully *instrumental*

W 112337-2	Hayden's Favorite-Reel	Co 33451-F
	vln solo, unk p	NY ca September 1930

Tully And Kelly

W 112501-2	Popular Reel	Co 33451-F
	acn, bj (it is not known who plays which), p	NY November 1930

36.210. Michael J. Twomey *instrumental*

BVE 38833-2	Ricketts Hornpipe; First Of May-Hornpipes	Vi rej
BVE 38834-2	Let Erin Remember The Days Of Old'	Vi rej
	acn solo, unk 2 vln, or 'bagpipe solo	NY May 24, 1927

36.211. Tyrone Pipers Band

68567-A	The Minstrel Boy; O'Donnell Abu; Let Erin Remember-Marches	De 12249
68568-	Major Norman Orr Ewing; Earl Of Mansfield-Marches	
		De 12248, DL8554(33)
68569-A	Men Of The West; Rakes Of Kildare; Hundred Pipers; Midlothian Pipe	
	Band-Marches	De 12250, DL8554(33)
68570-A	Wearing Of The Green; All The Way To Galway; Rakes Of Mallow-Marches	
		De 12249, DL8554(33)
68571-A	Farewell To Ballinascorney-March; Dolan's March; Marquis Of	
	Huntly-Strathspey; Macleod's Reel	De 12250, DL8554(33)
68572-A	Leaving Glen Urquhart-March; Dornie Ferry-Strathspey; Duntroon-Reel	
		De 12248
	d Pipe Major Thomas McSwiggan	NY January 9, 1941

De 12248-50 are in album 206.

36.212. Unknown Spoken

	The Inaugural Address Of Mayor MacSwiney-Pt. 1 Operaphone unnumbered
	The Inaugural Address Of Mayor MacSwiney-Pt. 2 Operaphone unnumbered
	NY ca 1920

Label note: By courtesy of the Irish Literary Society Of America, dedicated to Mrs. Terence MacSwiney.

36.213. Pakey Walsh *accordion*

C 90448-A   Fisherman's Widow; Tenpenny Bit-Jigs   De 12068
              Jim Donnelly-vln, Eleanor Kane-p   Chicago November 15, 1935

36.214. Pat White *vocal*

Padraig White

              On The Weather   Keltic 1002
              When Two Friends Meet   Keltic 1002
          spoken   NY   ca 1923

Pat White

BVE 38783-2   The Roundhouse (P. White)   Vi 20718, Yv K-501
BVE 38784-1   It's The Same Old Shillelagh (P. White)
                          Vi 20760, Bb B-4993, MW M-8635, Yv K-527, FL 9010(33)
BVE 38785-2   Duffy's Blunders (P. White)   Vi 20718
              c, vln, p, traps, d Leonard Joy   NY May 25, 1927

BVE 41523-1   Come Down McGinty (P. White)¹   Vi 21200, Yv K-510
BVE 41524-2   Raffle For A Stove (m: Pat White)   Vi 21200
              c, vln, alt sax, p, traps, d Leonard Joy, ¹band vo
                                                    NY   January 6, 1928

BVE 43178-2   I'm Leaving Tipperary (arr Pat White-Leonard Joy)   Vi 21663
BVE 43179-1   McCarthy's Mare (arr Pat White-Leonard Joy)   Vi 21663
              as before   NY   March 26, 1928

BVE 53831-1   Tim Toolin   Vi V-29048, Bb B-4962
BVE 53832-1   My Tipperary Girl   Vi V-29048
BVE 53833-2   Michael Mooney   Vi rej
              c, vln, fl, p, tuba, d Alfredo Cibelli   NY   June 12, 1929

37.1. Alcide Aucoin *violin*

B 39082-A   Key West; Caporal-Hornpipes   De 12021, Rex U321
         Elizabeth Mallett-p, unk percussion   Boston   November 18, 1934

37.2. Ken Mc Kenzie Baillie *bagpipes*

Pipe Major, 78th Pictou Highlanders

       Ross's Farewell To The Black Cat; Leaving Glenurquhart   Vi trial
       Nathaniel Shilkret-p   NY   May 5, 1922

B 26924-2   Ross's Farewell To The Black Watch-March; Elspeth Campbell   Vi 19107
B 26925-1   Balmoral Castle; Devil In The Kitchen; McDonald's Reel; Cameronian
         Rant; When You Go To The Hill Take Your Gun-Fling Eight Steps
         And Reel Eight Steps   Vi rej
B 26926-1   March Leaving Glenurquhart; Parker's Farewell To Perthshire-Marches
                                                       Vi rej
B 26927-1   The Lads Of The Kilt; Sword Dance; Cock O' The North   Vi 19107
         NY   October 4, 1922

Vi 19107 may only have been issued in Canada.

37.3. Boston Caledonian Pipe Band

B 39057-A   The Muckin' O' Geordies' Byre; The Bonny Dundee; Cock O' The North;
         The Campbells Are Coming-Quick Step
                 De 14007, 27882, DL8554(33), DL5379(33), ED2203(45)
B 39058-A   Athol Highlanders; March To Loch Katrine; Devil In The Kitchen; Miss
         MacLoud's Reel
                 De 14007, 27882, DL8554(33), DL5379(33), ED2203(45)
B 39059-A   Athol And Breadalbane-Highland March
                 De 14018, 27883, DL8554(33), DL5379(33), ED2203(45)
B 39060-A   Blue Bonnets Over The Border-Quick Step   De 14018, 27883, DL8554(33)
B 39061-A   The Forty-Second; Barren Rocks; Brown Haired Maiden; Highland
         Laddie-Quick Step
                 De 14025, 27884, DL8554(33), DL5379(33), ED2203(45)
B 39062-A   Bluebells Of Scotland; Wae's Me For Prince Charlie; Will You No Come
         Back Again-March
                 De 14025, 27884, DL8554(33), DL5379(33), ED2203(45)
        d Pipe Major George B. Smith   Boston   November 17, 1934

37.4. Bobbie Brollier *baritone*

8877-A	Tobermory	Sunshine 2
8878-A	Bella, The Belle O' Dunoon	Sunshine 2
	Royal Scotch Highlanders Band	St. Petersburg, FL ca January 1925

The Royal Scotch Highlanders Band also made recordings of non-Scottish material for Okeh and Sunshine.

37.5. Caledonia Band

W 109191-1	Caledonia's Farewell	Co 37022-F
W 109192-1	Miss Drummond Of Perth; Mason's Apron	Co 37022-F
		NY April 1928

37.6. William Cameron *bagpipes*

8175	Cock O' The North-March	Zon 5463, Ox 5463-A
		NY ca October 1907

37.7. Angus Chisolm *violin (1908-1979)*

B 39083-	Moonlight Clog; Hennessey's Hornpipe	De 14004, Sh 14001(33)
B 39084-	Rothermarches Rant; Braes Of Auchertyre	De 14004, Sh 14001(33)
	Elizabeth Mallet-p	Boston November 18, 1934

37.8. Columbia Scotch Band

W 109184-2	Jerome's Farewell	Co 37017-F
W 109185-2	Lord McDonald's Reel	Co 37017-F
		NY April 1928

37.9. William Craig *violin (d. 1911)*

	Lady Binnie-Strathspey; Shores Of Lake Erie-Reel	Ed 9893(2 min)
	Sterling Castle-Strathspey; Harvest Dance-Reel	Ed 10120(2 min)
	Farintosh-Strathspey; Jenny Dang The Weaver-Reel	Ed 10357(2 min)
	Highland Whiskey-Strathspey; Craig's Reel	Ed 10440(2 min)
	p	NY February 10, 1908

37.10. Donald Cumming And Eddy Holmes (Scotch Serenaders) *instrumental*

B 39027-A	The March To Embo-Highland March (MacFarlane)	De 14001
B 39028-	The Muckin' O' Geordies' Byre-Country Dance	De 14001
B 39029-	Auld Reckie Schottische	De 14002

B 39030-   Flowers O' Edinburgh-Country Dance; Green Fields Of America-Reel
                                                                        De 14002
B 39031-   Leaving Glen Urquhart-March; Inverness Gathering-Quick Step De 14015
B 39032-   Dornoch Links; Highland Wedding-Highland March   De 14003
        acn, dulcimer   Boston November 15, 1934

B 39049-A   Cock Of The North; Bonny Dundee; Pibroch O'Donald Dhua-Highland
                Marches   De 14016
B 39050-   Miss Stuart; Whistle O'er The Love O' It; What Wadna Fecht For
                Charlie-Sword Dance   De 14015
B 39051-   The Punchbowl; Triumph-Eightsome Reels   De 14003
B 39052-   High Road To Linton; Speed The Plough; Mason's Apron; Miss McLoud;
                Strip The Willow-Reels   De 14021
B 39053-A   My Nut Brown Maiden; Braes O' Benackie-Highland Marches   De 14021
B 39054-A   Moneymusk; Miss Drummond Of Perth; Devil In The Kitchen-Highland
                Fling   De 14016
B 39055-A   Braes Of Mar; Cawdor Fair-Highland Schottische   De 14022
B 39056-A   Barren Rocks Of Aden; Farewell To Kenmure-Highland March   De 14022
        as before   Boston November 17, 1934

37.11. John Cunningham *vocal; (from Harris in the Hebrides)*

AFS 4283A1   The Beata Beag {The Little Boat} (Alexander Cunningham)   LC
AFS 4283A2   S'truadh Nach Robh Mise A N'Eillean Mo Cridh
                {Oh I Wish I Were In The Isle Of My Heart}   LC
AFS 4283B1   Och On A Ri Se Mo Ribhim Donn {Oh My Dear, My Bonnie Brown Maid} LC
AFS 4283B2   Ho Horo Mo Mhairi Lubhrachd {Ho Horo My Bonny Mary}   LC
AFS 4284A1   S'truadh Nach Robh Mise A N'Eillean A Raoich
                {How I Wish I Were In The Isle Of The Heather}   LC
AFS 4284A2&3 A Teid Thu Leum A Ribbinn Mhaseach
                {Will You Come To The Isle Of Lewis?}   LC
AFS 4284B   Mo Chairtean S'mo Luchd Dubhchaodh {My Friends And Countrymen}
                (w: Dan McLeod)   LC
AFS 4285A1&2 'S'gann Gu Dirich Mi Chaoidh {I Can Hardly Climb The Mountain} LC
AFS 4285A3   Chi Mi Tir Sa Robh Mi Nam Bhalach {Song Of The Isle Of Harris} LC
AFS 4285B1   Insidh Mi Uille Na Tha Ma'n Mhuilean
                {I'll Tell You About The Old Mill}   LC
AFS 4285B2   Fa-la-la-lo   LC
                                            Berkeley, CA   June 20, 1940

37.12. David Ferguson *bagpipes*

A 1473-1   Caller Herrin'   Vi 1473(7")
A 1473-M-1   Caller Herrin'   Mon 1473
A 1474-2   The Cock Of The North   Vi 1474(7")
A 1474-M-1   The Cock Of The North   Mon 1474
                                                NY July 12, 1902

The files credit SGT. DAVID FERGUSON; he is announced as such and as a member of
the KILTIES' BAND OF CANADA.

37.13. David Ferrier *bagpipes*

272	Highland Fling	Phono-Cut	5053
273	Sword Dance	Phono-Cut	5053
		NY	1910s

37.14. Charlie Frank's Orchestra

B 39087-	I'm Eighty In The Mornin' (But Seventy-Nine Today)-Fox Trot		
	(Sandy MacFarlane)	De	14020
B 39088-	Granny's Highland Hame-Waltz (Sandy MacFarlane)	De	14014
B 39089-	Bella From Balloch-Myle-Fox Trot (Sandy MacFarlane)¹	De	14011
B 39090-	Silly Willie-Waltz (Sandy MacFarlane)¹	De	14011
B 39091-	Where The Blue Bell Grows-Fox Trot (Sandy MacFarlane)¹	De	14014
B 39092-	My Highland Rose-Waltz (Sandy MacFarlane)¹	De	14020
	¹Sandy MacFarlane-vo	Boston November 19, 1934	

Charles Frank's Famous Orchestra recorded standard dance band material for Grey Gull in 1920-1. Since that label was based in Boston, it is possible that they were by the same leader.

37.15. Angus Mac Millan Fraser *bagpipes*

W 108684-2	The Duke Of Edinboro	Co	37009-F
W 108686-2	Abercairney March	Co	37009-F
	Renfrewshire Militia March	Co	37010-F
	Athol Highlander's Farewell To Loch Catht'e	Co	37010-F
		NY	January 1928

37.16. Alick Gillis *violin (1900-1974)*

Alick Gillis And His Inverness Serenaders

B 39033-	Inverness Gathering-March	De	14005
B 39034-	John McNeil; Picnic Reel	De	14005
B 39035-	Joys Of Wedlock; Sheriff Muldoon; The Irish Jig-Jigs		
		De 12019, Rex U319	
B 39036-	Tin Wedding; Metropolitan-Hornpipes	De 12019, Rex U319	
B 39037-	White Clover; Time To Go; Put Out The Fire-Strathspey And Reels		
		De	14006
B 39038-	Devil In The Kitchen; Red Fiddle; Dancing Of The Fingers-Highland		
	Fling And Reels	De	14006
B 39039-	Lord McDonald; Harness The Old Grey Mare; The Fiddlers'		
	Favorite-Reels	De 14017, 12050	
B 39040-	Close To The Floor; Scholar; Gillis' Favorite-Reels	De	14017
B 39041-A	Go To The De'il And Shake Yourself; Margaree's Fancy-Jigs		
		De 12020, Rex U320	
B 39042-A	The Marchioness Of Tullybardine-Reel	De 14023, 12050	
	own, Alcide Aucoin-2 vln, Elizabeth Mallet-p, Paul Aucoin-bj, Hugh		
	Young-percussion	Boston November 16, 1934	

B 39079-A   Money Musk; Yon Toon; Go About Your Business-Fling And Reels
                                                                        De 14023
B 39080-A   Great Western Clog'   De 12021, Rex U321
B 39081-A   Irish American; Clydeside Lassie; Norton's Reel' De 12020, Rex U320
             as before   Boston November 18, 1934

Alick Gillis

B 39085-A   King George; George The VI; King's And Lochiel's Reels-Strathspey
                                                                        De 14024
B 39086-   Joe's Favorite; MacKinnon's Rant; Pigeon On The Gate; Broken
             Wheel-Reels   De 14024
             own vln, Elizabeth Mallet-p   Boston November 18, 1934

37.17. George Kennedy *tenor*

W 107944-1   Scotland Yet   Co 37016-F
W 107945-1   The Scottish Emigrant's Farewell   Co 37016-F
             orch   NY June 1927

37.18. Kilties' Band Of Canada (Regimental Band Of The Gordon Highlanders,
             Belleville, Canada)

All following issues are on a special plaid label; Berliner releases are
Canadian.

A 1477-2   The Bonnie Briar Bush March (Ord Hume)   Vi 1477, Ber 808(7")
A 1477-M-1   The Bonnie Briar Bush March (Ord Hume)   Mon 1477
A 1478-2   The Soldiers Of The Queen (Ellis)'   Vi 1478, Ber 807, G&T 0474(7")
A 1478-M-1   The Soldiers Of The Queen (Ellis)'   Mon 1478
A 1479-2   Reminiscences Of Scotland (Godfrey)   Vi 1479, Ber 803(7")
A 1479-M-1   Reminiscences Of Scotland (Godfrey)   Mon 1479
A 1480-2   Scotland's Pride (Godfrey)   Vi 1480, Ber 806, G&T 0428(7")
A 1480-M-1   Scotland's Pride (Godfrey)   Mon 1480
             d William P. Robinson, 'with chorus   NY July 16, 1902

A 1485-1   Ye Banks And Braes (Bonniseau)   Vi 1485, Ber 809(7")
A 1485-M-2   Ye Banks And Braes (Bonniseau)   Mon 1485
A 1486-2   Robert Bruce: Selections (Bonniseau) Vi 1486, Ber 804, G&T 0458(7")
A 1486-M-1   Robert Bruce: Selections (Bonniseau)   Mon 1486
A 1487-2   The Maple Leaf Forever (Muir); God Save The King'
                                                       Vi 1487, Ber 805(7")
A 1487-M-2   The Maple Leaf Forever (Muir); God Save The King'   Mon 1487
A 1488-1   John Anderson, My Jo (Burns)   Vi 1488, Ber 810(7")
A 1488-M-2   John Anderson, My Jo (Burns)   Mon 1488
             as before   NY July 19, 1902

C 266-   Reminiscences Of Scotland (Godfrey)   Deluxe 31062(12")
C 267-   Hiawatha (Neil Moret)   Deluxe 31061(12")
C 269-   United Empire March   Deluxe 31059(12")
C 272-   John Anderson, My Jo (Burns)   Deluxe 31060(12")

C 285-   Ephasafa Dill {Iffa Saffa Dill}   Deluxe 31063(12")
              as before   NY July 1902

37.19. Lovat Bag Pipe Band Of New York

"Detachment With Harry Lauder Co."

B 16787-1   74th Highlanders Farewell To Edinboro; Money Musk Strathspey; De'il
                  Amang The Tailors Reel   Vi 17920
B 16788-2   Midlothian Pipe Band; Lord Blantyre Strathspey; Alexander Duff Reel
                                                                        Vi 17920
                                                        NY November 20, 1915

B 17918-2   My Native Highland Home-March; Highland Harry Back Again-Strathspey;
                  Bonny Mary Of Lochgoyle-Reel   Vi rej
B 17919-2   Highland Light Infantry-Quick Step March; Aspen Bank-Strathspey; The
                  Braes Of Balquidder-Reel   Vi rej
                                                        NY June 22, 1916

              The 71st Highlanders March; The Braes Of Tullymet; Thomson's
                  Dirk-Medley Of Scottish Airs No. 1 Pat 20403, Operaphone 51106
              Medley Of National Airs   Pat 20403
                                                        NY ca 1917

Operaphone 51106 as HIGHLAND BAGPIPE BAND

718-1   The Highland Brigades; March To Alma; Jennies Bawbee; The Lass Of
                  Lowrie; My Love She's But A Lassie Yet-Scotch Regimental
                  Marches No. 1   GG L7001, Globe 4005
719-1   Leaving Glen Urquhart; Climbing Don Na Quaich; Duntroon-Scotch
                  Bagpipe Selections No. 1   GG L7001, Globe 4005
                                                          Boston 1920

37.20. Mary A. Mac Donald *vocal (b. 1848)*

AFS 4246A1   Notes On The Composition Of Songs Among The Scotch In Nova Scotia LC
AFS 4247A1   An Am Eiridh Sa Mhadainn {When He Got Up In The Nova Scotia Morning}
                                                                              LC
AFS 4247A2   Seann Brogan {The Out-Worn Shoes}   LC
AFS 4247B1   Na Cuperean {Cooperean} (1871)   LC
                                                Berkeley, CA April 11, 1939

37.21. Charlotte Mac Innes *vocal*

AFS 3857A1   The Four Maries   LC
AFS 3857A2   Hieland Mary   LC
AFS 3857A3   Ca' The Yowes   LC
AFS 3857B1   The Weary Pund O' Tow (w: R. Burns)   LC
AFS 3857B2   Cam' Ye By Athol   LC
                                              Oakland, CA February 15, 1939

AFS 4246A2   Flow Gently Sweet Afton

                                        Oakland, CA June 15, 1939

37.22. Donald Mac Innes *vocal*

AFS 3856A3&B3 Na Ghaidil Ann A Vancouver {The Highlanders In Vancouver}   LC
AFS 3858A1   Soiridh Leis An Aite {Farewell To The Country}   LC
AFS 3858A2&3 Chi Mi Fir Sa Robh Mi Nam Bhalach {Song Of The Isle Of Harris} LC
AFS 3858A4&B1 Thug Mi M'oichdhe Raoir Sa Bhata {Last Night I Spent On The Boat} LC
AFS 3858B2   Oran Mhairi Nighean Iain Bhan {Mary McDonald's Song}   LC
AFS 3859A1   Mo Nighean Ag Bhoidleach Uib Histeach {My Bonny Lass}   LC
AFS 3859A2   Eilean Leodhais {Praise Of Lewis}   LC
AFS 3859A3   Tha Bhuidh Air An Usige Bheadach {An Ode To Whiskey}   LC
                                        Oakland, CA February 15, 1939

AFS 4246B1   Sugradh Ris An Nighean Duibh {I Would Welcome The Black-Haired Lass}
                                                                            LC
AFS 4246B2   Mo Cheum {My Step Is Heavy}   LC
AFS 4246B3   Mo Chridhe Trom S'dulaich {My Heart Is Heavy, I Am Sad}   LC
                                        Oakland, CA June 15, 1939

37.23. Murdoch Mac Leod *bagpipes*

4858   79th Farewell To Gibraltar-March; MacKenzie Highlanders-March; Miss
                  Drummond Of Perth-Strathspey; Sleepy Maggie-Reel   Ed 51057
4859   Campbells Are Coming-March; Cock Of The North-March; Barren Rocks Of
                  Aden-March; My Brown Haired Maiden-March; The De'il In The
                  Kitchen-Strathspey; The Kilt Is My Delight-Reel   Ed 51057
                                        NY July 7, 1916

37.24. John Mac Phee *vocal*

AFS 3859B1   Chunnach Mi Damh Donn Sna Hailtean
                  {Hunting Song From The Isle Of Harris}   LC
AFS 3859B2   Cur Dhuit An A Cadal Is Toindeach Rhuim
                  {Put Off Your Sleep And Turn To Me}-Sailor's Lament   LC
AFS 3859B3   Soirdh Leis Na Gruaigichean {Farewell To The Maidens}-Sailor's Song
                                                                            LC
                                        Berkeley, CA February 14, 1939

37.25. Mary Mac Phee *vocal*

AFS 4248A1   Cailin Donn A 'Chualain Reidh {The Maiden With The Brown Hair} LC
AFS 4248A2   A Flaisgaich Oig A S'cheanalteadh {My Cheerful Young Man}   LC
AFS 4248A3   Fhille Duhinn S'tu Ga M'dhi {My Brown-Haired Lover,
                  I'm Without Thee}-Waulking Song   LC
AFS 4248B1   Hi Oró Na Horo Eile {Hi Oro Though We Must Sever}   LC
AFS 4248B2   Fa-la-la-lo   LC
                                        Berkeley, CA June 15, 1939

37.26. J.H. Mathieson *vocal*

AFS 3298A1	Thug Me Gaol Do'n Fhear Bhon	LC
AFS 3299A	An t-Eilean Muileach {Isle Of Mull}	LC
AFS 3299B	Eilean Leodhais {The Isle Of Lewis}	LC
AFS 3300A1	Mairi Mhin Mheall Shuileach {Mary Of The Bewitching Eyes}	LC
AFS 3300B1	Ho Ho Hiram-Dance Song	LC
AFS 3300B2	Mairi Mhin Mheall Shuileach {Mary Of The Bewitching Eyes}	LC
AFS 3301A1	Air Falmalalo-Waulking Song	LC
AFS 3301A2&3	Caidil Gu Lo {Sleep Till Morning} (lullaby for a child whose father is off to the Battle of Culloden)	LC
AFS 3301B1	Tha Mo Leannan-Dance Song	LC
AFS 3301B2	Bruthaichean Ghlinn Braoin {Braes Of Glen Braon}	LC
AFS 3302A1	Mo Cheunnaig Bhoidheach {My Pretty Girl}-Waulking Song	LC
AFS 3302A2	Galbhaidh Sinu An Rathed Mar {We Will Up And March Away}	LC
AFS 3302B1	Horo Mo Nighean Donn Bhoidheach {Horo My Nut Brown Maiden}	LC
AFS 3303A1	Mairi Laghach {Bonnie Mary}	LC
AFS 3303A2	Eriskay Love Lilt	LC
AFS 3303B1	Fear A'bhata {O, The Boatman}	LC

Duluth, MN September 18, 1937

37.27. New York Scottish Highlanders *bagpipes, drums*

8174	The 79th Farewell To Gibraltar-March	Zon 5463, Ox 5463-B

NY ca October 1907

37.28. Scottish Military Band

9922	Speed The Plough; Fairy Dance; The De'il Amang The Tailors; The Soldier's Joy-Eightsome Reels	Ed 51489
9923	Cameron's Got His Wife Again; Rachel Rae-Foursome Reels	Ed 51489

NY January 2, 1925

37.29. Pipe Major George B. Smith Of The Boston Pipe Band *bagpipes*

E 29811-	The Road To The Isles; The Skye Gathering-Slow Marches	Br 68009
E 29812-	Scotland The Brave; Soldier's Return; Wa'es Me For Prince Charlie-Airs	Br 68009
E 29813-	Campbells Are Comin'; Bonnie Dundee; Cock O' The North; Kenmores On, On, Awa'-Marches	Br 68010
E 29814-	Killicrankie; Devil In The Kitchen; Wind That Shakes The Barley-March, Strathspey And Reel	Br 68010

NY July 2, 1928

37.30. Sutcliffe Troupe *instrumental*

B 12157-2	Melody March; The Glendarual Highlanders; The Cock O' The North; Coming Through The Rye; Miss McLeod-Reels	Vi 17140
B 12158-1	The 79th Highlanders Farewell To Gibraltar	Vi 17408, HMV 6536

B 12159-2   Highland Lassie; My Love She's But A Lassie Yet   Vi 17408, HMV 6537
B 12160-1   The Battle Of Killiecrankie; Will Ye No Come Back Again   Vi 17140
        bagpipes, dm   NY July 5, 1912

SECTION 38. WELSH

38.1. Dan Beddoe *tenor*

14952-1-2   test recording   Co
                                                          NY   July 1909

85067-2   Bugeilio'r Gwyn   Co E4305
85068-3   Y Gwcw Fach   Co E4305
85126-2   Rhyfelgyrch Cadben Morgan   Co E4428
85237-2   Llwyn On   Co E4428
            orch   NY   April-May 1919

This artist also recorded material in English for Brunswick and Rainbow.

38.2. Festyn R. Davies *vocal*

7591   Mentra Gwen {The Stars In Heav'n Are Bright}   Ed 51046
            orch   NY   June 20, 1920

7952   O! Na Byddai'n Haf O Hyd {Oh! That Summer Smiled For Aye}   Ed 51046
            orch   NY   April 29, 1921

38.3. Henry Kirby Davies *vocal*

B 26232-2   Ar Hyd Y Nos {All Through The Night} (arr John Parry)   Vi 73317
B 26233-3   Bugeilio'r Gwenith Gwyn {Watching The Blooming Wheat}
                {Idle Days In Summertime} (Will Hopkin)   Vi 73317
            Francis J. Lapitino-harp, unk vln, fl, p, vc, d Nathaniel Shilkret
                                                    NY   March 3, 1922

38.4. Eleanor Evans *vocal*

P 16632-1   Y Gwen Ar Y Fedwen {The Cuckoo}   CMS 100
P 16633-1   Clychau Aberdyfi {The Bells Of Aberdyfi}; Y Bore Glas
                {The Early Dawn}   CMS 100
                                            NY   January 14, 1935

38.5. John George *baritone*

B 27545-3	I Fyny Fo'r Nod (w: Mynydog)	Vi rej
B 27546-2	Chwifiwn Faner {Fling Out The Banner} (w: Trebor Mai, m: W. Davies)	
		Vi 73761
B 27547-3	Gwlad Y Delyn {Land Of The Harp} (w: E. Jenkins-T.W. Griffith,	
	m: John Henry)	Vi rej
B 27548-3	Y Milwr Dewr {The Soldiers Brave} (w: D.R. Griffiths,	
	m: Dr. Joseph Parry)	Vi rej
	orch d Ted Levy	Camden, NJ February 13, 1923

B 27548-5	Y Milwr Dewr {The Soldiers Brave} (w: D.R. Griffiths,	
	m: Dr. Joseph Parry)	Vi rej
B 27549-2	Gwald Yr Hen Cheninen Werdd {Homeland Of The Old Green Leek}	
	(m: D. Emlyn Evans)	Vi 73761
B 27550-3	Pinad Anrhydedd (w: Nathan Wynn, m: R.S. Hughes)	Vi rej
	as before	Camden, NJ February 14, 1923

38.6. Glyndwr Mountain Ash Welsh Male Choir

B 23731-1	The Gypsies Laughing Chorus (Bell) [in English]	Vi 72812
B 23732-1	Rhyfelgyrch Gwyr Harlech {March Of The Men Of Harlech}	
	(arr Richards)	Vi 72812
B 23733-1	Bydd Myrdd O Rhyfeddodau {The Resurrection Hymn} (Babel)	Vi 72813
B 23734-1	Aberstwyth {Jesus Lover Of My Soul} (Dr. Joseph Parry)	
	[in Welsh and English]	Vi 72813
	4 1st ten, 3 2d ten, 3 1st bs, 3 2d bs, d T. Glyndwr Richards	
		NY February 11, 1920

Royal Mountain Ash Male Choir

W 98186-	Italian Salad (Genee) [in Italian]	Co rej (12")
	14 voices, d T. Glyndwr Richards, Rhys Thomas-ten solo	
		NY October 9, 1925

W 98187-	Crossing The Plain (T. Maldwyn Price)	Co rej (12")
	14 voices, p, d T. Glyndwr Richards	NY October 21, 1925

W 141183-2	To Arms	Co rej
	14 voices, d T. Glyndwr Richards	NY October 23, 1925

W 141742-3	Blue Danube Waltz (Johann Strauss)	Co rej
W 141743-2	The Gypsy's Chorus	Co 639-D
W 141744-1	Ar Hyd Y Nos {All Thro' The Night}	Co 986-D
	d T. Glyndwr Richards	NY March 2, 1926

38.7. Gwent Male Glee Singers

38452-1	Aberstwyth	Co E1243, E4306
38453-1	Cydgan Y Morwyr {The Sailor's Chorus}	Co E1242
38454-2	Hen Wlad Fy Nhadau {Land Of My Fathers}	Co E1242

38455-1   Ar Hyd Y Nos {All Through The Night}   Co E1243, E4306
                                                      NY November 29, 1912

38.8. Anthony Meuris Jones *vocal*

38728-   Eileen Alanna [in English]   Co A1324
38729-   Roses [in English]   Co A1324
38730-2   Nant Y Mynydd   Co E1419, E4307
38731-2   O! Na Byddai'n Haf O Hyd   Co E1419, E4307
            orch   NY March 25, 1913

38.9. John T. Jones *tenor*

CVE 40085-1   Blodwen: Mae Cymru'n Barod {The Martial Spirit} (Dr. J. Parry)'
                                                            Vi 68920(12")
CVE 40086-1   Gys I'r Gad {The Call To Arms} (Dr. Howells-R.S. Hughes)'
                                                            Vi 68920(12")
BVE 40088-1   Y Gwlad Garwr {Can I Denor} {A Patriot}
                (R. Cenydd Lloyd-R.S. Hughes)   Vi 80342
BVE 40090-1   Unwaith Etto'n Nghymrw Anwyl {Once More In Dear Old Wales}   Vi rej
              orch d Bruno Reibold, including Basil Fomeen-acn, 'with William A.
              Jones-bar   Camden, NJ November 18, 1927

BVE 41423-1   O! Na Biddai'n Haf O Hyd {Oh! That Summer Smiled For Aye}
                (William Davies)   Vi 21785
BVE 41424-1   Yr Hen Gerddor {The Old Minstrel} (Rev. B. Thomas-D. Pughe Evans)
                                                               Vi 21785
              orch d Bruno Reibold   Camden, NJ December 27, 1927

BVE 40090-3   Unwaith Etto'n Nghymrw Anwyl {Once More In Dear Old Wales} Vi 80342
              as before   Camden, NJ December 28, 1927

38.10. William A. Jones *baritone*

BVE 40087-1   Bryniau Aur Fy Ncwlad {The Golden Hills Of Wales}
                (T. Vincent Davies)   Vi 80321
BVE 40089-1   Fecrgyn Cymru {Men Of Wales} (Ap. Glaslyn)   Vi 80321
              orch d Bruno Reibold, including Basil Fomeen-acn
                                                Camden, NJ November 18, 1927

BVE 41425-2   Pa Le Mae'r Amen? {Where Is The Amen?}
                (Allen O. Gwyroswdd-Ap. Glaslyn)   Vi 21784
BVE 41426-2   Bendithaist Goed Y Meussyd {Blessed Are The Trees Of The Forest}
                (Daroh Thomas Hughes-D. Protheroe)'   Vi 21784
              orch d Bruno Reibold, or 'Charles Linton-p
                                                Camden, NJ December 27, 1927

38.11. Rhys Morgan *tenor*

BVE 38968-3	Ar Hyd Y Nos {All Through The Night}	Vi 20842
BVE 38969-2	Y Deryn Pur {The Dove}	Vi rej
BVE 38970-1	Yn Iach I Ty Gymru {Adieu To Dear Cambria} [in Welsh and English]	
		Vi rej
BVE 38971-1	Yn Iach I Ty Gymru {Adieu To Dear Cambria} [in Welsh and English]	
		Vi rej

        orch d Bruno Reibold   Camden, NJ June 28, 1927

BVE 38969-4	Y Deryn Pur {The Dove}	Vi 20842
BVE 38970-3	Yn Iach I Ty Gymru {Adieu To Dear Cambria} [in Welsh and English]	
		Vi rej

        as before   Camden, NJ July 18, 1927

38.12. Helen Protherol *vocal*

46222-1	Clychau Aberdyfi	Co rej
46223-	title untraced	Co rej
46224-1	Yny Y Plant	Co rej
46225-1	Medley Of Southern Songs	Co rej

        Chicago August 1915

38.13. Cor Meibion Rhondda (Rhondda Welsh Male Chorus)

BVE 32545-3	Gwyr Harlech {Men Of Harlech} (Hen Alaw Gymreig)	Vi 78148
BVE 32546-2	Y Delyn Aur {The Golden Harp} (D. Pugh Evans)	Vi 78149
BVE 32547-1	Gypsies' Laughing Chorus (J. Bell)	Vi 78148
BVE 32548-1	Hen Wlad Fy Nhadau {The Land Of My Fathers}-Anthem Genedlaethol	
	Cymru (Welsh National Anthem)	Vi 78149
BVE 32549-2	Mulligan Musketeers (Atkinson)	Vi rej
BVE 32553-2	Italian Salad-Musical Jest (Genee)	Vi rej
BVE 32554-2	The Song Of The Jolly Roger (Chandish)	Vi rej

        14 voices d Prof. Thomas Morgan, Emlyn Jones-p

        Camden, NJ April 28, 1925

38.14. Welsh Mountain Ash Party Of Wales (Glandwyn's Mountain Ash Welsh Male Choir)

B 6798-1	The Destruction Of Gaza (De Rille)	Vi 5687
B 6799-1	The Long Day Closes (Sullivan)	Vi rej
B 6800-1	Men Of Harlech'	Vi 5688
C 6801-2	Old Black Joe (S. Foster)	Vi rej (12")
C 6802-1	The Tyrol (Thomas)	Vi 31732(12")
B 6803-1	Faust: Soldier's Chorus (Act 4) (Gounod) [in English]	Vi 5689

        unaccompanied or 'p   NY February 15, 1909

38.15. Pedwarawd Wilkes-Barre (Wilkes-Barre Quartet) *vocal*

B 26153-3	Huddersfield (J. Newton)	Vi rej
B 26154-2	Crugybar {O Fryniau Caersalem} {From Salem's Hills Yonder In Glory}	
	(arr J. Cledan Williams)	Vi rej
B 26155-3	Y Delyn Aur {The Golden Harp} (arr D. Emlyn Evans)	Vi rej
B 26156-3	Ebenezer {Ton Y Botel}	Vi rej
	vln, org	NY March 13, 1922

B 26153-4	Huddersfield (J. Newton)	Vi 73316
B 26154-4	Crugybar {O Fryniau Caersalem} {From Salem's Hills Yonder In Glory}	
	(arr J. Cledan Williams)	Vi 73316, MS 45006(33)
B 26155-6	Y Delyn Aur {The Golden Harp} (arr D. Emlyn Evans)	Vi 73315
B 26156-6	Ebenezer {Ton Y Botel}	Vi 73315

Thomas W. Morgan-1st ten, David H. Jones-2d ten, Roger J. Howell-1st
bs, David E. Evans-2d bs, David John Williams-d/org, Gorodetzer-vln
NY April 5, 1922

39.1. Atilla The Hun (Raymond Quevedo) *vocal (1892-1962)*

Raymond Quevedo (Atilla The Hun)

14907-1	Graf Zeppelin (Atilla)	Ba B-731, Co 2004-F, Me M12961, Or O-731, Pe P-731, Ro R-731, Rounder 1039(33,C,CD)
	Gerald Clark-g, unk vln, cl, p, cuatro, sbs	NY March 7, 1934

14914-1	Landlord And Bailiff (Gorilla)	
	Ba B-734, Me M12964, Or O-734, Pe P-734, Ro R-734	
14915-	Young Man's Slave (Atilla)	Ba B-735, Co 2005-F, Me M12965, Or O-735, Pe P-735, Ro R-735
14917-1	Beef And Bone (Douglas)	
	Ba B-736, Me M12966, Or O-736, Pe P-736, Ro R-736	
	as before	NY March 12, 1934

14933-	Woman, Lovely Woman (Atilla)	
	Ba B-740, Me M13002, Or O-740, Pe P-740, Ro R-740	
14936-	Local Products (Atilla)	
	Ba B-739, Me M12998, Or O-739, Pe P-739, Ro R-739	
14938-	Bacchanal (Douglas)	
	Ba B-741, Me M13023, Or O-741, Pe P-741, Ro R-741	
	as before	NY March 13, 1934

39415-A	Good Will Flyers (Raymond Quevedo)	De 17252, Br 02625, FW RF4(33)
39417-A-B	History Of Carnival	De 17253, Br 04414, EC KA2(C)
	Gerald Clark And His Caribbean Serenaders: Gerald Clark-g, Berry Barrow-p, unk tp, vln, cl, p, cuatro, sbs	NY March 15, 1935

39421-A	Pomme Majais	De 17255
39425-A	Duke And Duchess Of Kent	De 17257, EC KA2(C)
	as before	NY March 18, 1935

39428-A	Vagaries Of Women	De 17259
39430-A	Sweet Elaine	De 17260
	as before	NY March 20, 1935

39449-A	Ramon Navarro	De 17263
39451-A	Iere Now And Long Ago	De 17264
39453-A	Women Will Rule The World	De 17265, Br 02627, EC KA1(C)
	as before	NY March 22, 1935

The Atilla

61956-A-B	Abdication (Raymond Quevedo)	De 17297
61960-A	Zingue Talala (Raymond Quevedo)	De 17299
61962-A	Intercolonial Tournament (Raymond Quevedo)	
		De 17300, Br 02624, EC KA2(C)
61966-A	Roosevelt In Trinidad (Fitz McLean)	De 17302, M30749, EC KA2(C)

Gerald Clark And His Caribbean Serenaders: Gerald Clark-g, unk tp,
vln, cuatro, sbs   NY February 16, 1937

61972-A	West Indian Federation (Raymond Quevedo)	De 17330, Rounder 1054(CD)
61974-A	Friends (Raymond Quevedo)	De 17307

as before   NY February 18, 1937

61976-A	Treasury Scandal (Raymond Quevedo)	De 17320, FL 9048(33)
61984-A	Man Man Biscoe (Raymond Quevedo)	De 17315
61987-	Josefita (Raymond Quevedo)	De rej

as before   NY February 19, 1937

61990-A	His Majesty King George The 6th {Coronation} (Raymond Quevedo)	
		De 17454
61995-A	Martiniquen (Raymond Quevedo)	De 17323
61997-A	Miss Bombilla Brown (Raymond Quevedo)	De 17329, RBF RF13(33)

as before   NY February 22, 1937

62023-A	Meet Me At Sangre Grande (Donald Heywood, arr Dr. Merrick)	
		De 17311, EC KA1(C)
62026-A	War (Hubert Raphael Charles-Raymond Quevedo-Rufus Callender)[1]	
		De 17328, FW FE4602(33), RBF RF13(33)

as before, [1]with The Lion, The Executor, The Caresser
                                                        NY February 25, 1937

68898-A	Woman Is Not The Weaker Sex (Atilla The Hun)	De 17470, 18143

Gerald Clark And His Caribbean Serenaders: Gerald Clark-g, unk vln,
cl, p, sbs   NY April 2, 1941

68948-A	Roosevelt's Election (Atilla The Hun)	De 17462, 18144

as before   NY April 8, 1941

68976-	Invasion Of Britain (Atilla The Hun)	De 17465
68981-A	If I Won A Sweepstake (Atilla The Hun)	De 17463, FW RF4(33)

as before   NY April 11, 1941

69006-A	The Red Cross Society (Atilla The Hun)	De 17474, 18144

as before   NY April 16, 1941

69024-	Gal Come Home With Me (Atilla The Hun)	De 17477

as before   NY April 18, 1941

39.2. Guy Barrington

62020-	Mango Man	De rej

                                                        NY February 23, 1937

39.3. Lionel Belasco *piano*

B 16404-1	Terecita-Waltz (Lionel Belasco)	Vi rej
B 16405-1	Buddy Abraham-Paseo (Lionel Belasco)	Vi rej
B 16406-1	Bajan Girl-Paseo (Lionel Belasco)	Vi rej
B 16407-1	Little Brown Boy-Paseo (Lionel Belasco)	Vi rej
B 16408-1	My Little Man's Gone Down De Main-Paseo (Lionel Belasco)	Vi rej
B 16409-1	Not A Cent, Not A Cent!-Paseo (Lionel Belasco)	Vi rej
B 16410-1	Licores De Borges-Vals Venezolano (Moreno)	Vi rej
B 16411-1	Poncha Crema-Vals Venezolano (Gómez)	Vi rej
B 16412-1	Belasco Trot-One Step (Lionel Belasco)	Vi rej
B 16413-1	Grande Fonde-Tango (Butcher)	Vi rej
B 16414-1	Junk Man Rag (C. Luckeyth Roberts)	Vi rej
B 16415-1	Chick A Biddy Rag (Lionel Belasco)	Vi rej

NY August 27, 1915

B 16404-2	Terecita-Waltz (Lionel Belasco)	Vi 67675
B 16405-2	Buddy Abraham-Paseo (Lionel Belasco)	Vi rej
B 16406-2	Bajan Girl-Paseo (Lionel Belasco)	Vi rej
B 16407-2	Little Brown Boy-Paseo (Lionel Belasco)	Vi rej
B 16408-2	My Little Man's Gone Down De Main-Paseo (Lionel Belasco)	Vi rej
B 16409-2	Not A Cent, Not A Cent!-Paseo (Lionel Belasco)	Vi rej
B 16410-2	Licores De Borges-Vals Venezolano (Moreno)	Vi rej
B 16411-2	Poncha Crema-Vals Venezolano (Gómez)	Vi rej
B 16412-2	Belasco Trot-One Step (Lionel Belasco)	Vi rej
B 16413-2	Grande Fonde-Tango (Butcher)	Vi rej
B 16414-2	Junk Man Rag (C. Luckeyth Roberts)	Vi rej
B 16415-2	Chick A Biddy Rag (Lionel Belasco)	Vi 67673

NY August 28, 1915

B 16405-3	Buddy Abraham-Paseo (Lionel Belasco)	Vi 67672
B 16406-3	Bajan Girl-Paseo (Lionel Belasco) Vi 67674, Harlequin HQ2016(33)	
B 16407-3	Little Brown Boy-Paseo (Lionel Belasco)	Vi 67685
B 16408-3	My Little Man's Gone Down De Main-Paseo (Lionel Belasco)	Vi 67674
B 16409-3	Not A Cent, Not A Cent!-Paseo (Lionel Belasco)	Vi 67673
B 16410-3	Licores De Borges-Vals Venezolano (Moreno)	Vi 67675
B 16411-3	Poncha Crema-Vals Venezolano (Moreno)	Vi 67676
B 16412-3	Belasco Trot-One Step (Lionel Belasco)	Vi 67676
B 16414-3	Junk Man Rag (C. Luckeyth Roberts)	Vi 67685
B 16459-1	La Belleza-Valse Venezolano (Lionel Belasco)	Vi 67676
B 16460-1	Shakes-Paseo (Gómez)	Vi 67692

NY September 7, 1915

Lionel Belasco String Orchestra

B 18873-1	Alfonso-Spanish Waltz (Gómez)	Vi 69306
B 18874-2	Anita-Spanish Waltz (Lionel Belasco)	Vi 69394
B 18875-2	Saucy Girl-Paseo (Lionel Belasco)	Vi rej
B 18876-1	Mammy Sent Me To Town-Paseo (Lionel Belasco)	Vi 69307
B 18877-1	Muchacho Alegre-Joropo (Cyril)	Vi rej
B 18878-1	Belle Sarah-Paseo (Whiterose)'	Vi 69308

own p, unk cl, md, vc, cuatro, bj, 'cl omitted   NY December 26, 1916

B 18873-3	Alfonso-Spanish Waltz (Gómez)	Vi rej
B 18875-3	Saucy Girl-Paseo (Lionel Belasco)	Vi 69307
B 18877-2	Muchacho Alegre-Joropo (Cyril)	Vi 69394
B 19001-1	Evelyne-Paseo (Lionel Belasco)	Vi 69308
B 19002-1	Sweety Maxwell-Paseo (Maxwell)	Vi rej
B 19003-1	La Favorita-Paseo (W. Gibbs)	Vi 72345
B 19004-1	Hallibelle-Paseo (N. Núñez)	Vi 72345
B 19005-1	Grande Fonde-Tango (B. Butcher)	Vi 69306
B 19006-2	Throw Me A Rose, from "Miss Springtime" (Emmerich Kálmán)	Vi rej
	own p, unk cl, banjo-mandolin, vc, cuatro	NY January 3, 1917

Belasco's Trinidad Orchestra

62092-1	Shim Me Sha Wabble-Jazz Fox Trot	Co test
62093-1	La Fiesta-Trinidad Waltz	Co test
		NY January 15, 1918

Lionel Belasco's Orchestra

| | Venezuela Waltz | Vi trial |
| | own p, unk vln, fl, cl, vc, g, cuatro | NY August 9, 1918 |

B 22096-2	Iris-Waltz (G.L. McKenzie)	Vi rej
B 22097-3	Miel Y Yo (G.L. McKenzie)	Vi rej
B 22098-2	Esperanzas (Lionel Belasco)	Vi rej
B 22099-2	Sinceridad (G.L. McKenzie)	Vi rej
B 22300-2	Kruger-Paseo (Lionel Belasco)	Vi rej
B 22301-2	Sweetie Charlie-Paseo (Lionel Belasco)	Vi rej
	own p, unk vln, fl, cl, vc, g	NY September 12, 1918

B 22098-3	Esperanzas (Lionel Belasco)	Vi 72193
B 22308-2	La Biesa-Paseo	Vi 72196
B 22309-2	Bay Road Sarah-Paseo (A. Lavine)	Vi 72196
B 22310-2	Port O'Spain Susie-Paseo (G.L. McKenzie)	Vi 72197
B 22311-2	Sally Lou From La Brea Town (G.L. McKenzie)	Vi rej
B 22312-2	Edna And Viola-Waltz (M. Creems)	Vi 72197
B 22313-2	Alhaja-Waltz (G.L. McKenzie)	Vi 72198
	own p, unk vln, fl, cl, vc, g, cuatro	NY September 19, 1918

B 22096-4	Iris-Waltz (G.L. McKenzie)	Vi 72193
B 22097-5	Miel Y Yo (G.L. McKenzie)	Vi 72194
B 22099-3	Sinceridad (G.L. McKenzie)	Vi 72194
B 22300-4	Kruger-Paseo (Lionel Belasco)	Vi 72195
	as before	NY September 27, 1918

Lionel Belasco

| | Grande Fonde-Tango | Vi trial |
| | p solos | NY September 27, 1918 |

Lionel Belasco's Orchestra

B 22301-4	Sweetie Charlie-Paseo (Lionel Belasco)	Vi 72195
B 22311-3	Sally Lou From La Brea Town (G.L. McKenzie)	Vi 72198
	own p, unk vln, fl, cl, vc, g, cuatro	NY September 28, 1918

Lionel Belasco

B 22322-3	The Caterpillar Walk-One Step (Lionel Belasco)	Vi rej
B 22323-3	Grande Fonde-Tango (Butcher)	Vi rej
	p solos	NY October 4, 1918

B 22322-5	The Caterpillar Walk-One Step (Lionel Belasco)	Vi rej
B 22323-5	Grande Fonde-Tango (Butcher)	Vi rej
	as before	NY October 11, 1918

B 22322-7	The Caterpillar Walk-One Step (Lionel Belasco)	Vi 72273
B 22323-6	Grande Fonde-Tango (Butcher)	Vi 72273
	as before	NY November 8, 1918

Belasco's Orchestra

B 23381-2	Cristina-Colombia Waltz (Morales Pino)	Vi 72567
B 23382-1	El Nada-Venezuelan Waltz (Miguel Rivas)	Vi 72568
B 23383-1	Reproches-Colombian Waltz (Emilio Murillo)	Vi 72567
B 23384-2	Idilo Eterno-Pasiilo Colombiano (S.M. Soto)	Vi rej
B 23385-2	Cocotero-Bambuco Colombiano (L. Calvó)	Vi rej
B 23386-1	Antioqueña-Danza Colombiana (Osbroja)	Vi 72569
B 23387-2	Sueños De Amor-Vals Venezolano (Cayetano Matucci)	Vi rej
	own p, unk 2 c, vln, fl, cl, bar hn, vc, cuatro	NY December 17, 1919

B 23388-2	El Pepe-Pasillo Colombiano (Pedro Morales Pino)	Vi 72594
B 23389-2	En El Acaso-Vals Colombiano (Alejandro Fernández)	Vi 72569
B 23390-2	Flor Del Tropico-Vals Venezolano (C. Matucci)	Vi 72568
	as before	NY December 19, 1919

B 23387-4	Sueños De Amor-Vals Venezolano (Cayetano Matucci)	Vi rej
B 23602-1	Tiesterito-Joropo Colombiano (E.M. Soto)	Vi 72595
B 23603-2	Brisas Del Pamplonita-Bambuco Colombiano (E.M. Soto)	Vi 72595
	as before	NY December 30, 1919

B 23611-2	Susie-Paseo (L. Belasco)	Vi 72596
B 23612-2	Prohibition-Paseo (Alberto Moroni)	Vi 72596
B 23613-2	Bessie Down-Paseo (J. Manderville)	Vi 72597
B 23614-2	Quejas Del Alma-Vals (Dr. A.M. Delgado Briceño)	Vi 72593
	as before	NY January 6, 1920

B 23623-1	Smile-Paseo (Vincent Padula)	Vi 72597
B 23624-1	Ingrata-Colombian Waltz (J. Manderville)	Vi 72594
B 23625-2	Nacional Joropo-Venezuelan (C.M. Ariata)	Vi 73340
	as before	NY January 12, 1920

B 24041-2	Fidelia-Danzón (Felipe B. Valdés)	Vi rej
B 24042-2	El Bobite-Danzón (Felipe B. Valdés)	Vi rej

B 24043-2   Claridades-Danzón (Felipe B. Valdés)   Vi rej
               c, 2 vln, 2 cl, tb, bar hn, tuba, dm   NY May 7, 1920

Belasco's South American Orchestra

               Marie-Venezuelan Waltz   BS 2047, Pm 12185
               Para Tí-Porto Rican Danza   BS 2047, Pm 12185
               Alma Mia-Cuban Waltz   BS 2048, Pm 12184
               Sweet Charlie-Jamaican Pasee   BS 2048, Pm 12184
               Lucille-Trinidad Waltz   BS 2050, Pm 12183
               Suspiro D Amor-Colombia Waltz   BS 2050, Pm 12183
                                                                    NY ca January 1922

Belasco Orchestra

BVE 39918-1   Violets-Venezuelan Waltz (L. Belasco)
                                         Vi 80076, Rounder 1054(33,C,CD)
BVE 39927-2   You Run You Run-Paseo (L. Belasco)   Vi 80075
BVE 39928-1   Caroline-Paseo (W. Houdini)   Vi 80076, Rounder 1039(33,C,CD)
BVE 39929-1   Good Night Ladies And Gents-Paseo (L. Belasco)   Vi 80075
               own p, Cyril Monrose-vln, Gerald Clark-g, unk cuatro
                                                                    NY August 1, 1927

BVE 46326-1   Big Man-Sweet Man (Lionel Belasco)   Vi 81847
BVE 46327-1   Gumbo Li Li (Lionel Belasco)   Vi 81501
BVE 46328-2   Girls And Old Women Of Today (Lionel Belasco)   Vi 46102
BVE 46329-2   Why Girls Are Fond Of Policeman (Lionel Belasco)   Vi 81848
BVE 46330-2   Blow Wind Blow (Lionel Belasco)   Vi 46102
BVE 46331-2   The Whey Whey (Lionel Belasco)   Vi 81848
BVE 46332-2   Anella (Lionel Belasco)   Vi 81502
BVE 46333-2   At The Break Of Day (Lionel Belasco)   Vi 46103
BVE 46334-2   Tell The Population (Lionel Belasco)   Vi 46103
BVE 46335-1   De Yo Devere (Lionel Belasco)   Vi 81847
BVE 46336-1   Sofia (Lionel Belasco)   Vi 81501
BVE 46337-2   One Cent Ah! Honeycomb (Lionel Belasco)   Vi 81502
               own p, unk vln, p, g, cuatro, vo   NY July 20, 1928

Lionel Belasco's Orchestra

E 28068-   Violets-Waltz (Lionel Belasco)   Br 7033
E 28069-   The Cross {Crucita}-Waltz   Br 7033
E 28070-   Sweet Man {Hombre Dulce}-Pasillo (Lionel Belasco)   Br 7034
E 28071-   Cecilia-Pasillo (Lionel Belasco)   Br 7034
E 28072-   Roses Of Caracas {Rosas Caraquenas}-Waltz (Lionel Belasco) Br 7035
E 28073-   Caracas-Waltz (Lionel Belasco)   Br 7035
E 28074-   The Moon Of Maracaibo {La Luna De Maracaibo}-Waltz (Lionel Belasco)
                                                                            Br 7036
E 28075-   Rosita-Waltz (Lionel Belasco)   Br 7036
E 28076-   Caroline-Pasillo (Lionel Belasco)   Br 7037
E 28077-   Anella-Pasillo (Lionel Belasco)   Br 7038
E 28078-   Casimir {Casimiro}-Pasillo (Lionel Belasco)   Br 7038
E 28079-   Blow, Wind, Blow-Pasillo (Lionel Belasco)   Br 7037
               with vo   NY August 14, 1928

W 96781-2	West Indian Sunshine-Waltz (Lionel Belasco)	Co 3283-X
W 96782-2	Amazon-Waltz (Lionel Belasco)	Co 3283-X, Harlequin HQ2016(33)
W 96783-2	The Women Of Today-Pasillo (Lionel Belasco)	Co 3285-X
W 96785-2	The Dog Catchers-Pasillo (Lionel Belasco)	Co 3284-X
W 96786-2	Justine-Pasillo (Lionel Belasco)	Co 3284-X
W 96787-2	Woman Sweeter Than Man-Pasillo (Lionel Belasco)	Co 3286-X
W 96788-2	Happy Days-Pasillo (Lionel Belasco-Bentham)	Co 3286-X
W 96789-	Sweet Sammy-Pasillo (Lionel Belasco-Bentham)	Co 3285-X
	own p, Cyril Monrose-vln, Gerald Clark-g, unk fl	NY October 1928

E 28520-	Gombolai-lai-Pasillo (Lionel Belasco)	Br 7039
E 28521-	Sophie-Pasillo (Lionel Belasco)	Br 7040
E 28522-	Toddy-Pasillo (Lionel Belasco)	Br 7040
E 28523-	The Dog Catchers-Pasillo (Lionel Belasco)	Br 7039
	with vo	NY October 8, 1928

261	Oh Rufus, Hold Me Tight	QRS R-7031
262	Bajan Girls	QRS R-7031
	own p, unk vln, g, vo	NY Autumn 1928

Orquesta De L. Belasco

E 30141-	Palais Royal-Vals (M.C. Palm)	Br 40754
E 30142-	Los Ojitos De Una Mexicana {Mexican Girl's Eyes}-Danza (J. Blassini)	
		Br 40754
E 30143-	Flores Curazoleñas {Flowers Of Curaçao}-Pasillo (R.H. Palm)	Br 40807
E 30144-	Ave De Paso {Passing Fancy}-Danza (Jac. Palm)	Br 40807
E 30145-	Feliz Encuentro {Happy Meeting}-Vals (Jac. Palm)	Br 40806
E 30146-	Tu Y Yo {You And I}-Danza (A. Mislan)	Br 40806
E 30147-	Bola Roja {Red Ball}-Pasillo Colombiano (Cipriano Guerrero)	
		Br 40757, 40837
	Café Santander-Rumba Colombiano	Br 40757
		NY ca June 1929

Lionel Belasco And His Orchestra

GEX 2318-	Venezuela-Waltz[1]	Ge 20356
GEX 2319-B	El Toro-Waltz	Ge 20355
GEX 2320-B	Leoncito-Waltz	Ge 20354
GEX 2321-	Katie-Paseo	Ge 20354
GEX 2322-A	Trinidad Obeah Man-Paseo[2]	Ge 20356
GEX 2323-B	Taffy, The Bogus Preacher Man-Paseo	Ge 20355
	own p, Cyril Monrose-vln, possibly Gerald Clark-g, unk vc, [1]fl, [2]vo	
		NY August 1929

Orquesta Belasco

BVE 57092-2	El Primer Beso-Vals (Lionel Belasco)	Vi 46586, 82013
BVE 57093-2	El Copey-Vals (Gómez)	Vi 46586, 82041
BVE 57094-2	Cocotte-Paseo (Lionel Belasco)	Vi 46710
BVE 57095-2	Esteline-Paseo (Lionel Belasco)	Vi 46710
BVE 57096-2	Matrimony-Paseo (Atilla)[1]	Vi 46818
BVE 57097-1	Volga Boatman-Paseo (Mentor)[1]	Vi 46819
BVE 57098-1	Warning To Mothers-Paseo (Atilla)[1]	Vi 46587

```
BVE 57099-2    Elaine-Paseo (García)'                                    Vi 46818
BVE 57100-1    In The Days Of Camboulay-Paseo (Mentor)'                  Vi 46587
               own p, unk vln, g, cuatro, 'Wilmoth Houdini-vo   NY  November 15, 1929


Vi 82013 and 82041 as ORQUESTA VENEZOLANA

BVE 57713-2    Woman, Sweet Woman-Paseo (W. Houdini)                     Vi 46711
BVE 57714-1    The Shango Dance-Paseo (García)                           Vi 46819
BVE 57715-2    Loretto-Paseo (Codallo)                                   Vi 46711
               as before, Wilmoth Houdini-vo                   NY  November 20, 1929
```

Lionel Belasco And His Orchestra

```
E 33575-A      The Palms Of Maracaibo (Belasco)                          Br 7172
               Las Palmas De Maracaibo-Vals                             Br 41161
E 33576-A      Maria Ranghell (Belasco)                                  Br 7173
E 33577-A      Big Mouth Bernard (Belasco)'                              Br 7172
E 33578-A      Mabel Give Me My Money Back (Belasco)'                    Br 7173
               'John Reid-vo                                   NY  August 12, 1930
```

Matrix numbers E 33275-78 were originally assigned to the above titles.

```
E 33938-A      That Man Of Mine (J. Giménez-L. Clark)'                   Br 7171
E 33939-A      Black Rose (Belasco)                                      Br 7171
               Rosa Negra-Vals                                          Br 41161
               as before                                      NY  August 13, 1930


B 11841-A      Esperanza-Waltz (C. Monrose)       Or O-702, Pe P-700, P-702, Ro R-702
B 11842-A      Adoración-Vals (Felix Mejías)          Br 7231, 41453, Lucky 5039
B 11843-A      Feliz Regreso {Happy Return}-Vals (Felix Mejías)     Br 7233, 41450
B 11844-A      Rayo De Luz {Ray Of Light}-Vals (Felix Mejías)       Br 7233, 41450
B 11845-A      Depression-Pasillo (García)            Br 7232, Me M12900, Pe P-722
               own p, Cyril Monrose-vln, unk cl, g, cuatro, sbs   NY  May 17, 1932


B 11860-A      Theresa-Pasillo (Belasco)          Or O-702, Pe P-701, P-702, Ro R-702
B 11861-       The Whe Whe Craze-Pasillo (Albany)'                      Pe P-701
B 11862-A      Single Tone-Calypso (Belasco)'         Br 7232, Me M12900, Pe P-722
B 11863-A      Three Little Girls (Douglas)'                            Pe P-700
B 11864-A      Mi Dulce Carmen {Sweet Carmen}-Waltz (Felix Mejías)
                                                       Br 7231, 41453, Lucky 5039
               as before, 'Fritz-vo                             NY  May 18, 1932


13340-1        The Treasury Fire-Pasillo (Beginner)'  Ba B-707, Me M12705, Or O-707,
                                                       Pe P-707, Ro R-707, Cr W-827
13341-1        Why Me Neighbour Vex-Pasillo (Douglas)'        Ba B-708, Me M12706,
                                                       Or O-708, Pe P-708, Ro R-708, EC KA3(C)
13342-1        The Pepper Sauce Woman-Pasillo (Atilla)'
                                                  Ba B-711, Me M12709, Or O-711, Pe P-711, Ro R-711
13343-1        Wash Pan Wash-Pasillo (Radio)'
                                                  Ba B-706, Me M12704, Or O-706, Pe P-706, Ro R-706
13344-1        Bournes Road-Pasillo (García)'
                                                  Ba B-709, Me M12707, Or O-709, Pe P-709, Ro R-709
13345-1        Cunumunu-Pasillo (Radio)'
                                                  Ba B-710, Me M12708, Or O-710, Pe P-710, Ro R-710
```

B 13346-1   Luna De Maracaibo-Valse (Belasco)   Ba B-708, Br 41556, Co 5065-X,
                                        2001-F, Me M12706, Or O-708, Pe P-708, Ro R-708
B 13347-1   Miraflores-Valse (Belasco)   Ba B-706, Br 41560, Co 5109-X, 2002-F,
                                        Me M12704, Or O-706, Pe P-706, Ro R-706
B 13348-1   Juliane-Valse (Belasco)   Ba B-710, Co 5065-X, 2000-F, Me M12708,
                                        Or O-710, Pe P-710, Ro R-710
B 13349-1   Carmencita-Valse (Belasco)   Ba B-707, Br 41561, Co 5108-X, 2002-F,
                                        Me M12705, Or O-707, Pe P-707, Ro R-707, Cr W-827
B 13350-1   Miranda-Valse (Belasco)   Ba B-709, Br 41561, Co 5108-X, 2001-F,
                                        Me M12707, Or O-709, Pe P-709, Ro R-709
B 13351-1   Rosa Roja-Valse (Belasco)   Ba B-711, Br 41560, Co 5109-X, 2000-F,
                                        Me M12709, Or O-711, Pe P-711, Ro R-711
            own p, unk cl, cuatro, sbs, 'E. Peters-vo   NY May 17, 1933

BS 76430-1   Conchita-Waltz (Lionel Belasco)   Vi 30893, Bb B-4991
BS 76431-1   Luna De Maracaibo-Waltz (Lionel Belasco)   Vi
BS 76432-1   Ensueños-Waltz (Lionel Belasco)   Vi 30894, Bb B-4992
BS 76437-1   Lucille-Waltz (Lionel Belasco)   Vi 30892, 26-6511, Bb B-4990
BS 76438-1   Miraflores-Waltz (Lionel Belasco)   Vi
BS 76439-1   Luengo-Waltz (Lionel Belasco)   Vi
BS 76440-1   Breach Of Promise-Paseo (Lionel Belasco)'   Vi
BS 76441-1   Dianee {The Lawyer's Dog And The Maid} (Lionel Belasco)'   Vi
BS 76442-1   Treasury Fire-Paseo (Lionel Belasco)'   Vi 30894, Bb B-4992
BS 76443-1   Why Me Neighbour Vex With Me-Paseo (Lionel Belasco)'   Vi
BS 76444-1   Wash Pan Wash-Paseo (Lionel Belasco)'   Vi 30892, 26-6511, Bb B-4990
BS 76445-1   Bournes Road-Paseo (Lionel Belasco)'   Vi 30893, Bb B-4991
            as before, 'E. Peters-vo   NY June 13, 1933

West Indian Serenaders

13595-1   Emancipation-Pasillo (Lionel Belasco)
                             Ba B-712, Me M12799, Or O-712, Pe P-712, Ro R-712
13596-1   Elsie-Pasillo (Lionel Belasco)
                             Ba B-715, Me M12809, Or O-715, Pe P-715, Ro R-715
13597-1   Hold Me Tight-Pasillo (Lionel Belasco)
                             Ba B-716, Me M12810, Or O-716, Pe P-716, Ro R-716
13598-1   Roaming At Night-Pasillo (Lionel Belasco)
                             Ba B-717, Me M12811, Or O-717, Pe P-717, Ro R-717
13599-1   Little May-Pasillo (Lionel Belasco)
                             Ba B-713, Me M12800, Or O-713, Pe P-713, Ro R-713
13600-1   Te Vi Primero-Vals (Lionel Belasco) [no vo]   Ba B-717, Co 2003-F,
                             Me M12811, Or O-717, Pe P-717, Ro R-717
            as before, E. Peters-vo   NY July 20, 1933

13610-1   San José-Valse (Lionel Belasco)   Ba B-715, Br 41583, Me M12809,
                                        Or O-715, Pe P-715, Ro R-715
13611-1   Mi Querida-Valse (Lionel Belasco)   Ba B-716, Br 41583, Co 2003-F,
                                        Me M12810, Or O-716, Pe P-716, Ro R-716
13612-1   Cuatro De Julio-Valse (Lionel Belasco)   Ba B-712, Br 41577,
                                        Me M12799, Or O-712, Pe P-712, Ro R-712
13613-1   The Last Rose-Valse (Lionel Belasco) Ba B-713, Br 41577, Me M12800,
                                        Or O-713, Pe P-713, Ro R-713
            as before   NY July 21, 1933

Lionel Belasco

13614-1	Manzanilla-Pasillo (Lionel Belasco)	Ba B-714, Br 41582, Me M12801, Or O-714, Pe P-714, Ro R-714
13615-1	Port Of Spain Carnival-Pasillo (Lionel Belasco)	Ba B-714, Br 41582, Me M12801, Or O-714, Pe P-714, Ro R-714
	p solos	NY July 21, 1933

Lionel Belasco And His Orchestra

BS 92468-1	Alma {Soul}-Valse (Lionel Belasco)	Bb B-4987
BS 92469-1	Mi Corazón-Valse (Lionel Belasco)	Bb B-4988
BS 92470-1	Serenade-Valse (Lionel Belasco)	Bb B-4988
BS 92471-1	Emaline-Danse Merango (Lionel Belasco)	Bb B-4987
BS 92472-1	The Jubilee Song (Lionel Belasco)[i]	Bb B-4989
BS 92473-1	War Song (Lionel Belasco)[i]	Bb B-4989
	[i]with vo	NY September 6, 1935

Lionel Belasco And His West Indian Orchestra

21016-2	Pensando En Tí-Waltz (Lionel Belasco)	Co 5648-X, Pe 788
21017-2	Año Nuevo-Waltz (T.A. Codallo)	Co 5595-X, Pe 774
21018-	Humberto-Waltz (Lionel Belasco)	Co 5618-X, Pe 789
21019-	A Tu Lado-Waltz (Lionel Belasco)	Co 5648-X, Pe 789
21020-	Venezuela-Joropo (Lionel Belasco)	Co 5618-X, Pe 787
21021-	Luna Blanca-Waltz (T.A. Codallo)	Co 5631-X, Pe 773
21022-	Agua Mansa-Waltz (T.A. Codallo)	Co 5573-X, Pe 772
21023-	Lindo Orinoco-Waltz (T.A. Codallo)	Co 5573-X, Pe 772
21024-	Me Avisas Cuando-Waltz (T.A. Codallo)	Co 5631-X, Pe 773
21025-	Amor Rechazado-Waltz (T.A. Codallo)	Co 5595-X, Pe 774
21026-	Flores De Mayo-Waltz (Lionel Belasco)	Co 5616-X, Pe 787
21027-	Santa María-Waltz (Lionel Belasco)	Co 5616-X, Pe 788
	own p, unk tp, 2 cl, g, sbs	NY April 21, 1937

Lionel Belasco's Orchestra

62601-A	After Midnight-Rhumba (Lionel Belasco)	De 17334, F40498
62602-A	Will You Sweetheart-Rhumba (Lionel Belasco)	De 17333, F40499
62603-A	Someday-Rhumba (Lionel Belasco)	De 17333, F40498
62604-A	Lola-Rhumba (Lionel Belasco)	De 17332, F40500
62605-A	Trinidad-Rhumba (Lionel Belasco)	De 17336, F40497
62606-A	Not Tonight Josephine-Rhumba (Lionel Belasco)	De 17337, F40496
62607-A	Butterfly-Rhumba (Lionel Belasco)	De 17336
62608-A	Thelma-Rhumba (Lionel Belasco)	De 17332, F40497
62609-A	Moonlight Carnival-Rhumba (Lionel Belasco)	De 17335
62610-A	Pompadour-Rhumba (Lionel Belasco)	De 17334, F40500
62611-A	Chiquita-Rhumba (Lionel Belasco)	De 17335, F40496
62612-A	Wait And See-Rhumba (Lionel Belasco)	De 17337, F40499
	own p, unk tp, 2 cl, g, sbs, percussion	NY September 12, 1937

22097-1	Torero-Valse (Lionel Belasco)	Co 5676-X, Pe 793
22098-1	The Dancer {Bailarina}-Pasillo (Lionel Belasco)	Co 5676-X, Pe 793
22099-	Shadows {Sombras}-Valse (Lionel Belasco)	Co 5672-X, Pe 796

```
22100-      Steamline Sue {Nana Guapa}-Calypso (Lionel Belasco)
                                                  Co 5672-X, Pe 796
22101-1     Daybreak {La Aurora}-Calypso (Lionel Belasco)     Co 5693-X, Pe 794
22102-      Dawn {La Madrugada}-Calypso (Lionel Belasco)      Co 5679-X, Pe 794
22111-1     Ensueño-Valse (Lionel Belasco)                    Co 5679-X, Pe 791
22112-1     Mama Catch Papa {Vuelve Para Casa}-Pasillo (Lionel Belasco)
                                                  Co 5693-X, Pe 791
            own p, unk tp, 2 sax, g, sbs, dm        NY  November 11, 1937

62762-A     El Démocrata-Vals (T.A. Codallo)¹          De 17340, 10349
62763-A     Patricia-Waltz (T.A. Codallo)¹                  De 17341
            Día De Fiesta-Vals                              De 10365
62764-A     Con Su Permiso-Vals (Lionel Belasco)¹     De 17343, 10349
62765-A     Sally You Not Ashamed? (Fitz McLean)     De 17339, FW RF4(33)
62766-A     Netty's Defense (Fitz McLean)                   De 17340
62767-A     Sa Gomes' Emporiums (Fitz McLean)               De 17338
62768-A     Trinidad Potpourri                              De 17338
62769-A     Mama I Don't Want To Get Married (T.A. Codallo)  De 17341
62770-A     Trinidad The Pearl Of The Caribbean (T.A. Codallo)  De 17339
62771-A     Zenith For Me (T.A. Codallo)                    De 17342
62772-A     Trinidad Carnival (Fitz McLean)                 De 17342
62773-A     Give Me An Ugly Girl (Donnie Moore)             De 17343
            own p, unk tp, 2 cl/sax, g, sbs, dm, ¹vln   NY  November 13, 1937
```

39.4. Harold Boyce And The Harlem Indians *vocal, instrumental*

```
65917-A     De Donkey Want Water (Thomas Boyce)³               De 7748
65918-A     De Bush To Boil Tea (Thomas Boyce)²                De 7636
65919-A     Sweet Willie (Don't Let The Neighbors Laugh At Me) {Little Willie,
                Don't Go From Me} (Fred Hall-Sam Manning)¹    De 7636
65920-A     Bajun Gal (Thomas Boyce)¹                          De 7748
65921-A     Knock Ya'self Out (Thomas Boyce)                   De 7696
65922-A     So What (Thomas Boyce)                             De 7696
            Harold Boyce-p/¹vo, Joe James-tp, Lem Davis-alt sax, Sidney Grant-ten
            sax, Gladstone Thomas-sbs/²vo, Arthur Herbert-dm/³vo  NY  July 5, 1939
```

Boyce's Harlem Serenaders

```
69799-      The Good Old Hometown Blues¹                       De 8602
69800-      Harlem After Midnight²                             De 8602
69801-A     'Long About Three In The Morning¹                  De 8585
69802-A     Get In The Groove²                                 De 8585
            Harold Boyce-p/¹vo, Harvey Davis-tp, Sidney Grant-ten sax, Gladstone
            Thomas-sbs, probably Joe Johnson-dm, ²group vo    NY  October 9, 1941
```

39.5. The Caresser (Rufus Callender) *vocal*

```
61959-A     Edward The VIII (Rufus Callender)     De 17298, M30748, RBF RF13(33)
61964-A     Paramaribo (Rufus Callender)             De 17301, FL 9048(33)
61968-A     Food Scandal (Fitz McLean)                         De 17303
            Gerald Clark And His Caribbean Serenaders: Gerald Clark-g, unk tp,
            vln, cl, cuatro, sbs                     NY  February 16, 1937
```

```
61970-B      Carnival Is We Bacchanal (Rufus Callender)
                                    De 17304, FW FP8(33), 6808(33)
61973-       Maracas Falls (Rufus Callender)          De 17478, M30736
             as before                           NY  February 18, 1937

61983-A      My Luxurious Life (Rufus Callender)                De 17306
61986-A      Theodore (Rufus Callender)            De 17308, FW RF4(33)
             as before                           NY  February 19, 1937

61991-A      Settle With An Old Queen (Fitz McLean)            De 17316
             as before                           NY  February 22, 1937

62004-A      The Rats (Rufus Callender)                           De rej
62007-A      Ah Gertie (Fitz McLean)                            De 17328
             as before                           NY  February 23, 1937

62011-A      Netty's Defense (Fitz McLean)                        De rej
62012-A      Selassie Is Held By The Police                     De 17314
62024-A      John Thomas (Fitz McLean)                          De 17330
             as before                           NY  February 24, 1937
```

39.6. Jack Celestain And His Caribbean Stompers *instrumental*

```
W 96742-2    Barbados Blues (Sam Manning)'                   Co 3268-X
W 96743-4    Lita-Calipso Song (Sam Manning)                 Co 3269-X
W 96753-3    Nancy-Dance Calipso (Sam Manning)   Co 3268-X, Harlequin HQ2016(33)
W 96754-2    I Am Done With That (Cyril Monrose)'            Co 3269-X
             own p, Cyril Monrose-vln, Gerald Clark-g, unk cl, alt sax, cuatro,
             'Sam Manning-vo                      NY  September 1928
```

39.7. Gerald Clark *guitar (d. 1976)*

Gerald Clark And His Night Owls

```
1587-2       No Woman's Man-Rumba Fox Trot (Wilmoth Houdini)   Cr 1002, Vars 7010
1588-1       The Better Woman Wins-Rumba Fox Trot (Wilmoth Houdini)
                                                 Cr 1001, Vars 7011
1589-2       The Man Without A Mind-Rumba Fox Trot (Wilmoth Houdini)
                                                 Cr 1001, Vars 7010
1590-3       Some More Scandal-Rumba Fox Trot (Wilmoth Houdini)
                                                 Cr 1002, Vars 7011
             Wilmoth Houdini-vo                   NY  December 31, 1931
```

Varsity 7010 and 7011 as WEST INDIAN NIGHT OWLS

```
BS 77446-1   Marguerite-Waltz (E. Peters)                      Bb B-4907
BS 77447-1   Carmelita-Waltz (E. Peters)       Bb B-4908, Rounder 1039(33,C,CD)
             John Lahoud-Vals                               Vi DS-109
BS 77448-1   Cocotte Medley-Paseo (E. Peters)                  Bb B-4909
BS 77449-1   Pauline Medley-Paseo (E. Peters)                  Bb B-4910
BS 77450-1   Cricketing Stars-Carnival Song (E. Peters)'       Bb B-4907
```

BS 77451-1   Iere's Defender-Carnival Song (E. Peters)[1]   Bb B-4908
BS 77452-1   The Minister-Carnival Song (E. Peters)[1]   Bb B-4909
BS 77453-1   Susan Medley {Cuban Medley}-Paseo (E. Peters)   Bb B-4910
              own and another-2 g, unk tp, vln, cl, p, sbs, [1]E. Peters-vo
                                                          NY August 10, 1933

Vi DS-109 (uncredited) is a soap company premium.

Gerald Clark And His Caribbean Serenaders

B 15204-A   Happy Days-Waltz (Edwards)   Ba B-767, Or O-767, Pe P-767, Ro R-767
              Alegrías-Vals   Co 5210-X
B 15205-   Shadows-Waltz (Green)   Ba B-766, Or O-766, Pe P-766, Ro R-766
              Sombra-Vals   Br 41659, Co 5150-X
B 15206-A   Under The Trinidad Moon-Waltz Ba B-767, Or O-767, Pe P-767, Ro R-767
              Castro Y Margarita-Vals   Co 5210-X
B 15207-   Darling-Waltz   Ba B-768, Or O-768, Pe P-768, Ro R-768
              La Favorita-Vals   Br 41644, Co 5197-X
B 15208-   Venezuela Moon-Waltz (Clark)   Ba B-766, Or O-766, Pe P-766, Ro R-766
              Luna De Venezuela-Vals   Br 41659, Co 5150-X
B 15209-   West Indies Lullaby-Merengue (Clark)
                                             Ba B-768, Or O-768, Pe P-768, Ro R-768
              Campanas Del Llano-Merengue   Br 41644, Co 5197-X
              own g, unk vln, cl, p, cuatro, sbs   NY May 14, 1934

All Br and Co issues as LOS CANTADORES DE ARAGUA

61267-A   Si-O-No-Valse   De 17291
61268-A   La Rosa-Valse (Julian Bernard)   De 17292
61269-A   La Ingrata-Valse   De 17293
61270-A   Christiana-Valse (Julian Bernard)   De 17294
61271-A   Flora De Mi Corazón-Valse (Julian Bernard)   De 17295
              Juliana-Vals   De 10364
61272-A   Flores De Trinidad-Valse   De 17296
              own g, unk tp, vln, cl, p, cuatro, sbs, dm   NY September 18, 1936

61273-A   Amor A La Luz De La Luna-Valse   De 17291, 10364
61274-A   Rosa Caraqueña-Valse   De 17292
61275-A   Las Campanas-Valse   De 17293
61276-A   Castro Y Margarita-Valse   De 17294
61277-A   Buenos Noches-Valse   De 17295, 10365
61278-A   Marguerite-Valse   De 17296
              as before   NY. September 20, 1936

De 10364 and 10365 as ROMANCEROS DEL CARIBE (Orquesta Criolla)

Gerald Clark And His Calypso Orchestra

US 1123-1   U.S.A. (Clark-Merrick)   Vars 8138
US 1124-1   Drusilla (Cecil Anderson)
                               Vars 8138, Savoy 5539, FW FP8(33), 6808(33)
US 1125-1   Walter Winchell (Clark-Taylor)   Vars 8130, Savoy 5539

US 1126-2   Maria (Cecil Anderson)   Vars 8130
             own g, Pacheco-vln, Gregory Felix-cl, Jack Celestain-p, Rogelio
             Garcia-sbs, Duke Of Iron (Cecil Anderson)-vo   NY December 1939

US 1324-1   G-Man Hoover (Clark-Merrick)   Vars 8188, RBF RF13(33)
US 1325-1   I Love To Read Magazines (Clark-Merrick)'   Vars 8195
US 1326-1   That Something Will Bring You Back (Clark-Taylor)   Vars 8195
US 1327-1   Camilla, The Jitterbug (Clark-Taylor)   Vars 8188
             as before, Sir Lancelot (Lancelot Pinard) or 'Macbeth The Great-vo
                                                          NY   January 1940

Gerald Clark And His Caribbean Serenaders

69027-   Chip Chip Water   De 17459
69028-   Woopsin   De 17459
             own g, unk tp, vln, cl, p, sbs   NY April 21, 1941

39.8. Timothy Dunn *vocal*

BVE 43612-2 Cordelia Brown (A. Johnson)   Vi 80778
             Donald Heywood-p, unk sax, g   NY April 5, 1928

39.9. The Executor (Phillip García) *vocal*

Later recordings by this singer are as LORD EXECUTOR.

61958-A-B   Three Friends' Advice (Fitz McLean)   De 17298, RBF RF13(33)
61965-A   I Don't Know How The Young Men Living (Fitz McLean)
                                                     De 17301, FL 9048(33)
             Gerald Clark And His Caribbean Serenaders: Gerald Clark-g, unk tp,
             vln, cl, cuatro, sbs   NY February 16, 1937

61969-A   Hold Up, Blackbird, Hold Up (Fitz McLean)   De 17303
61971-B   The Bells (Fitz McLean)   De 17304
             as before   NY February 18, 1937

61975-A   Shop Closing Ordinance (Fitz McLean)   De 17308
61985-B   Street Vendors (Philip García)   De rej
             as before   NY February 19, 1937

61994-A   Xmas Accident (Philip García)   De 17450
             as before   NY February 22, 1937

62002-A   Sweet Evelina (Philip García)   De 17316
62005-A   My Reply To Houdini (Fitz McLean)   De 17306, Rounder 1039(33,C,CD)
62006-   Arima Fete Santa Rosa (Fitz McLean)'   De 17318
             as before, 'with The Caresser   NY February 23, 1937

62014-A   Old Ginger (Fitz McLean)   De 17320, Rounder 1054(CD)
             as before   NY February 24, 1937

```
62021-A     Christmas Is A Joyful Day (Fitz McLean)                      De 17331
62022-A     Reign Of The Georges (Philip Garcia)            De 17314, FW RF4(33)
62025-      Lindbergh Baby (Fitz McLean)                                 De 17318
            as before                                    NY February 25, 1937
```

Several issues are credited to THE EXECUTER.

39.10. Felix And His Krazy Kats

This artist's full name is Gregory Felix.

Divit Et Son Orchestra

```
BS 78870-2  Tripotiezes-Biguine (R.H. Chauvet)                          Vi 32057
BS 78871-2  Zouzoune-Biguine (R.H. Chauvet)                             Vi 32055
BS 78872-1  Quaille, Qui Bagaille Ci La!-Biguine (R.H. Chauvet)         Vi 32056
BS 78873-1  Jeunesse Yo-Biguine (R.H. Chauvet)                          Vi 32057
BS 78874-1  Blanc Ca Yo-Biguine (R.H. Chauvet)                          Vi 32056
BS 78875-1  Ti Conseil-Biguine (R.H. Chauvet)                           Vi 32054
BS 78876-1  Moune Sotte-Biguine (R.H. Chauvet)                          Vi 32055
BS 78877-1  Erzulie-Voodoo Worship Song (R.H. Chauvet)                  Vi 32054
            Gregory Felix-cl, unk tp, p, g, Rick & Dido-vo   NY  December 19, 1933
```

The above is listed simply as "Felix Band" in the files.

Felix And His Krazy Kats

```
BS 89469-1  Chili {Pepper Pot}-Beguin (Gregory Felix)
                        Bb B-4950, Vi 83148, 26-6510, Cam CAL360(33)
BS 89470-1  Mademoiselle-Beguin (Gregory Felix)
                        Bb B-4950, Vi 83148, 26-6510, Cam CAL360(33)
            Gregory Felix-cl, unk tp, p, uke, sbs             NY  March 29, 1935
```

Vi 83148 as ORQUESTA FELIX Y SUS GATITOS

```
BVE 89840-1  Rubina {Ruby}-Son (G. Felix)                                 Bb B-4968
BVE 89841-1  Caricias {Caresses}-Son (G. Felix)                           Bb B-4968
BVE 89842-1  Shake It, But Don't Break It-Paseo (G. Felix)  Bb B-4951, Vi 26-6508
BVE 89843-1  Let My Wife Alone-Paseo (G. Felix)             Bb B-4951, Vi 26-6508
BVE 89844-1  Tropical Soiree-Beguin (G. Felix)                            Bb B-4952
BVE 89845-1  Bonheur-Beguin (G. Felix)                                    Bb B-4952
                                                            NY  May 21, 1935
```

```
63306-A     Josephine-Paseo (Wayne King-Burke Bivens-Gus Kahn)    De 1856, 17344
63307-A     Rosalie-Paseo, ftmp "Rosalie" (Cole Porter)                  De 17345
63308-A     The Dipsy Doodle-Paseo (Larry Clinton)                De 1856, 17346
63309-      True Confession-Paseo (Sam Coslow-Frederick Hollander)       De 17346
63310-A     Bob White (Whatcha Gonna Swing Tonight?)-Paseo
                        (Bernie Hanighen-Johnny Mercer) De 17344, Harlequin HQ2016(33)
63311-A     Bei Mir Bist Du Schön (Means That You're Grand)-Paseo
                        (Cahn-Chaplin-Secunda)      De 17345, Rounder 1054(33,C,CD)
            tp, vln, cl, p, g, cuatro, Duke Of Iron (Cecil Anderson)-vo
                                                     NY  February 21, 1938
```

2901

39.11. Ralph Fitz-Scott *vocal*

BS 95494-1	Last Ladies Night At The London (Ralph Fitz-Scott)	
		Bb B-4969, Vi 26-6504
BS 95495-1	Transfiguration (Ralph Fitz-Scott)	Bb B-4969, Vi 26-6504
BS 95496-1	Lego Me Man For Me (Ralph Fitz-Scott)	Bb B-4970
BS 95497-1	Alimony (Ralph Fitz-Scott)	Bb B-4970
BS 95498-1	Spin You Yo Yo (Ralph Fitz-Scott)	Bb B-4971
BS 95499-1	The Hawker's Song (Ralph Fitz-Scott)	Bb B-4971
	Felix And His Krazy Kats	NY October 28, 1935

BS 95592-1	Barbados And The MCC (Ralph Fitz-Scott)	Bb B-4972, Vi 26-6507
BS 95593-1	My Fair Sunshine (Ralph Fitz-Scott)	Bb B-4978
BS 95594-1	Parson Stop The Band (Ralph Fitz-Scott)	Bb B-4973, Vi 26-6503
BS 95595-1	Barbados Jubilee (Ralph Fitz-Scott)-Pt. 1	Bb B-4974
BS 95596-1	Barbados Jubilee (Ralph Fitz-Scott)-Pt. 2	Bb B-4974
BS 95597-1	Let Go Me Han (Ralph Fitz-Scott)	Bb B-4972, Vi 26-6507
	as before	NY October 31, 1935

BS 98012-1	The Musical Body Line (Ralph Fitz-Scott)	Bb B-4978
BS 98013-1	Not Me Referee Not Me (Ralph Fitz-Scott)	Bb B-4979
BS 98014-1	Fish Vendor (Ralph Fitz-Scott)	Bb B-4979
BS 98015-1	The Rays Of Your Eyes (Ralph Fitz-Scott)	Bb B-4983
BS 98016-1	The Sweet Man Parson (Ralph Fitz-Scott)	Bb B-4973, Vi 26-6503
BS 98017-1	The Land Of Pigtail And Metigee (Ralph Fitz-Scott)	Bb B-4983
	as before	NY November 1, 1935

BS 98024-1	The Four Sides Men (Ralph Fitz-Scott)	Bb B-4985
BS 98025-1	Woman's Passion (Ralph Fitz-Scott)	Bb B-4984
BS 98026-1	Flogology (Ralph Fitz-Scott)	Bb B-4984
BS 98027-1	Deuteronomy (Ralph Fitz-Scott)	Bb B-4985
BS 98028-1	Testification By Brother Two Mouths (Ralph Fitz-Scott)	Bb B-4980
BS 98029-1	Why Women Stick On With Me (Ralph Fitz-Scott)	Bb B-4980
	as before	NY November 4, 1935

39.12. Marcus Garvey *spoken (1887-1940)*

6453	Speech On His Return To The United States	See-Bee unnumbered
6454	Explanation Of The Objectives Of The Universal Negro Improvement	
	Association	See-Bee unnumbered
		NY ca 1924

39.13. George And Roscoe *vocal*

These artists' full names are George Gray and Roscoe Wickham.

81802-2	My Jamaica	Co 14024-D
81803-1	Black Star Line-A West Indian Chant	Co 14024-D
	uke	NY June 3, 1924

39.14. The Growler (Errol Duke) *vocal*

68899-A   Old Lady You Mashing My Toe (The Growler)
                                    De 17469, 18145, M30729, EC KA1(C)
               Gerald Clark And His Caribbean Serenaders: Gerald Clark-g, unk tp,
               vln, cl, p, sbs   NY April 2, 1941

68946-A   An Excursion To Grenada (The Growler)   De 17467, M30729
68950-   Britain Will Never Surrender (The Growler)   De 17465
               as before   NY April 8, 1941

68980-   The Fall Of France (The Growler)   De 17461
               as before   NY April 11, 1941

69008-A   Don't Hide Him Behind The Door (The Growler)
                                    De 17473, M30750, EC KA4(C)
               as before   NY April 16, 1941

69021-   Bore A Hole In My Constitution (The Growler)   De 17477
               as before   NY April 18, 1941

39.15. Slim Henderson *vocal*

S 72710-B   My Jamaica (Monrose-Grainger)   Ok 65001, Pa R3857
S 72711-B   Goofer Dust John (Monrose-Hogeben)   Ok 65001, Pa R3857
               Fred Hall's Orchestra   NY July 30, 1924

39.16. Donald Heywood *piano*

               Autumn Leaves   BS 60004
               Operatic Dream   BS 60004
                                                        NY 1921-2

The above is included only for the sake of completeness.

Donald Heywood's West Indian Band

BVE 38896-1   Il Me Désait {He Told Me So}   Vi 80776
BVE 38897-2   Baille Mono-Danzón Paseo   Vi 80776
               own p, unk sax, cuatro   NY June 9, 1927

39.17. Wilmoth Houdini *vocal (1895-1973)*

BVE 39919-1   Day By Day (W. Houdini-L. Belasco)   Vi 80077
BVE 39920-3   Cecelia (W. Houdini)   Vi 80077
BVE 39921-2   Caroline-Paseo (W. Houdini-L. Belasco)
                                    Vi 80078, Rounder 1039(33,C,CD)
BVE 39922-2   You Bob (W. Houdini)   Vi 80080
BVE 39923-1   Hit And Run Away (L. Belasco)   Vi 80080
BVE 39924-1   Woman Sweeter Than Man (L. Belasco)   Vi 80079

```
BVE 39925-1    Good-Night Ladies And Gents-Paseo (L. Belasco)           Vi 80078
BVE 39926-2    You Run You Run-Paseo (L. Belasco)                        Vi 80079
               Belasco Orchestra: Lionel Belasco-p, Cyril Monrose-vln, Gerald
               Clark-g, unk cuatro                             NY  August 1, 1927


W 401036-B     Song No. 99 (Houdini)                     Ok 8621, FL 9040(33)
W 401037-A     Uncle Jo' Gimme Mo' (Houdini)             Ok 8605, FL 9040(33)
W 401038-B     Sweet Like A Honey-Bee (Houdini)                         Ok 8621
W 401039-B     Sweet Like A Sugar-Cane (Houdini)                        Ok 8605
               Gerald Clark's Iërë String Band: Cyril Monrose-vln, Berry Barrow-p,
               Gerald Clark-g, unk bj                         NY  July 31, 1928


W 401740-B     Executor Doomed To Die                                  Ok 65011
W 401741-B     Trifling Men                              Ok 65011, FL 9040(33)
W 401742-A     March                                                   Ok 65010
W 401743-B     Constantine                                             Ok 65010
               Monrose-Barrow String Band: Cyril Monrose-vln, Berry Barrow-p,
               probably Gerald Clark-g                       NY  March 25, 1929


E 36077-A      No Mo' Bench And Board (Wilmoth Houdini)   Ba B-728, Br 7192, 80085,
                          BL58007(33), Me M12906, Or O-728, Pe P-728, Ro R-728,
                          FL 9040(33), CI CI-015(33), Festival CFR 10-568(33)
E 36078-A      Sweet Papa Willie (Wilmoth Houdini)      Ba B-727, Br 7201, 80087,
                          BL58007(33), Me M12905, Or O-727, Pe P-727, Ro R-727,
                          FL 9040(33), CI CI-015(33), Festival CFR 10-568(33)
E 36079-A      Honey, I'm Bound To Go (Wilmoth Houdini)   Ba B-727, Br 7201, 80087,
                          BL58007(33), Me M12905, Or O-727, Pe P-727, Ro R-727,
                          FL 9040(33), CI CI-015(33), Festival CFR 10-568(33)
E 36080-A      The Cooks In Trinidad (Wilmoth Houdini)   Ba B-728, Br 7192, 80085,
                          BL58007(33), Me M12906, Or O-728, Pe P-728, Ro R-728,
                          FL 9040(33), CI CI-015(33), Festival CFR 10-568(33)
               Gerald Clark's Night Owls: Walter Bennett-c, Walter Edwards-cl/ten
               sax, Berry Barrow-p, Joshy Paris-g, Gerald Clark-cuatro, Charlie
               Vincent-bj, Al Morgan-sbs                     NY  February 16, 1931


E 37021-A      Arima Tonight, Sangre Grande Tomorrow Night (Wilmoth Houdini)
               Ba B-726, Br 7219, 80086, BL58007(33), Me M12904, Or O-726, Pe P-726, Ro R-726,
                          FL 9040(33), CI CI-015(33), Festival CFR 10-568(33)
E 37022-A      Black But Sweet (Wilmoth Houdini)         Ba B-726, Br 7219, 80088,
                          BL58007(33), Me M12904, Or O-726, Pe P-726, Ro R-726,
                          FL 9040(33), CI CI-015(33), Festival CFR 10-568(33)
E 37023-A      I Need A Man (Wilmoth Houdini)       Ba B-725, Br 7224, 80086, 01228,
                          BL58007(33), Me M12903, Or O-725, Pe P-725, Ro R-725,
                          FL 9040(33), CI CI-015(33), Festival CFR 10-568(33)
E 37024-A      Stop Coming And Come (Wilmoth Houdini)    Ba B-725, Br 7224, 80088,
                          01228, BL58007(33), Me M12903, Or O-725, Pe P-725, Ro R-725,
                          FL 9040(33), CI CI-015(33), Festival CFR 10-568(33)
               as before                                    NY  August 13, 1931


Br 80085, 80086, 80087 and 80088 are in album B-1023.


B 11408-A      Sweet Lizzie And Joe-Rumba (Wilmoth Houdini)    Ba B-724, Br 7229,
                          Me M12902, Or O-724, Pe P-724, Ro R-724
```

B 11409-A   Keep Your Money Hot Daddy-Rumba (Wilmoth Houdini) Ba B-724, Br 7229,
                                        Me M12902, Or O-724, Pe P-724, Ro R-724
B 11410-A   Old Man You Too Old, You Too Bold, In Fact You Too Cold-Pasillo
                (Wilmoth Houdini)   Ba B-723, Br 7230, Me M12901, Or O-723,
                                                        Pe P-723, Ro R-723
B 11411-A   Tiger Tom Kill Tiger Cat, Damblay, Santapie And Rat-Pasillo
                (Wilmoth Houdini)   Ba B-723, Br 7230, Me M12901, Or O-723,
                                                        Pe P-723, Ro R-723
        tp, cl/alt sax, p, bj, sbs   NY March 5, 1932

Wilmoth Houdini And His Caribbean Orchestra

B 12602-A   You Will Pay For My Love Some Day-Waltz (W. Houdini)   Ba B-704,
                Co 2006-F, Me M12540, Or O-704, Pe P-704, Ro R-704, Cr W-824
B 12603-A   Johnie Take My Wife-Rumba (W. Houdini)   Ba B-704, Co 2006-F,
                Me M12540, Or O-704, Pe P-704, Ro R-704, Cr W-824
             Johnnie Take My Wife   Rounder 1054(33,C,CD)
B 12604-A   I Got What To Bring Her Back-Rumba (W. Houdini)
                        Ba B-703, Me M12539, Or O-703, Pe P-703, Ro R-703
B 12605-A   West Indian Sugar Crop (W. Houdini)
                        Ba B-703, Me M12539, Or O-703, Pe P-703, Ro R-703
B 12606-A   Man Sweet But Woman Sweeter (W. Houdini)
                        Ba B-705, Me M12541, Or O-705, Pe P-705, Ro R-705
B 12607-   That Big Black Woman-Pasillo (W. Houdini)
                        Ba B-705, Me M12541, Or O-705, Pe P-705, Ro R-705
        vln, fl, g, bj, sbs   NY November 17, 1932

Crown W-824 is a Canadian issue.

Wilmoth Houdini And His Humming Birds

14173-2   Sinners Get Ready For Glory-Carol (Houdini)
                        Me M12826, Or O-720, Pe P-720, Ro R-720, Co 2011-F
14174-1   Teacher Nose Gay The Shouter-Carol (Houdini)
                        Me M12826, Or O-720, Pe P-720, Ro R-720, Co 2011-F
14175-1   Tickling Charley (Houdini)   Me M12847, Or O-721, Pe P-721, Ro R-721
14176-1   Bernard King Of The Bamboo Band (Houdini)
                        Me M12847, Or O-721, Pe P-721, Ro R-721
14177-2   Trinidad Hurricane (Houdini) Me M12825, Or O-719, Pe P-719, Ro R-719
14178-2   Unfortunate Millie (Houdini) Me M12825, Or O-719, Pe P-719, Ro R-719
        vln, cl, p, bj, sbs   NY October 19, 1933

15381-1   Mickey Cipriani's Career   Me M13064, Or O-744, Pe P-744, Ro R-744
15382-   Memories To Trinidad Eagle (Wilmoth Houdini)
                        Me M13065, Or O-745, Pe P-745, Ro R-745
15383-1   Glorious Centenary (Wilmoth Houdini)
                        Me M13065, Or O-745, Pe P-745, Ro R-745, FL 9040(33)
15384-1   Cipriani's And Bradshaw's Death
                        Me M13064, Or O-744, Pe P-744, Ro R-744
15385-   Warning To Neighbors   Me M13063, Or O-743, Pe P-743, Ro R-743
15386-1   Bandsman Shooting Case
                        Me M13063, Or O-743, Pe P-743, Ro R-743, FL 9040(33)
        tp, vln, fl, cl, p, cuatro, bj/ten g, sbs   NY July 2, 1934

Wilmoth Houdini And His Shouting Congregation

16059-	He Was Born The King Of Kings (Wilmoth Houdini)	
	Ba B-746, Co 2012-F, Or O-746, Pe P-746, Ro R-746	
16060-	Come Ye Backsliders (Wilmoth Houdini) Ba B-747, Co 2013-F, Or O-747,	
	Pe P-747, Ro R-747, Lucky 5041	
16061-	Happy Land Of Canaan (Wilmoth Houdini)	
	Ba B-748, Co 2014-F, Or O-748, Pe P-748, Ro R-748	
16062-	Mary And Martha (Wilmoth Houdini) Ba B-747, Co 2013-F, Or O-747,	
	Pe P-747, Ro R-747, Lucky 5041	
16063-	The Foundations Of The Earth (Wilmoth Houdini)	
	Ba B-746, Co 2012-F, Or O-746, Pe P-746, Ro R-746	
16064-	Hold Me Lest I Fall (Wilmoth Houdini)[1]	
	Ba B-748, Co 2014-F, Or O-748, Pe P-748, Ro R-748	

cl, p, g, uke, sbs, or [1]org   NY September 26, 1934

Wilmoth Houdini And His Humming Birds

16375-1	Tropical Moon (W. Houdini) Ba B-749, Or O-749, Pe P-749, Ro R-749	
16376-1	Cousin Scratch Here So For Me (W. Houdini)	
	Ba B-749, Or O-749, Pe P-749, Ro R-749	
16377-1	War Declaration (W. Houdini)	
	Ba B-750, Or O-750, Pe P-750, Ro R-750, Rounder 1039(33,C,CD)	
16378-1	African Love Call (W. Houdini) Ba B-750, Or O-750, Pe P-750,	
	Ro R-750, LC LBC-10(33), FL 9040(33)	
16379-1	Lizzie Quit Joe (W. Houdini)	
	Ba B-751, Or O-751, Pe P-751, Ro R-751, Lucky 5048	
16380-1	Drunk And Disorderly (W. Houdini)	
	Ba B-751, Or O-751, Pe P-751, Ro R-751, Lucky 5048	

tp, cl, p, g, cuatro, sbs   NY November 30, 1934

Wilmoth Houdini

BS 89218-1	They Tired Talking About Me-Paseo (Douglas-Fitz McLean)	Bb B-4947
BS 89219-1	Alone Mable Why Not Leave Joe Laugher Alone-Paseo	
	(Douglas-Fitz McLean)	Bb B-4945
BS 89220-1	I'm Going To Chase The Young Girls Away-Paseo (Douglas-Fitz McLean)	
		Bb B-4945
BS 89221-1	The Old Man First Show Me His Love-Paseo (Douglas-Fitz McLean)	
		Bb B-4946
BS 89222-1	Tearing Up My Clothes-Calypso Singletone (Douglas-Fitz McLean)	
		Bb B-4946
BS 89223-1	Leave Me Business Alone-Calypso Singletone (Douglas-Fitz McLean)	
		Bb B-4947

c, cl, p, uke, sbs   NY March 19, 1935

BS 89465-1	Married Women Bad Bad Bad-Paseo (Johnny Walker)	Bb B-4948
BS 89466-1	Dingo Lay Oh-Single Tone Calinda (Fitz McLean)	Bb B-4948
BS 89467-1	They Are Lying On Me-Single Tone Paseo (Wilmoth Houdini)	
	Bb B-4949, Vi 26-6502, Cam CAL360(33)	
BS 89468-1	Don't Do That To Me-Calypso (Wilmoth Houdini)	
	Bb B-4949, Vi 26-6502, Cam CAL360(33), LC LBC-7(33)	

Felix And His Krazy Kats: Gregory Felix-cl, unk tp, p, uke, sbs
NY March 29, 1935

Wilmoth Houdini And His Calvary Bamboo Band

17251-1   Oh! Cinderella-Single Tone (W. Houdini)
                            Ba B-754, Or O-754, Pe P-754, Ro R-754
17252-1   Ble-O-Ble-Callindar (W. Houdini)
                            Ba B-754, Or O-754, Pe P-754, Ro R-754
17253-2   Miss Benard's Monkey-Single Tone (W. Houdini)
                            Ba B-753, Or O-753, Pe P-753, Ro R-753
17254-1   Call The Fire Brigade-Callindar (W. Houdini)
                            Ba B-753, Or O-753, Pe P-753, Ro R-753
17255-1   The Devil Behind Me-Leggo (W. Houdini)
                      Ba B-752, Or O-752, Pe P-752, Ro R-752, FL 9040(33)
17256-1   Way Down Sobo-Leggo (W. Houdini)
                            Ba B-752, Or O-752, Pe P-752, Ro R-752
        5 voices, 2 bamboo men, 2 gin bottle players, sbs, mar
                                        NY April 5, 1935

Wilmoth Houdini And His Humming Birds

18155-1   Loving Bonnie Jane-Double Tone (W. Houdini)
                            Ba B-765, Or O-765, Pe P-765, Ro R-765
18156-1   Ethiopian War Drums-Double Tone (W. Houdini)
                            Ba B-763, Or O-763, Pe P-763, Ro R-763
18157-1   Sweet West Indian Girl-Double Tone (W. Houdini)
                            Ba B-764, Or O-764, Pe P-764, Ro R-764
18158-1   Resisting Temptation-Single Tone (W. Houdini)
                            Ba B-763, Or O-763, Pe P-763, Ro R-763
18159-1   Lazy Mule-Single Tone (W. Houdini)
                            Ba B-765, Or O-765, Pe P-765, Ro R-765
18160-   Your Kisses Send Me Daddy-Single Tone (W. Houdini)
                            Ba B-764, Or O-764, Pe P-764, Ro R-764
        tp, vln, cl, p, cuatro, sbs   NY October 14, 1935

Wilmoth Houdini And His Night Owls

19099-1   St. Bernard Murder Case-Double Tone (Wilmoth Houdini)
                            Ba B-770, Or O-770, Pe P-770, Ro R-770
19100-2   Fire And Brimstone-Double Tone (Wilmoth Houdini)
                            Ba B-769, Or O-769, Pe P-769, Ro R-769
19101-1   They Put Him So-Double Tone (Wilmoth Houdini)
                            Ba B-771, Or O-771, Pe P-771, Ro R-771
19102-1   Man's Destiny-Single Tone (Wilmoth Houdini)
                            Ba B-770, Or O-770, Pe P-770, Ro R-770
19103-2   Daddy Turn On The Light-Single Tone (Wilmoth Houdini)
                            Ba B-769, Or O-769, Pe P-769, Ro R-769
19104-1   Gi' Me Mine In A Saucer-Single Tone (Wilmoth Houdini)
                            Ba B-771, Or O-771, Pe P-771, Ro R-771
        tp, vln, cl, p, g, sbs   NY April 24, 1936

Wilmoth Houdini

21053-   King George VI Address To Parliament-Ballad (Wilmoth Houdini) Pe 776
21054-   Executor The Homeless Man-Double Tone (Wilmoth Houdini)   Pe 785

21055-	I Like Bananas (Because They Have No Bones)-Ballad (Yacich)	Pe 784
21056-	Please Don't Quit Me Baby-Semi-Tone (Wilmoth Houdini)	Pe 785
21057-	Love, Sincere Love-Single Tone (Wilmoth Houdini)	Pe 775
21058-	Loyal Britishers-Semi-Tone (Wilmoth Houdini)'	Pe 776
21059-	Malnutrition Songsters-Single Tone (Wilmoth Houdini)	Pe 777
21060-	Sing Birdies Sing-Single Tone (Wilmoth Houdini)	Pe 784
21061-	I Owe Her Gratitude-Double Tone (Wilmoth Houdini)	Pe 786
21062-	Leave My Business Alone-Semi-Tone (Wilmoth Houdini)'	Pe 775
21063-	He Is A Very Good Boy-Semi-Tone (Wilmoth Houdini)'	Pe 786
21064-	High Priest Of Me Minor-Double Tone (Wilmoth Houdini)	Pe 777

Felix And His Krazy Kats, 'with vocal trio   NY   April 27, 1937

Wilmoth Houdini And His Royal Troubadours

22118-	Simón Bolívar-Calypso Waltz (Wilmoth Houdini) [no vo]	Pe 797
22119-1	Sweet Adeline-Singletone Calypso (Wilmoth Houdini)	Pe 797
22120-	Sweet Jamaican Girl-Singletone Calypso (Wilmoth Houdini)'	Pe 798
22121-1	Bad Habits-Singletone Calypso (Wilmoth Houdini)'	Pe 795
22122-1	The Way To Hold My Man-Singletone Calypso (Wilmoth Houdini)'	Pe 792
22123-1	Bajan Boy-Singletone Calypso (Wilmoth Houdini)'	Pe 792
22124-1	Radio-Radio-Double Tone Calypso (Wilmoth Houdini)	Pe 799
22125-	Trinidadian Advice-Double Tone Calypso (Wilmoth Houdini)	Pe 790
22126-1	Ship Without A Rudder-Double Tone Calypso (Wilmoth Houdini)	Pe 798
22127-1	As A Man Lives (So Shall He Die)-Singletone Calypso (Wilmoth Houdini)'	Pe 795
22128-1	Trifling Tina-Singletone Calypso (Wilmoth Houdini)'	Pe 799
22129-	You Are A Pretentious Girl-Singletone Calypso (Wilmoth Houdini)'	Pe 790

vln, cl, p, cuatro, sbs   NY   November 9, 1937

Wilmoth Houdini And His Royal Calypso Orchestra

66523-A	The Welcome Of Their Majesties-Calypso (Wilmoth Houdini)	De 18006
66524-A	Johnny Take My Wife-Calypso (Wilmoth Houdini)	De 18007, EC KA3(C)
66525-A	Roosevelt Opens The World's Fair-Calypso (Wilmoth Houdini)	De 18007, EC KA2(C)
66526-A	Monkey Swing-Calypso (Wilmoth Houdini)	De 18005, EC KA4(C)
66527-A	Hot Dogs Made Their Name-Calypso (Wilmoth Houdini)	De 18006
66528-A	He Had It Coming-Calypso (Wilmoth Houdini)	De 18005

NY   September 11, 1939

De 18005-18007 are included in album 78.

The Bamboo Orchestra, Featuring Wilmoth Houdini

BS 046813-1	Poor But Ambitious (Wilmoth Houdini)
	Bb B-10619, Cam CAL360(33), LC LBC-6(33), FL 9040(33)
BS 046814-1	Resisting Temptation (Wilmoth Houdini) Bb B-10619, Cam CAL360(33)
BS 046815-1	Cousin, Cousin, Scratch Here So For Me (Wilmoth Houdini)
	Bb B-10647, Cam CAL360(33)
BS 046816-1	Mama Call The Fire Brigade (Wilmoth Houdini)'
	Bb B-10647, Cam CAL360(33)

vln, cl, p, g, sbs, traps, or 'bamboo group   NY   January 31, 1940

Wilmoth Houdini And His Royal Calypso Orchestra

68116-A	Harlem Popcorn Man-Calypso (T. Lynch)	De 18102
68117-A	The Million Dollar Pair Of Feet-Calypso (T. Lynch)	
		De 18101, FW RF4(33)
68118-A	Harlem Alley Cats-Calypso (T. Lynch)	De 18100, EC KA3(C)
68119-A	Married Life In Harlem-Calypso (T. Lynch)	De 18100, EC KA3(C)
68120-A	Good Old Harlem Town-Calypso (T. Lynch)	De 18101
68121-A	Harlem Night Life-Calypso (T. Lynch)	De 18102
		NY September 17, 1940

De 18100-18102 are included in album 198.

39.18. Lord Invader (Rupert Grant) *vocal*

68900-A	Rate Rate Ray (Lord Invader)	De 17463, FW RF4(33)
	Gerald Clark And His Caribbean Serenaders: Gerald Clark-g, unk tp,	
	vln, cl, p, sbs	NY April 2, 1941
68947-A	Play The Tune On The Pianola (Lord Invader)	De 17464
	as before	NY April 8, 1941
68975-	Hitler's Moustache (Lord Invader)	De 17468
	as before	NY April 11, 1941
69004-A	Saga Boy's In Town (Lord Invader)	De 17460
	as before	NY April 16, 1941
69023-	Man Man Tee Way Tee Way (Lord Invader)	De 17472
	as before	NY April 18, 1941

39.19. Adrian Johnson *vocal*

BVE 43610-2	Gal You Want Fi Come Kill Me (Adrian Johnson)	Vi 80780
BVE 43611-2	Send Her Back To She Ma (Adrian Johnson)	Vi 80780
	Donald Heywood-p, unk sax, g	NY April 5, 1928

39.20. Keskidee Trio *vocal*

39410-A	Dingo Lay (Raymond Quevedo-Egbert Moore-Neville Marcano)	
		De 17250, Br 02626, SA1095, EC KA3(C)
	Raymond Quevedo (Atilla The Hun), Egbert Moore (Lord Beginner), The	
	Tiger (Neville Marcano)-vo, with Gerald Clark And His Caribbean	
	Serenaders: Gerald Clark-g, Berry Barrow-p, unk tp, vln, cl, cuatro,	
	sbs	NY March 15, 1935
39423-A	Trinidad-My Home (Raymond Quevedo-Egbert Moore-Neville Marcano)	
		De 17256

```
39424-A-B      Congo Bara (Raymond Quevedo-Egbert Moore-Neville Marcano)
                             De 17257, Rounder 1039(33,C,CD), EC KA1(C)
               as before                                 NY  March 18, 1935
```

Both reissues use matrix 39424-A.

```
39426-A        Go Down The Valley (Raymond Quevedo-Egbert Moore-Neville Marcano)
                                                                    De 17258
39433-A        War (Raymond Quevedo-Egbert Moore-Neville Marcano)     De 17261
39434-A        Shango (Raymond Quevedo-Egbert Moore-Neville Marcano)  De 17262
               as before                                 NY  March 20, 1935
```

```
39450-A        Marian Le' Go My Man (Raymond Quevedo-Egbert Moore-Neville Marcano)
                                        De 17263, M30746, EC KA4(C)
39454-A        Don't Le' Me Mother Know
                   (Raymond Quevedo-Egbert Moore-Neville Marcano)
                       De 17265, M30736, Br 02627, Rounder 1054(33,C,CD), EC KA1(C)
39456-A        Sa Gomes' Emporiums (Raymond Quevedo-Egbert Moore-Neville Marcano)
                                                                    De 17266
               as before                                 NY  March 22, 1935
```

39.21. Marcia Langman *vocal*

```
BVE 38894-1    Touch Me All About, But Don't Touch Me Dey            Vi 80777
BVE 38895-2    Mister Joseph Strut Your Stuff (D. Heywood)           Vi 80777
               Donald Heywood's West Indian Band: Donald Heywood-p, unk 2 sax,
               cuatro                                     NY  June 9, 1927
```

39.22. Lionel O. Licorich *vocal*

```
W 110131-2     Baijian Gal                                          Co 3360-X
W 110132-2     I Has The Blues For Thee, Barbadoes                  Co 3360-X
               One String Willie-one string vln, Jack "Sweet Willie" Celestain-p
                                                         NY  December 1928
```

This artist was quartermaster on the Vestris, which sunk off the Virginia coast on
November 14, 1928; he was credited with saving a number of lives.

39.23. The Lion (Hubert Raphael Charles) (Hubert Raphael De Leon) *vocal*

The Lion And Atilla The Hun

```
TO 1386        Psychology                                           Br test
                                                         NY  March 2, 1934
```

Hubert Raphael Charles (The Lion)

```
14904-         Psychology (Lion)¹ Ba B-732, Me M12962, Or O-732, Pe P-732, Ro R-732
14905-1        Dynamite (Johnnie Walker)¹ Ba B-731, Co 2004-F, Me M12961, Or O-731,
                                        Pe P-731, Ro R-731, Rounder 1054(33,C,CD)
14906-1        Wanga (Lion)     Ba B-732, Me M12962, Or O-732, Pe P-732, Ro R-732
```

14908-   Marry An Ugly Woman (Lion) Ba B-735, Co 2005-F, Me M12965, Or O-735,
                                                      Pe P-735, Ro R-735
             Gerald Clark-g, unk vln, cl, p, cuatro, sbs, ¹with Atilla The Hun
                                                      NY March 7, 1934

Rounder 1054 as ATILLA THE HUN

14911-1   Bad Woman (Lord Boniye)¹
                         Ba B-733, Me M12963, Or O-733, Pe P-733, Ro R-733
14912-1   Shango (Lion)   Ba B-733, Me M12963, Or O-733, Pe P-733, Ro R-733
14913-1   Mourner's Lullaby (Atilla)¹
                         Ba B-734, Me M12964, Or O-734, Pe P-734, Ro R-734
14916-   Where's Jonah Gone? (Atilla)¹
                         Ba B-736, Me M12966, Or O-736, Pe P-736, Ro R-736
             as before, ¹with Atilla The Hun   NY March 12, 1934

14932-1   Soucouyen (Lion) Ba B-740, Me M13002, Or O-740, Pe P-740, Ro R-740
14934-   Macafouchette (Gorilla)
                         Ba B-739, Me M12998, Or O-739, Pe P-739, Ro R-739
14935-   Hallelujah, When The Lion Roars (Lion)
                         Ba B-738, Me M12997, Or O-738, Pe P-738, Ro R-738
14937-   Trinidad Is Paradise (Radio)
                         Ba B-737, Me M12967, Or O-737, Pe P-737, Ro R-737
14939-   Grenadian Gal (Lion)
                         Ba B-742, Me M13024, Or O-742, Pe P-742, Ro R-742
14940-   Doggie, Doggie Look Bone (Lion)¹
                         Ba B-738, Me M12997, Or O-738, Pe P-738, Ro R-738
14941-1   Mamaguille (Lion)¹   Ba B-742, Me M13024, Or O-742, Pe P-742,
                                                      Ro R-742, LC LBC-11(33)
14942-1   Dorothy (Atilla)¹ Ba B-737, Me M12967, Or O-737, Pe P-737, Ro R-737
14943-   Matrimony (Atilla)¹
                         Ba B-741, Me M13023, Or O-741, Pe P-741, Ro R-741
             as before, ¹with Atilla The Hun   NY March 13, 1934

60953-A   The Rumba Dance   De 17270, Br SA1095
60955-A   Peggy Daniels   De 17290
60957-   Advantage Mussolini   De 17275
             Gerald Clark And His Caribbean Serenaders: Gerald Clark-g, unk tp,
             vln, cl, p, sbs   NY March 31, 1936

60966-A   Four Mills Brothers   De 17269, RBF RF13(33)
60970-A   Bargee Pelauri   De 17272
             as before   NY April 2, 1936

60986-A   Fall Of Man   De 17267, Br 02628, EC KA1(C)
             as before   NY April 4, 1936

60994-A   Bam See Lam Bay   De 17277, M30747
             as before   NY April 7, 1936

61004-A   Lavabo   De 17281
61005-A   Send Your Children To The Orphan Home
                                         De 17284, FW RF4(33), FL 9048(33)
61006-A   I Wouldn't Work   De 17285

61007-A	Life Of The Lion		De 17279
	as before		NY April 8, 1936

61022-A	Advantage Mussolini	De 17275, 17326, EC KA2(C)	
	as before		NY April 10, 1936

61957-A-B	Netty-Netty (Hubert Raphael Charles)		De 17297
61961-A	Love Thy Neigbour (Hubert Raphael Charles)		
		De 17299, Rounder 1054(CD)	
61963-A	Sally Sally Water (Hubert Raphael Charles)		
		De 17300, Br 02624, EC KA1(C)	
61967-A-B	Out The Fire (Fitz McLean)	De 17302, M30749, FW RF4(33)	

Gerald Clark And His Caribbean Serenaders: Gerald Clark-g, unk tp,
vln, cl, sbs   NY February 16, 1937

61988-A	Believes In The Land Of Glory (Hubert Raphael Charles)		De 17307
61989-A	Ho Syne No Day (Hubert Raphael Charles)		De 17331
61992-A	Power Of The Lion (Hubert Raphael Charles)		De rej
61993-A	Mi Ropa (Hubert Raphael Charles)		De rej
	as before		NY February 22, 1937

61996-A	King George The VI (Hubert Raphael Charles)		De 17321
62003-A	Bowl And Bat (Hubert Raphael Charles)		De rej
	as before		NY February 23, 1937

62008-A	Nora Darling (Hubert Raphael Charles)	De 17311, EC KA1(C)	
62009-A	I Will String Along With You		
	(Hubert Raphael Charles-Raymond Quevedo)'		De 17323
62010-A	Louis-Schmeling Fight (Hubert Raphael Charles-Raymond Quevedo)'		
		De 17329, RBF RF13(33)	
62013-A	Old Lady (Hubert Raphael Charles)		De 17315
	as before, 'with Atilla The Hun		NY February 24, 1937

The Lion And The Atilla

62018-A	Mrs. Simpson (Hubert Raphael Charles-Raymond Quevedo)		De rej
62019-A	Modern Times (Hubert Raphael Charles)		De 17321
	as before		NY February 25, 1937

The Lion

68897-C	Woopsin (The Lion)		De 17471, 18146

Gerald Clark And His Caribbean Serenaders: Gerald Clark-g, unk tp,
vln, cl, p, sbs   NY April 2, 1941

68945-A	Three Blind Mice (The Lion)	De 17469, EC KA2(C)	
	as before		NY April 8, 1941

69002-A	Winston Churchill (The Lion)		De 17462
69003-	A Little More Oil In My Lamp-Shouter (The Lion)		De 17475
	as before		NY April 16, 1941

69019-	Pappy Chinks (The Lion)		De 17461

| 69026- | If You Want Your Pardon (The Lion) | De 17475 |
| | as before | NY April 18, 1941 |

69029-A	Ugly Woman (The Lion)	De 18143, DL8519(33)
69030-A	Bing Crosby (The Lion)	De 18142
	as before	NY April 21, 1941

39.24. Lovey's Trinidad String Band

B 12118-2	Trinidad Paseo (Lovey)	Vi 63793, Harlequin HQ2016(33)
B 12119-2	Mary Jane {Mari-Juana}-Trinidad Paseo (Edwards)	Vi 63792
B 12120-1	666-Trinidad Paseo (Lovey)	Vi 63790
B 12121-1	Manuelita-Spanish Valse (Gomez)	Vi 63792
B 12122-1	La Leibre-Spanish Valse (arr Sucre)	Vi 63791
B 12123-1	Y Como Le Va-Tango Argentino (J. Valverde)	Vi 63791
B 12124-1	Oil Fields-Trinidad Paseo (Schneider)	Vi 63790
B 12125-1	Sarah-Trinidad Paseo (Lovey)	Vi 63793
		NY June 20, 1912

Lovey's Band, Trinidad, British W.I.

21601-1	Mango Vert-Paseo (Bernier)	Co L23, Rounder 1039(33,C,CD)
	Mango Verde	Co C2842
21602-1	Pauline-Paseo (Johnson)	Co C2727
21611-1	Manuelito-Vals (V. Cedeno)	Co L23, Harlequin HQ2016(33)
21612-1	Clavel Blanco-Vals (Ruiz)	Co C2727
	Grande Fando-Tango	Co C2842
		NY June 1912

Co C2727 as ORQUESTA TIPICA DE TRINIDAD, RONOCIDO POR BANDA DE LOVEY

39.25. Hubert Lucas And His Spiritual Rhythm Singers

BS 89846-1	Time Is Drawing Nigh-Negro Spiritual (Alice Cooper Grant)	Bb B-4953
BS 89847-1	Oh Day Yonder Come Day-Negro Spiritual (Alice Cooper Grant)	
		Bb B-4954
BS 89848-1	All My Sins Done Taken Away-Spiritual (Alice Cooper Grant)	Bb B-4986
BS 89849-1	Come And Go Wid Me-Negro Spiritual (Alice Cooper Grant)	Bb B-4953
BS 89850-1	Pure Religion-Negro Spiritual (Alice Cooper Grant)	Bb B-4954
BS 89851-1	The Army-Spiritual (Alice Cooper Grant)	Bb B-4986
	cl, p, g	NY May 23, 1935

39.26. Phil Madison *vocal, ukulele*

B 28371-2	Sly Mongoose (Phil Madison)'	Vi 77115
B 28372-1	Te-Le-Le (Phil Madison)'	Vi 77116
B 28343-1	I Send She Back To She Ma (Phil Madison)'	Vi 77425
B 28344-1	The Old Maid {Da Fu Lick You} (Phil Madison)	Vi 77425
B 28345-2	The Live Light (Phil Madison)	Vi 77115

B 28346-2   The Stuttering Parson (Phil Madison)'   Vi 77116
              Lionel Belasco-p, 'own uke   NY August 6, 1923

Matrices B 28371/2 are reumbered from B 28341/2 respectively.

B 28352-2   My Neighbor Next Door (Phil Madison)   Vi 77118
B 28353-2   Bow-Legged Liza (Phil Madison)   Vi 77542
B 28354-1   Pull Down (Phil Madison)   Vi 77118
B 28355-2   Somebody's Keeping Us Back (Phil Madison)   Vi 77426
B 28356-1   I Feel The Spirit Coming On (Phil Madison)   Vi 77117
B 28357-2   Caroni Swamp (Phil Madison)   Vi 77426, Rounder 1039(33,C,CD)
B 28358-1   Calaloo And Crab (Phil Madison)'   Vi 77542
B 28359-1   Too Much Bigger Than Me (Phil Madison)'   Vi 77541
B 28360-2   Frock Coats At Funerals (Phil Madison)'   Vi 77117
B 28361-1   Kiss Me A Little Bit More (Phil Madison)'   Vi 77541
B 28362-2   Corn Coo Coo And Flying Fish (Phil Madison)'   Vi 77543
B 28363-1   Susan (Phil Madison)'   Vi 77543
              as before   NY August 8, 1923

39.27. Sam Manning *vocal*

S 72672-A   Amba Cay La {Under The House} (Sam Manning)   Ok 65003, Pa R3853
S 72673-B   Susan Monkey Walk (Sam Manning)   Ok 65003, Pa R3853
              Palmer's Orchestra   NY July 18, 1924

S 72708-B   My Little West Indian Girl (Sam Manning)   Ok 65002, Pa R3852
S 72709-B   Baby-Carnival Song (Sam Manning)   Ok 65002, Pa R3852
              as before: vln, fl, p, cuatro   NY July 29, 1924

1864-   Africa Blues   Pm 12229
              orch d Fred Hall   NY ca August 1924

S 73485-A   Mabel (See What You've Done) (Manning)   Ok 65004, Pa R3850
S 73486-A   Camilla (When You Go Please Don't Come Back) (Manning)
                                                             Ok 65005, Pa R3851
S 73487-A   The Bargee (Belasco)   Ok 65004, Pa R3850
S 73488-A   Sweet Willie (Manning-Fred Hall)   Ok 65005, Pa R3851
              Cole Jazz Trio: cl/alt sax, g, uke   NY June 29, 1925

9268-B   Englerston Blues (Englerston Quartet)   Ok 65007, Pa R3856
9269-B   Home's Delight   Ok 65007, Pa R3856
              alt sax, g, uke   NY(?) August 1925

W 141020-1   Let Go My Hand   Co 2324-X, 14110-D, RBF RF13(33)
W 141021-1   Bungo   Co 2323-X, 14110-D
W 141022-   Mabel, Open Your Door   Co 2300-X, 2321-X
W 141023-   Lignum Vitae {Long Life}   Co 2300-X, 2320-X
              Cole Jazz Orchestra: alt sax, p, uke, dm   NY September 21, 1925

S 73881-B   Sly Mongoose (Belasco)   Ok 65008, Pa R3854, Rounder 1039(33,C,CD)
S 73882-A   Sweet Mama Ring-Ding-Ding (Sam Manning)
                                           Ok 65009, Pa R3855, CI CI-015(33)
S 73883-A   Barbadoes Blues (Sam Manning) Ok 65009, Pa R3855, CI CI-015(33)

S 73884-B   Brown Boy (Sam Manning)   Ok 65008, Pa R3854
             Cole Mentor Orchestra: cl, alt sax, p, bj   NY ca December 30, 1925

S 74031-B   Keep Your Hands Off That (Manning)   Ok 8302, CI CI-015(33)
S 74032-B   Go, I've Got Somebody Sweeter Than You (Manning)
                                                           Ok 8302, CI CI-015(33)
             Blue Hot Syncopators: c, cl, ten sax, p, bj   NY February 1926

Sam Manning's Orchestra

W 95118-2   Hold Him Joe {My Donkey Wants Water}-Mentor (Sam Manning) [no vo]
                                                   Co 2409-X, Harlequin HQ2016(33)
W 95121-2   ¡Oh Emily!-Trinidad Carnival (Sam Manning)   Co 2409-X
             Jamaica Blues-Mentor   Co 2410-X
             Buddy Eddy-Mentor   Co 2410-X
                                                           NY April 1926

Sam Manning

W 81104-A   Bongo (Manning-Grainger)   Ok 8488, CI CI-015(33)
W 81105-A   Pepper Pot (Manning)   Ok 8488, CI CI-015(33)
W 81106-A   Lignum Vitae (Manning)   Ok 8487, CI CI-015(33)
W 81107-B   Emily (Manning)   Ok 8487, LC LBC-2(33), CI CI-015(33)
             Adolphe Thenstead's Mentor Boys: Adolphe Thenstead-p, unk cl, ten sax,
             bj   NY June 23, 1927

E 26342   Bouncing Baby Boy (Sam Manning)   Br 7026
E 26344   Woman's Sweeter Than Man (L. Belasco)   Br 7026
             alt sax, p, g, uke   NY February 2, 1928

Sam Manning And Anna Freeman

E 27041   Nothin' But A Double Barrel Shotgun's Gonna Keep Me Away From You
                       (Porter Grainger)   Br 7027
E 27043   Goin' Back To Jamaica (Porter Grainger)   Br 7027
E 27046   The American Woman And West Indian Man (Porter Grainger)-Pt. 1
                                                                    Br 7028
E 27047   The American Woman And West Indian Man (Porter Grainger)-Pt. 2
                                                                    Br 7028
             Porter Grainger-p   NY March 19, 1928

W 400190-A   Sweetie Charlie (Manning)   Ok 8567
             Jack Celestain And His Caribbean Serenaders: Jack Celestain-p, Gerald
             Clark-g, unk alt sax, cuatro   NY April 3, 1928

W 400191-B   Lita (Manning)   Ok 8568
W 400192-A   Lieutenant Julian (Manning)   Ok 8567, Rounder 1039(33,C,CD)
W 400193-B   You Can't Get Anything Out Of Me (Manning)   Ok 8568
             as before   NY April 4, 1928

Sam Manning's Orchestra

W 703089-1   Talking To Myself (I. Ghee)   Co 3939-X, Harlequin HQ2016(33)
W 703090-2   I'm Going Your Way (I. Ghee)   Co 3939-X

```
W 703091-1    Caribbean Moonlight (Sam Manning)                    Co 3940-X
W 703092-1    B.G. Blues (Sam Manning)                             Co 3941-X
W 703093-2    Back To My West Indian Home (Sam Manning)            Co 3940-X
W 703094-2    Femme Martinique (Sam Manning)                       Co 3942-X
W 703095-1    Bacchanale (Sam Manning)                             Co 3942-X
W 703096-2    Land Of Humming Birds (Sam Manning)                  Co 3941-X
              own vo, unk cl, alt sax, p, sbs          NY   January 1930

W 703470-     Sinking Of The Kate Esau (Hector J. Dick)            Co 4414-X
                                                        NY   December 1930
```

Sam Manning & His West Indian Rhythm Boys

```
14129-        Sam's Advice (Sam Manning)    Me M12824, Or O-718, Pe P-718, Ro R-718
14130-        Clementina (Sam Manning)
                           Ba B-729, Me M12945, Or O-729, Pe P-729, Ro R-729
14131-1       Who Is Your Friend? (Sam Manning)
                           Ba B-729, Me M12945, Or O-729, Pe P-729, Ro R-729
14132-        High Brown (Sam Manning)
                           Ba B-730, Me M12946, Or O-730, Pe P-730, Ro R-730
14133-1       Hurricane (Sam Manning)       Me M12824, Or O-718, Pe P-718, Ro R-718
14134-1       Cuckoo Song (Sam Manning)
                           Ba B-730, Me M12946, Or O-730, Pe P-730, Ro R-730
              own vo, unk sax, p, g, cuatro, sbs, dm    NY   October 11, 1933
```

Sam Manning's Rhythm Boys

```
BS 78136-     Sweet Marie-Fox Trot (Sam Manning)         Bb B-4911, Vi 26-6509
BS 78137-1    Look Out Hurricane-Fox Trot (Sam Manning)  Bb B-4911, Vi 26-6509
BS 78138-1    Rico-Mentor (Sam Manning) [no vo]                    Bb B-4912
BS 78139-1    Din Din-Mentor [no vo]                               Bb B-4912
              own vo, unk fl, cl, p, g, cuatro, traps    NY   October 18, 1933
```

Sam Manning And His Orchestra

```
BS 81038-1    Great Men-Calypso (Sam Manning-Fitz Taylor)          Bb B-4923
BS 81039-1    Worthless Josephine (Sam Manning)                    Bb B-4923
              cl, p, cuatro, sbs                        NY   January 10, 1934

BS 81820-1    Doris-Calypso                                        Bb B-4925
BS 81821-1    Bad Woman-Calypso                          Bb B-4924, Vi 26-6501
BS 81822-1    Recuerdos Del Pasado-Waltz (Sam Manning-S.H. Vinas) [no vo]
                           Bb B-4924, Vi 26-6501, Harlequin HQ2016(33)
BS 81823-1    Inez-Fox Trot (Sam Manning-S.H. Vinas) [no vo]       Bb B-4925
              Gerald Clark-g, unk 2 cl, p, cuatro, sbs, percussion
                                                        NY   February 28, 1934

BS 82587-     Let's Call It A Perfect Day (Sam Manning)            Bb B-4926
BS 82588-1    Don't Interfere With Man And Wife (Sam Manning)      Bb B-4927
BS 82589-1    My Barbados Home (Sam Manning)             Bb B-4933, Vi 26-6505
BS 82590-1    If I Put That Thing On You (Sam Manning)             Bb B-4932
BS 82591-1    Cherie-Paseo (Sam Manning) [no vo]                   Bb B-4926
BS 82592-1    Belle Marchand-Paseo (Sam Manning) [no vo]           Bb B-4927
BS 82593-1    Petite-Paseo (Sam Manning) [no vo]                   Bb B-4932
```

```
BS 82594-1    Belle Femme-Paseo (Sam Manning) [no vo]
                         Bb B-4933, Vi 26-6505, Harlequin HQ2016(33)
              own vo, unk tp, p, g, traps              NY  June 4, 1934
```

Sam Manning

```
70003-A    Sweet Willie (Sam Manning)'                      De 18258
70004-A    Looking For Me Santa Claus (Sam Manning)'        De 18259
70005-A    Gambia Talk (Sam Manning)'                       De 18260
70006-A    Salt Lane Gal (Sam Manning-Sam Johnson-Oscar E. Johnson)  De 18258
70007-A    Iron Bar (Sam Manning-Sam Johnson-Oscar E. Johnson)      De 18260
70008-A    Medley Of West Indian Songs                      De 18259
70009-A    Papa Don't Want No Fish And Rice Again
               (Sam Manning-Sam Johnson-Oscar E. Johnson)   De 18257
70010-A    Go Back To You Ma (Sam Manning-Sam Johnson-Oscar E. Johnson)
                                                            De 18257
           Felix And His Krazy Kats, 'The Melodettes-vo    NY  December 5, 1941
```

De 18257-18260 are included in album 308.

39.28. Walter Merrick *piano*

```
              Rose Caraqueña; Come Down; Labor All Together       Vi trial
                                                  NY  April 29, 1921

B 25082-3    Kaiser William Run Away-Trinidad Carnival Paseo (C. Monrose)
                                                            Vi 73061
B 25083-2    Bing Bang-Estelline-Trinidad Carnival Paseo (C. Abdullah)  Vi rej
B 25084-1    Dis Thing Is A Funny Thing-Trinidad Carnival Paseo (A. Headley)
                                                            Vi 73061
B 25085-2    Let We Labour All Together-Trinidad Carnival Paseo (C. Monrose)
                                                            Vi rej
B 25086-2    Come Down Kuffie {Dame Lorraine}-Trinidad Carnival Paseo
               (Julian Whiterose)                           Vi rej
B 25087-2    Prince Of Wales-Trinidad Carnival Paseo (Jerry)  Vi rej
                                                  NY  May 17, 1921

B 25402-2    Rosa Caraqueña-Valse Venezolano (P. Gómez)     Vi 73209
B 25403-2    Come Quick, The Man At The Door-Grenada Paseo  Vi rej
B 25404-2    Amour D'Aimée-Valse Creole (W. Merrick)        Vi 73209
B 25405-1    Bull Dog Don't Bite Me-Tobago Paseo (Roy Rawlins)  Vi 73060
                                                  NY  May 19, 1921
```

Merrick's Orchestra

```
W 93971-1    Tres Bemoles-Vals (P. Eduardo)            Co 2297-X, 2320-X
W 93973-2    Married To You-Paseo (W. Merrick)  Co 2297-X, Rounder 1039(33,C,CD)
             Legnum Vital-Paseo                        Co 2298-X, 2321-X
             Crucita-Vals                                      Co 2299-X
             Esther-Creole Carnival Song               Co 2299-X, 2323-X
             own p, unk vln, cl, cuatro                NY  October 1925
```

Merrick's Trinidad Harmony String Band

BVE 33574-2	El Subido Al Cielo-Valse Creole (J. Tang)	Vi rej
BVE 33575-1	Tres Bemoles-Valse Creole (P. Edwardo)	Vi 78424
BVE 33576-2	Who You Voting For? Cipriani-Calypso Song (W. Merrick)[1] [3]	Vi 78425
BVE 33577-2	Carissima Mia-Tango Song (W. Merrick)[2]	Vi rej
BVE 33578-2	Esther-Creole Charleston (W. Merrick)	Vi 78426
BVE 33579-1	Stephanie-Creole Paseo (Cyril Monrose)	Vi 78426
BVE 33580-2	Married To You-Creole Calypso (W. Merrick)[1] [3]	Vi rej
BVE 33581-2	Cinderella-Waltz Song (W. Merrick)[2]	Vi rej
BVE 33582-2	Lignum Vitae-Creole Calypso (W. Merrick)[1] [3]	Vi 78425
BVE 33583-2	Ma Rose-Creole Paseo	Vi 78424

own p, unk vln, cl, sax, g, cuatro, dm, d Richard Owen, [1]Charles
Abdullah, [2]Richard Owen, [3]Lyle Willoughby-vo   NY October 19, 1925

Merrico's South American Troubadours

E 3787/8W	El Barquerita (Alfredo Cortez)[1]	Vo
E 3789/90W	Pamela-Tango (W. Merrico)	Vo

6 men, [1]Alfredo Cortez-vo   NY September 16, 1926

Orquesta Walt Merrico

E 4345/50W, E 21078/9 Quitate De La Bebida {Stop Drinking}-Tango Br 40180, Vo 8107
E 4351/2W, E 21080/1 Pobre Madre {Poor Mother}-Tango (L. Martínez Serrano)
                                                      Br 40180, Vo 8107
7 men, Martín Garralaga-vo   NY December 28, 1926

39.29. Dan Michaels *vocal*

BVE 41708-2	Mango Lane (Donald Heywood)[1]	Vi 80779
BVE 41709-2	Mongoose Hop (Donald Heywood)	Vi 80778
BVE 41710-1	Susanne (Donald Heywood)[1]	Vi 80779

Donald Heywood-p, [1]with Hilda Perleno   Camden, NJ December 27, 1927

39.30. Mighty Destroyer (Clifford Morris) *vocal*

68943-A	Night Hawks (Mighty Destroyer)	De 17464
68949-	Adolf Hitler (Mighty Destroyer)	De 17468

Gerald Clark And His Caribbean Serenaders: Gerald Clark-g, unk tp,
vln, cl, p, sbs   NY April 8, 1941

68978-A	High Brown Diplomacy (Mighty Destroyer)	De 17466

as before   NY April 11, 1941

69007-A	Police Diplomacy (Mighty Destroyer)	De 17476
69009-	Matrimony (Mighty Destroyer)	De 17460

as before   NY April 16, 1941

69020-	Cousin Family (The Growler-Mighty Destroyer)	De 17474
69025-A	Mother's Love (Mighty Destroyer)	De 17473, 18142

as before   NY April 18, 1941

39.31. Cyril Monrose *violin*

Monrose's String Orchestra

B 28240-2	Maysotis-Venezuelan Waltz	Vi 77052
B 28241-1	Trinidad Carnival Songs	Vi 77054, Harlequin HQ2016(33)
B 28242-1	Adelle-Trinidad Waltz (Belasco)	Vi 77053
B 28243-2	Old Lady, Old Lady-Trinidad Paseo	Vi 77053, Rounder 1039(33,C,CD)
	own vln, Gerald Clark-g, unk p, cuatro	NY July 5, 1923

B 28274-2	Marcelle-Vals	Vi 77054
B 28275-2	Sly Mongoose	Vi 77052
	as before	NY July 12, 1923

Monrose's String Band

S 73650-B	And She Run, And She Run (Walter Ernest Merrick)	Ok 65006, Pa R3858
S 73651-B	The Song Of Cecilia (Walter Ernest Merrick)	Ok 65006, Pa R3858
	own vln, unk cl, g, Lyle Lorieo-vo	NY September 1925

Pa R3858 as MONTROSE STRING BAND

Cyril Monrose Caribbean Serenaders

GEX 2537-A	Mama Put Your Dancing Shoes-Paseo	Ge 20359
GEX 2538-A	Coquette-Paseo	Ge 20359
GEX 2539-A	Play Mr. Headley Play-Paseo	Ge 20360
GEX 2540-A	The Shango Dance-Paseo	Ge 20360
GEX 2541-	See My Little Brown Boy-Paseo	Ge 20361
GEX 2542-B	Mongoose Hop-Paseo	Ge 20361
	own vln, Gerald Clark-g, Lionel Belasco-p, unk bj	NY December 1929

Gennett 20361 as LIONEL BELASCO AND HIS TRINIDAD ORCHESTRA; other issues may be similarly credited.

39.32. Egbert Moore *(Lord Beginner); vocal (1904-1981)*

39411-A	Young Girl's Touch¹	De 17250, Br 02626, EC KA3(C)
39412-A	One Morning	De 17251, M30745, Br 02625
39414-A	Anacaona	De 17252, Rounder 1054(33,C,CD), EC KA2(C)
39416-A	M.C.C. Vs. West Indies	De 17253, Br 04414, EC KA2(C)
	Gerald Clark And His Caribbean Serenaders: Gerald Clark-g, Berry	
	Barrow-p, unk tp, vln, cl, cuatro, sbs, ¹with Atilla The Hun	
		NY March 15, 1935

39419-A	Captain Cipriani	De 17254
39420-A-B	King George's Silver Jubilee	De 17255
39422-A	St. Peter's Day At Teteron Bay	De 17256, M30746, EC KA4(C)
	as before	NY March 18, 1935

| 39432-A | Young Boy's Scandal | De 17261 |
| | as before | NY March 20, 1935 |

| 39455-A | Women Are Good And Women Are Bad | De 17266 |
| | as before | NY March 22, 1935 |

All subsequent recordings (made In Trinidad) by this artist are as LORD BEGINNER.

39.33. King Radio (Norman Span) *vocal (d. 1971)*

60954-A	Concertina	De 17268
60956-B	Preacher Man	De 17270
	Gerald Clark And His Caribbean Serenaders: Gerald Clark-g, unk tp,	
	vln, cl, p, sbs	NY March 31, 1936

| 60968-A | Ma Mamaria | De 17274, Rounder 1054(33,C,CD) |
| | as before | NY April 2, 1936 |

60985-A	Ribs	De 17276
60988-	Warning The Children Towards Mother	De rej
	as before	NY April 4, 1936

60991-A	Ask No Questions	De 17267, Br 02628, EC KA1(C)
60992-A	Monkey	De 17271, Br 02623, EC KA1(C)
60995-A	Radio Maintain Your Child[1]	De 17273
	as before, with The Lion or [1]The Tiger	NY April 7, 1936

61008-A	Radio Fifty Wives	De 17290
61009-A	Texilia	De 17282
61010-A	Body Line	De 17278
61011-A	Neighbour	De 17288
61013-A	Frederick Street	De 17287
	as before	NY April 8, 1936

61015-A	Man Smart, Woman Smarter	De 17287
61018-A	Gold Diggers	De 17286
61020-A	Unfortunate Bridegroom	De 17286
61021-A	Warning The Children Towards Mother	De 17289
	as before	NY April 9, 1936

61028-A	Milly[2]	De 17275
61029-A	Abyssinian Lament[1]	De 17283
61030-A	War[1] [2]	De 17283
61031-A	We Ain't 'Fraid Nobody[1] [2]	De 17285, 17326, M30748, EC KA2(C)
61032-A	Don't Break It I Say[1] [2]	De 17280, 17327, M30747
61033-A	Miliington[2]	De 17279
	as before, with [1]The Lion or [2]The Tiger	NY April 11, 1936

68944-A	Chip Chip Water (King Radio)	De 17470, 18145
	Gerald Clark And His Caribbean Serenaders: Gerald Clark-g, unk tp,	
	vln, cl, p, sbs	NY April 8, 1941

```
68974-A      My Girl Mabel (King Radio)                                 De 17471
68977-A      Government House Dance (King Radio)                        De 17467
68979-A      Jitterbug (King Radio)                           De 17466, 18146
             as before                                   NY  April 11, 1941

69005-       Lovely, Noble Men (King Radio)                            De 17472
             as before                                   NY  April 16, 1941

69022-       Go And Sleep At Your Neighbor (King Radio)                De 17476
             as before                                   NY  April 18, 1941
```

39.34. Bill Rogers *(Augustus Hinds); vocal (d. 1984)*

```
BS 84982-1   A Constable Staff-Paseo (A. Hinds)                       Bb B-4934
BS 84983-1   Jimmy Black Pudding And Souse-Paseo (A. Hinds)  Bb B-4935, EC KA3(C)
BS 84984-1   Oh Dorothy-Paseo (A. Hinds)                     Bb B-4944, Vi 26-6506
BS 84985-1   Ugly Or Pretty Woman-Paseo (A. Hinds)                        Bb rej
BS 84986-1   International Cricket Tournament-Paseo (A. Hinds)         Bb B-4934
BS 84987-1   Down Tool Cloth (A Fashionable Dress Material)-Paseo (A. Hinds)
                                                                      Bb B-4965
          Felix And His Krazy Kats: Gregory Felix-cl, unk tp, p, cuatro, sbs
                                                     NY  November 14, 1934

BS 84996-1   The Troubles Of A Cook-Paseo (A. Hinds)       Bb B-4944, Vi 26-6506
BS 84997-1   That Rubbish Man-Paseo (A. Hinds)-Pt. 1                   Bb B-4936
BS 84998-1   That Rubbish Man-Paseo (A. Hinds)-Pt. 2                   Bb B-4936
BS 84999-1   Daddy Gone To Cove And John (A. Hinds)        Bb B-4935, EC KA3(C)
BS 86206-1   Jordanites Routey Feast (A. Hinds)            Bb B-4937, EC KA4(C)
BS 86207-1   Water Cocoanut Boys-Paseo (A. Hinds)                     Bb B-4943
             as before                                   NY  November 16, 1934

BS 86213-1   B.G. Bargee (A. Hinds)                                   Bb B-4938
BS 86214-1   Wire Wire Down Day-Paseo (A. Hinds)                      Bb B-4965
BS 86215-1   Unlucky Marriage {Creole Country Girl}-Paseo (A. Hinds)
                                                          Bb B-4941, Vi 26-6500
BS 86216-1   Sugar, Cent A Pound-Paseo (A. Hinds)          Bb B-4937, EC KA4(C)
BS 86217-1   West Indian Weed Woman (A. Hinds)    Bb B-4938, Rounder 1039(33,C,CD)
BS 86218-1   Silver Bangles Dipped In Gold-Paseo (A. Hinds) Bb B-4941, Vi 26-6500
             as before                                   NY  November 19, 1934

BS 84985-2   Ugly Or Pretty Woman-Paseo (A. Hinds)                    Bb B-4943
BS 86229-1   Boardin Policeman (A. Hinds)                             Bb B-4942
BS 86230-1   The Merry Mice And Happy Rats (A. Hinds)                 Bb B-4966
BS 86231-1   Fascinating Styles-Paseo (A. Hinds)                      Bb B-4942
BS 86232-1   Kingston Dead Cows (A. Hinds)                            Bb B-4964
BS 86233-1   Fire Craze In Albert Town-Paseo (A. Hinds)               Bb B-4966
BS 86234-1   Gibbs-Ortega Fight                                       Bb B-4964
             as before                                   NY  November 21, 1934

BS 86080-1   Garraway Stream-Fox Trot (A. Hinds)                      Bb B-4967
BS 86081-1   Demerara The Land Of The Sugar Stick (A. Hinds)          Bb B-4967
BS 86082-1   Leave Bad Women Alone-Paseo (Fitz McLean)                Bb B-4939
BS 86083-1   Standing By The Side Walk (Fitz McLean)                  Bb B-4939
```

```
BS 86084-1    I'm Looking For A Loving Wife-Calypso (Fitz McLean)
                                                    Bb B-4940, Vi 26-6512
BS 86085-1    The Girl I Love-Waltz (A. Hinds)              Bb B-4940
              as before                            NY  December 3, 1934
```

39.35. Jack Sneed And His Sneezers *vocal*

```
64608-        The Numbers Man (Jack Sneed)                        De 7522
64609-A       Sly Mongoose (The Dogs Know Your Name) (Lionel Belasco)
                                                    De 7566, 48058, M30950
64610-A       West Indian Blues (Jack Sneed)       De 7566, 48058, M30950
64611-        Big Joe Louis (Jack Sneed)                          De 7522
              Charlie Shavers-tp, Billy Kyle-p, John Kirby-sbs, O'Neill Spencer-dm
                                                    NY  September 9, 1938

65648-A       Jamaica Mama (Jack Sneed)                           De 2529
65649-A       Sissy In The Barn (Jack Sneed)                      De 2529
65650-A       Paul Revere (Sneed)                                 De 7621
65651-A       Ole Chris {Christafo Colombo} (Sneed)               De 7621
                                                    NY  May 25, 1939

66171-B       It's The Rhythm We Want (Norman Span)               De rej
66172-B       Woman's Headache (Hubert Raphael Charles)           De rej
66173-B       They Talk About Nora's Badness (Philip García)      De rej
66174-B       Don't Tickle Me Dorothy (Egbert Moore)              De rej
66175-B       Lyonaise Potatoes And Pork Chops (Jack Sneed)       De rej
                                                    NY  August 22, 1939
```

39.36. Grace Taylor *vocal*

```
1865-         Sweet Willie                                     Pm 12229
              orch d Fred Hall                       NY  ca August 1924
```

39.37. The Tiger (The Growling Tiger) (Neville Marcano) *vocal*

```
39413-A       Empty Pride (Neville Marcano)                     De 17251
              Gerald Clark And His Caribbean Serenaders: Gerald Clark-g, Berry
              Barrow-p, unk tp, vln, cl, cuatro, sbs   NY  March 15, 1935

39418-A       Money Is King (Neville Marcano)
                            De 17254, M30745, RBF RF13(33), FL 9048(33)
              as before                              NY  March 18, 1935

39427-A       Marabella Wedding (Neville Marcano)               De 17258
39429-A       Mannie Dookie (Neville Marcano)                   De 17259
39431-A       From Hell To Luxury (Neville Marcano)             De 17260
              as before                              NY  March 20, 1935

39448-A       Sadu Man (Neville Marcano)                        De 17262
39452-A       Emily (Neville Marcano)                           De 17264
              as before                              NY  March 22, 1935
```

```
60967-A        The Gold In Africa              De 17271, 17327, Br 02623, FW RF4(33),
                                                            FL 9048(33), EC KA2(C)
60969-A        Yaraba Shango                                          De 17269
60971-A        Sheila                                                 De 17274
               Gerald Clark And His Caribbean Serenaders: Gerald Clark-g, unk tp,
               vln, cl, p, sbs                                NY  April 2, 1936

60983-A        Delcina                                                De 17273
60984-A        Point Cumana                                           De 17276
60987-A        Movie Stars                                            De 17277
60989-A        Try A Screw To Get Through                  De 17268, EC KA4(C)
               as before                                     NY  April 4, 1936

60993-A        The Rats                                               De 17272
60996-A        Hell Yard And George Street Conflict        De 17284, FW RF4(33)
60997-A        Workers Appeal                              De 17288, LC LBC-7(33)
60998-A        Blue Basin                                             De 17280
               as before                                     NY  April 7, 1936

61014-A        They Couldn't Stop The Masquerade                      De 17289
61016-A        The Whe Whe Banker Wedding           De 17278, Rounder 1054(CD)
61017-A        The Mysterious Tunapuna Woman                          De 17281
61019-A        Bandandea                                              De 17282
               as before                                     NY  April 9, 1936
```

39.38. Johnny Walker *tenor*

```
               Pull Down                                              Vi trial
               Walter Merrick-p                              NY  April 29, 1921

B 25088-1      Argos Paper-Trinidad Kalendar (C. Abdullah)           Vi 73062
B 25089-1      Super Hay (Bunny Earl)                                Vi 73208
B 25090-1      Firearm De Fay (Henry Forbs)                          Vi 73062
B 25091-1      Zion Pony; Coming Down-Shouters Meeting (B. Nosegay)  Vi 73207
B 25092-1      Happy Land-Shouters Meeting (Brother Walters)         Vi 73207
B 25093-1      Go Way Gal-Trinidad Carnival Calypso (J. Maxwell)     Vi 73060
B 25094-1      I Want A Girl-Trinidad Ragtime Song (Johnny Walker-Walter Merrick)[1]
                                                                     Vi 73208
B 25095-1      Alexander's Jazz Band (Walter Merrick)[1]             Vi rej
               chorus, cuatro, or [1]Walter Merrick-p       NY  May 17, 1921
```

PART 9

AMERICAN INDIAN

40.1. Ignacio Alvarez *vocal; Yaqui*

3339   Coyote {Song Of Old War Society}   General 5012, Canyon CR 7999(33)
        dm, rattles   Pascua Village, near Tucson, AZ March 23, 1940

General 5012 is included in album G-18.

40.2. Chief Bull *vocal; Black Foot*

B 17169-1   A Dance Song Of The Black Foot Woman   Vi rej
        NY February 16, 1916

40.3. Chief Caupolican *baritone; Zuni*

        Zuni Sunrise Call; Zuni Blanket Song (Carlos Troyer)   Vi trial
        Camden, NJ September 21, 1927

BVE 39863-1   The Sunrise Call (arr Carlos Troyer)   Vi 20983, 45-5073
BVE 39864-1   Lover's Wooing {Blanket Song} (arr Carlos Troyer)   Vi 20983
        Myrtle C. Eaver-p   Camden, NJ September 29, 1927

Vi 45-5073 as CALVIN MARSH; both issues were in Victor's educational series.
William Moran reports that this Chilean-born singer's real name was Emile
Barrangon and that he sang briefly with the Metropolitan Opera.

40.4. Eagle Calf *vocal; Black Foot*

B 14857-1   Serenade   Vi rej
        NY May 23, 1914

Recorded for Victor's educational series; the other part of this matrix is by
MEDICINE OWL AND LAZY BOY.

40.5. Elsie L. Elms *soprano; Oneida*

7854-A   Appeal To The Great Spirit   Ed 77(33)
        unaccompanied   NY March 18, 1921

40.6. Chief Evergreen Tree *vocal*

Buffalo Song	Electra unnumbered
Imitation Of Animals And Birds Of The Forest	Electra unnumbered
	Chicago 1920s

40.7. Gregorio George García *flute, drum; Yaqui*

3333	Pascola {Masked Dance}	General 5012, Canyon CR 7999(33)
		Pascua Village, near Tucson, AZ March 23, 1940

General 5012 is uncredited, and is part of album G-18.

40.8. Glacier Park Indians *vocal; Black Foot*

B 14856-1	White Dog; Grass Dance	Vi 17611
B 14858-1	Gambler's Song	Vi 17635
B 14859-1	Medicine Song	Vi 17611
		NY May 23, 1914

B 14856-2	White Dog; Grass Dance	Vi 17611
		NY June 15, 1914

40.9. Big Chief Henry's Indian String Band

BVE 56382-2	Blue Bird Waltz²	Vi V-40225
BVE 56383-2	Choctaw Waltz²	Vi V-40225
BVE 56384-2	Indian Tom-Tom¹	Vi V-40281
BVE 56385-2	The Indian's Dream	Vi V-40281
BVE 56386-2	Cherokee Rag²	Vi V-40195
BVE 56387-2	On The Banks Of The Kaney²	Vi V-40195
	Henry Hall-vln/¹vo, Clarence Hall-g, ²Harold Hall-bj	
		Dallas October 14, 1929

40.10. Honauuh *(Chief Head of Snake Ceremony); vocal; Hopi*

The Gennett files give this name as HUNAWEU.

12527	Tacab Katcina (Navaho)	Ge 5761, FW FE4394(33)
12534	Tuwina'ay	Ge 5757, FW FE4394(33)
	El Tovar Hotel, East Mesa, Grand Canyon, AZ Summer 1926	

The other part of matrix 12534 is by TEUMA'EVY.

40.11. Ho-Nū-Ses *vocal; Iroquois*

A 1413-2	War Song	Vi 2855(7")
A 1414-1	Ghost Dance	Vi 2856(7")

```
A 1415-1    Song Of The Fish Dance                                  Vi 2857(7")
A 1416-1    Song Of The Green Corn Dance                            Vi 2858(7")
A 1417-1    Death Game Song-No. 1 {Moccasin Games}                  Vi 2859(7")
A 1418-1    Death Game Song-No. 2 {Moccasin Games}                  Vi 2860(7")
A 1419-1    Death Game Song-No. 3 {Moccasin Games} {Stick Burning}  Vi 2861(7")
A 1420-1    False Face Song                                         Vi 2862(7")
A 1421-1    Snake Song                                              Vi 2863(7")
A 1422-1    Social Dance Song {Woman's Dance}-No. 1                 Vi 2864(7")
A 1423-1    Social Dance Song {Woman's Dance}-No. 2                 Vi 2865(7")
A 1424-1    Social Dance Song {Woman's Dance}-No. 3                 Vi 2866(7")
                                                             NY   June 6, 1904
```

Vi 2864, 2865 and 2866 are described as having special labels.

40.12. Honyi (Head Of Antelope Priesthood) *vocal; Walpi*

The Gennett files give this name as HUNGI.

```
12529    Pawik {Duck}-Katcina                    Ge 5760, FW FE4394(33)
12531    Soyohim Katcina                         Ge 5759, FW FE4394(33)
12533    Powamu {Bean Harvest}-Katcina           Ge 5758, FW FE4394(33)
               El Tovar Hotel, East Mesa, Grand Canyon, AZ  Summer 1926
```


40.13. Hopi Indians (At The Hopi House, Grand Canyon) *vocal*

```
12536-A    Awatawi {Entry Song To The Buffalo Hut}                 Ge 5756
12537-A    Nakentawi {War Dance-Victory}                           Ge 5756
               El Tovar Hotel, East Mesa, Grand Canyon, AZ  Summer 1926
```


40.14. Hopi Snake Dancers *vocal*

```
              Chant Of The Hopi Snake Dancers                      Vi trial
                                            NY  February 17, 1926

BVE 35252-2    Chant Of The Snake Dancer          Vi 20043, FW FE4394(33)
BVE 35253-1    Chant Of The Eagle Dance    Vi 20043, 45-5072, FW FE4394(33)
          5 singers, dm                             NY  March 30, 1926
```


40.15. Kákapti *vocal; Hopi*

```
12526    Humis {Jemez}-Katcina                   Ge 5761, FW FE4394(33)
12530    Makwatu {Ma' Qutu} {Rabbit Hunt} {Rabbit Head}
                                                 Ge 5759, FW FE4394(33)
12535    Anga Katcina {Beard Dance}              Ge 5757, FW FE4394(33)
               El Tovar Hotel, East Mesa, Grand Canyon, AZ  Summer 1926
```

40.16. Chief Kiutus Tecumseh *vocal*

N 19518	Wi-Um-Indian Lullaby[1]	Ge
N 19519	Chant Of The Corn Grinders; Indian Prayer Song	Ge
	p, [1]fl	Richmond, IN July 26, 1935

40.17. Kutqa (Chief Of Walpi Pueblo) *vocal; Hopi*

12528	Malo Katcina	Ge 5760, FW FE4394(33)
12532	Mucaiasti Katcina {Buffalo Dance}	Ge 5758, FW FE4394(33)
	El Tovar Hotel, East Mesa, Grand Canyon, AZ Summer 1926 AZ	

40.18. Medicine Owl And Lazy Boy *vocal; Black Foot*

B 14857-1	Religious Song	Vi rej
		NY May 23, 1914

Recorded for Victor's educational series; the other part of this matrix is by Eagle Calf, q.v.

40.19. Charles Mooney *vocal*

There is considerable uncertainty surrounding the following recordings. Zinc copies of the unnumbered recordings are in the Library of Congress Archive of Folk Culture, where they have been assigned accession numbers; the titles with Berliner release numbers appear in the company's catalog. The identity of the performers is unclear. The zinc recordings seem to be sung by Charles (or possibly James) Mooney. Presumably the others are also, since there is little reason to believe that members of the various tribes represented were in Washington at the time. All of the following are on 7" discs.

Arapaho Nos. 44, 45-Ghost Dance	Ber (AFS 14034)
Commanche No. 1-Ghost Dance	Ber (AFS 14035)
Caddo No. 15-Ghost Song	Ber (AFS 14036)
Kiowa Mescal Song; Kiowa Daylight Song	Ber (AFS 14037)
Piute Gambling Song; Arapaho No. 67-Ghost Dance	Ber (AFS 14038)
Arapaho No. 73-Ghost Dance	Ber (AFS 14039)
Arapaho No. 1-Ghost Dance	Ber (AFS 14040)
Arapaho No. 9, 28-Ghost Dance	Ber (AFS 14041)
Kiowa No. 15; Caddo No. 12-Ghost Songs	Ber (AFS 14042)
Arapaho No. 52-Ghost Dance	Ber (AFS 14045)
	Washington July 5, 1894
Kiowa No. 12-Ghost Dance	Ber (AFS 14043)
Caddo No. 2-Ghost Dance	Ber (AFS 14044)
	Washington July 11, 1894
Three Melodies From The Ghost Dance	Ber 50
Three Melodies From The Ghost Dance	Ber 51

Three Melodies From The Ghost Dance	Ber 52
	Washington 1894

Arrapahoe No. 47	Ber 406
Arrapahoe Nos. 9 and 45	Ber 407
Arrapahoe No. 28	Ber 408
Caddo Nos. 12 and 2	Ber 409
Arrapahoe No. 73; Commanche No. 1	Ber 410
Arrapahoe Nos. 44 and 52	Ber 411
Mescal Song; Kiowa Daylight Song	Ber 412
Caddo No. 15; Piute Gaming Song	Ber 413
Kiowas Nos. 15 and 2	Ber 414
	Washington ca 1896

Berliner 406-414 are listed as "Songs From The Indian Tribal Ghost Dances" in the "Supplement List Of New Gramophone Records, June 1896," as "made for the U.S. Bureau of Ethenology (sic) by Prof. James Mooney, Indian Expert, Smithsonian Institute (sic) Reproductions Of The original copies filed with the U.S. National Museum at Washington D.C."

40.20. Mountain Chief *vocal; Black Foot*

B 17166-2	War Song Of The Mountain Chief	Vi rej
B 17167-1	White Dog Song	Vi rej
B 17168-1	Love Song; Love Song	Vi rej
	Mr. Dixon of J. Wanamaker's-announcements	NY February 16, 1916

File note for matrix B 17168: "This reminds me when I, Mountain Chief, sang this song around the camp when a boy of 18."

40.21. Chief Os-Ke-Non-Ton *vocal; Mohawk*

	Mohawk Love Song	Vi trial
		NY January 22, 1915
90098-1	Every Day Song	Co A3092
	tomtom	NY June 6, 1920
90099-2	War Song	Co A3092
	tomtom	NY June 8, 1920
90235-2	By The Waters Of The Minnetonka (Lieurance)	Co A3173
	orch	NY June 10, 1922
90258-1	Tribal Prayer; Mohawk's Lullaby; Happy Song	Co A3162
		NY March 1, 1923
90291-1	By The Weeping Waters (Lieurance)	Co rej
	orch	NY October 3, 1923
90291-3	By The Weeping Waters (Lieurance)	Co A3173
	orch	NY October 16, 1923

40.22. Chief Red Eagle

GEX 485R   title untraced   Ge rej
Santa Fe(?) ca 1926

File note: "Remake on Santa Fe Record"

40.23. Seneca Indians *vocal*

38957-1	Funeral Chant	Co S3057, A3057
38958-1	Children's Chorus'	Co S3057, A3057
38959-	Farewell To Minnehaha	Co rej
	'with tomtom	NY July 23, 1913

40.24. Juan Silvano *vocal; Yaqui*

3331	The Deer Dance-Pt. 1	General 5011, Canyon CR 7999(33)
3332	The Deer Dance-Pt. 2	General 5011, Canyon CR 7999(33)
	two additional voices, dm, rattles	Pascua Village, near Tucson, AZ March 23, 1940

General 5011 is uncredited, and part of album G-18.

40.25. Teuma'evy *vocal; Hopi*

12534   Tacheuktu {Mud-Head} {Clown}-Katcina   Ge 5757, FW FE4394(33)
El Tovar Hotel, East Mesa, Grand Canyon, AZ   Summer 1926

The other part of this matrix is by HONAUUH.

40.26. Porter Timeche And Hopi Group

Mud Head Katcina Song	Ge 1306, FW FE4394(33)
Butterfly Dance Song	Ge 1306, FW FE4394(33)
Hoop Dance Song	Ge 1307, FW FE4394(33)
Buffalo Dance Song	Ge 1307, FW FE4394(33)
vocal group with dm, gourd, rattles, bells	Richmond, IN(?) ca 1936

40.27. Anastacio Velázquez *vocal; Yaqui*

Señor Crucificado-Alabanza   Canyon CR 7999(33)
with Kapariam (women chanters)   Pascua Village, near Tucson, AZ   March 22, 1940

Señor Santa Ana-Alabanza   Canyon CR 7999(33)
as before   Pascua Village, near Tucson, AZ   March 23, 1940

40.28. Princess Watahwaso *contralto; Penobscot*

This artist's real name was Lucy Poolaw.

B 21014-1	By The Waters Of The Minnetonka (Thurlow Lieurance)[1] [2]	Vi rej
B 21016-1	By The Weeping Waters (Thurlow Lieurance)[1]	Vi 18418
B 21017-2	Sioux Serenade (Thurlow Lieurance)[1] [2]	Vi 18431
B 21018-2	A Song Of Greeting; Lullaby; Snail Song; Wedding Ceremonial Song-Four Penobscot Tribal Songs	Vi rej
B 21019-2	The Sacrifice; Pa Pup Ooh; Crow Maiden's Prayer (Thurlow Lieurance)	Vi rej

unaccompanied, or [1]Herbert Small-fl, Thurlow Lieurance-p; [2]"original Indian theme sung at the beginning by Thurlow Lieurance"

NY   October 30, 1917

B 21014-3	By The Waters Of The Minnetonka (Thurlow Lieurance)[1]	Vi 18431
B 21017-3	A Sioux Serenade[1]	Vi rej
B 21018-3	A Song Of Greeting; Lullaby; Snail Song; Wedding Ceremonial Song-Four Penobscot Tribal Songs	Vi 18444
B 21019-3	Two Indian Songs	Vi 18444

unaccompanied, or [1]Herbert Small-fl, Thurlow Lieurance-p

NY   November 16, 1917

B 24181-3	The Doe Skin Blanket (Cecil Fanning-Charles Wakefield Cadman, op. 66 no. 4)[1]	Vi rej
B 24182-3	Lover's Wooing {Blanket Song} (Carlos Troyer)	Vi rej

Joseph Pasternack-p, Wardwell-tomtom, [1]Clement Barone-fl

NY   June 25, 1920

B 24182-6	Lover's Wooing {Blanket Song} (Carlos Troyer)	Vi rej
B 25302-2	Apache Medicine Chant (Carlos Troyer)[1]	Vi rej
B 25303-3	Invocation To The Sun God (Carlos Troyer)	Vi rej

Joseph Pasternack-p, Francis J. Lapitino-tomtom, [1]William H. Reitz-rattle

Camden, NJ   May 16, 1921

B 25933-3	Her Shadow-Ojibway Canoe Song (Frederick R. Burton, arr Charles Wakefield Cadman)[1]	Vi rej
B 25934-3	Indian Spring Bird {Shi-Bi-Bi-La} (Alfred Fletcher-Thurlow Lieurance)	Vi rej

Clement Barone-fl, Joseph Pasternack-p, or [1]orch d Joseph Pasternack

Camden, NJ   January 5, 1922

B 25933-6	Her Shadow-Ojibway Canoe Song (Frederick R. Burton, arr Charles Wakefield Cadman)	Vi rej
B 25939-3	The Robin Woman (Frederick R. Burton, arr Charles Wakefield Cadman)	Vi rej

Agnes Quinlan-p

Camden, NJ   January 6, 1922

B 24182-9	Lover's Wooing {Blanket Song} (Carlos Troyer)[1]	Vi rej
B 25302-4	Apache Medicine Chant (Carlos Troyer)[2]	Vi rej
B 25303-6	Invocation To The Sun God (Carlos Troyer)[3]	Vi rej
B 25933-9	Her Shadow-Ojibway Canoe Song (Frederick R. Burton, arr Charles Wakefield Cadman)[4]	Vi rej

B 25934-6   Indian Spring Bird {Shi-Bi-Bi-La}
                (Mildred Fletcher-Thurlow Lieurance)[5]   Vi rej
B 25939-6   The Robin Woman (Frederick R. Burton, arr Charles Wakefield Cadman)[3]
                                                                       Vi rej
             [1]Rosario Bourdon-p, William H. Reitz-tomtom, [2]Rosario Bourdon-p,
             William H. Reitz-dm/rattle, [3]Myrtle C. Eaver-p, [4]Rosario Bourdon-p/dm,
             unk 2 vln, fl, vc, bsn, [5]Clement Barone-fl, Rosario Bourdon-p
                                                            NY   July 7, 1924

Princess Watawaso

BVE 21015-3   A!-O!-Ah-Love Song From The Red Willow Pueblos (Thurlow Lieurance);
                Her Blanket-Navaho (Thurlow Lieurance)   Vi 22316
BVE 21016-4   By The Weeping Waters-Chippewa Indian Mourning Song   Vi 22316
BVE 21018-6   A Song Of Greeting; Lullaby; Snail Song; Wedding Ceremonial
                Song-Four Penobscot Tribal Songs   Vi rej
BVE 58624-2   Her Shadow[1]   Vi rej
             Mary Ann Williams-p, [1]Mayer-fl   NY   January 27, 1930

A file note says that the artist's name was changed to correspond with her
signature on a 1929 letter.

40.29. Lester Williams *(Star Eagle); spoken; Santee Dakota*

BVE 38707-1   Star Husband Story-Beginning   Vi rej
                                                            NY   April 29, 1927

40.30. Yaqui Indians *instrumental*

3333   Pascola {Unmasked Dance}   General 5012, Canyon CR 7999(33)
3340   Chapayeka Procession[1]; Matachini Dance[2]
                                                   General 5013, Canyon CR 7999(33)
             vln, harp, rattles, or [1]vln, fl, dm, rattles, [2]2 vln, g, rattles
                                     Pascua Village, near Tucson, AZ   March 23, 1940

General 5012 and 5013 are part of album G-18. Canyon CR 7999 does not include
"Chapayeka Procession".

PART 10

INTERNATIONAL

SECTION 41. INTERNATIONAL

41.1. Accordion, Clarinet And Guitar

| 44713-2 | Over The Waves—Waltz | Co E4173 |
| | | NY ca February 1917 |

41.2. Ray Jack Bankey And Tony Lombardo *of Station KQV, Pittsburgh*

W 403612-B	Pennsylvania Polka[1]	Ok 11467
W 403614-C	Gody Weselne-Polka[1]	Ok 11467
W 403616-	Melodie Italiane-Valzer[1]	Ok 9496, Co 14658-F
W 403620-B	Bella Donna-Mazurka[1]	Co 14651-F
W 403621-B	Lombardo-Polka[1]	Ok 9496, Co 14658-F
W 403622-	Mio Padre[1]	Co 14651-F
W 403623-A	I Still Have A Place In My Heart For You[2]	Ok 45422
W 403624-A	Since I Gave My Heart To You[2]	Ok 45421
W 403625-A	You're My Old Fashioned Sweetheart[2]	Ok 45421
W 403626-B	The Burial Of The Miner's Child[3]	Ok 45422

        [1]acn-g duets, [2]singing (in English) with acn, vibraphone, g, or [3]hca, g
                                            NY ca January 14, 1930

All issues as JACK & TONY except Co 14651-F, as BANKEY & LOMBARDO

Bankey and Lombardo recorded eight popular songs in English for Gennett on March 25, 1929 in Richmond, IN.

41.3. Dominic Bartol *accordion*

B 29656-2	Schottische Tirolese	Vi 77656
B 29642-2	Tyrolean Characteristic Dance	Vi 77415
B 29643-3	Canzone Tirolese-Valzer	Vi 77656
B 29644-2	Repasz Band March (Charles C. Sweeley)	Vi 77415
		NY March 11, 1924

Vi 77656 is an Italian release.

B 31257-2	Grandfather's Polka	Vi rej
B 31258-3	Grandmother's Polka	Vi rej
B 31259-2	Lithuanian Waltz	Vi 77885
B 31260-1	Lithuanian Mazurka	Vi 77885
		NY December 5, 1924

BVE 38583-2	Caro Papà {Father, Dear}-Valzer	Vi 80561
BVE 38584-2	Bartolina Polka	Vi 80203
BVE 38585-2	Melodia D'Amore {Strains Of Love}-Valzer	Vi 80203
BVE 38586-2	Father Luchi's March (Bartol)	Vi 80461
BVE 38587-2	City Of Progress {Città Del Progresso}-March (Bartol)	Vi 80461
BVE 38588-2	Distaccato-Schotticshe (Bartol)	Vi 80561
		Camden, NJ September 22, 1927

Vi 80561 (as DOMENICO BARTOL) is an Italian release.

41.4. Bellson Novelty Trio *instrumental*

GE 13131-A	Beautiful Brunette-Polka	Ge 6301, 40130, Univ 4099
GE 13132-A	Camille-Mazurka	Ge 6301, 40130, Univ 4099
	acn, g, bj	St. Paul October 1927

41.5. Raoul Biais Belgian Orchestra

58854-2	Belgian Potpourri-Pt. 1: Two Step	Co E3708
58857-1	Belgian Potpourri-Pt. 2: Waltz	Co E3708
	Belgian Potpourri-Pt. 3: Two Step	Co E3709
	Belgian Potpourri-Pt. 4: Fox Trot	Co E3709
		NY 1917

41.6. The Calophone Serenaders *instrumental*

W 107041-2	Humming Bird-Walzer, aus "Der Vorschuss Auf Die Seeligkeit"	
		Co 12044-F
W 107042-2	The Bewitching Waltz	Co 12046-F
W 107043-2	Goldenlocks-Mazurka	Co 12046-F
W 107044-2	Rio-Waltz	Co 12044-F
		Chicago July 1926

41.7. Clarinet Orchestra

85872-1	One Evening With A Jolly Bunch	Co E4614
85874-1	Red Heart Sweetheart	Co E4614
	Kur Tu Eini	Co E4647
		NY ca January 1920

Co E4647 (Lithuanian) as KLARNETŲ ORKESTRA

41.8. Lawrence Duchow And His Red Raven Orchestra

BS 029277-1	Kacka Polka (Karel Vacek)	Vi V-712, 25-1011
	Lesacka Polka	Vi V-1086, 25-2020
BS 029278-1	No No Polka (Karel Vacek)	Vi V-713, 25-1013
	Ale Ne Polka	Vi V-1086, 25-2020

```
BS 029279-1  Green Grove {Red Raven}-Polka (Grill)
                            Vi V-715, 25-1014, LPM2563(33), Cam CAE421(33)
             Maryana Polka                            Vi V-1088, 25-2022
             Pod Gazem Polka                                    Vi V-16455
BS 029280-1  Emilia {Laughing}-Polka (L. Vitak)   Vi V-714, V-1087, 25-1001,
               25-1013, 420-0127, 53-1218(45), 447-0127(45), EPA-5067(45)
BS 029281-1  Hot Clarinet Polka    Vi V-716, 25-1002, 25-1015, 20-3226, 420-0127,
                      53-1219(45), 447-0127(45), EPA-5067(45), SPD-17(33)
             Leśniczówska Polka                                Vi V-16455
BS 029282-1  Wisconsin Polka {Jolly Coppersmith Polka}¹
                            Vi V-6393, 25-4061, Cam CAE421(33)
BS 029283-1  Jolly Coppersmith Polka
                            Vi V-716, 25-1015, 53-1210(45), Cam CAE421(33)
BS 029284-1  Old Timers Waltz {In Red Raven Inn}         Vi V-717, 25-1016
BS 029285-1  Skoda Laendler {Laendler No. 1} (Vitak-Elsnic)
                            Vi V-712, V-1088, 25-1011, 25-2022, LPM2563(33)
BS 029286-1  Juice Clarinet Laendler No. 1              Vi V-713, 25-1012
BS 029287-1  Juice Clarinet Laendler No. 2 {Marianne}   Vi V-715, 25-1014
BS 029288-1  Clarinet Polka In Waltz Tempo
                (Regards To Norbert Ecker And Howard Wolff)
                            Vi V-714, 25-1013, 53-1218(45), EPA-5067(45), LPM2563(33)
BS 029289-1  Schottische Medley                                        Vi
BS 029290-1  Morning Star Polka (Karel Echtner)                        Vi
             ¹Lawrence Duchow-vo                    Chicago  December 15, 1938


Vi V-1086, V-1087, V-1088, 25-2020, 25-2022 and 25-2027 as VICTOR ČESKÁ KAPELA


91717-       Hopeless Polka                         De 2592, Vo VL3739(33)
91718-       Red Raven Polka              De 2543, 3681, 45005, Vo VL3739(33)
91719-       Merry Month Of May Polka       De 2785, 45066, Vo VL3739(33)
91720-       Hortensie Polka                                   De 2654
91721-       Adrian Polka                                      De 2986
91722-       Jager March Waltz                                 De 2785
91723-       Heartaches Waltz                       De 2986, Vo VL3739(33)
91724-       Innocence Waltz                                   De 2654
91725-       Maybe Lonesome Waltz          De 2543, 45041, Vo VL3739(33)
91726-       Auf Wiedersehen Schottische   De 2592, 3722, Vo VL3739(33)
             tp, 3 cl/sax, acn, bbs, dm             Chicago  May 9, 1939


91804-A      Zelena Polka (Elsnic)          De 3022, 45005, Vo VL3739(33)
91805-       Old Comrades Polka                     De 3075, Vo VL3739(33)
91806-       Lonesome Musicians (C. Hopfensperger)             De 3115
91807-A      Graceful Polka                         De 3192, Vo VL3739(33)
91808-       Faded Rose Waltz                                  De 3115
91809-A      Medley Of Old Time Waltzes             De 3192, Vo VL3739(33)
91810-       Clarinet Joy Laendler                  De 3075, Vo VL3739(33)
91811-A      Red Raven Waltz (Duchow-Hopfensperger) De 3022, Vo VL3739(33)
                                            Chicago  September 25, 1939
```

41.9. Elite Ensemblers *instrumental*

86151-2	Happy Hours In Golden West-Schottisch-Pt. 1	Co E4639
86152-1	Happy Hours In Golden West-Schottisch-Pt. 2	Co E4639
		NY April 1920
86473-1	Peppy Steps	Co E4791
		NY July 1920
	Josephine Polka	Co E4859
	Kleine Kokette-Polka	Co E4859
		NY 1920

41.10. Elite Orchestra

BVE 49222-2	The Suitor's Waltz {Friare-Valsen} (D. Hellstrom)	Vi V-4
BVE 49223-2	The Barn Dance {På Logbotten-En Norrlandsvals}; Sorunda-Valsen	
		Vi V-4
BVE 49224-2	Veronica-Waltz (Leon Witkowski)	Vi V-7
BVE 49225-2	Dear Grandma {Cara Nonnia}-Polka (Leon Witkowski)	Vi V-7
	c, fl, cl, acn, tb, p, tuba, traps, d Alfredo Cibelli	
		NY December 4, 1928

41.11. John Fischer's Band

84651-1	Hudson River Waltz	Co E4143
84652-1	Recreation In Camp-Polka Mazurka	Co E4143
84653-1	Circus Clowns-Gallop	Co E4173
		NY ca September 1918

41.12. Fisher's Dance Orchestra

W 205536-1	Gold And Silver-Waltz	Co 59038-F(12")
W 205537-2	Vienna Life-Waltz	Co 59038-F(12")
	Memories From Home-Waltz	Co 59037-F(12")
	Blue Danube-Waltz	Co 59037-F(12")
		NY ca March 1927
W 205610-2	Czardas Princess-Waltz	Co 59041-F(12")
W 205611-1	Just A Kiss-Waltz (J. Kasick)	Co 59042-F(12")
W 205612-2	Luna-Waltz (Paul Lincke)	Co 59042-F(12")
W 205613-1	Cavalier-Waltz	Co 59041-F(12")
		NY July 1927

41.13. Derk Gootjes *violin*

44837-4	Gipsy Airs (Pablo De Sarasate, op. 20)	Co E3475
58160-2	Andante (C. Gluck)	Co E3475
	Kanarek {Country Bird}	Co E3343

Madrigal	Co E3343
Menuett	Co E3379
Fifth Hungarian Dance	Co E4039
p	NY 1917

41.14. David Grupp's Orchestra

W 109242-3	Dolores Waltz (E. Waldteufel)	Co 12080-F
W 109243-2	American Patrol (F.W. Meacham)	Co 12080-F, RZ G9399
		NY April 1928

41.15. Gypsy Trio *instrumental*

B 29142-1	Galitzianer Zigeuner Chusid'l (The Galician Gypsy Dance)	
	(Wolf Schildkraut)	Vi 77281
B 29143-2	Polka Mazurka	Vi 77281, 77288, 77289, 77371
B 29144-2	Warszawska Polka (arr W.K. Grigaitis)	Vi 77288
	Jolly Companions-Polka	Vi 77289
	Polka Brio (Lively Polka)	Vi 77308
	Moscow Polka	Vi 77371
	vln, cl, acn, p	NY December 19, 1923

Vi 77281 is a Jewish release; 77288 (Polish) as CYGAŃSKIE TRIO; 77308 (Italian) as TRIO ZINGARO; 77371 is Russian.

41.16. Fred Handte *violin*

W 110119-3	Gypsy Love Song, from "The Fortune Teller"	Co 12102-F
W 110120-4	Sweet Mystery Of Life, from "Naughty Marietta"	Co 12102-F
		NY December 1928

41.17. Harry Harden And His Orchestra

67414-	The Woodpecker Song-Polka (Reginella Campagnola, Italian lyric and music by Eldo Di Lazzarow, tr Harold Adamson)	
		De 3130, Vo VL3612(33)
	El Pájaro Carpintero-Polka	De 10462
67415-	The Tavern Waltz (w: Teddy Demey, m: Herms Niel)	
		De 3130, 45054, Vo VL3612(33)
	La Taverna-Vals	De 10462
67416-	Put Your Little Foot Right Out-Waltz (Larry Spier)	
		De 3131, 45031, Vo VL3612(33)
	Déjame Verte-Vals	De 10463
67417-	Pizzicato Polka (Johann Strauss-Josef Strauss)	
		De 3131, 45032, 45129, DL5140(33), Vo VL3612(33)
	Pichicato-Polka	De 10463
		NY March 28, 1940

De 10462 and 10463 as ORQUESTA DECCA INTERNACIONAL

"Happy" Harry Harden's Musette Orchestra

67923-	Bartender Polka (H. Gerlach-Teddy Demey-Sam Ward)	
		De 3308, 3681, 45004
67924-	Emilia Polka	De 3308, 3681, 45004
		NY July 9, 1940

68380-	Karlstad Ball-Schottische	De 3564, 45034
68381-	Mate's Waltz	De 3564, 45032
	Amigo-Waltz	De 10509
		NY November 20, 1940

68554-	Bring Out The Little Brown Jug {Good Fellow's Polka}	
	(Gloria Franklin-Melvin Franklin)	
	De 3629, 45020, DL5240(33), Vo VL3612(33)	
68555-	All Pals Together-Polka March (T. Reg Sloan)	De 3650
68556-	Titana's Tavern-Oriental Polka	
	(Lew Brown-Malcolm Johnson-Thomas Loustin)	De 3650, 45033
68557-	The Zoompa-Polka (w: Hugo Mariani, m: Lew Brown)	
	De 3629, 45017, DL5240(33), Vo VL3612(33)	
		NY January 7, 1941

De 45017 and 45020 are in album 557.

68884-	Aurora-Fox Trot (Mario Largo-Roberto Roberti)	De 3741, 10509
68885-	Beer Barrel Polka {Roll Out The Barrel}	
	(Lew Brown-Vladimir A. Timm-Jaromir Vejvoda)	
		De 3767, Vo VL3612(33)
68886-	Keep Hoping-Polka (Harry Harden-Mart Fryberg)	De 3741
68887-	Bowling Alley-Polka (Harry Harden-Mart Fryberg)	
	De 3741, Vo VL3612(33)	
		NY March 28, 1941

69466-	Tinkle Polka-Swing Polka (Paul Abraham-Emery H. Holm)	
	De 3909, 45129, DL5140(33)	
69467-	Laughing Polka-Swing Polka (Bert Reisfeld)	De 3909
69468-	Flight Of The Bumble Bee-Swing Polka (Rimsky Korsakov,	
	arr Harry Harden) De 4296, 45034, Vo VL3612(33)	
69469-	Music Box Schottische (Mart Fryberg-Harry Harden)	De 4296, 45033
		NY July 8, 1941

69774-	The Kiss Polka, ftmp "Sun Valley Serenade"	
	(Harry Harden-Mack Gordon)	De 4091
69775-	All American Polka (Emery H. Holm-Artie Jones-Faith Breslau) De 4091	
69776-	The Elbow Song-Swing Polka (Paul Abraham-Emery H. Holm-Kim Gannon)	
		De 4322
69777-	· What Will My Mommie Say Now? (Mart Fryberg-Jules Loman)ˡ De rej	
	Murray Garun or ˡduet-vo NY October 3, 1941	

69776-C	The Elbow Song-Swing Polka (Paul Abraham-Emery H. Holm-Kim Gannon)ˡ	
		De 45019
69777-C	What Will My Mommie Say Now? (Mart Fryberg-Jules Loman)² De 45019	
69901-	Set 'Em Up Polka (Richard Howard) De 4335, Vo VL3612(33)	
69902-	Let's Pack Our Things And Trek-Polka (Josef Marais) De 4322	

69903-   If I Could Only Play A Concertina-Polka (Joe Burke-Al Stillman)[1]
                                                                     De 4110
69904-   The Man With The Lollypop-Polka, ftmp "Weekend In Havana"
                 (Harry Warren-Mack Gordon)[1]   De 4110
            [1]Jerry Burton or [2]unk-vo   NY   November 3, 1941

De 45019 is in album 557.

70033-   All American Polka (w: Artie Jones-Faith Breslau, m: Emery H. Holm)[1]
                                                 De 45020, DL5240(33)
70034-   The Kiss Polka, ftmp "Sun Valley Serenade" (w: Mack Gordon,
                 m: Harry Warren)[1]   De 45018, DL5240(33)
70035-   Tic-Tac-Toe-Polka (Paul Abraham-Emery H. Heim-Albert Gamo)
                         De 4421, 45017, DL5240(33), Vo VL3612(33)
70036-   Pick Pick Pick A Little Polka (Mart Fryberg)
                               De 4347, 45018, Vo VL3612(33)
70037-   It Takes A Kiss To Catch A Kiss-Conga Polka
                 (Paul Abraham-Emery H. Heim-Albert Gamo)[1]   De 4421
70038-   One More Stein-Polka (Bert Reisfeld)
                         De 4347, 45019, DL5240(33), Vo VL3612(33)
            [1]Jerry Burton-vo   NY   December 11, 1941

De 45017-45020 are in album 557.

71211-   I'd Rather Stay Home And Be Lonely
                 (Than Go Out With Somebody Else)-Fox Trot (w: Benny Davis,
                 m: Ted Murry)[1]   De 4376
71212-   It's The Lover's Knot-Fox Trot, ftmp "Iceland" (w: Mack Gordon,
                 m: Harry Warren)[1]   De 4376
71213-A   My Marietta-Fox Trot (Mart Fryberg-Harry Harden-John Redmond-James
                 Cavanaugh)   De 4386
71213-B   My Marietta-Fox Trot (Mart Fryberg-Harry Harden-John Redmond-James
                 Cavanaugh)[1]   De rej
71214-   I Was Leaning On Lena-Waltz (Mart Fryberg-Mickey Stoner)
                                     De 4386, 45031
            [1]Jimmy Blair-vo   NY   July 28, 1942

Harry Harden also recorded several titles for the World Transcription company around 1942.

41.18. International Band

59953-1	Tralala-Hopsasa-Polka	Co 50009-F(12")
59954-3	The Dancing Tailor	Co 59017-F(12")
	Wenn Der Schneider Tanzen Geht	Co 55005-F(12")
	A Tantz Far Die Schneiderlach	Co 57012-F(12")
	La Danza Del Sarto	Co 60007-F(12")
	Šokiko Kriauciaus-Šokis	Co 61000-F(12")
	Tanczacy Krawczyk	Co 63003-F(12")
	Ko Krojač Plesat Gre	Co 68001-F(12")
59955-1	Cobbler Polka	Co 59017-F(12")
	Schusterbuben Polka	Co 55005-F(12")

	Shuster Polka	Co 57012-F(12")
	Polka Del Ciabattini	Co 60007-F(12")
	Kobler'o Polka	Co 61000-F(12")
	Szewska Polka	Co 63003-F(12")
	Polka Čevlijarskih Vajencev	Co 68001-F(12")
		NY April 1925

Co 50009-F as KOLÍNSKÁ SELSKÁ KAPELA, 55005-F as SCHWOBISCHE VETERANEN KAPELLE, 60006-F as BANDA DEL VETERANI, 61000-F as TARPTAUTINĖ KAPELIJA, 63003-F as KAPELA WOJSKOWA, 68001-F as KRANJSKA VETERANSKA KAPELA

59966-4	Ellis Island-Polka Potpourri	Co 59021-F(12")
	'Raus & 'Rein-Polka	Co 55013-F(12")
59967-3	Der Kleine Kohn-Polka Potpourri	Co 55011-F(12")
59968-4	Rundgesang-Marsch Polka	Co 55013-F(12")
59974-3	Die Grossmutter Tanzt-Walzer Potpourri	Co 55011-F(12")
59975-4	At The Actors Ball-Waltz Potpourri'	Co 59017-F(12")
	Pod Háječkem-Valčik	Co 50009-F(12")
		NY ca May 1925

Co 50009-F as KOLÍNSKÁ SELSKÁ KAPELA, 55011-F as SCHWOBISCHE VETERANEN KAPELLE, 55013-F as DEUTSCHE VETERANEN KAPELLE

41.19. International Dance Orchestra

W 112147-1	Sweet Memories-Waltz	Co 12133-F
	Vals "Sladkiya Metchty"	Co 20229-F
	Kauniita Unelmia-Valssi	Co DI173
W 112148-1	All Is Quiet-Waltz	Co 12133-F
	Krugom Vsio Ticho-Vals	Co 20229-F
	Hiljaisuus-Valssi	Co DI173
W 112149-2	The First Kiss-Waltz	Co 12134-F
W 112150-1	European Memories-Waltz	Co 12134-F
		NY June 1930

Co 20229-F as RUSSKYJ ORKESTR "MOSKVA", DI173 as VENÄLÄINEN ORKESTERI

41.20. International Peasant Band

85222-1	Los Dos Hermanos-Vals	Co C3797
85223-1	Ice Skating Waltz	Co E4359
85226-3	Happy Wanderers-Polka	Co E4359
		NY ca May 1919

Co C3797 as ORQUESTA SUIZA

41.21. International Rhythm Boys *instrumental*

29468-1	Lover's Lane-Polka (V. Cesarino)	Ok 16006, Cq 9744
	Callejuela Del Amor-Polka	Ok 9386
29469-	Merry Go Round Polka (A. Libardo)	Ok 16005

	Carnera Polka	Co 15095-F
29470-1	Little Brunette Polka (E. Rossi)	Ok 16005
	Brunettina-Polka	Co 15095-F
29471-1	Army Hostess-Polka (A. Libardo)	Ok 16006, Cq 9744
	Alma Mia-Polka	Ok 9386
		NY January 15, 1941

Ok 9386 as EL TRÍO CON RITMO, Co 15095-F as I MONTAGNOLI ALLEGRI

41.22. Jerry Jaros *instrumental*

Jaros Olympians

BVE 35071-2	Rio-Waltz (Chas. Kovacs)	Vi 78801, HMV R4941
BVE 35072-3	Gay Widow-Schottische (Chas. Kovacs)	Vi 78801
	vln, md, acn, sax, p, g	Chicago May 28, 1926

HMV R4941 as ORCHESTRINA JASILLI

Jaros Novelty Orchestra

BVE 36250-3	Happy Days {New York}-Medley Waltz	Vi 20308
	Happy Times-Waltz	Vi V-746
BVE 36251-1	Good Old Days {Turkey}-Polka	Vi 20308, V-746
BVE 36252-3	Waltz Melodies	Vi rej

6 persons: vln, md, hca, 2 sax, acn, autoharp, jews harp, shake
chimes, g   Webster Hotel, Chicago September 17, 1926

BVE 36425-3	Hot Time In The Old Town	Vi rej

6 men: vln, md, sax, acn, hca, zither jews harp, g   Webster Hotel,
Chicago September 28, 1926

41.23. A. Jellinek *accordion*

85733-1	A Brilliant Time-Landler (A. Jellinek)	Co E4505
85737-2	Mazurka Characteristique (A. Jellenek)	Co E4505
	g	NY ca November 1919

Co E4505 is uncredited.

85957-2	Peasant Feast-Waltz	Co E4615
85960-1	Girls From The West-Schottisch	Co E4615
		NY ca February 1920

41.24. Stephan Kautz Orchestra

W 401505-A	Staro Krajska Polka	Ok 11410
	Staro Krajova-Polka	Ok 18071
	Tėvynės Polka	Ok 26085
W 401506-B	Moderne Polka	Ok 10523

	Novo Svecka Polka	Ok 18071
	Nauja Polka	Ok 26086
W 401507-A	Kiss Waltz	Ok 3516, 10523
	Un Beso-Vals	Ok 16350, Od ONY 16350
	Bučkio Valcas	Ok 26086
W 401508-A	Cuckoo Waltz	Ok 3516, 11410, 16350, 26085, Od ONY 16350
		NY January 8, 1929

Ok 3516 as OKEH INTERNATIONAL ORCHESTRA, 11410 as ORKIESTRA NARODOWA, 18071 as SLOVENSKA ORKESTRA, 26085 and 26086 as OKEH TARPTAUTINĖ ORKESTRA

41.25. Laughing Record

88778-5	Laughing Record	Co E7796, 12118-F
	Rise Sensacional	Co C4168
		NY October 1922

This performance consists of a cornetist who plays "The Last Rose Of Summer," while a man and woman laugh. Co C4168 as RISE SENSACIONAL

41.26. Walt Leopold And His Orchestra

BS 75134-1	Mimi-Fox Trot, ftmp "Love Me Tonight" (Lorenz Hart-Richard Rodgers)	
		Vi 24251
BS 75136-1	Was Willst Du Haben?-Fox Trot (Al Bryan-James V. Monaco) Vi 24251	
	2 tp, 3 vln, 3 sax, acn, p, tuba, traps NY February 20, 1933	

BS 062842-1	Bluffer {Szubranecka}-Polka (Walt Leopold)	Std T-2003
BS 062843-1	My Emily {Moja Emcia}-Polka (Walt Leopold)	Std
BS 062844-1	Foxy {Liser}-Polka (Walt Leopold)	Std T-2003
BS 062845-1	Jeannine {Janeczka}-Polka (Walt Leopold)	Std T-2029
BS 062846-1	Free Jokes {Wolne Żarty}-Polka (Walt Leopold)	Std
BS 062847-1	Don't Fool Me {Nie Bujaj Mnie}-Polka (Walt Leopold)	Std
BS 062848-1	Red Head {Ruda Głowka}-Polka (Walt Leopold)	Std
BS 062849-1	Hunting {Mysliwska}-Polka (Walt Leopold)	Std T-2029
	2 tp, vln, acn, p, sbs NY March 17, 1941	

41.27. Liggy And Schoenberger *violin duet*

85717-2	Young And Old-Mazurka	Co E4504
85718-	Skoczny Taniec-Mazur	Co E4512
85719-1	Home Again	Co E4504
85720-	Po Żniwach	Co E4512
	p	NY November 1919

Co E4512 (Polish) as DUET NA SKRZYPCACH

41.28. Lyric Gypsy Band

714	Marche Rakoczy	Lyric 3782
715	Gypsy Waltz	Lyric 3782
	vln, fl, cl, cym	NY ca 1919

41.29. Nicolas Matthey *instrumental*

Nicolas Matthey And His Gypsy Orchestra

64648-A	Doină Oltului-Roumanian Shepherd Song And Dance	De 2118
64649-A	Hora Staccato (Dinicu)	De 2119, 25045
64650-A	Țuică-Drinking Song	De 2121
64651-A	Transylvania-Regional Dance	De 2122
64652-A	Steluta {Star}; Ciocărlia {Nightingale}	De 2120
64653-A	Țața Marița {Aunt Maritza}-Peasant Song And Dance	De 2121
64654-B	Sărbă	De 2122
64655-A	Hora Țăgăziniasca-Gypsy Dance	De 2118
64656-A	Sava Chavo {The Gay Fellow}	De 2119
64657-A	Hora Calului	De 2120
		NY September 14, 1938

The above are in album 21.

64808-A	Snowshoes; Riding The Troika	De 2369
64809-A	Little Bricks; A Glass Of Vodka	De 2371
		NY December 14, 1938

The above are in album 42.

Nicolas Matthey And His Oriental Orchestra

65294-A	The Stork {Krounk}	De 2718
65295-A	The Sweet Vendor; Dawn In The Valley-Slow Dance	De 2718
65296-A	Hail To Antranic	De 2715
65297-A	Rangui; Tasn Tchors-Armenian Dances	De 2717
65298-A	Armenian Air; Little House	De 2719
65299-A	The Morning Thea; The Fruit Vendor	De 2716
65300-A	Lullaby	De 2717
65301-A	Sweetheart	De 2716
65302-A	Wedding Dance	De 2715
65303-A	Bosphorus	De 2719
		NY March 28, 1939

The above are in album 68.

66096-A	Misirlou-Turkish Song (N. Roubanis)	De 3205, 25045
66097-A	Skutari-Turkish Song	De 3206, F7763
66098-A	Zembek	De 3207
66099-A	Taxim-Turkish Street Song	De 3208, F7754
66100-A	Sheker Oghlon-Turkish Dance	De rej
66101-A	Chanabali {Chanak Clalais}-Turkish Song	De 3205

66102-A	Constantinople-Turkish Dance For Two	De 3207
66103-A	Smyrna	De 3206, F7763
		NY August 15, 1939

The above are in album 105.

66210-A	Mravel Jamier	De 3220
66211-A	Kasbek-Caucasian Folksong	De 3220
66212-A	Trngi I Kintauri-Georgian Karaban Dance	De 3221
66213-A	Allah Verdi-Georgian Song	De 3221
66214-A	The Prayer Of Shamil-Georgian Dance	De 3222
66215-A	Haitarma-Caucasian Glass Dance	De 3222
66216-A	Tcherkes Dance, from "Demon" (Rubinstein)	De 3223
66217-A	Nothcinka-Caucasian Song	De 3223
66218-A	Kunak-Caucasian Dance	De 3224
66219-A	Georgashvili-Georgian Song; Lesginka-Caucasian Dance	De 3224
		NY August 28, 1939

The above are in album 106.

66541-A	Allah-Turkish Prayer	De 3208, F7754
66542-A	Nighara-Oriental Sketches (N. Kotchteff)	De 3241
66543-A	Zuleika-Persian Dance (Francis Salabert)	De 3242
66544-A	Kuraoglou-Persian Sketches	De 3241
66545-A	Berceuse Persane	De 3242
66546-A	Omar Khayyaim-Persian Dance	De 3240
66547-A	Song To Persian Girls (Serge Orlanski)	De 3243
66548-A	Scharaschub-Traditional Persian Song And Dance (Karaglen)	De 3243
66549-A	Kyrat (Karaglen)	De 3240
		NY September 12, 1939

The above are in album 107, except for De 3208, which is in album 105.

41.30. Montmartre Orchestra

BS 041178-1	Let's Have A Drink-Polka (Zarkevich)	Vi V-736
BS 041179-1	Let's Dance (Zarkevich)	Vi
BS 041180-1	For Your Black Eyes-Polka (Vella)	Vi V-736
BS 041181-1	Oompah-Pah-Fox Trot (Ricardi)	Vi V-744
BS 041182-1	Ta Ta Ta Polka (Zarkevich)	Vi V-735
BS 041183-1	Harasho {South American Dance} (Zarkevich)	Vi V-735
BS 041184-1	Funny Face-Fox Trot (Ricardi)	Vi V-744
BS 041185-	Peggy One Step (Zarkevich)	Vi
	vln, acn, 2 sax, xyl, p, 2 g, sbs	NY August 4, 1939

41.31. Samuel Nafshun's Orchestra

W 113872-2	"Kazbek"	Co 12183-F, 20313-F
W 113873-1	Potpourri Of Russian Melodies	Co 12183-F, 20313-F
W 113874-1	"Doina"	Co 12182-F
W 113875-2	Hungarian Fantasy	Co 12182-F
		NY February 1934

41.32. Oldenburg's Concertina Band (From Henderson, Minnesota)

C 1846-, E 7275W	St. Paul Waltz	Vo 15679
C 1847-, E 7276W	Tinker Polka	Vo 15678
C 1848-, E 7277W	The Love Dream-Waltz'	Vo 15680
C 1849-, E 7278W	Minneapolis Waltz	Vo 15681
C 1850-, E 7279W	Norwegian Schottische	Vo 15680
C 1851-, E 7280W	Peggy-Quadrille	Vo 15682
C 1852-, E 7281W	Louise-Mazurka	Vo 15677
C 1853-, E 7282W	Hunter's March	Vo 15679
C 1854-, E 7273W	Henderson Waltz	Vo 15677
C 1855-, E 7274W	Mayflower Waltz	Vo 15678
C 1856-, E 7283W	Grace-Polka	Vo 15681
C 1857-, E 7284W	Christiana Waltz	Vo 15682

7 men, or '2 vln, concertina (as OLDENBURG'S TRIO)

Chicago   April 2, 1928

41.33. Oriental Orchestra

87429-2	Pekin Peeks (H.A. Wade)	Co E7160
87431-1	Egyptian Dancer {The Ghawazei} (J.C. Breil)	Co E7160

NY   May 1921

Some copies of Co E7160 as ORIENTAL WOODWIND ORCHESTRA

87500-1	Danse Arabe (Egon Putz)	Co E7258, 12031-F
87501-2	Danse Orientale (Egon Putz)	Co E7258, 12031-F

NY   ca June 1921

Co 12031-F as COLUMBIA ORCHESTRA

41.34. Peasants' Orchestra

761	Rustic Polka	Lyric 4132
762	The Return From The Park-Polka	Lyric 4132
	A Happy Couple-Polka	Lyric 4110

NY   ca 1919

41.35. Plehal Brothers (Paul Filmore-Douglas Nash) *harmonica duet*

M 1	Springtime Polka	De 1773
M 2	Farewell Blues	De 1956
M 3	Ellen Polka	De 1773, 45030
M 4	Wedding Of The Winds	De 1956

g, sbs   Minneapolis(?)   1938

65275-A	Beer Barrel Polka {Roll Out The Barrel}	
	(Lew Brown-Wladimir A. Timm-Jaromir Vejvoda)	De 2393

	El Barrilito-Polka	De 10429
65276-A	Jolly Crowd Polka	De 2485
65277-A	At The Mill March	De 2485
65278-A	Muziky, Muziky	De 2393, 45052
	Vamonos Con La Musica-Polka	De 10429
	as before	NY March 20, 1939

De 10429 as ORQUESTA PLEHAL

91745-A	W.P.A. Polka (Curt Mahr-W.A. Timm)	De 2576, 45028
91746-A	Cuckoo Waltz	De 2576, 3750, 45008
91747-	Home Coming Waltz	De 2742, 3746, 45028
91748-	Jolly Lumber Jack-Polka (J.F. Wagner)	De 2742, 45052
91749-	Under The Window-March	De 2663
91750-	Vanda Polka (E. Stolc)	De 2633
		Chicago May 22, 1939

91795-B	When It's Lamplightin' Time In The Valley (Sam C. Hart-Joe Lyons)	De rej
91796-	It Makes No Difference Now (Jimmie Davis-Floyd Tillman)	De 2960, 3746
91797-	Let's Say Goodnight To The Ladies {Beer Chaser's Polka} (Bill Gale-Lew Brown)	De 2960
91798-	Railway Waltz	De 3012
91799-	Low Down Polka	De 3012
91800-	Le Secret-Schottisch (L. Gauthier)	De 3096, 3728
91801-	Lena Schottische	De 3060, 3728
91802-	Hot Pretzels-Polka (Will Glahe-Sam Ward-W.A. Timm)	De 3060
91803-B	Oh Dem Golden Slippers (James Bland); Down Home Rag (Wilbur C. Sweatman-Roger Lewis)	De rej
		Chicago September 24, 1939

93019-A	Pokey Polka (Toby Prin-Plehal Bros.)	De 3296
93020-	Saturday Waltz {Lordags Valsen}	De 3353
93021-	Barbara Polka	De 3372
93022-	Dalbacktrallen Polka	De 3353
93023-	Swing Me Round-Polka (Wolmer Beltrand-Teddy Demey)	De 3372
93024-	Lokkoren {The Callers}-Valsen	De 3265
93025-A	Emilia Polka	De 3296
93026-	Ferry Boat Serenade {La Piccinina} (E. Di Lazzaro-M. Panzeri-Harold Adamson)	De 3265
		Chicago June 5, 1940

93524-	Cherry Pickers-Polka	De 3820
93525-	Life In The Finnish Woods-Waltz	De 4324
93526-	Red Wing; Silver Bell-Two Step	De 4150
93527-	Fireman's Polka	De 4150
93528-	Two Canaries-Polka	De 4324
93529-	Sweet Corn Polka (Plehal Bros.)	De 3717, 45060
93530-	Hoiriger Schottische (Will Grosz-Sam Coslow)	De 3717, 45030
93531-	Jenny Lind Polka	De 3820, 45029
		Chicago March 3, 1941

```
93825-     Finska Waltz (Olaf Bergstrom)                    De 4401, 45029
93826-     Night Off Polka                                         De 4419
93827-     Der Harmony Schottische (arr K. Echtner)                De 45001
93828-     Black Hawk Waltz                                 De 4419, 45060
93829-     Happy Hour Polka (Thomas and Edward Plehal)             De 4355
93830-     Midnight Schottische (Thomas and Edward Plehal)         De 4355
93831-     Our Katy Polka (arr Louis Vitak)                       De 45001
93832-     In The Green Grove Polka (arr A. Grill)                 De 4401
                                           Chicago   April 24, 1941
```

41.36. Polka Four (Polka Dot Four) *instrumental*

```
93839-A    Tickling The Accordion-Polka (George Hovan)      De 4260, 45044
93840-A    Tip Top Polka (George Hovan)                     De 4260, 45044
93841-A    The Mad Polka (I. Podgorski)                            De 4396
93842-A    Judy Polka                                              De 4396
                                           Chicago   November 24, 1941
```

41.37. Posadas *instrumental*

Posadas And Monaku

```
85479-3-4  Christmas Eve                                          Co E4752
85480-3    Edelweiss And Violets                                  Co E4469
                                           NY   ca September 1919
```

Posadas And Nova

```
85490-1    My Loving Star                                         Co E4469
85491-1    Clarinet Waltz                                         Co E4557
                                           NY   ca September 1919
```

Co E4469 as HAWAIIAN GUITAR DUET

```
85764-1    Summer Night                                           Co E4641
85765-1    Alpine Violet                                          Co E4641
87567-1    A Bohemian Party                                       Co E4557
                                           NY   ca November 1919
```

```
86193-1-2  Hedwig Waltz                                           Co E4752
86194-2    Adelia Waltz                                           Co E4676
86195-1    Tyrolian Lake Waltz                                    Co E4676
                                           NY   April 1920
```

41.38. Henri René *instrumental*

This artist's real name is Harold M. Kirchstein.

René Musette Orchestra

```
BS 050629-1   Windmill Tillie-Polka (H. Kirchstein)              Vi V-756, 25-1032
BS 050630-1   Let's Step High, Baby (You And I)-Polka (H. Kirchstein)
                                                                 Vi V-756, 25-1032
BS 050631-1   Sea Breezes-Polka (F. Marx)                             Vi V-759
BS 050632-1   Chicken Coop-Polka (F. Marx)                            Vi V-759
              2 acn, 2 sax, p, sbs, traps                     NY  May 1, 1940
```

Vi V-759 as ANDRÉ MUSETTE ORCHESTRA

```
BS 050668-1   I Wonder What You Are Doing-Fox Trot (Pierre Beaucaire)¹   Vi V-760
BS 050669-1   Perlita-Fox Trot (J. Fouskas-T. Demey)¹                Vi rej
BS 050670-1   Giddy Up Horsie-Polka (T. Demey)            Vi V-758, 25-1033
BS 050671-1   Valse Musette (M. Souyoul-T. Demey)                    Vi V-760
              2 acn, sax, p, g, sbs, traps, ¹Pierre Beaucaire-vo   NY  May 17, 1940
```

```
BS 051447-1   Giggling Girlies (G. Constant-T. Demey)                Vi V-770
BS 051448-1   Polka Musette (G. Constant-T. Demey)        Vi V-763, 25-1034
BS 051449-1   Catch Me Quickly-Fox Trot (G. Constant-T. Demey)       Vi V-192
BS 051450-1   Dear Little Swiss-Polka (G. Constant-T. Demey)         Vi V-767
              2 sax, acn, Hammond org, traps                 NY  June 18, 1940
```

```
BS 050669-    Perlita-Fox Trot (J. Fouskas-T. Demey)¹                Vi V-765
BS 051461-1   Burning Cheeks-Polka (Henri René)           Vi V-195, 25-0051
BS 051462-1   Never Say No-Fox Trot (Henri René)                     Vi V-199
BS 051463-1   Week End Polka (Nick Grabowsky)             Vi V-763, 25-1034
              2 vln, acn, sax, p, g, sbs, ¹Pierre Beaucaire and chorus-vo
                                                             NY  June 20, 1940
```

```
BS 054955-1   Rolling Wheels-Polka (N. Grabow-T. Demey)              Vi V-765
BS 054956-1   Zig Zag-Polka (N. Grabow-T. Demey)                     Vi V-775
BS 054957-1   Triangle Polka (N. Grabow-T. Demey)                    Vi V-766
BS 054958-1   Ting Ling Ling-Polka (N. Grabow-T. Demey)              Vi V-773
BS 054966-1   Come With Me To The Booneville Ball-Polka
                   (Mart Fryberg-B. Goldsmith)                       Vi V-781
BS 054966-2   Come With Me To The Booneville Ball-Polka
                   (Mart Fryberg-B. Goldsmith)¹                      Vi V-767
BS 054965-1   Lucky Bird-Polka (M. Fryberg-B. Goldsmith)             Vi V-781
BS 054965-2   Lucky Bird-Polka (M. Fryberg-B. Goldsmith)¹            Vi V-767
BS 054967-1   Tip Top Polka (Nick Grabowsky-T. Demey)                Vi V-812
BS 054968-1   Puppet's Birthday-Fox Trot (Nick Grabowsky-T. Demey)   Vi V-201
              vln, acn, sax, p, g, sbs, ¹vo                  NY  August 1, 1940
```

```
BS 056350-1   Lo-Lo-Lita-Polka (M. Fryberg-F. Allen)           Vi V-771, 25-1035
BS 056351-1   Cannibal's Polka (Jessnicka Polka) (M. Fryberg)  Vi V-776, 25-1037
BS 056352-1   My Guitar And I (M. Fryberg)                          Vi V-777
BS 056353-1   Here Comes Baby-Polka (T. Demey)                 Vi V-771, 25-1035
              acn, sax, p, g, sbs, dm                        NY  October 1, 1940
```

```
BS 056352-2   special for Tetos Demetriades                         Vi test
BS 057305-1   Come Along To Hobohemia-Polka (Fryberg-Wood-Cavanaugh-Redmond)
                                                                     Vi V-775
BS 057305-2   Come Along To Hobohemia-Polka (Fryberg-Wood-Cavanaugh-Redmond)¹  Vi
BS 057306-1   Tinkling Glasses-Polka (N. Grabow)       Vi V-795, V-209, 25-1041
BS 057307-1   Rookie Playing Hookie (T. Demey)                      Vi V-777
```

BS 057308-1   Puppy Love {Birds Of Paradise}-Polka (N. Grabow)   Vi V-776, 25-1037
               acn, sax, p, g, sbs, dm, 'vo   NY October 23, 1940

Vi V-795 as ANDRÉ MUSETTE ORCHESTRA

BS 058321-1   Jumping Puppets {Daredevil}-Polka (F. Allen-T. Pic)
                                                        Vi V-779, 25-1038
BS 058322-1   Hocus Pocus {Tick Tock}-Polka (A. Ellis)   Vi V-788
BS 058323-1   At Chiquita's Café {Rinaldo Rinaldini}-Valse Musette (M. Fryberg)
                                                                    Vi V-791
BS 058324-1   One Up {Follow The Band} (A. Ellis)   Vi V-782, 25-1039
BS 058325-1   Stop Crying (Mart Fryberg)   Vi V-787
BS 058326-1   Turn The Lights Down Low {Give Me Another Dance} (Mart Fryberg)
                                                                    Vi V-784
BS 058327-2   Fiddle, Fife And Squeezebox {I'll Tell Mama} (Joe Lazarz)   Vi V-778
BS 058328-1   Old Fashioned {Gay 90's}-Polka (Harold M. Kirchstein)
                                                        Vi V-779, 25-1038
               vln, acn, cl, sg, p, sbs, traps   NY December 6, 1940

Vi V-788, V-782, V-787 and V-791 as ANDRÉ MUSETTE ORCHESTRA

André Musette Orchestra

BS 058344-1   Fatty's Dream {Steno's Dream} (T. Demey)   Vi V-780
BS 058345-1   Whis-Whis-Whistle {Whistling Joe} (Harold M. Kirchstein)   Vi V-787
BS 058346-1   In The Barracks (Harold M. Kirchstein)   Vi V-789
BS 058347-1 . Happy-Go-Lucky (Harold M. Kirchstein)   Vi V-780
               tp, cl, acn, p, g, sbs   NY December 10, 1940

BS 058166-1   Double Talk-Polka (Harold M. Kirchstein)   Vi V-791
BS 058167-1   Hop And Skip {Military Polka}-Polka (M. Grabow)   Vi V-800
BS 058168-1   Bubbing Over {Shoe Shiner's}-Polka (M. Grabow)   Vi V-799, 25-1043
BS 058169-1   Seven Come Eleven {Jolly Crackpot}-Polka (Harold M. Kirchstein)
                                                                    Vi V-778
               acn, cl, p, g, sbs, traps   NY December 11, 1940

Vi V-778 as RENÉ MUSETTE ORCHESTRA

Henri René Musette Orchestra

BS 058681-2   Hy'a Susie {The Nightingale Polka} (Nowicki-Fiedler)   Vi V-790
BS 058682-1   Quintuplets (H. René)   Vi V-783, 25-1040
BS 058683-1   Fly A Kite {Crazy Cat} (D. Zattas)   Vi V-789
BS 058684-2   Waltz Of The Sparrows {Java Musette Des Pierrots} (Pierre Beaucaire)
                                                                    Vi V-785
BS 058685-1   Johnny Peddler {I Got} (Lew Brown-De Almeida-Nesdan)
                                                        Vi V-782, 25-1039
BS 058686-1   Nickel-A-Polka {Crazy Girl} (D. Zattas)   Vi V-788
BS 058687-1   Chicken Farm (H. René)   Vi V-784
BS 058688-1   Right On The Spot-Polka (George Torke)   Vi V-794
                                                         NY January 2, 1941

Vi V-784 and V-785 as RENÉ MUSETTE ORCHESTRA, V-782, V-788, V-789, V-790, V-794
and 25-1039 as ANDRÉ MUSETTE ORCHESTRA

René Musette Orchestra

```
BS 058762-1   Pound Your Table {Village Tavern} {Crazy Wolf}-Polka
                  (H. Lenk-E. Drake-D. Zattas)           Vi V-783, 25-1040
BS 058763-1   Come And Get It {Don't Forget} (D. Zattas)    Vi V-795, 25-1041
BS 058764-1   Jeanette-I'll Get You Yet {Go Away} (Mart Fryberg)     Vi V-785
BS 058765-1   Give Me A Lift {Marching Feet} (H.M. Kirchstein)       Vi V-790
                                                    NY   January 7, 1941
```

Vi V-790, V-795 and 25-1041 as ANDRÉ MUSETTE ORCHESTRA

```
BS 063467-1   Sicilian {Short Of Breath}-Polka (H. Grant)   Vi V-818, 25-1051
                                                    NY   April 8, 1941

BS 065723-1A  Shoemaker's Serenade-Polka (D. Zattas)                Vi V-794
BS 065724-1   Drugstore Cowboy {Don't Cry, Susie} (Mart Fryberg)   Vi V-801
BS 065725-1R  Oh Daisy! {Crosseyed}-Polka (D. Zattas)              Vi V-792
BS 065726-1   Croaking Frogs-Polka                                 Vi V-793
                                                    NY   May 15, 1941

BS 065781-1   Toy, Toy, Toyland (H. Grant)                         Vi V-801
BS 065782-1   Boy Chases Girl {Pink Milk Polka} (D. Zattas)
                                              Vi V-803, V-815, 25-1048
BS 065783-1   I Won't Go Home Tonight-Polka (M. Fryberg)           Vi V-793
BS 065784-1   Hiccup-Polka {Pardon Me} (H. Grant)                  Vi V-792
              2 sax, acn, Hammond org, g, traps          NY   June 2, 1941

BS 066638-1   Tattooed Lady {From Abroad} (D. Zattas)              Vi V-802
BS 066639-1   Jumping Beans {Two Kittens}-Polka (B. Fiedler)       Vi V-800
BS 066640-1   The Scissor Grinder (H. Lenk-H. Grant)        Vi V-799, 25-1043
BS 066641-1   She Knows What's What (M. Fryberg)                   Vi V-803
              Ohio Polka                               Vi V-815, 25-1048
                                              NY   September 17, 1941

BS 068957-1   Calling All Cats {Happy Days Polka} (Paul Abraham)   Vi V-807
BS 068958-1   Abra-Ka-Dabra {Fee-Del-Dee Polka} (H. Grant)         Vi V-808
BS 068959-1   Pancho Bought A Rancho {Fiesta In Savannah Polka} (M. Fryberg)
                                                                   Vi V-807
BS 068960-1   Tonight Or Never {Holding Hands Polka} (Paul Abraham)  Vi V-808
                                                    NY   January 22, 1942

BS 073671-1   Pennsylvania Polka (Lester Lee-Zeke Manners)   Vi V-810, 25-1047
BS 073672-1   Shoot The Chutes {Jodel Polka} (William F. Schulze)   Vi V-811
BS 073673-1   Pretzel Bender Serenade {Parade Of The Hobgoblins} (M. Fryberg)
                                                          Vi V-810, 25-1047
BS 073674-1   From Soup To Nuts {One Two, Three} (N. Roubanis)      Vi V-811
                                                    NY   April 1, 1942
```

Matrix BS 073671 was re-recorded on February 23, 1950.

René Musette Orchestra

BS 075039-1   Pit-A-Pat Polka {Don't You Realize It's Fun} (M. Fryberg)
                                                          Vi V-818, 25-1051
                                                          NY May 20, 1942

BS 075587-1   Over The Hilltops {I'll Wait For You} (Paul Abraham)
                                                          Vi V-814, Cam CAL270(33)
BS 075588-1   Down The Hatch (D. Zattas)   Vi V-813, Cam CAL270(33)
BS 075589-1A   See Saw Rhythm {Moonbeams} (M. Fryberg)   Vi V-813
BS 075590-1   Crackerjack {Children Polka} (Paul Abraham) Vi V-814, Cam CAL270(33)
                                                          NY July 28, 1942

Henri René Musette Orchestra

BS 075366-1A   Tick Tock Serenade (Leo Corday-H. Grant)   Vi V-812
                                                          NY July 29, 1942

41.39. Ricci Musette Orchestra

BS 062802-1   The Village Band {Dorfmusik} (Fryberg)   Continental C-1111
BS 062803-1   Snappy-Pappy {Accordeon Polka} (E. Ricci) Continental C-1111
BS 062804-1   Hopsassa {Bohemian Polka}   Continental C-1112
BS 062805-1   Wine Barrel Polka {Polish Polka Ja Radu} (J. Vejvoda)
                                                          Continental C-1112
               acn, sax, p, g, sbs   NY March 6, 1941

41.40. Jolly Jack Robel *instrumental*

Jolly Jack Robel And His Radio Band

19955-	Picnic Polka	Vo
19956-1	Boom Tarara Polka	Co 18629-F, Vo 15945
19957-2	Ti-Ri-Um-Tum Mazur	Co 18628-F, Vo 15951
19958-2	Tavern Dance	Co 18627-F, Vo 15946
19959-1	Kolomejka	Vo 15953
19960-2	Kozak	Vo 15953
19961-2	Jolly Jack Robel's Theme Song	Vo
19962-2	Okey Dokey-Polka	Vo 15944
19963-2	Charlie In The Box-Polka	Vo 15946
19964-2	Laura Polka	Co 18627-F, Vo 15944
19965-2	Do You Remember-Polka	Vo 15945
	tp, vln, 2 sax, acn, tb, p, sbs, dm	NY September 28, 1936

Jolly Jack Robel And His Orchestra

65279-A	At The Outing-Polka	De 2527
65280-	Duck Polka	De 2661
65281-A	Earbender Polka	De 2527, 3679, 45015
65282-	World's Fair Polka	De 2444, 45013
65283-	Beer Barrel Polka {Roll Out The Barrel} (Lew Brown-Vejvoda) De 2384

	El Barrilito-Polka	De 10428
65284-	Jitterbug Polka	De 2444, 3679, 45050
65285-	Robel Polka	De 2670, 45036
65286-	The New Okey Dokey Polka	De 2384, 45048
	Los Brinquitos-Polka	De 10428
65287-A	Ping Pong Polka {Jumping Jack Polka}	
	De 2755, 45035, 45128, DL5140(33)	
65288-	Martha Waltz	De 2661
65289-	Dutch Waltzes-Medley	De 2670, 45035
65290-A	Harvester-Polka	De 2755, 45036
	NY March 26, 1939	

De 10428 as ORQUESTA ROBEL

67549-	Wilkes Barre Polka	De 3276, 45038
67550-	On The Accordeon-Polka (arr Curt Mahr)	De 3181
67551-	Let's Say Goodnight To The Ladies-Polka	De 3230, 45016
67552-	Golden Gate Polka De 3230, 45037, 45128, DL5140(33)	
67553-	Mountain Belle-Schottisch	De 3278, 3729
67554-	Point Breeze Polka	De 3344, 45051
67555-	Meet Me Tonight In Dreamland-Waltz	
	(Leo Friedman-Beth Slater Whitson)	De 3181, 3747, 45038
67556-	Nanticoke Waltz {Petala Sie Pani}	De 3344, 3747, 45037
	NY April 16, 1940	

69037-	Bridgeport Polka	De 3809, 45050
69038-	Rock And Rye Polka (Larry Wellington-Richard Colby)	De 3829, 45049
69039-	Doghouse Polka (E.P. La Freniere-Charles French-Walter Bishop)	
	De 4062, 45014	
69040-	Milkman Polka	De 3809, 45049
69041-	Evening On The Lehigh-Waltz	De 3829, 45048
69042-	Moonlight Schottische (Emil Ascher)	De 4062
69043-	Mama's Pajamas Polka (Bert Reisfeld)	De 4323
69044-	Chicago Polka	De 4323
	NY April 23, 1941	

69846-	Down At Polka Joe's-Polka (Russ Ball-Claude Herltier)'	De 4121
69847-	Brooklyn Polka (F. Zarkevich)	De 3805
69848-	The Farmer Took Aother Load Away! Hay! Hay!-Polka	
	(Edgar Leslie-Charles O'Flynn-Larry Vincent)	De 4382
69849-	Philadelphia Polka	De 4382, 45016
	Jerry Burton-vo	NY October 22, 1941

70016-	Now All Together-Polka	
	(Jack Robel-Horace Jones-Harry Pule-George Sumner)	De 4404
70017-	Scranton Polka (F. Zarkevich)	De 3805
70018-	Ring Those Bells {Steel City Polka}	
	(Joseph Zarnich-Mack David-Abner Silver)	De 4121, 45013
70019-	Phoenixville Polka	De 4404, 45014
	NY December 8, 1941	

De 45013-45016 are in album 556.

41.41. Bela Schaeffer *instrumental*

Hungarian Rhapsody Orchestra

CVE 42500-2 A Night In Vienna-Medley Waltz (Bela Schaeffer-Gustav Paepke)
$\qquad$ Vi 35886(12")
CVE 42501-2 A Night In Budapest-Medley Waltz (Bela Schaeffer-Gustav Paepke)
$\qquad$ Vi 35886(12")
$\qquad$ Vito La Monaca-org, unk 2 1st vln, 2d vln, 2 cl, vla, vc, p, sbs
$\qquad$ Camden, NJ February 8, 1928

CVE 42593-2 Hungarian Flower {I Tender You Roses}-Waltz (C. Kovacs,
$\qquad$ arr Bela Schaeffer-Gustav Paepke) Vi 35929(12")
CVE 42594-2 Gypsy Souvenir-Medley Waltz (arr Bela Schaeffer-Gustav Paepke)
$\qquad$ Vi 35929(12")
$\qquad$ 2 1st vln, 2d vln, 2 cl, vla, vc, p, org, cym, sbs, traps
$\qquad$ Camden, NJ April 3, 1928

CVE 45243-2 Dreams Of Schubert-Medley Waltz
$\qquad$ (arr Bela Schaeffer-Gustav Paepke)-Pt. 1 Vi 35925(12")
CVE 45244-3 Dreams Of Schubert-Medley Waltz
$\qquad$ (arr Bela Schaeffer-Gustav Paepke)-Pt. 2 Vi 35925(12")
$\qquad$ 2 1st vln, 2d vln, 2 cl, vc, p, org, sbs Camden, NJ June 6, 1928

Polska Narodowa Orkiestra

CVE 48044-2 Noc W Warszawie-Walc (arr Gustav Paepke) Vi V-66000(12")
CVE 48045-2 Noc We Lwowie-Walc (arr Gustav Paepke) Vi V-66000(12")
$\qquad$ Vito La Monaca-org, unk 2 1st vln, 2 2d vln, vla, 2 cl, vc, p, sbs
$\qquad$ Camden, NJ November 9, 1928

Hungarian Rhapsody Orchestra

CVE 49382-2 Life In Hungary {Hungarian Fantasia} (arr G. Paepke)-Pt. 1
$\qquad$ Vi 35973, V-50004, V-502, 38-2003(12")
CVE 49383-2 Life In Hungary {Hungarian Fantasia} (arr G. Paepke)-Pt. 2
$\qquad$ Vi 35973, V-50004, V-502, 38-2003(12")
$\qquad$ Vito La Monaca-org, William H. Reitz-traps, Feri Sarközi-cym, 2 1st
$\qquad$ vln, 2 2d vln, fl, 2 cl, vla, o, vc, bsn, p, sbs, played by S.
$\qquad$ Jacobinoff, L. Angeloty, D. Nowinski, G. Paepke, H. Camposky, G. Klug,
$\qquad$ A. Hirschberg, R. Crueger, J. De Matteis, E. Sepentini, L. Morris, N.
$\qquad$ Cerminara Camden, NJ December 26, 1928

Valaskij Chor (Bela Schaeffer Group)

CVE 50666-1 Pletke Pri Studencu {Gossips At The Well}-Pt. 1[1]
$\qquad$ [in Slovak or Ukrainian] Vi V-72021(12")
CVE 50667-2 Pletke Pri Studencu {Gossips At The Well}-Pt. 2[1] [2]
$\qquad$ [in Slovak or Ukrainian] Vi V-72021(12")
CVE 50668-1 Jnivo {Harvest Feast}-Pt. 1[3] [4] [in Slovak or Ukrainian]
$\qquad$ Vi V-71015, V-72015(12")
CVE 50669-2 Jnivo {Harvest Feast}-Pt. 2[3] [4] [in Slovak or Ukrainian]
$\qquad$ Vi V-71015, V-72015(12")

CVE 50670-1   Jnivo {Harvest Feast}-Pt. 3³ ' [in Slovak or Ukrainian]
Vi V-71016, V-72016(12")
CVE 50671-2   Jnivo {Harvest Feast}-Pt. 4³ ' [in Slovak or Ukrainian]
Vi V-71016, V-72016(12")
¹Julia and Elizabeth Selvasi-talking, ²Rev. Iszak, Mr.
Selvasi-talking, ³6 women, 8 men-vo, ⁴2 vln, cl, acn, sbs
Camden, NJ April 1, 1929

Vi V-71015 and V-71016 as KARPATKI-RUSSKI SPEVOKOL, V-72021 as UNGVARSKA BESEDA

Bela Schaeffer's Orchestra

CVE 51807-2   Medley Of Russian Waltzes-Pt. 1   Vi rej (12")
CVE 51808-2   Medley Of Russian Waltzes-Pt. 2   Vi rej (12")
William H. Reitz-traps, unk 4 vln, 2 cl, fl, o, vla, vc, p, sbs
NY April 17, 1929

41.42. Emilie Schneid *contralto*

38356-1	Cat Team Iubit [in Roumanian]	Co E1179
38359-1	Suspine Crude [in Roumanian]	Co E1178
38360-1	Pentru Tine Jano¹ [in Roumanian]	Co E1175
38362-1	Am Un Leu Si Vreau Să'l Beau¹ [in Roumanian]	Co E1176
	vln, p, ¹with Jean Schneid	NY October 23, 1912

38624-1	Na Vršacu [in Slovene]	Co E1328
38625-1	Slepec [in Slovene]	Co E1329
38626-1	Na Gorenjskem Fletno Je [in Slovene]	Co E1330
38627-1	Odpri Mi Kamrico; Prišla Bo Pomlad [in Slovene]	Co E1331
	orch	NY February 10, 1913

38628-1	Što Se Bore Misli Moje [in Slovene]	Co E1333
38629-1	Nevjerni Dragi [in Slovene]	Co E1334
38630-1	Tam Kjer Lunica [in Slovene]	Co E1332
	orch	NY February 14, 1913

Emilia Schneid

38962-1	To Sladko Zlato Vince [in Slovene]	Co rej
38963-1	Sezidal Sem Si Vinski Hram [in Slovene]	Co E1609
38964-1	Oj Zlata Vinska Kaplja Ti [in Slovene]	Co E1633
38965-2	Povsod Me Poznajo [in Slovene]	Co E1632
38966-1	Natočimo V Čaše Svoje [in Slovene]	Co E1631
38967-1	Tiček In Tičica [in Slovene]	Co E1630
	orch	NY July 25, 1913

39055-1	To Sladko, Zlato Vince [in Slovene]	Co rej
	p	NY October 17, 1913

39055-2	To Sladko·, Zlato Vince [in Slovene]	Co
	p	NY December 5, 1913

Milka Schneid

39854-1	Nestiskaj Mi, Suhaj Ručku [in Slovak]		Co rej
39855-1	Prijdi Janik Primilený [in Slovak]		Co E2293
39856-1	Dolun Branu Zapat Rockov Stavali [in Slovak]		Co rej
39857-1	Mala Som Frajera [in Slovak]		Co E2293
39858-1	Sadela Som Bobovnicok; V. Nukul As Key Kompanu [in Slovak]		Co rej
	orch	NY	February 11, 1915

Milka Šnaidova

43671-	Luna Sije [in Slovene]		Co E2779
43672-	Sladko Je Vince, Ne Bon Se Možila [in Slovene]		Co E2779
	Po Jezeru [in Slovene]		Co E2778
	Domovini [in Slovene]		Co E2778
	orch	NY	1916

Mrs. Schneid

61613-	test recording		Co
		NY	May 4, 1917

Milka Polancer Šnajd

B 20109-2	Cekat Cú Ga [in Croatian]		Vi 69507
B 20110-2	Ej Vrbniče! [in Croatian]		Vi 69507
B 20111-2	Na Te Mislim [in Croatian]		Vi rej
	King's Orchestra	NY	June 13, 1917

B 20111-4	Na Te Mislim [in Croatian]		Vi rej
B 20162-2	Ah Kad Tebe Ljubit Nesmjem [in Croatian]		Vi 69703
B 20163-2	Pridi Janík Premilený-Hymn [in Slovak]		Vi 69620
	as before	NY	June 26, 1917

B 20212-2	Datelinka V Lese [in Slovak]		Vi 69620
	King's Orchestra d Rosario Bourdon	NY	July 10, 1917

Vlado Korić I Milka Polancer Šnajd

B 20272-2	Svračanje [in Serbian]		Vi 69623
B 20273-1	Ti Većaspavaš Milko Moja [in Serbian]		Vi 69623
	with Obrad Djurin (pseudonymously), King's Orchestra		
		NY	August 1, 1917

B 20278-2	Sveta Noč {Sveti Večer} (m: V. Klaica) [in Slovene]		Vi rej
	Edward T. King-org	NY	August 6, 1917

Milka Polancer Šnajd

B 20516-2	Zujte Žice [in Croatian]		Vi 69703
	King's Orchestra	NY	August 15, 1917

Milka Polancer Šnajd-Vlado Čorič

B 20278-4	Sveta Noč (m: V. Klaica)		Vi 69694
	Sveti Večer		Vi 69698
	with Obrad Djurin (pseudonymously), Edward T. King-org		
		NY	August 27, 1917

Vi 69694 is described as Croatian-Serbian, 69698 as Slovene (with Djurin's name as Ianez Gorenc).

Milka Polancer Šnajd-Emil Blažević

B 20567-3	Isus Se Rodi {Jesus Is Born} [in Croatian]		Vi 69706
B 20568-2	Došao S Neba {Angel Came From Heaven} [in Croatian]		Vi 69706
	Edward T. King-org	NY	September 17, 1917

Milka Polancer Šnajdova

| B 20580-2 | Ne Bom Se Možila [in Slovene] | | Vi 69802 |
| | King's Orchestra d Rosario Bourdon | NY | September 20, 1917 |

| B 20587-2 | Ljub'ca Povej Povej [in Slovene] | | Vi 69802 |
| | King's Orchestra | NY | September 21, 1917 |

Milka Polancer Schneid

B 20780-2	Tărăncuţa [in Roumanian]		Vi 72053
B 20281-2	Fă Mă Doamne Ce Moi Face [in Roumanian]		Vi 72053
	as before	NY	October 17, 1917

B 20797-2	In Raristea [in Roumanian]		Vi rej
B 20798-2	Venček Na Glavi [in Slovene]		Vi rej
	as before	NY	October 19, 1917

| B 20797-5 | In Raristea [in Roumanian] | | Vi rej |
| | King's Orchestra d Rosario Bourdon | NY | November 9, 1917 |

B 21105-2	Ko Dan Se Zaznava [in Slovene]		Vi rej
B 21106-2	In Pădurea [in Roumanian]		Vi rej
	orch d Nathaniel Shilkret	NY	November 22, 1917

B 21129-2	V Milknlasskej Kompann [in Slovak]		Vi rej
B 21130-2	Sadila Som Bobovnicok [in Slovak]		Vi rej
	King's Orchestra	NY	November 30, 1917

Mila P. Šnajdova-Franjo Potočnik

B 21312-2	Al Me Boš Kaj Rada Imela {I Am Sure You Will Like Me} [in Slovene]	
		Vi 72206
B 21313-2	Oj Ta Polončica {Oh My Polončica} [in Slovene]	Vi 72206
	with Emil Blažević (pseudonymously), orch d Nathaniel Shilkret	
		NY December 27, 1917

Milka Polancer Šnajdova

B 21130-4	Sadila Som Bobovnicok [in Slovak]	Vi rej
B 21331-2	Na Gorenjskem Je Fletno' [in Slovene]	Vi 72364
B 21332-2	Tiček In Tičica' [in Slovene]	Vi 72364
	orch d Nathaniel Shilkret, 'with Emilio Blažević	NY January 3, 1918

Vi 72364 as MILKA POLANCER ŠNAJDOVA-FRANJO POTOČNIK

B 21362-2	Vsi So Prihajali [in Slovene]	Vi rej
B 21363-2	Sem Slovenska Deklica [in Slovene]	Vi 72232
	orch d Nathaniel Shilkret	NY January 11, 1918

B 21517-2	Pod Klančkom Sva Se Srečala [in Slovene]	Vi rej
B 21518-2	Bom Šla Na Planince [in Slovene]	Vi 72232
	as before	NY February 14, 1918

B 21556-2	Oj Djevojko Nevaraj Junaka [in Croatian]	Vi rej
	as before	NY February 28, 1918

B 21517-3	Pod Klančkom Sva Se Srečala [in Slovene]	Vi rej
	as before	NY March 14, 1918

B 21556-4	Oj Djevojko Nevaraj Junaka [in Croatian]	Vi rej
	as before	NY March 28, 1918

Milka Polancer Šnajd

B 21825-2	Kad Djevojka S'Kuče Ide [in Croatian]	Vi 73024
B 21826-1	Visoka Je Gora [in Slovene]	Vi rej
	as before	NY May 3, 1918

B 21826-3	Visoka Je Gora [in Slovene]	Vi rej
	as before	NY May 31, 1918

Milka Polancer Šnajdova

B 22048-2	Na Planincah Solnce Sije [in Slovene]	Vi 72472
	as before	NY June 27, 1918

B 22055-1	Barčica Po Morju Plava [in Slovene]	Vi 72472
	as before	NY June 28, 1918

	Duhni Vjetre [in Bulgarian]	Vi trial
	Nathaniel Shilkret-p	NY April 5, 1919

Milka Polancer Šnajd

B 22768-1	Narodi Nam Se-Christmas National Song (Franjo Dungan) [in Croatian]	
		Vi 77109
B 22769-2	Radujte Se Narodi-Christmas National Song (Franjo Dunjan)	
	[in Croatian]	Vi 77109
	Edward T. King-org, unk chimes	NY May 20, 1919

```
B 23201-2    Marijo O Mili Glas-National Church Song [in Croatian]      Vi 73220
B 23202-2    Marijo Svibnja Kraljice-National Church Song [in Croatian]  Vi 73220
             Nathaniel Shilkret-org                           NY  August 9, 1919

B 23329-2    Za Horami, Za Dolami Ku Ku [in Slovak]                      Vi rej
B 23330-2    Oj Djevojko Nevaraj Junaka [in Croatian]                    Vi 73024
             King's Orchestra d Nathaniel Shilkret           NY  August 15, 1919

B 23337-1    Medzi Horami Lipka Zelena [in Slovak]                       Vi rej
             as before                                   NY  November 15, 1919
```

Milka Polancer Šnajd-Emil Blažević

```
B 23395-2    Tuga-Sorow [in Bulgarian]                                   Vi rej
             as before                                   NY  December 23, 1919
```

Milka Polancer Šnajd-Obrad Djurin

```
B 23395-4    Tuga-Sorow [in Bulgarian]                                   Vi rej
B 23631-2    P'lna Ta Luna {Full Moon} [in Bulgarian]                    Vi rej
             as before                                    NY  January 13, 1920
```

Milka Polancer Šnajd

```
B 23863-2    Grmni Rose [in Bulgarian]                                   Vi rej
B 23865-3    Duhni Vjetre (Rada Boianoff) [in Bulgarian]                 Vi rej
             as before                                      NY  March 20, 1920

B 21105-4    Ki Dan Se Zaznava [in Slovene]                              Vi rej
B 23329-4    Za Horami, Za Dolami Ku Ku [in Slovak]                      Vi rej
             orch d Nathaniel Shilkret                     NY  August 4, 1920

B 21362-4    Vsi So Prihajali [in Slovene]                               Vi rej
B 21517-6    Pod Klančkom Sva Se Srečala [in Slovene]                    Vi rej
             as before                                    NY  October 3, 1921
```

41.43. J. Serebroff's Orchestra

```
W 109276-2   The International Railroad Express           Co 12081-F, RZ G9399
W 109279-    Polka Frieda                                          Co 12081-F
                                                              NY  May 1928
```

41.44. Joseph Soukup And Joseph Peroutka *instrumental*

```
GE 12819-A   Mariechen Waltzer                     Ge 6193, Ch 15314, Univ 4100
                                                   St. Paul, MN  June 3, 1927

GE 12911-A   Polka                                           Ge 6246, Univ 4097
GE 12912-A   Grandpa's Courtship Waltz  Ge 6207, 20295, Ch 15314, Sil 5114, 8279,
                                                                 Supertone 9098
GE 12913-A   Mice Parade                      Sil 5114, 8279, Supertone 9098
             acn, concertina, tuba                     St. Paul, MN  July 2, 1927
```

41.45. Sam Stern's Viennese Orchestra

59894-1	Amoreuse Waltz (Berger)	Co 50009-D(12")
59897-1	Acclamations Waltz (Waldteufel)	Co 50009-D(12")
	Wine, Women And Song	Co 59009-F(12")
	Tales From The Vienna Woods	Co 59009-F(12")
	Manon	Co 59014-F(12")
	Sirenes {Sirenezauber}	Co 59014-F(12")
		NY early 1925

41.46. A.F. Thaviu *instrumental*

Thaviu Military Band

	Victorious America	Co E3567
	Spanish Bolero	Co E3567
		NY 1917

Thaviu's Concert Band

85408-1	Circus March	Co E4867
	Concours-Marcha	Co C3597
85409-1	Serenata Española	Co C3597
85412-	Mazur Ebana	Co E4564
85413-1	Santa Barbara-Habanera de Concierto	Co C3596
85415-	Svietit Miesiac	Co E4701
85416-1	Český Legionál	Co E4450
	Legión De Cesky-Marcha	Co C3598
85418-1	Garibaldini Del Mare-Marcia	Co E4455
85419-2	Svenska Paradmarschen	Co E4537
85421-1	Doughboys To The Front	Co E4467
85423-1-2	Svensk Byvals	Co E4537
85425-1	Número Uno-Marcha	Co C3596
85426-1	Queen Of The Mountains-March	Co E4503
85427-	Kukuh In The Woods-Waltz	Co E4442
85428-	Jedność-Polka	Co E4457
	Cerca-Polka	Co C3598
85430-2	Si, Lo Perdi-Tango	Co C3685
85431-2	On Tip Toe-March	Co E4503
85432-	Marcia Orientale	Co E4871
85433-1	Turin Gallop	Co E4867
85434-1	Our Boys Of The 69th	Co E4467
85435-	Na Polskiej Sali-Mazur	Co E4457
85436-	Kowal-Mazur	Co E4564
85438-	An Old Timer-Waltz	Co E4442
85441-1-2	Ice Skating Waltz	Co E4468
	Pantinado En Hielo-Vals	Co C3685
85442-1	Trans-Atlantic March	Co E4441
85443-1	Flag Parade March	Co E4441
85444-2	Fiume Italiana-Marcia (Nomaro Nomari)	Co E4455
85445-1	Clarinet-Peasant Waltz	Co E4468

Česká Společnost	Co E4450
Pod Polska Chorag Wią	Co E4456
Zbiór Polskich	Co E4456
Tango Espagnol	Co E4632
	NY September 1919

Co   C3596, C3597, C3598 and C3685 as BANDA DEL TROCADERO, E4564 (Polish) as KAPELA
KONCERTOWA Z CHICAGO ILL., E4867 as THAVIU MILITARY BAND, E4450 as THAVIU KAPELA

Banda Thaviu

509-1-2	Tannhäuser: March (Wagner)	Em 02039P(12")
510-2	Blue Danube Waltz (Strauss)	Em 02039P(12")
4561-2	Tango Argentino {Y Como Le Va} (Valverde)	
		Em 02034XP, Symphonola 4266
4562-1	Two Hungarian Dances (Brahms)	Em 02034XP, Symphonola 4266
	Il Barbiere Di Siviglia: Sinfonia	Em 19043XX(12")
	Carmen: Fantasia	Em 19043XX(12")
	Guglielmo Tell: Sinfonia-Pt. 1	Em 20047
	Guglielmo Tell: Sinfonia-Pt. 2	Em 20047
		NY ca October 1919